SUFFERING AND SMILING

A Diagnosis of African Impoverishment

Sterling Johnson

AF739133

University Press of America,® Inc.
Lanham · Boulder · New York · Toronto · Plymouth, UK

University Press of America,® Inc.
4501 Forbes Boulevard
Suite 200
Lanham, Maryland 20706
UPA Acquisitions Department (301) 459-3366

Estover Road
Plymouth PL6 7PY
United Kingdom

Printed in the United States of America
British Library Cataloging in Publication Information Available

Library of Congress Control Number: 2008935276
ISBN-13: 978-0-7618-4351-1 (paperback : alk. paper)
ISBN-10: 0-7618-4351-5 (paperback : alk. paper)
eISBN-13: 978-0-7618-4352-8
eISBN-10: 0-7618-4352-3

™ The paper used in this publication meets the minimum requirements of American National Standard for Information Sciences—Permanence of Paper for Printed Library Materials, ANSI Z39.48—1984

Table of Contents

Acronyms

AAAA	Accelerated Action against Aids in Africa
ADB	African Development Bank
ACPG	African Caribbean and Pacific Group
ACRI	Africa Crisis Response Initiative
AEC	African Economic Commission
AFRC	Armed Forces Revolutionary Council
AFRICOM	Africa Command (AU)
AGRA	Alliance for a Green Revolution in Africa
AI	Amnesty International
AMREF	African Medical and Research Foundation
ARV's	Anti-Retrovirals
ASPA	American Service Members Protection Act
AU	African Union
AGOA	African Growth Opportunities Act
AgriSA	Agriculture South Africa
ASGISA	Accelerated & Shared Growth Initiative
ANC	African National Congress
APSC	African Political Security Council
ARPS	Aborigines Rights Protection Society
BASCO	British South African Company
BBC	British Broadcasting Corporation
BEE	Black Economic Empowerment
BICC	Bonn International Center for Conversion
BPO	Business Process Outsourcing
CAFTA	Central American Free Trade Association
CBC	Congressional Black Caucus
CCFR	Chicago Council on Foreign Relations
CMB	Cocoa Marketing Board
CCPP	Counter Cyclical Payments Program
CDB	China Development Bank
CFA	Commonuate Financiére Africaine
CMI	Chieftaincy of Military Intelligence (Uganda)
CFU	Commercial Farmers Union
COSATU	Congress of South African Trade Unions
CNPC	China National Petroleum Company
CPI	Corruption Perception Index
CRG	Control Risk Group
DFA	Development Fund for Africa
DICON	Defense Industries Corporation (Nigeria)
DMG	Democratic Monitoring Group
DNDI	Drugs for Neglected Diseases Initiative
EBRD	European Bank Reconstruction Development
ECA	Economic Commission for Africa
ECLA	Economic Commission for Latin America
ECGD	Exports Credits Guarantee Department (UK)

ECOMOG	Economic Community Monitoring Group
ECOWAS	Economic Community of West African States
EDF	Environmental Defense Fund
EO	Executive Outcomes
EPLF	Eritrean Popular Liberation Front
EPRDF	Ethiopian Peoples Revolutionary Dem. Front
EURODAD	European Network on Debt and Development
EU	European Union
FAO	Food and Agriculture Organization
FDC	Forum for Democratic Change (Uganda
FEWSNET	Famine Early Warning Systems Network
FDLR	Forces for the Dem. Liberation of Rwanda
FHI	Family Health International
FLC	Congolese Liberation Front
FNI	Nationalist and Integrationist Front (DRC)
FRELIMO	Liberation Front of Mozambique
G8	Group of Eight Industrialized Nations
GATT	General Agreement on Trade and Tariffs
GEMAP	IMF/ Liberian Economic Plan
HDI	Human Development Index
HES	Household Expenditure Surveys
HIPC	Highly Indebted Poor Country
HRFOB	Human Rights Field Operations in Burundi
HRFOR	Human Rights Field Operations in Rwanda
IEA	International Energy Agency
ICC	International Criminal Court
ICDP	Immune Compromised Disease Positive
ICIPE	Intl. Center for Insect Physiology and Ecology
ICJ	International Court of Justice
ICTR	International Criminal Tribunal for Rwanda
IDP's	Internally Displaced Persons
IFF	International Financial Facility
IFPRI	International Food Policy Research Institute
ILO	International Labor Organization
IMF	International Monetary Fund
ISI	Import Substitution Industrialization
ISP's	Internet Service Providers
ITN's	Insecticide Treated Nets
ITU	International Telecommunications Union
JAG	Justice for Agriculture Group (Zimbabwe)
KACC	Kenyan Anti-Corruption Commission
KANU	Kenyan African National Union
KP	Kimberley Process
LAFTA	Latin American Free Trade Association
LRA	Lords Resistance Army (Uganda)
MAP	Millennium Action Plan
MDC	Movement for Dem. Change (Zimbabwe)
MEND	Movement for the Emancipation of the Niger Delta
MJP	Movement for Justice & Peace (Cote d'Ivoire)
MONUC	UN Mission in the Dem. Republic of Congo
MOSOP	Movement for the Survival of the Ogoni People

MPIGO	Ivorian Popular Movement of the Far West
MPLA	Popular Movement Liberation of Angola
MSF	Medicines Sans Frontiéres
NAFcoc	National Fed. Chamber of Commerce & Industry
NFTC	National Foreign Trade Council (US)
NLF	National Liberation Front
NASI	Nigerian Aviation Safety Initiative
NATO	North Atlantic Treaty Organization
NEEDS	National Economic Empowerment Development Strategy
NEPAD	New Partnership for African Development
NIH	National Institute of Health (US)
NMOG	Neutral Military Observer Group
NNPC	Nigerian National Petroleum Corporation
NCP	National Congress Party (Sudan)
NPFL	National Patriotic Front of Liberia
NSE	Nairobi Stock Exchange
OAU	Organization of African Unity
ODM	Orange Democracy Movement (Kenya)
OECD	Organization for Economic Cooperation Development
OPIC	Overseas Private Investment Corporation
PAC	Pan-African Congress
PAYO	Pan-African Youth Organization
PCC	People's Caretaker Council (Zimbabwe)
PDGE	Democratic Party of Equatorial Guinea
PDP	People's Democratic Party (Nigeria)
PIPA	Pıogram on International Policy Attitudes
PPI	Private Sector Participation in Infrastructure
RBZ	Reserve Bank of Zimbabwe
RCD	Congolese Rally for Democracy
RENAMO	National Resistance of Mozambique
RUF	Revolutionary United Front (Sierra Leone)
SAIRR	South African Institute of Race Relations
SACP	South African Communist Party
SADC	Southern African Development Community
SAS	Small Arms Survey
SLPP	Sierra Leone People's Party
SOFA	Status of Forces Agreement
SPDC	Shell Petroleum Development Company
STAMICO	State Mining Company (Tanzania)
SWAPO	SouthWest African Peoples Organization
TAC	Treatment Action Campaign (Aids)
TASO	The Aids Support Organization
TI	Transparency International
TPLF	Tigrayan People's Liberation Front
TWP	True Whig Party (Liberia)
UGCC	United Gold Coast Convention
UN	United Nations
UNCTAD	UN Conference on Trade and Developmen
UNAMIR	UN Mission in Rwanda
UNAMSIL	United Nations Mission in Sierra Leone
UNESCO	United Nations Economic and Social Council

UNHCR	The UN High Commission for Refugees
UNICEF	UN International Children's Emergency Fund
UNDDC	UN Drylands Development Center
UNDP	UN Development Program
UNITA	Union for the Total Independence of Angola
UNMIL	UN Mission in Liberia
UPC	United People's Congress
UPDF	Ugandan Peoples Defense Forces
USAID	US Agency for International Development
WAMCO	West African Mining Company (Liberia)
WDC	World Diamond Council
WFP	World Food Program
WGM	World Gospel Mission
WTO	World Trade Organization
WHO	World Health Organization
ZANU-PF	Zimbabwe African National Union-Patriotic Front
ZAPU	Zimbabwe African Peoples Union
ZEC	Zimbabwe Election Commission

Foreword

These are indeed puzzling times and if you have not noticed, you a part of the puzzle. In *Killing the Nerve*, G.K. Chesterton, the Catholic theologian and philosopher wrote: "It is now generally agreed, with great cheerfulness and good temper that one of the chief features of the state of peace we now enjoy is the killing of a considerable number of harmless human beings." Since ancient times, physicians have been known to do whatever it takes to treat you, even if it kills the patient. This philosophy pays. One such patient on the world wide ward is Africa. The doctors are there, but these physicians do not want, expect or hope the patient will recover. They just want to get paid. Picture this. Dressed in their usual doctor's garb of scrub suits, white lab coats and surgeons' caps, they surrounded the emaciated, groaning, half-naked man. He was covered with bedsores, and smelled foul with diarrhea and vomit. The hovering and buzzing flies paid him the notice that these learned healers in their seeming sterile attire would not. The flies were at least willing to touch him and even plant their maggot larvae into his wounds to eat the decaying flesh. This does help cleanse the wounds that the doctors fear to touch. They hemmed and hawed about this and that. 'What if, we tried this new therapy on him? It couldn't hurt too much, it might help and at least we could appear to be doing something!' Their duty was not to cure, nor to care. Their duty was to order the appropriate diagnostic tests, apply the current modes of therapy, and await either the desired result, or the insurance payment, whichever came first. These are 'forgers of lies..., physicians of no value'. As Job describes his friends in the Biblical account (Job 13:4): The doctors discussed the man's illness at length, at arms' length to be exact. They neither made eye nor physical contact with him as if they might become infected with the illness and diseases with which he was stricken. The donors, do-gooders and dominating forces within Africa find themselves stuck with the same dilemma. How can they meet their interests first while appearing to be meeting the needs of the patient before them, when the two goals may be mutually exclusive?

Starvation, disease, and death are as much part of the African landscape, as the rainforests, deserts and mountainous terrains. Death of indigenous African humans however, does not generate tourist interest (they are not yet on the endangered species list), as there is no way to make it novel, no matter where on the continent it is found. They want a Disney vacation, not a look at desperation. From Niger to Ethiopia, and from Malawi to Kenya, hunger and poverty are the continent's common denominators. The HIV/AIDS crisis is looked upon as the 'window of opportunity' to address these problems by Oxfam and other agencies. Without the devastation of this illness, Africa's problems might go unnoticed.

It started well before the immoral, church and state sanctioned trade of human beings in the 15th century, and continues to the present day extraction of gold, platinum, copper, tin diamonds, bauxite, cocoa, coffee, and myriad other resources. It is nearly impossible to develop the socio-political will and conscience to make a difference when it might interfere with the comfortable hedonistic lifestyles of the donor and investor nations.

Overstuffed people sitting on overstuffed pillows in front of overflowing tables have no interest in what ails Africa. As some European nations propose a micro-credit fund to be managed by the World Bank, other nations continue to siphon off billions of dollars by well vested family empires and banks. The poorest of the poor in Africa subsist while eating tree bark, roots, and leaves, completely unaware of these complexities. These poor know nothing of the flow of assistance from the donors as it moves to the coffers of their capital cities to its principal recipients; the governments and their corrupt associates.

Other nations, including the United States of America, abide by United Nations sanctions when it meets their interests and adhere to them when it harms their opponents. These proxy economic wars are fought by African politicians, using the military hardware purchased on loan from nations far away and exploiting Africa's growing population of orphaned children who serve as combatants. Even the patient's distant relatives, those of the African Diaspora, don't want the patient to recover, as it will negatively impact their lifestyles in their new homelands. These sons and daughters of Africa will allow the world powers to dig through the hole-filled pockets of the emaciated patient. This allows them to not be seen as beneficiaries of this suffering and to choose the moral high ground while directly blaming those of other skin pigments. They are quick to point fingers at the Chinese who are the new economic colonialists in Africa. It is easy to criticize the Arab slave traders who not only operated in ancient times but continue to engage in this sordid cartel of human trafficking which promotes and the extermination of indigenous people of the continent 21st century. Such is the medical, political, technological and scientific approach to Africa. Historically, this approach has been and continues to be completely devoid of the human touch while ignoring the spiritual depths and longstanding traditions and strength of this continent. The physicians are the technocrats, the non-governmental organizations, the mission agencies and the world-wide web of donors, do-gooders and even some of the "bottom feeders" who are there to observe, consult and treat the patient. Thus, Africa is in what seems to be the last throes of death. Come make rounds with us as we journey from bed to bed, room to room, patient to patient, nation to nation.

The world must recognize that it is in the interest of the entire global population to seek a cure for the ailments of this continent. Destruction of natural resources, including the rain forests, the destruction of the lakes and rivers, help foment rebellion and serve to solidify the forces of global terrorism. Who wouldn't join these gangs of poor to terrorize the rich? The diseases and desperation of the poor know no boundaries just as the passage of microbes on a plane or boat from an infected passenger is not detectable by metal detectors or body cavity searches. Let us see how we as a world community have been part of making suffering a part of the African smile. When you finish reading you can answer whether if you are merely puzzled or part of the puzzle.

Michael D. Johnson, M.D.

Acknowledgements

This work would not have been possible without the valuable advice of Dr. Lawrence R. Poree, who helped me to frame the diagnostic theoretical framework and to Dr. Michael D. Johnson for allowing me to participate in his consulting and operating theaters in order to appreciate the intensity of pain and suffering involved. A special acknowledgement to Dr. Tom Catena who allowed me to accompany him on his rounds of the HIV/Aids ward of St. Mary's hospital and explained the disease's symptoms and processes and to Keturah Johnson for acquainting me with the orphanages of Nairobi. I wish to thank Dr. Ronald Swan for his insight into the psycho-social analysis of pain tolerance. Thanks to Jackie Robert, Hao Sun, Joe Lewis, Robert Bucholz, John Dinse, Benjamin Machar, Lee Fleming. To Samuel and Eliud Mambo for their assistance in Kenya. Thanks to Lisa Aubrey National Conference of Black Political Scientists for her feedback. Thanks to Del Ringquist for material on African agricultural policy. Thanks to Ronald Thompson, Nicholas Bagalay, and Andrew Price for valuable assistance with printing the CRC manuscripts. Thanks to Petra Klinkenberg and William Sartore for their valuable and editorial suggestions. Thanks to o Kay, Michael and Elizabeth Johnson and Helen and Grady Dale for their support. Finally, I am indebted to my students of African Political Systems for their questions which helped to inform the development our theoretical framework. Any errors are my own. Finally, thank you to Maya, who tolerated my long absences at the keyboard and became a teen-ager during the writing process.

Introduction

"Suffer, suffer, suffer, suffer, suffer suffer for world, now your fault be that".

"Shuffering and Shmiling" From a song by the late Nigerian Artist/Activist; Fela Kuti.

If you are reading this you are concerned about Africa and her people. As the title suggests, something is wrong there. To investigate further may reveal the something about our moral and political choices. To add to this consternation, the book is about poor Africans. So you think, yet another set of horror stories from the "dark continent"? Stories of suffering Africans who continue to slaughter one another with impunity, corrupt and greedy leaders who with external assistance steal from their people, live ostentatious lifestyles and foment ethnic, religious and linguistic conflict, civil-war, genocide, rape, superstition and sorcery. Why read more tales of starvation, ecological devastation hurricanes, locusts, drought, famine and of parasitic diseases widely unknown in the West? Why investigate such human horror? This is what we seek to understand. The patient is a continent and the indigenous people who inhabit it. Africans have suffered in the name of Imperialism, Colonialism, Racism, Chauvinism, Euro-centrism, Islam, Catholicism, Protestantism, Marxism, Corporatism, Capitalism, Fascism, Scientific Socialism, Pan-Africanism, Communism, Maoism, DeGaullism, Fidelism, Nkrumahism, Senghorism, Habariyamanism, Mandela-ism, Nyerere-ism, Idi Aminism, Charles Taylorism, Mobutuism, Cleintelism, Milton, Friedmanism, Reaganism, the Cold War, Globalism and the "War on Terrorism." The historic, political and economic impact of these interventions and experiments have manifested in myriad forms of suffering and death. If the patient, the African continent, walked or was carried into an emergency room, wounded, bleeding, starving and near death most Americans would avert their eyes in horror and disgust.

Although *CNN* Journalist Anderson Cooper frequently focuses on the daily struggle of Africans for survival, the question remains, why should Americans concern themselves with the problems of Africans half a world away? Are they not sufficiently burdened with the plight of their fellow citizens who are of African descent? In Washington D.C., half of all African-American live below the poverty line. where the infant mortality rate rivals that of many African states and the life expectancy of African-American males is shorter than that of a citizen of Bangladesh and the HIV rates among African-American women rival those of the most poverty stricken African countries. Besides, as good and compassionate "Christians," they give to African missions through their churches and dutifully pay their taxes. This missionary impulse and largesse alleviates any sense of guilt that might be attached to the behavior of their government or US-based corporate activity in Africa. Why be concerned with the use of Africans as guinea pigs for the pharmaceutical industry or for the dumping of obsolete, dangerous and untested drugs on impoverished Africans? After all they are going to die any way. Why be concerned about the testing of weapons systems or viruses for that matter. For is not the African less?

How healthy is any nation? How well-trained, intelligent, and professional are its political leaders prepared to defend it? How strong are its supporting limbs in flexibility and dexterity? How does it feed itself and from where does it derive nutrition? How strong is it's capability to adapt to change in the external environment? How strong are its capabilities to control or challenge the external environment? We must answer these questions to understand the political and economic maladies that plague African states and impoverish African people. These are the questions examined in this work.

The late historian John Henrik Clarke often observed that Africa has always had something that others in the world could not do without and did not want to pay for. This includes: human beings, gold, platinum, copper, tin, diamonds, bauxite, cocoa, coffee and myriad other resources used to simultaneously strengthen the West and weaken Africa. After several centuries of such asymmetric exploitation, the debt has come due. The US State Department refused to attend the 2002 Durban, South Africa conference on the Trans-Atlantic Slave Trade and Racism. The balance due is of course, incalculable in misery, human lives and for Christians in whose names these costs were incurred perhaps souls. The year 2005 was to be an historic year in the economic and physical well-being of the African people. It was not. In 2007 the debate on the affects of the slave trade has begun in the UK while in the US, the state of Virginia made a masked apology for that "peculiar institution." All the physicians need to do is wait for the patient to die and West can escape paying the bill. Africans are dying thousands by the minute from starvation, disease, war and genocide. On a slow night their suffering might make the evening news.

In a renewed push for progress on development targets the UN focused international attention and the Group of Eight responded in part to a list of recommendations by the Commission for Africa. These efforts were eclipsed when the 2003 massive Tsunami devastated the countries of Asia killing over 70,000 people. The outpouring of public donations and governmental pledges to the tsunami victims from the international community, revealed an what was described as an embarrassment of riches. The $5 billion pledged calculates to about $1,000 for each of the estimated 5 million people affected, much more than the average income of an African peasant. The pledges were five times greater than the $977 million appeal launched by Kofi Annan. Asked about the contrast, Kofi Annan replied: "That's a dilemma we live with...The crisis has generated an incredible amount of resources, whilst other crisis do not get the response that we will need."

The widely applauded UN and G8 efforts went largely unnoticed in Africa, where the cost of a newspaper is beyond the budget of the average citizen. The economic promises rang hollow and were received with skepticism by others. Perhaps that is because all the attendant hype was directed at western not African publics. Pressure from high-profile campaigners led to the cacophonic sound bites that poverty could be eliminated with a single stroke without eliminating the structures of impoverishment. The optimism reflected the confusion between humanitarian relief aid and aid for long term-development. It reflected the western tendency to bundle 53 diverse countries into one category and misdiagnose the symptoms of what is commonly portrayed as the sick, staving and mendicant continent.

The EU pledged to "begin the process of unlocking" $540 million in development funds. A UK-led international initiative to help with Sudan's $26 billion debt was delayed. Prioritizing Africa issues seemed ever more critical as John Prendergast of the *International Crisis Group* warned that: "If the international community is not diligent, [the process] will go off line so quickly our heads will spin because there was so much unwillingness to do the things they have made concessions on. There's a tremendous gulf between expectations and reality." In May 2006 the Organization for Economic Cooperation and Development's (OECD), annual African Economic Outlook reported improvement in African economic performance. Growth for the continent as a whole was estimated at 4.9 percent and projected to rise to 5.8 percent within the year. Inflation hit historical lows and trade balances in many countries have improved from the windfall gains of oil and commodity prices. However, the report found that despite new poverty reduction strategies, progress toward the reduction of poverty was limited and that most would fail to meet the Millennium Development Goals of halving poverty by 2015. Negligible progress has been made in combating hunger. Only a quarter of African countries are likely to fulfill the goal of universal primary education. Only North Africa and Mauritius are on schedule to meet the poverty reduction target. The OECD reports that Africa has benefited the most from a recent rise in development aid, but most of the increase comes from a "temporary surge" in debt relief and emergency assistance.

Speaking on the tenth commemoration of the Rwandan genocide, Kofi Annan spoke of his "deep sense of foreboding" about the Crisis in Darfur. That should not be allowed to happen again, he implied, as he launched an "action plan" to prevent genocide. He warned that the international community could not "stand idle" as the violence escalated there. As the former head of UN peacekeeping, Annan reminded the world that it did nothing as more than 500,000 Rwandans were slaughtered within 100 days. He expressed a legitimate concern that the UN had transferred responsibility for Darfur to the fledgling African Union without sufficient economic or security support. "There are many other situations, some comparable to Darfur, where we are not getting the kind of support we need." Appeals for African disasters have generated as little as 14 percent of the funds requested. Nevertheless, the failure of humanitarian aid and intervention are not the only reasons Africans are suffering. Much has gone wrong in Africa, a combination of historic, economic and political forces have reduced the people of the "Dark Continent," to Frantz Fanon's *Wretched of the Earth*.

Imagine the continent of Africa as an emergency room patient. Using a human biological and anatomical analogies, this work seeks to examine and explain an underlying dimensions of African dis-ease i.e., impoverishment. Socio-economic maladies such as ethnic conflict, land distribution and use, exploitation of inert resources, starvation, the arms trade and refugee flows are examined as symptoms of impoverishment. Political maladies such as ethno-partisan conflict, communal instability, military instability and political corruption. Selected patients (state-level analysis), are discussed with respect to the persistence of these maladies. Chapter one describes of the health crisis in Africa. The continent's myriad health issues are discussed by examining several individual clinical cases, the distribution of health care and the role of the international community in providing assistance to the African health infrastructure. Chapter two considers the patient's "chief complaint," impoverishment. Africa's economic marginalization, issues of fair trade, the failure of multilateral aid and the debt management crisis are examined with respect to the 2006 failed round of Doha trade talks. Chapter three queries: What is Africa? This chapter is a geographic description of the African continent. The European misperceptions of the Africans and their political and spiritual systems are also examined for European prescriptions impact contemporary African political conflict. Chapter four explores the major diseases decimating the African people including, efforts to treat, arrest or eradicate these maladies. Chapter five, HIV+Africa examines the devastating impact of HIV/Aids on the lives and the economies of Africa. Chapter six, a history of the present illness, is a description of the patient's history focusing on the trauma of the slave trade and colonialism and the African Liberation Movements.

Part Two (chapters 7-16), presents a case history and patient by patient examination of selected states including: The Democratic Republic of Congo, Cote d'Ivoire, Kenya, Liberia, Nigeria, Rwanda, Sierra Leone, South Africa, Uganda and Zimbabwe. Some of the conversation among the global corporate economic elite; who control Africa's wealth and largely determine Africa's economic health, is reported in *The Financial Times*. This public conversation among those who control African wealth provides much of our diagnosis, because FT journalist often present the perspectives of Africa's impoverished. Chapter seventeen considers the impact of the arms and the arms trade on Africans. The role of small arms on the militarization of refugees by state and non-state actors and the efforts of the international community to control the flow of arms to Africa are also examined.

Part Three, the laboratory investigation, is a diagnosis of the patient. This includes an examination of the role of the media on Africans in terms of media input into their eyes and ears. Chapter eighteen is an examination of the input-symptoms including the Head Eyes Ears Nose and Throat (HEENT). The HEENT examination is part of the basic diagnosis.

Chapter nineteen examines of the patient's cardiovascular system, the education infrastructure. Lack of educational infrastructure plagues most of Africa. Chapter twenty examines the gastrointestinal system focusing on hunger and starvation. Because they threaten to prolong the African hunger crisis, the impact of climate change on food and water insecurity and population growth are examined. Chapter twenty-one examines Africa's respiratory system by exploring the issues of African resource usage including diamonds, platinum and gold and other minerals. Chapter twenty-two is an examination of Africa's compromised auto-immune systems. Because they are critical the defense of the state, the roles of the military and police are examined with respect to their function in peacekeeping and nation-building. Also examined are the roles of the OAU and the African union and AFRICOM. Chapter twenty-three, the skeletal system, examines the African infrastructure. The costly economic impact of poor roads, schools, hospitals and the prospects for telecommunications growth and increased air and rail travel, development and health are considered. Chapter twenty-four examines the central nervous system(s) and addresses issues of African leadership with respect to succession, political corruption and the problematic role of political parties. Chapter twenty-five provides a psychological profile of a people suffering myriad maladies and symptoms including psychological enslavement, impoverishment and self-negation. Also examined are the devastating psychological and attitudinal effects of political corruption on the African body-politic. Chapter twenty-six concludes our examination and prescribes some policy treatments to address the economic and political roots and manifestations of African impoverishment. In the West any dire medical diagnosis usually requires a secondary opinion. This the differential diagnosis, offers or recommends alternative treatment. Unfortunately, there are no simple treatments or remedies.

Sterling Johnson

1: A Continental Medical Crisis

In March 2005, an outbreak of the hemorrhagic disease known as Marburg fever struck the village of Uige, in north-west Angola. In the aftermath of the disastrous Asian tsunami and the death of Pope John Paul II, the catastrophe received little media attention. Marburg hemorrhagic fever is similar to Ebola; it causes high fever, diarrhea and vomiting followed by bleeding. The disease is spread through infected blood saliva, feces or other bodily fluids. Arresting its transmission requires patients to be hospital-isolated, and hospital staff wearing and protective clothing and equipment. It also requires systematic tracing and the quarantining of all those whom with the patient has been in contact. Most victims die within a week of contracting the illness. The virus was first identified in 1967 in Marburg, Germany, after an outbreak among laboratory workers was traced to green African monkeys from Uganda. In 1998 and in 2005 there were outbreaks in Africa. The source of the outbreaks remains unknown. Viral hemorrhagic fevers are a group of illnesses that are caused by several distinct families of viruses, arena viruses, filoviruses, bunyaviruses and flaviviruses. Some of these cause relatively mild illnesses, while others cause severe life-threatening disease. Examples include Lassa fever, Marburg and Ebola. Because the viruses depend on their animal hosts for survival they are usually restricted to the geographical areas inhabited by germ carrying rats, cotton rats and house mice. These viruses are endemic in areas of Africa.[1] According to the World Health Organization's alert and response director Mike Ryan, 174 people died in the immediate outbreak. Like Africans in cities all over the continent, most people in Angola's capital city of Luanda live in slums or poor townships, where sanitary and medical facilities are poor or non-existent. According to the WHO, low levels of education contributed to spread of the disease. A scarcity of WHO testing facilities complicated the accurate counting of casualties and the number surpassed the outbreak in the Democratic Republic of the Congo in 1998-2000, where 123 people died. This was the first outbreak of Marburg fever in an urban area. A team of fifty international experts went to Angola to help the government contain the disease. An emergency appeal for $3.5 million was launched by the United Nations and the WHO and other agencies sent protective and logistic equipment. The villagers in Uige had to be convinced that WHO workers were not practitioners of witchcraft, vampires, body snatchers, or traffickers of vital organs. At first, this mistrust and superstition may seem strange. This mistrust is understandable when one recalls covert US and Apartheid South African governmental plans to create toxins and diseases to destroy individuals or groups of Africans. In February 2004, the WHO rushed to the Democratic Republic of Congo to help combat the outbreak of pneumonic plague at a diamond mine in a remote north-eastern part of the counrry. Most of the miners and their families fled, raising fears they would spread the disease. If untreated, pneumonic plague can kill within 48 hours. Controlling an outbreak requires tracing and quarantining the infected and their contacts and treating them with antibiotics. WHO officials said more than 60 people died and that several hundred more could have been infected. In September 2004, the WHO urgently launched an appeal for $5.7 million, which was needed "within a few days," to purchase 6 million doses of a new meningitis vaccine before the annual outbreak of meningitis in the so-called "meningitis belt" which stretches from Senegal to Ethiopia. *Glaxo-Smith-Kline,* which developed the vaccine against s new strain of the disease that had emerged in 2001, offered the drug at €1 Euro per dose. *Médecins Sans Frontiéres* promised to buy 1 million doses.

Africans grow up in a culture where learning to suppress pain is part of life. They learn to tolerate pain. Boys are made to feel like less it they wince at the pain of circumcision or they can't stand still in the cold morning air at age 13. The results of some of this handy work are amputated penises and other mutilations. Many young girls must endure the pain and suffering of a clitorodectomy or female circumcision, which involves the quick swipe of a knife as they are held down by the elder women. The results are less than predictable as the knife may not be sharp and could be rusty. It has been used on others that night and the hepatitis passed from one girl to the next is later passed from child to child. The resulting scar at the vaginal entrance often makes these girls unable to have sexual intercourse and thus, once married, they are beaten and displaced by their husbands. It is a cycle of pain leaving both their bodies and psyches scarred. However, they learn to persevere because it is part of being African. Africans learn to persevere. It is routine to perform a tubal ligations without local anesthesia. A woman lies on the table and pretends to not be in pain as the physician put his hand on her belly. There is not enough sedation, but when asked if she wants her something for her pain, she grimaces and says 'no!' The Doctor's Kenyan staff laughs at her as she begins to cry. "She is weak" they say! "She should be able to get through this without more pain medication." She is ridiculed because she hasn't learned to persevere. Suffering is an art Africans have mastered well. They accept that the schools will have no books and that the few dilapidated hospitals built by foreign money will have no water in the water faucets, no drugs in the pharmacy and no electricity to run the broken down x-ray equipment. According to the United Nations, there is a direct link between malnutrition and HIV-infection.

Simon Robinson, of *Time* Magazine's European bureau, provides a vivid description of the painful decisions of survival that individuals Africans confront daily. The Alupe sub-district hospital in western Kenya is like most hospitals in Africa; patients wait on wooden benches or lean against the yellow and blue-painted concrete walls. Insects and small lizards crawl out of cracks in the floors, up wooden beams and onto the underside of the corrugated iron roofing. In the midday heat, mothers jostle their crying babies. The patients arrive on the backs of bicycles, in taxis or in rattling old buses. Many others stayed at home, unable to afford the fare, the patient's share of the operation's cost (between $3.50 and $7), or the time away from the fields. "Many people fear the bills so they tend to stay at home," says Bramwell Wafula, a nurse. "It's a hard decision, but in rural areas people know that if they take their child to the hospital the family will starve."

Some believe that illnesses are caused by curses. "Some have to be brought here by force," says George Matete, who, as head of the Kenya Trypanosomiasis Research Institute, studies African sleeping sickness. "But even if you get them here, if they've been told by relatives that they are going to die they may just give up." On the final morning of his stay, a missionary surgeon lectures local staff on forearm injuries, covering everything from fractures to telling a patient that a limb must be amputated. You have to ask yourself: "Is my patient able to understand and accept the outcome?". Such concern for a patient's mental state is an integral part of medical practice around the world. In rural Africa it is a luxury.

Patients must often provide their own medication and often share the limited bed space. Medicines are in short supply and patients are often prescribed a drug that they have to buy themselves at a chemist in Busia, which is 9 kilometers away down a dirt road. "It's a daily battle," notes Jackton Kisivuli, the medical officer in charge of the hospital. Within two hours they will treat 46 patients. During the three-day surgical safari at Alupe, a former leprosy hospital, not far from the Ugandan border, they perform 28 operations, varying from straightening malformed bones to removing a breast lump. Consultations are brief by western standards, but patients in rural Africa are lucky to see a doctor at all. According to the World Bank, there is just one doctor practicing for every 10,000 Kenyans. In the US the ratio is 25 per 10,000, in Germany, 35.

AMREF foundation is a Nairobi-based non-governmental organization that provides health care to some of the most remote areas in Eastern and Southern Africa. Founded in 1957 by three western surgeons, the African Medical and Research In addition to providing a regional flying doctor service, The organization's efforts were recognized and awarded the $1 million Conrad N. Hilton Humanitarian Prize, the world's richest humanitarian award.

Annual public and private health spending in Kenya totals a mere $8 a person compared to nearly $1,500 in the U.K. or over $4,000 in America. The story in other African countries is similar or worse. Nigeria spends $5 a person on health. Ethiopia spends just $3, while Tanzania, which has fewer than one hospital bed per 1,000 people, spends nine times more on servicing its national debt than it does on providing basic health care for its citizens. In Burundi, patients unable to pay for their care are often detained in the hospital or their treatment is terminated.

The scenario is worsened by the fact that Africa's health care human resources are diminishing. African health care is undermined by the "poaching" of nurses and doctors by the United States and Europe. The Physicians for Human Rights reports that the public-health care of most sub-Saharan African countries suffer significant shortages of health professionals because hospitals in Europe and the United States have lured many trained African doctors and nurses with prospects of higher wages and better working conditions. According to the report, 50 percent of medical school graduates in Ghana emigrate within five years of qualifying to practice and 75 percent leave after ten years. Zimbabwe trained 1200 doctors during the 1990s, but only 360 of those were there still in 2001. There were 5,334 doctors trained in African medical schools practicing in the US in 2002. The flow of African nurses and pharmacists to the West has also risen. Ghana and Zimbabwe offer financial incentives to retain their medical professionals. The benefits include subsidized mortgages and car loans." We have to find ways of keeping health care workers in their countries," says Jim Kim, director of HIV/Aids for the World Health Organization. In Botswana, the migration of nurses to UK is a problem. Botswanan Minister of Health, Lesego Motsumi notes, that despite having adopted a code of practice forbidding National Health Service from recruiting nurses from Africa, they leave to work in private British nursing homes.

Much of Africa is fighting what can be termed "the other war on drugs," the fight against the trade in illegal medicines. By the end of the millennium, Nigerians were among the world's most frequent victims of counterfeit drugs. Counterfeit drugs yield a faster return of capital to pharmaceutical criminal enterprises and don't occupy much shelf space. Nigeria's reputation for producing counterfeit pharmaceuticals is so bad, neighboring states refuse to import medicines that have crossed Nigeria's borders. A 2001 analysis of 2,060 drug samples taken from large wholesale markets, where most medicines are easily purchased, revealed that 62 percent were not registered with Nigeria's National Agency for Food and Drug Administration and Control (Nafdac). These included: multi-vitamins, injectable ketamine (an anesthetic); phenylbuzatone (a painkiller banned in Nigeria because of its severe side effects); *Gynotab* (vaginal tablets that failed laboratory quality tests); *Tamoxifen* (a powerful treatment for breast cancer) and *Viagra*. Among the counterfeit drugs available in Lagos' Idumota market are antibiotics, anti-malarial drugs, painkillers and asthma treatments. Many, if not most, of the legal drugs have false expiration dates. They are not stored at the specified temperature and are sold by illiterate street hawkers who often administer the wrong drug.

According to Nafdac director-general, Dora Akunyili, the worst counterfeiters s are the hardest to target: "The drug people were like gods here. Since independence, they became progressively entrenched and terrorized everyone unchallenged. Outside oil, there's no business as lucrative as drugs." After taking the job she was constantly threatened with arson and assassination. She angered powerful people by reprimanding *Nestlé* for importing out of date baby milk. She closed the bakery of a former president's wife for using a carcinogenic bread-enhancing chemical. She even terminated the contract with one of President Obasanjo's farms for importing chemicals without a permit. She's fired 300 of the 3,000 Nafdac staff members stating that: One of her directors suggested we stop posting men to the ports and drug registration department because the men were too tempted and women were less corrupt. She was guarded by ten armed men, two of whom followed her physician husband. Her children were sent to study in the US, following the attempted to kidnapping of her son. After an assassinations attempt in 2003, Foudeh Darwish, the managing director of *AfrabChem,* a Lebanese manufacturer of antibiotics and other drugs, joined with other drug companies to provide Dora Akunyili with a bullet-proof BMW. "I would never do her job," said Darwish. "It's too dangerous."[2]

Each day is a long one for the medical staff at Saint Mary's hospital in Nairobi. Over twelve hours, they will treat over 1,000 people for myriad maladies that are unmanageable to western medical practitioners, and they do so without the medicines and technology commonly used by their western counterparts. People travel from all over the country to visit the facility; which is far superior to the Kenyatta and Nairobi national hospitals. Kikuyu, Masai, Luo, Kipsigis, Muslims and Christians; arrive seeking treatment for their chief complaint pain, from a missionary facility that will seek to relieve both their physical suffering spiritual pain. They will each receive one diagnosis, and one "halafu" or treatment of an additional complaint. On the second floor of the hospital, a boy no more than four or five years old lies on his knees and elbows, his badly burned buttocks and entire waist area is elevated to avoid the pain of contact. Despite his pain, he does not complain. Like the others, he is only here because can no longer tolerate his acute or chronic pain.

A young man enters Dr. Michael Johnson's examination room with a badly swollen hand. He claims the injury was sustained during a robbery. There are broken bones in his hand, the pain is treated and he will wear a sling for a few weeks.

A Somali woman is unable to swallow due to a tumorous growth in her throat. She is told that radiotherapy will burn her lungs and heart and that surgery will result in certain death. The best treatment available is the insertion of tube down her throat to her stomach that will circumvent the tumor and allow her to eat and gain weight.

A man pushes his brother into the office in a wheelchair. He suffers from a spinal tumor which originated in the prostrate. Suffering severe pain in his legs, he wears a colostomy bag to collect his waste. He is not hyper-reflexive (no reflex response), so a CAT-scan is recommended. The $200 cost for the procedure precludes such diagnosis. His brother, a truck driver, will have to find additional work because as the Xhosa of South Africa say "Asinimali" (we have no money). The Dr. will seek to find work for the walking brother so that he can pay for the treatment.

Six-year-old Jonathan's parents bring him to have the burn injuries to his face and head in sustained a bus accident examined.

Walter, described by hospital staff as a recurring "nuisance patient," comes in with a case of constipation and hemorrhoids. His treatment should be easy, the doctor tells him to eat some mangoes, bananas, and drink two liters of water per day. Even though he is told it will reveal nothing, he insists upon having another unnecessary x-ray.

A mother and daughter who have been referred by a Muslim agency, the Social Service League, come in with the most sullen faces. The mother's histology includes an ulcerated lip and vitiligo, (loss of pigmentation). She complains of a itching all over. A steroid cream prescribed to alleviate her suffering.

The next woman suffers from a calcium problem because her body produces too much thyroid supply hormone (TSH). The doctor schedules surgery and tells her to continue to her medication. Kenya's rich volcanic soil grows vegetables which can contribute to increased TSH levels.

Manute, a Sudanese refugee who fled to Kenya through Ethiopia, has not seen his family in six years. He complains of constant inexplicable stomach pain. In the Kenyan refugee camp he is allocated 15 kilos of maize, wheat, and flour every fifteen days by the UN Refugee Commission. The doctor suspects Manute's pain may be largely psychological.

A 30 year-old woman with a badly swollen leg and infected knee requires admission and antibiotics. This will cost $3000 Kenyan shillings, less than $30 US. Her suffering is visible as she considers the choice between saving her leg and feeding her family. She weeps in fear.

The next woman complains of the pain, and it is revealed that her bile ducts are badly clogged. Dr. Johnson suspects she has more than stones blocking her bile ducts because her eyes are so jaundiced. He sends her for tests.

Benedetta Kisike, an intelligent, dignified, handsome, but poor woman, complains of intense stomach pain. Many Kenyan women are victims of sexual predators. Their beauty and their poverty make them vulnerable to sexual exploitation and rape by relatives, teachers and strangers alike. She has thus far survived her beauty.

Accompanied by his cousin, a young man with a soccer-ball sized tumor on the right side of his face, a "mandibula mass," struggles in. This is his second facial tumor. The first was removed a few year s ago he says and this new tumor has been growing for sixteen months. Dr. Johnson seems concerned about but not surprised by this fact. The patient has no paperwork with him concerning previous diagnosis and treatment. There is an x-ray of this facial tumor, but he has left it at home. After all, the doctor should know what the problem is and how to fix it. He and his cousin go home to retrieve the x-rays and return just before the hospital closes it doors for the day. The doctor tells him that he can remove the tumor, but that there is a high-probability he will bleed to death during the operation. The surgery will cost 10,000 Kenyan Shillings and the hospital bed 350 shillings per day. At this point, money is less of a concern than life to the boys and they say they are willing to purchase blood for the surgery. The doctor tells them that blood availability is less a factor than blood loss, and schedules surgery.

John Ayoti enters the office accompanied by his daughter. His expensive MRI scan reveals some spinal damage due to a disc squeezing his spinal cord. The doctor examines the X-ray and finds something eating away his L4 vertebrae. In consultation with his colleague, the diagnosis could be tuberculosis, but they suspect cancer. They tell him the news and John and his daughter exchange a glance of hope and misery.

A young man follows with complaints of stomach pain when he drinks hot tea or puts pressure on his stomach. His self-diagnosis is that he has an ulcer, they run in his family, and he insists on an x-ray. The doctor tells him an x-ray would reveal nothing and that an endoscopy is required. The young man persists in his demand for an x-ray. The doctor tells him he will not waste his money on an x-ray. The doctor suspects constipation and tells him to eat more mangoes, bananas and to increase his intake of clean water. He leaves, angry that he did not get the treatment he dictated. Contaminated water is the primary of stomach ulcers here.

A seventeen year-old girl with an intestinal cyst is diagnosed with what is commonly called "Sheep shit's" disease spread from the fecal matter of sheep to dogs and humans.

Twenty year-old grace delivered a still born baby who eroded her vagina into her bladder. She constantly leaks urine and will likely die soon

A mother and father bring in their one-year boy old with a badly infected his leg re-to have it examined. It is not healing well and they are told who will return on for another follow up. Each time possible or certain death is an issue, the doctor takes an opportunity to treat the patient and the spirit through prayer. Christian, Muslim, and Animist alike, they join him in prayer and seem to leave the room comforted despite the prognosis.

This is the patient, a suffering people and continent whose suffering many prefer to ignore. A people enriched by nature but impoverished by slavery, colonialism, corruption and globalization. Their misery is multiplied by the millions of impoverished people across the continent in orphanages, rural villages, slums and shanty-towns. They have been sentenced to poverty, pain and death so that we might enjoy cheaper, beef, tea and coffee, drive more technologically advanced vehicles, wear diamonds, access to affordable health care, communicate at accelerated speeds, and develop more destructive and accurate deadly weapons systems.

We visit the University of Nairobi Hospital and Medical School, which trains most of Kenya's physicians and provides government subsidized health care. The multi-story complex surges with pedestrian traffic as thousands of patients and their family-members, medical students, nurses, doctors and visitors seek their appointed destinations. The halls are dreadfully crowded and the smell of death fills the air. We walk rapidly for anyone recognizing Dr. Michael Johnson will request an immediate expert consultation and as the former chief surgical consultant, he finds it difficult to deny such requests. A security guard randomly stops the odd person walking with insufficient deliberate purpose. A few people wait for the elevator doors to open the stairwells are literally crawling with sullen and silently faces filing down. Dr. Johnson notes that he always avoids the elevators because should the power fail, as it does several times a day, one could spend hours trapped in the elevator and as a result of the trauma, have to be rushed to the emergency room. He is recognized by two medical students, he inquires into their studies and classes and their well-being.

The tour includes a visit to the pediatrics wards which covers two floors. Each room has 10-30 children. Thus, there are hundreds of children and their mothers sharing beds. Ninety students are on rotation in one years' class of medical students. The children suffer from all types of illnesses. They and their parents are suffering but not smiling. They have long waited and the medical staff is exponentially overwhelmed by their numbers. The emergency room overflows with victims of trauma in acute pain, burst appendices, victims of traffic accidents, severe burns, rape victims beating victims, stabbings victims and many broken bones. There are not enough doctors or enough medicine. There is no health insurance because these are the poor, the physically broken and their families. Many face immediate and irreversible decisions of life and death. This suffering has negative implications for Africa's future. The poor health conditions prevailing on the continent raise labor costs and discourage foreign investment.

Medical training in Africa focuses on fixing the patient. Physicians learn to treat illness and *dis-ease*. They do not have the luxury of the specialized western liberal arts curricula of religion, philosophy, ethics, psychology, politics, sociology and family medicine by which to inform their practice of medicine. Later that evening, Dr. Johnson invites two students to discuss their studies and curricula. Their spiritual growth is also part of his mission. After sharing with him the nature and difficulty of their course work he uses Biblical text to explore questions about hypothetical scenarios involving life choices of euthanasia, resuscitation death and reacting to family and patient concerns. How do you tell someone that he or she or a loved one will likely die soon? How do you tell them to put their personal affairs in order How do you counsel someone considering euthanasia choices? Is it the family's will? Is it the patients will? Is it God's will? What can they tell the dying and their relatives about Christ or Muhammad that will prepare them for death? The students whisper their answers, for they fear responding incorrectly. They have been largely taught by rote method and such abstract thought about existential and spiritual issues makes them uncomfortable. Dr. Johnson prays with them for their families and asks them to bring something they know of how their elders traditionally death with death. They look puzzled, as if they have been so long estranged from their traditions they do not know of which he speaks.

Diagnosing a Continent

A useful diagnosis must include the patient's biological and psychological strengths and weaknesses. Certain questions and issues must be explored such as:

1. What are the patient's psychological strengths and weaknesses?
2. How do the historical, social and cultural structure(s) impact current structures?
3. What proportion of people are immigrants, refugees, nationals and non-state nations?
4. What roles have the media and missionaries played on the African self-image?
5. How great is Africa's addiction to foreign aid?
6 What is the nature of the co-dependency syndrome on NGO's and Missionaries?
7. Where does the patient place the *Locus of Control,* internally or externally?
8. What impact did the suppression of national institutions and their replacement with culturally incompatible patterns of governance, worship and consumption have on the psychological trauma?
9. What basic medicines to resolve Africa's life-threatening acute and long-term chronic pain are available? They are Africa's people, resources, plant and animal life and precious minerals. Can they be utilized effectively to serve African development goals?

Journalist, Martin Mbugua Kimani asked; does this reflect the state of traditional healing in Africa? Is African pain and suffering rooted in nature and not the social domain? Is it inexorable and elementary? Is the African befuddled by politics because politics consists of actions driven by the innate conviction that circumstances and destiny can be changed? Is the solution to this pain and suffering and the locus of control in the hands of western humanitarian sentiments, missionary, and NGO intervention? [3] Africans have embraced western modernity at the cost of their own spiritual and cultural well-being. The Nigerian health insurance and hospital management company, Hygeia, operates a high-tech clinic called the Lagoon Hospital, where white coated doctors traverse the immaculate sanitized corridors. Most Nigerians cannot afford to be treated there. Most of Africa's health care services cater to the elite, while neglecting the impoverished millions.

African death through disease and violence is beamed into western living rooms as a function of humanitarian outreach. The world knows of this suffering via the BBC. Sir Trevor McDonald a British journalist noted for his professional integrity hosted a documentary using Joseph Conrad's racist title 'Heart of Darkness' for the purpose of soliciting public contributions to help UK charities in the Africa. The documentary followed a young English volunteer at a humanitarian camp for Darfur's refugees. It showed wrinkled bags of bones; withered breasts, hungry mouths; glassy eyes caked with flies and hands extended in silent supplication.

Another channel reports the story of a 15 year-old rape victim who recounts how her father was killed in front of her and she was continuously raped by three men for eight hours. The interviewer nods sadly and probes for more gory details. She said that she wants to be helped by the people of the UK. However, this answer is not sufficiently graphic to solicit pledges of financial support from the viewing audience. Rosita Chibrolee of Mozambique became famous for being born in a tree during the floods. Six-month old Liketsu of Lesotho became famous for being cradled on television by Prince Henry, after she had been raped by an HIV positive man on the advice of a witch doctor.

In December 2007, the World Bank's International Finance Corporation planned to coordinate a $1 billion dollar package of debt and equity designed to strengthen Africa's private health sector. Supported by the Bill and Melinda Gates Foundation, the IFC's strategy reflects a belief that donors, health insurers, medicine distributors and clinics should be supported in fighting Africa's diseases. An IFC study showed that half of the funding, provision and distribution of healthcare in sub-Saharan Africa is conducted by the private sector which serves poor and rich as well as urban and rural areas. The report predicts that healthcare expenditure in the region would increase from $16.7 billion in 2005 to $35.4 billion by 2016. It estimates that another $25-30 billion was needed for infrastructure such as clinics, warehouses and manufacturing facilities.[5]

The IFC launched an effort to attract foreign investors and expand private medical services for the poor in Africa. Advocates of private sector provision of affordable health care point to the R-Jolad clinic in the Gbagada neighborhood of Lagos, Nigeria. The IFC reports that about half of the health expenditure on the continent has already been captured by an array private sector providers. Nigeria's R-Jolad clinics and Hygeia health insurance may provide models for other African countries. Similar to Health Maintenance Organizations coverage plans in the US, subscribers pay into the Hygeia plan. Hygeia signs contracts with hospitals which treat its members at one of its three sites or at some 300 clinics in its network. The hospitals benefit because the contracts guarantee a steady flow of patients and payments. The Nigerian government contracted Hygeia to insure its workers and 115,000 state employees. Hygeia is owned by family members and local insurance companies. The Dutch government purchased a 20 percent stake in the company, and subscribed about 120,000 new members who could not afford annual premiums between $100-$500. It is hoped that this pilot project will spread across the continent.[6] The International Medical Group in Uganda operates 10 profitable clinics throughout the country and a 100 bed hospital in Kampala. The hospital funds half of its budget for its non-profit work. In short, millions of uninsured Americans should be able relate to a health care systems where one's life or death may depend on whether family and friends can raise enough money to pay for treatment.

1.http://www. Wickipedia HPA-Infections Viral Hemorrhagic Fever.htm

2. Andrew Jack. 'A dose of courage,' The *Financial Times*, April 7-8, 2007, pp 19-20.

3. Martin, Mbugua Kimani, "Of Darfur and Western Navel-gazing" *Iko Magazine*, October-December 2004. pp. 16-17.

4. Andrew Jack, 'Funding sought for Africa's private health sector, *The Financial Times*, December 7, 2007, p. 3.

5. Matthew Green and Andrew Jack, 'The fatal cost of illness in Africa," *The Financial Times*, Dec, 18, 2007. p.8.

2: The Chief Complaint: Impoverishment

In a book published in 1924, *The clash of color: A study in the problem of race*, Basil Matthews wrote: "The white man owes the soil of Africa and the laboring hands of the black "an inexhaustible catalogue of necessities, ranging from the cup of coffee or cocoa, the box of chocolates and the bunch of bananas on the dinner table, to the timber for office furnishings, the ivory on knife handles and billiard balls and rubber on balls and tires, the leather for shoes, bags, and jackets, and much of the gold used as currency." Will this debt be paid? Chinua Achebe provides one key to the problem noting that: "Because the white man has both the yam and the knife, he refuses to call for price indexation and thereby guarantees unequal exchange." [1] In other words, the African has little power to negotiate.

Kibera, a massive Nairobi slum, is one of the largest in Africa. Within its' boundaries live three percent of Kenya's population. We visited Kibera to administer health care to an orphanage and to the children of the slum. From the high road the slum is a vision of corrugated metal roof tops that comprise a self-enclosed small city. The residents of these chicken wire and mud huts pay rents to occupy this squalor. They are plagued by hunger, disease, rats and criminals. Despite their impoverishment, these people carry themselves through the trash strewn streets, open sewers and mud trenches running with human and animal feces with great dignity. The absence of indoor toilets and the absence of insecurity in the slum has necessitated the phenomena of the "flying toilet." Since there are no sidewalks, in the evening while walking past windows, one risks being hit with tossed human waste. Fear of venturing to an outside facility at night requires wrapping human waste in paper and tossing it through an open window. One in five children here is an Aids orphan. Many children are now the head of household. If they grow up, the boys will likely become scavengers and the girls will turn to prostitution.

In Guinea-Bissau, one of the world's poorest countries, the poor are truly getting poorer. One of the bottom countries, according to Human Development Index (HDI) rankings, the country has suffered repeated political crisis, troubled relations with aid donors, chronic backlogs in paying state employees and insignificant savings investment. Mangos literally fall from the trees but the only mango juice for sale in Guinea-Bissau is imported from the Netherlands.[2] As elsewhere in Africa, mothers sleep two to a bed in the hospitals central maternity ward and the fire department often has no water to combat blazes. For example, according to the government's figures, poverty rates have increased since 2002, with the proportion of the people living on less than $2 per day rising from 64.7 to 65.7 percent and those living on less than $1 per day rising from 20.8 to 21.7 percent.[3] A 2005 UN report described Guinea-Bissau's economic symptoms as a "structural emergency," a result of having had "a dysfunctional and weak state, bad and inefficient governance, a fractured political elite and a highly divided and interventionist military..[4]

Guinea-Bissau's infrastructure was destroyed in the civil war. The 9,000-strong military force is notoriously poorly paid, housed and equipped. The defense minister calls army conditions "almost inhuman", and a foreign expert described the army barracks as "easily the worst I have ever seen."[5]

The process of impoverishment has not impoverished all Africans. Many Africans have grown rich in the impoverishment process. The huge development gap, parasitic economic relations, cancerous corruption, religious and ethnic conflict, military spending, debt, unfair trade regulations are all factors perpetuating their economic reality. The result for far too many is impoverishment. Despite reduced US aid, most African countries made progress during the 1990s, with average economic growth rates of 4 percent between 1994 and 1999. However, forty-five percent of sub-Saharan Africans still live on less than $1 dollar a day. In 2000, thirty-three of the countries categorized as Highly Indebted Poor Countries (HIPC) by the IMF were sub-Saharan states. The debt of African countries increased from $234 billion in 1990 to $288 billion in 1996 and $360 billion by 2005.

Economic Marginalization

African states inherited rules of law established by Western international conferences and treaties; that pre-exist their status as nation-states. Only European states participated at the Congress of Vienna. However, Ottoman representatives attended the Paris Peace Conference of 1856. Chinese delegates took part in the 1870s creation of the Universal Postal Union, the International Institute of Agriculture, and the Association for the Reform and Codification of the Law of Nations. The Hague Conference of 1899 brought European Ottoman and Chinese diplomats together with those of Mexico, the United States, Japan, Persian and Siam. At the 1907 Hague Conference forty-four states sixteen were Latin American states including Haiti and the

Dominican Republic. As late as 1935, Italy manipulated Ethiopia's position as a sovereign state by using the rhetoric of the League of Nation's Mandate system distinction between "civilized and "uncivilized" people to justify its invasion of the only sovereign African state.[6]

Throughout history, Africa has played two economic roles making it at times central to and at other times marginal to the world economy. Africa's current economic marginalization is both economic and politic-strategic. In the current era of state and non-state terror and warfare, Africa is important to the major actors in the global economy. The end of the Cold-War served to further marginalize African countries with respect to their strategic importance to the United States and Russia. For example, Africa's per income levels and growth rates declined after the 1973 oil crisis, but its percentage of worldwide official development assistance rose from 17 percent in 1970 to 38 percent in 1991. However, despite the poor global economic climate, other developing countries outperformed Africa. For the period 1982-1992, average GDP growth for Africa was 2.0 percent, for South Asia, it was 5.2 percent; and for East Asia, it was 8.0 percent.

The most startling contrast between Asian and African economic performance was the level and the quality of investment. Africa's investment as a percentage of GDP declined in the 1980s as South Asia continued to increase despite the decades difficult economic conditions. South Asia pursued better economic policies and provided a much more propitious socioeconomic and politico-administrative environment for investment. This disparity is vividly revealed in the comparative rates of return of investment: Africa's fell from 30.7 in the 1960's to 2.5 percent in the 1980's, whereas South Asia's increased slowly but steadily from 21.3 to 22.4 percent in the same period. In 1965, manufacturing accounted for 9 percent of economic activity in Africa, rising to only 11 percent by the late 1980s. As a result, by 1990 there was little interest on the part of major global economic actors in lending or investing in Africa.[7]

In the 1980s, Africa was linked to the global economy in two respects. First, Africa became extremely dependent on the IMF and the World Bank Second, the liberal or neoclassical nature of this economic policy of 'conditionality' pushed the continent to a more intense dependency on integration into the global economy. Both these actions were linked to the ensuing debt crisis. Thus, in 1974 total African debt was an estimated $14.8 billion; by 1992 it was $150 billion, or more than 100 percent of Africa's total GNP. Some referred to this dependency on the IMF and the World Bank as the as the new neocolonialism, intended to design economic reform packages and the resources needed to implement them. Debt would be leveraged into economic policy conditionally-specific economic policy changes in return for borrowed mineral and petroleum resources. The main object was to more fully integrate African economies into the global economy by resurrecting the primary-product export economies that existed at independence and this time making them work "correctly" by creating a more "liberal" political economy.[8]

By the early 1980s, the question was not whether Africa faced a crisis, but what could be done about it. Many African leaders failed to realize just how important Africa was becoming to the world economy and sought to avoid integration into emerging global economic regime. Many sought and still seek shortcuts and quick fixes to their national economic dilemmas. Many responded by railing against the external locus of control and the prescriptions of external actors such as the World Bank and the IMF. Throughout the 1980s and early 1990s, large and small economic reforms were made, but there were few instances of multi-sector, sustained reform. In fact, Ghana and Uganda were the only clear examples and they encountered significant domestic resistance. They were forced to choose between those who disdained any talk of financial discipline and the dogma of monetarism. As the Rawlings regime in Ghana and the Museveni regime in Uganda discovered, neither position provides any guarantees. Policy incentives do not ensure that markets will work well and revenue is imperative.[9] Jerry Rawlings kept his options open by resisting pressure to liberalize politically until he was ready; then he launched a controlled liberalization process. Uganda was the first country to enter the complicated HIPC process.

Africans have long argued that substantial resource flows and debt relief are prerequisites for sustained reform. One of the lessons of Ghana and Uganda is that these are necessary but not sufficient conditions. By the early 1990s, external actors began to realize that increased flows of debt relief would be required for Africa. As this realization sank in, the enormous obstacles to economic reform and the possibility of widespread economic failure became alarmingly apparent. Meanwhile, a larger problem increasingly linking Africa to global economic marginalization emerged. An implicit bargain struck between western countries and African leaders. The provisions of the bargain were that it African countries successfully reformed their economies in a neo-orthodox direction with the help of the IMF and the World Bank, then new international private bank and bond lending and equity plus direct foreign investment would be made available to support and sustain the reform efforts. Proponents of neo-orthodox reform in Africa argued Africa's poor economic track record could be overcome, if Africa provided relatively predictable environments for investment. Michael Camdessus, the managing director of the IMF, called it an "unwritten contract," and in a March 1990 speech stated that:

> Every country has responsibility for its own destiny and the main source of its future posterity lies in its own efforts. Foreign investment and other assistance can only supplement the actions of the country itself...In view of the rapid growth in Africa's debt-servicing burden, strenuous efforts to reduce the debt overhang must continue. For the future, African countries will need to be prudent about their borrowing, both as regards its scale and terms, and be careful to use new resources wisely and efficiently, so that

> they will contribute to growth and external viability...You all know that the Fund also has heavy ongoing responsibilities in the global debt strategy, and new challenges in helping Eastern Europe countries to reform. Despite these demands on our resources, we shall be able to continue to support all African countries that are prepared to persevere with far-reaching reforms and that back up these reforms with financial discipline.[10]

Camdessus' message was clear. The international economic system is based on self-help and resources would flow only to those who helped themselves. By the early 1990s, one or both parties had violated the terms of the contract. The World Bank and the IMF could not reverse the legacy of Africa's history of poor economic performance. Structural shifts in the global economy and nation-state systems made other areas of the world more attractive to investors. This "unwritten contract" was based on carefully constructed rules of economic conditionality that reflected the degree of Africa's marginalization, major changes in the international division of labor and the international political economy. Between 1985 and 1987 for example, President Kenneth Kaunda of Zambia, implemented a half-hearted and unpopular IMF-World Bank economic reform package. Kaunda terminated the program in May 1997 after a series of deadly riots, strikes, and protests, announcing that Zambia would formulate and implement its own reform package without external resources and the conditionality that came with them. The capacity of African states to absorb new resources effectively is easily and often overlooked. Certainly more resources are needed to increase the likelihood of sustained economic reform, but there is a point of marginal utility both politically and technically. Inefficient and redundant programs and renewed rent-seeking are but two negative outcomes, as the post-Kaunda Zambian government of Frederick Chiluba demonstrated. A striking expatriatization, led by Nigerians elites, quietly took place in many African countries. In the mid-1990s, the head of the World Bank noted "the extraordinary fact that there are more expatriate advisors in Africa today then at the end of the colonial period."[11]

By the mid-1980s IMF and World Bank officials began to realize that the stop and go cycles of economic reform were a slow process and that reform would fail unless changes were made in how the programs were designed and implemented. These institutions and their African government proxies became more attuned to the need for the politics of fine tuning and carefully calibrating the instruments, timing, and sequencing of their policy measures with respect to sensitive issues of health, fuel and wages in order to minimize the pain of the socioeconomic and political impact of their structural adjustment programs. One result of IMF structural adjustment and WTO trade liberalization programs is that across Africa, disease, malnutrition and hunger have grown by leaps and bounds.

The policy impact of denying basic daily nutrition to Africa's hungry, while simultaneously using African resources to feed global markets, is but one of the inhumane side effects of globalization. African governments are unable to feed their hungry citizens because this involves making laws, policies and financial commitments that their western benefactors consider "protectionist." From the perspective that it places profit above life and commerce above justice (i.e., international finance capital seeks profit and puts the latter above all else, including social justice), globalization is another form of economic warfare against nature, women, children and the poor. Agent Orange, the military herbicide used to defoliate Vietnam, is now being sprayed on farms in Africa along with *Round-Up* and other poisons. Plants and animals are being genetically engineered, thereby making Africa's fields targets of biological warfare. According to a 1990 report by Pesticide Action Network of North America, life cycles and future food growth are threatened by genetically-engineered, sterile terminator seeds. Who benefits from such parasitic financial arrangements? The volatility of global money markets in part reflects the self-interest that international commercial banks, investment banks, hedge funds and other financiers exercise in manipulating capital.

Oxfam issued a stinging attack on structural-adjustment in early 1993 entitled, *Africa Make or Break: Action for Recovery*,[12] which was complemented by criticism from the Environmental Defense Fund, Development Gap and Christian Aid. Oxfam International and the European Network on Debt and Development (Eurodad) formed a coalition of NGO's from fifteen European countries, funded in part by the European Community. Oxfam boldly declared that IMF reform had failed in Africa and that if the Fund did not undergo reform it should withdraw from Africa. In early 1998, another African renaissance was proclaimed. After three years of continued economic growth, key external actors stated that Africa had "turned the corner" and that growth would continue. President Clinton made his historic trip to Africa. A *Financial Times* headline trumpeted that "Fast Growth Forecast Targets Asia and Africa." *Time* Magazine ran a cover story entitled "Africa Rising: After Decades of Famine and War, Life is Finally Looking Up For Many Africans." The economic realities were quite different. In mid-1998 the IMF noted that real GDP growth for 1990-1994 was 1.6 percent; and for 1995-1997, 4.3 percent. The per capita growth figures for the respective periods were -2.0 and 1.4 percent. The IMF reported that in 1996, twenty-one African countries had growth rates of over 5 percent; and eleven over 7 percent. By October 1998, the *Financial Times* had refined its optimism and reported that the "Renaissance Train Has Been Delayed."[13] The Afro-pessimism and victim blaming continued in a 2000 issue of *The Economist*, which ran a cover story entitled 'The Hopeless Continent'.

Another result of structural adjustment in Africa is the rising level of external debt. In 1998 Africa's long-term debt was $176 billion. Unlike other regions of the world, this was mostly "official" debt owed to major western countries, the IMF and the World Bank. In fact, Africa owed an incredible 6 percent of this to bilateral and multilateral creditors (44 percent and 32 percent respectively), a major indicator of marginalization.[14] The rising debt burden of poor countries was of increasing concern to creditor states and institutions. The structural inequality underscored the emergence of an international underclass of weak states and economies that have been unable to benefit from economic reform and democratization. The Paris Club became the official debt management regime, i.e., the actors, norms, processes and mechanisms which focused around countries unable to service their public and public guaranteed debt.

The Paris Club, a powerful hybrid international financial organization; illustrates much about the evolution of the international political economy and the nature of transnational governance in Africa. The Paris Club is one of the most powerful international organizations affecting the lives of millions of people although technically it does not exist. It is not a formal organization with a charter, legislated set of rules, fixed membership, a large bureaucracy; rather it is described as an ad hoc "forum" of creditor states. Since the 1970s, the Paris Club has been embedded in a complex web of interactions with other important actors of the international political economy including the IMF, the World Bank, regional development banks, consultative groups, the UN Conference on Trade and Development (UNCTAD), the Organization of Economic Cooperation and Development (OECD), the Bank for International Settlements and the private debt rescheduling forum of international banks known as the "London Club".

The Paris Club's innovative debt menu signaled that the major actors of the international debt regime were beginning to recognize the existence of the underlying structural dilemma of bilateral debt. By 1992, the G7 and several NGOs had focused their activities on multinational debt. At the IMF and World Bank annual meetings in Madrid in 1994, the US and Britain proposed that the two institutions conduct a study of multilateral debt. A critical juncture was reached in June 1995 when James Wolfensohn became the ninth president of the World Bank. After visiting Africa, Wolfensohn became more amenable to the views of debtor governments. He was less worried about the financial market consequences of altering the Bank's preferred creditor status; and he needed major policy initiatives to mark his arrival as head of the Bank. He saw debt relief as one of those initiatives and empowered sympathetic elements of the World Bank staff to accelerate working on a new debt initiative. Just before the joint IMF-World Bank 1995 annual meeting, a World Bank staff report was leaked to the *Financial Times*. Many in the NGO community believed the report was leaked by staff opposed to the proposal. The leak galvanized opposition to the plan among the hard line G7 governments and some of their legislatures. Despite support for multilateral debt relief, the US expressed reservations about the cost of the initiative. Planning shifted to a proposal that eventually became the dysfunctional and complicated HIPC mechanism that is the current debt regime.[15]

The effects of these policies have been quite consistent. Budget cuts depressed the effective demand of African economies, which led to declining growth. The implementation of privatization often failed to distinguish which state enterprises may have been strategic in nature and too often accompanied by corruption, and often suffered from the hostile acquisition of domestic industries by foreign capital with little concern for maintaining local employment or production levels.

Trade, Aid, Debt and Development: The Locus of Control

For many African leaders foreign aid provides an incentive and excuse to maintain the status quo. These leaders are only too happy to continue their roles in the political charade which mortgages their inert and their human resources for debt relief and military assistance packages. Placing the locus of control on forces beyond the control of Africa's political leaders diminishes the impact of decades of failed economic planning, wholesale looting, the manipulation of ethnic conflict, the waging of proxy war and the loss of millions of lives to political repression.[16] Focusing on the external locus of control ignores the pervasive and ubiquitous links between privatization, foreign aid and political corruption.

In 2002, African finance ministers criticized the World Bank's debt relief program for failing to keep step with goals to reduce poverty in some of the poorest African countries. They called for the Heavily Indebted Poor Countries (HIPC) initiative to be brought in line with the UN's Millennium Development Goals, which seek to halve poverty levels by 2015. African governments want the World Bank and donor countries to offer greater debt relief and to extend relief to non-HIPC countries. "It is clear that the HIPC initiative is not working well enough. Only six African countries have reached their completion points and for some of them the debt remains unsustainable;" the ministers observe.

The ministers met in Johannesburg under the aegis of the UN Economic Commission for Africa to seek ways of implementing the New Partnership for Africa's Development (NEPAD), a plan to promote good governance and greater aid and investment flows. The ministers wanted deeper and faster measures of debt relief within the NEPAD framework. At the heart of their debate was a voluntary mechanism of review by African countries of each other's governance and economic policies. Those countries submitting to the review expected to receive benefits from donor countries. Only Ghana and Tanzania submitted to review.[17]

The World Bank HIPC initiative is a package of comprehensive measures to provide developing countries relief from unsustainable debt levels. The initiative, agreed to in 1996, was reviewed in 1998 and was heavily championed by western governments and the anti-poverty activist and U-2 musician, Bono. Under the program debt relief is awarded in return for the implementation of poverty reduction and economic reform. Donor country policies and African political leaders share the blame for Africa's impoverishment. While necessary, debt relief only serves as a palliative that diverts attention from the disease to the symptoms such as arms sales and the mutually corrosive corruption of the free-market-system of capitalist states.

Rodrigo Rato, the managing director of the International Monetary Fund, advocates giving African countries more representation on the board and on the staff of the fund. Rato, after consultations with African finance ministers in Madrid, said he would include proposals for greater African representation in governance reforms that he would present at the September 2006 meeting of IMF directors in Singapore. "Governance reforms are at the heart of the continued legitimacy and effectiveness of the fund;" Rato observed. "No one group will achieve all its priorities, so there will have to be a compromise. But I am confident that we will be able to put forward proposals in September that will be acceptable to all." At the April 2006 IMF spring meeting, a consensus emerged on an ad hoc increase in the representation of China, South Korea, Turkey and Mexico, but there was no agreement on broader reform, with the US supporting wider-ranging options than many European countries. Trevor Manuel, South Africa's finance minister, said the priority of African IMF governors was to arrest the decline in the continent's voice and representation because of Africa's declining share of world economic output. "As Africans, we have an interest in arresting this trend of diminishing African representation on the board. The fight is partly mathematical, and partly political. We are at a serious disadvantage and want a bigger voice for Africa on the IMF executive board;" he declared." Rodrigo Rato promised to address the under-representation of Africans on the staff of the fund in order to make it a "more diverse institution".

After consultations with governors in Europe, Asia and the US, Rato announced that there was a "clear sense among governors that representation on the IMF board needed to reflect changes in the world economy and the need to give low-income and emerging countries bigger representation in the fund". These comments were made the week that the IMF published its latest work highlighting the priority it was giving to multilateral surveillance of global trade imbalances. Its proposal to start negotiations between the US, China, the Euro zone, Japan and Saudi Arabia went before the board that same month. The slimming down of the IMF's article IV bilateral surveillance exercise was scheduled on a trial basis in "non-systemic and stable economies", with the aim of providing "more selective analysis and sharper policy advice".

Foreign Aid Flows

Foreign aid to Africa began at modest levels in the 1960s and rose rapidly during the early 1970s and 1980s. They peaked in the 1990s and have declined steadily since 1994, . In fact the level of aid to Africa in 1997 was equal in real terms to the level of aid in 1983. Every country in Africa received some aid, if only relief assistance. The countries that received the largest amount of aid relative to the size of their economies; were not the same as those receiving the largest overall aid flows. In 1997 the African countries with the largest aid to GNP ratios were São Tomé and Principe (117 percent) Guinea Bissau (71 percent), Rwanda (49 percent), Mozambique (43 percent) and Cape Verde (29 percent). These figures indicate that smaller countries in Africa and elsewhere tend to receive larger amounts of aid relative to the size of their economies, reflecting a tendency on the part of aid donors to provide aid to countries above certain minimum amounts regardless to the size of the country's population. About one-third of all bilateral and multilateral aid to Africa is used to fund social and administrative infrastructure (including education, health, water supply and sanitation) as well as government, civil society and other services. About 15 percent is used to fund activities in agriculture, industry, mining, construction, trade and tourism. The remainder funds a variety of activities, including multi-sector programs and projects, program assistance, debt relief and emergency aid.[18]

Carol Lancaster identifies five purposes for which aid is given. First, aid is to promote development in recipient countries, although ideas about what development is and how to promote it varies. During the 1960s, the focus was on promoting economic growth through funding the expansion of infrastructure, social services and health. In the 1970s the emphasis shifted toward using aid to benefit the poor directly by funding projects in rural areas that addressed "basic human needs" such as primary education, health care, clean water and sanitation i.e., the promotion of "integrated rural development," It was hoped this would enable small farmers to expand their production and income.

Second, states utilize foreign aid as a tool of a diplomacy and foreign policy. During the Cold War, competition between the NATO and the Warsaw Treaty Organization courtiers of the Soviet-bloc, aid was used to secure foreign policy objectives in Africa. The Cold War motivated these states to give aid to Africa as an instrument of "high Politics." For most aid-granting governments, there was also the "low politics" of aid in exchange for particular benefits from the recipient government. These benefits included, for example, votes in the UN or access to prominent government officials. This aid serves as a source of lobbying recipient government officials and is a source of corruption.

A third reason states give aid is strictly for commercial proposes. Aid packages of mixed credits (export credits on relatively hard terms), serve as an inducement for African governments to purchase goods and services from enterprises in donor countries. These packages of mixed credits are often tied to particular projects, such as dam construction, and the import of heavy equipment such as trains or aircraft. Too often they include military equipment and ordnance. The most avid practitioners of aid for commercial advantage have been the French and Italian governments.[19]

The fourth purpose of aid is political and cultural, including the spread of a particular, language, religion or value system. The French have been the most successful at tying aid to the maintenance and spread of language and culture. The fifth reason is aid is used for collective humanitarian purposes: to relieve suffering, promote rehabilitation and recovery in the wake of man-made and natural disasters and to alleviate the suffering of the impoverished. Nearly all donors of aid to Africa provide a portion of their aid for this purpose.

African political leaders have their own motives for accepting foreign aid. It is a symbol of development and thus very important to the many African governments whose legitimacy and support rest on promises of economic prosperity. Additionally, these leaders place a priority on issues of security and nominal sovereignty. Foreign aid provides additional resources to governments, thereby freeing up domestic resources to be used for security purposes. In several cases donors provided governments with economic assistance for just this purpose. It is certain that many African governments exploited the "fungibility" (i.e., substitutability) of foreign aid for domestic resources to fund additional military expenditures or other activities related to their personal political security. Under these circumstances, many economists believe aid is in effect financing not the apparent projects or programs to which it is tied but, rather, other activities, such as military expenditures or luxury imports, that are not the purposes for which the aid was intended.[20]

With the decline in diplomatic motives for providing aid and relatively high levels of aid on which many African governments depend, aid donors began to examine the impact of their aid packages on development in the region. In a study conducted by Craig Burnside and David Dollar of the World Bank, the results were not reassuring. They found that: (1) there was little systematic relationship between aid and development (this had been observed in other econometric studies of aid and development); (2) aid was effective where good policies, defined in terms of fiscal and monetary policies, were in place; (3) aid was not effective in persuading African governments to adopt good economic policies.[21]

NGO's and Debt Relief

During the past two decades several hundred religious, humanitarian, labor and environmental nongovernmental organizations (NGO's) have focused on the issue of debt and its negative impact on millions of impoverished people. Their activities revolve around a moral discourse and employ powerful concepts of justice, representation, accountability, transparency and equity. It challenges the notion of who should have authority over such issues in the global community, calls for intervention to rectify injustices and the end to what is considered blatant exploitation of the poor. [22]

Pop star-producer, Sir Bob Geldof, found himself at the center of the media's attention when he stated that he was "profoundly" bored by Africa. In a *Radio Times* magazine interview he stated "the pace of change is far too slow and Africans excuse their own complicity in exactly the same way as our politicians." Geldof said he had been as blunt with African leaders as he was "with our lot" but that he "knew the consequences of saying 'fuck off', so I'm more patient." He expressed his frustration with being "Mr. Bloody Africa" and with society's confusion about the roles of celebrities and politicians. His remarks followed the appearance of a string of celebrities and politicians at the World Economic Forum in Davos, Switzerland, campaigning to combat African poverty including; Sharon Stone, Angelina Jolie, Richard Gere, U2 singer Bono, Thabo Mbeki, Tony Blair, Bill Gates and former President Bill Clinton.

Geldof did much to bring the suffering of Africans to the world's attention with projects such as the "Live Aid" concert which brought food relief to famine-stricken Ethiopians. Geldof is a member of the Africa Commission, the high-profile initiative established by Tony Blair to promote African development. "Who's interested if the leader of Niger goes on *Newsnight*. Its get Geldof," he said of a popular BBC current affairs program. Of course, his comments drew criticism form South Africa where some characterized them as "racist." "Here's a Tarzan who trapezes into the continent to save it with his good works," said Francis Kornegay of the Center for Policy Studies, a Johannesburg-based think tank. There was truth in Geldof's comments, which made them all the more distasteful to African leaders and painful for Africans. Stronger governance, an improved infrastructure and access to long-term capital are clearly needed.

For many Americans, Africa and the issues of African Development are not foreign policy priorities. The end of the Cold war signaled a decline in Africa's geopolitical importance to the West. Development aid declined from $32 per capita in 1990 to $19 in 1998. During the 1990s, India and China made substantial progress in the reduction of poverty. According to United Nations Development Program director, Mark Malloch Brown, a significant number of hard core of countries ended up further behind. Fifty-four countries (many from Africa and the former Soviet bloc) grew poorer, and 21 saw a decline in their human development indicators such as life expectancy, education and daily caloric intake. Globalization has more than tripled international trade.

In June 2005, British finance minister, Gordon Brown announced that the G8-Britain, Japan, US, Canada, France, Italy, Germany and Russia-would cancel all multilateral debt to eighteen of the world's poorest countries upon their completion of an IMF initiative. The $40 billion G8 offer is enough to wipe out debts owed to international organizations by: Burkina-Faso, Ethiopia, Ghana, Guyana, Honduras, Madagascar, Mali, Mauritania, Mozambique, Nicaragua, Niger, Rwanda, Senegal, Tanzania, Uganda and Zambia. The completion point is the date when the scheme's debt write-off becomes effective. Analysts said the debt stock remained too large and that canceling the entire debt was preferable. "We need the entire debt written off to make an impact on economic growth and development and to accelerate spending in social sectors like health and education;" said Isaak Ngoma, of the think-tank, Economics Association of Zambia. In return, African governments would use the aid wisely, stamp out corruption and promote democracy.

The G8's record of keeping promises has been comprehensively analyzed, but exactly one year after the June 10 meeting in Gleneagles Scotland, a debt-forgiveness agreement was signed. "Experts" stated that the African record of promises had fallen short of expectations. African governments made individual and collective promises to improve the conditions of their people, pledging action through forums and the African Union. They noted that it is hard to conclude that a renaissance of freedom, honesty and prosperity is sweeping the continent. Richard Dowden, the director of the Royal African Society, went as far as to state: "We can't really say that the whole of Africa is going the right way." There was concern that countries close to the G8 process and to the UK (Ethiopia, Kenya and Uganda) are regressing on these issues. On the other hand, countries which were already governing well, Ghana Mozambique and Tanzania, continue to do so. Dowden noted that a sense of collective responsibility has grown and that: "Presidents are much more willing to interfere in each other's business."[23] Judging Africa collectively rather than nation-by nation is a limited measurement of development progress. Or, as Bono, the activist/rock star is fond of saying: "We must be careful not to keep treating a continent like a country."

Speaking of Africa's mixed performance on the G8 Africa compact, Geldof stated: "There's the good, the OK and there's the ugly." The "ugly" piece to which he referred was the doomed round Doha trade talks scheduled for July 2006, where there was no basic agreement on what would constitute a good trade deal for poor countries. The good to which Geldof refers is the debt relief granted to the 18 poorest qualifying countries. The "ok" is the uncertain aid which the G8 promised to increase by $50 billion a year by 2010, half of which was to go Africa. The 33 day war in Lebanon, the ongoing and intensified civil-war in Iraq and the prospect of a protracted and expanded Middle East conflagration precluded any non-security related US and UK commitments to Africa. The general consensus was that both Africa and the G8 countries are off track to meet specific aid targets by 2010.[24] "The entire system is dysfunctional and there is nothing the WTO can do about it;" observed Susan Sechler, US director for trade and development at the German Marshall Fund. "It used to be that you first got a deal at the WTO and then used it to discipline domestic agricultural spending. That doesn't work any more, partly because developing countries in the WTO won't accept a post-dated check."[25]

The promises made at the Gleneagles summit were broken at the June 2007 G8 talks. To the disappointment of African leaders, the G8 leaders refused to be specific on when they would meet pledges made to boost development assistance by $50 billion by 2010 at the Gleneagles summit. Senegalese president, Abdoulaye Wade, expressed this disappointment with the G8 and stated that Senegal had "not received an extra dollar in aid since the Gleneagles pledge" and Bono condemned the G8 for 'broken promises.[26]

By December 2007, the rising price of petroleum had wiped out the benefits promised African countries at the Gleneagles Summit, and threatened a repeat of the Africa's debt crisis. An International Energy Agency (IE) survey of 13 non-oil-producing African countries, including South Africa, Ghana, Tanzania and Senegal, found that the increase in the price of oil was equivalent to 3 percent of their combined gross domestic product. This is more than the sum of debt relief and aid received by the countries, which have a combined population of 270 million, of whom 104 million live on less than $1 a day. Senegalese President, Abdoulaye Wade, said: "There is a growing understanding that the most urgent need in Africa today is the challenge of providing affordable energy," and he warned that the crippling oil prices threatened to provoke "unrest and violence" in Africa. [27]

Fair Trade? The Banana War

In his 2007 address to the Africa-US business summit in Capetown, Ugandan president, Yoweri Museveni, caustically described the record of western businesses in Africa by noting that Uganda received $1 per kilogram of coffee it grows before the beans are roasted and ground in London and then sold for $20. "For each 1 kilogram of coffee we are donating $19. We have been doing this for a long time. But we are fighting it. We are going to change." Uganda's unfair trade experience with the West is common.[28]

American cotton farmers have long resisted the call for fair trade from cotton-producing African countries. Just before US treasury secretary, Paul O'Neill went on a tour of Africa with Bono, the White House backed a farm bill that further distorted global agriculture and hurt African farmers. He advised farmers to dig more wells and to plant better tomatoes while ignoring the hypocrisy of US trade policy.[29] A meeting of the WTO's goods council in October 2004 failed to produce an agreement over how to help African and Caribbean countries. The US moved to secure restrictions on Chinese imports into the US market while continuing to subsidize US farmers. The suspension of the Doha round of trade talks removed some of the pressure for the US to agree to a new farm bill or farm support program.

Africa's share of global exports declined from nearly 5 percent in 1980 to less than 2 percent in 2004. Africa's textile and clothing exports to the US are estimated at $17 billion. But African farmer's manufacturers now struggle to survive competition from China for American markets. Few African farmers are equipped to transform their own cotton into fabric. West and Central African cotton farmers are estimated to be losing $1 billion annually in foreign earnings because exports of subsidized US cotton have squeezed their sales by lowering world cotton prices. US subsidies helped to reduce world cotton prices by fifty percent between 1997 and 2002. Thus, in February 2004, government ministers from a dozen African countries met in Kenya with assistant US trade Representative, Floriezelle Liser to signal their intention to "lobby hard" to secure a White House commitment to push through congress legislation extending the African Growth and Opportunities (AGOA).

AGOA, one of the latest instruments of globalization, spelled out a new US economic policy for Africa. AGOA authorized the US government to pursue a policy that promotes stable and sustainable economic growth in Africa through trade, investment, debt-reduction, technical assistance, and infrastructure development. Promoted as trade-oriented legislation to promote trade-led African development, AGOA is likely to boost the exports sectors only of the African countries eligible for participation.

AGOA emerged as legislation by liberal Democratic Representative Jim McDermott from Washington state and members of the Congressional Black Caucus (CBC), who portrayed it as a way to ensure Africa its share of US trade and investment. It was then sold as a bipartisan plan and developed in conjunction with conservative Illinois Republican Representative Phil Crane, one of the bills principle supporters. Republicans were comfortable signing on because the bill strongly supported US exports and corporate investment. Sponsors of the draft legislation presented the it as a "paradigm shift" from aid to trade. During the legislative session, American companies with interests in Africa joined African ambassadors, Clinton administration officials, and congressional backers to lobby for AGOA. But there was growing resistance from critics who opposed the bill's simplistic pro-market bias and from textile state representatives, who argued that import quota reductions would ultimately hurt US manufacturers.[30]

These issues divided the CBC. Some CBC members supported the bill hoping it would give Africa a larger share of global markets by promoting "equal opportunity" among exporting nations, while others saw little benefits for ordinary Africans who argued the emphasis on free-market policies would result in even more economic damage to their fragile markets. CBC Chair, Maxine Waters commented during the floor debate, that both proponents and opponents should recognize that the bill is neither the "best thing nor the worst thing" that could happen to Africa.

AGOA eligibility requires African states to restructure their domestic economies and to make them more market driven by adopting the US practices of market capitalism. With unrealistic hopes of rapid development, Africans are expected to embrace more tightly the consumer patterns of the market-based economy. Moreover, AGOA focuses on opening African markets to US exports not vice versa. If Africans open their markets to US exports and the United States subsequently reduces or eliminates tariffs on African cotton for example; the likely result is that US goods will out compete goods produced in Africa in both price and quality, in both African and US markets. The result, US producers will become dominant in African markets, forcing most African producers into bankruptcy while maintaining their dominant positions in the US economy.

The debate heated up when Jesse Jackson Jr., introduced alternate legislation, the Human Rights Opportunity, Partnership and Empowerment (HOPE) Act, calling on the United States to cancel all approximated $4.5 billion in bilateral debt with sub-Saharan Africa. This provided a positive initiative behind which the critics of AGOA could rally. However, continued division within the CBC left the fate of the two bills unresolved. Neither AGOA nor HOPE provided a viable comprehensive framework for expansion of mutually beneficial US African economic relations. [31]

At a September 2003, World Trade Organization meeting in Cancún, Benin, Burkina-Faso, Chad and Mali, which are among the poorest nations on earth, asked for a timetable eliminating cotton subsidies. The US pays $3.3 billion in subsidies annually to 25,000 American cotton farmers This makes the US the worlds largest cotton exporter, despite high production costs, which are passed on to the American taxpayer. US trade Representative, Robert Zoellick, met with the ministers of the four countries to offer assistance in building their textile and clothing industries.

The Bush administration argued that cotton subsidies should not be treated as a separate issue at the Cancún meeting, but should be part of broader agricultural negotiations of the in the Doha global trade round in Qatar and hoped to persuade the Africans to drop their demands in return for promises of US investment in their budding textile industries. This conciliatory gesture was spurred by the European Unions' Africa Initiative which had recently gained the support of Germany, France, Sweden and the UK. Robert Zoellick cleverly avoided questions about ending US subsidies by stating: "We recognize the importance of cotton to Africa. The African proposal highlights the need for ambitious results in all areas."

For Lesotho, US economic policy in Africa is a disaster. "Two thousand people work here, and unfortunately last week I had to retrench 500 people, because there are no orders;" Boodia Heman, director of the *Ever Unison* Garment factory, said in a recent interview. "The American buyer is not coming to Lesotho to buy." If one buys fleece sweats at *J. C. Penney* or *Hanes* panties anywhere in the United States, there's a likely chance that they were stitched together in Lesotho, in an acre-size garment factory crammed with thousands of frantically working sewing machines. Virtually all of *Ever Unison's* output, 25,000 items of clothing daily, is exported to the United States. [32]

While American shoppers complain of the dollar's fall and an irritating rise in the prices of imported goods, for the people of Lesotho, the impact of the devalued maloti is potentially fatal. Garment makers represent more than 9 in 10 manufacturing jobs in this impoverished nation. Unable to match the prices of foreign competitors and still make a profit, six of 50 clothes factories had to shut down eliminating 5,800 of the 50,000 garment-making jobs. Layoffs claimed at least 6,000 more. Garment workers who might otherwise decide to ride out the dollar's slide; "are starting to realize that they're losing their shirts," said Mark Bennett, who advises the government on textile issues for the nonprofit *ComMark Trust*, based in South Africa. The government stepped in, seeking to resurrect three of the closed factories and offered incentives to others. Those efforts largely depend on the vagaries of the dollar. Most garment manufacturers in Lesotho are foreign-owned. They reported that if the dollar dropped another 20 percent against the South African rand, as some economists predicted, a new wave of factory closings was inevitable.

Actually, the problem is not so much the buyers from America but the drastic drop in the value of the American dollar. In 2002, Lesotho's garment factories had to sell only $56 worth of clothes to stores in the United States to cover the monthly wage of 650 maloti for a sewing-machine operator. By 2005 that same salary consumed $109 in sales. When the dollar is worth 8.5 maloti or more, said Heman, "we break even and we are satisfied." Right now, the weak dollar fetches less than 6 maloti. The dollar could not have shrunk at a worse time for the economies of southern Africa.

In January, China's powerful apparel industry was freed from the international multi-fiber arrangement, which for decades set nation-by-nation quotas and capped its garment exports to the developed world. China, which keeps its currency tightly pegged to the dollar, has thoroughly penetrated African markets. Across southern Africa, industries that depend on American customers or compete with American producers are feeling the effects of the falling dollar. South Africa, which surrounds Lesotho, has lost an estimated 30,000 textile jobs since 2002. In neighboring Swaziland, nearly three in four textile factories report that they have no firm orders. South Africa's fabled gold-mining industry lost 11,000 jobs between January 2003 and June 2004, in part because income from its dollar-denominated exports fell sharply. Botswana's budget tipped from a surplus to a $325 million deficit last year as its dollar income from diamond sales was diluted by a 10 percent rise in its currency, the pula.

All these nations, and nearby Namibia, share a common problem: their currencies are pegged one-to-one to South Africa's rand, which recorded a big rise against the dollar (Botswana's pula is pegged to a basket of currencies dominated by the rand.) The Euro had risen 52 percent against the dollar since February 2002, but the rand, driven by a boom in commodities like gold, had nearly doubled in value. According to Anthony Twine, a senior economic analyst at *Econometrix,* a Johannesburg consultant firm; "The weak dollar is bad economic news for countries that are not on a dollar-parity system." .

On February 2, 2006, the US House of Representatives voted to eliminate some subsidies to cotton farmers. The House repealed the "Byrd Amendment," which gave US companies the duties paid on imports that competed unfairly with their business. The European Commission welcomed the abolition of the Byrd Amendment but was critical of the transition period which was extended until 2007. African countries welcomed this development during the first "Doha round" of global trade talks. Benin, Burkina-Faso, Chad and Mali had threatened to veto a deal unless the US agreed to dismantle the harmful cotton subsidies.[33] After Brazil and Canada secured a WTO investigation of US farm subsidies, which they claim exceeded permitted limits, a panel ruled that the US must do more to eliminate $3-$4 billion dollars in illegal subsidies lavished on US cotton farmers. These subsidies unfairly boosted US exports while depressing prices on world markets hurting poor farmers in Africa and in Latin America.

Banana production is critical to the economic diversification of Cameroon and the Cote d'Ivoire. They are the two biggest suppliers in banana-producing countries in the African Caribbean and Pacific Group (ACPG), which is mostly, comprised of former colonies. They would like a larger share of the EU market as part of a new import regime. Under a 2001 settlement the EU abandoned quotas on non-ACP bananas. In order to sell larger quantities to Europe ACP countries had to buy quota licenses from Caribbean producers at $150 a ton, in effect subsidizing richer countries. Market experts noted that two African countries were paying 20-25 million Euros a year for licenses covering about 30 percent of their exports to the EU. This is the equivalent of twice the current tariff paid by Latin American producers within the European Union's import quota system.

Bananas from Central and South America are controlled by US corporations such as *Dole Food, Del Monte* and *Chiquita Brand.* They supply about 60 per cent of EU consumption, with 20 per cent coming from ACP countries. *Dole Food* has investments in Cameroon and Cote d'Ivoire through the French-controlled *Compagnie Fruitière*, the leading banana producer in both countries. Latin American producers, scheduled to be released from quota restrictions, would enjoy tariff-free access for a fixed amount of their production. Luc Magliore Atangana, Cameroon's trade minister, complained that the growth potential for African exporters was being thwarted by Brussels. He stated that: "It wasnot possible to resolve the difference over tariffs for non-ACP bananas even though European Commission proposals were already well below the levels African and Caribbean producers wanted." The resulting WTO trade dispute underscored the problem of opening trade in a sector that pits two groups of developing countries against one another. European import rules were designed to favor their former African and Caribbean colonies thereby linking them to European capital and markets, not to Latin America, where the US corporations *Dole*, *Del Monte* and the *United Fruit Company* control vast banana plantations.[34]

In October 2005, the WTO ruled against the EU's plans to expand trade with former colonies of Africa and the Caribbean. This was the second WTO ruling against the EU on bananas in one year. A spokesman for the EU agriculture commissioner called the ruling surprising and stated disappointingly that: "We need to read this ruling very carefully and study its implications." The EU then shelved a policy for improved agricultural market access offer to African and Caribbean banana producers. Dacio Castillo, the Honduran ambassador to the WTO, said the ruling should mark the end of any preferential treatment toward ACPG exporters, which benefited from the expiring guaranteed export quotas and waiver.[35] Peasant banana producers in both regions suffer under the current regime and Africans farmers would now become even poorer.

In November 2007, a draft copy of a proposed economic partnership agreement between the EU and the East African Community (EAC) called for Kenya, Uganda, Burundi, Tanzania and Rwanda to cut import tariffs on two-thirds of their trade within two years. The Interim Goods Only Agreement provides for a 25-year transition period for cutting tariffs. But the EAC objected to the 25-year transition period because it covers just five percent of all EAC trade. The proposal was criticized for strong-arming developing countries into signing the agreements which will replace the preferential policy for the ACP former colonies. Tetteh Hormeku, adviser for Third World Network Africa, argued that the text of the proposal had been arrived at in haste...and the costs for development are likely to be very high." Paul Collier, director of Oxford University's Centre for the Study of African Economies recommended that the EU give the ACP countries more time. "Africa should not liberalize to abruptly;" Collier wrote in a paper with a fellow Oxford economist. Only half the countries of Africa have signed the interim goods-only deals to preserve their trade privileges.

When African and European leaders met in Lisbon during December 2007, they clashed again over the EU trade proposal. Led by South Africa, some countries delayed signing the agreement. Senegalese President, Abdoulaye Wade, warned that the tariffs could create a "seismic" rupture between Europe and Africa at a time when China was wooing Africa with loans, new infrastructure and cheap goods. "African has other suitors now;" he warned in comments reflecting widespread African frustration at Europe's response to Africa's changing realities. "Europe has nearly lost the battle of competition in Africa. With the price of one European car you can but two Chinese cars;" Wade stated. Western dominance on aid and trade was threatened because; "If I want to do five kilometers of a road with the World Bank or one of the international financial institutions it takes at least five years. One year of discussions. One year of back and forth. One year of I don't know what. With the Chinese it is a few days and I say yes or no, they send a team and we sign."[36] The EU offered deals to individual countries concerning goods only. The East African community was the first to sign: Zimbabwe, Seychelles, Botswana, Lesotho, Swaziland and Mozambique and Angola followed their lead. South African and Namibia refused to sign because the trade deal would compromise their sovereignty.[37]

The UN Report called for rich countries to make a serious commitment to development goals. In September 2000, the UNDP "Millennium Development Goals" to include reducing poverty by half by 2015, and to create a "non-discriminatory trading and financial system" were agreed to. The UN and the international community have been establishing development goals for over forty years. "Do the goals give any sense of priorities, or are they just another wish list?" asked Nancy Birdsall, director of the Center for Global Development. "Development is a complex business. This is useful as a way of getting more people engaged." Jeffrey Sachs, head of the Earth Institute at Columbia University, observed that though the list of goals may seem daunting it is the reality-and it is simpler than it appears. "You can't address health without water; you can't address water without education. The nature of the investments that need to be made are rather straightforward...Any serious calculation shows this can be done for less than 1 percent of GNP for the rich world; said Sachs." Almost fifty percent of the African population subsists on one dollar a day. The 2002 Monterey conference on development produced promises of an extra $16 billion a year by 2006, bringing total assistance to 0.26 percent of OECD countries incomes.[38] The UN Development program reported that at the current pace of growth, sub-Saharan would not reach international poverty reduction goals until 2147, a century behind schedule. These findings clarified the challenges faced by George W. Bush during his first tour of Africa.

The first Doja, Qatar Round of world trade negotiations placed African aspirations for economic growth and development squarely in opposition US protectionist policies. Washington demanded that African states dismantle their trade barriers. Africans respond that they could hardly be expected to do this when industrialized countries impose tariffs on their meat, fruit and vegetables often exceeding 100 percent or when western states spend $1 billion dollars a day on agricultural subsidies. US subsidies to cotton growers more than triples US aid to sub-Saharan Africa. The reluctance of G8 nations to make concessions on domestic agricultural subsidies has disappointed and frustrated African producers, who say the payments serve as anti-competitive barriers to African commodities. Hans van der Merwe, Deputy executive director of AgriSA, a South African farmers association, summarized their sentiment stating that the G8 countries spoke "with a forked tongue." Take for example, the issue of market access. Despite preferential access agreements, including Washington's African Growth and Opportunity Act and the "Everything but Arms" agreement, Africans are still denied gain free access to OECD markets. According Executive Secretary of the UN Economic Commission for Africa K.Y. Amoako, unrestricted access would stimulate trade and African economic growth and a provide a sustainable approach to development. "If the EU were to abandon the idea of symmetry in the final agreements to accept non-reciprocity, it would demonstrate a commitment to a new pro-development approach to trade;" he argues" For Amoako, the spirit of the Doha Declaration was clear: Africa should integrate into the global economy and would benefit from world trade. Africa is committed to trading its way out of poverty, but cannot do so with international trade arrangement stacked against it.

The marathon 2004 global trade negotiations of the Doha round brought no immediate cuts in trade barriers. The biggest achievement was to win EU commitment to the elimination of its agricultural export subsidies, which many blame for distorting global farm trade by encouraging the dumping of surplus products on global markets. Washington and other rich WTO members agreed to negotiate reductions in the domestic subsidies they use to support farm incomes. However, in contrast to previous trade rounds, this time the African countries were better disciplined and well prepared to negotiate the minute and critical details of international trade policy. This time, rather than using the Doha round as a forum for political grand-standing, African negotiators won a crucial reduction of US cotton subsidies.

African delegates and their supporters celebrated in the conference center when the 2003 global trade talks collapsed in Cancun. However there was no celebration among the delegates from Africa when WTO director-general, Pascal Lamy, announced an indefinite suspension to the 2006 Doha round. Although, economic models suggest that an agreement would accrue trade benefits to a relatively few competitive exporters such as China and Brazil, but many African nations will suffer the consequences of failure.

The failure at Doha risked weakening the multilateral rule-based trading system giving impetus to a burgeoning network of preferential trade deals. The 250 extant accords are estimated to account for more than half of world trade making regional and global trade increasingly difficult for African exporters. Trade analysts say that bilateral and regional trade deals allow powerful trading nations to strong-arm weaker nations. Thus, the US insistence that countries comply with strict intellectual property laws protecting US software, music and films, goes well beyond WTO requirements and expectations. Prior agreements may also be withdrawn, including the "development package" painstakingly pieced together at the WTO's ministerial meeting in Hong Kong. Moreover, an opportunity to reform the global trading system out of fairness in favor of poor and developing countries, and to reduce distortions in agricultural trade, was lost.

The World Trade Organization categorizes farm subsidies by dividing them into three "boxes of ascending harmfulness"- green, blue and amber. A fourth notational red box would contain completely banned subsidies. Green box subsidies such as paying farmers to protect the environment are defined as trade distorting and are unlimited. Blue box subsidies which often base payments on fixed output or the size of farms and try to limit output are more trade distorting. Amber boxes payments are linked to current production or prices. To further complicate things, countries are allowed "*de minimis*" subsidies if payments are a small share (5 percent) of the value of agricultural production, either "product specific (PS) *de minimis*" linked to a single crop or non-product specific (NPS) *de minimis*, if not.

Under current WTO rules, there is a ceiling on amber box payments but none on blue. During the final Doha round the US proposed cutting its amber box limit by 60 percent from $19.1 to 7.6 billion a year; capping the blue box at $4.8; and halving the PS de minimis to 2.5 percent of production or $4.8 billion a year each. This, US trade representatives argued, that the US would reduce the most distorting and easiest to use subsidies such as price supports. Since the US does not use the blue box, it sought to protect its controversial counter-cyclical payments program (CCPP) which compensates farmers for low prices, by opening a blue box and shifting and them from amber. EU trade minister Peter Mandelson said the US was merely "box shifting" and playing a shell game of reducing national limits while protecting actual subsidies. The US demands the opening of agricultural markets which would coincidentally helps its heavily subsidized agricultural sector. The EU demands exempting poor countries from tariff cuts, which would strengthen European agricultural protectionism. Peter Mandelson urged George W. Bush to veto any attempt by the Congress to extend the costly farm bill which was due to expire in 2007. He also sought to portray the EU as the friend of the poor countries, and argued that the seven development issues of the Doha round should be adopted and implemented.

Transatlantic hostility escalated after the collapse of the Doha trades talks when the new US trade representative, Susan Schwab accused her European counterparts of spreading lies to divert the blame. She claimed that the US had so far "refrained from responding to finger-pointing by some," in order to preserve prospects for reviving the Doha round and that the notion that the US had shown a lack of flexibility in the negotiations was "false and misleading. In reality, the US could have signaled a willing to compromise earlier. However, in order to appease Congress, both US trade representative Robert Zoellick and his last minute replacement, Schwab, continued to promise farmers new, but unlikely agricultural export markets.

The so-called "commodity groups" of the US agricultural sector- those growing rice, corn, wheat, soybeans and cotton received more than three-quarters of all US farm subsidies over the last decade. Sixty percent of US farmers receive virtually nothing from the farm bill and 93 percent of the subsidies go to five crops. The collapse of the Doha round meant the US would not have to cut, but might increase the billions spent on farm subsidies.

African producers will require increased aid to become competitive in the global marketplace. "You don't put a bantam-weight against a heavy-weight in the ring;" said Ghana's President John Kufuor following a World Bank report on the UN's 2015 development goals for Africa. "If you do that you are sending the bantam-weight to slaughter, and it's the same with the market. To help build the muscle, Africa needs aid as well as trade." The New Partnership for African Development (NEPAD) seeks to change both internal and external attitudes on African development. The program of peer review would enable African countries to learn by example of the benefits flowing from better (less corrupt) governance, argued President Kufuor. Ghana, Nigeria, Sierra Leone, Gambia and Guinea plan to create a monetary union by July 2005 and subsequently merge with the CFA franc into a single currency area. By diversifying the economy, John Kufuor hopes that Ghana will be able to lift its average income from $400 to $1000 a year within a decade.

In 2004, International aid agencies looked to the UK to lead the rich nations in the global struggle to alleviate poverty. Chancellor of the Exchequer, Gordon Brown, outlined the British government's plans for increasing government spending to reach the United Nations target of devoting 0.7 per cent of its national income development aid within a decade. Brown stated that 2005 was the year where... "the needs of Africa would be the focus of the UK's G7 presidency as a presidency for development. Britain has really upped the ante with this budget, and that makes it hard for other countries to look the other way;" observed Lucy Matthew of the campaign group Debt, Aids, Trade and Africa. Justin Forsyth of Oxfam said the combination of all these meetings with Britain's leadership means they will be able to put some ambitious proposals on the table. If Britain's plan is internationally accepted, the objective of 0.7 percent could be achieved by 2008-09. Only France accepted Brown's proposed International Financing Facility (IFF) to borrow up to $50 billion from global capital markets to fund development. The United States, which gave only 0.14 percent of its national income in 2003, made no such commitment.

Not waiting for the European Union to alleviate African poverty, South African President Thabo Mbeki announced a plan for a series of big industrial projects to accomplish the same. Addressing June 2002 NEPAD summit in Durban, he announced that at its core the organization would have a number of mega-projects designed to bring development to the continent. The plan identified industrial projects intended to attract private sector investments in energy, infrastructure and telecommunications. An example is the hydroelectric project at Inga Falls on the Congo River. The Inga project, which has the potential to export electricity to Europe, has been on the drawing board for decades and is typical of the type of project favored by the World Bank. Earlier regional instability in central Africa and the civil war in the Democratic Republic of Congo derailed such development plans. The G8 gave a qualified blessing to Africa; however, they expressed reservation about providing the $64 billion a year in investment aid required to halve African poverty by 2015.

Frustrated African finance ministers have long argued that the World Bank's debt relief program for Africa failed to keep step with poverty reduction goals in the poorest countries. At a three day meeting in October 2002 hosted by the UN, the finance ministers called for the Heavily Indebted Poor Countries (HIPC's) initiative to align with UN Millennium Development Goals, to cut poverty by half poverty by 2015. They called upon the World Bank and donor countries to move beyond HIPC to offer greater debt relief to non-HIPC countries. Since the mid-1990s, two-dozen countries have received $35 billion in commercial and official debt reduction under the HIPC initiative. Government officials and bankers gathered at the 2004 World Bank-IMF meeting endorsed a scheme combining greater debt forgiveness with the creation of new international and domestic securities access.

By 2006, many sub-Saharan stock exchanges were leading performers and awarded sovereign ratings from the main global agencies. But the continent's main stock exchanges are dominated by South Africa's $330 billion capitalization program, which was upgraded 15 percent by *Standard and Poor's* IFCI index in the first three quarters reflecting 3.5 GDP growth.

In Botswana the investment grade rating benefited from an 8.5 percent advance by the Standard and Poor's IFC Frontier Index. This was boosted by inflation and falling interest rates with annual price rise targets at 7 percent and benchmark one year bond returns of 12 percent. The diamond industry accounts for half of government revenues and has endured recurring devaluation, strikes and reform shake ups.

In March 2005, Nigerian President Obasanjo challenged Britain to live up to its commitments to Africa, to take the lead in writing off Nigerian Debt and do more to recover stolen money held by international banks. Addressing the UK-led Commission for Africa, President Obasanjo said: "Mr. Blair's government would be telling the rest of the world that you believe in the report and you are willing to do something about it." Nigeria's $35 billion foreign debt is the largest in sub-Saharan Africa, but the country falls outside the HIPC debt relief plan. Prime Minister Blair also called for a new "debt compact," covering Nigeria and other countries, but Nigeria's creditors were skeptical.

The Group of Seven industrialized countries moved slowly toward a compromise but failed to reach a detailed agreement in preparation for the forthcoming G8 summit that July. The G7 statement acknowledged the need for additional funds. UK Chancellor of the Exchequer, Gordon Brown stated that he preferred to proceed with proposals for writing off the debt of poor countries rather than continue to pay interest on their behalf. US Treasury Secretary, John Snow, stated: "The momentum is toward the US proposal for 100 per cent debt cancellation and then using grants forward in lieu of debts." The US refused to take part in the UK's International Finance Facility to borrow money against future aid flows, but France and Germany planned to support the IFF pilot program in return for UK support for an airline tax to repay the IFF.

The ancient north-African trade routes of Mali and Songhai and Timbuktu have long passed into history, disrupted by colonialism and the Arab and the European slave trades. However, Africa is the most populous part of the Islamic world and trade between Arabic countries and Africa played an historic role in the development of both regions. Iranian-African Cooperation was established in 2004. In January 2005, Iran's deputy commerce minister for international trade, Mojtaba Khosrowtaj, expressed his regret over the low level of Iranian-African trade. Addressing a session of the joint Iran-Africa Economic Cooperation Council, he reported that bilateral trade was a meager US $280 million in 2004. He noted that Africa's total international trade in 2003 was only US $338 billion and of which Iran's share was very low. There are plans establish four free trade zones in Africa, develop banking ties, form an Iran-Africa merchants council and a five-year program of the Africa Research Center affiliated with Iran's Teacher Training University.

There is a little economic optimism. According to the World Bank, International Finance Corporations' *Doing Business Report*, two-thirds of African countries, led by Ghana and Tanzania implemented at least one pro-business reform between 2005 and 2006. Other pro-business reforms were initiated in Benin, Burkina-Faso, Cameroon, Gambia, Madagascar, Malawi, Mali, Mozambique, Niger, Nigeria and Zambia. The annual report indicated that despite these advances, Africa ranks as the world's most regulated region. But Africa is not alone here. The report found that France, which has long scored poorly on *Doing Business Report* indicators, also ranks among the top 10 reforming nations.[39]

By the late 1980s, it became quite evident that neo-liberal prescriptions were killing the patient. A debate raged about whether two World Bank reports (*Africa's Adjustment and Growth in the 1980s* and *Sub-Saharan Africa: From Crisis to Sustainable Growth*, both published in 1989), adequately explained the continent's dramatic declines in standards of living, terms of trade and ability to service debt. There was great doubt about the truth of a World Bank claim that during the late 1980s countries which adopted orthodox macroeconomic reforms grew more rapidly. World Bank prescriptions were embraced by several African leaders who saw no feasible alternative policy. Their adoption of the cynically named 'home-grown' structural adjustment programs could only be understood against the need the World Bank expressed for 'legitimacy'.[40]

As the UK debated whether it should begin atoning for its role in the trans-Atlantic slave trade by offering an apology, the Organization for Economic Cooperation and Development announced they would break their promises to increase aid to poor nations unless they radically changed their spending habits. The OECD reported that a 2006 partial survey of the development committee's 23 member states showed that their spending plans fell short of pledges. Some academics and development campaigners point to the misleading figures which count as aid the writing off of almost worthless defaulted commercial debt from a middle income country such as Iraq. Reported aid levels for 2005 received a huge one time boost from the cancellation of debts owed by Iraq and Nigeria.[41] Unfortunately, debt relief offers very little long-term hope. Africa's share of world exports fell from 2.1 percent in 1987 to 0.9 percent on 2007 making it difficult to address Africa's perpetual impoverishment.

Table: 2.0 African GDP per capita & % Children in Labor Force 2000

Country	2000	2000
Angola	506.07	26.08
Benin	414.16	26.47
Botswana	3951.1	14.39
Burkina-Faso	252.05	43.46
Burundi	140.69	48.5
Cameroon	675.15	22.96
Cape Verde	1519.11	13.55
Central African Republic	338.56	
Chad	217.83	36.64
Comoros	435.78	37.56
Congo Dem. Rep.		28.6
Congo Rep.	841.41	25.41
Cote d'Ivoire	742.52	18.65
Equatorial Guinea	1598.55	32
Eritrea	155.04	38.42
Ethiopia	115.88	41.1
Gabon	4377.99	14.07
Gambia The	370.47	33.83
Ghana	413.25	12
Guinea	603.39	31.09
Guinea-Bissau	209.75	36.73
Kenya	328.19	39.17
Lesotho	551.43	20.73
Liberia		15.39
Madagascar	245.79	34.07
Malawi	168.63	31.49
Mali	287.73	51.13
Mauritania	495.67	22.1
Mauritius	4429	2
Mozambique	191.07	32.41
Namibia	2407.57	17.37
Niger	202.79	43.57
Nigeria	253.6	23.91
Rwanda	241.76	41.35
Sao Tome and Principe	340.64	
Senegal	609.23	27.3

Seychelles	7000.37	
Sierra Leone	147.38	13.9
Somalia		31.3
South Africa	3985.14	0
Sudan	319.08	27.41
Swaziland	1476.4	12.25
Tanzania	190.48	36.9
Togo	326.61	26.82
Uganda	347.95	43.78
Zambia	392.38	15.61
Zimbabwe	620.7	27.04

Source: The World Bank, 2002.

1. Achebe, Chinua. *Things Fall Apart.* New York: Anchor Books. 1959.

2. David White and Peter Wise, 'Fragile state appeals to rich donors,' *The Financial Times* Special Report Guinea-Bissau October 31, 2006, p. 2.

3. David White, 'Where the poor get poorer,' *The Financial Times*, Special Report Guinea-Bissau October 31, 2006. p. 2.

4. David White, 'People tired of senseless upheaval,' *The Financial Times*, Special Report Guinea-Bissau, October 31, 2006. p.3

5. See Hedley Bull and Adam Watson (eds.), "Europe and Africa," in *The Expansion of International Society.* Oxford: Clarendon Press. 1984, p. 109.

6. Callaghy, Thomas M, "Africa and the World Political Economy: More Caught Between a Rock and a Hard Place" in John W. Harbeson and Donald Rothchild, eds., *Africa in World Politics: The African State System in Flux.* Oxford :Westview Press. 2000 pp. 44-45.

7. Ibid. p. 48.

8. Ibid. p. 50.

9. Ibid. p. 51.

10. Ibid. p 53

11. Oxfam, *Africa Make or Break: Action for Recovery*, London. 1993

12. Callaghy, Op. Cit. p. 60.

13. Ibid. p. 63.

14. Ibid. pp. 72-74.

15. Marian Tupy, 'Africa's war on poverty begins at home.' *The Financial Times* December 20, 2005.

16. James Lamont. 'African censure for World Bank over drive to reduce poverty,' *The Financial Times,* Comment, October 22, 2002.

17. Lancaster, Carol, "Africa in World Affairs," In John W. Harbeson and Donald Rothchild, eds., *Africa in World Politics: The African State System in Flux.* (Oxford: Westview Press, 2000), 209.

18. Ibid. p. 215.

19. Ibid. pp. 222-232.

20. Craig Burnside and David Dollar. Assessing *Aid: What Works, What Doesn't and Why.* The World Bank Policy Research Report. (Washington, D.C. : Oxford University Press), 1998.

21. Callaghy, Op. Cit. p. 71.

22. Alan Beattie, 'Africa also strains to keep its side of G8 bargain,' *The Financial Times,* July 8-9, 2006 p.5.

23. Alan Beattie,' Promises pledged to end poverty are not kept,' *The Financial Times,* June 30, 2006 p.4.

24. Frances Williams and Alan Beattie, 'Poor nations left swimming in 'spaghetti' bowl of rules,' *The Financial Times,* July, 26, 2006, p. 2.

25. Andrew Ward, Hugh Williamson, Bertrand Benoit and Fiona Harvey, 'Russia-US tensions mare end of summit," *The Financial Times*, June 9-10, 2007 p.1

26. Ed Crooks and William Wallis, 'Africa aid wiped out by rising cost of oil,' *The Financial Times*, December 29-30, 2007. p. 1

27. Alec Russell, US business frets over China's Africa Expansion, *The Financial Times,* November 20, 2007, p. 6.

28. *The Financial Times,* 'O'Neill's African Tour,' Editorial, , *June*, 6, 2004.

29. Minter, William, "America and Africa: Beyond the Double Standard," *Current History*, (May, 2000 202-203.

30. Emmanuel Nnadozie, "Africa at the Crossroads of Globalization" In *Africa at the Crossroads*, by John Mukum Mbaku and Suresh Chandra Saxena eds., London: Praeger Press (2004) 29-30.

31. Michael Wines. 'Dollars' Fall Silences Africa's Garment Factories,' *The New York Times*, March 12, 2005.

32. Alan Beattie, 'Qualified welcome for US cotton move,' *The Financial Times* February 3, 2006.

33. David White, 'Banana exporters fight EU market,' *The Financial Times* September 25, 2005.

34. Raphael Minder, 'EU loses final round in long WTO banana battle,' *The Financial Times,* October 28, 2005.

35. Andrew Bounds and Peter Wise, 'Africa warns of rupture over European tariffs,' *The Financial Times*, December 12, 2007 p.6

36. Andrew Bounds, 'Two African nations refuse to join EU trade deal,'
The Financial Times December 4, 2007 p.4.

37. Alan Beattie, 'African nations off track in reducing poverty,' *The Financial Times*, October 9, 2003.

38. Guha Krishna, 'World Bank praises pro-business reforms in many African countries,' *The Financial Times*, September 6, 2006.

39. Patrick Bond, Against *Global Apartheid: South Africa meets World Bank, IMF and International Finance* (Cape Town, London and New York: Zed Books. 2003) 23.

40. Alan Beattie, 'Rich nations risk breaking aid pledges,' *The Financial Times,* February 23, 2007. p. 4.

3: What is Africa? A Continental Profile

Africa is the second-largest and second most populous continent. Covering about 30,244,050 square kilometers (11,677,240 square miles) including its adjacent islands, it covers 20.3 percent of the planets total terrain. With over 800 million human inhabitants in 54 countries, it is home to about one seventh of the planets human population. The name ''Africa'' was adapted into western use through Roman usage. Ancient used the name "Africa-terra'' "land of the Afri" (plural, or "Afer" singular) - for the northern part of the continent, as the province of Africa (Rome's Bread Basket) and its capital Carthage, which is modern-day Tunisia. The Afri were a tribe, possibly Berber, who dwelt in North Africa in the Carthage area. The origin of "Afer'" may be connected with Phoenician languages Phoenician "afar", dust (also found in most other Semitic languages); some other etymologies that have been postulated for the ancient name 'Africa' that are much more debatable include: The Latin word "aprica", meaning "sunny"; the Greek language Greek word "aphrike", meaning "without cold." Historian, Leo Africanus 1495-1554, attributed the origin to the Greek word "phrike"; meaning "cold and horror", combined with the negating prefix a-, thus meaning a land free of cold and horror. However, the change of sound from "ph" to "f" in Greek is dates to about the first century, so there is doubt surrounding the origin of the name.

Egypt, considered part of Asia by the ancient historians, was assigned to Africa by the Egyptian geographer and astronomer Ptolemy (85 -165 A.D.), who marked Alexandria as the Prime Meridian and made the Isthmus of Suez and the Red Sea the boundary between Asia and Africa. As Europeans came to understand the real size of the continent, their understanding of "Africa" expanded.

Africa is the largest of the three great southward projections from the main mass of the Earth's surface. Separated from Europe by the Mediterranean Sea it is joined to Asia at its northeast extremity by the Suez Canal Isthmus of Suez (transected by the Suez Canal, (130 km 80 miles wide).

Geopolitically, Egypt's Sinai Peninsula east of the Suez Canal is often considered part of Africa, as well. From the most northerly point, Cape Blanc (Ra's al Abyad) in Tunisia (37& deg; 21& prime; N), to the most southerly point, Cape Agulhas in South Africa (34 ° 51& prime; 15 & Prime; S), is a distance of approximately 8,000 km (5,000 miles); from Cape Verde 17 & deg; 33 & prime; 22& Prime; W, the westernmost point, to Ras Hafun in Somalia, 51& deg; 27& prime; 52 & Prime; E, the most easterly projection, is a distance of approximately 7,400 km (4,600 miles). The length of coast-line is 26,000 km (16,100 miles) and the absence of deep indentations of the shore is shown by the fact that Europe, which covers 9,700,000 km (3,760,000 square miles), has a coast-line of 32,000 km (19,800 miles).

Africa is the only continent to extend from the northern to the southern temperate zone, while encompassing some of the world's driest deserts, largest tropical rain forests, and highest equatorial mountains.

Africa is the cradle of the human family i.e., it is the only place in the planet where the bones found allow us to uninterruptedly reconstitute the human genealogy. Our ancestors *Homo sapiens* originated there about 7 million years ago. The human family's mitochondrial DNA mother, Eve originates from this continent. During the mid 20th century, anthropologists discovered fossils and evidence of human occupation perhaps dating to as early as 7 million years ago. The Leakey family discovered several species of early ape-like humans thought to have evolved into modern day man, such as "Australopithecus afarensis" (radiometrically dated to 3.9-3.0 million years BCE), "Paranthropus boisei " (2.3-1.4 million BCE) and "Homo ergaster" (c. 600,000-1.9 million BCE). These were among the most significant research findings in the pursuit of the study of human evolution.

Throughout humanity's pre-history, Africa (like all other continents) had no nation-states, and was inhabited by groups of hunter-gatherers such as the Khoi and San (formerly known as Bushmen). Around 3300 BC, the historical record opens in Africa with the rise of literacy in Egypt, which continued with varying levels of influence over other areas until 343 BC. Other prominent civilizations included Ethiopia, the Nubian kingdom, and the kingdoms of the Sahel Ghana, Mali, Songhai and Great Zimbabwe.

Most Americans and many Europeans equate native Africans with blacks, white Africans with recent intruders, and African racial history with the story of European colonialism and the slave trade. The obvious reason for these historic misperceptions is that they focus on specific facts: blacks are the sole native Africans familiar to most Americans, because they were transported in large numbers as slaves to the United States and their political and economic dilemma is ongoing. But very few humans may have occupied much of modern sub-Saharan Africa as recently as a few thousand years ago, and the so-called African blacks are heterogeneous. Prior to the arrival of white missionaries and colonialists, Africa was home to five of the world's six major divisions of humanity, and three of them remain natives of Africa. One quarter of the world's languages are spoken in Africa. No other continent contains such human diversity.[1]

European Misperceptions and Prescriptions

In a paradigm shaking article on the European view of Africa, Katherine George described European perceptions as an "antagonistic fantasy." She referred primarily to Dutch, Italian and Portuguese literature while making minimal references to English writers. However, her work indicated that all European countries were equally prejudiced about Africa, and that their literature reflected these biases. The British view of Africa appears to have been, at best, absurd and at worst, the product of malice and cynicism.[2]

From the first recorded British voyage of William Hawkins in 1530, to the early nineteenth-century voyages of exploration, English relations with Africans were shaped by mercantile interests. Nowhere does British writing during this era indicate an interest in the lives of Africans equal to that of the Dutch or the Portuguese. British traders did not engage in polemics or cultural comparisons; when they expressed distaste at what they saw, it was for moral judgment. In their view, the Africans were savages, but one could trade as profitably with savages as with anyone else; and these particular savages were just as eager as the British to engage in commerce".[3]

Today, scientists and scholars accept that the concept of race is a social construct and of little value in distinguishing genetic variance in people. A century of European scholarship seeking to classify Africans culminated with the publication in 1930 of C.G. Seligman's *The Races of Africa*, which "measured" hair types, skin color, head form, nasal width, lip size, etc. An American, Seligman attributed the rise of Africa's great civilizations of Mali, Songhai, Kush and Axum to the long-term emigration of light skinned "hamites' from the Middle East. It was inconceivable to the Eurocentric mind that the dark skinned "Negroid" race could have produced such remarkable civilizations. Seligman's "hamitic hypothesis" was widely accepted and taught throughout the colonial era. The subsequent Egyptian carbon dating and genetic research by Cheikh Anta Diop and the UNESCO and the research of Ivan van Sertima[4] ended the scientific debate on the African origins of the linguistic and techno-complex of these civilizations.

Cheikh Anta Diop found that in fifteenth century, the first Portuguese, Dutch, English, French, Danish contact with Africans were via small trading posts on the West African coasts. These exploring Europeans considered the political organization of the African superior to that of their own states. Because historic forces disrupted their equilibrium with the environment, Africans developed a new equilibrium without social political and moral organization. With economic resources assured by means that did not require perpetual inventions, Africans became indifferent to material progress.[5]

In their book on eighteenth century writing about Africa, *The Africa That Never Was,* Dorothy Hammond and Alta Jablow found that the literature on Africa placed inordinate emphasis upon the sanguinary aspects of West African cultures. In West Africa, British missionaries were presented as the vanguard of commerce, "enlightenment" and philanthropy. African behavior, institutions, and character were not merely disparaged but presented as the negation of all human decency. African religions were but vile superstitions; governments were a cruel form of despotism; polygyny was not marriage but an expression of innate lust. Enslavement of such people was thus, not only desirable, it was justifiable. The character of Africans could be improved through contact with their European masters. Slavery, in effect, became the means of the Africans' salvation for it would introduce them to Christianity and civilization. Those opposed to the enslavement of Africans were of diverse belief and background. People such as James Fox, John Wesley, Harriet Martineau, Hannah More and Sir Charles and Lady Middleton protested and eventually achieved abolition in the early 19th century. They too wrote tracts, made speeches and took political action. They produced a literature of abolition, but their writings did little to contribute to correct distorted European images of Africa. The anti-slavery writers created a pseudo-Africa. Contrary to the "beastly savage" image promoted by the slavers, theirs was a "noble-savage," a literary device often used in criticism of the writer's society. The explorers Sir Francis Drake and Sir Walter Raleigh, seemingly with an eye toward promoting colonization, praised the virtues of the "noble-savage". European attitudes toward nobility were therefore pivotal in selecting those virtues granted the "noble-savage". He was depicted as the counterpart of the contemporary English aristocrat. The "noble-savage" and the "beastly savage" were conventions equally lacking in realism; both represented opposite poles on a scale of English values.[6]

Traditional African Spirituality

The study of religion is a growing yet largely unexplored field of inquiry. Nowhere is this more obvious than in the contemporary debate between evolutionist and the advocates of "intelligent design." Basil Davidson observed that it is understandable that scientists have cared little to delve into the topic; since Galileo was bullied into saying the earth was flat. Professor Evans-Pritchard wrote that for many of the anthropologists of the 19th century, 'religious belief was....absurd, and it is so to most anthropologists yesterday and today'. Davidson notes that modern society has torn the means and ends of science apart; and that the price of our progress is a divided consciousness, Science tells us what can be done but not what ought to be done or why it ought to be done.[7]

According to Davidson, the European scientific taxonomy of all systems of thought and belief which existed in Africa under the catch-all label of 'religion' is misleading and used only for want of a better social analytical concept. "We cannot begin to understand the drift of logic of African apprehension of reality unless, for example, we have grasped the reasons why appointed ancestors should become the jealous guardians of the highest moral values...the axiomatic values from which all ideal conduct (has been) deemed to flow'. In this sense the study of religion is the study of social fact."[8] Davidson refers to these belief systems as a 'science of social control'.

Religion is also indigenous to Africa. Africans are a deeply spiritual people, however one of the least understood facets of African life concerns their religious traditions and belief systems. European and American missionaries who visited Africa became obsessed with African concepts of ancestral spirits and spirits in general as though there was nothing more to African spirituality. Since their mission was to convert the African to Christianity, they were not obliged to learn of and had little interest in the origins of African spirituality.

The spiritual beliefs of a people are determined by the social and cultural conditions and the physical environment they inhabit. The overwhelming majority of Africans traditionally believed in the concept of a Supreme Being, who created the universe and everything in it. Some Africans had an anthropomorphic image of God and used human terms to describe who God was. Some described God in masculine terms, others used feminine terms, and still others used no image at all.

These belief structures were mandatory in a social sense, explanatory in a material sense, and therefore the basis for rational thought. They reflected a developed awareness of the practical possibilities of prediction based upon observation: what anthropologist Lévi-Strauss termed 'the science of the concrete.' In fact, traditional African thought was quite empirically sound in its approach to natural phenomena. Experimentation dates to these societies. Nothing else explains such detailed knowledge of the environment.[9]

The Dogon of the Western Sudan classified plant life into twenty-two species and eleven sub-species. The Karimajong can distinguish 'as precisely as any professional observer the topographical features of predictable water supply.' Lévi-Strauss noted that the many known classifications such as these 'are not only methodical and based on carefully developed theoretical knowledge. They are also comparable, from a formal point of view to those used in contemporary zoology and botany.'[10]

African dance and art were an expression of their religious world views and a part of the superstructure of their societies. In early Africa, most religious beliefs were associated with the mobilization and discipline of large numbers of people in order to facilitate state formation and ensure social justice. However, religion imposed a rigidity which precluded the rapid adaptation to technological change.[11]

There were many conceptions of God, because in each locale, the concept took its emphasis and complexion from the regional sociological structure and climate. Thus, there are several variations on a theme. For example, the Ibo and the Yoruba of Nigeria believe in a Supreme Being who was assisted by lesser deities. The Yoruba held the idea of an almighty God whom, they named *Olurun*. This supreme being was assisted by lesser deities called *Orishas*. Each *Orisha* had a name and was responsible for a specific function among the humans. The *Orishas* were God's assistants who looked after God's creation. There was the God of Rain, the God of Fertility, the God of the Forest, the God of the Sea, the God of Agriculture etc...When women were not producing children for the community, the people prayed to the God of Fertility to make the women more fertile. When hunting, prayers were offered to the special deity of hunting to protect the hunters and to make their efforts bountiful. When fishermen went to sea, the God of the Sea was invoked to provide safety and a bountiful catch.[12]

The Kipsigis (a subgroup of Kenya's Kalenjin people) also believed in one God called *Asis* or *Asista*. Because he Kipsigis used many terms to refer to God, some scholars assumed that there were many Gods, when most probably the names referred to the variety of functions or activities the *Asis* performed. In his study of the Kipsigis of Kenya, Robert Manners suggests that they were not particularly religious in terms of holding many formal religious gatherings, but when their community faced a crisis, special appeals were made[13]

The Kikuyu of Kenya also believed in one God, Ngai, the creator and giver of all things. In *Facing Mount Kenya,* Jomo Kenyatta describes Ngai: "He has not father, mother, or companion of any kind. His work is done in solitude. He loves and hates people according to their behavior. The Creator lives in the sky, but has temporary homes on earth, situated on mountains, where he may rest during his visits. The visits were intended as a kind of 'general inspection,' and to bring blessings and punishments to the people."[14]

In his study of African religions, John Mbiti notes that the universe created by the Kikuyu God existed on several levels: the heavens (where God resides with the sun, the planets and the stars); the earth with its bounty and the underworld (where some spirits may reside). Man is the link between the Universe and God. The Kikuyu universe is orderly and order must be maintained on at least four levels. 1) The Natural level, governed by the laws of nature, as revealed through science; 2) the Moral level , which consists of the moral code as given by God for societal harmony and peace; 3) The Religious level refers to man-made institutions such as churches, temples and shrines, whose duty it is to advise people how to live their lives as God instructs; and 4) The Mystical level deals primarily with magic and witchcraft given to specific individuals and spirits to communicate with supernatural forces.[15]

Most groups have their own myths or legends of how the universe came into being, or how their community originated. One of the more interesting "creation myths" is that of the Abaluhya people of western Kenya. In short, the World was created by *Wele Xakaba* who first created heaven. To prevent heaven from falling in he supported it all around with pillars. He then created two assistant's *wele muxobe* and *wele murumwa*. After creating the heavens he decided to put in the moon the sky, the sun and then put clouds in the sky. He created a big rooster *(engoxo enjahi)* from which lightning originates. Whenever it shook its wings there was lightning and whenever it crowed there was thunder. Having created the sun and given it the power or resplendence, *Wele Xakaba* asked himself, "for whom will the sun shine?' This led to his decision to create man.

The Vugusu believe that the first man was called Mwambu. God created woman because Mwambu needed someone he could see and with whom he could talk. Therefore, God created the first woman, *Sela*, to be Mwambu's partner. After providing the earths surface with water, God created all plant life. He then said that all the plants are useless unless there was something to eat them. So animal's birds and other creatures living in the water, on the surface of the earth, and in the soil were created.... God created the whole work of creation in six days. On the seventh day he rested because it was a bad day. The Vugusu have all sorts of beliefs and taboos referring to this day and the number seven.[16]

African 'totems' and 'taboos' were long regarded as mystical projections of the 'primitive mind' or phantoms derived from aboriginal fears and suspicions. Or they were explained as more or less mystical aids to solving material problems: such as sharing available food. For example, one clan ate buffalo but not eland, while its neighbor ate eland not buffalo.[17]

A story in the January 19, 1968 edition of *The Times* of London reported that fifteen Africans had been gaoled after being found opening the grave of an African baby and eating the body. In statements made to the police the accused said: 'We are witches and this is the food of witches'. A few days before this incident, President Kenyatta had urged a crowd of 40,000 Kenyans...to give up witchcraft. Confessions such as these are not rare in 21st century African courts. A winner at the film 2005 Cannes film festival, *Delwende* is based on the story of a woman driven from her village after being accused of witchcraft. Much of the film uses real footage including a visit to the witches' asylum in Ouagadougou.

Then, as now, across modern Africa, there are people who believe in witches and who sometimes plead guilty to charges of witchcraft. There are even more who believe in the power of wizardry for good or for evil; who are encouraged or dismayed by a host of signs and omens; and who spend money they can ill afford on spells and counter-spells.[18] However, this is should not seem strange given that many Americans admittedly believe in angels.

Basil Davidson posed the question: how can magical beliefs and confessions of doing things such as eating a dead baby, remain possible within a moral order which is derived from the empirical observation of real phenomena? The sociological and anthropological response is to view these beliefs in their cultural context. They are common to all "pre-scientific societies. He cites an early but typical European example that occurred in 1080 A.D. when King Harald of Denmark was told by Pope Gregory VII that 'he must no longer tolerate among his people the gruesome superstition according to which Christian priests or wicked women are held answerable for bad weather, storms unfruitful year, or outbreaks of plague.' But King Harald had to tolerate these practices because his people continued to believe these superstitions for centuries.[19]

The 'Black Death,' which in the 14th century killed almost a quarter of the European population and led to panic, was largely attributed to the work of diabolical power. A report in the 1484 *Rhineland Clergyman* claimed that magic potions for general protection against 'Black Death' were brewed at secret, nocturnal banquets where 'the occult and magic arts and flights of witches gained increased strength'.[20]

Citing Janssen's *History of Germany*,[21] Davidson notes that after the great Christian religious schism, belief in the power and the arts of the devil became universal and the resulting demoralization from the social and political struggle, was particularly favorable to the development of the witch-superstition. Large quantities of books on magic and mysticism were published. Magicians roamed the countryside as 'wondermen, ring slippers, mist makers, illusionists, mandrake hawkers, quacks, howlers, spider-eaters, conjurors, benison-healers, hare-catchers, bullet-stoppers, sure-shots, stab-proofs, sword-dancers, love-compellers, mice-drivers or rat-leaders and spear and sword doctors.[22] As late as 1967-68, the European Christian community in Rhodesia was exhorted by the clergy to pray for rain.

In 1969, most observers agreed that witchcraft fears had increased in Africa over the past 150 years, and that these fears were less controlled than in the traditional era of built-in protective mechanisms. Pre-scientific Europe mirrored pre-scientific Africa. Or as Davidson notes: "What appears certain is that the understanding of witchcraft beliefs in historical Europe can be illuminated by the study of witchcraft beliefs in contemporary Africa."[23]

A typical example of African witchcraft comes from the beliefs of the Ga people of Ghana. The spirits of witches were said to leave their bodies during sleep, glide through the air on the back of an owl or some other creature, often accompanied by brilliant balls of fire, and cluster in a warlock's meeting where the personalities of chosen victims are ritually eaten after which these victims die. The worst witches are believed to have had hooks or spurs growing from their heels. This cannot be disproved any more than the 'evidence' of European or African witch-persecuting courts could be or can be denied, since only an accredited 'witch finder' could know about witches.[24]

Ancestral Worship

The Akan have a saying, *Onipa ne asem,* meaning "it is mankind that matters." The meaning in this context is that any man can always be responsible for himself. Within the God-given community of the dead, the living and the yet unborn, it is the living that face the real problems of life, and therefore take priority. The ancestors promised that the living could solve these problems only if they obeyed the rules. However, the ancestors are also obliged to play by the rules. Thus, if African spirits became the servants of men, the proper manipulation of these spirits became a preoccupation of these societies. For example, among the Kalabari of the Niger Delta, if a spirit becomes too demanding the living will tell him where the wood his 'totem' (his carved wooden image) is located. In other words, the spirits cannot be expected to do what they are told; but they can be expected to behave according to reliable prediction.

Not all ancestors were important, only those who were recognized as standing in the line of succession back 'to power without beginning'. These were the appointed ancestors who channeled that power to the living, and by doing so provided the means of protecting the present, guaranteeing the future, and generally assuaging the doubts and worries of wandering groups.[25] Among the Konkomban, when a man or group of men wished to move and settle on unoccupied land, they first consulted a diviner who advised them whether or not it was advisable to move based on the location of the shrines, usually groves of trees in the new area they proposed to occupy. From the beginning, this established a relationship between a group of kinsmen and the territory they occupied and between this new group and Konkomban society. They had also connected with their ancestors and adjusted their new settlement to the ideal balance and could face life safely on their own.[26] Whenever a kinship group decided to move away from the parent group, they were faced with the harsh realities of breaking with their lineal ancestors. This often meant breaking with their moral order.[27]

Among the Karimajong, obedience to the elders brings good fortune through their beneficence. Ultimately, it is the elders who guard and impose the rules, whether individually or collectively. On the other hand, disobedience and disrespect bring individual punishment or suffering, or collective calamity. The attributed the ability of the elders to intercede with deity on the community's (or individual's) behalf or to refuse in time of need was powerful. Elders enjoyed a number of punitive sanctions applied in varying degrees of doom. A curse thrown by the elders was the major punitive sanction. More drastic were collective curses which multiplied individual or communal woes. The offending Karimajong was deeply and immediately concerned with averting wrathful retribution. He or she had to plead or pray for remission.[28] Thus, an offender's remission depended upon forgiveness by the powers that underpin society. The belief connotes someone who is struggling with a force greater than himself that may only be removed on the force's behalf. But this occurred only when the forces of good are enabled by appropriate individual action and voluntary acceptance to overcome the forces of evil.

Traditional Medicine

An examination of community level social therapy among the Mbugwe people of northern Tanzania reveals a pattern of 'sorcery between chiefs'. Disasters and damage to entire villages rather than to individuals were attributed to the workings of chiefly witchcraft. These beliefs reinforced the existing political structures by creating tensions and attitudes of hostility between chiefdoms, and stimulating loyalties within the group. Therapy at the individual level was quite diverse. The Kaguru believed that no one should seek unusual wealth or power, and that anyone who did so might well have helped himself by witchcraft, because, intentionally or not, he had disturbed the ideal balance.[29]

Marital conflicts drew on similar beliefs. Children belonged to one wife's clan, and a man believes that his wife taught the children to favor her brothers rather than her husband. Kaguru men often accused their wives of witchcraft because they felt great insecurity toward them and saw them as independent or even secretly hostile.

It seems as though the Africans anticipated the work of Sigmund Freud and the neo-Freudians. Modern day psychiatric workers in Africa seem to agree that suggestive therapies of this kind were practiced by witch doctors that were deeply familiar with their milieu and with positive results. In 1969, Adoeye Lambo, M.D., M.R.C.P., D.P.M., a Nigerian psychiatrist, and former Chancellor of Ibadan University who was much respected for his clinical work; reported that witch doctors scored almost sixty percent success rates in the treatment of neurosis. At the time, western psychiatrists were scoring less than forty percent rates of success . A long-experienced European psychiatrist in Central Africa noted that; "If not for the traditional healers we should be flooded out here with anxiety-neurosis cases."[30]

The training of doctors was a very serious affair. The traditional African healer went through many years of training and was less a secular than a religious person. The doctor's authority was vested in his access to the explanations which lie beyond common reason, the explanations by which Africans searched for the roots of causality. The medical practice seems to have been divided into two major sections; practicing herbal cures and practicing divination or other forms of religious treatment. In modern Africa the lines between these two have become blurred. African cities and towns are dotted with clinics and in East Africa, *duko la dawa's* (pharmacies) offer herbal cures for every ailment or disease and the newspapers are full of advertisement for faith healers. It is not uncommon to see signs reading "We cure HIV/Aids" or "We cure Insanity" or as "We Specialize in Everything." In many African towns and cities, where there is widespread superstition, the absence of a coherent religious system is not uncommon.[31]

The Home of Human Language

By most estimates Africa contains well over a thousand languages. There are four major language families native to Africa. The Afro-Asiatic language family of about 240 languages spoken by 285 million people is widespread throughout North Africa, East Africa, the Sahel, and Southwest Asia. The Nilo-Saharan language family consists of more than a hundred languages spoken by 30 million people. Nilo-Saharan languages are mainly spoken in Chad, Sudan, Ethiopia, Uganda, Kenya, and northern Tanzania. The "Niger-Congo" language family covers much of Sub-Saharan Africa and is probably the largest language family in the world in terms of the number of different languages. A substantial number of them are the Bantu languages spoken in much of sub-Saharan Africa.

Africans may be grouped according to whether they live north or south of the Sahara Desert; these groups are called respectively; North Africans and Sub-Saharan Africans. Arabic-speaking Berber/Arab-Berber peoples predominate in North Africa. Joseph Greenberg classified Semitic languages as part of the Afro-Asiatic family. The most widely spoken language in the northern third of Africa is Arabic. Glottochronologists hypothesize that an original Afro-Asiatic mother tongue existed about 10,000 years ago, probably somewhere near the confluence of the Blue and White Nile, before the original speakers of Semitic ancient Egyptian, Cushitic, Berber, and Chadic subfamilies separated and began to disperse in different directions. As the ancient Egyptians moved north, Berbers and Chadic (including Hausa) speakers moved west, Cushitic people speakers (including Amharic, Somali and Galla) inhabited the Horn. The ancestors of these ancient Semites moved into what is now called the Middle East.[32]

Sub-Saharan Africa is dominated by a number of disparate populations often grouped according to their language, Niger-Congo predominately in West Africa. Greenberg originally identified a dozen Niger-Congo subfamilies and estimated that about 400 different languages with Bantu origins now spoken south of the Sahara. According to the estimates, these hundreds of Bantu languages probably began differentiating from one another about 3,000 years ago.

A large language group identified by Greenberg as Nilo-Saharan is spoken in the Eastern highlands. Several subfamilies and dozens of different modern languages with Nilo-Saharan roots have been researched and are spoken by people living in the areas bounded by Lake Chad and the Nile River, the Sahara Desert and Lake Victoria-Nyanza including the Luo, Masai, the Nuer and the Dinka.

Speakers of Bantu languages (part of the Niger-Congo family are the majority in southern, central and east Africa; but there are also several Nilotic groups in East Africa, and a few remaining indigenous Khoisan San' (sub-click language family) or (Bushmen) and Pygmy peoples in southern and central Africa, respectively. The Khoisan languages are currently spoken only by isolated groups of hunters and gatherers living on marginal lands of southern and central Africa. The distinctive "clicks" of the language seem to be the surviving remnants of earlier speech patterns. Some of these clicks have been incorporated into neighboring Xhosa and Zulu languages.

In 1956, Joseph Greenberg, published his work the *Classification of African Languages* which proposed that hamites were a fiction, a confused intermixing of obscurely known physical characteristics lacking linguistic-cultural empirical evidence. Language differences based on Greenberg's classification demonstrated not only that culture and civilization have nothing to do with pigmentation, but that the more than 800 languages currently spoken in Africa can be related to one another in only four major language groupings. Using lexicostatistics, historical linguists have modified Greenberg's model, added newly researched languages, and rearranged the language subfamilies.

Bantu-speaking Africans predominate in Gabon and Equatorial Guinea, and are found in parts of southern Cameroon and southern Somalia. In the Kalahari Desert of Southern Africa, the distinct people known as the Bushmen (also "San", closely related to, but distinct from "Khoikhoi Hottentots) have long been present. The San are physically distinct from other Africans and are the indigenous people of southern Africa. "Pygmies" are the indigenous people of central Africa.

The peoples of North Africa are primarily Arab-Berber. The Arabs who arrived in the 7th century assimilated the indigenous Berber people. Semitic Phoenicians and ancient Greeks and Romans settled in North Africa as well. Berber peoples remain a significant minority within Morocco and Algeria and are present in Tunisia and Libya. The Tuareg and other often-nomadic peoples are the principal inhabitants of the Saharan interior of North Africa. Nubians also developed civilizations in North Africa during ancient times. In the seventh century, parts of Africa were captured in the name of Islam. Ali Mazrui observes that three factors accelerated the Arabization of North Africa and the Lower Nile Valley. The first was Africa's cultural receptivity and remarkable assimilability. The second was the Arab lineage system and the way it defined the offspring of mixed Arab-African marriages. The third factor was the spread of the Arabic language and its role in defining what constitutes an Arab. Thus, the cultural capital of the Arab world is in Africa, Cairo. The population of Cairo is larger than the population of Saudi Arabia. Over 60 percent of the Arab world is west of the Red Sea on African soil. The headquarters of the Arab League is in Africa. Between 1979 to 1989 it was relocated from Cairo to Tunis only to return to Cairo in 1990.[33]

Some Ethiopian and Eritrean groups (like the Amhara and Tigrayans, collectively known as "Habesha") have Semitic (Sabaean) ancestry. The Somalis originated in the Ethiopian highlands, but most Somali clans can trace their Arab ancestry as well. Sudan and Mauritania are divided between a mostly Arab north and a native African south (although many of the Arabs of Sudan clearly have African ancestry, and differ in appearance from Arabs in Iraq or Algeria). Some areas of East Africa, particularly the Tanzanian island of Zanzibar and the Kenyan island of Lamu, received Arab and Asian Muslim settlers and merchants throughout the Middle Ages.

Over the past several millennia, the human family has expanded and settled in different ecozones throughout the continent developing different customs and vocabularies to describe their existence. Some archaeologists and linguists posit that "language" and "culture" are synonymous. Each language culture or subculture is best understood by the particular language or dialect that characterizes it.

Traditional Political Systems

Democracy is indigenous to Africa. To prevent the abuse of power by one person the traditional political systems were based on the consent of the governed and striking a balance between centralized and decentralized power. There were systems of checks, balances and accountability. Most traditional political systems represented a union of heterogeneous groups or clans with its own history language and identity. They established these systems to centralize authority, ensure clan cohesion and to realize their common interests. The head of state in these societies was a territorial ruler, but power often devolved to chiefs who functioned as the administrative and judicial officials of specified territories. The chiefs were vested with powers of economic and legal control over their divisions.

Stability was based upon a balance of political forces, which included chiefs, queens, queen-mothers, courts and democratic councils committed to the norms of tradition and vested the with power to depose the head of state when necessary. Power was further diffused to regional, zone and district chiefs. Local chiefs represented the interests of the central authority as well as the interests of their people, thus their powers were commingled.

Balancing these competing interests required a certain degree of wisdom on the part of the chief. The structure of political organization ensured that at any level of government a chief and his council ruled with the consent of those below and above him and with the consent of the people as a whole.[34]

The responsibilities of a traditional political ruler went beyond normal secular functions, he or she embodied the values and mystical beliefs that constituted the ideological superstructure society. Basil Davidson notes that first and foremost kings were the repositories of the ritual power of the kingship. Their authority rested mainly and consistently upon its place in a people's belief about themselves and their world. Kings were ritual specialists who accumulated power in societies which had gone beyond the subsistence level and had developed, whether in isolation or by migratory-stimulus, the need for centralizing institutions. In the many types of centralized systems, which emerged over a thousand years ago, and whose customs have become known over the past two centuries, the rulers were never supposed to appear in public in any manner that would make them appear as ordinary human beings. They had to eat privately, and were rarely seen except by their servants.

The greater kings were provided with stone or clay palaces. Each possessed the sacred objects of rule and office: spears of copper, ornaments of gold and other ritual-related objects. In many cases they presided over sacral fires from which it was believed that all other fires were symbolically derived. When a king became senile or otherwise unfit to rule, he was killed- or at least it said in the rules that they ought to be killed or quietly deposed in order to preserve the ritual virtues of the office.[35]

African kings were not 'divine' in the sense of that they were regarded as gods. They were political and therefore earthly beings as well as ritual and therefore spiritual beings. These qualities were inextricable and only separated when failure in the first appeared to threaten the second, but their spiritual quality always remained paramount.[36] Divinity was accented because the king's existence as a political or military leader was secondary. Above and beyond these secular functions, he was responsible for maintaining harmony between a society and its natural environment by means of ritual actions which he alone could undertake. His duties in this sphere were threefold: 1) to perfume the daily rites for which he was uniquely qualified by office; 2) to provide for and direct the activities of other cults; and 3) to sustain and control his own spiritual potency. Davidson notes that although the forms of kingship varied: the role of kings in Africa and Europe were the same.[37]

Title was correlated with the king's character and the 'peoples good'. As Davidson writes; "Ideally, the king should be strong and comely, generous of mind, bold in warfare, cunning in council and devout in everyday life. He should epitomize a people at one with its moral order, at peace with itself, at every point in harmony with the ancestors 'who brought us into our land and gave us life'" From this it followed that he should never continue to rule once his powers had failed or when he became tyrannical and departed from the rules of justice.[38] Kings might have embodied the will of God; but this did not guarantee their hold on power. As among the European monarchies, there were also rivals and pretenders to the throne.

Other clues to the nature of kings and kingships are revealed by examining the traditions of succession. Even when succession was the outcome of warfare and the killing of rival clans, great care was taken to prevent any formal or obvious break in the line of transmitted power. 'The King is dead, long live the king!' was the ruling sentiment. This was primarily in order to avoid disturbances based on the demand to preserve the integrity of ancestral descent. If the kings' person embodied the spiritual and therefore the material welfare of his people, the king must never die.[39] Some people believed that the king must never 'die' but they also went to great lengths to prepare for that inevitability. It is said that when a king was approaching death the Dinka traditionally buried their chief ritual priests, their 'Masters of the fishing Spear.'

> "The Master of the Fishing Spear was not afraid of death; he will be put in the earth while singing his songs, Nobody among his people will wail or cry because their man has died. They will be joyful because their Master of the Fishing Spear will give them life, so that they shall live untroubled by any evil...and nobody will say alas he is dead. They will say, It is very good".[40]

Whenever the emperor or Oyo died in Nigeria's Yorubaland, appointed officials cut off his head, cleaned his skull, and took out his heart. During the inaugural or installation rite, the next Oyo was obliged to sacrifice to *Shango*, a senior God, and he was given a dish containing the heart of his predecessor which he was obliged to eat'. A little later he was required to swallow a potion of corn gruel from his predecessor's skull. These rites were occasioned by the need 'to open his ears to distinguish truth from falsehood,' to give 'his words compelling power,' and to assign 'to him alone the authority to execute criminals and domestic enemies and to make war'. The point was not the grotesquerie, but the mobilization of chartered power behind the granting of solemn office, thereby guaranteeing legitimacy, i.e., accountability for the exercise of power.[41] These traditional African political and religious systems persist in some forms and may serve to heal Africa in the future.

---

1. Jared Diamond, *Guns, Germs and Steel: The Fates of Human Societies* (New York, W.W. Norton, 2005) 377.

2. Dorothy Hammond and Alta Jablow. *The Africa That Never Was: Four Centuries of British Writing About Africa* (Prospect Heights IL: Waveland Press, 1992) 15.

3. Ibid pp. 19-20.

4. Van Sertima, Ivan. *They Came Before Columbus: The African Presence in Ancient America.* (New York: Random House, 1976).

5. Cheikh Anta Diop. *The African Origin of Civilization Myth or Reality*, (Chicago: Lawrence Hill Books, 1974) 23.

6. Ibid pp. 25.26

7.Davidson, Basil (1969) *The African Genius: An Introduction to African Social and Cultural History*, Boston: Little- Brown. p. 109

8. Ibid. p. 114

9. Ibid p. 111

10. Ibid. p 112

11. Rodney, Walter, *How Europe Underdeveloped Africa*. (Washington, D.C., 1982, Howard University Press) . Pp. 35-36.

12. (Vincent Khapoya, *The African Experience: An Introduction*. (New Jersey: Prentice Hall, 1988) 53-54.

13. Robert A. Manners, "The Kipsigis of Kenya: Culture Change in a 'Model' East African Tribe" in *Contemporary Change in Traditional Societies,* ed. Julian H. Steward Vol. I (Urbana, IL: University of Illinois Press, 1976).

14. Jomo Kenyatta, *Facing Mount Kenya*. (New York: Vintage Books, Random House, 1965) 225.

15. John Mbiti, *African Religions and Philosophy (* Garden City: Anchor Books, Doubleday & Co., 1970) 36-37.

16. Gunter Wagner," The Abaluyia of Kavirondo :Kenya," in Daryll Forde, ed., *African Worlds* (New York: Oxford University Press 1968).

17. Davison, Op. Cit. p.116.

18. Ibid. p. 121

19. Ibid. p. 122

20. Ibid. p. 123

21. See: J. Janssen, *History of the German People at the Close of the Middle Ages1896-1910,* 16 vols., London: Kegan Paul International .

22. Davidson, Op Cit. 124.

23. Ibid. p. 126

24. Ibid.

25. Ibid. p. 48

26. Ibid. p. 78

27. Ibid p. 148

28. Ibid. p. 88

29. Ibid pp 147-49

30. Ibid. p. 150

31. Ibid. p. 154

32. Khapoya, Op. Cit. pp. 14-25

33. Ali A. Mazrui, "Africa and Other Civilizations" In John Harbeson and Donald Rothchild, eds., *Africa in World Politics: The African State System in Flux*. (Oxford University Press: London, 2000)

34. Daniel Osabu-Kle, *Compatible Cultural Democracy: The Key to Development in Africa* (Peterborough, Ontario, Canada : Broadview Press, 1985) 80.

35. Basil Davison, *The African Genius: An Introduction to African Social and Cultural History* (New York: Little Brown and Company, 1969) 190-91.

36. Ibid.

37. Ibid. p. 193

38. Ibid

39. Ibid p. 196

40. Ibid. p. 118

41. Fortes, Meyer and E. E. Evans-Pritchard. *African Political Systems* London: Oxford University Press New York: Kegan Paul International, 1940

4: The Major Maladies

Throughout recorded history, the major killers of human beings have been infectious diseases, such as smallpox, influenza, tuberculosis, malaria, the plague and cholera. These diseases evolved from animals, even though they are paradoxically confined to humans. Questions about the animal origin of diseases such as H5N1 and HIV/Aids are behind the broadest pattern of human history, and thus lie behind the most important issues confronting humanity.

In his Pulitzer prize winning work, *Guns, Germs and Steel*, Jared Diamond examines why some microbes evolved to "make us sick," whereas most other species of living things do not make us sick.[1] Microbes evolve like other species. The germ that spreads better and leaves more babies is favored by natural selection. Evolution selects those individuals most effective at producing babies and helps them spread to suitable places to live. For a microbe, spread may be defined mathematically as the number of new victims infected per each original patient. That number depends on how long each victim remains capable of infecting new victims, and how efficiently the microbe is transferred from one victim to the next.

The easiest way for a germ to spread is to wait to be passively transmitted to the next victim. In this manner, microbes are somewhat analogous to a parasitic invasion of corruption; they destroy the system from within. This strategy is employed by microbes that wait for one host to be eaten by the next host. For example in the salmonella bacteria, which is contracted by eating infected eggs or meat; or the worm responsible for trichinosis, which migrates from pigs to humans by waiting for humans to slaughter and improperly cook the animal. Another example is the worm causing anisakiasis, with which sushi lovers are often infected for consuming raw fish. For Diamond, the award for sheer physical effort goes to worms such as hookworms and schistosomes, which actively burrow into a host's skin from the water or soil into which their larvae had been excreted in a previous victim's feces.[2]

Other germs are much more aggressive, modifying the anatomy or habits of their host in order to accelerate transmission. For modification of the host's behavior, the rabies virus is most efficient, it not only gets into the saliva of an infected dog but drives the dog into a biting frenzy, thus infecting new victims. The open sores of genital venereal diseases serve as useful devices to enlist the host's help in inoculating microbes into a body cavity of a new host. Skin lesions caused by smallpox similarly spread microbes by direct or indirect body contact (occasionally very indirect), as when some in the US government, bent on wiping out "belligerent Indians," sent the Natives gifts of blankets previously used by smallpox patients).[3] From the human perspective, genital sores, diarrhea, and coughing are "symptoms of disease." From the microbe's perspective, they are clever evolutionary strategies to spread the germ. It is in the germ's interest to make us sick. Diamond asks; "Why should a germ evolve the apparently self-defeating strategy of killing its host"? From the germs perspective, death is an unintended by-product of host symptoms promoting the efficient transmission of microbes.[4]

In September 2003, the World Health Organization urgently appealed for $5.7 million to purchase 6 million doses of a new meningitis vaccine to preclude the annual outbreak in Africa's meningitis belt from Ethiopia to Senegal. *Glaxo-Smith Kline*, which developed the vaccine, offered the medicine at about $1.40 per dose. This is of course beyond the means of most Africans.

Aids, tuberculosis and malaria are three of Africa's major killer diseases. However, the focus on these diseases diverts resources from half a dozen easily treated illnesses that have a greater impact on healthcare and economic development in Africa. David Molyneux of the Liverpool School of Tropical Medicine, Peter Hotez of George Washington University and Alan Fenwick from Imperial College London called for the launch of "small costs, huge impact" public health program in sub-Saharan Africa. Backed by research and political support, the study, was published in the online journal *PLoS Medicine* and pointed out the high costs of and the failure to significantly reduce disease transmission. "We are not saying give less to the other diseases but lets have a balance," said Professor Fenwick." [5] Their study posits that only $200 million a year over five years to distribute four existing drugs could effectively treat 500 million people. This would rapidly reduce poverty and help to achieve seven of the Millennium Development Goals and the targets of the Commission for Africa. With pills that are already offered cheaply or free by existing manufacturers, Fenwick, Hotez and Molyneux estimate that 40 US cents per patient per year would cover the cost of medicines and wide-spread distribution for lymphatic filariasis, schistosomiasis, intestinal helminthes, onchorcerciasis and trachoma. Current treatment costs $200 annually per person for HIV/Aids and tuberculosis and $7 for each case of malaria, which can recur five to ten times each year. Efforts to raise short-term funding in order to implement proven treatments reflects the support provided by the International Financial Facility (IFF). Fenwick stresses the safety and effectiveness of these drugs which he claims can be "given" in combination throughout the population. *Mectizan* is donated by *Merck*, *Albendazole* by *Glaxo-Smith-Kline*, Zithromax by *Pfizer*, and *Praziquantel* which is produced cheaply by companies in China. Ironically, several of these drugs are already manufactured for profit in rich countries for the multi-billion dollar treatment of animal infection industry .

Malaria

Malaria, or "bad air" (formerly called *ague* or marsh fever in English) is an infectious disease which in humans causes about 350-500 million infections and approximately 1.3 million deaths (mainly in the tropics), annually. Sub-Saharan Africa accounts for 85% of these fatalities.[6] This disease kills an African child every thirty seconds. Malaria is caused by the protozoan parasites of the genus *Plasmodium* (one of the Apicomplexa), and the transmission vector for human malarial parasite is the female *Anopheles* mosquito. The *P. falciparum* variety of the parasite accounts for 80% of cases and 90% of deaths. Pregnant women and children under the age of five are most vulnerable. A French army doctor, Charles Louis Alphonse Laveran, was awarded the Nobel Prize for Physiology or Medicine in 1907 for his discovery of the cause of the disease. In 1902, Britain's Sir Ronald Ross also received a Nobel Prize for describing the life cycle of the malaria parasite as it develops in the bodies of its mosquito and in human hosts. It is thought that humans have been affected by malaria for about 50,000 years, and that several human genes responsible for blood cell proteins and the immune system have been shaped by the body's struggle against the parasite.[7]

In malarial-endemic African countries, between 25 and 40 per cent of all outpatient clinic visits are for malaria and between 20 and 50 per cent of hospital admission are for malaria-related illnesses. Understanding precisely how mosquitoes in a particular area resist insecticides may allow for the selective use of formulations that can overcome these defenses. The infected female *Anopheles* mosquito carries *Plasmodium* sporozoites in her salivary glands. If she bites a person, which they usually do starting at dusk and continuing throughout the night, the sporozoites enter the person's body via the mosquito's saliva, migrate to the liver where they multiply within hepatic liver cells. There they develop into merozoites which then enter red blood cells, where they further multiply, periodically breaking out of the red blood cells. The classical description of waves of fever coming every two or three days arises from simultaneous waves of merozoites breaking out of red blood cells.

The parasite is relatively protected from attack by the body's immune system because for most of its human life cycle it stays inside liver and blood cells. However, circulating infected blood cells are destroyed in the spleen. To avoid this fate, the parasite produces certain surface proteins, which infect blood cells present on their cell surface, causing the blood cells to stick to the walls of blood vessels. These surface proteins known as PfEMP1 are highly variable (there are at least 50 variations) and they do not serve as a reliable target for the immune system.

Malaria affects the lives of almost all in sub-Saharan Africa. The majority of infections are caused by *Plasmodium falciparum*, the most dangerous of the four human malaria parasites. The infection rate, according to statistics, is influenced by the imposing presence of the Anopheles mosquito, which is most difficult to control.

Carriers of the sickle cell anemia gene are protected against malaria because of their particular hemoglobin mutation; this explains why sickle cell anemia is particularly common among people of African origin. They have a specific variant of the beta-globin gene. Some scientists hypothesize that another hemoglobin mutation, which causes the genetic disease thalassemia, may also give its carriers an enhanced immunity to malaria. The choice of drug for prevention and/or treatment largely depends on the geographic area where infection is likely to occur.

In most parts of the world, *Chloroquine* was the antimalarial drug of choice for many years. However, resistance of *Plasmodium falciparum* to *Chloroquine* has spread from Asia to Africa, making the drug ineffective against the most dangerous *Plasmodium* strain in many affected regions of the world. There are several other substances which are used for treatment and partially for prophylaxis. Their deployment depends mainly on the frequency of resistant parasites in the area where the drug should be used.

The disease is a heavy burden on Africa which undermines future socio-economic well-being. According to the World Health Organization's weekly epidemiological records, the disease is most devastating among Africa's poor. According to WHO data, malaria kills between 1-2 million children each year Africa. Between 15 and 40 per cent of children with cerebral malaria, associated acidosis and anemia will die. Half will die within 12 hours of arriving at the hospital.

Children under the age of five and pregnant women are most at risk. Data show that over 90 per cent of all malaria deaths in Africa occur in young children who most often, are infected during within two years of life with cerebral malaria, anemia, diarrhea, respiratory infections and other treatable infections. The two per cent of children who recover from cerebral malaria infections suffer from learning impairment, disabilities, epilepsy and spasticity.

In November 2005, some 1,500 scientists, policymakers, African ministers, health care workers, community members and other experts on malaria gathered for the fourth Multilateral Initiative on Malaria Pan-African Malaria conference and the "Roll Back Malaria Global Partners" forum in Yaoundé. The MIM Pan African Malaria conference "Focus on Malaria," highlighted the African effort to empower communities, battle complacency and eliminate the barriers of effective prevention and treatment for the most vulnerable.

East African scientists are sharing new findings on the anti-mosquito properties of indigenous African plants as a low-cost and effective mosquito repellent that could play a role in reducing malaria transmission.

Scientists at Nairobi's Kenyatta University and The International Center for Insect Physiology & Ecology (ICIPE) are working with scientists from other East African research institutions. They have tested oils extracted from 150 East African plants for their properties to repel malaria-carrying mosquitoes and found that 20 of them appeared to be effective. They have formulated a mixture of the oils into a topical cream that is now being marketed under the brand name *Mozigone*. Their tests show the cream was more effective than DEET, the chemical found in most widely used consumer brands of mosquito repellent and cheaper to produce as well. The discussion of the scientific process that led to the development of this new, plant-based repellent was one of many presentations made at the MIM conference exploring how modern research is turning to traditional plants to find new weapons for the fight against malaria.

Scientific efforts to derive new malaria medicines from indigenous plants have intensified since an extract of the wormwood plant, artemesinin, emerged as the leading drug for fighting the disease. "There are certainly many opportunities for the use of traditional herbal medicines for malaria control;" said Merlin Wilcox, coordinator of an international network known as the *Research Initiative for Traditional Anti-malarial Methods* (RITAM). But there are obstacles as well. "The main problem is that policy makers are not open to this idea, because they are trained only in modern medicine." Also, they demand strong evidence, but it is hard to find funding for the research needed to produce this evidence.

In Mozambique, doctors tested the most advanced vaccine, RTSS, to combat Africa's greatest child killer, malaria. Malaria is a blood parasite spread by mosquitoes. Traditional drugs such as chloroquine are no longer effective and newer drugs lose their effectiveness as the plasmodium parasite develops resistance. RTSS produced a short-term immune response in seven out of ten volunteers when tested in the Gambia. Recent efforts to decode the malaria parasite's genome have provided researchers with 5,000 potential targets for new vaccines. According to Melinda Moree director of the Malaria Vaccine Initiative, funding even a few of them will be impossible.

The Malaria Vaccine Initiative, a public-private partnership plan to inoculate 2,000 children in an 18-month trial. RTSS, also developed by *Glaxo-Smith-Kline*, is one of 16 potential vaccines in clinical testing for use against malaria. Adrian Hill, an Oxford University scientist, observed that if RTSS protected only half the children of Mozambique it would be a significant breakthrough. If successful, it would be the first demonstration that a vaccine can control malaria in real world conditions. If it fails, more products are waiting for trial. The partnership has only $65 million; a figure dwarfed by the $360 million budget of the US National Institute of Health spends on Aids vaccine research. "Aids kills a lot of people too, but if Mr.

Bush mentions malaria during his visit that would be nice;" Melinda Moree lamented.

The situation in Cameroon is equally alarming, where malaria accounts for 40 to 45 per cent of all medical consultations, 57 per cent of hospitalization and 26 per cent of all sick leaves. Cameroon is often described by scientists as "Africa in miniature" due to its diversity of climatic and ecological conditions. An extensive study conducted on a malaria-carrying mosquito in differing ecological zones of Cameroon reveals a widespread and varied resistance to insecticides. This is part of an alarming trend across Africa that could ultimately jeopardize efforts to control malaria with treated bed nets and indoor spraying. The study was presented at a special session on insecticide resistance at the Fourth Multilateral Initiative on Malaria (MIM) Pan-African Malaria Conference. It illustrates a growing body of research in Africa that is finding increasing mosquito resistance to pyrethroid insecticides, which are used for insecticide-treated bed nets and to DDT, which has been used successfully in household spraying programs.

Scientists at Cameroon's Institute of Medical Research and Study of Medicinal Plants (IMPM) and the Organization for Endemic Disease Control in Central Africa (OCEAC), believe their findings are applicable to the other malaria endemic regions of Africa because they analyzed mosquito populations at 32 different sites located across the country. The IMPM/OCEAC study illuminates how mosquitoes in different areas of Africa employ a variety of biological weapons to fight off insecticides. For example, in the northern cotton and rice fields of Cameroon, malaria vectors rapidly detoxify or "metabolize" pyrethroids, effectively neutralizing their killing capability.

In western Cameroon's tropical gardens, mosquitoes survive both pyrethroids and DDT through forming what is called a "knock-down response" or KDR, a genetic mutation and modification of the target site. This mutation desensitizes the target of the DDT and pyrethroids insecticides in the mosquito's nervous system. In coastal and inland equatorial areas of Cameroon, some mosquitoes have developed both resistance mechanisms. "The range of mechanisms involved in resistance is likely having an impact on the effectiveness of treated bed nets," said Josiane Etang, the lead researcher. "Overall, we need to rethink management strategies, especially in areas where the KDR mutation and detoxification are coupled." He also noted that research is needed to understand which of the two KDR mutations is most prevalent in Cameroon. One is more common in the West, the other in the East, but both may be present in Cameroon. Andreas Heddini, the MIM secretariat coordinator, noted; "The potential for insecticide resistance to interfere with promising malaria interventions requires urgent attention. But if we have scientists in the field throughout Africa regularly monitoring mosquito populations then we will have the up to date evidence we need to guide an effective response."

African cooperation with China on health issues is developing with a small group of African investors and farmers seeking to relieve the shortage of Artemisia, a Chinese herb that is a critical new therapy in the battle against malaria. The herb is mainly grown in China and Vietnam, but increasing demand requires greater production for use in artemesinin-based combination therapies (ACTs). Artemisia has been used for medicinal purposes in China for more than 1,500 years and was developed as an anti-malarial drug in the 1970s to help the North Vietnamese army. Despite its low cost, effectiveness and the absence of side effects associated with combination therapy, there is growing international consensus that Artemesinin should be taken in combination with other drugs in order to prevent the development of resistance.

Health officials are trying to diversify the cultivation of Artemisia and the production of the extract artemesinin with projects in Kenya and Tanzania, where the climate facilitates the growth of the plant in six to nine months. African farmers have been growing the herb on a small scale for ten years through two micro-companies: African Artemisia in Arusha, Tanzania and its Kenyan counterpart, East African Botanicals (EAB). During most of that time these companies struggled in isolation with little capital, shared office space and enjoyed or created little demand. However, since the shortage of Artemisia in Asia, EAB has been approached by some of the world's largest producers of anti-malarial drugs. The US Agency for International Development (USAID) and the WHO are considering working with EAB on the Kenyan and Tanzanian projects. Allan Schapira, a WHO malaria expert said: "We want Artemisia to be grown in Africa as soon as possible, but we want a strong market and market growth in the future."[8] There are an estimated 500 million cases of malaria around the world every year, and growing drug resistance, combined with failing health systems in Africa mean an increase in those suffering symptoms and death, approximately 1 million per year.

The WHO does not endorse monotherapy treatment, but in 2005 it issued guidelines urging any remaining countries to ban such treatment in their national health systems. Most countries complied by officially renouncing monotherapies-with the possible exceptions of China and Vietnam. "Drug resistance is a huge problem and we have to pre-empt resistance with artemesinin because it could take 10 years before another alternative drug could emerge," said Dr. Arata Kochi senior malaria official of the World Health Organization. The marketing and sale of single drug "monotherapy" to treat malaria could lead to increased drug resistance. Dr. Kochi identified 18 pharmaceutical companies whose production of medicines risked triggering drug resistance and jeopardizing the fight against malaria. Among those named were *Sanofi-Aventis,* a Paris-based group and *Cipla*, the India-based generic manufacturer, which are often praised by aids activists for their role in producing cheap antiretroviral medicines. *Sanofi-Aventis,* one of the world's largest pharmaceutical houses, announced it would withdraw it monotherapies. Dr. Kochi threatened that if these companies failed to withdraw monotherapies for malaria, he would consider other measures, including urging organizations, including the World Bank and the Global Fund to Fight Aids, TB and Malaria. He would also consider removing the "pre-qualification" status given by the WHO to companies which produce monotherapies for malaria as well as combination therapies.

Dr. Yusuf Hamied, head of *Cipla*, the Indian generics maker, acknowledges producing some monotherapies as well as combination therapies for malaria. Dr. Kochi said those drugs were often supplied for use with a range of different second treatments depending on local circumstances.[9]

Dafra, the world's most important supplier of artemesinin-based monotherapy to the private market in Africa recently came under scrutiny by public health experts. Herwig Jansen, a chemist who worked for *Dafra* before starting his own company, estimates that 75-80 percent of *Dafra's* $18 million in annual sales come from Arinate, its artesunate tablets and related products including Artesian, an injectable equivalent. Jansen, who sees himself as a pioneer in the field of developing the drug in a range of forms, claims to have owned the first factory producing artemesinin in China in the 1990s. "China and Vietnam have successfully used monotherapy for 20 years without a problem of resistance. It has saved the lives of so many people; he states."[10] Jansen claims a study in Africa has shown to be effective in 24 hours, rather than in the three days scientist argue is necessary. Jansen has a 100-strong sales force in Africa and factories in Nairobi and Lusaka. He claims that he would like to see the world shift toward combination treatments for malaria. He says that his company provides such medicine, but that the side effects associated with the second drug "put people off." Some African importers refused one combination therapy he offered with *amodiaquine*. "They said the doctors told them they wouldn't see their patients again if they prescribed it." Critics are nervous about *Dafra's* plans to launch a combination therapy.

For the WHO, *Dafra* is part of the problem, preying on desperate Africans by selling them a monotherapy that runs the risk of triggering resistance. The adaptability of the malaria parasite has rendered single drugs such as chloroquine all but useless. This same principle applies to drugs for tuberculosis and HIV, which are always given in combination. Pascal Ringwald, of the WHO, warns: "If we wait for the full evidence we will be too late." There are already signs of malaria resistance to artemesinin in laboratory tests.

In some areas efforts to eradicate malaria by eliminating mosquitoes have been successful. Malaria was once common in the United States and southern Europe, but the draining of wetland breeding grounds and improved sanitation, in conjunction with the monitoring and treatment of infected humans eliminated it from more affluent regions. Malaria was eliminated from the northern parts of the USA in the early twentieth century and with the use of the pesticide DDT during the 1950s, it was eliminated from the south.

A major public health effort to eradicate malaria worldwide by selectively targeting mosquitoes in areas where malaria was rampant was launched in the 1950s and 1960s.[11] However, these efforts ultimately failed to target malaria in the developing world. Thus, the disease indiscriminately kills African infants and children.

DDT, the first of the modern insecticides, was developed and initially used with great effectiveness to combat malaria spreading mosquitoes. It was banned for use in many countries in the 1970s due to its negative environmental impact. There remains great controversy regarding this impact and the use of DDT to fight human diseases. Some claim that the ban is responsible for malaria deaths counted in the tens of millions in tropical countries where the disease had been under control. The WHO recently recommended that the walls of village huts in infected areas be sprayed with DDT because there would be minimal environmental effect.

The World Bank estimates that malaria costs Africans about $12 billion a year in lost productivity. Yet international funding for malaria control only totals $100 to $200 million a year.[12] It is argued that, in order to meet the Millennium Development Goals, the money should be redirected from HIV/AIDS treatment to malaria prevention, which for the same amount of money would provide a much greater stimulus to economic development.[13]

Insecticide-treated bed nets (ITNs) offer great potential to dramatically reduce malaria infections in Africa and campaigns to ITN use have met with some success. According to research findings presented at the Fourth Multilateral Initiative on Malaria (MIM) Pan-African Malaria Conference, issues of inadequate supply, lack of funding, apathy and lack of empathy, complex community attitudes and disagreement about the threat and role of mosquitoes as the cause of malaria, challenge efforts to provide sufficient anti-malaria controls. African leaders meeting Abuja, Nigeria in 2000 agreed that 60 percent of vulnerable groups-mainly pregnant women and children under 5-should be sleeping under ITNs by 2005.

NetMark is a public-private partnership working to increase both the supply and demand for ITNs. Martin Alilio, *NetMark* senior policy advisor and research director and his associates held a session to discuss the results of the extensive five-country survey that sought to gauge ITN ownership and use since 2000. *NetMark* conducted surveys in Nigeria, Senegal, and Zambia in 2000 and in 2004. In 2004, Ghana and Ethiopia were also surveyed. "One thing that is clear is that while there has been admirable progress in using ITNs, the research points to several areas where additional work is needed. There have been increases-sometimes dramatic-in awareness, ownership, and use of insecticide-treated nets to prevent malaria. And we've found that those most vulnerable to malaria are given priority for using the nets;" said Alilio". Continued efforts are needed to keep expanding the accessibility and affordability of nets, especially to poor households.

What the survey reveals is that by the end of 2004, there was a considerable boost in ITN ownership. In Zambia, ITN household ownership climbed from

6 percent to 35 percent. In Nigeria household ITN ownership more than doubled jumping from 12 to 27 percent. In Zambia household ownership increased from 25 to 50 percent. In Senegal household ownership went from 34 to 56 percent. Although more people are using ITNs, usage varies from country to country. Generally, the proportions of children under five and pregnant women under ITN's rose substantially. The *NetMark* study notes that perceptions of ITN's are very favorable overall and surpass perceptions about other insect control products such as aerosols and coils. Soori Nnko of the National Institute for Medical Research in Tanzania, reported on research from a two-year field study in rural northwestern Tanzania. The study found that despite extensive national public health campaigns, the majority of people contacted failed to re-treat their nets with insecticides even though cost was not an issue. Tanzanians cited concerns about toxicity and doubts about the effectiveness of ITNs

The study also revealed concern that pregnant women using nets treated with insecticide dropped to negligible levels in 2004. It points to areas needing continued emphasis by malaria control programs. Although ITNs are used in a significant proportion in some countries, they are not used when it is hot. The programs emphasize that nets are to be used year-round, even when there are few mosquitoes.

Andreas Heddini, the secretariat coordinator for MIM, said the findings from the *NetMark* research and other ITN related research shows that scientists are moving aggressively throughout Africa to identify and explore any obstacles that may prevent widespread adoption of ITN's for malaria control. "The fact that so many researchers are going into African communities, urban and rural, rich and poor, and probing what it will take to get more people sleeping under ITN's is a sign of progress;" observes Heddini. "The science demonstrating their effectiveness at killing malaria-carrying mosquitoes is quite strong. Now we need researchers on the ground in Africa telling us precisely what we need to do to realize the potential of this powerful tool."

In Mozambique, doctors tested the most advanced vaccine, *RTSS*, to combat Africa's greatest child killer. Traditional drugs such as chloroquine are no longer effective and newer drugs lose their effectiveness as the plasmodium parasite develops resistance. The *RTSS* vaccine produced a short-term immune response in seven out of ten volunteers when tested in the Gambia. Recent efforts to decode the malaria parasite's genome have provided researchers with 5,000 potential targets for new vaccines. However, funding even a few of them will be impossible according to Melinda Moree, director of the Malaria Vaccine Initiative, a public-private partnership plan to inoculate 2,000 children within an 18-month trial period. RTSS, also developed by *Glaxo-Smith-Kline*, is one of 16 potential vaccines in clinical testing for use against malaria which kills 1 million Africans each year. Adrian Hill, an Oxford University scientist, observed that if *RTSS* protected only half the children of Mozambique it would be a significant breakthrough.

If successful, it would prove the first time that anyone has demonstrated a vaccine that can control malaria in real world conditions. If it fails, more products are waiting for trial. The partnership had only $65 million; a figure dwarfed by the $360 million budget of the US National Institute of Health spends on Aids vaccine research. "Aids kills a lot of people too, but if Mr. Bush mentions malaria this week that would be nice," Ms. Moree commented. George W. Bush's 2006 Presidential Malaria Initiative pledged to spend $1.2 billion by 2010 and promised to stimulate private-sector donations.[14]

In March 2007, The British All Party Parliamentary Malaria Group issued a report on financing mechanisms for tackling malaria calling for immediate action to increase funding and for more effective deployment of resources. The Global Fund to Fight Aids, TB and Malaria, the World Bank's Booster Initiative and George W. Bush's Malaria Initiative committed $767 million by 2010. But this is far short of the $3.2 billion required to substantially reduce the impact of the disease.[15]

New and encouraging medical developments have contributed to the treatment of malaria. In March 2007, a French pharmaceutical company and a Swiss Charity launched production of a low-cost malaria drug for Africa. *Asaq,* named after its two constituent drugs artesunate and amodiaquine combined in a single pill offers a relatively affordable and simple treatment. *Asaq* is the first product of a growing number of "product development partnerships," combining the Drugs for Neglected Diseases Initiative (DNDI) in Geneva, a non-profit organization that coordinates academic research groups with *Sanofi-Aventis* the French pharmaceutical manufacturer.[16]

Bird Flu

Humans have been challenged by another mutating disease, Bird Flu or the H5NI strain. There are more than 1 billion domestic fowl in sub-Saharan Africa. In February 2006, the deadly H5N1 strain of Bird flu was confirmed on several farms in northern Nigeria. Tens of thousands of birds were destroyed in culls supervised by the government. In a country where millions depend on birds as a source of food, some officials feared the virus had already spread beyond the reach of the government. This outbreak of bird flu in Nigeria is the first known in Africa, but the disease had already killed 90 people in Asia. Neighboring countries quickly banned poultry imports from Nigeria. However, government restrictions and sealing off national borders cannot arrest the spread of disease.

The Nigerian government's response was undermined by a lack of technical expertise, administrative delays and bureaucratic conflicts between myriad ministries and authorities. Culling at some farms was performed by farm workers who used their bare hands to throw sick and dead chickens into the flames. The government dispatched small clean up teams, equipped with 2,000 safety suits donated by the United States. The UN sent teams of experts to offer technical assistance on quarantining, culling and testing laboratories and mapping the spread of the virus. The teams faced the difficult task of overseeing safe culling and looking for ways to stem the spread of the virus to remote rural areas where chickens run freely in villages and backyards. "It is a disaster. We are concerned for Nigeria, but also for the region as a whole. We do not want to spread any more panic:" said Juan Lubroth, a senior official of the UN Food and Agriculture Organization (FAO).

The FAO recommended that the government control the movement of poultry resulting in a wave of poultry panic selling in some markets. This underscores the difficulties associated with enforcing emergency policies in a country of 130 million people who travel with their chickens on public transportation. The Nigerian government has promised a small compensation to the farmers for each bird lost to H5N1, but many local and state authorities were reluctant or unable to close down poultry markets. While the World Health Organization and other UN agencies offered technical assistance and worked to raise awareness of H5N1, they expected Nigeria to implement its own national program.[17] Nigerian officials claimed illegally imported poultry could be the source of the virus. Others say the virus arrived in Nigeria via migrations of wild birds, many of which travel to Nigeria from other parts of the world. The outbreak stemmed from three distinct strains that entered the country at different times. Research findings published in the journal *Nature*, found that different strains closely resembled those identified in Egypt, Russia and Mongolia. The genetic analysis of the Nigerian viruses was led by the Institute of Immunology and Luxembourg's National Public Health Laboratory. The analysts found that one Lagos strain was genetically found in a chicken in Egypt. "If there are multiple introductions, that means there are several risks in the way the virus can get into Nigeria," said Juan Lubroth, of the FAO's infectious diseases group.[18]

There is an additional economic risk posed to families who will lose vital income derived from selling the eggs and poultry raised in their backyards, and the resultant malnutrition. For example, in Uganda, almost half of all rural families own three or more domestic birds. Most chickens are kept for their eggs, which are a valuable source of vitamin A (which protects children from blindness) as well as protein. One egg can supply 20 percent of a five-year olds child's daily protein requirement. The loss of one egg may not sound like much, but it can be critical for nutrient-deprived individuals exposed to many kinds of viruses.

Cholera

Cholera is a disease that is transmitted through contaminated food and water. Left untreated, the mortality rate can reach 50 percent. It is an infectious disease, caused by bacteria that are usually ingested by drinking water contaminated by improper sanitation or by eating improperly cooked fish, especially shellfish. Cholera was first described in a scientific manner by the Portuguese physician Garcia de Orta in the 16th century. Symptoms include explosive diarrhea, abdominal cramps, nausea, vomiting, and dehydration. Death is generally due to the dehydration caused by the illness. Treatment typically consists of aggressive rehydration. With treatment, death rates plummet.

Cholera produces potentially lethal secretory diarrhea through a pathway that involves the Cystic Fibrosis Transmembrane conductance Regulator or CFTR. This discovery led to the hypothesis that carriers of cystic fibrosis, who have lower levels of functional CFTR, are protected from the severe effects of cholera because they don't lose water as quickly as others. This might explain the high incidence of cystic fibrosis among populations which were formerly exposed to cholera. However, no evidence of resistance (*in vivo*)has been observed in humans.

Recent genetic research has determined that a person's susceptibility to cholera (and other diarrheas) is affected by their blood type. Those with type O blood are the most susceptible. Those with type AB are the most immune. Between these two extremes are the A and B blood types, with type A being more resistant than type B.[20] In 2005, several West African countries, including Liberia, Guinea, Mauritania, Guinea Bissau, and Burkina-Faso, have suffered horrific cholera outbreaks. In most countries, a large number of patients were from the capital cities. Doctors of Medicine Without Borders/*Médecins Sans Frontières* (MSF), actively fought the outbreak of cholera across the region, sending additional staff and supplies in response. After an initial assessment in Guinea Bissau, where the epidemic was quickly expanding, *MSF* chartered a flight with more than 70 tons of medical and logistical supplies including 3,000 cholera kits and first aid first kits, 2,400 meters of plastic sheeting, 12 dispensary tents to serve as treatment centers, 1,200 jerry cans, water tanks and spraying equipment.

"*MSF* is increasing its response capacity to face the cholera outbreak all over West Africa," said Stephan Goetghebuer, the Brussels-based regional operational coordinator. In Burkina-Faso *MSF* treated 282 patients, in Liberia's capital Monrovia 2,337 severe cases and in Guinea Conakry MSF treated 7,291 suspected infections, where they set up three treatment centers and provided support to another two. In Mauritania they have treated over 1,000 people. They planned to open cholera centers in Guinea Bissau, and hope to reach Kachek Island in Guinea Conakry. Overall figures show that the number of cases are growing across many countries in West Africa."

Patients had to be rehydrated with oral re-hydration salts. Many of the outbreaks occurred in Africa's capital cities such Monrovia, Conakry, Ouagadougou, and Nouakchott. In Guinea, of the 1,779 cases reported more than 1,000 were in the capital's Donka Hospital. According to Charlotte Bohot, head of mission for *MSF* in Guinea; "Many people arrive at the hospital from the poor and marginalized areas of Ratoma and Matoto. That is why we decided to open two more cholera centers there and start a public awareness campaign." Her colleague in Liberia, Miles Kemplay, witnessed a similar pattern. "In Monrovia, living conditions are incredibly poor; all over the city people are vulnerable to communicable disease." In one week there were 153 severe cases and 306 suspected infections. The heavy rains and terrible sanitation helped to spread the disease.

Public awareness is an important element in the efforts of *MSF* and other organizations. They try to explain to the population how to protect themselves from being infected and where to go to receive medical assistance. In Liberia, *MSF* commissioned a 'cholera song' in collaboration with the ministry of health. During the entire month of August, the song was played on ELBC Radio and Radio Veritas, two of the most popular stations in Liberia. *MSF* planned to open its first cholera treatment center in Guinea Bissau within days. [21]

MSF has been operating in Chad for 20 years. Part of the organization's role there is supporting the ministry of health in fighting cholera, meningitis, and measles epidemics. The last major *MSF* cholera intervention was in 2001 when 5,000 cases were registered.[22] In June 2004, another cholera epidemic emerged in Chad, with more than 2,000 infections and 100 deaths. A new *MSF* cholera treatment center was built by in the capital city, N'Djamena. One week later, it was full. The cholera treatment center was constantly filled to 80-patient capacity. "Treatment is relatively easy if patients are found early enough. Patients usually stay two or three days in the treatment center. We currently have a turnover of some 35 people each day. The local population is well aware that cholera is related to a lack of hygiene. So, people wait for the last moment to come to our center. When these patients arrive, the disease is already in a well-advanced stage;" explains Stéphane Heymans, head of the *MSF* mission in Chad.

MSF cholera treatment includes consultations and hospitalization. The center is staffed by local ministry of health personnel, with the help of an *MSF* team of three international volunteers (one medical coordinator, one nurse, and one specialist in water and sanitation). *MSF* also provides supplies, such as standard kits for treating cholera. Of the 221 patients, eight died. One of the main problems with cholera is the stigma linked to the disease. Controlling the spread of the disease is the essential factor. In addition to treatment, it is important to isolate patients and disinfect their homes. "As soon as a sick person arrives at the treatment center, one of our three mobile teams is sent to the person's home to spray chlorinated water inside the house and on clothes. This should protect the people still living on the premises," explained a local *MSF* nurse. The primary objective of building the treatment center was to relieve some of the pressure on Chadian health facilities, such as the "HÃ´pital Liberté," which only has a capacity to treat 100 patients and receives 70 new cholera cases a day. The situation is extremely worrying in N'Djamena, which has over one million inhabitants, many of whom live in unsanitary conditions. [23]

Dengue Fever, Diarrhea & Diphtheria

Dengue fever or (DHF) once emerged of as a major public health problem in the America's. In a 1950s-60s effort to prevent urban yellow fever, the Pan American Health Organization (PAHO) launched a campaign that eradicated the *Ae. Aegypti germ* in Central and South America. As a result, epidemic dengue occurred only sporadically in some Caribbean islands. The eradication program was officially discontinued in the United States in 1970, and steadily weakened elsewhere.

In 2002, mosquitoes began to reinfest countries from which diarrhea had been eradicated. The result was wider geographic spread of the *Ae. Aegypti* germ.[24] DHF broke out in East Africa, where major epidemics were reported for the first time: Kenya (1982), Mozambique (1985), Djibouti (1991-92), Somalia (1982, 1993), and Saudi Arabia (1994). Epidemic DHF has not been reported recently, but sporadic outbreaks have been reported from Mozambique, Djibouti and Saudi Arabia.

Diarrhea (from the ancient Greek word διαρροή = leakage; i.e.,"to run through"), is a condition of frequent watery, chunky, or loose bowel movements. In the Third World, it is the most common cause of death among infants, killing more than 1.5 million per year. It can be symptom of injury, disease, or a food borne illness and it is usually accompanied by abdominal pain, nausea and vomiting. There are other conditions which involve a combination of these symptoms. The medical definition of diarrhea is defecation of more than 200 grams per day (though formal weighing of stools for diagnosis is rarely done).

Diarrhea occurs when insufficient fluid is absorbed by the colon. As part of the digestion process, or due to fluid intake, food is mixed with large amounts of water and food is liquefied prior to reaching the colon. The colon absorbs the water, leaving the remaining material as a semisolid stool. If the colon is damaged or inflamed, absorption is inhibited and watery stools result.

Diarrhea is commonly caused by myriad viral infections, but is also often the result of bacterial toxins. In sanitary living conditions and with ample food and water available, an otherwise healthy patient typically recovers from common viral infections within a week. However, for malnourished individuals diarrhea can lead to life-threatening severe dehydration. It can also be a symptom of more serious diseases, such as dysentery, cholera, or botulism and be indicative of a chronic syndrome such as Crohn's disease. Although appendicitis patients don't generally have diarrhea, it is a common symptom of a ruptured appendix. This is also an effect of severe radiation sickness or be caused by excessive alcohol consumption, particularly among people who don't eat enough.

Diphtheria is a highly contagious disease spread by direct physical contact or inhaling the secretions of the infected. It is an upper respiratory tract illness characterized by sore throat, low fever and a sticky membrane on the tonsils, pharynx and nose. A milder form of diphtheria is limited to the skin. It is caused by *Corynebacterium diphtheriae*, an air-borne or *aerobic* bacterium.

The respiratory form of diphtheria has an incubation time of 1-4 days. Symptoms include fatigue, fever, a mild sore throat and problems swallowing. Children have symptoms that include nausea, vomiting, chills, and a high fever, although some do not show symptoms until the infection has progressed further. The disease is manageable, but in severe cases, lymph nodes in the neck may swell and breathing and swallowing will become difficult. People in this stage require immediate medical attention for obstruction of the throat may require a tracheotomy. In addition, an increase in heart rate may cause cardiac arrest. Diphtheria can also cause paralysis in the eye, neck, throat, or respiratory muscles.[25] Patients with severe cases are put in Intensive Care Units and given anti-toxins and bactericidal drugs such as penicillin and erythromycin. Physical activity should be limited, especially in cases where there is inflammation of the heart muscles. Recovery is slow.[26]

Once quite common, diphtheria has been largely eradicated in developed nations. In the US for example, there have been fewer than 5 cases reported a year since 1980). The Diphtheria-Tetanus-Pertussis (DPT) vaccine is given to all school children. Booster shots are recommended for adults because the benefits of the vaccine decrease with age. Booster shots are recommended for those traveling to areas where the disease has not been eradicated. Few in sub-Sharan Africa can afford these shots.

Meningitis

Meningitis, is an infection of the meninges membrane, which covers the brain and the spinal cord. According to Paul van Haperen, MSF director in Chad, without treatment the disease kills between 50 to 80 percent of those who contract it. In January 2005, there was a small outbreak in the Darfur refugee camps in Bredjing and Treguine of Chad. High population density in the refugee camps makes the spread of meningitis more likely. Chad is located within an area spanning sub-Saharan Africa known as the "meningitis belt," where epidemics affecting many thousands of people occur frequently.[27] In Chad alone, outbreaks occurred in 1998, 2000 and 2001. MSF has worked along Chad's eastern border since September 2003 and is providing medical and surgical relief, nutritional support, water and sanitation facilities to over 85,000 Sudanese refugees. After several years, the living conditions in these camps remain deplorable. The outbreak was caused by the relatively rare "W135" strain of the meningococcus bacterium.

In July 2005, Without Borders/*Médecins Sans Frontiéres* launched a meningitis vaccination campaign in eastern Chad, following an outbreak among refugees from Sudan's Darfur region. The campaign focused on protecting thousands of people in the overcrowded camps. MSF mobilized its vaccination teams as quickly as possible. Mobile teams covered a number of vaccination sites in addition to the refugee camps and three sites in Adré town and other outlying areas. MSF improved the surveillance system in the district and treated patients who had contracted the disease with antibiotics.

MSF worked with local health authorities and the International Federation of Red Cross and Red Crescent Societies. Within two weeks, MSF vaccinated about 70,000 refugees and local residents in the border town of Adré. [28]

A meningitis vaccine is available, including one effective against the W135 strain, largely due to the combined efforts of MSF, the WHO, the International Federation of the Red Cross and Red Crescent Societies (IFRC), the United Nations International Children's Emergency Fund (UNICEF) and other international donors. This is a more sophisticated type of vaccine that provides longer protection against bacteria, but unfortunately there are no such vaccines against meningitis in the research and development pipeline.[29] In 2003, a campaign to pressure *Glaxo-Smith-Kline* (GSK) to produce this vaccine at an affordable price, one dollar per dose. MSF was instrumental in funding the pre-purchase of 6 million doses of the vaccine by mobilizing donor governments and individuals to raise the necessary funding.

While the situation in Chad was ameliorated, the remaining 5.7 million doses of the vaccine is insufficient should a larger epidemic involving many countries, or one big country like Nigeria occur. Since production of the vaccine takes 6 months, it is important to monitor the situation and, if necessary, for *GSK* to produce sufficient vaccine at the same affordable price. In the long term, there is a strong need for a vaccine that is effective for all strains of meningitis endemic in Africa.

African Trypanosomiasis or Sleeping Sickness

Human African trypanosomiasis, known as sleeping sickness, is a vector-borne parasitic disease of the genus *Trypanosoma*. The parasites concerned, are protozoa transmitted to humans by tsetse flies (*glossina*). Tsetse flies live in Africa, and they are found in the vegetation by rivers and lakes, gallery-forests and vast stretches of wooded savannah. Another human form of trypanosomiasis (Human American Trypanosomiasis) occurs in the Americas and is known as Chagas disease.

Sleeping sickness or African trypanosomiasis is a parasitic disease. The disease is endemic in Sub-Saharan Africa, covering about 36 countries and 60 million people. An estimated 300,000-500,000 people are infected, and about 40,000 die each year. Three major epidemics have occurred within the past one hundred and ten years, in 1896-1906, 1920, and 1970. 3-10% of those infected have a reactive encephalopathy (convulsions, progressive coma, or psychotic reactions) a perhaps 50% die. Encephalopathy can cause brain damage in survivors. Another serious effect of sleeping sickness is blindness.[30]

The disease occurs in two forms, depending on the parasite, either *Trypanosoma brucei gambiense* or *Trypanosoma brucei rhodesiense*. The *T. b. gambiense* parasite is found in central and western Africa; it causes a chronic condition that can extend in a passive phase for months or years before symptoms emerge. A person can be infected for months or even years without obvious symptoms of the disease emerging. When symptoms do emerge, the disease is already at an advanced stage. The *T. b. rhodesiense* parasite is the acute condition of the disease but it has a much more limited range. The condition is found in southern and eastern Africa where it develops faster, is more virulent and therefore more quickly clinically detected.

The trypanosome can cross the placenta and infect the fetus causing abortion and perinatal death. Accidental infections can occur in laboratories, through the handling of blood of an infected person, although this is rare. Early symptoms include bouts of fever, headaches, pains in the joints and itching. The second phase, known as the neurological phase, begins when the parasite crosses the blood-brain barrier and infests the central nervous system. At this stage the characteristic signs and symptoms of the disease appear: confusion, sensory disturbances and poor coordination. The sleep-cycle is disturbed giving the disease its name, is the most important symptom. Without treatment, the disease is fatal. If the patient is not treated before the onset of the second phase, the neurological damage is irreversible.

Sleeping Sickness has been present in Africa at least the 14th century. The cause and the vector of the disease were identified in 1902- 1903 by Sir David Bruce. But the differentiation between the protozoa was not made until 1910. An arsenic based drug, atoxyl, developed by Paul Ehrlich and Kiyoshi Shiga in 1906, was the first effective treatment. In 1920, *Suramin* was introduced to treat the first stage of the disease. Later, it was generally combined with *Tryparsamide* in the treatment of the second-stage. Tryparsamide, an pentavalent organo-arsenic drug entered the market in 1922. It is effective in treating the second stage of the disease of the *gambiense* strain. It was used during an epidemic in West and Central Africa on millions of people and remained the primary therapy until about 1960.

After 1939, *Pentamidine*, another drug for treatment of the first stage of sleeping sickness, was effectively used as a prophylactic agent in Western Africa, leading to a sharp decline in infection rates. At the time, it was thought that eradication of the disease was near. An organo-arsenical medicine, *Melarsoprol* (Arsobal), which is widely-used currently, was developed in the 1940s, was effective for patients with second-stage sleeping sickness.

In the past the two centuries, there have been three serious epidemic outbreaks of sleeping sickness in Africa: The first, between 1896 and 1906, occurred mostly in Uganda and in the Congo Basin. The second, in 1920 struck several African countries. In 1923, shortly upon returning from a visit to South Africa, A British statesman, Lord Alfred Milner, died of the disease. The epidemic was controlled after mobile teams systematically screened millions of people at risk. The disease practically disappeared between 1960 and 1965. After successful screening and effective surveillance were relaxed, the disease reappeared in an endemic form. The current outbreak, began in 1970.

Strangely, there are many regions where tsetse flies are found, but sleeping sickness is not. Rural populations that live in such environments and depend on them for agriculture, fishing, animal husbandry or hunting, find that their livestock are most exposed to the bite of the tsetse fly. Sleeping sickness affects remote and rural areas where health systems are least effective, or non-existent. It spreads with socio-economic misery such as political instability, displacement of populations and war. It develops in areas ranging in size from a single village to an entire region. Within a given area, the intensity of the disease can vary considerably from one village to the next. Human African trypanosomiasis takes two forms, depending on the parasite involved. .

Almost 45,000 cases of the disease were reported in 1999, the WHO estimates that the number of people affected to be ten times greater. The 45,000 figure does not reflect reality, but rather the lack of screening. The real number of cases was estimated to be between 300,000-500,000. Reported cases in come from countries where surveillance coverage is no more than 5 percent. In certain villages and many provinces of Angola, the Democratic Republic of Congo and southern Sudan, the prevalence of the disease is between 20 and 50 percent. Only 3 to 4 million people at risk are under surveillance, with regular examination or access to a health centre that can provide screening. According to the WHO estimates for 2000, Africans lost 2 million Disability Adjusted Life Years (DALYs) due to sleeping sickness. In 1998, the WHO indicated that over 60 million people were at risk of contracting the disease with about 300,000 new cases each year. In response to this resurgence, the WHO coordinates activities in endemic countries and mobilized the Program for Surveillance and Control of African Trypanosomiasis (PSCAT) several national control programs, non-governmental organizations, donor countries, private foundations, regional institutions, research centers universities and a wide range of partners.

Detection of the disease requires a major investment of human and material resources, such as well-equipped health centers and qualified staff. Because such resources are lacking, most victims of sleeping sickness die before they can be diagnosed. The WHO places countries in four categories in terms of prevalence. In each country the spatial distribution of the disease is highly diverse; it is found in both foci and micro-foci. 1) Countries where there is an; Epidemic of the disease, in terms of a very high cumulated prevalence and high transmission (Angola, Democratic Republic of Congo and Sudan); 2) Highly-endemic countries, where prevalence is moderate but increase is certain (Cameroon Central African Republic, Chad, Congo, Côte d'Ivoire, Guinea, Mozambique, and United Republic of Tanzania; 3) Low Endemic countries (Benin, Burkina-Faso, Equatorial Guinea, Gabon, Kenya, Mali, Togo and Zambia); and 4) Countries whose status is not clear (Botswana, Burundi, Ethiopia, Liberia, Namibia, Nigeria, Rwanda, Senegal and Sierra-Leone).

There are three stages of disease management; 1) Screening is the initial sorting of people who might be infected. This involves checking for clinical signs or the use of serological tests. 2) diagnosis, which reveals whether the parasite is present. The only sign, one that has been known for centuries, is swollen cervical glands; and 3) a diagnosis revealing the progression of the disease involving the examination of cerebro-spinal fluid, obtained by lumbar-puncture is used to determine the course of treatment.

The long asymptomatic first phase, is one of the factors that make treatment so difficult. Diagnosis must be made early in order to preclude the onset of irreversible neurological disorders and to prevent transmission. Case detection is difficult. The disease is endemic in rural areas among the poor with little access to health facilities.

Tuberculosis

Tuberculosis is the world's most common major infectious disease infecting two billion people or one-third of the world's population; with nine million cases of disease detected annually and two million deaths. Mostly in poor and developing countries.

Tuberculosis is an infection with the bacterium *Mycobacterium tuberculosis*, which most commonly affects the lungs (pulmonary TB), but it can also affect the central nervous system (meningitis), the lymphatic system, the circulatory system (miliary TB), the genitourinary system, bones and joints. Ninety percent of those infected have asymptomatic latent TB infection or (LTBI). There is a ten percent lifetime chance that LTBI will become TB disease. Untreated, TB kills more than 50 percent of its victims.

The neglect of TB control programs, the impact of HIV/AIDS, and accelerated refugee immigration has caused a resurgence of the disease. Multiple extremely drug-resistant strains of TB (MDR-TB) are emerging. The WHO declared TB a global health emergency in 1993.[32] These drug resistant strains (XDRs) of TB are now spreading both in Africa and globally. In 2006 XDRs were detected in South Africa, where 52 of the 53 diagnosed patients, died. XDRs have been identified in 34 countries including all of the G8 nations The spread of XDR triggered a fierce debate among specialists over the policy of isolating patients against their will, if necessary, to avoid the spread of infection. [31]

A number of philanthropists have contributed to the fight against TB. George Soros' Open Society made a $3 million grant supporting international efforts to fight the problem of drug-resistant tuberculosis. Soros stated: " I believe that we need to support efforts to urgently create a workable model to treat this deadly disease. My contribution is intended to catalyze other donors-governments, foundations and individuals to respond to this emergency and show that every person with XDR can be treated." Bill Gates, the founder of *Microsoft* also made a large contribution. Failure to quickly diagnose and access to existing drugs are major challenges. South African and Lesotho authorities are fast-tracking two new classes of drugs. Some cases resist all six existing medicines. The disease is widespread in the urban slums of Africa and the overcrowded habitations of migrant workers, immigrants and prisoners. Some question whether if this one reason the international community has failed to adequately respond.

Yellow Fever

Yellow fever (also called yellow jack, black vomit or "American plague"), is an acute viral disease. It is a major cause of hemorrhagic illness in several African and South American countries despite the existence of an effective vaccine. In the past, it was the source of several devastating epidemics. In 2005, the World Health Organization estimated that yellow fever causes 200,000 illnesses and 30,000 deaths every year among unvaccinated populations.

The disease is caused by an *arbovirus* of the family *Flaviviridae*, and is one of the smallest RNA viruses isolated by man. Mosquitoes are the primary vector in transmission of the disease from forest monkeys to humans and in person-to-person transmission. The transmitting mosquitoes in Africa are *Aedes simpsoni*, *Aedes africanus*, and *Aedes aegypti*; and the *Haemagogus* and *Sabethes genera.* [32]

The disease can remain undetected in humans for long periods, and then suddenly break out in epidemic fashion. In Central America and Trinidad it is due to a form of the disease ("Jungle Yellow Fever") which is kept alive in the Red Howler monkeys, which live in the canopy of the rainforests and transmitted by *Haemagogus* mosquito species. It is passed to humans when rainforest trees are cut down. Infected woodcutters pass on the disease to others via species of *Aedes* mosquitoes, which typically live at low altitudes, thus triggering epidemics. The course of the disease varies from no symptoms of infection to an intense feverish illness with high mortality rates. After a 3 to 6 day incubation period, the typical symptoms are fever, muscle aches, headache and backache. Other symptoms include a red tongue, flushed face, and reddening of the eyes. In a proportion of cases there is also involvement of internal organs (liver, kidneys and the heart). There may be hemorrhage from the digestive tract (bloody vomit). Later, the disease is complicated by jaundice with liver failure, or renal insufficiency with proteinuria. If the disease progresses, delirium, seizures and coma follow. Hypotension and dehydration are also common. The mortality rate is about 5%; although historically it has been much higher. Patients who die usually do so within six to seven days of being infected.[33]

There is a difference between disease outbreaks in Africa's rural areas and forest areas and in cities towns. Disease outbreaks in cities and towns and among non-native people are usually more serious. Mandatory mass preventive vaccinations programs between 1925 and 1953 in French West Africa, kept the number of cases quite low. In 1980 there was an increase in the frequency number of outbreaks. One reason for this is the build-up of susceptible populations that followed the cessation of the preventive vaccination programs. There is no definitive treatment, but Yellow Fever can be effectively prevented by vaccination given in preventive immunization programs such as EPI or during mass Yellow Fever vaccination campaigns organized in response to an epidemic.

Despite the efforts of governmental and non-governmental organizations, corporate and individual donors, the pharmaceutical and humanitarian agencies, These preventable illnesses continue to kill millions of Africans each year. Why ?

---

1. Jared Diamond, *Guns, Germs and Steel: The Fates of Human Societies* (New York, W.W. Norton, 2005) 198.

2. Ibid.

3. Ibid. 199.

4. Ibid.

5. Andrew Jack, 'Call to focus on Africa's easily treated diseases,' *The Financial Times*, October 11, 2005.

6. Scott P. Layne, M.D. UCLA Department of Epidemiology, "*Principles of Infectious Disease Epidemiology* / EPI 220."

7. http://www.Wikipedia. the free encyclopedia.htm

8. Andrew England, 'African farmers prepare to relieve shortage of Chinese malaria remedy,' *The Financial Times,* November 18, 2004.

9.Andrew Jack, 'Malaria fight hurt by drug companies WHO claims,' *The Financial Times,* January 20. 2006, p.6.

10. Andrew Jack, 'Monotherapy saves the lives of so many,' *The Financial Times January*, 20, 2006, p. 6

11.*The New Yorker*, "The Mosquito Killer." 2001-07-02. PDF of the same article. Also available in PDF.

12. Sarah Boseley, "Malaria crisis may doom Africa progress, MPs say." *The Guardian*, June 9, 2005.

13." *The Economist*, "The $25 billion question," July 2nd-8th, 2005. 24

14. Andrew Jack, 'US talks aim to reverse malaria failure,' *The Financial Times,* December 14, 2006 p. 7.

15. Andrew Jack, 'Africa urged to boost spending to fight malaria, *The Financial Times,* March 16, 2007. p. 5

16. Dino Mahtani, 'Corners are cut in order to bring drugs to Africa,' *The Financial Times,* March 30, 2007 p.9

17. Dino Mahtani, 'Nigeria struggles to contain bird disease,' *The Financial Times* February 17, 2006. p.3.

18. Jia Rui Chang. 'Nigerian bird flu came from strains in Asia, Europe Africa.' *The San Francisco Chronicle* July 6, 2006.

19. http://www.Wikipedia cholera

20. http://www.Wikipedia .htm

21. http://www.doctorswithoutborders.org/news/2005/09-19-2005.cfm

22. http://www.doctorswithoutborders.org/pr/2005/01-28-2005.cfm

23. http://www.doctorswithoutborders.org/news/2004/08-31-2004.cfm

24. http://www.CDC/Dengue Fever Fact Sheet - CDC Division of Vector-Borne Infectious Diseases DV(BID).htm

25. http://en.wikipedia.org/wiki/Diptheria

26. http://en.wikipedia.org/wiki/Diptheria

27. Ibid.

28. http://www.doctorswithoutborders.org/pr/2005/01-28-2005.cfm

29 . http://www.doctorswithoutborders.org/pr/2005/01-28-2005.cfm

31 Ibid

32. http://en.wikipedia.org/wiki/Tuberculosis"

33. http://en.wikipedia.org/wiki/Yellow Fever

5: HIV+ Africa

In 2008, there were 22.5 million Africans living with the HIV/Aids virus. The virus has affected over 60 million Africans. Over 20 million Africans have died and 11 million children have lost one or both parents. Global funding to fight Aids increased from $2.1 billion in 2001 to $6.1 billion in 2004. The global epidemic spreads differently making it difficult develop preventive strategies. In Eastern Europe and much of East Asia, intravenous drug use is the primary agent of transmission. In the developed world intravenous drug use and sexual contact remain the primary means transmission. In Africa, exclusive hetero-sexual contact is the primary means of transmission.

The relatives of the women on the Aids ward of Saint Mary's hospital, in Nairobi, refer to HIV/Aids as "slims disease." Out of respect for the taboo and humiliation to families associated with disease, The ward physician, Dr. Tom Catena, refers to the symptoms as "ICDP" (Immune Compromised Disease Positive). Dr. Catena took me on a tour of the ward. In an HIV infected person, an immune system with a Compromised Disease or "CD4" count of 1000 is stable, A patient with a "CD4" count of 500 is treatable. A lower count compromises the immune system's ability to resist this disease. These women represent the suffering accompanying a disease that is decimating generations and nations. Most of Dr. Catena's patients are very ill and all require some type pharmaceutical intervention. Many have lesions covering their bodies and suffer complications of tuberculosis, meningitis and diarrhea. The pungent smell of illness and death mixes with an awful sense of serenity. When you look into the eyes of these suffering women you and feel a mixture of anguish and anger.

A young woman with a pelvic infection from STD's and a dangerously low CD4 count of 78 is told that she must return with her boyfriend before she can be placed on Anti-Retroviral drugs (ARV's). If not, his virus will likely mutate into a new more resistant strain.

For far too many, ARV's are either not affordable or they are not ready to commit to treatment. Even if they could afford treatment, the supply of ARV's is erratic and the hospital is often out of stock. In an adjoining bed, lies an HIV positive woman in fifties with a CD4 rate of 240. She is coughing blood from complications of pneumonia. A year ago she was given a blood transfusion and placed on ARV therapy. The physician, Dr. Catena questions her about her compliance to the drug treatment regime. She has not been able to afford her medication.

Another bed is occupied by a 32 year-old woman with severe anemia. Her legs are being eaten away by severe wounds. Her bandages are carefully removed to prevent ripping the newly stapled skin graft. She has a CD4 rate of 240 and her pain is palpable. She is placed on iron supplements to assist the healing process.

A woman in her thirties complaining of severe headaches is admitted by her family. She has Cryptococcal meningitis, an immune deficiency disease, and she has a CD4 rate of between 15 and 20.

A woman with a soul piercing smile is walking skin on bone and quickly wasting away. As she walks through the ward she seems to personify the disease for there is an oral yeast infection on her mouth, she has tuberculosis, diarrhea and is constantly vomiting. She has a CD4 rate of 38.

A 19-year old with a five year-old child and cystic pneumonia has a CD4 rate of 48. She tells the nurse and Dr. Catena that she first went to a street healer. She is immediately placed on steroids, antibiotics and drugs for treating tuberculosis.

A 28 year-old woman treated for tuberculosis a few years earlier has returned. With a CD4 count of 35, she is now on a 3 month positive spectrum for TB and HIV as an outpatient and must take ten pills a day (4 sulfa and 6 Anti Retroviral drugs). She is the victim of rape by a predatory school teacher. Such crimes by authority figures are quite common. Physical beauty can be literally be a deadly curse in Africa.

HIV Politics

HIV was first identified in Africa on the shores of Lake Victoria in 1982. The following year it was diagnosed in the United States. An estimated 20 million Africans have died, a toll approaching that of the "Black Death" in Europe during the mid 14th century. Most die at the prime of their working and parental lives, children must leave school, skills are lost, poverty increases, the ratio of workers to dependants increases and key institutions such as education, health and security are eroded.

According to the UN, there are 32.7 million living with Aids. Though new infection rates have dropped in sub-Saharan Africa, two-thirds of all HIV infected people are African. A disproportionate number of those are in the more developed and urban southern part of the continent, with its large transient workforce and migrant population. Africans and the highly infected female African-American community must compete for US governmental sympathy and treatment for the virus. According to UN reports, India and South Africa have the highest number of people living with HIV in the world, where an estimated 600-1000 people die of the disease each day. The Mbeki African government has been widely criticized for doing too little to fight the epidemic, including refusing to provide life-prolonging, anti-retroviral drugs in public hospitals.

An overwhelming majority of Africans (92 percent) identify HIV/Aids as their country's most serious problem. This pandemic disease outranks poverty, jobs, and terrorism. Only in Nigeria and South Africa is HIV/Aids not perceived as the most serious problem. Seventy-five percent of Africans polled, think that solving health problems in Africa is the shared responsibility of all governments. Eighty-two percent think that the "Rich countries have a moral responsibility to ensure that poor countries receive affordable drugs for serious diseases." Lloyd Hetherington, executive vice president of *GlobeScan* commented that; "Clearly Africans are looking to the developed world to support them in their struggle against HIV/Aids." The World Health Organization's "3 by 5" campaign to get 3 million people on to HIV treatment by the end of 2005. He called for the creation of a "humanitarian corridor," in which leading anti-retroviral manufacturers would allow rival companies to produce drugs at low prices for modest royalties.[1]

The prevalence of the disease in these countries is typically above 20 percent, reaching 35 percent in countries such as Botswana. South Africa the regions economic engine had the highest infection rate in the world at 4.7 million. South Africa's largest HIV/Aids lobby group, Treatment Action Campaign for affordable HIV treatments (TAC), reacted to South Africa's absence from the summit with disgust. "There is a gross failure of political leadership in most southern African countries when it comes to Aids," TAC spokesman, Mark Heywood observed. Only four of the 14-member Southern African Development Community leaders; Angolan president and SADC chairman José Eduardo dos Santos; Zimbabwe's president, Robert Mugabe; Botswana's President, Festus Mogae; and Ling Letsie III of Lesotho, attended a July 2003 summit in Maseru Lesotho, to create a plan to unite their efforts and fight the disease. Noticeably absent, was a representative of the Bush administration, which was planning a visit the region the following week with plans to visit Botswana and South Africa where Aids would be a focus of discussion. SADC countries are among the states worst hit by HIV/Aids, which is also the single greatest impediment to regional development.[2] In July 2005, Nelson Mandela, hoping to illuminate awareness of the HIV/Aids crisis, announced that his son had died from the disease.

Southern Africa shows only faint hope of declining infection rates. With just 10 percent of global population, Africans are more than 60 percent of the worlds HIV infected people. Sisonke Msimang, the UN/Aids gender advisor for Eastern and Southern Africa, noted that: "We've reached a stage in the epidemic where we have very high death rates and very high infection rates. The combination of the two almost cancels each other out so it looks like we're stabilizing… It's not good news, but it's not entirely horrible news." In 2000, the UN reported that of the 30 million Africans infected with HIV/Aids, only 30,000 had access to anti-retroviral drugs. A UN report predicted that by 2010, twenty-million children in Africa would be orphaned by HIV/Aids. This is equivalent to 6 percent of all African children. Nine million of all 13.4 million "Aids orphans" are in sub-Saharan Africa. The ratio of people requiring treatment who actually received ARVs was about 1: 40, and was likely to increase dramatically.

Desmond Cohen, of the International Labor Organization noted that the macro-economic impact of the crisis, the loss of human capital, is often ignored. Forty percent of the nurses and doctors and 20-30 percent of the teachers in Botswana and other countries could die of Aids within the decade. Bernard Schwartlander, director of Aids programs at the WHO noted that more than 20 percent of adults in seven sub-Saharan countries were infected with HIV. This will have a devastating impact on their economic performance. He warned that by 2020, more that 25 percent of the work force in some countries may be lost to Aids, he warned. World Health Organizations director general, Lee Jong-Wook, announced a plan to train "barefoot" doctors to deliver Aids drugs in Africa and other poor countries. The plan is reminiscent of the Chinese health programs which utilized non-doctors to deliver rudimentary health care services to impoverished rural China.

Resistance to existing Aids drug therapies is growing at a rapid rate, underscoring the importance of continued research and development of anti-retroviral drugs. Frederick Hecht, one of the authors of a report in the *Journal of the American Medical Association* (JAMA), stated: "I think we are going to see continued resistance over the next two years." The report warned that the increase in drug resistance, which in some cases was witnessed before treatment had begun, showed that western countries could not be complacent in combating the disease. In another *JAMA* report, Doctors Joel Trachtenberg and Merle Sande warned that: "Wide distribution of ARV's without development of an adequate infrastructure is a recipe for the emergence of a drug-resistant virus."

A scandal in the US pharmaceutical industry over the manipulation of clinical trials became a source of legitimate concern among Africans. In late 2004, Jonathan Fishbein, a former research scientist with the US National Institutes of Health (NIH) blew the whistle about serious errors in the conduct of NIH drug trials of the Aids drug *nevirapine* (HIVnet021) in Uganda. Fishbein accused the NIH of keeping such sloppy records and that the doctors were uncertain which patients had been given the drug. Investigators were often absent from the clinic, relying on unqualified staff for reports of serious side effects. Dosing was haphazardly administered and the investigators failed to follow guidelines for toxicity. Some patients continued to take the drug despite negative reactions. Jonathan Fishbein's allegations led to charges of double standards in clinical trials, reflecting a pharmaceutical industry pattern of using lower standards for African test subjects. What seems clear, is that NIH officials concealed these concerns for economic and political reasons.

In addition to diverting attention from the crisis, the event has serious implications for the conduct of medical research and health care policy in the

United States. "It's enormously disconcerting for those with a life-threatening illness who are beginning to feel well and suddenly worries if they're killing themselves off;" observed Zackie Achmat of TAC. Nonetheless, doctors in Africa are less concerned about the possibility that the drugs potential could have side effects than the risk that the scandal may deter HIV-infected women from seeking a treatment that could stop the virus from infecting their unborn. In 2002, *Merck*, the US pharmaceuticals group reduced the price of its Aids drugs by 20 percent, and announced the introduction of *Storicin*, a daily dosage drug. Priced at $0.95 a day per patient, *Storicin* is still beyond the budget of most African HIV patients.

In March 2005, a series of cutting edge research developments on the Aids drug *Tenofovir* were also compromised. Nigeria was the fourth developing country in which the *Tenofovir* trial experiments faced difficulty. Family Health International (FHI), a US-based non-governmental cancelled trials on Nigerian prostitutes after local researchers failed to comply with the necessary scientific standards. Another trial was threatened after the government of Cameroon suspended research following a political debate over the ethics of the procedure.

The US Senate Finance Committee sought an investigation of conflict of interests at the NIH. Data obtained by the Associated Press under the Freedom of Information Act, suggested that 916 current and former NIH researchers were paid $8.9 million in royalties for drugs and inventions while working for the government.

As African leaders' debated and the US Senate investigated, HIV/Aids destroyed decades of economic, progress in Africa. The US Census Bureau reported that a number of African and Caribbean countries will experience dramatic reversals in life expectancy and population growth. In Botswana, the country with the highest rate of infection, life expectancy was projected to fall to 27 years old by 2010, to 33 in Swaziland and to 34 in Namibia. The annual death rate of five per 1,000 people was projected to rise to 42 per 1,000 by 2010. Many African countries are only beginning to see the impact of these high rates of HIV prevalence. According to the US Census Bureau, African life expectancy will decline to levels not seen since the end of the 19th century.

In 2005, African countries received only a fraction of the funds needed to pay for treatment and prevention programs, jeopardizing the UN drive to halt the spread of the virus. A 2005 report by Accelerated Action against Aids in Africa (AAAA) and by UNAids, estimated that sub-Saharan Africa required $5 billion for basic services and $1 billion more for more anti-retroviral treatment for 2.5 million HIV/Aids sufferers, a sum more than ten times the 2000 spending levels and twice the funds available.

The disease forced the United World Food Program to shift its humanitarian aid effort in southern Africa from traditional emergency food supplies to a greater response to HIV/Aids. To put this in perspective the American Pet Manufacturers Product Association (APMPA) quotes that:

"After tracking pet industry statistics for more than a decade, APMPA announced new figures today demonstrating a continued rise in pet expenditures. Pet spending has more than doubled from $17 billion in 1994 to an estimated $38.4 billion in 2006." In 2006, Americans' spending on their pets was estimated to be higher than ever:

$15.2 billion for food

$9.3 billion for supplies and over-the-counter medications

$9.4 billion for veterinarian care

$1.8 billion for live animal purchases

$2.7 billion for other services

From another perspective, Americans spend enough on chocolate to combat this crisis. According to *New York Times*, in 2005, chocolate sales in the US exceeded $3 billion. In December 2005, the UN sponsored Global Fund to Fight Aids, Tuberculosis and Malaria, faced a $400 million shortfall. By December 2006, it was $2 billion. Launched in 2002, the Global Fund was created entirely independent from existing agencies such as the World Bank and the World Health Organization. Funding is demand driven and while most donors decide on which programs they will support, the requests from 136 recipient countries are prioritized. The Global Fund channels and monitors grants, but has no involvement in program implementation. Its 237-strong staff is headquartered in Geneva and backed by auditors on the ground, reflecting the principle that projects should be performance-based. "The Global Fund is marvelous;" notes Derek von Wissell, head Swaziland's National Emergency Response Council on HIV/Aids. "We don't have many bilateral donors so we're getting money we would not otherwise have."

At the July 2001 meeting of the G8 in Genoa, participants offered encouraging words on development aid along and promises of contributions to a small global HIV fund. There was much rhetoric about forcing pharmaceuticals to reduce the price of ARVs for the world's poor. Outside the proceedings thousands of protestors criticized G8 inaction on the debt burden, poverty and Aids in countries such as Zambia. Zambia which spends a quarter of its national budget on debt repayment ($100 million) funded by ten percent of government expenditures. One-fifth of Zambia's population is believed to be HIV positive.

While addressing a UN conference on Aids in Barcelona in July 2002, former president Clinton,, urged the Bush administration to give nearly $2 billion a year to stem the tide of the Aids epidemic. The former president said that poor countries should buy cheap generic Aids drugs from India or Brazil since they could not win satisfactory price cuts from multinational pharmaceutical producers. Characterizing the Aids epidemic as a global security threat, Clinton called on rich nations to provide the lion's share of the $10 billion a year requested by the UN for prevention and treatment programs. "I pledge that in every speech I give and in every private meeting I have I will raise this issue." President Clinton was often criticized for inaction over continuing a ban on needle-exchange programs and for bullying poor countries that ignored multinational pharmaceutical patents. In the last month of the Clinton administration, the US issued a formal complaint at the WTO against the patent law in Brazil, the only country to provide free generic Aids drugs produced in government plants. The US claimed the complaint, which was subsequently withdrawn by the Bush administration, had nothing to do with Brazil's free generics program.

In March 2007, health experts called on countries with high HIV prevalence to consider offering adult male circumcision to stop the stop the pandemic. An expert committee of the WHO and UNAids, said that the evidence was "compelling" that circumcision reduced sexual transmission of HIV from women to men. The data confirmed a ground-breaking 2005 French study in Orange Farm, in South Africa, as well as long standing "ecological" studies showing a lower incidence of HIV among circumcised populations. Increased circumcision offers particular scope in southern and eastern Africa where it has become a widespread and generalized among heterosexual couples, and where circumcision is traditionally accepted. Kevin De Cook, director of the WHO's HIV/Aids department, said: "Male circumcision should be considered as an additional strategy that offers important but incomplete protection against HIV."[3] Reports from the Congo in March 2008 of penis shrinking "witch doctors" only complicated the problem.

HIV+ Mozambique

In Mozambique, millions of Africans seeking physical relief or spiritual care, first turn to traditional healers. About 14 percent of Mozambique's population is HIV positive. The WHO estimates that perhaps 80 percent of Africans use traditional medicine. These practitioners of the healing arts use the traditional healing methods of appeasing angry ancestors. Traditional healers are an ancient and enduring part of Africa's social fabric. They are trusted for their expertise in bewitchment, where ancestral anger is believed to be the cause of maladies. Mozambique's newspapers are full of advertisements promising to "cure "incurable diseases." The use traditional medicine has become a contentious issue among Aids activists.

John Reed of the *Financial Times* provides the account of Ibrahim Soba, a traditional healer who sees patients in his one-room practice on the outskirts of Maputo. For patients recently infected with the HIV/Aids virus, Mr. Soba prescribes a thrice-daily regimen of palm oil, rock salt, and an indigenous herb called tondulo dissolved in water. He also slices their arms with a razor blade and administers a vaccine made of HIV-infected dried blood-burned, first "to avoid re-infecting people." He claims he can purge the virus from his patients' bodies. Mozambican authorities are trying to reign in these unscrupulous practitioners who charge exorbitant prices for quack cures. In extreme cases, they are found endangering patients' health by re-using razor blades and concocting remedies with untreated water. Most traditional healers try to follow basic health rules. But, director of Mozambique's National Institute of Health, Dr. Joao Manuel Carvalho Fumane, stated: "We also realize we have charlatans, people who claim they are a kind of god that can save people and solve their problems."

Authorities are also trying to use the trust that many Africans place in traditional healers, to encourage their patients to see a doctor after their traditional treatment. The government runs a training program for traditional healers which covers basic hygiene and safety and an approved a policy on the use of traditional medicine. It plans to build a legal framework for the field of traditional healing similar to that of South Africa. Unlike many African countries, Mozambique has an Aids treatment plan to place up to 400,000 people on ARV's within five years. However, given the constraints of the nation's health infrastructure, ARV's will only reach half of them.

HIV+ Nigeria

Nigeria was late to confront the rise of HIV/Aids. There was with no real governmental response until the advent of civilian rule. Nigerian President, Olesegun Obasanjo, made fighting the spread of the disease a national priority and intensified efforts to beat the stigma attached to those infected. Figures showed a rise in HIV prevalence among Nigerians over 15-18 years of age of 1.8 percent in 1991, rose to 5.8 percent a decade later. According to the US Agency for International Development factors that contribute to the spread in Nigeria include polygamy, poverty, low literacy rates, a high level of untreated sexually transmitted infections, and poor health in general. However, these official data mask the extent of HIV infection. "The figures are not realistic;" says Pat Matemilola, who heads the Network of Nigerians living with HIV/Aids. Matemilola is HIV positive and he kept his condition secret for seven years. "The incidence that all of us are seeing is much higher," Instead of 3 to 4 million infected indicated by the official data, the total is really 5 million or more, surpassing South Africa and making Nigeria the nation with the largest HIV+ population.

Official prevalence rates vary from 1 to 13 percent among Nigeria's 36 states. Some states have their own anti-retroviral programs but receive smaller treatment subsidies. The Nigerian health ministry projected that between 300,000 and 400,000 people would require ARV treatment by 2007 and announced plans to manufacture of the drugs locally.

The central eastern state of Benue is the worst afflicted. The main transport routes, with their concentrations of sex workers, are the primary corridors of HIV transmission. The south-west as a whole is less infected because of its more-highly educated population. In some states, the infection rates are higher in rural than in urban areas. Nigerian officials say public awareness has increased dramatically within the past several years. Nigeria is typical of the of slow pattern change in Africa sexual behavior. Condoms are sold in large numbers (supplied mainly through UK/aid) but remain unpopular, and experts fear that prevention efforts will loose priority to the need to provide treatment. Another concern is the burden of anti-aids therapy, with its strict monitoring requirements, that threaten to overburden a public health system where many hospitals do not have running water.

In 2002, a pilot scheme for treating adults with anti-retroviral drugs began at 25 testing centers supplying drugs for the equivalent of about $7 a month. This was a 75 percent subsidization of the medicine by the government. "The essence of the pilot program is to demonstrate the do-ability of it;" said Babatunde Osotimehin, chairman of the Obasanjo's National Action Committee on Aids. The program suffered a major setback in late 2003, when patients stopped receiving supplies of the drugs bought from Indian manufacturers. This was in part attributable to the large number of participants taking part (14,000 instead of the planned 10,000), and to "delays in the process of release of government funds," according to Nigerian officials. "It is not just bad for the people under treatment," said Colonel Matemilola, warning that the interruption in supply could lead to the development of new drug resistant strains. "The way we're going about it, we'll have a lot of problems. The fear is that it will spill out of the country. It's not going to be easy at all. The infrastructure is not there. The trained people are not there. But we have to start somewhere."[4]

HIV+ South Africa

South Africa has the second largest HIV-positive population: an estimated 4.7 million or 11.7 percent of the total population. In December 2001, the South African government lost a land-mark court decision, when the Pretoria High Court ordered it to provide *Nevirapine* to all pregnant mothers. The WHO and UNAids endorse *Nevirapine.* South African President, Thabo Mbeki, who had denied the link between HIV and Aids, seized upon the *Nevirapine* drug trial allegations to further his argument against the value of Aids treatment. *Boehreinger Ingelheim* offered to supply the drug for free, but received no response from the Mbeki's government. *Nevirapine* can prevent mother to child transmission of the HIV virus. The court ruled that the government must provide formula milk to prevent the infection of babies by breast-feeding and devise a comprehensive national plan to prevent mother-to-child- transmission.

Old Mutual, South Africa's largest financial services company warned that rising death benefit costs could within ten years severely erode the country's retirement savings. This macro-economic threat of the Aids pandemic was not lost on corporate mining interests. The mining sector stepped up to protect its long-term interests. *Anglo-American*, the largest employer in southern Africa was the first to provide its 134,000 workers free Aids drugs in an attempt to stem the pandemic. *Anglo-American* negotiated with *Glaxo-Smith-Kline, Merck* and *Boehreinger Ingelheim* to supply the drugs. *Anglo-American* supplied about $4.3 million worth of medicine over three years, to

"Lovelife," an HIV-prevention program for youth. The Global Fund to Fight Aids TB and Malaria offered $12 million in further funding along with the Nelson Mandela Foundation and the Henry J. Kaiser Family Foundations. According to Brian Brink, *Anglo-American'* spokesman on corporate efforts to fight the pandemic; "We do not live in isolation in the mining community. If we are serious about tacking Aids, we can't limit treatment to a privileged few." This moved Thabo Mbeki's government to announce that it would finally draft a plan to provide ARVs.

In the battle to fight the pandemic, the South Africa government turned to an old ally, Cuba. South Africa's ties with Cuba date to Fidel Castro's initial support of the African National Congress in the struggle against minority rule and apartheid. Nelson Mandela established diplomatic ties with Cuba the day after his inauguration, calling Cuba a "good friend." The medical assistance agreement, which irritated Washington, strengthened Cuban investment in South African minerals and energy and built on a previous bilateral agreement that sent thousands of Cuban doctors and teachers to assist in South Africa.

In November 2003, the South African government approved the provision of free ARVs in the nation's public hospitals. The cabinet instructed the department of health to proceed with implementation, making it the largest anti-retroviral program in the world. Aids activists, doctors and nurses around the country had been urging for years. South African Minister of Health, Manto Tshabalala-Msimang, who along with President Mbeki, had earlier questioned the effectiveness and safety of ARVs, describing them as poisons, noted: "to deliver this kind of care across the country, with equitable access to all, will require a major effort to upgrade our national health care system...This will cost over half the total budget." Several years later, Mbeki unofficially excused himself from the debate allowing his deputy Phumzile, Mlambo Ngcuka to address the issue. He claims he is "not a denialist" and rejects that he ever said there was no connection between Aids and HIV maintaining that, he was misunderstood and just wanted a more comprehensive approach to immune deficiency by looking at other factors such as poor nutrition, syphilis and tuberculosis.

HIV+ Uganda

Replicating a pattern across sub-Saharan Africa, Uganda was one of the countries first and worst hit by the pandemic. In 1992, Ugandan HIV prevalence was calculated at 18 percent. Some antenatal clinics equipped with monitors, reported infection rates of more than 30 percent among adults. By 1993, the WHO ranked Uganda number one, with the world's largest proportion of Aids cases per capita. The disease is primarily transmitted through unprotected heterosexual sex, reinforced by poverty, underdevelopment and ignorance. But, official figures for Uganda in 2001, showed the rate had declined to 6.5 percent. The World Bank's Aids

Campaign Team for Africa reported that Uganda is one of only two countries in Africa where HIV infection prevalence has been demonstrably reduced. Atypical of the disease in Africa, was the Ugandan pandemics rapid peak and decline. Other countries have yet to see the worse. Uganda's 25 million people include 1.6 million Aids orphans. Perhaps 1,000,000 people have died from the disease; more than in the 1994 Rwandan genocide. Health experts attribute Uganda's success in arresting the epidemic to several factors including Museveni's protracted leadership and the social structure of a largely rural population. This is in marked contrast to other southern African countries, where infection is spread by the dense urban interaction and the concentration of migrant workers.

Following a period of prolonged chaos and bloodshed, Yoweri Museveni took power in 1986. He made Uganda a model of governmental anti-Aids leadership. Museveni launched a campaign to break taboos, spread awareness and overcome the popular stigma attached to the disease. Museveni's efforts were backed by non-governmental initiatives such as The Aids Support Organization (TASO), a community-based initiative experts consider critical to dealing with the disease and its long-term consequences. TASO has seven centers and a training facility run by sixteen volunteers, many of whom have died. TASO director, Alex Coutinho, warned that Uganda's rural structure and success combating HIV/Aids will prove difficult to duplicate in other countries.[5] Uganda's Aids Information Center provided free HIV counseling and testing in the early 1990s. *Straight Talk*, a widely imitated monthly newsletter, was distributed to adolescent girls, who are estimated to be four to six times more vulnerable to infection, than males the same age. Protestant, Catholic, Orthodox Christian and Muslim leaders cooperated in the campaign. In October 2003, George W. Bush stopped at an Ugandan support center for Aids victims and the world of the diseased African came face to face with the "compassionate conservative." Ironically or not, Bush pledged the largest sum of money to the country which had most effectively fought the virus.

HIV+ Zambia & Zimbabwe

Almost fifty years after independence in 1964, Zambia struggles with the legacy of colonial rule, underdevelopment and poverty. Zambia's economy contracted by 1 percent per year during the 1990s. The education system is chronically under funded and many Zambians never attend school. Zambia owed over $6 billion to the IMF and the World Bank, which is twice its national income. Almost all national wealth flows abroad through systemic mismanagement of the state-owned mining companies. Half the country's exports are copper and the landscape is deeply scarred by massive mud-built shanty settlements around the mining "copper belt." There are mountains of waste and vast open pits of abandoned excavation.

Zambia received early warning about the potential impact of HIV when the son of Kenneth Kaunda, the former president, died of the disease. By 1986, the Anglican and Catholic churches were cooperating in combating the pandemic. No one knows for certain how many Zambians are infected with the virus, because HIV/Aids is never listed as the cause of death. It is reported as whatever opportunistic infection that deals the death blow.[7]

Kitwe, the center of the copper belt, provides an ideal environment for spreading the virus. Desperate poverty and poor education conspire to transmit the disease. A company town, Kitwe is part of the trucking route to central Africa. The transient miners are highly paid and thousands of rural Zambians are lured to Kitwe by mining money. The miners are forced to sell this valuable commodity to foreigners, including the South African colossus, *Anglo-American*, at relatively low prices, in exchange for generous tax benefits. Bars frequented by the copper miners draw prostitutes. And, at the end of the month, there is no shortage of local women who are forced by poverty to sell their bodies. When impoverished parents can no longer afford to provide the basic necessities for their children, the children are turned into the street. Sex becomes a source of family income and these children contract the virus. Alan Beattie, of the *Financial Times* described Kitwe's market where hovered gangs of distressingly young and beautiful women "small girls" in the local usage, some as young as thirteen work as prostitutes. One told him she charges 20,000 kwacha ($5) a time or 40,000 kwacha for all night. Condoms are not considered macho by many men and prostitutes charge more for unprotected sex.

Zimbabwe has the fourth highest prevalence of HIV/Aids, with an estimated infection rate of 1.8 percent of its 13 million people. But Zimbabwe receives only $14 per capita in overall donor support, compared with $68 per capita in neighboring Namibia, and $111 per capita in Mozambique.

In the border town of Livingstone, Mary Mukwanza, a volunteer Aids worker, related the story of organized volleyball games to teach the participating prostitutes about HIV and the causes of Aids. Later, that same evening on a rowdy street of "shebeens" or liquor houses, some of the girls returned still clad in their uniforms, drinking cheap beer and looking for customers. Long distance truck drivers call these teenage prostitutes "village chickens." The price of sex starts at about $1. Unprotected sex can be negotiated for $2-$3. Experts attribute the spread of infection among young people to peer pressure and low self-esteem, combined with poverty, inequality and ignorance. Chief executive of Lovelife, David Harrison, notes that 60 percent of people who contract the virus, do so before the age of nineteen. By 1986, the Anglican and Catholic churches began cooperating to combat the disease.[8] An article published in *Science,* by Simon and Gregson of the Imperial College London, reported that changes in behavior are reducing the rate of HIV infection in Zimbabwe. The study examined a representative sample of 9,500 people in Manicaland (eastern Zimbabwe) between 1998 and 2003. Overall HIV prevalence declined from 23 percent to 20.5 percent in the adult population, the decline was even sharper among younger age groups. .

In March 2005, UNICEF executive director, Carol Bellamy, warned against "penalizing the world's poorest." The country has over 1 million Aids orphans. She asked the world to look beyond the Mugabe regime and focus on the country's humanitarian problem. "The world must differentiate between politics and people in Zimbabwe," Bellamy noted.

As the Global Fund approached its fifth anniversary, there was growing debate over how to best utilize the money raised and about its governance model which pioneered balancing the voices of donor governments to dictate how their aid money is spent with recipient countries and non-governmental organizations. The World Bank's donor roundtable failed to fill a $200 million funding gap. Moreover, Western donors are hesitant to assist Zambia until they are assured there is a efficacious program. For many, the failures of the Zambian government are to blame. Botswana's foreign minister, Shiela Tlou, was pressured by donors to switch her support for Mali's Michel Sidipe, a top official at a UN/Aids offshoot, as executive director, in favor of Michael Kazatchkine, France's UNAids ambassador. "It was disappointing. The writing is on the wall for institutions in which someone in the west tells us what to do, and we must do it ;" She warned.[9]

While these diseases have a devastating affect on Africa and Africans, they are but symptoms of a continent and peoples suffering much deeper economic and political maladies. To fully appreciate the challenge Africans face we must examine how the patient came to such be in such desperate state of impoverishment and dependency. This requires exploring the history of the present illness.

---

1. Andrew Jack and Jo Johnson, 'WHO says Aids battle still being lost,' *The Financial Times,* November 22, 2005.

2. Andrew Jack, 'Aids epidemic undermining African Development,' *The Financial Times*, October, 12 2002.

3. Andrew Jack, 'Circumcision case compelling,' *The Financial Times* March 29, 2007 p. 5.

4. David White, 'An epidemic fed by polygamy, poverty and poor health.' Special Report Nigeria, *The Financial Times,* February 24, 2004 p. 4.

5. David White, 'Bush begins African tour with UN warning of continent in crisis,' *The Financial Times*, October 9, 2003.

6. *The Financial Times,* Special Report: 'Zambia's Deadly Virus,' July 5-6, 2002.

7 Ibid.

8. Ibid

9. *The Financial Times,* Comment and Analysis: 'Fund divided-tensions rise between rich and poor in the fight against disease,' December 4, 2006, p. 11.

6: A History of the Present Illness

The Atlantic Slave Trade

The number of persons engaged in the slave trade and the amount of capital embarked in it exceeded our powers of calculation. The city of New York has been of late (1862) the principal port of the world for this infamous commerce; although the cities of Portland and Boston are only second to her in that distribution.

Dr. W.E.B. DuBois. Quoting a report of 1862 in a study of the African Slave Trade.

The attending physician will usually ask the patient three questions: When did you last feel well? When did the change occur from your feeling of well-being to feeling ill? Was there a sense of urgency or did your symptoms change over time? The physician asks if the patient is in pain. Their facial expressions seem to say what pain? I've been traumatized, humiliated, robbed, raped and betrayed. The look in the patient's eyes seem to say that they are in so much pain, they have surrendered to suffering. A psychologist is required to examine if the patient has changed the emotional component of the pain by de-linking physical suffering from their ability to function. What internal control system facilitates the tolerance of high thresholds of suffering and pain? A history of the present illness is critical to the diagnosis for it reveals the patient's health history from the absence of illness to the present maladies. This is necessary to make a realistic prognosis and offer prescriptions.

The history of the present illness involves an examination of pre-colonial Africa, the impact of the slave trade and colonialism and how that history contributes to impoverishment? In the streets of Africa there are millions of patients. They are people struggling off to earn an existence as bus drivers, policemen, soldiers, security guards, maids, salesmen, vendors, beauticians, rag collectors, metal workers, tire recycling workers, furniture makers, gardeners, secretaries, lawyers, doctors, nurses, medical workers, insurance salesmen, doormen, communications workers, cooks, clerks, janitors, teachers, garbage collectors, garbage pickers, entrepreneurs, artists, carpenters, iron workers, students, the unemployed, street gangs, prostitutes, beggar women with small children on their backs and orphaned children with their younger siblings in tow. In too many of their faces, there is a visible determination to tolerate pain.

Cheikh Anta Diop incisively observed that; the memory of recent slavery is cleverly kept alive in Black minds and often affects Black consciousness negatively. From that history an attempt has been made to construct, despite all historical truth, a legend that the African has always been reduced to slavery by the superior white race with which he has lived, wherever it may have been. This enabled whites to easily justify the presence of Africans in Egypt, Mesopotamia or Arabia, by decreeing they were enslaved.[1]

The Slave Trade

Prior to the Portuguese era, the slave trade was an overland trade, and not confined to any one continent. In 1482, the Portuguese established the first of many trading stations along the Guinea coast at Elmina. The chief commodities were Africans, gold, ivory and spices. Christopher Columbus' '"discovery" of America in 1492, was immediately followed by the trans-Atlantic slave trade.

Beginning in the 16th century, the Portuguese and the Dutch began to establish trading posts and fortifications along the coasts of western and southern Africa. Eventually, many Dutch, augmented by French Huguenots and Germans, settled in what is now South Africa. Their descendants, the Afrikaners and the 'Coloreds,' constitute the largest European-descended groups in Africa today.

By the time slavery was ending in Europe in the early 19th century, the European powers were engaged in the "scramble for Africa." They occupied most of the continent creating colonial states, leaving only two so-called independent nations; Liberia and Ethiopia. This occupation continued until after World War II, when most colonial states gradually obtained formal independence.

In the 19th century, a second phase of colonization brought a large influx of French and German English, Irish to Africa. The Portuguese settled what are now Angola and Mozambique. The French in large numbers in Algeria where they became known collectively as "Pied-noirs," and on a smaller scale in other areas of North and West Africa as well as in Madagascar. The British settled primarily in South Africa, the colony of Rhodesia, and in the highlands of what is now Kenya. Germans in what are now Tanzania and Namibia

In the 1490s, during the reign Nzinga a Nkuwu, the Mani-Kongo (King) of the Bakongo people, the Portuguese decided to Europeanize the Bakongo. The Bakongo people lived on the southern bank of the River Congo. Impressed with the missionaries and the trade goods they offered. Nzinga a Nkuwu, decided to Europeanize his kingdom. He abandoned his ancestral "superstitions" and embraced Christianity. He was baptized and his name was changed to "Dom Alfonso I, King of Congo and Lord of the Ambundos." He dropped his traditional African titles. With the help of Portuguese women who taught domestic arts to the ladies of his court; his court was Europeanized in etiquette and dress. He sent some of his relatives to study in Portugal and Rome. One relative, Dom Henrique served as Bishop of Utica on the Mediterranean and retuned to serve as Bishop of Bukongo.

Dom Alfonso I built several European-style schools and churches. The capital, Mbanza Kongo, was renamed São Salvador and he filled the city with so many churches it was renamed *Ekongo dia ngungo* or "city of the bells." From 1506 to 1543, the Europeanized African Prince persistently requested economic, technical and religions assistance to help transform his country and people and please his fellow Christians. Dom Alfonso I wanted help for autonomous development, but the Portuguese wanted only slaves. So, while he was sent a few masons, printers, blacksmiths, other assorted artisans, and some books; he was over run with slave traders. Determined to save his society and his throne, he to wrote King John III of Portugal complaining of his treatment. His complaints fell of deaf ears.

Portuguese "slaving priests, traders and assorted adventurers," now undermined Dom Alfonso's royal monopoly on Bukongo's foreign trade. His vassals, by now, "Europeanized", were greedy for European trade goods, which they could only get in exchange for slaves. They rejected Dom Alfonso's injunctions and joined in on the profits of the slave trade.[2]

Slave raids and political revolts fomented by the Portuguese to stimulate the slave trade increasingly destabilized the Bakongo and the social decay was irreversible. In 1665, the reigning Mani-Kongo denied the Portuguese permission to prospect for gold and copper in his kingdom, and he raised an army to enforce his policy. In the wars that followed, both sides went into battle waving the banner of the cross. The Bakongo were summoned to battle "to defend our lands, wares, children, women and our own lives and freedoms, which the Portuguese nation wants to conquer and dominate..."[3] They were eventually defeated, their army destroyed and their Mani-Kongo killed. For the next two centuries they were enslaved.

By the 1520s, Portuguese ships began transporting West Africans across the Atlantic into enslavement in the Americas. This devastating event began a long epoch of trading Africans which lasted at least until 1870. By 1600, many West African coastal-trading cities such as Lagos and Bonny were trading directly with European slavers, trading Africans for guns. These African prisoners of war, were often those who refused to render tribute to higher authorities and asserted their independence from Kingdoms like Benin, Segu and Kongo. Between the 15th and 19th centuries, Spain, Portugal and England traded alcohol, firearms and textiles for captured Africans and shipped them to North and South America where they became the foundation of agricultural and industrial economies.

At the beginning of the eighteenth century, the Dutch were falling behind the Spanish in the profitable trade of Africans. In order to regulate mercantile conflict in the capture and export of Africans, *The French Guinea Company* acquired a Spanish contract or *assiento* and became the *Assiento Company*. The contract called for the delivery of 38,000 Africans to the Spanish colonies (or 48,000 if, the war between France and England ended within twelve years). The tax was fixed at 33.3 silver coins per captured African and the company was required to pay the King of Spain in advance. Britain was awarded an *assiento* in 1713 and immediately proceeded to take the trade to the America's away from the Spain. Under a monopoly contract, the British were to provide 144,000 Africans over 30 year period averaging 4,800 a year. Britain paid the king of Spain 200,000 crowns, and agreed to pay a 33.3 tax for each African landed alive in the Americas.[4]

Having lost most of its former colonies to its Anglo-Saxon rivals, and humiliated in its conflict with Germany in the Franco-Prussian war in the eighteenth and nineteenth centuries, France lost prestige and power in the European balance of power. Now, France embarked upon a policy of acquiring colonies in North and West Africa where, at least, it had military superiority over the Africans. The French presence further undermined African society and development. The consequent loss of African freedom and land, was followed by a loss of valuable human resources.

In an 1879 alliance with Belgium, France dispatched explorers Henry Morton Stanley and Savorgnan de Brazza to sign treaties with African Kingdoms in the area of the Congo River. Stanley was scorned by Britain's scientific and geographical establishment and ridiculed by the press. Critics decried his association with slave merchants and his decision to become an agent of the mass murdering imperialist, Leopold II of Belgium. Stanley's exploits earned him the reputation as the most brutal explorer of the 19th century.

The circumstances and scenarios that led to the signing of these treaties are important. The Africans had minimal knowledge, if any, of treaty tables and other forms of European diplomatic protocol, nor of the languages in which the treaties were written. However, they did have a vivid memory of the slave trade and the European capability for violence and cruelty. They also knew that the Europeans were conflicted over the issue of the slave trade. The European debate over ending the slave trade, convinced some Africans rulers that, some Europeans were genuinely interested in protecting Africans against the onslaught of other Europeans. Their leaders recognized the European advantage in weapons, such as the maxim gun, which signified that the outsiders, could and would always use force as a means to achieve their political end in Africa.[5] The signing of these treaties marked the beginning of the formal transplantation of alien ideologies and political practices into African political culture. It is a significant health altering event in the history of the present illness.

From East Africa and the Sudan many Africans were taken by Arabs and sold to Arab slave-traders. This trade should not to be confused with the European slave trade from Africa. The latter were shipments of Africans made by Europeans, to markets controlled by Europeans. Based on the surviving records, the number of Africans imported to the Americas, is an underestimation. Any estimation of Africans landed live, is dubious. The Atlantic crossing or "Middle Passage" was notorious for transshipment mortality rates which averaged 15 to 20 percent. There were also innumerable deaths, in Africa, between the time of capture and time of delivery. The captives were forced to walk hundreds of miles to the coast. Since warfare was principal means of obtaining captives, it is also necessary to estimate the true number of people killed or injured in order to extract the millions landed alive outside of Africa. That figure represents the number of Africans stolen and forced to build the infrastructure and capital of the US and Europe economies.[6]

Many African kings and chiefs acquiesced to the European slave trade for what they probably reasoned, were their self-interest. However, none of them could have predicted the disastrous consequences. African state development and economic activity were arrested by this population loss. As Walter Rodney observed: "In effect, enslavement was causing these people to lose their battle to tame and harness nature, a battle which is at the basis of development."[7] Captives were shipped out of Africa to create wealth for Europeans, not to other parts of the continent to create wealth from nature. The economic opportunity offered by the slave trade, to engage in raiding and kidnapping, became a major catalyst for social violence between African communities and a source of insecurity within every community. Among the Shambala of Tanzania, the feeling was expressed in the saying "A king is people." Among the Balanta of Guinea-Bissau, the family's strength was represented by the number of hands available to cultivate the land. Across continent there are examples indicating that people, the communities most vital factor of production, were stolen.

Early in the 19th century, the Kingdoms of Oyo and Yorubaland began exporting large numbers of slaves obtained through military campaigns outside Yorubaland, and by also kidnapping locals, which involved armed raids. Around 1830, these activities, in addition to internal constitutional tensions, and threats from the Islamic north, brought about the downfall of the Oyo empire. While politics were being the militarized in Yorubaland, changes were taking place in the structure of society. Many prisoners of war were retained locally, under conditions ranging from slavery to serfdom. Sometimes, refugees were forced to provide service to their new overlords by farming the land in return for armed protection. Serfs became soldiers, which meant they now had access to a means of production, land. This sharpening of class stratification further weakened the traditional kinship system. The Yoruba extended the division of labor with the use of professional soldiers, or "war-boys," as they came to be called. They were the sons of aristocrats, who scornfully left farming to the prisoners of war and the serfs.

The Kingdom of Dahomey was long involved in the European slave trade. Dahomey had a stagnant if not declining population and nothing but slaves to export. Europeans in Africa in the 18th and 19th century's referred to Dahomey as the "Black Sparta". Like the Spartan's, Dahomey's leaders focused on military prowess and development. Their value system rewarded bravery while despising and liquidating the cowardly and those who failed on the battlefield. They encouraged young boys to study war and to become apprentices of warfare. By the age of eleven or twelve a boy was attached to a veteran soldier to carry his supplies and to observe battlefield tactics. Dahomey introduced governmental refinements such as census taking and conducted widespread diplomacy, with all the niceties of protocol associated with the "civilized" states of Europe. [7]

The slave trade destroyed Dahomey. Slaving campaigns were not always profitable, but they were always costly. The invisible hand of the market also regulated the slave trade. European buyers often failed to show up during certain years. For example, when market conditions were down. During the American War of Independence and the French Revolution, there was a drop in human exports. Fewer slave sales meant fewer guns. Fewer guns meant fewer slaves captured. As Dahomey's glory and military honor receded, her leader's turned to human sacrifice to symbolically compensate for the diminishing reputation of the state and its monarch.

The shift by Africans to warlike activity and kidnapping adversely economic activity. This was particularly true for agriculture. Many Africans can still remember the colonial era, when able-bodied men left home to become migrant laborers. The farming routines of home districts were disrupted often resulting in famine. European slave trading was, in effect, a much more brutal and disruptive migration of labor. The areas which were most adversely affected by the slave trade are: West Africa (from Senegal to Angola along a belt extending two hundred miles inland) and the East Central Africa (which today covers Tanzania, Mozambique, Malawi northern Zambia and the eastern region of the Democratic Republic of Congo). [8]

Most of the European slave trade focused on the United States, with its dominant European population and it capitalist institutions transferred from Europe. The profits from this trade in humans went to the commercial ports and industrial areas of New England; to Massachusetts, Connecticut, New York and New Jersey. In a study of the 1862 American Slave trade, W.E.B. Dubois wrote:

> The number of persons engaged in the slave trade and the amount of capital embarked in it exceed our powers of calculation. The city of New York has been until of late (1862) the principal port of the world for this infamous commerce; although the cities of Portland and Boston are only second to her in that distribution.

While slavery was perhaps one of the quickest means of accumulating capital, it was too rigid for industrial development. Slaves had to be issued crude non-breakable tools, which slowed the development of agriculture and industry. Many slaves resisted by breaking these tools. Thus, the northern states gained far more industrial benefits from slavery than did the south. When the leading capitalist states of Europe determined that the American slave trade was no longer in their economic interest, they abandoned the trade. Britain made this decision early in the 19th century, and was later followed by France. In 1807, Britain abolished the international trade in Africans and began actively interdicting the trade by other states. This was less due to a moral impulse than to systemic economic change. If, history equals economics over time, then England's slave-based economy was no longer efficient and thus, a new historic epoch began. The new economy was based on a manufacturing and industry, with accumulated capital and inert resources such as coal and iron ore for exporting finished products.

By the end of the legal African slave trade, Europe had to find another rationalization for exploiting Africa's labor and natural resources. A readily available pretext was to call to arrest the Arab slave trade in the Sudan.

Centuries later, although banned by international law, slavery is practiced in Niger. There are no statistics on the exact numbers of slaves even though, it is blatantly manifest. The Nigerien government is a signatory to ILO conventions against forced labor and adopted new anti-slavery provisions to be included in the country's penal code. These provide for prison terms of 10 to 30 years and fines of one million CFA francs (US $1,375), to five million CFA francs (US $6,875) for those found guilty of enslavement. The presence of slavery suggests that so many Africans are impoverished malnourished and ill because African life has been made and remains cheap.

Colonialism

The most serious blow suffered by the colonized is being removed from history and from the community. Colonization usurps any free role in either war or peace, every decision contributing to his destiny and that of the world, and all cultural and social responsibility.

Albert Memmi, Tunisian Scholar

Africa is home to 54 independent countries, all but two still have the borders imposed during the Berlin Conference of 1885, the dawn of the European colonization of Africa. The Conference was essentially a conspiracy. No African ruler was invited to participate in these discussions concerning the future of Africa. Daniel Osabu-Kle has astutely observed that no meaningful conspiracy would let the targeted victim participate in the planning of their destruction. Strategies for colonization were drafted, approved and ratified by all participating states. The continent was to be economically, politically and ideologically partitioned. The economic partitions enabled imperialist countries to share the economic resources of Africa based upon how much each of those countries invested in the exploitation process. The political partitions placed, identified and demarcated areas of Africa under the control of specified European countries. Europe's advancement to industrial capitalism drastically increased demand for Africa's resources. The European settlers took the best land and created a new world order using African labor and resources. Those African communities which lay outside the immediate white settler sector were regulated along tribal lines. In 1943, one of the many British Royal Commissions on colonialism published the following report:

> The Commission's recommendations, which were accepted by the British government, implied that Kenya was to be partitioned into two racial blocks, African and European. And in the African sector, all economic, social and political developments were to be conducted on tribal lines. Racialism thus became institutionalized.

Human activity within small groups connected by kinship patterns such as tribes represents a very transient phase through which all continents passed in the phase of communalism. With colonialism this phase ceased to be transient and became institutionalized, thereby interrupting African development. That is what is implied in Memmi's reference to Africans being removed from history. Frantz Fanon and Amilcar Cabral expressed the same sentiment when they spoke of colonialism having made Africans into objects of history.[10]

Pre-colonial trade sparked the disintegration of African economies and their technological impoverishment. Colonial rule accelerated that process. Trading companies such as the *Dutch East India Company* and the *Royal Niger Company* banded together, obtained charters from their national governments, and moved to seize African markets from the very same African merchants with whom they had traded for centuries. The means by which British traders encroached upon the sovereignty of the Niger Delta states and the origins of the present-day conflict in that area, serve as a case in point. British traders complained that the people of the Niger Delta sold the produce of the interior to them "at a very much higher price than they had paid for it originally even after they paid for transport; so they had made a good profit on this trade in other people's produce."[11] As Chinweizu notes: "These coastal states, they whined, went even further. They were in the habit of collecting customs from Englishmen! And more: with guns and ammunition bought from the English, these black savages dared to interfere with the free-trading liberties of English monopolies by blocking access to the hinterland markets. British profits were too important to be allowed to suffer"[12]

In response to African resistance, the colonizing powers began to systemically interfere in the sovereignty of African states. The practice of helping one faction to depose a ruler and install another was the precursor to the modern African *coup d'etat.* They bestowed recognition upon those whom they could control or those rulers they found it in their interest to support. Violence was the major instrument of British policy in Africa. In 1807 a British squadron of four ships with ninety-eight guns patrolled some three thousand miles of the West African coast. Its mission was to enforce the 1801 British ban on the slave trade and to "protect" British "legitimate" traders, i.e., those that did not deal in slaves. One of the first cases in international law and examples of British naval and consular interference in Africa's internal affairs occurred at Bonny, a Niger Delta city-state. The British seized a Spanish ship it accused of waiting to board a cargo of slaves. The Regent of Bonny imprisoned the British officers for intruding upon his domain. The British squadron threatened to raze Bonny unless their officers were released.[13]

In the Niger Delta during the 1850s, Dr. W.B. Baikie, a missionary trader and Foreign Office agent traveled the region spying out the land. He was followed by armed British merchants. British merchant-warrior, Macgregor Laird, brought his trading steamers up the River Niger, but he encountered opposition from African traders protecting their markets. With large cannon strategically placed along the banks, the Africans fired at his steamers, sank some, ran others aground and boarded them. In retaliation, long range British gunboats opened fire. Towns and villages as far as seventy miles from the coast were shelled. Military escorts were then provided for the merchant steamers which traveled beyond the range of the gunboats.

In the 1880s, Sir George Goldie, another merchant adventurer, equipped a private fleet of twenty gunboats and sailed up the River Niger, bombarding every town that resisted his monopolist penetration. Brass, Akassa, Aboh, Asaba, Onitsha, Idan and Petani are but a few of the towns which suffered from the violent onslaught of mercantile trade.[14] However, such armed trade proved not only too risky and too costly, it precluded the establishment of peaceful and orderly markets. The merchant warriors thus turned to their governments to suppress African resistance and to impose a European peace. Africa, they argued, could not be left barren. It had to be developed for the 'Good of Europe, civilization and the world'. Realizing that white men could not settle the tropics with white labor as had been done in Australia, New Zealand and the America's, they proposed a scheme to utilize a minimal white presence to conquer, organize and supervise African labor for the development of Europe.[15] In the words of Cecil Rhodes of the British South Africa Company, national interest demanded that England; "deal with these questions of expansion and retention of the world."[16]

The Berlin Treaty outlined the rules for their scramble for Africa. At the time of the signing, Spain occupied the Canary Islands and Fernando Po Island; Portugal held São Tomé and Principe, occupied the coast of Mozambique and had settlements at Luanda and Benguela on the coast of Angola; Italy held onto Assab on the Red Sea and the coast of Ethiopia; Germany had trading post sand settlements on the coasts of Southwest Africa, Cameroon's, Togo, Tanganyika; France colonized Algeria and Tunisia and also had trading and military posts in Saint Louis and Goree on the Senegal coast and at Grand Bassam, Assinie, Porto-Novo and Libreville, and on the west coast of Africa. Britain had trading posts in the Niger Delta, settlements on the Gambia River, in Sierra Leone, the Gold Coast and the Cape Colony in South Africa and exercised protectorate powers over Egypt and the Upper Nile.[17]

The implementation of religious-ideological partitions allowed the "Christian" church to "tame" Africans to accept European rule as ordained by God. James S. Coleman notes that Christian missionaries were "the front troops of the Government to soften up the hearts of the people and while the people look at the Cross white men gather riches from the land."[18] Not surprisingly, the first slave ship, *Jesus,* sailed with the blessings of the Pope. Coleman's view of the Roman Church's historic role is confirmed by evidence of the staunch resistance of many bishops and other religious leaders to the abolition of the slave trade and colonialism.

The French also used the suppression of the slave trade as a pretext for their aggression. In 1791, Bishop Maury of France told the French National Assembly:

> "If you were to lose each year more than 200 million *livres* that you now get from your colonies: if you had not the exclusive trade with your colonies to feed your manufactures, to maintain your navy, to keep your agriculture going, to repay your imports, to provide your luxury need, advantageously balance your trade with Europe and Asia, then I say clearly, the Kingdom would be irretrievably lost."[19]

The French used varied military and economic tactics to undermine African sovereignty and to seize African markets. For example, they acquired land on the estuary of the River Ogowe and in 1843 and built blockades for the inevitable conflicts with African traders. From this beachhead they established trading posts up the valley of the Congo to promote "legitimate" trade. The French used their naval squadrons to blockade ports, shell towns and intimidate African kings into submission. This was the era of Gunboat diplomacy.[20]

Colonialism's devastating and destabilizing impact continues to debilitate African political and economic development. Prior to European penetration, national borders were not much of a concern. A group's territory was congruent with its military or commercial influence. The European insistence on drawing borders around territories to isolate them from the other colonial powers often had the effect of separating otherwise contiguous political groups, or forcing traditional enemies to live side by side with no territory to buffer them. For example, the Congo River, although it appears to be a natural geographic boundary, was inhabited by several ethnic groups that shared a language, culture or other similarities and resided on both sides.

The division of the land between Belgium and France along the Congo River isolated these ethnic-groups. Those who lived in Saharan or Sub-Saharan Africa and who had traded with one another across the continent for centuries, found themselves crossing "borders" that existed only on European maps. The exclusion of African rulers from the Berlin Conference was built upon a Eurocentric world view and certainty that the Africans had neither history nor right to make their own history. The economic political and ideological administrative structures established in the colonial era were to accommodate the interests of Europe. While The French benignly referred to *La Mission Civilatrice* and their willingness to *dominir pour server*, while the English spoke of the *Dual Mandate* or Rudyard Kipling's famous "*white man's burden.*" For these reasons, the Africans were subject to enslavement, mass murder, theft and brutality. According to Lord Lugard, author British policy of the *Dual Mandate*: "The partition of Africa was due primarily to the economic necessity of increasing the supplies of raw materials and food to meet need of the industrialized nations of Europe."[21]

The British policy of "indirect rule" demoted African kings to the status of chiefs, and emperors to the status of paramount chiefs. They were often kidnapped and coerced into serving the interests of imperialism. Under colonialism, whole nations including their kings, queens, emperors and other rulers, were captured and enslaved in their own lands. Whole societies were subject to collective humiliation along with their rulers. In 1897, Bechuanaland, a small local riot involving a few drunken "natives" was deliberately ignited and used as a pretext to expel 8,000 of the "natives" from land "inalienably" secured by the *Bechuanaland Annexation Act of 1895*.

After the First Matabele War, the British confiscated all of the Matabele's cattle for the purpose of stocking the farms of the white settlers thereby, provoking the Second Matabele War. The defeat of the Matabele led to further confiscations of their cattle and the Matabele diagnosed their condition thusly: "Our country is gone and our cattle; we have nothing to live for. Our women are deserting us; the white man does as likes with them. We are the slaves of the white man; we are nobody; and we have no rights of any kind"[22].

In nations that had substantial European populations, such as Rhodesia and South Africa, systems of second-class citizenship were established in order to give Europeans inordinate political power. Colonization also brought large groups of Asians to the British colonies, particularly people from the Indian subcontinent. Large Indian communities are found in South Africa and smaller Asian communities are present in Kenya, Tanzania, and other Southern and East African countries. A large Indian community in Uganda was expelled by Idi Amin in 1972, though many have since returned. The islands in the Indian Ocean are populated primarily by people of Asian origin, often mixed with Africans and Europeans. The Malagasy people of Madagascar are a Malay people, but those along the coast are generally mixed with Bantu, Arab, and Indian and European blood. Malay and Indian ancestries are important components in the group of people known in South Africa as Coloreds (people with origins in two or more races and continents).

The political calculus of colonialism required that African societies remain weak enough so that they could be methodically subjugated. That policy would fail if different ethnic groups within the artificial colonial states were to unite. Therefore, the Europeans changed the balance of power, created ethnic divides where they did not exist, and introduced a cultural dichotomy psychologically injurious to the native inhabitants in the areas they controlled. The colonial policy of divide and rule tribalism set various African Kingdoms against one another. Tribalism was first created and used to facilitate the slave trade and later to serve colonial interests. More importantly, the words tribalism and tribe exist in no African language for there is no word for such phenomena. In the absence of such an African word for essentially a discriminatory distinction, the colonists adapted the words tribe and tribalism to describe artificial groups of humans that they were creating. These de-humanizing terms supported the imperialist rationalization for the African slave trade.[23]

In what is now Rwanda and Burundi, Hutus and Tutsis were merged into one culture by the time Belgian colonists who took control of the region during the nineteenth century. They were no longer divided by ethnicity as intermingling, inter-marriage, and the integration of cultural practices over the centuries had long since erased visible signs of any culture divide.

Since race-based categorization and philosophy was a fixture of European culture of that time, upon taking control of the region, the Belgians instituted a policy of racial categorization. The term Hutu originally referred to the agricultural-based Bantu speaking tribes that moved into present day Rwandan and Burundi from the west. The term Tutsi referred to North Eastern cattle-based tribes that later migrated into the region. These terms for the indigenous peoples eventually came to describe a person's economic class. Those individuals who owned 10 or more cattle were considered Tutsi, and those with fewer were considered Hutu, regardless of ancestral history. This was not a strict line but a general rule of thumb, allowing individuals to move from Hutu to Tutsi and vice versa.

The Belgians introduced a racialized system. Africans who had characteristics which the Europeans admired (fairer skin, ample height; narrow noses, etc...), were given more power then other Africans. The Belgians determined these features, which were more ideally Hamitic, thus more ideally European, belonged to those of Tutsi ancestry. They instituted a policy of carrying identity cards based on this racist philosophy. Those closest to this ideal were proclaimed Tutsi, and those not were proclaimed Hutu. The historic result is a series of genocidal events based on imported racial biases.

King Leopold II of Belgium vigorously professed his Christianity. But within twenty years his colonial policies reduced a population from over twenty million half that number. Leopold simply declared the people of the Congo Free State his personal property and they were enslaved. He confiscated the produce of their land, destroyed all internal trade and made a slave of virtually every Africans he did not kill.

One of Leopold's agents, a Lieutenant Tilkens, wrote Brussels telling of how the quantity of rubber production had increased from 360 to 1500 Kilograms within one month.

> "Am I not a luck fellow?" he wrote. "If I go on like this, within two years I shall have earned premiums of 12,000 Fcs. S.S. Van Kerkhoven is coming down the Nile and will demand 1500 porters. Unlucky niggers! I can hardly bear to thin of them. I am asking myself how on earth I shall be able to hunt up so large a number...Marshes, hunger, exhaustion. How much blood will be shed because of this transport! Three times, already, I have had to make war upon the chiefs who would not help me to get the men I needed. The fellows would rather die in their own forests than as members of a transport train."[24]

A Belgian senator and jurist, Edmund Picard, recorded what he saw while traveling in the Congo Free State:

> "The inhabitants have disappeared. Their homes have been burned; huge heaps of ashes amid neglected palm hedges and devastated abandoned fields. Inhuman floggings, murders, plundering and carrying offs... The people flee....A continual succession of blacks, carrying loads upon their heads; worn-out beasts of burden. With projecting joints, wasted features, and staring eyes, perpetually trying to keep afoot despite their exhaustion. By thousands they pass, in the service of the State, handed over by the chiefs, whose slaves they are and who rob them of their wages. They totter along the road, with bent knees and protruding bellies, crawling with vermin, a dreadful process across hill and dale, dying from exhaustion by the wayside, or often succumbing even should they reach home after their wanderings."[25]

Each European power hypocritically justified its "mandate" in Africa. Whether it was the French proclamations of a "civilizing mission" and "dominance to serve," or the British "Dual Mandate" and "White Mans Burden," the impact was the same, the devastation of African people, cultures and civilizations.

Colonial Africa fell into the sector of the international capitalist political economy from which "surplus" was extracted to feed western capitalist societies. The object of colonialism was to repatriate profits to the so-called mother country. From the African perspective, this meant the consistent expatriation of surplus produced by African labor from African resources. The colonial employer paid wages that were usually insufficient to sustain the workers, thus they had to grow their own food in order to survive. This was particularly true for plantation-type farm laborers, mine workers and certain types of urban employment. There were many reasons why African workers were more crudely exploited than their European counterparts. Firstly, the European colonial state had a monopoly on violence. Secondly, the African working class was small, dispersed and unstable due to migratory policy and practice. Thirdly, while capitalism exploited workers everywhere, European capitalists in Africa used racial justifications for exploiting African labor. For example, the 1955 records of the American shipping company, *Farrell Lines*, reveals that of the total amount spent on labor for loading and discharging cargo moving between Africa and the US, 83.3 percent went to American workers and 16.7 percent to African workers. In the period preceding World War II, European civil servants in the Gold Coast (Ghana) received an average of £40 per month along with quarters and other privileges, while Africans were paid an average salary of £4 per month.[26]

Between 1884 and 1906, King Leopold II of Belgium made at least $20 million exploiting African labor, ivory and rubber. The total capital inflow into the Congo from 1887 to 1953 was estimated by Belgium at over $10 billion. In the five years preceding independence the net outflow of African wealth to Belgium reached massive proportions. Most of the expatriation of this African wealth was handled by one major European finance monopoly, *Société Générale*, and its main subsidiary the *Union Miniére de Haute-Katanga*. *Union Miniére* made profits reaching as high as $43 million per year. In Katanga, *Union Miniére* had the reputation for leaving some of the profits behind in the form of housing and maternity services for African workers. But the other Rhodesian copper belt companies expatriated their African profits without moral compunction.[27]

In Guinea, Sierra Leone and Liberia, Ghana and Nigeria, Tanganyika, Uganda and Congo-Brazzaville, the diamonds, gold, iron ore, manganese and bauxite were extracted by African labor to create European wealth. Walter Rodney noted that in each case, an understanding of the situation begins with an inquiry into the degree of the exploitation of African resources and labor and by proceeding to follow the surplus to its external destinations into the capitalist bank accounts that control majority shares in the major multinational mining corporations. Their profits depended on the incredibly low wages and harsh working conditions imposed on African workers in mining and agriculture. They invested little capital in obtaining the source of production, the land. For example, when the Kenyan highland were declared "Crown Land," the British government sold Lord Delamore 100,000 acres of the best land at one penny per care. This stolen African land was then sold to whites at nominal prices. Lord Sir Francis purchased 350,000 acres, the East African Estates Ltd and the East African Syndicate took another 100,000 acres adjoining Lord Delamore's estate.[28] In 1926 colonial Liberia, the *Firestone Rubber Company* acquired one million acres of forest land at a cost of 6 cents per acre and 1 percent of the value of the exported rubber.

Harvey Firestone, a friend and business colleague of Henry Ford, acquired Liberian plantations because Britain and The Netherlands were raising the price of rubber which came from their colonies of Malaya and the Dutch East Indies. In Liberia, Firestone had secured a cheap and reliable source during both peace and war. The demand for rubber and the profits "expatriated" from Liberia's land and labor made the *Firestone Rubber Company* one of the most powerful corporations in the United States.[29] Between 1940 and 1965, *Firestone* took $160 million worth of rubber out of Liberia The caretaker "citizen" Liberian government received only $8 million.[30]

Apologists for colonialism argued that African farmers benefited western of agricultural policy such as the opportunity to create surplus by growing or collecting produce such as cocoa, coffee or palm oil. African peasant farmers growing cash crops or collecting produce had their labor exploited by a long chain of individual, starting with local businessmen. Sometimes they were Europeans, but usually they were an imported ethnic group such as Syrians, Lebanese or Indians who served as intermediaries between the white colonialist and the exploited African peasant. The Syrians, Lebanese or Indians did the work that Europeans could not be bothered with. They owned the cotton gins which separated the seed from the lint. The Europeans concentrated on marketing to the cotton mills back home. While the Europeans preferred to conduct business in towns, their Asian middlemen went into the villages and did all the buying and selling. They channeled most of the profits to the Europeans in the towns and to Europe.

Cash-crop peasants rarely, had capital of their own. The African peasant went into cash-crop farming for many reasons. A minority began farming in order to continue acquiring the European trade goods which they became accustomed do during the pre-colonial era. Others, all over the continent took up farming in order to pay taxes or because they were forced to, as in the Portuguese territories, French Equatorial Africa and French Sudan during the 1930s. Peasants in Tanganyika under German rule, were literally forced to do farm work under whip and gun. They had to exist from one crop to the next, depending on good harvests and good prices. A bad harvest or a drop in market prices meant peasants had to borrow in order to eat and pay taxes. As security, they mortgaged their future crops to foreign moneylenders and middlemen. The rate of interest on the loans was always usurious. In East Africa, this legal extortion of Africans got so bad the colonial government had to enact a "Native Credit Ordinance" in order to protect Africans from exploitative Asian businessmen.

Colonial trading companies also took full advantage of expropriated labor. trading companies such as *Compagnie Française d'Afrique Occidentale* (CFAO) and *Société Commerciale Ouest Africaine* came into direct contact with African peasants. [31] Many trading companies merely recycled the profits accumulated during the slave trade. The slave trading port of Liverpool, was the first to switch from trade in humans to the trade in palm oil. Throughout the 19th century and right into the colonial era, Liverpool firms focused on importing peasant produce. The British-controlled *United Africa Company* (UAC) is another well known concern borne of exploiting African peasants. The UAC was a subsidiary of the giant Anglo-Dutch monopoly, *Unilever*. *Unilever*; and its agencies exploited labor in all of Britain's West African colonies as well as in East Africa. *Unilever* also controlled *Compagnie du Niger Française,* and *Compagnie Française de la*

Côte d'Ivoire, SCKN in Chad, *NOSCO* in Senegal, *NCSA* in Portuguese Guinea and *John Walken & Co. Ltd.* in Dahomey.

In 1885, while Africa was being partitioned in Berlin, William H. Lever began manufacturing soap in Liverpool. Ten years later, Lever was selling 40,000 tons of soap per year in England and building an export business in other part of Europe, America and the British colonies. Soon, he was producing and selling 60,000 tons *Lifebuoy*, *Lux* and *Vim* in Canada, the United States, South Africa, Switzerland, Germany and Britain.

The basic ingredient in the manufacture was stearin, obtained from oils and fats. Other than animal tallow and oil, the desirable raw materials; palm oil, palm kernel oil, groundnut oil and copra, all came from the tropics. West Africa was the world's greatest palm produce zone and a major grower of groundnuts. By 1902, William Lever had dispatched his own "explorers" to Africa. They decided that the Congo was the best area to exploit because the Belgian government offered huge concessions of land with innumerable palm trees. Lever obtained the concessions, brought in machinery and began work in Africa extracting oil from palm kernels. In 1910, Lever purchased a small Liverpool firm in Nigeria. That was followed by the purchase of two small companies in Sierra Leone and Liberia. By 1920, *Lever Bros.* had a foothold in every colony of West Africa and had purchased the *Niger Company* for £8 million.

During the 1914-1918 war, *Lever Bros.* began making margarine. The major European corporations producing soap and margarine were the Dutch firm *Jurgens* and *Van der Bergh* and two Austrian firms, *Schicht* and *Centra.* In 1929, the Dutch firms merged with *Lever Bros. creating Unilever* registered in Britain and *Unilever N.V.* registered in the Netherlands. Some of *Unilever's* profits went into the research and development of colonial raw materials to make detergents. Two of the firms which dominate the detergent business are *Unilever* and *Proctor and Gamble.* By 1960, *Unilever* had four main laboratories, two in the UK, one in the Netherlands and one in the United States. The firm employed over three thousand people of whom one third were qualified scientists and technologists. Most of this employment, research and development was made largely possible through the expropriation and expatriation of African labor and resources.[32] Colonialism further debilitated African society and people by weakening the poltical cultures that bound people together and destroying their economic systems. Sometimes, a patient with a strong immunity system begins to show signs of resistance to an infection. The infection of European colonialism encountered such resistance, and as the patient mutated the infection, the auto- immune system began to fight back.

Resistance & Liberation

The Africans always resisted their European conquerors, and the perennial issues of land and taxes eventually sparked struggles for sovereignty. British possessions in Africa were of two "legally" distinct types, colonies and protectorates. The colonies were technically British territory; the protectorates were technically African territory under British protection. The former could legally demand the rights of British citizens, the latter could not. On the other hand, the obligations of British citizenship could be imposed on the colonials, but not on the protected persons.

When the governor of the Gold Coast sought to transfer Fanti lands to the British Crown, opposition crystallized under the leadership of the Cambridge-educated, Fanti lawyer and journalist, J.E. Casley-Hayford. He formed the Aborigines' Rights Protection Society (ARPS) to protest the governors' scheme. They discovered a sound legal principle for challenging colonial abuses and reclaiming African sovereignty. Casley-Hayford and his ARPS colleagues argued that since British rule over the Gold Coast was legally based on numerous protectorate treaties with African rulers, the Gold Coast was not "legally" a British colony. Since it its people were British-protected persons rather than its citizens or subjects, their lands could not be taken away by the very crown whose treaty obligation it was to protect them.

The colonization of the protectorates forced African nationalists to choose between an anti-colonialism aimed at national liberation and the restoration of sovereignty to protectorates This was an anti-colonialism that focused on reforming foreign-rule and winning civil liberties for the colonized.[33] Another option, while pragmatic under the circumstances, amounted to tacitly accepting forced inclusion in the British empire. This meant assimilating into European culture, history and traditions in exchange for dominion status or local autonomy within the empires, not real sovereignty. Conscientious African nationalists such as Casley-Hayford were reluctant to retreat from the principle of African sovereignty and merely settle for the limited prize of civil liberties. Therefore, they reluctantly accepted an indefinite colonization. Many had been born into a sovereign Africa and accepted the fact that independence would be a long time coming . They reasoned that someday the Europeans would have to leave and their sovereignty would be returned.[34]

This generation of leaders was comprised of essentially civil libertarians, and the politics of national liberation was not part of their world view. Unlike their predecessors, rather than being preoccupied with rule by aliens, they were primarily concerned with how they were ruled. They criticized the absence of democracy in colonial society. Their education focused on vocational skills that would make them useful to their colonial masters. However, they did learn enough about the libertarian ideals of the colonizers to find racial dominance and segregated rule insulting to their sensibilities and ambitions. They learned to criticize and eventually to defy, the absence of democracy under colonial rule. They demanded that such libertarian principles as one man-one vote; liberty; equality; fraternity;, no taxation without representation; and all men are created equal; be applied within Africa.

Lacking poltical experience, and with insufficient knowledge of the pre-colonial sovereignty of Africans, and trained with a Eurocentric world view, they only questioned colonial-rule because it denied them civil liberties. "People can say what they want, but to the African mind, to imitate Europeans is civilization," declared Samuel Chiponde, who was the president of the Tanganyika African Civil Servants Association.[35]

In Senegal, Blaise Diagne defended French rule in the hope of alleviating the oppressive weight of colonialism on French imperial African subjects. In 1917, as the deputy from Senegal to the French National Assembly, Diagne was asked by Georges Clemenceau to recruit troops from to help defend France from rapidly advancing Germans troops poised along the Marne River. Diagne complied and sent to France with nearly a million black laborers and soldiers hoping that France would reciprocate with more liberal policies toward her African colonies. Like Casley-Hayford, he accepted the reality of empire and dutifully served it. But Diagne's ultimate objective was to create the preconditions for the restoration of African sovereignty.[36] They anticipated Frantz Fanon's 'maxim' to Africans the world over that "each generation must out of relative obscurity, discover its mission, fulfill it, or betray it."

> This meant the assumption of the status and power symbols of the white conqueror. He already had their education "so he demanded full admission to their privileged society: wanted to be admitted to exclusive white clubs and residential areas; he wanted to hold jobs heretofore, reserved for whites, and at white scales of pay; he wanted the higher-echelon jobs in the colonial civil service; he wanted to be represented and consulted at the policy-making deliberations of conquerors." This preoccupation with dignity and symbolism proved a flaw in this brand of nationalism.[37]

This legal campaign for rights and privileges within the colonial structure represented the interests of those with ties the colonial metropole, the *petit bourgeoisie*. Within colonial society, the lawyers, doctors, teachers, journalists, clerks and businessmen found themselves caught between their responsibilities as the administrative and commercial representatives of Europe on the one hand, and the interests of the African masses on the other. As Walter Rodney observed, for them, colonialism was not really a problem, for they were not poor and at least they could look down upon their non-Europeanized countrymen. In his works *Black Skin White Mask*, and in the *Wretched of the Earth,* Frantz Fanon diagnosed the distorted mentality of the colonized. He identified the secret desire to replace the colonizer and the psychological value of violence to destroy both the colonizer and the colonized. The *petit bourgeoisie* derived much of their domestic prestige from their positions in colonial society. And this position cultivated contempt for them in the eyes of their colonial masters. Men of high standing in African eyes were perceived as mere mannequin functionaries in the eyes of the Europeans. Their local prestige was met with disdain and indignities from their white masters. They were grossly underpaid relative to their white counterparts, and they were consistently humiliated, bullied and patronized. They lived between two worlds, and to a degree, shared the psychological experience that W.E.B. Dubois described as the "double consciousness" of the American "Negro."

This class of Africans was caught between the reverence and adulation of their less-privileged and illiterate relatives, and the abrasive contempt and discrimination of their white masters. "His Education, he believed, put them a class above the rest of the Africans; but his color, he believed, denied him the full privileges due to persons with his education. For him the indignities he endured were due to racism and the colonizers malice; he could not construe them as the normal lot of the conquered." They eventually found the psychic pain intolerable.[38]

Obafemi Awolowo, one of the leaders of the *petit-bourgeois* Nigerian freedom movement, declared: "The educated minority...are the people who are qualified to lead their fellow nationals into higher political development."[39] This minority represented their interests as universal African interests. But, his presumption angered the traditional African elite, who looked upon them as nothing more than educated clerks from low traditional backgrounds.

This competition between the traditional elite and the stewards of colonialism continues to deter African political stability. In Nigeria, the antagonisms between petit-bourgeois nationalist and the Emirs is exemplified the ongoing conflict over sovereignty and petroleum resources. Such class conflict delayed Nigerian independence and contributed to the disorders that plunged the nation into the 1967 civil war. In Ghana, there was antagonism between Kwame Nkrumah's Convention People's Party (CPP), the "Party of the New Men" and the various alliances of the traditional ruling class interests. The traditional ruling elite contemptuously referred to CPP men as "veranda boys." This class enmity and ideological division created the political atmosphere which led to the coup that over through Nkrumah.

When the African National Congress was formed to agitate for the political aspirations of the Gold Coast's black bourgeoisie in 1920, it was opposed by the traditional ruling elite, led by Nana Sir Ofori Atta. In 1934, they sent rival delegations to London to protest sedition laws they both found unacceptable. Sir Ofori Atta and his relative Dr. J.B. Danquah, represented the chiefs and the unofficial African members of the Gold Coast Legislative Council. The other delegation was sponsored by the Gold Coast Aborigine's Rights Protection Society.

Nnamdi Azikiwe was one who represented the aspirations of the Gold Coast *petit bourgeoisie*. According to K.A.B. Jones-Quartey: "Azikiwe had decided that the traditional leaders of Africa had outlived their usefulness...and must be reformed or removed. They, their old minds, and the calcified conditions of yesterday which surround them, constituted the Old Africa....The Old Africa must be destroyed because it is at its death grips with the New Africa."[40] In his Biography, Azikiwe wrote of how his study of political science at Howard University in the US, prepared him for his life's work: "I absorbed the following as part of my equipment for the battle of life; in political science, to seek for the good life, by fighting for individual freedom, under the rule of law, in a liberal democracy...to regard no race as superior or inferior...in economics to safeguard property."[41] Of course, traditional rulers reacted negatively to this challenge, and Nana Sir Ofori Atta replied:

> We have heard so much of the 'New Africa' coming to birth. The protagonists of the New Africa are spreading doctrines which can only tend to cause trouble in this country. But if the youth are to be taught and educated to show open contempt to their Chiefs and Elders and leading public figures with whose views or with whose persons those teachers" are not in agreement, or for whom they have an animosity, then there is real danger. [42]

The outbreak of World War II further provoked the dismantling of territorial empires and weakened European hegemony the world over. Germany and Italy, which had both lost out in the nineteenth century scramble to colonize the world, declared war in the 1930s to seize a share of the British, French, Belgian and Dutch empires. The temporary defeat of the French, English and the Dutch by the Japanese in Indochina destroyed the international myth of white supremacy. African soldiers fighting for the Allied colonial powers were told that they were fighting for freedom and democracy. The European were surprised, when they found that the Africans were also fighting freedom and democracy, for Africa. World War II war was not merely a war between the capitalist powers. The Axis powers were fascist states that subscribed to an ideology or racial superiority. Fascism is a deformity of capitalism that strengthened the institutional racism already being bred by against Jews and Africans in places like Portugal and Spain by the Catholic church and in South Africa by the Boers and the Dutch Reformed Church. Fascism is the result of centuries of capitalist exploitation, beastiality, domination and racism exercised mainly outside of Europe.[43]

The Americans came to the rescue of their Anglo relatives, but the British paid a price, by acceding to the Atlantic Charter. The Atlantic Charter affirmed the rights of all peoples to self-determination. It provoked the dismantling of European-style territorial empires, weakened European hegemony and opened their empires to a US form of neo-colonialism; the type of nominal political sovereignty territorial rule the US perfected in Latin America. American capitalists acquired considerable assets in the colonies.

For example, the US assisted the Liberian government with loans, but used the opportunity to take control of Liberian customs revenue, to plunder thousands of square miles of rubber-bearing forest land and in general to dictate to the weak Liberian government. The US-controlled International Bank for Reconstruction and Development became an important vehicle of American influence in Africa and a major tool for the economic repartitioning of the continent. Dr. Kwame Nkrumah revealed that between 1945 and 1958, private direct American investment in Africa increased from $110 million to $789 million, most of it drawn from *Firestone* profits. Official estimates of profits made by US companies between 1946 and 1959 are estimated at $1,234,000,000 million.

The Marshall Plan, the resurrection of Western European capitalism with US capital following World War II, also involved sending American agricultural and geological experts to Africa in search of wealth. Marshall Plan money (through the Economic Commission for Africa) went to firms like *Zellidja*, which mined lead and zinc in North Africa allowing Americans to buy controlling shares in the company. By 1954, the American industrialist J.P. Morgan and the Rothschild's of Europe, controlled most of the stock in *Zellidja*.[44]

At the end of the war Churchill refused to concede that the "all peoples" in Atlantic Charter really meant all peoples, and that the Charter applied only to those European people Germany had overrun. US pressure to decolonize, helped determine the form African independence would take and US interpretation of the charter prevailed. The European empires fell apart piece by piece, not to the Axis challengers, but to the emerging American empire.[45] For the first time in the former British and French colonies, African trade unions were not only tolerated but officially encouraged in order to prevent their grievances from festering and sabotaging war production. African post-war aspirations had to be accommodated, for if widespread resistance broke out, loss of empire soon would follow.[46]

The USSR provided support for the African liberation movements. The Soviets reasoned that if they provided emerging anti-colonial forces arms, troops and Marxist-Leninist (primarily Stalinist) propaganda, the colonized might realize independence more rapidly and join the international community of socialist states. From the perspectives of the colonizers, this had to be prevented at any cost. They reasoned that it was better to implement reforms, liberalize and obscure European control by sharing it with the US, than to lose everything to the Africans and the communists.[47]

Portugal's neutral status guaranteed that control over its African subjects remained secure and it's colonial policy unchanged. Any African daring to question Portuguese colonial policy could be arrested and tortured by well known police methods. The Portuguese raided villages in Angola, Mozambique and Portuguese Guinea capturing and enslaving their inhabitants. Portuguese-ruled Africans were prohibited from participating in political affairs and any signs of nationalism were brutally crushed. All organizations were banned and the *cardeneta,* passport system, designating racial identity, was brutally enforced.

Perhaps the closest analogy to Africa with respect to the negative impact of colonialism is found in the Middle East. The partition of the Ottoman Empire and the consequent political repercussions are the roots of conflict in the region. Thrones had to be found for Great Britain's Hashemite allies; the duplicity of incompatible wartime promises to Arabs and Zionists bore the seeds of inextricable and protracted conflict over the Palestinian mandate awarded to Britain by the League of Nations. Britain invented Jordan as a territory for its wartime ally Prince Abdullah; Lebanese borders were drawn in order to maximize the zone of dominance for Maronite Christians. Sunni Arab nationalism in Syria was countered with heavy recruiting of Alawites for the colonial militia; and demands for a Kurdish state were denied so that oil-rich zones could be attached to the British-Iraqi mandate.[48]

The scars of European geographic mapmaking, continue to distort African geo-political and economic realities. In the 1970s, a wave of seizures of foreign assets with compelling neo-colonial connotations swept across Africa: Idi Amin's "economic war" against the Asian community(1972); Mobutu Sese Seko's "Zairianization" and radicalization campaigns(1973-1974); Tanzania's Ujamaa socialization measures after the Arusha Declaration (1967); the Nigerian "indigenization decrees" and the nationalization of copper mines in Zambia and Zaire (1972 and 1976) were all symptoms of rejecting colonial history.

Many Post-colonial political African leaders were poorly educated and ignorant of the mechanics of governance. Political instability was the result of the marginalization of other ethnic groups and corrupt governance under these leaders. Many leaders used their positions of power to ignite ethnic conflicts that were created during colonial rule. In many countries, the armed forces were controlled by the only ethnic groups that could effectively maintain order. Between the early 1960s to the late 1980s, Africa had over 70 coups and 13 presidential assassinations.

Cold War proxy conflicts between the United States and the Soviet Union played another role in African political instability. When a country became independent it was often expected to align with one of the two superpowers. Many countries in Northern Africa received Soviet military aid, while many in Central and Southern Africa were supported by the United States and or France. The 1970s witnessed an escalation of tensions in Africa as newly independent Angola and Mozambique aligned with the Soviet Union and the West and South Africa sought to contain Soviet and Cuban influence in the region. In the challenge to defeat socialism as a competing mode of production and way of life, Africa played at least two critical roles. One as a source of strategic minerals for the growing US armaments industry. The most vital of these strategic materials were uranium and other substances used to produce nuclear and thermonuclear weapons. The second role was geostrategic. With pre-positioned military infrastructures in each colony it was relatively easy for the US and NATO to establish a continental military presence. [49] Virtually all of North Africa was turned into a sphere for NATO operations against the Soviet Union. When the US agreed to build a port at Monrovia in 1943, the Liberian government conceded to the US "the right to establish, use, maintain and control such naval air and military facilities and installations at the site of the port, and in the general vicinity thereof, as may be desired for the protection of the strategic interests of the USA in the South Atlantic.

A legacy of colonialism are the series of political and humanitarian crisis left in its wake. In Southern Africa, the roots of conflict can be traced to the British and transfer to the white minorities in Rhodesia and South Africa in 1910. Virtually every concession to African interests was in order to retain colonial sovereignty or concession over Basutoland, Bechuanaland and Swaziland protectorates. Decolonization swept Portuguese Africa following the 1974 army coup in Lisbon. Portugal, backed by NATO, created UNITA and RENAMO to counter the popular Marxist liberation movements of the Popular Movement for the Liberation of Angola (MPLA) and the Liberation Front of Mozambique (FRELIMO). The resulting 16-year civil-war destroyed the infrastructure of both states and cost millions of lives.

Sudanese-Arab nationalism in the north forced the pace of decolonization. In the 1950s, the primary British objective of the British decolonization negotiation process was to guarantee that Sudan became independent from its "condominium partner," Egypt. In 1960, simultaneous revolts broke out in several zones of the south of Sudan. The violence was temporary ended in 1972 with a creative peace settlement. However, by 1983 the terms of the peace were violated and guerilla warfare resumed. This time the violence was more intense and was driven by a widespread famine-induced starvation, which took 250,000 lives in 1988.[50] But the mere indictment of decolonization policy and colonial policies that encouraged regional division in Sudan does not explain the myriad miscalculations, insensitivities, and repression that followed initial independence in 1956. This colonial legacy is nonetheless an essential element to understanding the ethnic-religious war waging in Darfur.

Border and territorial disputes are common along the European-imposed borders of many nations and contested through armed conflicts. Failed government policies and political corruption have resulted in widespread famine and significant portions of Africa have poor no infrastructure to disseminate enough food or water for their populations to survive. Despite these numerous hardships, there are signs of hope. Democratic governance is slowly spreading. Many states have at least nominally recognized basic human rights for all their citizens and many and have created reasonably independent judiciaries.

There is also evidence of increased political cooperation among African states and organizations. In the civil war in the Democratic Republic of Congo (formerly Zaire); rather than rich, non-African countries intervening, about half-a-dozen neighboring African countries got involved in this contagious war. The death toll in this regional war is estimated at 3.5 million people. This conflict could play an historic role for African similar to that played by World War II for Europeans. Following the war, the people of the neighboring countries decided to integrate their societies in such a way that war between would be as unthinkable as a war between France and Germany would be today.

For investors, South Africa is a major economic success is, with the developed a mature *Johannesburg Stock Exchange.* This is largely due to the nations wealth of natural resources, It is the world's leading producer of both gold and diamonds, and has a well-established legal system. South Africa also has more access to capital, markets and skills.

Another promising country is Nigeria which holds one of the world's largest proven oil reserves and the largest and fastest growing population in Africa. However, most of Nigeria's oil industry is foreign owned, and is rife with corruption. Very little of the oil revenue remains in the country, and benefits a very small percentage of the population. The slave trade and colonization left the Africans psychologically dehumanized, culturally, politically and economically compromised and impoverished. In search of treatment, African states have been prescribed incompatible forms of both capitalism (political democracy) and socialism (economic democracy) which have frequently been hampered by instability, corruption, violence, and authoritarianism. The majority of African nations are republics that operate under some form of the presidential system of rule. Some are weak or failed states. Few nations in Africa have been able to sustain western-style democratic governance. Instead, they have been weakened by a series of brutal coups, counter-coups and corrupt civilian and military dictatorships.

---

1. Cheikh Anta Diop, *The African Origin of Civilization: Myth or Reality,* (Chicago: Lawrence Hill Books, 1974) 26.

2. Chinweizu The *West and the Rest of Us: White Predators Black Slavers and the African Elite.* (New York :Vintage Books, 1975), 28-29.

3. Basil Davidson,. *The African Slave Trade.* (Boston, Atlantic: Little Brown, 1961), 147-48.

4. Ibid. 81.

5: Osabu-Kle, Daniel. *Compatible Cultural Democracy: The Key to Development in Africa.* (Broadview Press, Hertfordshire, UK. 2000), 38.

6. Rodney, Walter. *How Europe Underdeveloped Africa.* (Washington, D.C., 1982, Howard University Press) 96.

7. Ibid. 98.

8. Ibid 99-101.

9. Ibid. 229-230.

10. Ibid

11 . C.R. Niven, *A Short History of Nigeria.* (London: Longmans Green and Co., 1952). 156.

12. Ibid.

13. Chinweizu, Op. Cit. 37-38.

14. Ibid. 41.

15. Ibid.

15. Quoted in Hannah Arendt, *Imperialism* (New York: Harcourt, Brace, 1968) 12.

16. Chinweizu, Op. Cit. 12-13.

17. James S. Coleman, *Nigeria: Background to Nationalism.* (Berkeley: University of California Press, 1958), 108.

18. Osabu-Kle, Op. Cit. 40-41.

19. Ibid. 39.

20. Sir Frederick D. Lugard, *The Dual Mandate in British Tropical Africa.*(Edinburgh and London: Blackwood and Sons, 1923) 613.

21. Chinweizu, Op. Cit. 57.

22. Ibid. 42.

23. André Gide, *Voyage au Congo* (cited in Chinweizu Paris: Librairie, 1927) 62.

24. Quoted in Ludwig Bauer, *Leopold the Unloved.* (Boston: Little Brown and Company, 1935), 263. hinweizu, Op. Cit. 63.

25. Rodney, Op. Cit. 150-151.

26. Ibid. 153.

27. Ibid. 153.

28. Ibid.

29. Ibid. 192-193.

30. Ibid. 155.

31. Ibid. 180-184.

32. Chinweizu, Op Cit. 80-82.

33. Ibid. 84.

34. Quoted in Ralph A. Austen, "Notes on the Prehistory of TANU," *Makarere Journal, #9* March, 1964.) 2.

35. Ibid. 85.

36. Frantz Fanon, *The Wretched of the Earth*. (New York: Grove Press, 1968) 167.

37. Chinweizu, Op. Cit. 94.

38. Obafemi Awolowo, *Path to Nigerian Freedom*. (London: Faber and Faber, 1964) 64.

39. K.A.B. Jones Quartney, *A Life of Azikiwe*. (Baltimore, Penguin Books, 1965) 119.

40. Nnamdi Azikiwe, *My Odyssey*. (New York, Praeger, 1970) 252.

41. Ibid. 124.

42. Rodney, Op Cit. 196-200.

43. Ibid.

44. Ibid. 193-194.

45 Ibid. 102.

46. Ibid. 103.

47. Ibid.

48. Crawford Young, "The Heritage of Colonialism." in John Harbeson and Donald Rothschild eds. *Africa in World Politics: The African State System in Flux.* (Oxford, London, 2000), 23.

49. Ibid.

50. Wai, Dunstan M, *The African-Arab Conflict in the Sudan* (New York: African Publishing House; 1968) and Mohamed Omar Beshir, *The Southern Sudan: Background to Conflict.* (London: William Blackwood and Sons, 1978).

Part II: Patient Examinations

7: The DRC: A Diarrheatic State

Each day in the Democratic Republic of Congo (DRC formerly Zaire) over 1,200 people die of war, famine and disease. The HIV/Aids rate is estimated at five percent meaning 1.1 million people living or dying with HIV/Aids, but other diseases take their toll including: malaria, sleeping sickness, protozoal disease, diarrhea, river blindness and hepatitis A. The life expectancy for men at birth is forty-seven years, for women it is fifty-one. Ninety-eight out of every one thousand infants dies at birth. There is one physician for every 16,000 people. Over 3.5 million people have died in the ongoing conflict.

During the Cold War, the DRC was the principal US client state in Africa. For thirty-two years President Mobutu Sese-Seko, who was installed by the CIA and the Pentagon and backed by western corporations; ran a brutal military dictatorship which destroyed the country's economy. The fact that the Congo holds nearly 70 percent of the world's known cobalt and other vital resources was rarely, if ever, mentioned to Americans by the electronic or the print media.[1] But fear of a world war in Africa escalated when eight weeks of peace talks to end the civil war collapsed in April 2002.

In February 1960, King Baudouin of Belgium invited eighty-one Congolese political leaders to a pre-independence conference in Brussels. They were there to formulate a plan for the colony's independence which was scheduled for June. Populist leader, Patrice Lumumba was released from jail, where he had served three months for inciting a crowd, so that he would be allowed to attend the conference. According to the Encyclopedia Britannica's, *Biography of Lumumba*, Lumumba and his Belgian political contacts in the Liberal Party were more oriented toward the socialist-bloc countries than were his political rivals. The Belgians had created a parliamentary system in the Congo and elections were held that May. Most Congolese people owed their political loyalty to their village and tribal chiefs, and the largely illiterate peasant population was beyond the reach of the media. The Belgian supervised elections gave Lumumba a majority of the popular vote and his party won 35 of 137 seats in parliament.

History reveals that the 1960 election was much more fair and honest than the one-party elections held during Mobutu's long rule. In 1982, Madeleine G. Kalb used the US Freedom Action Act to reveal the cable traffic between Leopoldville and Washington and gave an account in her book, *The Congo*

Cables. The cables illustrate the racism and provincialism of US foreign policy in Africa Kalb wrote:

> Accustomed to the context of big-power diplomacy, no one in the policy-making chain of command could see the Congo for what it was: a couple of hundred mini-nations, whose people were consumed with the daily chore of warding off hunger. These nations had long been occupied against their will by white people and occasionally forced to do slave labor for whites. Suddenly, under rules laid down by whites, they were proclaimed to be one "country," with common leadership. [2]

Whether in the Congo, Vietnam, Iraq, Panama, Afghanistan or Iran, Americans are forced learn geography during warfare. American knowledge of Africa is framed to facilitate the pursuit of elite US foreign policy interests. For example, the cartoonist for the *Indianapolis Star* frequently used his talent to wage the Cold War in Africa. Frequently the front page featured caricatures of Soviet Premier, Nikita Khrushchev cavorting with the natives in a jungle setting under the caption of a popular 1940s song, "Bingo, Bango Bongo, I don't want to live in the Congo." In another, cartoon Khrushchev peered at the reader through tall grass, flanked by natives adorned with bones in their noses. The drawing was shown around the *Stars* office with its original caption: "Ain't nobody here but us niggers." It was published under the caption "Ain't nobody here but us natives." [3]

Time magazine portrayed the Belgians as heroes whose occasional interventions interrupted human sacrificial rituals.[4] Under the headline "Freedom Yes, Civilization Maybe," *Time* reported that "Once Belgian control ends, the self-rule everyone seems to want will bring barbarism and strife." The June 30, 1960 *New York Times* story on Congolese independence noted that "the Kingdom of the Congo flourished from the fourteenth century and even exchanged envoys with Portugal, the Vatican, Brazil and the Netherlands." The story went on to say that independence brought the country "lost greatness that would only be found with the coming of the Belgians, who set out to substitute the carpenter's hammer for the tribal drum, introducing the twentieth century overnight to a primitive people divided by many warring tribes." [5]

Cold War in the Congo

One of the most bizarre civil wars in history took place in Africa during the mid-1960s when Cubans faced Cubans on Congolese battlefields. Upon independence, the United States and Belgium introduced CIA recruited

Cuban mercenaries to the Congo. According to the *Senate's Select Committee to Study Government Operations With Respect To Intelligence Activities* (the Church Committee), seeking a way to employ the veterans of its failed 1961 Bay of Pigs invasion, the CIA brought anti-Cuban pilots to the Congo in early 1964. Their mission was to bomb railroads, bridges and other infrastructure in areas threatened by or under rebel control. The rebels were organized around Patrice Lumumba's lieutenant, Antoine Gizenga, who had ended his Secession long enough for Joseph Kasavubu and Mobutu Sese-Seko to appoint a replacement government in Stanleyville.[6]

Cyrille Adoula, who was on the CIA payroll, controlled the trade unions. When Kasavubu and Mobutu demanded that Adoula be appointed prime minister or that the parliament would be dissolved, Gizenga felt betrayed and announced the formation of an anti-western political party. He accused the US of replacing the Belgians as colonialists. The CIA planned his assassination and almost succeeded.

Responding to Gizenga's dilemma, Fidel Castro dispatched several hundred Cuban troops to the Congo, under the personal command of Ernesto "Che" Guevara. There is no proof as to which contingent of opposing Cubans arrived in Congo first, but dates in evidence suggest the CIA mercenaries entered first. What is clear is that Guevara and his men went to the Congo to help Gizenga establish his "People's Republic" and to escalate the Simba rebellion. Jonathan Kwitty surmises that when Che Guevara entered the Congo, he expected to find a heroic and impassioned people fighting for liberty and human dignity. What he found was Laurent Kabila and a barbaric rag-tag army of starving farmers turned vicious killers who were incapable of being organized into the disciplined militia he was accustomed to leading. In 1967, Castro pulled Guevara out of the Congo. In September 1981, a reporter for the *Wall Street Journal* raised the subject with Castro at a cocktail party in Havana. Castro thought a moment and said, "He went to help them with a revolution. He spent a short time there, and he succeeded, and he left."[8]

Congolese soldiers, barred from leadership under Belgian colonial rule felt stronger loyalty to their tribes than to the abstraction called Zaire or the concept of a state called 'Congo,' have never constituted a cohesive national military. The Balunda people were basically excluded from the debates and campaigns for national leadership. However, they occupied the land with all the copper and cobalt deposits and therefore decided to deal directly with western investors. Three western multinational industrial concerns persuaded Moise Tshombe, leader of the Lunda tribe in Katanga (Shaba province), to secede. They promised to supply mercenaries and to defend the secessionist province against Lumumba's central government. According to a CIA report from Elizabethville dated January 17, 1961, the mercenaries included Belgian paratroopers, former members of the German SS and former Italian fascist troops."

Lumumba naturally, opposed the secession and he called upon the United Nations to intervene and help establish the authority of his government. On

July 21, the UN Security Council, with US and Soviet support, demanded Belgian withdrawal. Lumumba conferred with Ghana's President Kwame Nkrumah, the advocate of African socialism and pan-Africanism, offered Ghana's support. Convinced the Belgians would not withdraw when the UN peacekeepers arrived, Lumumba and Kasavubu asked the USSR to monitor the situation and consider sending assistance if "certain western countries didn't halt their "aggression." In the view of CIA director John Foster Dulles, Lumumba was not only "a spy in Soviet pay," but a "global threat". In reality, Lumumba, Kasavubu, Adoula, Mobutu, Tshombe and Kasavubu were all on Soviet, US and Belgian payrolls.

US Ambassador Claire Timberlake, said that Lumumba was acting on the direction of his "anti-white, pro-communist" Ghanaian advisors. She recommended that the US instigate a coup to remove him CIA. As deputy director for operations, Richard Bissell recalled: "The Agency had put top priority, probably, on a range of different methods of getting rid of Lumumba in the sense of destroying him physically, incapacitating him, or eliminating his political influence."[9] CIA scientist, Dr. Stanley Gottlieb, was assigned to produce a poison that in his testimony to the Church Committee was to: "Produce a disease that was indigenous to the area that could be fatal...either kill the individual or incapacitate him so severely that he would be out of action." The Church Committee learned of a plot to have someone inject poison into Lumumba's toothpaste.[10] Here, a rudimentary knowledge of Africa might have saved the CIA some trouble. Toothpaste was not needed nor widely used in Africa.

The Soviets were hypocritically selective in their support for liberation movements. Soviet imperialism, albeit less distasteful than Belgian colonialism, would probably have proven equally disastrous for the Congo. The arrival of Soviet planes and advisors, the continuing violence in Kasai and prompting by the US government, persuaded Kasavubu's to make a national radio address on dismissing Lumumba as prime minister. In response, Lumumba appeared before both houses of parliament which had given him their overwhelming support, insisted on maintaining constitutional democracy and fired Kasavubu. According to Jonathan Kwitty, two unnamed State Department officials working on US-Congo policy, told him that the US planned Lumumba's coup and selected Mobutu Sese-Seko to do the job. The State Department's official document, *Analytical Chronology of the Congo Crisis*, tacitly admits this by referring to a plan "to bring about the overthrow of Lumumba and install a pro-western government."

On September 12, 1961 Lumumba was arrested, held for three days by troops loyal to Mobutu and released. On the night of September 27, he sneaked past the troops guarding with hopes of regrouping his political forces. However, was re-captured and returned to Stanleyville. CIA station Chief, Lawrence Devlin, helped Mobutu's government set up roadblocks. Captured without UN protection, Lumumba was returned to Leopoldville, where US news agencies took photographs of a savagely beaten and bloodied man. Devlin requested the help of a stateless soldier of fortune, former bank robber and forger code named WI/ROGUE. The CIA instructed Devlin that WI/ROGUE "is indeed aware of the precepts of right and wrong, but if he is given an assignment which may be morally wrong in the eyes of the world, but necessary because his case officer ordered him to carry it out, then it is right, and he will undertake appropriate action for its execution without pangs of conscience."[11] The last reliable accounts of Lumumba alive were reported by Swedish UN troops at the Elizabethville airport that day. They reported seeing the Prime Minister Lumumba being kicked and beaten by a group of Moi, Tshombe's soldiers and their Belgian advisors.[12]

The State Department and the CIA considered their US operatives far more capable of choosing a prime minister than were the Congolese voters. This US policy of political penetration would be repeated across Africa. Ambassador Timberlake objected to State Department plans to reconvene parliament as a vehicle for legitimatizing Cyrille Adoula. He stated that the Congolese lacked the "ability to produce anything resembling democratic government until they have been taught...They obviously cannot practice something they do not understand...Furthermore, I do not believe democracy can be imposed on any people over night."[13] For resisting foreign intervention, Lumumba became Africa's most widely recognized hero. To this day, across The DRC, people in cities and villages await the return of this legendary champion to govern the country.

Mobutu

To say that Mobutu Sese-Seko enriched himself at the expense of his people is an understatement. To please the IMF, in 1979 Mobutu imposed tough financial restrictions by abolishing peoples rights to spend their savings or to convert the $Z dollar to foreign currency. Meanwhile, he personally withdrew 364.3 million francs from Zaire's National Bank. Between 1977 and 1979, Mobutu's cronies withdrew $2.8 million in US currency, 132.1 million in Belgian francs, 6.4 million in French francs and 268 million in Swiss francs from the Zimbabwe National Bank.

In 1980, reporters for the Belgian weekly, *Humo*, documented the real estate holdings of Mobutu and his inner circle. The records revealed that Joseph Desiré-Gbiatwa-address: Kinshasa: occupation: chief of state; owned two houses, a chateau, a park, stables, and an undeveloped property in Belgium. Just twenty five miles outside of Brussels, Mobutu had a castle surrounded by a moat. Mungul-Diaka, the former head of Mobutu's political apparatchik, released an itemized list of Mobutu's European holdings. The Belgian real estate holdings were valued at about $100 million. The list included a Swiss bank account which contained $143 million and a $5.4 million chateau on Lake Geneva. There were villas in Paris and Nice valued at $1.1 and $1.3 million. There were chateaus in Spain, Italy and the Central African Republic which he gave to President Valery Giscard d'Estaing and each of his family and friends.[14] Three pages were required to itemize Mobutu's Zairian property and another page and half to name the companies he and his family allegedly controlled. Among these was a majority-share in the diamond buying *Comptoirs*, (agencies) in western Kasai, where Maurice Tempelsman, an *Oppenhiemer* associate and contributor to both US political parties and the wife of the Belgian foreign minister who was on Mobutu's payroll, received diamonds via a special Mobutu government concession.

Mobutu established an appalling record for human rights abuses. On November 1, 1980, a group of dissident parliamentarians anonymously published a fifty-page open letter to Mobutu. The letter accused him suppressing liberty and going back on his promise to improve their economic situation. The parliamentarians challenged Mobutu's account of the 1979 killing of 97 civilian diamond scavengers outside Mbuji-Mayi, the diamond center of Kasai province. Just before the letter was disseminated in Europe, thirteen parliamentarians were arrested and charged with its authorship. They were flown to their homes in outlying Zaire and placed under five-year house arrest. A 1980 *Amnesty International* memorandum presented to President Mobutu evoked no response. In a March 11 Communiqué from Brussels, Mobutu claimed that *Amnesty International* had congratulated him on his country's human rights record.[15]

Mobutu was a long-standing ally of the United States and a particular friend of CIA director William J. Casey, who reportedly visited Zaire in early 1986 to arrange the covert transshipment of Stinger antiaircraft missiles and other weaponry. These arms transfers were part of the CIA's aid to the Angolan rebels of UNITA who attacked MPLA through Zairian territory. The relationship began in the mid 1970s when the CIA began supporting pro-western UNITA rebels struggling for control of Angola. This US geo-strategic hypocrisy encouraged Mobutu to violate human rights with impunity. Mobutu demonstrated a sharp understanding of power politics and a willingness to use harsh measures against his people. According to the State Department's *Country Report on Human Rights Practices:* "There is question that mistreated detainees, particularly beatings at the time of arrest and preliminary interrogation is the rule rather than the exception....abuses of all kinds are endemic in Zaire's jails and prisons."

In early 1985, *Amnesty International* received reports of human rights violations committed by the Zairian armed forces in the southeastern part of the country. These included torture, severe beatings, whippings with barbed wire and extra-judicial killings. In early 1986, supporters of a second political party were shot and wounded by security forces as they celebrated the release from prison of one of their leaders. As a one-party state, Zaire offered little, if any, protection of civil or political rights. The Constitution of the Republic of Zaire illustrates the inadequacy of domestic law protections stating:

> If serious circumstances imminently threaten the Nation's independence or integrity or cause an interruption in the regular functioning of the organs of the Popular Movement of the Revolution or jeopardize State

> interests, the President of the Republic, may proclaim a state of emergency, with the consent of the Political Bureau. "He shall so inform the Nation by message. (Article 48: 1974 amended in 1978).[16]

Nowhere in the Constitution is defined the phrase "serious circumstances imminently threatening the nation's independence or integrity." Such lack of definition of the type of action deemed to jeopardize a vital state interest rendered the phrase dangerously vague. Furthermore, the Constitution permits the suspension of guarantees during a state emergency. Since the Constitution provides insufficient guidelines for the interpretation of its provisions and permits derogation from guaranteed human rights, it is viewed as an inadequate tool for construing the provisions for human rights established under the newly created *Banjul Charter on African Human Rights*. As in other African states, the US State Department largely ignored human rights violations by Zaire's armed forces, but in the mid 1980's, the took symbolic measures to demonstrate US concern through diplomatic channels. President Mobutu never responded positively to the criticism of *Amnesty International* or of the United States.[17]

Since 1978, *Amnesty International* had documented evidence of detentions without charges or trials, the use of torture, frequent death from torture, ill-treatment, harsh prison conditions, the use of the death penalty and extrajudicial executions, all practices currently utilized or tolerated by the United States. In one year, *Amnesty International* reported the deaths of 2,309 prisoners from malnutrition and disease. The report stated that; "Detention without trial occurs frequently, and is used by authorities to suppress political opposition. Detainees frequently 'disappear' after their arrest. They are either transferred to another prison or they die in custody...Most people killed for political reasons have...been summarily executed by members of the security forces without being given any sort of trial."

In April 1982, Mungul-Diaka, a former Mobutu political aid, issued a compilation of massacres in Zaire showing that the Mbuji-Mayi incident was part of a pattern. He cited fourteen incidents including: the hanging of four cabinet ministers without the right of legal defense for allegedly plotting a coup in 1966; the killing of several thousand Katangese soldiers by burning, live burial, or being thrown from helicopters in 1967; the killing of several hundred peaceful demonstrators at the National University near Kinshasa in 1969; the massacre of 500 people in villages in reprisal for killing a soldier who stole a chicken in 1970; the massacre of 2,000 to 2,500 members of a sect in Kitawala in January, 1978; and the massacre of 150 people in Eastern Kasai on October 6, 1981 after some villagers challenged army officers illegally dealing in ivory. Mobutu also harassed Cardinal Joseph Malula, the Archbishop of Kinshasa, for criticizing his government. He also held a grudge against the Cardinal because when Pope John Paul II visited Zaire in 1980, Mobutu wanted the Pope to marry him to a new wife. Unfortunately, the Cardinal had to tell Mobutu that the Pope had refused the request.[18]

Thus, the United States, with its admirable restrictions on conflicts of interest, belief in open government and rhetoric of fighting monopoly trusts, chose to undermine Zairian democracy. The CIA and the US State Department taught the people of Zaire governance by means of duplicity, bribery, thievery, torture and assassination. American support for the Mobutu regime was usually justified before Congress in terms of anti-communist national security interests and access to Zaire's minerals riches. A civil war in this neo-colony would jeopardize the supply of cobalt, diamonds, copper and other strategic minerals.

The family of former president Valery Giscard d'Estaing controls the banks that siphoned billions of dollars from African economies. The family has extensive business dealings in Gabon, Morocco, Chad, the Central African Republic, Cameroon, Cote d'Ivoire, Niger and Benin. The governments of these countries were forced to acquiesce to French demands in order to maintain domestic stability and remain in power.

French banks loaned the Mobutu family money secured by the mineral riches Zaire and other African countries. As a rule, this borrowed money never reached Africa. It was transferred to European manufacturing companies connected to the Giscard d'Estaing family. These companies in-turn, built over-priced showpiece items of questionable economic or infrastructural value. Mobutu signed contracts with d'Estaing family corporate interests to build skyscrapers and other ostentatious structures including a billion dollar satellite and microwave communications system with studios. The French manufacturer proudly announced that Zaire was now "one of the first countries in the world to possess its own domestic satellite-communication network." The president of that company was Philippe Giscard d'Estaing, first cousin of the former French president who twice deployed French troops to Zaire to protect his own economic interests.

Control of the Belgian mining company *Société Géněral,* was transferred from Belgian to Mobutu's control and renamed *Gecamines* with the legal intervention of US diplomat, Theodore Sorensen. Between 92 to 93 percent of *Société Géněral* stock was to be held by the public, the other 7-8 percent would be controlled by the company. In 1981, Mobutu broke his contract with *De Beers* to sell all of Zaire's industrial diamonds to the *DeBeers* syndicate. He then contracted Herman DeCroo, the minister of telephone and telegraphs to buy all other mining companies. At the time his government was $1 billion in debt to the Belgian-owned Zimbabwe telephone company. A World Bank review of *Gecamines* accounts indicated a number of special transactions undertaken after the 1979 transfer of ownership that reduced the *Gecamines* cash flow by $49.4 million. Mobutu had spent $59 million for improvements on his farm which received half of all national fertilizer imported and 85 out of 125 of a shipment of *Jeeps* sent by Belgium for development.

In 1980, the IMF and the World Bank reported that the 1.8 percent positive growth rate meant the deterioration of Zaire's economy "was arrested." It characterized Mobutu's wiping out of his peoples private savings as a "comprehensive stabilization program." Manadou Touré, the Senegalese economist who ran the IMF team in Zaire, resigned in frustration telling a reporter; "I can't control" the illegal outflow of wealth from the country. We are under the supervision of the Zairian authorities. I have to take for granted what they tell me." Meanwhile, Mobutu was embezzling and siphoning the countries natural resources: 200 tons of cobalt to on the "spot" markets in Switzerland; ten thousand tons of copper to South Africa; and 20,000 tons of copper to China.[19]

Historically, mining contributes 25 percent of the DRC's gross domestic product, but the weakening mining sector collapsed in the 1990's. With a crushing debt of $1.6 billion, *Gecamines* produced only 14,000 tons of copper and 600 tons of cobalt before going bankrupt in 2005. *Gecamines* was restructured under a World Bank program. When it was fully operational the company employed 30,000. After 12,000 lay-offs, the company now has a $4.5 million monthly payroll and expenses of $150,000 for hospitals and $100,000 for schools. Other companies are building schools and clinics realizing they cannot rely on government to develop the region. "We run the risk of being viewed as a substitute for the government and there's a lot of challenges managing the expectations of local communities;" explained Bill Turner, CEO of *Anvil Mining*, an Australian mining company operating in Katanga .

In 2006 *Phelps-Dodge*, a US mining group acquired a 57.75 percent stake in the country's Tenke Fungurume Mining operation (TFM), which it described as "the largest and highest-grade undeveloped copper and cobalt project in the world today." *Phelps-Dodge* anticipates producing 100,000 tons of copper and 8,000 tons of cobalt annually by 2008. Within 5-10 years, copper production could rise to 400,000, tons per year and that this level of production could be sustained for twenty years. This brings little consolation to the DRC's impoverished masses. Not all the mining groups operating in Katanga are reputably listed on the world markets. Like parasites on a weak or dying host, companies from the US, Australia, South Africa, Canada and China have interests in Katanga including *First Quantum, BHP Billiton, OM group and* China's *Covec*. However, under the new constitution, 40 percent of a province's revenue will be returned to the region. Mining companies should pay 30 percent corporate tax, 2 percent royalty on net sales and 1 percent tax on exports. The problem is the absence of an enforcement mechanism and the rule of law.[20]

Between 1990 and 1997, war destroyed most of country's business sector arresting economic growth and stability. [21] In 1994, the economy shrank 7.4 percent and inflation reached 23,700 percent. [22] The state mining sector declined to 10 percent of it post-colonial output and spending for primary education and health care dropped precipitously. According to an internal World Bank report, while doubling in population the DRC economy had contracted to its 1958 size.[23] Mobutu's plans for political transition failed.

from the outset. Since there was no effective government independent of his personal will, the process went through four phases and half a dozen interim governments. In August 1992, he consented to the convening of a Sovereign National Conference, a broad-based assembly of nearly 3,000 participant's intent on planning the nation's future. The Sovereign National Conference effectively functioned between April and December of 1992. Resistance to Mobutu's authoritarian style resulted in the 1993 dismissal of Prime Minister Etienne Tshisekedi's government. French Ambassador Philippe Bernard was shot and killed in January 1993, by Mobutist troops who in an attempt to kill Tshisekedi had strafed the embassy.

National resistance was further weakened during a third phase, when Mobutu revived the discredited National Assembly and formed a "parallel government." A fourth phase began in 1994, when the opposition entered a compromise with Mobutist forces and consented to a merger of the "parallel institutions." The opposition agreed to merge the National Assembly into the High Council of the Republic and create a 738-member transition parliament. Most of these parliamentarians were hand picked by Mobutu. The unity government was short-lived. Unity behind prime minister Tshisekedi dissolved when Leon Kengo wa Dondo, another Mobutu puppet, presented himself as a reformer and was elected prime minister by the transitional parliament with 45 percent of the vote. Kengo wa Dondo threatened to resign if he was not able to fulfill the transition mandate, including reform of the armed forces. He achieved nothing.[24]

The Kabila Regimes: Contagious Conflicts

Laurent Désiré Kabila, a Muluba from Lumumba's mineral-rich Shaba province, was a major player in the 1964-1965 insurrection. He disappeared from the political radar and retreated to an enclave near Lake Tanganyika, where he engaged in gold smuggling. When young male Banyamulenge refugees in Rwanda began asking General Paul Kagame of the Revolutionary Patriotic Forces (RPF) for permission to return home to fight Mobutu, he joined them. The DRC was now host to armed and politically active refugees and guerillas from Burundi. Guerrillas infiltrated from Rwanda with the help of their kinsmen in Uvira. These were member of the Bashi, tribe living around near Bakuvu who disdained Mobutu's rule. In contrast to their previous genocidal activities during the 1994 Rwandan genocide, these young men trained with the RPF fighting the local militias that were still engaging in ethnic pogroms. In 1996, Kabila and the Banyamulenge ruthlessly targeted Burundian refugee camps between Uvira and Bukavu scattering the refugees and escorting them to the border under arms. Within ten days Kabila forces eradicated the refugee camps and the Hutu refugees were escorted to the border where they were met by the Burundian army for 'clearing'. Many ware killed outright and the remainder were placed in concentration camps. More than 100,000 remaining refugees moved deeper into the rainforests of Zaire. According to Gérard Prunier, the battle yielded an unexpected result: two thirds of the refugees suddenly regrouped and crossed into Rwanda *en masse*. For the refugees, the sudden exodus presented a triple dilemma. First, they feared the cadres of the former Hutu regime who had been intimidating and threatening the refugees and preventing them from returning. Second, fear vengeful Tutsis who might kill them if they returned. Third, fear of fleeing deeper into the forests of the DRC.[25]

The next campaign was launched against the Rwandan camps located in the same area up the coast of Lake Kivu. These attacks were synchronized with strikes on Rwandan refugee camps in North Kivu and Kahindo by "mysterious armed men." In each case, the attacks were ruthless, targeting even hospitals where patients were killed in their beds.[26] These mysterious attackers were not the Banyamulenge, who were busy fighting in South Kivu, but Tutsi from North Kivu who had survived the genocide, escaped to Rwanda and been trained and rearmed by the RPF. Some of these were Bahunde and Banyanga who had been among those killing Tutsi only a year earlier. They merely switched allegiances and were now killing Hutu refugees in order to earn support from Kigali. After herding the refugees into Mugunga camp, Kabila and his forces joined an advance party of Banyamulenge and their allies in the north. When the combined force attacked Mugunga, the town fell in less the 24 hours. President Mobutu's forces fled as they had done in previous battles.

Kabila started his war with about 1,000 guerilla fighters but quickly realized he needed more. He solved this recruitment problem by integrating a large number of Zairians living in the East African diaspora. Mobutu, who once denounced Kabila as a "stooge of foreigners," was in Europe undergoing surgery for prostate cancer when the war broke out. Etienne Tshisekedi, who remained in Zaire after the transition began, broke his long-standing refusal to deal directly with Mobutu, and went to France to meet with the ailing president. Upon his return he surprisingly announced that Mobutu had agreed to name him as prime minister. Just as before, the claim was denied and proven to be untrue. Tshisekedi then broke ranks with the government and defying popular opinion called for negotiations with Kabila. On December 17, 1996, Mobutu returned home for one last hurrah to enthusiastic crowds. He officially appointed Kengo wa Dondo prime minister which not only further disappointed Tshisekedi supporters, but the opposition who wanted real reform.

It is unclear how much Kabila was supported by Uganda and Rwanda in the campaign to overthrow Mobutu or whether they were creating a buffer zone along their own borders. France, Belgium and the United States each had interests in the conflict but only France had reconciled with Mobutu. Mobutu's foreign assets were frozen and many sanctions imposed. Mobutu's old cohorts became international pariahs, his visas were restricted, his wife was not allowed to shop in Paris and his entourage could not travel freely. When France refused to back Mobutu, old allies including Morocco, Togo and Chad also refused to provide overt support. Eventually, mercenaries from Serbia, Belgium, France were hired to defend his embattled regime.

To the French government, Kabila's invasion was part of the same historic Anglo-American "plot" which brought the Tutsi's to power in Rwanda and extended Ugandan president Museveni's reach into West Africa. French officials accused the US of supporting the rebellion and providing Kabila with advisors. A group of African leaders, including: Yoweri Museveni, Nelson Mandela, Daniel Arap Moi and Secretary-General of the OAU, Salim A. Salim, met to discuss the war. At the last minute, prime minister Kengo wa Dondo canceled the meeting denouncing it as an Anglo-Saxon conspiracy.[27] The uncritical US response to the attack was interpreted in Paris as support for Kabila. However, US ambassador to Zaire, Daniel Simpson, publicly denounced the attack as a foreign invasion. The US eventually attempted to establish negotiations between Kabila and Mobutu's allies. The February meetings in South Africa provided a public relations coup to Kabila, who presented himself as a statesman with Nelson Mandela at his side.[28]

After a long and brutal guerilla campaign, Kabila's forces eventually defeated Mobutu and Zaire became the Democratic Republic of Congo. The strategic city of Kisangani fell to Kabila's forces eliminating all hope of military resistance. Laurent Kabila and his advisers used their *de facto* rule to invite humanitarian groups to return to the region and hinted at the creation of transitional government that would exclude political parties for one year. Laurent Kabila and the rebel Congolese Liberation Movement (MLC) forged an agreement excluding the Rwandan-backed Congolese Rally for Democracy (RCD) and other opposition parties. Shortly thereafter, Laurent Kabila was ambushed and killed by his bodyguards. He was replaced by his son, Joseph.

The proposed all-party talks to resolve differences with smaller delegations were postponed. The RCD controlled the eastern part of the Congo fiercely resisted the new Kabila presidency. The pact that was agreed to on the sidelines was not recognized by the facilitator, Ketumile Masire, former president of Botswana, who described the talks as taking the peace process "back to square one."

Etienne Tshisekedi, a veteran opposition leader and head of the Union for Democracy and Social Progress, formed an alliance with the RCD to encourage the international community to increase its pressure to resolve the civil war. The agreement between Kinshasa and MLC that devastated the .ongoing 50-day European Union backed talks in Sun City. Tshisekedi said the Sun City agreement "was a private one struck in a hotel room." Most delegates left the South African casino-resort for home days before. It was Tshisekedi complained; "An entirely unexpected coup d'état of the inter-Congolese dialogue." He claimed that Joseph Kabila's government and its regional backers had little incentive to pursue peace. Upon departing the Congo, Kabila government officials warned that the transitional government would be established without the RCD if it continued to reject the peace proposals. Tshisekedi said the father and son had established a dictatorship worse than Mobutu's and that comparing them was like comparing cholera with the plague. He added; "Kabila is not in control of Congo. He's a stooge of Zimbabwe and Angola, who are looting the country."

South African President, Thabo Mbeki, mediator of the Lusaka accords, proposed a power-sharing agreement, allowing Joseph Kabila to remain in office, while MLV leader Jean-Pierre Bemba and his RCD counterpart would serve as joint vice-presidents. Mbeki referred to the desertion of the peace talks as an "adjournment" and insisted the only remaining obstacle was the composition of the transitional government, which he expected to soon be resolved.

The peace talks also were intended to arrange for the withdrawal of 20,000 Rwandan troops from the DRC. Rwanda refused to withdraw its troops as long as the cross-border incursions by Congolese militias continued. During the civil war, five neighboring countries established and maintained a military presence in Congo. Angola, Namibia and Zimbabwe were backed by Mobutu, while Uganda and Rwanda supported rebel movements. Rwanda, Uganda and Zimbabwe committed to troop withdrawals following a peace accord in July 2002. By early October, Rwanda had withdrawn about 22,000 troops leaving Zimbabwe with the largest foreign military presence in the DRC.

Like a patient with severe diarrhea who is being dehydrated of life-sustaining nutrients and proteins, the DRC is leaking inert resources and mineral wealth to mercenary corporations and neighboring states. The Rwandan, Ugandan and Zimbabwean occupations involved the widespread theft of Congo's resources. The foreign armies financed their military campaigns by cooperating with foreign mining and timber operations to steal the wealth of Congo. They established a military-industrial complex stretching across east Africa with links to Greece, Belgium and Sri Lanka. Although the intensity of the conflict has diminished, the elite network linked to the armies maintain their control over the mining operations and the arms trade flows they established.

A UN panel report to the Security Council found that the withdrawal of foreign armies facilitated the continued plunder of the DRC's natural resources. The panel amassed evidence of how Rwandan, Zimbabwean and Ugandan armed forces had collaborated with Congolese government and rebel officials to rob the country of billions of dollars worth of minerals, gems and other resources. The report describes organizing pillaging and theft on a scale unrivaled since the rule of King Leopold of Belgium, who made the Congo his private fiefdom, utilized a brutal system of slavery to exploit the resources and killed millions of Africans in the process. The systemic looting previously conducted by the armies, was replaced with organized systems of embezzlement, tax fraud, extortion, the use of stock options, kickbacks and the diversion of state funds by groups of organized criminal entrepreneurs. The researchers called upon the UN to impose financial restrictions on the 29 companies and 54 individuals involved in abuses. The eradication of the sources of corruption could provide salaries to teachers, doctors and public servants allowing them to do their jobs, and grow the economy.

Most of these enterprising criminals are Africans but the list includes four Belgian diamond companies and the Belgian Group *George Forrest Mining Operations*. The US-based *OM Group* in partnership with the *Forrest Group*, allegedly defrauded the DRC out of benefits derived from processing of 3,000 tons of germanium and a $25 billion stockpile of cobalt and copper tailings. The report identifies 85 other multinationals in South Africa, Europe and the United States that violated OECD guidelines. Seven African countries were drawn into the Congo. As a result, the state was stripped of $5 billion worth of assets. In one example, a company fronting for the Zimbabwe Defense Force paid only $400,000 for mining licenses valued at more than $1 billion.

The report estimated that Rwanda earned as much as $20 million a month from the sale of stolen coltan, a rare mineral used in making mobile telephones and in the aerospace industries. Large quantities of illegal coltan were exported from Kigali, Rwanda to Europe and the United States. The Rwandan government also levied a tax on diamond sales, and a share of the revenue was used to support the Rwandan-backed rebels of the Rally for Congolese Democracy (RCD), which controlled much of the territory vacated by Rwandan government forces. The report estimates that RCD-controlled areas produced about 720 kg of gold a year and about 29 tones of coltan. RCD gold diamond and timber passed through the port of Dar-es-Salaam, Tanzania. Rwandan president, Paul Kagame denied this trade was state-sponsored, stating that if the allegations could be proven he would not hesitate to act.

War crimes, crimes against humanity and other atrocities are a tragic part of the civil war. Tens of thousands of young girls and women were raped or subjected to sexual violence during five years of conflict according to international investigations. Some of the victims were as young as three. A report by Human Rights Watch noted that; "On occasion military commanders and the heads of armed groups seem to have encouraged the use of sexual violence as a way to terrorize civilians." In October 2004, at least 10 women were being raped every day in the eastern town of Bunia, according to the report. The French medical aid organization, *Médecins sans Frontiéres* treated more than 2,500 rape victims, ranging in age from four months to 80 years at its hospital in Bunia by June 2003.

Sheltered in a refugee camp protected by UN peacekeepers with tanks and machine guns, 32 year-old Therese Yeda, reported that a militia group gang-raped her as she walked between two villages. "Ten of them had guns, the other two had machetes. All 12 of them raped me," she said. "I am eight months pregnant but the baby doesn't seem to be moving any more." An assessment by the WHO, which examined victims in the provinces of South

Kivu and Maniema and the cities of Goma and Kalemie, concluded that up to 40,000 people had been raped. "Combatants of most armies and armed groups in eastern Congo committed acts of sexual violence both before and after the establishment of the 2003 transitional government;" Human Rights Watch reported. "Alleged perpetrators include fighters of the former rebel movements; the RCD-Goma, the MLC, RCD-ML, and soldiers of the former national army, the Federal Army of Congo. All were supposedly part of an integrated Congolese army. In Ituri province, armed groups of different ethnicity have fought each other for years. Combatants often used sexual violence to target other ethnic groups seen as the enemy. In some areas, women and girls stopped working in the fields or going to the market and went into hiding in the forest at night instead of sleeping in their homes. Civilian and military judicial authorities rarely punished the perpetrators of these crimes.

More damning than the international community's response were allegations that the UN Mission in Congo, "Often failed to protect civilians, including those targeted for sexual violence." The report further stated that: "Worse, some MONUC peacekeepers and civilian staff have discredited the operation by committing crimes of sexual violence and by sexually exploiting women and girls. MONUC peacekeepers, from different military contingents, have sexually exploited Congolese women and girls who were in desperate need of food, money or other items."

In July 2003, European Union foreign policy chief, Javier Solana, committed EU peacekeepers to "making a difference" in the DRC. Solana planned to make the European Security and Defense Policy "concrete by stopping talk about theory and capabilities and instead carry out a mission," announced Steven Everts, of the Centre for European Reform in London. The EU went into the Congo without US support.

Some in Washington suspected that the French pushed the EU to intervene in Bunia where 1,400 French-led EU troops, free of US influence; were involved in their first African peacekeeping mission.[29] The "Berlin Plus" rules, allowing the US certain control over any EU led peacekeeping in return for NATO assets, were removed for MONUC mission. European diplomats insisted that EU peacekeeping operations were not about the Europeans becoming independent of the US, but were about Europe's long-term defense strategy. A strategy based on the prevention of conflict. That failing, and taking a lesson from the US policy failure in Iraq, the EU wanted to intervene quickly and restore civilian institutions with strong a back-up of police and judges. The role of civilians, a key dimension of Solana's security doctrine, calls for utilizing civilian resources in crisis and post-crisis situations. The EU wanted this strategy to be applied in the Congo and an EU policy analysis explained how both political and civilian intuitions in the Congo might be restored if the Congolese parties established a transition government, and trained and integrated the police and judiciary per agreement during the Sun City peace talks.

The UN emphasized the effectiveness of the private sector in promoting the DRC's economic development. Doubtful the fragile peace would hold, bankers remained reluctant to promote investment in the high-risk country. Analysts advised caution on the grounds of contractual uncertainty and enduring military interests, noting that the late president, Laurent Kabila was notorious for overriding existing contracts in favor of clients linked to military interests. Ross Herbert, senior researcher at the South African Institute for International Affairs stated: "Congo isn't a stable legal environment. There is still concern that contracts can be changed willy-nilly. You would also have to check who is being left behind. Are the Zimbabweans really moving out or are they leaving paramilitaries there to tend to their interests?"

Following the withdrawal of foreign armies from the eastern part of the country, the UN approached investment banks to reappraise mining projects and encourage international mining investment. Seeking to attract corporate investment, the UN wanted the capital assets relinquished by the fighting armies brought under the legitimate corporate entities which had for the most part fled the country. The South African mining companies were expected to be the first to respond, but there was little investor interest. *Anglo-American* withdrew its copper interest in neighboring Zambia arguing that the cost of development was higher than expected. "Some large mining companies were wary of investing in the DRC because it is impossible to operate there without becoming entangled in a complex web of political alliances. Others were more optimistic," Geoffrey White, vice chairman of the *Oryx* diamond mining company said: "In the last six months, there's been radical change. It's possible to get bank debt. And there are mechanisms for entrepreneurs to put projects together." *De Beers,* the global diamond group, signaled its intention to return to Congo in 2002, and began negotiating exploration agreements with *MIBA*, the semi-private *Congolese Diamond Company*. The US-based *American Mineral Fields of Toronto* took over *Kolwezi Copper Development* from *Anglo-American*.

Determined not to let continuing instability in the east derail the peace process, Joseph Kabila warned of "shadows still lurking behind us," suggesting that "foreign hands" were playing a role in destabilizing the mineral-rich east. Joseph Kabila's role in negotiating an end to formal foreign involvement in Congo's war and in bringing Congolese players together starkly contrasted that of his father whose three-year rule merely exacerbated regional conflict. Kabila told the *Financial Times* that there was no going back on the power-sharing government installed in July 2003, which had followed five years of war. A government, whose institutions had been destroyed, infrastructure devastated and people impoverished, faced the task of establishing its authority across a territory four times the size of France. If necessary, peace would be imposed on opponents to the South African-UN-brokered peace agreement. Expressing his determination Kabila said: "We have come so far. We have achieved so much. Is it really true that one, two three, four, five individuals are going to pitch the whole nation back into crisis? I say no. There is no way back and we will have to make these understand this the hard way, maybe."

Congo watchers pointed out that power-sharing in the regions and at lower levels of government proceeds very slowly, that the transitional government was fragile and that parts of the eastern DRC where rival militias continued to fight were unstable despite the presence of UN peacekeepers. Joseph Kabila was anxious to bring diamond exports under government control, but was unable to exert governmental authority over the east where diamonds and other strategic minerals were traded through Uganda and Rwanda.

Kabila acknowledged the political weaknesses that allowed neighboring countries to exploit Congolese resources, emphasizing the importance of forming an army of combined former rebel and government forces. "The success of the transition lies in the government putting in place a national army capable of defending its borders, taking care of the security of the people of the Congo and their institutions." He added: "People should not come and politicize the army. That could be the most dangerous thing because in one day the whole process can go up in flames." Kabila recognized the need to decentralize power to the Congo's regions, but favors a strong unitary state. "One way or another, federalism will always lead to secession," he warned. He was referring to Congo's not too distant history, the Kantangan secessionist movement which manipulated by western interests. He noted that it was the politicization of the army that led to the CIA-backed coup and murder of the country's first Prime Minister, Patrice Lumumba which led to a 32-years Mobutu dictatorship.

The Kabila government reviewed all mining contracts drafted during the years of war in order to finance the combating parties. The new contracts would rehabilitate that sector of the economy and encourage future investment. However, diplomats and UN officials expressed concern that corrupt hardliners associated with Laurent Kabila's retained too much influence. Joseph Kabila spoke of his concern for potential corruption; "Considering the past activities of quite a lot of people constituting the government itself... Our defense should be: let's get the people involved, let's get the population asking questions each every time there is a problem, and let's take people to court, let's take people to jail." Many of the key players in Congo's political drama are the sons of men who played leading roles in the Congo's disastrous post-independence years.

Between 60 and 80 percent of customs revenues were embezzled, 25 percent quarter of the national budget was not properly accounted for and more than $3 million was stolen from the army payroll. Despite such ravenous theft, not a single DRC official was convicted on corruption charges during the three years of transitional rule. The degree to which corruption has permeated the military is exemplified in a story by Jason Stearns and Michela Wrong of the *International Crisis Group*. Three women, each weighed down by a 100 pound sack of flour, were walking on a dirt trail. Sitting in front of them on the path with an AK-47 between his legs, was a soldier. The women dumped their bags on the ground and without being asked handed over the equivalent of 20 cents, almost half their daily wages. As they lifted their bags, the soldier said: "*Chai yangu*-my tea." Multiply this single incident by tens of millions of Congolese facing the same petty, devastating corruption, and it becomes clear why many DRC citizens see themselves as victims of a predatory state. According to Kabila, "You have got generations that grew up within the system. They didn't know anything except the system. The question is will they change their ways?" He said he wanted to only attract investor's with no "close ties" to the former dictator. Under Mobutu, Zaire was synonymous with corruption; the country's mineral wealth was siphoned off by a sleazy elite who let the country's infrastructure deteriorate. "It is not always good to see the same names, the same investors. Investment needs to be diversified as much as possible," Kabila argued. A 2006 survey conducted by the World Bank asked the Congolese people how they would treat the state it were a person. "Kill him," was a frequent reply.[30]

Just days after eleven heads of state signed a declaration to promote peace, security and development in Africa's great lakes region, threats of a renewed war in the east escalated when it was reported that Rwandan troops had crossed the border to attack rebels based inside the DRC. Rwanda had previously invaded its giant neighbor in 1996 and 1998 in pursuit of rebels. One week earlier, the UN had announced that it would send more peacekeepers and warned Rwanda against using force, but found no evidence of the reported incursion. Rwandan President, Paul Kagame hinted that the threatened attack against ethnic Hutu extremists in the DRC might had already began: "It will not take long, or could even be happening now" he told the Rwandan senate. The Kabila government announced that within two weeks it would send at least 6,000 troops to the border area to repel the rebel forces. DRC officials suspected Rwanda of using the rebel presence as a pretext to continue to control and exploit the mineral and timber wealth of the east.

In July of 2004, students rioting in Kinshasa expressed their disgust with the chaos and crisis by chanting and painting a graffiti slogan, "One plus four equals zero," to describe the power sharing arrangement between 33 year-old president Kabila and his four vice presidents. Two of the vice-presidents achieved their positions through force of arms at the head of rebel movements. In the east, insurgents under the command of Tutsi leader Laurent Nkunda, captured and terrorized the town of Bukavu. Students were not alone in their disappointment. Across the country people began to discuss doomsday scenarios reminiscent of the 1960 UN Operation in the Congo. "Everywhere we feel there is need for a change;" said Kyungo wa Kumwanza, the president's uncle and former governor of Katanga." Quite naturally, Mr. Kumwanza is displeased that he has not been restored to his former position. "We have a president who is not free;" Kumwanza lamented. Some demanded the "one plus four" power-sharing arrangement be changed.

The RCD-Goma, the rebel faction, backed by Rwanda and which held one of the vice-presidencies, effectively split because some in the movement benefited from the positions of the transitional government, while others did not. Those left out had little to gain by submitting to Kinshasa , disarming and relinquishing control of local inert resources.

Pessimism abounds with respect to the role played by the UN, which was to reinforce security in the Congo. MONUC leaders warned of military activity and political unrest in South Kivu. Certainly the CIA station chief and political officers in Kinshasa had reported the imminent crisis to the State Department desk officer in Washington. However, the report provided UN headquarters with "little or no indication" that tensions were rising. The report states "The desire to show the outside world that everything is in order is a natural and common mistake made by the organization in challenging situations. A more serious problem is the lack of understanding of the dynamics of the situation itself."

The June 2004 humiliation of UN forces at Bukavu humbled the former US ambassador to Congo and UN envoy William Swing, who was distrusted by many Congolese. The fighting erupted in the strategic town Bukavu in South Kivu region when forces loyal to Colonel Jules Mutebutsi, a suspended Congolese army officer, clashed with government troops. The fighting intensified when another renegade commander, General Laurent Nkunda marched on Bukavu in support of Mutebutsi. A Ugandan battalion commander surrendered control of Bukavu airport to General Nkunda despite orders to defend it "with force if necessary." On June 2nd General Nkunda captured Bukavu and killing, rape and looting ensued until the renegade commanders withdrew a few days later. MONUC's failure to stop the renegade army's advance sparked violent anti-UN protests in Kinshasa and many senior officials left MONUC. However, ambassador Swing remains determined to complete his term.

The steps required to restore the UN's credibility include reinforcing the 10,800 strong peacekeeping force and more aggressive use of the UN Charters' Chapter 7 mandate to intervene. In March 2005, the MONUC operation in the eastern Congo again came under fire when an internal report charged the mission was tainted by the perception of "cowardice." The report says that UN troops failed to aggressively defend civilians against renegade Congolese army commanders during fighting in a province south of Kivu which called into question the "very purpose of the mission." It further criticizes MONUC for poor leadership, providing misleading statements and failure of a commander to follow orders.

The report charges MONUC with failure to use force during the crisis "smeared the mission" with the taint of impotence and cowardice and giving the perception "that it had failed the Congolese people at a critical moment," MONUC is the UN's most expensive peacekeeping operation. A UN spokesman described it as "part of the lessons-learnt process," because MONUC provides unprecedented insight into the problems of modern peacekeeping operations. The United Nations announced that it was considering the use of force against the 10,000 Rwandan rebels in the eastern Congo as part of an effort to stabilize the region. MONUC used decisive force in March 2005 following the deaths of nine Bangladeshi peacekeepers in the Ituri region when UN forces killed at least fifty militia members. UN Secretary-General Kofi Annan warned peacekeeping efforts were badly stretched and called for new strategic reserves.

Ross Mountain, deputy head of the UN Mission, said UN peacekeepers would disarm and arrest the insurgents if they continued to threaten civilians. MONUC was criticized for failing to protect civilians who were terrorized by both Rwandan rebels and their allies and an estimated 15,000 Congolese militia fighters. These clashes are the remnants of the bloody proxy- war between Kinshasa and Kigali that should have ended with the civil war in 2003. This potential continent-wide war has drew intervening combatants from six African countries. Inviting perhaps another round of genocide, the UN argued that it has no mandate to disarm the Rwandan rebels but only assist in a voluntary disarmament program. "The mandate says we are able to respond directly to civilians under threat and I'm not sure that we have understood it in as quite an active way in the past as we understand it now;" explained Ross Mountain noting that in the future, MONUC would interpret its mandate to protect civilians in a more "active" fashion. "We don't have to invent excuses; civilians are being attacked, particularly in the east, by the militias. They are killing in the thousands, burning, pillaging and above all raping." The United Nations peacekeeping reputation was dealt another blow when Head of UN peacekeeping, Jean Marie Guehenno called for a systematic-wide overhaul of staff discipline after revelations of sexual harassment reached the UN headquarters forcing the resignation of Ruud Lubbers, the UN Commissioner for Refugees. In November 2004, a French civilian working for MONUC was arrested and deported in connection with pedophilia. Two Tunisian soldiers were sent home for sexually abusing women in Kinshasa. There were widespread reports of sexual abuse by UN peacekeepers in the town of Bunia. According to Marie Guehenno, the sexual exploitation of prostitutes or minors by troops and civilians was endemic. He observed that the large size of the mission meant some morally weak individuals crept into the ranks and found themselves in positions of unchecked power. He told the *Financial Times*: "That problem has been there for years, but as we stir the pot, we see things coming up which give a real sense of dimension. I went to Congo three times to sensitize MONUC from the top down, and shake the tree. Now things are beginning to happen in a serious way."

In October 2005, Kofi Annan asked the Security Council for additional peacekeeping troops to suppress violence by the Mayi-Mayi militia in the lawless and strategic north and center of Katanga province. A UN report of the situation stated that; "An enhancement of the mission's military capacity will be required to address the threat posed by armed groups in Katanga."

Most of the 16,000 peacekeepers in the DRC are in the east and there are only 77 unarmed military observers in Katanga. After denying the request, a US official advised the UN to use troops from missions in neighboring countries if needed adding; "We cannot do everything. We have advocated sharing troops for the election." Meanwhile, Ross Mountain, optimistically stated; "We will do the best we can with what we have. There are security concerns related to our own people and the population and access issues, but clearly whatever the Security Council decides we have to live with." Another UN official reluctantly speculated there was some back-up capacity in the mission to deal with emergencies but, "if all went badly wrong, quite clearly we would have to look for assistance outside."[31]

Holding elections in the wake of a civil war that by now had cost 3.8 million lives was a political nightmare. The DRC's interim government announced that plans for elections the scheduled for June 2006 when the postwar transition period had ended. In March 2005, Jean Pierre Bemba, one of the four vice-presidents suggested drawing up the electoral register in late May and early June and holding elections in December Bemba noted that only a small part of assistance promised by the EU and other international donors to cover elections costs-estimated at $285 million (€ 213m, £148m) had been received and that "elections will not be the end of the story of the transition." Former belligerent organizations needed to develop into real political parties, he advised.[32] Widespread dissatisfaction with the transition, led many to vote against the Charter referendum for a new constitution, even though very few realized that a negative vote could extend the term of the regime in power. Approval of the referendum also promised to pave the way for the first genuine multi-party elections since independence in 1960. A no vote would be a setback for the peace process that formally ended the war in 2003. Ross Mountain stated that: "We are not planning for a "No" vote at this point. We realize there have been a number of parties and individuals calling for a "No" vote, which has been somewhat surprising. The logic applied is of some concern."

On December 18th 2005, the people of the DRC took a step toward ending years of conflict and gross misrule, when they voted on a referendum for a new constitution. If approved, parliamentary and presidential elections would follow in June. Approval also meant more than doubling the number of provinces, which would increase from 10 to 26, thus providing for greater devolution of power and enabling the provinces to retain 40 percent of their revenue. The UN provided logistical support to move the constitutional referendum forward and 25 million citizens of the DRC people prepared to vote. Despite numerous political crises, including two alleged coup attempts and military mutinies in the east, with the help of $1.5 billion in donor aid, the Laurent Kabila administration survived. However, the Kabila regime was widely criticized for graft, failing to improve conditions for ordinary Congolese and for moving too slowly to establish a new national army and police force. Voters approved the new constitution and the electoral commission reported the referendum turnout at 60 percent. Results from 58 percent of polling stations showed that about 80 percent of the votes supported the new charter. The new constitutional mandate set the stage for the presidential and parliamentary elections in June 2006.

The EU had established a rotational system of multinational "battlegroups" to provide regional security in the DRC In 2004. The following year, the UN asked the EU to send troops. Berlin maintained that EU foreign policy chief, Javier Solana should have done more to clarify the nature of the mission, but some EU officials insisted Germany should have done the planning. Reacting to criticism of the EU's slowness in creating the small force of 1500 soldiers for the elections, Germany offered to lead a European pre-election military mission to the DRC, if other countries agreed to contribute troops.

The German government faced opposition from within its governing coalition over the deployment of up to 500 German troops to the DRC to protect a polling process. But foreign minister Frank- the Walter Steinmeier told the parliament that: "Germany could not abandon the DRC at the time of its first free elections in 45 years." If passed by parliament, it marked the first full-scale deployment of German troops in Africa since 1943. German Chancellor, Angela Merkel, questioned whether Germany should play a military role in Africa, after political controversy over German Afghan and Balkan deployments.[33]

On July 30, 2006, the people of the DRC took the prescribed treatment for democracy and went to the polls for the first time in 45 years. The election marked the culmination of three years of negotiation between 35-year old president Joseph Kabila, those who oppose him and various rebels formerly backed by Rwanda and Uganda forming a power sharing government. Kabila took much credit for putting the power-sharing government together, by promoting himself as "The Quiet Force." For the UN, which maintains an 18,000-strong peacekeeping force and spends $1.1 billion a year presence in the DRC, successful elections meant a step towards fulfilling its mandate of helping to rebuild a failed and shattered state. Over 1,800 tons of paper ballots marked with 33 presidential candidates, over 9,000 candidates for 500 parliamentary seats were flown from South Africa at a cost exceeding $450 million, making this the most expensive UN-assisted election. Profit hungry CEO's, prepared to pour billions of dollars into the large DRC copper and cobalt concessions, eagerly watched the elections while calculating their risk and profit strategies.

The electoral process was contested by a segment of the Catholic community which called on people to abstain from voting because of the risk of "manipulation, cheating and fraud". The church's appeal was taken up in Kinshasa where thousands of eligible voters boycotted registration after former prime minister, Etienne Tshisekedi appealed to them to do so. The boycott increased voter turnout of Kabila's opponents set the stage for prompt opposition challenges to the election results. On the eve of the election, demonstrators at a rally in Kasai hurled rocks at Kabila's entourage. In Kinshasa, thousands of Tshisekedi supporters protested Kabila's rule by throwing Molotov cocktails at riot police as the police backed by Kabila's armed presidential guard used tear gas to beat them back.

In much of Kinshasa and Kasai the perception was that Kabila had used his incumbency to dominate the electoral process. "Everything has been done to ensure Kabila has been imposed. The international community wants polls at all costs because they've spent so much organizing them:" said Pierre-Celestin Mulumba, one of 800 worshipers at St. Joseph's church in Kinshasa. The usual political intimidation was reported and the UN condemned the government for blocking the campaign activities of Oscar Kashala, a US-trained doctor whose popularity was perceived as a threat by Kabila. Jean Peirre Bemba, a the well-educated son of a businessman and friend of Mobutu, is also a former Uganda-backed rebel leader, one of four vice-presidents and presidential candidate. He warned of a "fire" if the election was rigged and Kabila emerged the winner. Meanwhile, the neighboring Central African Republic requested that the International Criminal Court investigate human rights violations by Bemba's troops allegedly committed when they intervened to stop a coup attempt in the CAR. Analysts reported that between 2003 and 2006 much of the $8 million per month allocated for soldier's salaries was embezzled.

Another problem concerns the level of military integration of soldiers into the brigades of the eastern province of North Kivu, which is controlled by the CAR. One brigade in North Kivu is dominated by several thousand RCD soldiers loyal to renegade commander, Laurent Nkunda. In South Kivu, it is unclear to whom soldiers attach their loyalties. The RCD participated in the transitional government but made no signs of progress toward reconciliation. Although the RCD did not interfere with the elections, their continued presence poses a threat to post-election stability. "If the cause of the war is not finished, the war is not finished;" warned Nkunda. "The purpose of the transition was to reconcile people but it did not do that;" he noted. Nkunda enjoys the support of regional Hutu majority politicians and businesses. His refusal to be integrated into the national army placed an obstacle to Kabila's efforts to extend federal power in the east. Nkunda claimed that he would use force only as a last resort.[34] Preliminary results indicated that Kabila had won an estimated 80 percent of the votes in the east and the west largely sweeping away the RCD's political power base.[35]

The DRC's Hutu and Tutsi population in the DRC is estimated at between 600,000 and 1 million and they are a significant part of the military force, due to support from Kigali. Members of other Congolese tribes are often openly hostile toward the Kinyarwanda-speaking Tutsi and Hutu communities, accusing them of being agents of Kigali. The role of Kigali is critical to a lasting peace. Under international pressure Rwanda softened its stance toward Kabila's government and signaled intentions to work with him if won the election.

Electoral hostility erupted in violence just hours before Kabila's victory was announced, even though a run-off was scheduled for October. Gun battles raged in the streets of Kinshasa forcing the EU to add an additional 200 reinforcements to its peacekeeping operation. Diplomats meeting with Jean Pierre Bemba were pinned down by the gunfire from the presidential guard. This targeting obviously shook Bemba's confidence in the possibility of a peaceful run-off election. The final count threatened to create a new class of disenfranchised politicians willing to utilize any means, including ethnic conflict, to regain power. The following day, three of the four vice-presidents in the power-sharing government, including Bemba, voiced concern over alleged irregularities in the election process stating: "Perhaps we are heading for a masquerade or a parody of elections."[36] Analysts observed that a run-off between Kabila and Bemba could exacerbate the country's fundamental political divisions and that any fall-out would come after the second round results were declared. Both candidates resolved to maintain their private armies. The Bemba camp's portrayal of Kabila as a western stooge resonates in the western part of the country and in Kinshasa. Kabila takes credit for compromising with the rebels and bringing peace and elections under the power-sharing government. But some in his coterie are less accommodating. "If we win we must rule without interference," said one of them. "Refusing to recognize that the supposed loser is a force to reckon with will only be opening the door to anarchy and refusing really an opportunity to unite the country," said former president of Ghana, Jerry Rawlings during a visit to Kinshasa.[37]

Diplomats and UN officials predicted that a first-round win for Kabila would spark mass riots in Kinshasa and other parts of the country. Some diplomats hoped a Kabila victory would support a request by the neighboring Central African Republic to the International Criminal Court to investigate Bemba's involvement in a counter-coup plot there.[38] Angola, a key ally to the Kabila government, stationed troops near the border in what was described as a "routine exercise".

Several months after the election violence again erupted when gunmen opened fire outside the Supreme Court in Kinshasa, which was meeting to confirm the election results. Police used tear gas against Bemba supporters in the streets. Hundreds of UN peacekeeping troops brought in to bolster the peacekeeping operation were scheduled to withdraw within ten days. UN armored vehicles were sent to disperse some 200 protestors who ransacked the court, set fire to the annex and burned electoral documents. Fear rose that hard-liners in Kabila's camp would push the president into pre-emptive strike against Bemba and a weak UN response would provide justification for deploying his private presidential guard.[39] A few days later Troops loyal to Bemba began withdrawing from Kinshasa in response to a 48-hour ultimatum from President Kabila.

The UN monitoring force reported that 600 of Bemba's soldiers had moved to a camp outside of the capital. Diplomatic efforts had yet to convince Bemba to accept Kabila's 42 percent electoral victory. Moreover, efforts to persuade Bemba's to take diplomatic asylum had failed. Bemba described his choice between exile and ICC prosecution as "nothing but blackmail."[40] Diplomats feared Bemba would provoke a mass uprising in Kinshasa or face pre-emptive action from Kabila's hard-line military factions and Presidential Guard forces. Ringed by heavily armed UN peacekeepers and DRC anti-terrorist police, the court resumed hearing the appeal election results in a small room in the foreign ministry. After pitched battles in the streets of Kinshasa, the state prosecutor issued an arrest warrant for Bemba. Analysts speculated that either Bemba would either be forced into exile or stand trial for treason. "Democracy is the largest loser in all this;" said a Kinshasa banker, who during the fighting had taken refuge with a dozen employees inside his bank vault.[41] Leon Kengo wa Dondo, a former minister Under Mobutu Sese Seko who spent a several years exiled in Belgium and upon his return campaigned for Bemba, was elected president of the Senate, the second most powerful position in the DRC. Some thought his election might impede Kabila's authority and control over all institutions of state. .[42]

In March 2007, the DRC state prosecutor issued an arrest warrant for Bemba whose militia was cornered in pitched firefight on the banks of the River Congo. Bemba slipped into the capital seeking asylum in the South African embassy. There was speculation that he would either be forced into exile or handed over to the Kabila government to stand trial for treason.[43]

A November 2006 IMF memo indicated that the DRC was heading for an economic meltdown requiring urgent government and international donor measures to avoid a prolonged crisis. The IMF, noted that economic mismanagement preceding the presidential election could "durably jeopardize" stability in the country. "The mismanagement under the power-sharing arrangement is unacceptable but ultimately not surprising. Now we have no money, but we need to reinforce the legitimacy of the Congo," said Olivier Kamitatu, a Kabila ally; "Without support, any new government risks collapsing."[44] To make matters worse, the World Bank withheld the findings of an inquiry into the mismanagement of funds. An audit by the integrity department, which answered directly to former assistant secretary of defense and former World Bank president, Paul Wolfowitz, was launched in early 2006 when the allegations of mismanagement were made. Some donor nations accused Wolfowitz of selectively targeting certain states with his anti-corruption campaign. A draft report was completed that autumn, but the World Bank was reluctant to cause controversy by publishing the findings. Some experts contend that the World Bank failed to exercise sufficient oversight of the DRC loan. In keeping with its policy of "not to punish the poor twice when there is government corruption," World Bank officials argued that if normal procedures had been applied in the DRC, where the state was in advanced collapse, no funding would have been possible. A senior European diplomat and a DRC government appointee said that they believed the report was held back so that Wolfowitz, who was caught in a personal World Bank corruption scandal, would not lose the support of DRC leaders.[45]

Despite this negative prognosis, the world's leading mining companies quickly returning to the DRC. Meeting in Cape Town, *Anglo-American, Rio Tinto*, and *BHP Billiton* announced an increase in their mining activities for the DRC's copper, iron ore, nickel, gold, bauxite, diamonds, uranium, coltan and cobalt. *BHP Billiton* is planning to build an aluminum smelter which could take advantage of the hydroelectricity generated by dams on the river Congo. *Gecamines* and *Miba,* the near-bankrupt state-owned copper and diamond companies, began reviewing some of their joint ventures.[46] Twenty-six new provincial legislative assemblies are planned that could, if endowed with the necessary checks and balances, make the president more accountable. The national parliament launched an audit of state companies and a review of mining contracts.

The courts, which presently serve as an appendage to the executive branch, could perform their function as a check on power, eventually returning the system to homeostasis. Building the infrastructure would facilitate all of this but first peace must prevail and that requires a healthy auto immune system. Barely 6 percent of the population of the DRC has access to electricity and at night the slums of Kinshasa are lit by candle light. Repairing the DRC's military (auto-immune system), requires not only reforming the corrupt and compromised army, but commanding its absolute loyalty to the leader of a fragile government, a major challenge faced by too many African states.[47] MONUC helped the DRC's army's plan a military solution to the eastern war and transported soldiers and ammunition to the frontline. However, this time UN headquarters in New York refused to grant MONUC forces permission to take part in the fighting. The effectiveness of the multi-billion dollar MONUC operation was questioned, but the Security Council renewed the peacekeeping mandate after Laurent Nkunda's outnumbered rebel forces, humiliated and scattered Kabila's forces. Using small non-uniformed groups, the rebels killed dozens of government soldiers. Many surviving government soldiers either sold or gave their arms and ammunition to Nkunda's forces. Outgoing head of MONUC, William Swing admitted that mission goals had not been met stating: " Of all the crises in Africa, the one that if solved offers potentially the greatest benefits to the whole continent is the Congo."[48] When Nkunda finally signed a peace treaty in January 2007, over 5,400,000 people had been killed in the war.

Sixty one years after Nuremberg, Thomas Lubanga Dyilo, a Congolese citizen accused of conscripting children to fight, faced history-making charges in The Hague, making him the first African to face justice in the ICC. On November 9, 2006, a tribunal at the ICC was asked to rule on whether there was sufficient evidence that Lubanga enlisted and conscripted child soldiers, for a full trial to proceed. Prosecutor, Fatou Benosuda, told the judges the case against Lubanga was "a key step" in realizing the hope that impunity for war crimes could be ended.[49] The DRC continues to bleed out its life sustaining inert resources in what can best described as severe form of economic diarrhea. Parasites both internal and external are dehydrating the patient and the evidence is clearly seen in the pain, hunger disease and suffering of the Congolese people.

---

1. Andrew England, 'Peace deal' with Congo leaves talks in limbo,' *The Financial Times*, April 27, 2002.

2. Jonathan Kwitty, *Endless Enemies: The Making of an Unfriendly World.* (Congdon and Weed: New York, 1984) 51.

3. Ibid.

4. Ibid

5. Ibid.

6. Ibid. 84.

8. Ibid. 85.

9. Ibid. 55.

10. Ibid. 65.

11. Ibid.

12. Ibid. 69.

13. Ibid. 68.

14. Ibid. 87.

15. Ibid. 88.

16. *The Universal Declaration of Human Rights*, Article 2; *The International Covenant on Economic, Social, and Cultural Rights*, Article 2; International and Article 2 of *The Covenant on Civil and Political Rights.*

17. Richard Gittleman, "The Banjul Charter On Human and Peoples Rights: A Legal Analysis" in Claude E. Welch, Jr., and Robert Meltzer, eds., *Human Rights and Development in Africa* Albany: State University of New York, 1984), 318.

18. Ibid. 90.

19. Ibid. 97.

20. Andrew England,, 'Concession to history: when miners in Congo must look beyond the bottom line,' *The Financial Times*, August 21, 2006. p.7.

21. *The Financial Times,* Ibid

22. The Financial Times, Ibid

23. Rosenblum, Peter "Endgame in Zaire." *Current History,*, Vol. 96, no. 610. (1997): 202.

24. Ibid.

25. Ibid.

26. Prunier, Gérard "The Great Lakes Crisis." *Current History,* Vol. 96, No. 610. (1997): 196-197.

27. Ibid p. 204.

28. Ibid p. 205.

29. Andrew England, 'Congo the test for EU peacekeeping skills,' *The Financial Times*, October 15, 2003.

30. Jason Stearns, and Michela Wrong, 'The struggle for a functioning Congo,' Comment: *The Financial Times*, August 4, 2006. p. 11.

31. Mark Turner, 'US rejects call form more troops to Congo, *The Financial Times,* October 2, 2005.

32. David White, 'Congo vice-president admits elections likely to be delayed,' *The Financial Times,* March 18, 2005.

33. Hugh Williamson, 'German troops will lead mission to protect Congo poll,' *The Financial Times,* March 18-19, 2006, p. 2.

34. Andrew England, 'Congo's rebel leader watches and waits,' *The Financial Times,* August 8, 2006, p.2.

35. Dino, Mahtani, "Army's factional loyalties jeopardize Congo poll success,' *The Financial Times*, July 29, 2006 p. 3.

36. Dino, Mahtani and Andrew England 'Congo Opposition raises election concerns,' *The Financial Times,* July 31, 2006.

37. Dino, Mahtani, 'Presidential poll unlikely to end Congo's schism as strongmen hold sway,' *The Financial Times.*

38. Dino, Mahtani, 'Congo poll figures point to Kabila-Bemba run-off,' *The Financial Times*, August, 21, 2006. p.3.

39. Dino, Mahtani, 'Violence hits hopes of Congo deal between presidential rivals,' *The Financial Times*, November 22, 2006, p.6.

40. Dino, Mahtani, 'Troops loyal to Bemba start Kinshasa pull-out,' *The Financial Times,* November 4, 2006, p.4.

41. William Wallis, 'Congo seeks to arrest Bemba,' *The Financial Times*, March, 24-25, 2007 p.4.

42. William Wallis and Dino Mahtani, 'Mobutu enforcer back to haunt Kabila,'
The Financial Times, May 14, 2007, p 4.

43. William Wallis, 'Congo seeks to arrest Bemba,' *The Financial Times*, March 24-25, 2007 p.2.

44. Dino, Mahtani. 'Donor partners face dilemma as Congo heads for meltdown,' *The Financial Times,* November 27, 2006, p.6.

45. Dino Mahtani, Eoin Callan and Wallis, William. 'Anti-corruption doubts as Congo report withheld,' *The Financial Times,* May 1, 2007 p. 3.

46. Rebecca Bream, 'Stability tempts mining companies back to Congo,' *The Financial Times*, February 21, 2007 p.5.

47. Dino, Mahtani. 'Poll offers Congo chance to step out of darkness,' *The Financial Times*, July 26, 2006, p. 4.

48. William Wallis and Fred Robarts, "UN sees its Congo Peacekeeping operations descend into disarray,' p. 1. and Fred Robarts and David Lewis, 'Rebel raid snuffs out army move to end Congo conflict,' *The Financial Times*, December 22-23, 2007 p. 5.

49. 18. Nikki Tait, 'ICC opens with child soldier hearings,' *The Financial Times,* November 11, 2006 p. 6.

8: The War-Traumatized Côte d'Ivoire

Between two mountainous heaps of garbage in Abidjan stands a woman who is, balancing scrap wood on her head and choking on toxic waste, covers her mouth with a head scarf and laments: "I have no choice. But I hope this mess will be cleared away soon." Weeks after 400 tons of toxic waste were discharged from a ship at a dozen sites around Abidjan; the residents of the city once known as the Manhattan of West Africa, were still choking on toxic and poisonous fumes. The poisoned air killed ten people and sent tens of thousands in search of respiratory treatment, prompting the government to offer its resignation. "This crisis is a problem of the unconsciousness of our leadership," said a young student doctor at the university hospital in Cocody, an upscale section of Abidjan.[1] *Trafigura*, a privately owned commodity trading group agreed to pay $200 million to settle claims about dumping toxic waste of the coast of West Africa. The payment represents one of the largest fines for environmental damage in Africa.[2] The country's environmental and economic health is threatened by criminal deforestation and water pollution. The health standards for people are not much better. They suffer from hepatitis A, yellow fever, typhoid fever, malaria, tuberculosis, cholera, leprosy and schistosomiasis. Life expectancy for males is a mere 43 years and for females 46 because 92 out 1,000 thousand infants dies at birth. The HIV/Aids infection rate is 10.76 percent and there is one physician for every 11,800 people. Since the death of the first president Félix Houphouët-Boigny, the people of Cote d'Ivoire, once considered model of West African political stability and economic growth have been traumatized by a series of military calamities and sustained economic deterioration.

Peace in the Cote d'Ivoire collapsed in 2000 over contested election results. The government of Laurent Gbagbo insisted that it had been democratically elected while opponents charged the election was flawed because Alassane Ouattara, a former Prime Minister who enjoyed strong support in the largely Muslim populated north, had been excluded from the ballot. The rebels demanded that the government resign the recognition and participation of opposition parties and new elections. The existing agreement to disarm rebel movements and to draft a new constitution was never fully implemented.

The July 2002 elections brought renewed violence after thousands of voters were barred from the polls because they had not been issued the required new identification papers.[3] Fights broke out at polling stations between security forces and supporters of the opposition demanding the right to vote. The dispute over identity cards led to opposition party accusations that the government was complicit in voter fraud manipulation.

Muslims from the north, primarily supported the Rally of the Democratic Republicans (RDR) complained of discrimination by polling officials who denied identification cards to people with Islamic or northern-sounding names. There are three main rebel groups: the New Forces Movement (formerly the Ivory Coast Patriotic Movement; (MPCI) an obscure group whose leadership and agenda were vague; and the Movement for Justice and Peace (MJP) and the Ivorian Popular Movement (MPIGO). The opposition parties claimed that at least twenty percent of the country's 5 million voters were denied the vote, but the government claimed the figure was only 250,000.

In November 2002, the Gbagbo government accused the rebels of breaking the truce, raising fears of renewed violence and further regional destabilization. French Foreign Minister, Dominique de Villepin, was dispatched to Abidjan to assist in an international effort to revive peace talks. France, which keeps more than 1,000 troops in the Cote d'Ivoire, offered to provide logistical support to the government and to evacuate French expatriates. After deciding that President Gbagbo was capable of implementing the agreed to peace accords, Dominique de Villepin chose to support him, while simultaneously responding to the hostility of his militant supporters.[4]

Senegalese President, Abdoulaye Wade, recommended that the internationally-backed elections be abandoned until hostilities ended. He offered George W. Bush and Jaques Chirac administrations an alternative plan, governance by technocrats. A transitional government, run by technocrats with no party affiliations, would lend the process legitimacy, while allowing Laurent Gbagbo and the parliament to remain in power until their mandate ended in 2005. "My view is that the Ivorian political class has failed," President Wade observed.

In July 2003, at a ceremony held at Gbagbo's presidential palace, the military chiefs and the rebels declared that the war had ended. In September they promptly withdrew from the transitional unity government accusing Gbagbo of failing to honor the peace agreement.

The Gbagbo government claimed that neighboring countries were involved in the insurrection and were nurturing hostility toward the large immigrant population, which provides invaluable labor to the cocoa producing economy. The UN High Commissioner for Refugees (UNHCR) reported processing 800 immigrant cases in Abidjan alone. Most of these immigrants were Liberians, whose homes were subsequently burned by police or military forces.

On October 14, 2003, fighting broke out in Bouaké, Cote d'Ivoire's second largest city, when forces loyal to the Gbagbo attempted to extricate rebels who had seized control of much of the north during an uprising that September. With the collapse of the ceasefire plan, ECOWAS (Nigeria, Ghana, Niger, Mali, Togo and Guinea-Bissau), put pressure on Gbagbo to negotiate with the Patriotic Movement of the Cote d'Ivoire. Gbagbo refused to negotiate with the rebels on equal terms. A presidential spokesman warned that military operations would continue "until law is re-established over the entire national territory." Ammedou Ould Abdallah, the UN secretary-general's special representative for West Africa, underscored the frustration of trying to avert civil war, and outlined Kofi Annan's plan to share these concerns with presidents Obasanjo of Nigeria and Wade of Senegal.

Liberia, the other nation in this saga, was slowly emerging from 14 years of civil-war with the help of a UN peacekeeping force. Liberian militias fought for both sides in the Cote d'Ivoire's civil war. The area near the Liberia's western border, where these militias once terrorized the local population, remains a dangerous and unstable region. The coup attempt left rebels in control of the northern city of Bouaké, making travel around the country increasingly difficult. In November 2003, Liberia's transitional leader, Gyude Bryant, held talks with President Gbagbo about securing their troubled border. This was Bryant's first visit to Abidjan after becoming the leader of a broad-based coalition government. The talks involved high-level contacts between the rival Ivorian warring factions and West African leaders determined to put the Cote d'Ivoire's peace process back on track.

The Security Council scheduled a session to consider the situation after West African states called for the 5,300 French and West African peacekeeping troops in the country to be given a full UN mandate. The French presence was considered essential to avoiding total chaos and perhaps regional war. The rebels sent a convoy to attack a bridge 65 kilometers from Man, a large town in the northwest. The battle resulted in hundreds of deaths and cut off a vital regional supply route from the country's ports.

Tensions rose again, after Gbagbo's allegedly refused to devolve effective power to the ministers of the broad-based government of national reconciliation. The rebels withdrew their ministers in protest. Repeated diplomatic attempts by ECOWAS leaders to persuade Gbagbo to be more flexible, failed. Gbagbo' spokesman, Alain Toussaint, reported that they had discussed the ongoing peace processes in both countries and of ways of preventing the movement of armed insurgents across their porous border. In search of peace, Gbagbo also held talks with President Omar Bongo of Gabon and French Foreign, Minister Dominique de Villepin, but there was no breakthrough in the intractable and complex negotiations to end the increasingly tense but violent stalemate.

The Political-Economy of Cocoa

In the West, "death by chocolate," is culinary cliché really only occurring due to complications associated with over consumption. In the Cote d'Ivoire death by chocolate refers to the wars fueled by the global demand for chocolate-based products. Three times each week, a train leaves the rebel capitol of Bouaké for the government capital of capitol Abidjan. The railway is one of few remaining symbols of the country's infrastructural integrity. The railway runs the length of the country north to south. It rumbles through cotton fields and winds its way through cocoa plantations crossing the front lines of the civil war. According to *Global Witness*, after diamonds and timber, chocolate exports funded most of the conflict in Cote d'Ivoire. The country's economy was built in part on the labor of neighboring West African immigrants, who estimatedly accounted for at least one quarter of the population before the conflict. Cote d'Ivoire produces about 40 percent of the world's cocoa beans. According to *The Economist's*: Intelligence Unit; cocoa exports reached $1.3 billion in 2001, accounting for one-third of the nation's export earnings and 13 percent of its gross domestic product. The country's cocoa earnings suffered in 2003; due to lower prices, poorer agricultural conditions, the poor infrastructure and production problems related to the civil war. An excellent cocoa crop in 2002 helped fund government military spending. In 2005, cocoa exporters reported that despite market disruptions, 90 percent of the season's main cocoa crop reached the ports.[5]

The number of people involved in growing and buying cocoa for export declined significantly, raising concerns that farmers were abandoning their land and turning to smuggling. "The situation is serious because people are working but not getting the returns;" observed Raphael Zogbo, president of *Awane*, a cocoa-producers cooperative. Speculators predicted a 10 percent production decline from the 1.3 million tons shipped in 2002-2003. Buyers in the western cocoa town of Daloa, reported that their cocoa purchases declined by 60 percent during the September to January harvest season. Buyers and producers complained that the "farm gate" cocoa price had been cut by half that year to FCFA 375 per kilogram i.e., by (68 US cents, 57 euro cents, 40 UK pence). However, the benchmark London cocoa price fell by only a quarter during the same period. The decline was a disincentive to production and encouraged smugglers to seek higher prices in neighboring Ghana. One exporter estimated the illegal cocoa trade could amount to tens of thousands of tons.

An audit published in 2004 and sponsored by the European Union, indicated that despite the introduction of a trade liberalization plan providing a complex web of cocoa boards for regulating and financing the cocoa sector, conditions for farmers had failed to improve. The farmers found alternative export markets and some cocoa was smuggled out through neighboring countries. They complained of middlemen, who take their cut before taxes are levied. Many of these middlemen pay farmers much less than the standard price of $0.75 a kilogram. Farmers and immigrants from other parts of West Africa reported being harassed by security forces because the government claimed the rebels controlling the north received backing from abroad. [6]

Ghana, backed by an internationally syndicated loan worth several hundred million dollars, guaranteed a minimum price of around a $1.00 per kilogram. The result was an exploitable price discrepancy between Ivorian and Ghanaian cocoa prices, which only encouraged more smuggling. To the joy of western cocoa speculators, cocoa futures soared. *Global Witness* proposed that cocoa exporting companies exercise due diligence by publishing information on the origin of the cocoa they purchased. Many cocoa exporting countries argued they had no control over the use of cocoa revenues by the government of Cote d'Ivoire. Susan Smith, a spokesperson for the Chocolate Manufacturers Association, a US-based trade group, which includes *Nestlé* and *Hershey's* said; "Tracing or labeling individual beans is, as a practical matter, impossible." She argued that having to provide the origin of cocoa would damage the industry. [7]

In an effort to prevent money laundering and the costly destabilization of West Africa's trading system, an African Franc Zone was created. The West African franc zone includes: Benin, Burkina-Faso, Cote d'Ivoire, Guinea-Bissau, Mali, Niger, Senegal and Togo. In 1992, a new currency was issued to replace the CFA 800 billion in circulation. Banknotes in the eight countries were replaced with new currency. Designed and printed by the Bank of France, the new currency depicted local flora and fauna, banana trees, dromedaries, satellite dishes and aircraft. However, they lacked color fastness and begin to fade almost immediately. The new bills proved problematic because among the masses of poverty stricken people who are used to hustling cash for a daily existence, there is great suspicion of banks.

The franc zone and its central African counterpart are the legacy of French colonialism. At the end of the colonial era, France pegged the African currencies to the franc in order to cement trade links with their former colonies and protect them from currency devaluations suffered by the other West African countries. The CFA Franc was devalued again in 1994. In 2004, it traded at a equal value with the French franc and kept pace with the rapidly appreciating Euro. This exchange rate delighted the country's elite who could purchase expensive imported goods, but horrified and further impoverished of the country's cotton farmers and workers.

Neo-Colonial War

The fragile peace collapsed in November 2004, when government forces launched air attacks on rebels in the north. France responded by destroying the nation's air force. National Assembly leader, Mamadou Koulibaly stated that France's retaliation marked the start of; "a long hard war...Vietnam will be nothing compared with what we are going to do here." The US, Canada,

Spain and the UK began to evacuate about 2200 of their citizens. Several hundred British troops were placed on standby and a small military team was deployed to review "contingency plans" and to meet with French authorities. Inflammatory anti-French sentiment, on state television, accused France of declaring war on the Cote d'Ivoire. However, state television failed to mention, that the Gbagbo government had breached the internationally brokered ceasefire by bombing rebel-held territory, killing nine French peacekeepers and an American citizen.

For France, the nation's former colonial ruler and for decades its closest African ally, the mass protests marked the end of one its most enduring post-colonial Africa's relationships. Their neo-colonial status is not lost on the people of the Cote d'Ivoire. There is widespread sentiment that Paris never stopped playing the role of "master" and continues to exert political and economic control over their lives. The capitol city, Abidjan is a geopolitical tribute to neo-colonialism. The main bridges are named after Charles DeGaulle, the Former French Premier, and Félix Houphouet-Boigny, Cote d'Ivoire's francophile head of state, who ruled from independence in 1960 until his death in 1993. The benefits of his rule accrued to France were so lucrative that his funeral was attended by both right-wing and left-wing French politicians, including Jacques Chirac and Francois Mitterrand. There are more than 14,000 French citizens living in the Cote d'Ivoire, of whom 8,000 have dual nationality. The 14,000 French expatriates and French companies account for more than half of the foreign investment and are prominent players in key sectors such as power supply, water supply and telecommunications.

Reacting to hostilities in its neo-colony, France launched an evacuation of its citizens from the Cote d'Ivoire. Four French airliners were dispatched to Abidjan to collect some 1,000 French citizens. President Jacques Chirac said that France would defend the interests of French citizens and continue to work with the UN and the African Union to help stabilize the country. He called on the Gbagboto restore Public order.

Although government ministers appeared on state television, urging Ivorians to return to work, the violence continued. Loyalist and militant Gbagbo supporters set up roadblocks and searched passing cars in the garbage strewn streets of the upscale Abidjan's Plateau and Cocody districts. The city was economically strangled. The loyalist's demanded the departure of French troops, who they accused of killing dozens of protestors outside the *Hotel I'voire*, which was used by French troops as temporary barracks. "We will make them leave;" said a protestor named Guede Severin. "Even if they kill us, we will be here. We want France to leave in 48 hours;" shouted a young protester named Anon Dgoro Pierre. "It's France that is attacking us now not the rebels;" he said, responding to claims that French troops had fired on the crowds. French foreign minister, Michael Barnier replied that French troops had fired shots to cover the departure of French tanks and armored vehicles from the hotel. He told French television audiences that:

"We have no intention of destabilizing Cote d'Ivoire. We have no intention other than stability and peace, within the framework of the United Nations mandate." A spokesman for UNICORN, a French force of more than 4,000 troops, replied that: "We are not against the Cote d'Ivoire. It is out of the question that we will replace President Gbagbo, who is democratically elected." [8]

More than 10,000 peacekeepers from France and the UN intervened to prevent a return to civil war because peace was essential to the peacekeeping efforts in Liberia and Sierra Leone. of UN Head peacekeeping, Jean-Marie Guehenno, warned that no attempt to resolve the political crisis by military means would be successful. He told *The Financial Times*; "We all hope leaders have seen the abyss. The policy of brinksmanship is extremely dangerous. We hope the possibility of extreme violence will convince all the key players that the military option is definitely dead." A return to civil war would mean the further destabilization the West Africa, where conflicts have a tendency to spill over the porous borders. In order, to preclude the Gbagbo government purchasing more arms, France called upon the Security Council to impose an immediate arms and travel embargo and to impose financial sanctions on both sides. The Senegalese president cited "sources from a western power," that Gbagbo had already sent a mission to purchase weapons from Libya and China. Nigerian President, Obasanjo sought and received assurances from both countries that they would not sell arms to the Cote d'Ivoire. Rebel leaders persistently emphasized that they would not disarm until their people received voter registration cards.

Conflict over land ownership worsened when ethnic communities from other parts of the country began migrating to the western region to grow cocoa. A wave of ethnic violence drove farmers from their villages leaving over 100 people dead. Violence in the ethnically diverse western region, threatened the cocoa crop. If the farmers were unable spray pesticides they could not meet western market demands. "If the conflict takes root in the west, it could really hinder the normal functioning of the commercialization of cocoa;" said Jean Luc Agkpo, director of the Cote d'Ivoire's National Bureau for Technical and Development Studies. According to *Saga*, a French transport company with a dominant presence in Cote d'Ivoire ports, exports of cocoa beans and products fell 11.7 per cent between October 2004 and April 2005. Down 922,725 tons from the previous season due to a poor harvest and smuggling. There was also a 13 percent decline in cocoa arrivals at the ports between 2003 and 2005.[9]

Comprehensive media coverage of the violence and of the French response eclipsed the work of the more than 6,000 UN peacekeepers. It also obscured the already clouded perspectives of many Ivorians. This was particularly true in rebel-held areas, which regarded the militant loyalists as violent, xenophobic and opportunistic looters, who wanted the French to remain. For some Ivorians, the conflict with France was both a shocking and bitter new reality. Kobena Alomo, a businessman who studied in Bordeaux stated:

"Before, I used to have a feeling in my heart when France played football. Now, I don't feel anything for France." The International Committee of the Red Cross estimated that 600 people were wounded during the Abidjan violence and the Security Council considered a draft motion proposed by France to impose a general arms embargo.

The April 2004, an AU peace-deal brokered by South African President, Thabo Mbeki, averted renewed conflict and opened the way to elections in October. Under the peace accord, signed in Pretoria, the parties declared "the immediate and final cessation of all hostilities." The signatories; President Gbagbo, rebel leader Guillaume Soro and opposition politicians Alassane Ouattara and Henri Konan Bėdiė agreed to meet for a disarmament program. The UN and African leaders backed a new prime minister, Charles Konan Banny, who was mandated to organize the elections and a disarmament plan. Banny, who is widely seen as an unbiased technocrat, unnerved Gbagbo supporters with his choice of ministers and those who argued that the internationally mediated solution amounted to a political coup.

A political impasse between Gbagbo and the rebels occupying the northern part of the country over Gbagbo's reluctance to implement the peace agreement, led to danger of renewed conflict. Amadou Kone, a senior aide of Guillaume Soro, the Ivorian rebel leader, indicated that rebels, officially known as "The New Forces," were willing to attend an internationally-sponsored meeting to put the peace process back on track by establishing a "consensual roadmap" of action. However, Soro reiterated that the rebels would not renegotiate the French-brokered peace agreement. He told reporters in Niger that the "The New Forces" wanted the African Union and the United Nations to become more closely involved in international efforts to break the deadlock, stating; "Today we would wish to see the African Union and the UN coming in to reinforce all the peace initiatives launched by ECOWAS (Economic Community of West African States) so that Cote d'Ivoire can rapidly find peace and unity."

By June 2005, President Gbagbo had not passed critical bills on nationality and a new electoral commission. "There is a lot of foot dragging which cannot be tolerated for long," commented Pierre Schori the UN's top envoy to the Cote d'Ivoire. Laurent Gbagbo's term of office would end in October 2005 and if scheduled elections were not held, the country would face a constitutional crisis.[11]

Diplomats estimated that three months were needed for electoral lists to be prepared in order to prevent a flawed election process. There were concerns whether 10,000 UN and French troops could effectively monitor an arms embargo near the border with Liberia, which also scheduled elections for October. Liberia is the home of thousands of former fighters. Western militia groups, many created there by Gbagbo, are scheduled to disarm. As of June 2005, the rebels had only handed over one Kalashnikov rifle.

Private companies in the north pay informal taxes to rebel authorities while transporting their goods across the front-line to pay official export taxes, even if the good are exported via the rebel zone. Rebels raise funds in 60 per cent of the territory by taxing transporters and by controlling smuggling routes for cocoa and other goods. In March 2005, The *International Crisis Group* published a report called *The Worst is Yet to Come*, warning that if elections could not be held, Gbagbo would continue the war of attrition, or face a popular uprising or an attempted coup. However, in the OAU tradition of non-interference, African leaders backed Gbagbo's claim to power beyond the October 30, 2005 mandate.

The October elections were postponed because the political stalemate continued. Thousands took to the streets of Abidjan calling for Gbagbo to step down, while thousands of his supporters lined the waterfront to witness a military exercise. The military exercise was widely perceived as a warning to the opposition not to challenge the UN resolution extending Gbagbo's mandate for another year. The UN resolution was based on AU recommendations; it mandated a new prime minister with extensive powers with respect to disarmament and elections processes. An international working group was to monitor progress toward the unimplemented, 2003 French-brokered peace deal. An *International Crisis Group* report stated; "If the UN Security Council does not use the 12-month transition period to impose shock therapy, the machetes and AK-47 assault rifles will resume service quite fast."[12]

Northern rebels control half of the territory of Cote d'Ivoire's. They refuse to disarm, citing among their reasons the government's failure to disarm its loyal militia, the manipulation of important laws on nationality and the creation of an electoral system manipulated by Gbagbo. After a former chief of staff urged the armed forced to remove Gbagbo by "any means," the president agreed to pay his soldiers $200 million in back pay. Gbagbo then asked his supporters to "vaccinate the country" with preventative measures to resist challenges to his authority.

Cote d'Ivoire sustained serious damage to its auto immune system but quickly began to recover. The UN arms boycott severely compromised the country's internal security. Several disarmament deadlines were missed. A UN panel study reported that the government sought to repair, maintain and rebuild the air force to demonstrate the government's superiority in the. The study corroborated reports that foreign technicians were seen working on military aircraft at Abidjan airport. According to the report, the Cote d'Ivoire air force prepared a helicopter to respond to an alleged attack in Anyama. The flight was stopped after the French commander gave warning that the flight would be considered a hostile action. Kadet Bertin, special envoy to the president, protested that repairing an aircraft was not in violation of a Security Council resolution. In October 2004, the government of Togo grounded four Cote d'Ivoire aircraft passing through Abidjan. The aircraft were being repaired at a hangar company that supplied aircraft to the Cote d'Ivoire government. Togo was already on a Security Council list of countries identified as sources of arms smuggling into Angola.[13]

For several days in January 2006, destruction and violence was widespread, as youth militia controlled of the streets of Abidjan. A UN base in the town of Guiglo near Abidjan, where Bangladeshi troops were stationed, was attacked by "young patriots" and pro-Gbagbo militia, leaving four UN troops dead. France renewed prospects of international sanctions against the Cote d'Ivoire and began drafting a UN Security Council statement to that effect. The ruling party announced its intention to withdraw from the peace process and called for the departure of the 10,000 UN and French peacekeeping troops after international mediators recommended that the parliament, which is dominated by supporters of President Gbagbo, not be allowed to reconvene. The Security Council considered a resolution to deploy an extra 34,000 soldiers. However, a US diplomat cautioned that the recommended troop increase was unlikely given the Bush administration skepticism about the efficacy of the mission. The rebels announced they would abandon their separate administrative system and accept central government centered authority once their demands were met and a peace was secured.

AU leaders met in October 2006, to make a recommendation to the UN Security Council about a second extension Gbagbo's presidency. Meanwhile, the country's economy deteriorated, farmers went on strike as both rebels and government officials continued to exploit national finances and the nation's cocoa, oil and diamond resources. Plans to implement World Bank recommendations to tighten control over revenues began and the government pledged to open the hydrocarbon industry to international auditors. But as long as the political stalemate continues, Ivorians will continue to suffer.

---

1. Dino, Mahtani, 'Toxic waste is the least of Cote d'Ivoire's Troubles,' *The Financial Times,* October 3, 2006, p. 6.

2. Morrison, Kevin, 'Cote d'Ivoire wins $200m payout over toxic waste,' *The Financial Times,* February 15, 2007. p 7.

3. Dino Mahtani, 'Tension mars Cote d'Ivoire polls as some voters barred,' *The Financial Times,* July 8, 2002.

4. Dino, Mahtani, 'Cote d'Ivoire in peril.' *The Financial Times,* 'November 18. 2002.

5. Dino, Mahtani and Mark Turner, 'UN set to consider sanctions on Cote d'Ivoire,' *The Financial Times,* January 19, 2006. p 6.

6. Ibid

7.William Wallis and Dino Mahtani, 'Cocoa exports fund conflict in Ivory Coast,' *The Financial Times,* June 8, 2007, p. 9.

8. Daniel Dombey, "NATO to provide support in Darfur mission," *The Financial Times*, April 28, 2005.

9. Dino Mahtani, 'Ethnic Violence threatens cocoa harvest,' *The Financial Times,* June 16, 2005.

11.Dino, Mahtani, "Foot-dragging threatens Cote d'Ivoire stability," *The Financial Times*, June 21, 2005.

12. Dino Mahtani, 'Crowds call for Ivorian president to stand down,' *The Financial Times*, October 31, 2005.

13. Dino Mahtani, 'Cote d'Ivoire seeks to rebuild air force as political statement says UN,' *The Financial Times*, November 4, 2005.

9: Kenya: Cancerous Corruption & Poisonous Politics

In September of 2005, Kenyan President, Mwai Kibaki optimistically told investors, that he expected economic growth to rise to 5.5 percent by the years end. He reaffirmed his electoral pledge to create jobs promising his government would strive for higher rates that would affect poverty. According to the IMF, Kenya's economic growth had dropped to less than 1 percent during the previous decade. Aid agencies estimated that 60 percent of Kenyans live in poverty. A bloated and corrupt civil service and capital losing, parastatal enterprises consume most of the public resources. Life expectancy is short, at 46 years for males and 48 years for females. Sixty seven out of every thousand Kenyan infants dies at birth. The adult HIV/Aids infection rate is 13.5 percent and there is one only doctor for every 6,000 people, a relatively high ratio among African nations. Kenyans routinely die from malaria, bacterial and protozoal diarrhea, hepatitis A, typhoid fever, schistosomiasis, tuberculosis, bilharzias (worm disease), sleeping sickness and protein deficiency. Only 49 percent of the population has access to safe drinking water and only 8 percent have access to adequate sanitation facilities.

Kenya's social structure is burdened by the influx of over 300,000 refugees from war-torn Ethiopia, Somalia and Sudan. In August 1998, the world's attention focused on the bombings of the American Embassies in Nairobi and Dar es Salaam. For most Kenyans, the bombing was an unprecedented act of international terrorism dealt another blow to the already troubled tourist industry, which was declining due to increased criminal and political violence.

Pre-colonial Kenyans lived in relatively small, but economically linked societies. Predominantly pastoral people, such as the Masai and Turkana, exchanged cattle for the crops of the Kalenjin, Kamba, Kikuyu, Luo and others. Swahili city-states developed on the Indian Ocean coast and in the

1800s caravans of Arab and Swahili traders' stimulated economic and political change in these societies. However, the European impact on these societies and cultures was devastating.

Modern day Kenya was born out of violence. The Europeans began to arrive in the first decade of the twentieth century and by the 1930s much of the temperate hill country around Nairobi had become the "White Highlands." More than 6 million acres of Masai pasture and Kikuyu and Kamba farmland was stolen by European settlers. African communities were frequently displaced and forced onto overcrowded reservations. Laborers, mostly Kikuyu migrants from these reservations, worked for the Europeans, sometimes on the very land they had once farmed.

By the 1950s, African grievances reached a crescendo with the increased European encroachment and the removal of African "squatters" from European "estates". Armed resistance by a secret society known as Mau Mau, began in 1951, by launching isolated attacks on white settlers. In response, the British proclaimed a state of emergency, which lasted for ten years. Without outside support, the Mau Mau held out by using the highland rainforests as sanctuary. Using US-supplied Lincoln aircraft, the British attacked the rainforests with saturation bombing. By 1955, Mau Mau military resistance had been crushed. For most Westerners, the name Mau Mau became synonymous with anti-white terrorism. In reality, only 32 European civilians lost their lives during the rebellion, while over 1 million Kenyans were killed; 80,000 were incarcerated by colonial authorities; and more than 1 million were resettled in remote isolated villages. Although the Mau Mau were neutralized by ruthless counterinsurgency measures, they did achieve an important political victory. They forced the British to realize that the long-term preservation of Kenya, as a white-settler-dominated colony, was militarily and politically untenable.[1] Jomo Kenyatta, the charismatic leader of the nationalist movement who without any evidence, was detained and accused by the British of leading the Mau Mau, became president at independence in 1963. Through his Kikuyu-based party, he remained in power until his death in 1978. Following the death of Jomo Kenyatta (a Kikuyu), Kenya, long praised for stability, experienced great political upheaval. The Moi government quickly built a record of alarming police practices that damaged the countries reputation as a stable place for foreign investment. Moi (a Luo) had successfully blocked any challenge to his 24 year-rule by fomenting inter-ethnic hostility and distrust, by bribing or silencing would be dissenters, by manipulating the judiciary and electoral systems and by making money from a western-styled, dysfunctional political system.

The Uhuru Revolt

Kenyatta's The Kenyan African National Union (KANU), which ruled Kenya for forty years, faced its first serious challenge in January 2002, when a dissident wing joined forces with opposition parties and formed a grand coalition to stop the electoral ambitions of Uhuru Kenyatta. In October, several high profile dissidents of KANU, announced they could no longer work with President Moi. This announcement, effectively split the KANU party. The disagreement grew fiercer, after President Moi personally handpicked as his successor, Uhuru Kenyatta (the son of Jomo Kenyatta). "This is the end of the road as far as KANU is concerned;" said party secretary-general Raila Odinga. Moi insisted that KANU had not really split and warned that if the party rebels took power "Kenya would be in a ditch."

Raila Odinga attended university in East Germany and was imprisoned for eight years for his alleged involvement in a 1982 coup attempt against Moi. There were fears that his election would lay the political groundwork for a radical redistribution of wealth. Odinga' s name became synonymous with the Luo tribe's legacy of unrewarded struggle. His father, Oginda Odinga, was instrumental in the fight for independence and served as vice president for three years in the 1960s. But after a disagreement with Jomo Kenyatta, he resigned. Promised the post of Prime Minister, Raila Odinga played a central role in Mwai Kibaki's 2002 presidential campaign. To his surprise, he was dismissed in 2005. Many believed that Moi picked Uhuru Kenyatta as his successor in order to guarantee himself a peaceful retirement. Uhuru Kenyatta pledged to fight corruption.

Tens of thousands of opposition supporters gathered in Nairobi's Uhuru Park singing "Without Moi, anything is possible." KANU leaders, known as the "Rainbow Alliance;" held hands with members of the opposition National Alliance and Kenya (NAK) and the Peoples Coalition parties. This confederacy of former rivals proclaimed the end of cronyism and poor government in Kenya. Rainbow Alliance leader, Raila Odinga, resigned from the cabinet along with other opposition leaders, signaling a dangerous shift to multi-party and ethnic politics. Charity Ngilu, Kenya's senior female opposition leader observed that: "All of us would have been interested in being president: all leaders who stand in front of you realize the need to come together. Nothing from today can separate us again: we have come with one voice to liberate our nation." The Kanu rebels formed a new political party, the Liberal Democratic Party and merged with the People's Coalition. There were talks with the National Alliance of Kenya (NAK) about the possibility of fielding a single candidate for the presidency. Michael Wamalwa of the NAK insisted that no one would repeat the abuses of the past and that: "The introduction of Uhuru (unity) has brought many diverse parties together. They'll have to change because circumstances have changed."

The alliance of Kenya's ruling party dissidents and major opposition party members, signaled the death of the single-party rule in Africa. In 1997, Mwai Kibaki won only 31 percent of the vote as candidate for the Democratic Party. The 74 year-old president pledged to end the one-man rule era of Daniel Arap Moi, to dispense with ethnic-politics and to reignite Kenya's dormant economy with foreign investment and sound governance. "We have gone through a very long period of dictatorship by an individual. We must create leadership by a team that works closely together. We must all commit ourselves to denouncing corruption and exposing those who practice it, starting from the top;" Kibaki boldly stated. The stage was set for a runoff a presidential election between two candidates from Kenya's largest tribe, the Kikuyu. Uhuru Kenyatta, and 74 year-old, Mwai Kibaki, graduate of the London School of Economics, former finance minister, health minister and Moi's vice president.

In December 2002, the National Rainbow Coalition (NARC) won the elections, effectively ending Moi's two decade kleptocratic regime. Many Kenyans saw Moi's backing of Kenyatta as a transparent attempt to install a puppet government. When Moi left office at the end of 2002 he had an deposited an estimated $1 billion in foreign bank accounts. A 110 page secret report into high-level corruption produced by the security group *Kroll*, claims that Moi's sons Gideon and Phillip are worth over $1.5 billion. And that they own properties and stakes in companies around the world. [2]

One week before George W. Bush was scheduled to meet with President Moi, car bombs explosions outside an Israeli-owned hotel in Nairobi, reminded him of al-Qaeda's presence in the Horn of Africa. Bush had come to meet with President Moi and Ethiopian Prime Minister, Meles Zenawi, to discuss their roles in the regional "war on terror." In a 2002 National Security Strategy Report, Bush had labeled both countries as "vital African partners in global anti-terrorism." A Somali Islamist group, *al-Ittihad*, connected to al-Qaeda, was "known" to have operatives in both Nairobi and Mombassa. The US central command established a sub-regional center in neighboring Djibouti to attack possible terrorist cells in Yemen, capture al Qaeda operatives and to guarantee that commercial and military sea lanes remained open.

Both Presidents Moi and Zenawi had atrocious human rights and domestic governance records. Both countries struggled with famine, economic failure, rising HIV infection rates and political instability. When Bush invited Moi to visit the White House, he calculated (as Moi certainly must have), that the visit would bolster Moi's political stature and political base by distracting the international community from the forthcoming Kenyan elections. Moi, who personally controlled almost all political power and wealth in Kenya, was closely-tracked by the foreign press when he traveled abroad.

Reports of tortured confessions from people accused of being political dissidents were common. In 1986, sixty-six people were sentenced to death for sedition, after having been detained or held incommunicado; all 66 confessed. A single prosecutor and judge handled most of the cases. When charged with allegations of human rights abuses, Moi embarked on a counteroffensive ballet that sidestepped the substance of the allegations, by accusing his critics of anti-Kenyan bias.

Government policy was that if they felt someone is a security risk, such as a member of the Mwakenya, the underground political organization and a primary target of the government, they were a security threat and the government had to crackdown on them. Under the Preservation of Security Act, such police actions were consistent with the way government has always dealt with those it perceives as security risks. According to one senior official; "the West sees these people as dissidents, we see them as subversives." An April 1989 report by *Amnesty International* charged that more than 75 Kenyan political opponents had been imprisoned after "unfair trials."

The New York-based Lawyers Committee on Human Rights, issued a report alleging torture and unfair trials in Kenya. In 1987, the US Congress, for the first time, conditioned aid to on improvement of Kenya's human rights record. This was largely a symbolic gesture. The US depends on naval facilities at the Kenyan port of Mombassa to project power in the region. Kenya provided a base for US aircraft during the Persian Gulf War. By 1988, President Moi began to take corrective measures. Kenyan human rights lawyers speculated that he took these steps because he wanted to begin his new administration with a clean slate. While continuing to deny allegations of government-sanctioned detentions and mistreatment of prisoners, Moi released several "political" prisoners. He also appointed a new police commissioner, and spoke out against "errant police officers." But, for the most part, Moi's response to outside criticism was an indignant rage. In December 1988, he told *Amnesty International*, which had written a documented report on torture in Kenya, to "go to hell".

Corruption permeates Kenyan politics. Hundreds of officials were fired when Kibaki's coalition was elected under the pretense of dismantling a patronage system blamed for the institutional decay, bureaucratic lethargy and the for deterioration of East Africa's largest economy. Following the release of a report investigating corruption among Kenya's judges and magistrates in November 2004, Mwai Kibaki's nine-month-old government moved to introduce sweeping reforms. The British revoked the visa of one of Kibaki's closest allies, Chris Murungaru, because of his "character, conduct and associations." Arund Devani, Chairman of the Kenya Association of Manufacturers stated; "We are looking at a great opportunity, the experience of the past three years showed us the ministers spent more time politicking that giving attention to the economy."[3] A government committee found extensive evidence of "corruption, unethical conduct and other forms of misbehavior," among 5 of Kenya's nine appellate court judges; 18 of 36 High Court judges; and 82 of 254 magistrates. The offenses detailed by Justice Aaron Ringera, included accepting bribes in return for partial judgments, manipulating evidence, stealing exhibits and the pursuit of sexual favors. "We are apprehensive that in handing this to you we are presenting a dragon. It is bound to snort, jump, kick and even attack, for corruption always fights back. Your Lordship will have no option but to seize it by the horns and slay it;" Ringera told the Chief justice upon submitting his report.

A few months later, The Kibaki government sabotaged its war on corruption, by failing to pay the *Kroll*, the consulting firm hired to track state graft. In 2003, the Kibaki administration employed *Kroll*, the international risk consulting firm, to locate funds siphoned out of the country by the Moi government. By April 2004, Kenyan officials with the help of *Kroll* investigators, were reportedly closing in on more than $1 billion (€ 528m, £775m), and were taking steps toward freezing other expatriated assets. The government missed a second payment to *Kroll*, settling the account six months later, and endangering the investigation at a critical stage. The late payment, which possibly allowed more theft of state assets, was blamed on a "bureaucratic delay." Justice minister Kiraitu Murungi told the *Financial Times*: "I wouldn't say the investigations were suspended but they kept reminding us for payment." Donor attacks slowed with the resignation of John Githongo, Kenya's widely respected top anti-corruption official, over his frustration with Kibaki's unwillingness to tackle high-level graft.

Kenya emerged from the 2003 donor conference with more limited support from its creditors. Twenty-five multilateral and bilateral donors met with Kibaki's cabinet, opposition leaders and members of civil society to demonstrate the government's determination to stimulate the economy and curtail corruption. The World Bank, IMF and numerous other participants expressed doubt about the ability of the coalition government to deliver on its commitment of economic reform. The IMF approved a $252.8 million loan towards a three year recovery plan. This, ended a three-year freeze on direct aid to Kenya imposed by foreign donors due to the corruption and Moi's resistance to market-oriented reforms. News of renewed donor support reversed years of declining private sector investment and Nairobi's main stock exchange rebounded to a four -year high the next day.

In an April 2004 corruption probe of former government officials, Kenyan authorities took the initial steps required to freeze over $1 billion worth property and other assets in the UK, Switzerland and other countries. A previous investigation uncovered a link to $3 billion, alleged to have been channeled abroad by the late Nigerian dictator Sani Abacha and his family, during the 1990s. Kenyan and *Kroll* officials, said they had identified a "key Geneva-based individual," who was central to money laundering operations in both cases. Switzerland promised cooperation in freezing the assets which included residential properties in London and south-east England. Justice, Minister Kiraitu Murungi, queried senior UK officials about the UK government investigation. Kenya also engaged an international law firm to start investigations in the several countries where the funds have been traced. Destinations included South Africa, the Netherlands, Luxembourg, Italy, the Gulf states and New Jersey. Kenyan officials said illegally obtained funds may also have been used to purchase real estate in the United States and Australia. The money trail leads to a dozen people still in government as Justice Minister Murungi observed: "We are aware that some of the tentacles might come even into the current government. I don't expect to be a popular minister." He accused some involved of using their illegal funds to foment political friction in order to increase the opposition to the Kibaki administration.

Kibaki introduced universal primary education and resumed relations with multilateral donors in an effort to revive economic growth and re-build primary institutions. However, revelations of scandal and murder investigations plagued his government. The death of the vice-president, allegations of corruption among the factious cabinet and the government's handling of the murder of prominent constitutional reform activist, Odhiambo Mbai in October 2003, are but a few examples. The arrest of a senior editor at the *Sunday Standard* newspaper, who was charged with stealing a videotape by a suspect in a extra-judicial killing, added fuel to the fires of suspicion. Odhiambo Mbai had editorialized that the near-dictatorial powers of the presidency accumulated under Moi, should be reduced. Such outspokenness is not tolerated.

For most Kenyan's, political corruption is a reality that damages their daily lives. Greed and the fruits of corruption are primary reasons for practicing politics. In October 2005, their political leaders disappointed the Kenyan people yet again. This time, the issue was a referendum for a new constitution. The draft constitution was hotly debated for weeks. The debate was divisive with little discussion of the merits of the charter, which would replace the 1963 Independence Constitution. Opponents criticized the document because it was purportedly based on a version drafted by pro-Kibaki ministers of parliament. They accused the government of reneging on promises to reduce the all-encompassing powers of the presidency, to decentralize government and to create an independent and powerful prime minister's office.

Obscured in the debate was the fundamental question about how to restructure the Kenyan state. Some opponents said the proposed devolution of power did not go far enough. "The constitution process was supposed to bring us together but it's divided us further. This tells us maybe our expectations were too high...What we are seeing is the fruits of "Moiism," the policies of divide and rule, the policies of patronage;" said Maina Kiai, chairman of the Kenya National Commission on Human Rights.

Kibaki's cabinet reportedly had not met for two month's and the weak Kibaki's coalition government lost seven ministers to the opposition's anti referendum campaign. The campaign was marked by provoking rhetoric, sporadic violence, ethnic tensions and death. Two schoolboys were shot dead in clashes in Kisumu. According to Kenyan political scientist, Musambayi Katumanga; "Politicians are instrumentalizing ethnicity for their own ends-it's the elite trying to control resources. As long as there is no leadership it doesn't matter what constitution you have."[4]

Following popular rejection of proposed constitution, Kibaki responded to the people's mandate by firing his entire cabinet. Some considered this an act of desperation, designed to convince Kenyans he would deliver change.

Kibaki then announced the formation of a new cabinet, which would be formed within two weeks, be more cohesive and "better able to serve the people." But Kenyans immediately questioned whether the new cabinet would deliver efficient government or just be another disillusioning collection of presidential sycophants and cronies. Analysts observed that new faces in a more inclusive cabinet might help to allay the ethnic and political tensions ignited by the constitutional debate.

Kenya's fight against corruption suffered another setback when, in early January 2006, the World Bank approved a $25 million loan to Kenya to "strengthen the capacity of key ministries." The head of the Kenyan chapter of Transparency International criticized the timing of the loan for sending the wrong messages at a time when government officials were implicated in corrupt deals. The World Bank announcement came just days after a leaked dossier produce by John Githongo, Kenya's former anti-graft Czar, alleged that senior government officials and presidential aides were involved in corrupt schemes that could have cost the country more than $270 million. Those named in the dossier included vice-president Moody Awori, finance minister, David Mwiraria and energy minister Kiraitu Murungi. They all of course, denied any wrongdoing.

The Anti-Corruption Commission announced plans to summon the three for questioning in connection with a multi-million dollar scandal known as "Anglo Leasing". Kenya director for the World Bank, Colin Bruce, said it was; "an historic moment for the government to signal where it stands on the issue of political accountability." However, Maina Kiai, Chairman of the Kenya National Commission on the Human Rights, said the timing of the loan was "insulting to us Kenyans in the midst of these revelations." Kiai stated that the integrity of any investigation would be surrounded by doubt as long as officials tainted by graft allegations remain in office.[5] Colin Bruce retorted that the government should be allowed to respond and that it would be inappropriate for the World Bank to second guess what the government would do stating; "Meanwhile the government continues to function...are going to wait until a person is dealt with? What happens in the interim? How do we call ourselves supportive partners and do nothing?"

Executive director of Transparency International (TI) Kenya, Mwalimu Mati, said the World Bank should have waited until there were clear signs that President Kibaki was taking action to fight corruption before disbursing new funds. "We think that when the vice president, cabinet ministers, and the head of public service are being mentioned as either being involved in corrupt deals or of covering up investigations, the bank is sending out the wrong signals...by approving the loan. They need to be more careful about the subtext of the message-that nothing is wrong."

John Githongo, who had resigned from the government in February 2005, after becoming frustrated with its failure to tackle graft, left Kenya for exile in the UK. A group of Ministers promising the government was now committed to tacking corruption, called upon Githongo requesting his return to Kenya to testify before the country's anti-corruption body. Githongo agreed to return. According to a report by TI and Kenyan's National Commission on Human Rights, the government wasted millions of dollars on luxury vehicles for the use of senior officials, despite pledges that it was committed to tackling poverty and more efficient administration. The report said the spending was an example of "wasteful expenditure and conspicuous consumption which seriously undermines any commitment to reform." Between January 2003 and September 2004, the government purchased 57 *Mercedes*, 42 *Land Cruisers*, 3 *Range Rovers* and numerous other four-wheel-drive vehicles, valued at $12 million. It was enough money to purchase anti-retroviral drugs for 147,000 people; or to have paid for eight years of education for 25,000 children. Mwalimu Mati, of TI Kenya, said the money spent on the luxury cars was corruption in another form. It was a definite abuse of power for personal convenience."[6]

The Kenyan government was forced to confront face civil service greed, when it was disclosed that billions of shillings in irregular personnel allowances had been lost over the years. The Secretary of the Permanent Public Service Remuneration Review Board, Mark Bor, reported that 40 per cent of the total Public Service wage bill went to allowances. Senior officials at the Directorate of Personnel Management (DPMI) expectedly reported that some claimed allowances were not genuine. Kenya's total public service wage for more than 600,000 personnel was over 120 billion shillings. According to Secretary Bor, of the 80 different types of allowances, "some are duplications", and that the perks were stopped to achieve "a real salary increase." Perks enjoyed by civil servants include, "special duty," meals, hardship and medical allowances, field trainers, and "entertainment and responsibility allowances." The Government hired a consulting firm to review and reduce wasteful allowances. Pauline Nginye, an auditor at the DPM, said the practice amounted to waste of funds, which denied key priority areas, like staff motivation. "The Government should give priority to areas that are lean and save the money for priority areas," she said. She admitted that some new officers had asked for new models of cars, carpets, and furniture instead of using what they found in the offices and that her department authorized the procurement of the materials, although they knew it was wrong.[7]

In response to the new politically damaging allegations, Kibaki finance minister, David Mwiraria, was sacrificed as fodder to anti-corruption forces. One day after assertively dismissing allegations linking him to suspect deals, ubiquitous media coverage of the charges, forced Mwiraria to resign. In this country with a history of misrule, endemic corruption, systemic graft, and government lethargy, a resignation stemming from financial scandals was unprecedented. The long-time Kibaki ally, insisted he was merely stepping aside to facilitate investigations and to protect the integrity of the government.

Many remained doubtful of Kibaki's resolve to move against those named in the dossier with little more than a cabinet reshuffling. The often criticized Kenya Anti-Corruption Commission (KACC), also lacked the political will to conduct genuine investigations. There were threats of a vote of "no confidence" against the government. This required a simple majority in parliament, but was not likely since they would then have to surrender their lucrative salaries, benefit packages and luxury automobiles. The bloated Kibaki government included more than 60 cabinet ministers and assistant ministers and 222 members of parliament. KACC member, Maini Kiai, warned that if the government continued down the path of inaction, it would be up to civil society groups to force MPs to heed people's demands. "Serious questions about whether the government can survive will remain unless they take action, because the pressure and clamor will continue;" Mani cautioned.[8]

A few days after detaining three journalists, armed police raided the offices of *The Standard* newspaper and blocked the broadcast of the *Kenyan Television Network* (KTN), reinforcing fears of a return to the draconian-style rule of the Moi era. The journalists were arrested in connection with an article published a week earlier which alleged that President Kibaki had met secretly meeting with Kanlonzo Musyoka, a former cabinet minister who was dismissed in a cabinet reshuffle. Both Kibaki and Musyoka denied the meeting took place and the government demanded an apology. The journalists were charged with "publishing an alarming statement" and released on bail. The incident was seen as another attempt by Kibaki to intimidate an increasingly outspoken press. The raids came at a time the when the government was under intense pressure over high-level corruption allegations and political scandals.

The Standard's main newspaper competitor, human rights officials, opposition leaders and diplomats all condemned the police action. Tom Mshindi, the *Standard Group's* chief executive, reported that masked police "roughed up" *KTN's* security staff, stole equipment and burned thousands newspapers ready for distribution. The government's response to the criticism was well coordinated. Kenya's internal security manager, John Michuki, described the events as a national security matter. "When you rattle a snake, you must be prepared to be bitten;" he observed. When asked about the incident, President Kibaki echoed Michuki's words. Police spokesman, Jasphar Ombati, said the raids were conducted to collect evidence on an intended act whose perpetuation would have posed a major threat to national security. "Evidence pointed to an intention of inciting ethnic hate and animosity." Small publications have been closed before, but this was the first time a major media group had been so blatantly targeted. "We deplore the current campaign of vilification and harassment of selected media. Clearly the intent is to intimidate journalists. These acts of thuggery have no place in an open democratic society," said a source at the US embassy.[9] The World Bank also condemned the raid. World Bank Country director, Colin Bruce, said that the bank was awaiting an explanation for the raids. "I recognize there have statements made about internal intelligence and matters of that sort but frankly I cannot think of a scenario under which that kind of action as it turned out can be excused".[10]

A panel of inquiry into what is known as the 1990s "Goldenberg" financial scandal that cost Kenya hundreds of millions of dollars, recommended that former president Moi face further investigation and former minister of education, George Saitoti, face criminal charges for their alleged roles in the scandal. Saitoti was both finance minister and vice-president when the alleged fraud took place. The case involved payments of by the government to a company called *Goldenberg International,* to subsidize gold and diamond jewelry exports during the 1990s. The prosecution alleged that the exports were non-existent. Kenya has a negligible gold deposits and no diamonds. "It can be reasonably inferred that Saitoti supported the activities of *Goldenberg International*," reads the report. President Kibaki appointed a board of inquiry into the Goldenberg affair and again hired *Kroll* international consultants to track down more than $1 billion believed to have been siphoned out of the country during Moi's 24-year rule. The 81 year-old former president denied allegations that he was aware of the scam and he was not charged with any of the alleged abuses. However, the inquiry states: "We doubt whether the former president, as chief executive officer of the country was completely unaware."

The long delayed *Kroll* report was suppressed when the government failed to pay the *Kroll*. Kibaki appointed Saitoti despite allegations of his involvement with Goldenberg. He came under even more pressure following the release of the so-called Githongo dossier. "We have been waiting for the Goldenberg report but we are also still concerned about reports on current scandals and this will not deflect our attention from what is going on;" said Mwalimu Mati of Transparency International Kenya.[11]

Despite all real and the alleged corruption, the Kibaki government underscored its economic confidence and optimistic electoral prospects by seeking to capitalize on Kenya's burgeoning economic growth. In 2006, the gross domestic product expanded by 5.8 percent. Kenya joined a small group of African countries led by Ghana, Nigeria and Zambia that were exploring ways to tap into international debt markets. In April 2007, Amos Kimunya, the finance minister, announced the launch of a dollar-dominated bond valued a $73 million. Additionally, to the Kibaki government's credit an economic truth council was proposed.

Kenyan Women's Rights

In neighboring Uganda, thousands of women rallied for the Domestic Relations Bill which would provide them with specific legal rights should their husbands decide to take a second wife. In Rwanda, eleven years after the genocide, women, many of them war widows, hold 49 percent of the seats in the lower house of parliament. They were compelled to rise in protest, after their male leaders presided over the 1994 massacre of 800,000 Tutsis and Hutus by the Hutu majority. Across the continent, because men had failed to govern properly, women agitated and lobbied for the nomination of more female politicians, including a presidential candidate for 2007. At the June 2005, Scotland G8 meeting, female activists expressed their hopes that international aid would include funding for women seeking rights in their court systems and more representation in their state legislatures. The election of Liberian President Sirleaf Johnson, offered a renewed era of gender balanced leadership in Africa.

In Kenya, for three decades Professor Wangari Maathai, the first African woman to win the Nobel Prize, battled political corruption in Kenya. Awarded the Peace Prize in 2004, for her contributions to sustainable development, environmental protection and democracy, Maathai was praised for courageously standing up against the oppressive Moi regime and inspiring the fight for democratic rights and for the environment. Under Moi's autocratic rule of (1978-2002), she led the struggle to protect the countries dwindling indigenous forests; that were being destroyed by international developers and illegal loggers connected to corrupt Kenyan politicians. In 1977, professor Maathai founded the Kenyan-based Green Belt Movement, an organization comprised mainly of women which has planted more than 25 million trees. According to the Green Belt Movement, a mere 1.7 per cent of the country's indigenous forests remains. "It's more than tree planting. The world should focus its attention, particularly in the African context, on the relationship between environmental security and human security;" observed Davinder Lamba, a Kenyan activist seeking to highlight the relationship between environmental degradation and political instability in Africa.

In 2002, Maathai was elected to parliament where she also serves as assistant minister of environment. Based on the conditions of most of their lives, Maathai's election sent an inspiring message of empowerment to Kenyan women. Many women have been undergone hardships that few women in the West can imagine. One ethnic group practices courtship by having the man and woman wrestle in hand to hand combat. If the woman wins, the man is considered unworthy of her hand in marriage. This is tradition, and the people living in this desolate wilderness, believed that if the man cannot defeat his wife, it is unlikely that he can defend her. Once a Kenyan woman is married, she ceases to be a part of her own family. The husband purchases her with a dowry of cattle or other livestock. Out of respect for what the family has invested in this young bride, sometimes money or property is exchanged. This too is tradition. If she has been educated and been taught a trade or profession, the dowry even has greater value. This tradition can obviously be corrupted. Like the couple mentioned earlier, the government of Kenya is wrestling with a corrupt system where some families are forced sell their young daughters to old men. It is widely rumored and equally ignorantly believed, that if a man with a sexually transmitted disease sleeps with a young virgin, he will be cured of the disease. Families desperate for money have been known to give their young daughters (as young as 12 years) up for marriage. The circumcision of females was abandoned in 2001.

Even under the best of circumstances, women have no real say in most Kenyan homes. They have no property, no education and no rights. They don't worry over trivialities. They just want to know "Is life worth living?" A Kenyan wife is often one of the husband's children. When you greet the husband on the street and ask him; 'How are the children?' You don't need to ask, how is the wife? A man can do what he wants with this wife in many communities and clans as long as he does not kill her. It is only then that he may suffer the consequences of the law. He is the law in his home. If she does not abide by his law, produce children, or service him well, she can be dismissed. In response to extreme sexual violence, the battle against HIV/Aids and the aftermath of warfare, a mix of female self-assertion and external influences has generated an African feminist movement. New laws give women unprecedented rights to refuse marriage proposals; fight sexual harassment in the workplace; refuse genital mutilation; and prosecute rape. Rape is so prevalent, many Kenyan leaders call it the nation's biggest human rights issue. Newly drafted legislation against rape includes a "chemical castration bill," with life imprisonment for repeat offenders.

Many such women often come to the World Gospel Mission's Tenwek hospital in Bomet, southeast Kenya. A woman who was six months pregnant by her husband, who decided he no longer wanted her, since he had found another wife. In this situation as she relates the story she no longer satisfied him. Therefore, he sent her to live with her parents. He is allowed by law and tradition to have many wives. Each new wife is subject to his rule and law. Of course, she no longer belongs to her parents. The parents agree to take her in only if she will get rid of the baby. Abortion is illegal. Someone will perform it however, and she will probably die as a consequence. Several days later she was admitted to the hospital in toxic shock, confused, anemic, bleeding, and near death. The required surgery, an emergency hysterectomy, was performed and she survived.

There can be serious ramifications for adhering to tradition. Among the Lou, the tradition is that the brother inherits the wife of his late sibling. When a man dies of HIV/Aids, this tradition becomes deadly. Tradition also dictates, that before the deceased can be buried, the surviving brother must sleep with the widowed wife. The pandemic, coupled with tradition, is decimating the Luo people. Most deaths in the region are no longer attributable to malaria, cholera, typhoid, meningitis, dehydration and starvation but to HIV/Aids. Whole families have been wiped out and 50-60 percent of the population, in certain regions of the country, are dying from the disease.

An April 1999 edition of the Kenyan, *Daily Nation* published a story of a history-making anti-Aids campaign in Nyanza, province in western Kenya. A groups of widows decided to openly rebel against long held cultural practices blamed for the spread the disease. In the city of Kisumu, thirteen HIV/Aids widows met with US envoy, Prudence Bushnell for 30 minutes as she listened to the heart-breaking personal, social and economic problems they faced. None had formal employment, a business or any other means of steady income. Among the 13 was an 80-year-old grandmother caring for 63 Aids orphans. She spoke of how she had lost four sons and six in-laws to the HIV/Aids epidemic within three years. Most of her age group had between two and nine children in their charge. Many of their children were forced to drop out of school because they lacked fees.

When Prudence Bushnell, asked what message they would like to convey to Kenyans about their plight and dreams, one widow emotionally replied: "I would like to say that I have accepted that Aids is really here because it claimed my husband, other relatives and friends. I advise the public to keep off irresponsible sex... let us not kill others knowingly." According to one Kenyan official: "The death of a husband usually renders the women vulnerable to accepting relatives' demands, including ritual sexual cleansing which is often the most risky. If she completely rejects these practices, the woman may lose ownership or access to some of the family property."

Emily Wax, of *The Washington Post* reported the story of Rebecca Lolosoli, the matriarch of the woman's village of Umoja, who gave sanctuary to a 13 year-old girl seeking to avoid forced marriage to Lolosoli's brother. "You are a small, he is an old man," she told the girl. Over ten years ago, a group of women established the village of Umoja on an unwanted field of dry grasslands. The women claimed that after being raped, they were abandoned by their husbands for bringing shame upon the community. About three dozen women live in Umoja and no men are allowed to live in their circular village of mud and dung huts. They run a cultural center and a camping site for tourists visiting the nearby Samburu National Reserve. Umoja is so successful, that troubled women, some beaten and seeking divorce, come from afar to join the female settlement.

Rebecca Lolosoli was invited to the New York to attend a UN conference on gender empowerment. "That's when the very ugly jealous behavior started. They just said frankly, that they wanted to kill me;" she recounted. Prior to her departure, her life was threatened by local men. Lolosoli's efforts reflect the difficulties of changing the rhythm and structure of village life. Before going to New York, she went from house to house in the nearby town telling women that they had rights; such as the right to refuse to have sex with their husbands if they were being beaten or treated poorly. "A woman is nothing in our community," she said, referring to the members of her tribe and in the village men across the road. "You are not able to answer men or speak in front of them whether you are right or wrong."

At the UN conference, Lolosoli and women from around the world, bonded during an episode of *Oprah* that focused on women, verbal abuse and cheating husbands. She returned to Kenya armed with ideas, empowerment training workshop books, and she stood her ground. "I just ignore the men when they throw stones at me and ask, 'Are you OK? Are your children OK? Are your cows OK?" Her tactical calm is disarming and she adamantly states, "After everything, they weren't going to stop us."

In an amusing reaction, the men of her tribe started their own village near Umoja in order to monitor the women's activities. The men's attempt to build a cultural center failed. Thus, what began as a group of homeless women seeking a place of their own, became a thriving village attracting so many women seeking assistance that they now hire men to do traditional woman's work, such as hauling water and firewood. Empowered by revenue generated from their camp site and the cultural center, the women for the first time, can send their children to school, eat well, and reject male demands that their daughters be circumcised and marry. Sebastian Lesnik, chief of the male village, describes the division between men and women thusly: "The man is the head the lady the neck. A man cannot take, let's call it advice, from his neck." "We are at the start of something important for African women;" remarked Margaret Auma Odhiambo, a leader of Western Kenya's largest group of widows. The male village chief admitted that he is a little jealous, and painfully observed; "She has been successful, it's true. Maybe we can learn from our necks a little bit."[12]

Kenyan women have embraced opportunities to build businesses through micro-financed loans. Pauline Mwangi is an example of this emerging female entrepreneurial class. She created a pilot program called "Young Women in Enterprise" for Technoserve, a non-profit, international development organization funded by the *Nike* Foundation. The objective of the program is to equip young women from the slums of Nairobi with the life and business skills to start small businesses. Each woman was given 100 hours of training in entrepreneurship and life skills. They also received mentoring from leading female entrepreneurs, and coaching from business schools such as the UCLA Anderson School of Management. At the end of the program, the women participated in a business plan competition. Of the 260 who completed the training, 40 were awarded a small amount of seed money to start their own businesses.[13]

Prosperity For The Few

As Kibaki had predicted, by 2005, the Kenyan economy expanded rapidly. Investing in the Nairobi Stock Exchange (NSE) became the latest economic trend.. The investment run began after the 2002 election, when the main NSE index, soared 432 percent in Kenyan shillings to a peak of 6000 by January 2003. The total capitalization of the 48 companies listed on the NSE climbed to $12 billion. Kenyan newspapers began printing large headlines applauding the machinations of the market, and banks began to offer "share loans" to their novice investors. Farmers, reportedly sold cattle to raise a few thousand shillings to invest. The NSE estimated that 700,000 Kenyans owned shares.

NSE chairman, Jimnah Mbaru observed: "We have a new generation of young people. In the old days people used to invest in land. Now young people understand and want financial assets. It's a paradigm shift". Robert Gichuru, a young bank worker, who invests Ksh 5,000 into equities each month, observed that the NSE is not driven by rigorous analysis: "If you ask a person why he's buying it's often because his neighbor is buying. A number of people are entering the market on a gut feeling."[14]

The history of the post-colonial Kenyan government is confounding. Kibaki's election brought lofty hopes of reform, but these hopes have not been realized. Kibaki failed to launch any sweeping reforms. However, the government has tackled the bureaucratic quagmire of rules and regulations that stifle productivity and innovation. Most notably, with the reduction of the number of required business licenses from 1,325 to 400.[15] A certain degree of macroeconomic stability and fewer economic shocks, have made Kenyan currency more stable. *Barclays* and *Unilever* maintain large operations in Kenya. "You have asked me to lead this nation out of the present wilderness and malaise to the promised land. And I shall;" Kibaki told thousands of people squeezed into Nairobi's Uhuru park. The 75 year-old was expected to run for re-election. Despite 6.1 percent economic growth in 2006, many Kenyans were unhappy that the benefits of that growth were not widely felt.[16] Thus, the "Uhuru Revolt" gained renewed momentum, when Raila Odinga threatened to topple Kibaki in the 2008 elections and become the "people's president," by rebuilding Kenya's infrastructure and removing deterrents to foreign investment.

Both Kibaki and Raila Odinga promised big budget infrastructure investments. The business community feared that Kibaki's reelection would bring little improvement, and that an Odinga victory would bring economic uncertainty. "Is he a socialist, a communist, a social democrat?" asked James Wangunyu, vice chairman of the Kenyan stock exchange. "Is he likely to nationalize privatized organizations? Is he likely to take wealth from others? How certain are we with a Raila leadership."

Poisonous Politics

The Kikuyu, who have dominated Kenyan politics since independence, are only 22 percent of Kenya's population. The 2007 presidential election results, traumatized and divided Africa's exemplary democratic state. Raila Odinga's Orange Democracy Movement, won 95 of the 210 directly elected seats. Twenty members of Kibaki's cabinet were defeated. Joshua Odihiambo Nyamori, the campaign coordinator of ODM noted that: " In 2002 we thought we'd done away with the ghost of tribalism because Luos voted for Kibaki almost to the man, but I think Kibaki betrayed this." The Lou, the Kalenjin and some fifty smaller tribes were shocked and angered when after the closest election Kenyan history, Kibaki, after trailing Odinga by a wide margin, was suddenly declared the winner.

Raila Odinga was narrowly favored in the polls but there were widespread rumors of the use of pre-marked ballots and of policeman disguised as KANU party agents, in order to commit voter fraud. Samuel Kiyuitu, Chairman of the Electoral Commission, dismissed the allegations as baseless. The enthusiasm and support of Odinga's Luo ethnic-group, was matched by anti-Luo sentiment among Kibaki's politically and economically dominant Kikuyu. For many Kikuyu, the prospect of an Odinga presidency was alarming for the Luo are stereotyped as aggressive, boastful and chaotic. "Raila wants to finish the Kikuyu. His tribe are lazy, so lazy. They are jealous of the success we get from working hard;" said a Nairobi taxi driver. To divide the Kenyan people, Kibaki engaged in the poisonous politics of manipulating fear and stereotypes.[17]

Vote counting was stopped in Kajiado, where violence erupted after charges of ballot stuffing. Raila Odinga accused Kibaki of stealing the election and anti-riot police were deployed to the massive Kibera and Kajiado slums, where many of Odinga's supporters reside.[18] This time text messaging technology was used to target the victims. In the Kibera slum, Gangs of Luo attacked Kikuyu with sticks, machetes, knives, bows and arrows. Rioting broke out across the country, and over a thousand people were killed in the ensuing inter-ethnic violence. Fleeing women and children were targeted. Some, seeking refuge in churches, were burned alive. The UN Food and Agriculture Organization warned that 100,000 people in the Rift Valley were threatened by violence and hunger. The crisis threatened regional trade with Uganda, Rwanda, Burundi, Sudan and the Democratic Republic of Congo; all rely on the Kenya's port of Mombasa for fuel supplies. A quarter of Uganda's and Rwanda's GDP and one third of Burundi's GDP transits through Kenya. The 100% increase in the price of petroleum also made it more difficult for commuters in the region to get to work.

US assistant secretary of State, Jendayi Frazier urged Kibaki to postpone forming a cabinet until the crisis was resolved. Kibaki responded by immediately forming a 17-member all Kikuyu cabinet that excluded any members of Odinga's ODM party.[19] After four weeks of negotiations, in February 2008, Kofi Annan struck a tentative power-sharing deal between Kibaki and Odinga. The political crisis was resolved when Kibaki agreed to share power and appoint Odinga Prime Minister. Power sharing among the ethno-political elite will not save Kenya's politically rotten body-politic. As long as the epidemic corruption and the poisonous use of ethnic violence continues, the economic and social wounds of the impoverished Kenyan masses will continue to fester.

---

1. Wayne Edge, *Africa: Kenyan Country Report,* Africa Global Studies with Annual Editions (Dubuque McGraw-Hill/Dushkin 2002), 70.

2. Barney Jopson, 'Leaked report puts Kenya graft in spotlight,'

The Financial Times, September 1-2, 2007 p.2.

3. Andrew England, 'Kenyans get a taste for the power of the ballot box,' *The Financial Times*, November 25, 2005.

4. Andrew England, 'Fruits of democracy slow to ripen in Kenya,' *The Financial Times*, November 17, 2005.

5. Andrew England, 'Watchdog criticizes World Bank loan to Kenya,' *The Financial Times*, January 27. 206. p.2

6. Andrew England, 'Kenya accused over spending,' *The Financial Times*, January 31. 2006, p.14.

7. Oreyo Ochieng, 'Kenya: Billions Lost in Allowances.' *The East Afriçan Standard*, Nairobi March 28, 2006 Posted to the web March 27, 2006.

8. Andrew England, 'First Kenyan scalp fails to appease public clamour for action on corruption.' *The Financial Times*, February 3, 2006. p.3

9. Andrew England, 'Kenya police 'thugs' target media group in midnight raids.' *The Financial Times*, March 3, 2006. p. 6.

10. Andrew England, 'Kenya pushed into cycle of 'crisis appeal and aid.' *The Financial Times*, February 14, 2006. p.6.

11. Andrew England, 'Moi caught up in Kenyan corruption inquiry.' *The Financial Times*, February 7, 2006. p.4.

12. Emily Wax, 'Kenyan village is sign of burgeoning feminism in Africa,' *The New Mexican*, July 15. 2005.

13. Rebecca, Knight, 'fortuitous paring has been life transforming,' *The Financial Times*, December 17, 2007 p. 14.

14. Barney Jopson, 'Investing craze takes hold in disorderly environment,' Special Report: Kenya, *The Financial Times*, June 13, 2007, p. 2.

15. Barney Jopson, "uneven spoils of economic revival, Special Report Kenya: *The Financial Times*, June 13, 2007 p.1.

16. Barney Jopson, 'Kenyans promised action on economy,' *The Financial Times*, December, 15, 2007. p.5

17. Barney Jopson, "Kibaki faces tough test in tight race,' *The Financial Times* p. 4; and "Odinga aims to rise above tribal allegiances," *The Financial Times* December 27, 2007, p. 4

18. Barney Jopson, 'Business supports continued separation of Kenya's powers,' *The Financial Times,* December 25-26, 2007 p. 3.

19. Michela Wrong, 'Violence bars gateway to heart of Africa, p.6; and Barney Jopson, 'Rally called off as death toll rises' *The Financial Times,* January 8, 2008. Barney Jopson 'Kenya shuns effort to resolve crisis' January 5-6, 2007 p. 4 and Barney Jopson and Michela Wrong, 'Mediation hopes hit a Kibaki names Kenya cabinet,' *The Financial Times,* January 9, 2008 .

10: Liberia: Political Schizophrenia

Africa's oldest republic was not colonized by Europeans, but by ex-slaves who were "repatriated" from the United States in 1847. The Liberian flag is a flattering imitation of the American flag. Liberian currency is the US dollar and much of the culture, a mirror of African-American popular culture. The average life expectancy for Liberian males is 50 years and for females 53. One-hundred and thirty out of every thousand infants dies at birth. The HIV/Aids infection rate is 9 percent and there is one doctor for every 8,333 people.

Ghana's fragile democratic institutions have been devastated by tyrannic rule, ethnic-conflict, corruption and war. While thousands of innocent civilians were being slaughtered during the long civil war, the United States, which bears responsibility for the failed "51st state," essentially looked the other way. During the reign of Samuel K. Doe and Charles Taylor, the country exploded with ethnic and fratricidal warfare. The conflict caused a humanitarian crisis, created a generation of child soldiers and exacerbated regional instability. Between 1989 and 1996, over 300,000 Liberians were killed.

In 2001, Liberia had an estimated population of 2.7 million and a gross domestic product of $500 million. The country has few sources of income. Central Bank Statistics report the government revenues of L$1.94 billion during the last six months of 2002. The real value is difficult to assess because Central Bank Data is compiled by the World Bank for future IMF loans against Liberia's few resources. The Liberian dollar is pegged to the US$ one-for-one, but in practice trades at anything from L$45 to L$70 per dollar. Three quarters of total revenues are derived from a combination of customs duties, petroleum taxes; the country's forestry and shipping registry.

Among the African states, Liberia shares with Ethiopia the distinction of not having been ruled by Europeans. Between 1847 and 1980, Liberia was governed by an elite class comprised primarily of descendants of American ex-slaves who settled along its coastline two decades earlier. Most Liberians belong to indigenous ethno-linguistic groups, such as the Kpelle, Bassa, Grio,

Kru, Krahn and the Vai, who were conquered by the"Americo-Liberians." Some accepted this subjugation which included conversion to Christianity and literacy. The ability to speak English was imposed in order to advance in this class-based system. The natives had to accept the social hierarchy and become a "client" of an Americo-Liberian or a "patron."[1] Americo-Liberians constituted only 5 percent of the population, but they dominated Liberian politics for decades by controlling of the electoral process and fixing elections through their True Whig Party (TWP). The only real "citizens," of Liberia were the descendants of American slaves. This political system, designed by ex-slaves, lasted for over 100 years gave the "citizens" and the natives to the area, roughly equivalent legislative power, despite the fact the natives outnumbered the citizens 10:1. The inspiration for this unequal division of power was the US Senate, which had balanced the power of free and slave states despite the much larger populations of the free states.

Samuel K. Doe

In 1980, following the assassination of William Tolbert, Samuel K. Doe, an army staff sergeant, seized power to become Liberia's first indigenous president. Doe used the military to rule and was reportedly was never seen without his two way radio and machine gun. The leadership of the Tolbert administration and their allies were publicly executed. Those suspected of plotting against him, and there were many, were summarily executed either by military court or during interrogation. Under Doe's rule, Liberians suffered horrific human rights abuses. Despite all guarantees, the constitution was suspended, martial law was imposed, and political activities were banned. The roots of the Liberia's civil war are buried, in part, in the abysmal human rights record of the Doe regime. But US complicity in Liberian history also shares blame.

The coup d'etat roundly condemned, but those in Washington, who felt that US aid to Liberia was important, argued that the country's position on the coast of West Africa was critical to US interests and that political and economic instability there would invite external interference. This geo-strategic yet, neo-colonial perspective, was adopted by the Reagan administration, which took a geo-strategic approach to maintaining US influence in the region. In 1981, on the first anniversary of the coup, President Reagan sent a naval destroyer to Monrovia on a training exercise along with one hundred Green Berets, to train Doe's elite troops.

After staging a commemorative parachute jump, the Green Berets remained for one month to administer a basic training program for the Liberian infantry. The Reagan administration implemented a previously existing plan granting the $7 million in military assistance, allocated by the Carter administration, and adding $2 million more for the following year, Reagan also granted Liberia an additional $25 million in economic support. In exchange, Doe re-established diplomatic relations with Israel, traveling there in 1983, for talks on trade, military and technical aid and intelligence sharing. Doe, reportedly fearful of the rise of Islamic fundamentalism in some of Liberia's rural areas, was eager to enlist Israeli help in monitoring Libyan activities in West Africa. Armed with millions of dollars worth of military aid by the Reagan administration, he could now curtail the threat of Islamic influence in the region.

Reports of human rights violations included: massacres of majority Gio tribe members, by Doe's (Krahn) group; and a number of ritual murders conducted by the so-called "heart-men," who were asked to provide body parts for mystical ceremonies on the behalf of those seeking election to public office. These abuses, combined with the abuse of power by the military, contributed to the unrest that eventually destroyed Liberia. In 1984, Doe called for elections and took a symbolic steps toward returning Liberia to civilian rule the following year. In the 1985, elections, Doe claimed to have won the presidency with 80 percent of his ethnic Krahn vote, and 50.9 percent of the popular vote.

Liberia's civil war began in December 1989, when Libyan backed leader, Charles Taylor and 200 guerrillas invaded the country from the Cote d'Ivoire. The guerrillas ignited a rebellion between members of the Gio and Mano tribes against Doe's ruling Krahn tribe. As they advanced on Monrovia, they split into two factions. In February 1990, Africa Watch reported fighting in Nimba County between insurgents and government forces. The mainly Mano and Gio refugees, provided testimony about indiscriminate killings of unarmed civilians, rape, looting and the burning of homes by government forces. They spoke of soldiers coming into Nimba County and opening fire on unarmed civilians with mounted machine guns and burning entire villages to the ground. Some of the refugees belonged to the Krahn ethnic group. They spoke of abuses by rebel forces that targeted Krahn civilians in retaliation for the army's brutal counterinsurgency tactics.

One incident occurred at the UN compound. Where many Mano and Gio people sought refuge. On May 31, 1990, eight soldiers entered the compound where they stripped and abducted 40 refugees. The following morning the bodies were found in different areas of the city. The year that the Doe regime celebrated its tenth anniversary, the civil war fully erupted. Rebel armies led by Charles Taylor, Prince Johnson and disaffected military officers turned political conflict into ethnic-warfare destroying the countries infrastructure devastating the political institutions and eventually taking over 300,000 lives.

Perhaps American arms support made Doe feel invulnerable. During the first Reagan administration, the US provided $500 million in military assistance to his government. In the aftermath of the fraudulent elections of

1985, and a subsequent coup attempt, Reagan administration spokespersons tried to explain away or deny the reports of gross human rights abuses and election fraud. Despite active opposition from the Congress, the Reagan administration pursued a policy of "quiet diplomacy," in Liberia which was continued by the George H.W. Bush administration. The drastic decline in US aid assistance to Liberia, was largely due to Congressional action.

Toward the end of the war, Doe sought US intervention. In August of 1990, he and his troops were isolated in Monrovia and under siege by rebel troops. On September 8, Doe was wounded and captured by rebels loyal to Johnson. Two days later he was found castrated and shot dead with his penis in his mouth; reportedly killed while being interrogated about huge hidden sums of money. The war had turned half of the nation's 2.4 million people refugees.

Charles Taylor

As a member of Liberia's elite "citizen" class, Charles Taylor was able to study economics in the US in the early 1970s. Like many of his generation, he was influenced by the ideologies of Pan-Africanism and Marxism. As a student, he confronted and defeated Liberian President, William Tolbert, during a debate in the United States. Upon graduation, he was invited by Samuel K. Doe to run a government agency. In 1983, he was charged and with embezzling $900,000 in Liberian government funds. Taylor fled to the US, where he was arrested. Charles Taylor's escape from Massachusetts's Walpole prison, remains a mystery. Allegedly, he was able to saw through the bars and escape down knotted sheets. In another conspiratorial story, while President Doe was at the height of cordial diplomatic relations with the Reagan administration, he escaped with the collusion of the CIA. He resurfaced in Libya, training in guerilla camps sponsored by Muammar Qadhafi.

In Libya Taylor became acquainted with Foday Sankoh, leader of the Revolutionary United Front RUF (rebel movement) of Sierra Leone. Crossing the border from neighboring Cote d'Ivoire in 1989, Taylor launched a rebellion against Doe. Initially, the rebellion was popular because Taylor claimed to be an avenger for the pogroms against certain tribes committed by Doe's death squads. On orders from Taylor, when captured, Doe's was to be tortured before he was murdered.

Taylor exchanged his military fatigues for white safari suits. Like Doe he exchanged his rifle for a carved cane and Like Doe, Taylor's eyes remained behind trademark aviator sunglasses. He won a landslide election against Ellen Sirleaf-Johnson in 1997, after battling other armed groups for control of the capital. The slogan of his supporters was: "He kill my ma he kill my pa. I vote for him."[3] Just as his predecessor had done, he subcontracted national assets to personal business acquaintances. The economic decay that accompanied his rule fed a scramble for the country's natural resources. "Taylor had a tremendous amount of financial assets at his fingertips and did business with a wide range of presidents, arms dealers, smugglers and other nefarious types;" said Corinne Dufka, of Human Right Watch. During Taylor's seven-year rule, a rebellion broke out with one group backed by neighboring Guinea and another by the Cote d'Ivoire.

As the war in Sierra Leone ended in 2002, Taylor began losing his grip on power. In 2003, he was persuaded by several African leaders to step down and accept asylum in Nigeria.[4] Upon his resignation and departure in 2003, Taylor said: "I will always remember you wherever I am. I say to you, God willing, I will be back." Regional leaders gathered in Monrovia to mark Mr. Taylor's exit from office and discuss the terms of his refuge in Nigeria.

Appeals from Liberians, the UK and United Nations to the Clinton and Bush administrations to restore the peace in the quasi-American colony fell on deaf ears. 250,000 Liberian lives later, Bush said his administration was carefully monitoring the situation and working with the ECOWAS, on plans for a UN peacekeeping force. ECOWAS, the 15-member union, met to discuss the deployment of 1500 Nigerian soldiers and other contingency forces to restore the peace.

Resisting calls for a US intervention, the Bush administration announced plans to send a team of experts to Liberia in July, 2003. White House Press Secretary, Ari Fleischer said that Bush had instructed the Pentagon team to assess how to bring peace to the country. The presence of an indicted war criminal, Charles Taylor, presented a dilemma for US commanders because of the mounting international pressure for his arrest. Taylor had requested 40 days to consider Nigeria's offer of asylum, and said he welcomed the prospect of US participation in restoring the peace stating it would be; "essential for stability." He told a gathering of religious leaders at his presidential mansion that: "I see myself as stepping down to turn power over to a transitional regime, I have no problem with that. Any time, any day." Bush urged Taylor to back up his encouraging words with deeds so that stability of the region could be achieved.

The truce between the Taylor government and the Liberians United for Reconciliation and Democracy (LURD) rebels, collapsed during the heavy fighting around Monrovia in October 2003. Taylor, the former warlord who had won election in 1997 after a devastating fourteen year civil war, was charged with war crimes by a UN-backed court in Sierra Leone. The crisis was complicated by uncertainty over the intentions of Charles Taylor, who had agreed to resign by August 11, 2004, had a reputation for making promises under political pressure, and later reneging on them. "No one believes what Charles Taylor says;" stated a foreign government official. According to Vaanii Paasewe, Charles Taylor's press secretary, the president planned to leave but would do so at the time of his choosing and did not see his departure as part of the peace process. Asked if Taylor was considering remaining in the country, Paasewe responded: "Why shouldn't he? This is his home and to the best of my knowledge the President prefers to live and die here." [5]

Secretary General, Kofi Annan urged ECOWAS and the US (including by writing and telephoning Colin Powell), to stop prevaricating, warning that Liberia was "poised" between hope and disaster." The Security Council agreed to a US-sponsored resolution to approve the deployment of an international peacekeeping force and a UN stabilizing force.[6]

During his first Presidential campaign, Governor W. Bush, heaped disdain on his predecessor's interventionist policy of "nation-building" and distinctively ruled out any such US action in Africa, which he saw as void of interests for US security policy. Secretary of State, Colin Powell, pierced this position, adding: "You can't ignore it." We will have to wait to see exactly what that phrase means when, and if, the US intervenes militarily in Liberia." In seeking to explain why Liberia should be the exception, Powell raised other questions. If Liberia qualified, what standard would be used to judge US participation in other African political and humanitarian crisis in places such as the Ethiopia, Somalia, Sudan, or the Democratic Republic of Congo?[7]

Moral foreign policy values aside, the reasons for US caution in Liberia were transparently obvious. The Pentagon, overstretched in Iraq did not want a repeat of the humiliating humanitarian peacekeeping experience of Somalia. Moreover, Liberia had little value in the new geo-political calculus of American strategic doctrine. The Clinton administration had been constantly attacked for alleged military frivolity, which risked American lives for unclear goals, and abstract values associated with human rights and freedom. Like president Carter, it was now former president Clinton, who asserted the need for US foreign policy to represent not just the strategic calculus of experts, but the moral values of the American people, where so could be done reasonably.

According to a Gallup poll conducted in July 2000, US within two weeks public support for the contribution US troops to a UN peacekeeping operation in Liberia increased from 57 to 63 percent. This increased support was in response to the intense reporting (*CNN* effect), on Liberia's deteriorating security situation. The US began to positioning troops for some form of intervention. Historically, The American media, and therefore the US public, pays little to Africa. The American attention span increases and the media focuses on US troops deployed abroad. But, lessons from the UN Mission in Somalia and the desecration of the corpses US soldiers in the streets of Mogadishu were not soon forgotten. Other polling, conducted month's later, revealed striking variant responses suggesting that support for Liberia was soft and flexible. A *Program on International Policy Attitudes* (PIPA) Knowledge Networks poll with 1,066 respondents, conducted in July 2000, found that 48% of the respondents supported contributing US troops. Other polls found support ranging from a high of 63% in a *Gallup* poll to 35% in a *Fox News* poll.[8]

The highest level of support was found on poll questions that made it clear that other countries would also be contributing troops; that this was a peacekeeping operation; and that it would be under the auspices of the United

Nations. The lowest level of support was found in polls that failed to mention these facts and that used ambiguous phrases to avoid the specifics about the operation and its political implications. These polls, failed to describe exactly what US soldiers would be doing, or implied that the troops would be actively involved in enforcement activity in the midst of a civil war. Support was lower when the questions about Liberia were followed a series of questions that required thinking about the costs and risks of the war in Iraq. The research suggested that support might solidify if the Liberian operation was clearly perceived as a multilateral operation under the United Nations; and to erode if it involved the risk of American life.

The Pentagon sent three warships to Liberia's coast for limited involvement and for emergency evacuation. The marines flew in by helicopter to defend the US Embassy, which had been struck by mortars aimed at the heavily populated US civilian area. Two hundred marines were sent ashore to demonstrate the commitment to restoring stability. One of their first tasks was to transport a shipment of *Heineken* to the Embassy. Eventually, about 100 US military personnel remained in Monrovia to protect the Embassy. The Pentagon confirmed it would send 4500 troops to the Mediterranean as part of "prudent planning" exercises for a possible intervention. After 3,500 Nigerian peacekeepers eventually restored order to Monrovia, the US withdrew its warships, renewing security concerns. After weeks of heavy fighting, the Nigerian troops were, "re-hatted" as UN peacekeeping troops, while reinforcement from other nations assembled. The Nigerian and other West African peacekeepers concentrated their efforts on Monrovia and the southeast road to Buchanan, Liberia's second port.

Kofi Annan implored the US to extend its presence, by leaving behind 2,300 marines and lending symbolic support to the UN peacekeeping effort. Two of the three warships left within a week, the third left shortly thereafter. The 15,000 strong UN stabilization force in Liberia was the organizations largest African deployment. An interim administration, agreed to by the warring factions, was scheduled for installation in October, 2004 and elections were scheduled for 2005.

By August of 2003, Charles Taylor was in exile, and much of Monrovia had been reduced from ruins to rubble. The Liberian Parliament had been looted of all but a few chairs by Taylor supporters. Above the debris, hung a plaque displaying the national seal and motto: "The love of liberty brought us here;" a reference to the freed slaves who settled Liberia.. The documents scattered in the corridors of the looted parliament attested to an abuse of that liberty as was indicated by the 2002-2003 budget of the Ministry for Presidential Affairs. The ministry's staff of 1,261 included a 127-member choir. The chief executive officer of *Airwing Aerospace* reported taking orders for delivery of five helicopters including pilots and engineers.

The terms of Taylor's exile were outlined in a warning issued by the Nigerian government preventing Taylor from "engaging in active communications with anyone engaged in political life, illegal or governmental activities in Liberia." Concerned with possible political repercussions for granting Taylor asylum, President Obasanjo met with Taylor and warned him to comply with these terms.

The August 18, 2003 international peace agreement divided control of the important economic ministries and agencies including: the Liberian Petroleum Refining Corporation, the National Ports Authority and the Bureau of Maritime Affairs; among Taylor loyalists and the two rebel groups. This shaky peace was criticized for undermining the credibility of the government's commitment to transparency and accountability. Supporters of the peace agreement argued that domestic safeguards such as new contracts and a monopolies commission, would be supplemented by significant outside supervision.

The Liberian people suffered the consequences of Taylor's status as an international pariah. In July 2003, the UN compounded an existing embargo on diamond sales, by adding a travel ban on Liberian government officials and their allies and imposing sanctions on timber exports. Concerned over the country's $2.7 billion foreign debt and the lack of financial controls in such areas as shipping and forestry, the International Monetary Fund suspended Liberia's voting rights. "We are down to zero," stated Charles Bright, Liberia's outgoing finance minister. The economic damage reflected an historic 'benign-neglect' policy of nation-building and the lack of responsibility toward a *defacto* US colony. "I don't think the task is possible;" stated Jacques Paul Klein, Kofi Annan's special UN representative to Liberia. Klein asked how quickly international investment could be generated to employ the people of country destroyed by a 14 year civil war? "We have a limited population, we have resources here-we have to find out who owns them." According to the Roman Catholic Archbishop of Monrovia, Liberian despair over the destruction of their country and gratitude for the belated international interest, outweighed any fear of renewed neo-colonialism.

Taylor's alleged links to al-Qaeda made US intervention in Liberia were made consistent with the "war on terror," only in that terrorists took advantage of Liberia's political chaos. Bush's Liberian policy proved to be an open and shut case. US forces would go and install a new president via constitutional methods, followed by a transitional government and finally elections. This, in short, is nation-building. Leon Fuerth notes that, as in Iraq, Bush's Liberia policy reflected a lack of thoughtful planning based upon over-confident presumptions of US capability and commitment. It neglected the fact that the country is divided into three areas controlled by former government militias and two rebel movements. Aid and Human rights organizations reported continued harassment and abuse of civilians including public beatings, executions, widespread rape and extortion by armed gangs.

UN experts reported that the Taylor regime spent $30 million dollars to purchase weapons, in violation of a Security Council resolution. After the UN imposed an embargo on Liberian diamonds, the ruling class turned to the maritime industry to fund the war in neighboring Sierra Leone. Liberia earns some $18 a year million from its maritime business, providing between 25-50 percent of total government revenues. Excluding Panama, Liberia has the second largest maritime fleet in the world. Under growing international sanctions, many companies stopped using Liberia's flag of convenience. This had serious repercussions for such companies as *Royal Caribbean*, *Carnival Cruise*, *ExxonMobil*, *Chevron*, and *Cosco*, the Chinese bulk carrier. Experts warned of a profound impact on the shipping industry because 1,734 vessels were registered under Liberia's flag of convenience including 35 percent of all oil tankers.

The 135-page UN report found that the Liberian International Shipping and Corporate Registry (LISCR), the US based company that manages Liberia's maritime registry, facilitated Charles Taylor's illegal purchase of weapons. In response to requests from Liberia's commissioner of maritime affairs, LISCR made four money transfers to non-government accounts. At least two of these were $1 million transfers to purchase arms in violation of the UN embargo. The payments were made in violation of the company's agreement with the Liberian government and according to one UN official showed a complete lack of due diligence. To stop the misuse and the flight of corporate funds, the experts recommended that the Security Council establish an escrow account for development. The financing of terrorism in Africa by a US corporation was never addressed. The Security Council ignored the experts' recommendation to strip Charles Taylor of the right to manage the Liberian economy despite the political and economic devastation wrought by his rule.[9]

In April 2005, a UN panel and the Liberian government released details of a mining deal, signed under "extremely opaque" circumstances, creating ten year a de facto monopoly over much of Liberia's diamond-producing region. Experts described the deal, which was signed by Liberian officials from different political factions with the *West Africa Mining Corporation* (Wamco); as symptomatic of the secretive nature of Liberia's transitional government. A draft contract, identified Liberia's Minister of Mines, Jonathan Mason, of the Model rebel group, finance minister Lucinee Kamara, Justice minister, Kabineh Ja'neh of the LURD rebel faction, and Roosevelt Quaiah of the Liberian National Investment Commission as signatories to the deal.

Michael Saint Yrian, a *Wamco's* signatory to the deal, was Liberia's representative to the United Nations Educational Scientific and Cultural Organizations (UNESCO). He was also economic advisor to the Equatorial Guinean government and to the *Samsson Group*. Yrian brokered a contract was with the representatives of the armed factions waging violent campaigns of torture, mutilation, slaughter and rape in order to control large portions of mineral-rich and forested territory. Under the *Wamco* deal, they would share wealth and power with the former government officials in Monrovia.Under the deal, *Wamco* had the right to establish cooperatives and purchase all minerals not already under contract in western Liberia.

Wamco's majority shareholder, *London International Bank* (LIB) is an investment house, run by David Aim, a French businessman who approached Saint Yrian and proposed the scheme. *London International Bank* manages a $200m fund with Lehman brothers, and has millions of dollars invested in real estate. The draft contract generously set aside a 10 percent equity share for the government of Liberia. Paul Majmander, *LIB* strategic operations manager, said that the *LIB* would ensure that the deal would be managed openly. To the contrary, the UN panel found, an avoidance of transparency because the *London International Bank* circumvented the Liberian Monopolies and Contracts Commission. The top UN envoy called the Liberian government, a "coalition of the unwilling."

During the civil war, the harbor at Buchanan, Liberia largest port was stripped by the rebel army. The port, part of the government-owned Liberian Mining Company (LIMINCO), was offered to *Mittal Steel* the world's largest steel producer for revitalization. LIMINCO employed a private security service, that during the 14-year war, functioned primarily as a death squad. the worlds richest steel magnate and billionaire investor, Lakshmi Mittal, is expected to invest $900 million to develop iron ore deposits near Liberia's border with Guinea, to refurbish the destroyed port and the 250-kilometer railway line. The Liberian government planned to take a 30 per cent equity stake in the project.

A conflict between *LIMINCO, Mittal Steel* and *Global Infrastructure Holding Limited* (GIHL), which is run by Lakshmi Mittal's younger brother Pramod, further complicated the deal. A document from Liberia's National Investment Commission revealed that the *GIHL* deal was approved in December 2004 and that *GIHL* had outbid other mining giants such as *Rio Tinto, BHP Billiton* and *LNM Holdings*, by forming a joint venture with the Liberian Government. Only days after the joint venture was incorporated,

US ambassador to Liberia, John Blaney, wrote Bryant urging him to improve the transparency of government contracts. Gyude Bryant, Liberia's interim president, sent instructions to ministry officials to stop the negotiations with *GIHL*, and transparently advertise the project. Gyude Bryant's instructions for greater transparency were ignored.[10] That September, *Ispat Inland*, a *Mittal Steel* subsidiary with a heavy US investment, wrote Bryant asking for his assistance in facilitating discussions with the government. The letter mentioned that *LNM Holdings* could guarantee "30,000 jobs in the Chicago area if it had access to Liberian iron ore. Blaney urged Gyude Bryant to review the contract process stating that: "Rumors are circulating the members of the review committee have been approached to sell their support." A sworn affidavit signed by a labor ministry official alleged that Bryant said the US would "slow down their support of the peace process in Liberia" if the government followed though with the *GIHL* deal. US government officials declined to comment on the affidavit, but those in favor of the *Mittal Steel* deal dismissed such statements as politically motivated.

The US Department of Commerce had previously signed a commercial advocacy agreement with Pramad Mittal. By March, *Mittal Steel* was again negotiating with the Liberian government, while *GIHL* was lobbying to have its deal validated. *GIHL* mounted a legal challenge in the Liberian Supreme Court but withdrew the challenge for "commercial reasons" just before Mittal announced he had won the concession. The law firm representing *Mittal Steel* is run by Varney Sherman, a presidential candidate from Bryant's political party. The two leading presidential candidates, Ellen Johnson Sirleaf, a former World Bank official, and George Weah, a populist international soccer star, vowed that if they won the presidency, they might review the contract.

In April 2005, the chief prosecutor of the UN war crimes court in Sierra Leone, accused Charles Taylor of masterminding an assassination attempt on the president of Guinea, Lasana Conté. Former Defense Department attorney, David Crane, testified to having evidence linking Charles Taylor to the gunmen who fired on President Lasana Conté's convoy in Conakry, the capital of Guinea. Many, considered Guinea the weakest link in the chain of countries of the region. Some suspected that Taylor was searching for a base from which to reignite regional conflict. Court documents concluded that Taylor was plotting to overthrow the Cote d'Ivoire government as part of a master scheme to plunge West Africa into further chaos and return to power. The Sierra Leone, UN-backed war crimes court indicted Taylor on 17 counts of crimes against humanity, for his role in supporting Sierra Leone's rebels in a war that cost hundreds of thousands of lives. The special court to lobbied for his extradition, but the Nigerian government refused to do so until a request was made by an elected Liberian government.[11]

Taylor promised not to further interfere in Liberian politics. The US House of Representatives passed a resolution calling upon Nigeria to hand the former warlord over to the Sierra Leone war crimes court. Some Senators wrote Secretary of State Condoleeza Rice, urging her to pressure Nigeria for Taylor's return. "Allowing Nigeria to shield Charles Taylor from the special court would set an unfortunate precedent. Permitting an indicted war criminal to escape economic justice from a UN and United States supported tribunal, undermines Security Council resolutions and damages our country's efforts to promote human rights around the world;" read the letter which was signed by four Republican and four Democrat Senators.

In August 2004, Human Rights Watch interviewed 60 former fighters involved in the various conflicts throughout the region. Noticeably, a third of them had been solicited by different recruiters to fight either for or against Lasana Conté. *Financial Times* correspondent, Dino Mahtani, obtained a special court document alleging that Charles Taylor broke the conditions of his asylum, when he traveled from Nigeria to Ouagadougou, Burkina-Faso's capital, to meet collaborators including; Francois Galawolo, a Liberian lawyer and presidential candidate. The Nigerian government claimed it would never have allowed Charles Taylor to leave his exile in the port city of Calabar. "There is not a single iota of truth in that allegation," said presidential spokeswoman, Remi Oyo. The Human Rights Watch document further alleged that Taylor's grand scheme included overthrowing the government of the Cote d'Ivoire. Government official said that Taylor and the government of Guinea supplied arms to the Ivorian rebels, which had conquered large parts of the rainforest. With an estimated third of the world's known bauxite reserves, Guinea could provide its rulers with sufficient resources to finance a protracted war. Taylor had financed his previous military campaigns by selling timber and diamonds from Liberia and Sierra Leone.

The October 2005 elections brought hope that Charles Taylor would finally be extradited, tried for war crimes, and held responsible for over 1.2 million deaths. Shortly before the election, Desmond de Silva, prosecutor of the special court for Sierra Leone met with US National Security Council senior director for African affairs Cindy Courville. Prosecutor de Silva pressed the Courville to convince the Bush administration to hand Taylor over to the special court which was trying nine other people accused of war crimes in Sierra Leone. The US and the UK played key roles in encouraging Nigerian president Obasanjo to grant Mr. Taylor exile in 2004. In prosecutor's de Silva view, since Bush supported the special court he should also provide political support for Taylor's extradition. Wary of the Bush administrations reluctance to jeopardize its relationship with petroleum-rich Nigeria, de Silva stated: "It is very important that his principle of accountability is put into effect."[12] He claimed that the deposed warlord continued to foment regional instability from exile, using the vast sums he plundered from Liberia's diamond and logging industries, and expressed concern that Taylor would flee to Zimbabwe to avoid extradition.

Salih Booker, of Africa Action, a Washington-based lobbying group, questioned the newly-elected governments' ability to prioritize extradition proceedings and the impact it might have on aid from major donor countries. The recent history of warlords plundering natural resources to sustain their patronage systems and militia groups, suggested that a failure to deliver would bring renewed protracted conflict. Despite the presence of 15,000 UN peacekeepers, many of Liberia's most lucrative diamond mines, timber forests and rubber plantations were occupied by officially disarmed, unmonitored former fighters. Contracts awarded Taylor's ministers included diamond concessions, rubber plantations, oil blocks and a $900 million iron ore project. The contracts raised questions about how much control the new government would really have over the country's most valuable resources.

Anticipating this scenario, international donors pushed an intrusive package of binding reforms, known as the General Economic Management Assistance Plan (GEMAP), on the interim and newly elected governments. GEMAP would use externally appointed co-signatories within the revenue generating branches of the government; the Ministry of Finance and the Central Bank, to tightly monitor all procurement and concession contracts. Many members of the interim power-sharing government, who were constitutionally barred from standing for election, objected to the new regulations calling the GEMAP policy an attack on Liberian sovereignty.

In the October 2005 elections, Liberia's 1.3 million registered voters chose from 22 presidential candidates including former rebels, warlords, ministers and a soccer champion. The winner faced the task of rebuilding a failed state and reversing the polarizing tide of ethnic politics. Liberia needs a new electricity grid, drivable roads, piped running water, a public education system, a healthcare system, a judiciary and a dependable internal security apparatus. The 2005 national budget was a mere $80 million. A private US security firm was tasked with training a 2,000 member strong national army. GEMAP's $520 million pledge, for donor-implemented projects over a 36 month period, depended on successful, effective and transparent fiscal management by the newly elected government.

George Weah, a former AC Milan millionaire soccer superstar, waged a campaign that drew large crowds of Liberia's young and poor he drove through the destruction of post-war Monrovia. His popularity mirrored their hopes that this election would mark a new chapter in Liberian and West African history. Raised in a shanty town, many questioned George Weah's qualifications and political experience to be president. But his supporters chanted; "You know book, you don't know book, we vote for you." Many of his supporters are disillusioned former rebels who supported him despite his minimal political skills and poor education. Weah based his campaign on a slogan of "elitism versus grass-rootism." It was an appeal to youth who feel the country had been dominated by the descendants of the ex-American slaves who colonized in 1847 and who ruled thereafter.[13]

Weah's principal opponent, Ellen Sirleaf-Johnson, was a former World Bank economist and *Citibank* director who first ran for the presidency in 1997. She inspired confidence among many Americo-Liberians, despite her association with Charles Taylor's war to oust Samuel K. Doe. Known as the "iron lady," for her tough political style, Sirleaf-Johnson campaigned on her experience. The contrast between the two candidates reflected a deep political cleavage defined by a complex mixture of ethnic and social alliances between indigenous Africans and the descendants of repatriated American slaves. She emphasized her strong management style and the value of technocratic meritocracy required to rebuild the country. George Weah's supporters' pointed out that professionals, like Sirleaf-Johnson, had done little to help ordinary Liberians during the past two decades.

Central to the ability to govern Liberia was maintaining a balance of power in the newly elected 30-seat Senate and 64-seat House of Representatives. "The government will have to be inclusive. If it isn't the old nightmares will come back to haunt them;" observed Alan Doss, the UN's top envoy in Liberia. Samuel Kofi Woods, a human rights lawyer in Monrovia noted: "If there were clear ideological lines in this election bid, you wouldn't have such a similar-looking group of people who have committed human rights violations backing both candidates." The GEMAP deal received the backing of both Sirleaf-Johnson and George Weah. Sirleaf-Johnson said the external management, good governance plan was meant to "save us from ourselves."[14]

Under the protection of UN peacekeepers, thousands of Liberians, voting for the first time, lined up at churches, school and rural huts to elect a better future for a county destroyed by civil war. Many walked miles over long mud soaked roads and some spent the night at polling stations. Expressing the hope of many, a 19 year old voter, Willie Moore stated: "We will get a leader who will help us go to school and who will give our parents work."

The first-round of balloting left George Weah and Sirleaf-Johnson as finalists. The resentment against the old ruling elite known as "Congo's" (because of their lighter complexion), attracted votes for "King George," who took 29 percent of the first round vote. Sirleaf-Johnson, who served in the administrations' of president's William Talbert and Samuel Doe, but also stressed her working class roots, won only 19.8 percent of first-round votes. Both candidates were supported by tainted political figures who were deemed critical to galvanizing an election victory. These included Charles Taylor's estranged wife and one of his former deputies.

On November 8 2005, Liberians elected 67 year-old Ellen Sirleaf Johnson Africa's first female president. With 97 percent of the polling stations reporting, she won almost 60 percent of the vote. Sirleaf-Johnson's victory relied on appealing to many chiefs and warlords to turn out the vote in their appointed fiefdoms.[15] In protest, angry Weah supporters marched on the US embassy in Monrovia. UN police guarding the embassy, used batons and tear gas to beat them back. Alleging ballot-stuffing and intimidation at polling booths Weah's party accused the election commission of bias, filed a Supreme Court writ to stop vote-counting and for an official declaration of the results. International observers found insufficient evidence to support these allegations.

Ominous implications of post-election conflict were expressed by former child soldier, Junior Russ, who fought for three different militia groups during the war. "I want a neutral person to rule this country, not Ellen Johnson Sirleaf, who has ruined this country by backing revolutions. We have been used by people like her;" he bitterly observed. President-elect Sirleaf-Johnson said she would welcome George Weah into her government as part of a process of reunification stating; "I'd like him to play an important role. I think working together we can do a lot to respond to the needs of our country, particularly the young people." Weah called upon his frustrated supporters to remain calm, but his control over them was questionable.

Twice imprisoned by Samuel Doe and accused of treason by Taylor, Sirleaf-Johnson has her share of political enemies. Legal challenges to the results not withstanding, her real challenge was to convince opposition supporters that she was not partisan to the "citizens" or to the "Congo" elite.

"The composition of the government will be a strong signal that we are committed to this;" she told a reporter. Her ability to keep her corrupt allies in the background would depend on how well she implemented the GEMAP reform package. Asked about the future of Charles Taylor, she speculated that he was unlikely to face trial in Liberia, but probably would be prosecuted in Sierra Leone.

In a cynical show of support, on January 16th two US Navy warships were parked offshore Monrovia for presidential swearing in ceremonies, which were attended by Laura Bush and Condoleezza Rice. In her inaugural address, Africa's first female president said: "We know that your vote was a vote for change, a vote for peace, security...and we have heard you loudly. We recognize this change is not a change for a change's sake, but a fundamental break with the past, therefore requiring that we take steps to address the problems that have for decades stunted our progress." Kofi Annan congratulated Sirleaf-Johnson, saying that she had a "historic mandate to lead the nation toward a future of lasting peace and stability."

On November 11, 2005, The Security Council adopted Resolution 1638, calling for the apprehension and transfer of Charles Taylor to the UN backed Special Court in Sierra Leone on charges of war crimes and crime against humanity. Taylor and 11 others indicted by the court were charged with war crimes, crimes against humanity and other serious violations of international humanitarian law. All but two of the indicted, including Taylor, were in custody of the Special court in Sierra Leone. According to the release covering the Council's decision, the return of Charles Taylor to Liberia would; "constitute an impediment to the country's stability and a threat to its peace."

The Security Council expressed appreciation to President Obasanjo for his country's contribution to restoring stability to the sub-region. The Council acknowledged that Nigeria had acted with broad international support in its decision to provide for Taylor's temporary asylum. The Security Council gave an additional mandate to the UNMIL, to keep the governments of Liberia and Sierra Leone and the Security Council fully informed should they have to transfer or facilitate Taylor's transfer. The Brazilian and Argentinean Security Council Ambassadors explained their votes in support of the resolution as votes for enforcing the rule of domestic and international law and as punishing impunity.

Responding to President Sirleaf-Johnson's request for "closure" under Security Council resolution 1638, Nigeria agreed to extradite Charles Taylor. "I appreciate the decision he made regarding Charles Taylor," George W. Bush stated. Preparations were made to transfer Taylor to Sierra Leone, but that he had escaped custody after hearing of the agreement. The lapse in security was a source of embarrassment for president Obasanjo who was scheduled to conduct bilateral talks with Bush. State Department officials expressed their dismay at Taylor's escape from his luxury seaside villa and demanded an explanation. The Bush administration considered canceling a

White House meeting with President Obasanjo upon hearing of Taylor's disappearance. Condoleeza Rice called Obasanjo to reinforce the White House message that, the President was waiting to hear from Nigeria on the whereabouts of Mr. Taylor.

Some in the US Congress were outraged that Nigeria had let Taylor slip away and suggested that Liberian officials should go and seize him. California representative, Ed Royce declared that: "Nigeria reportedly has let a mass murderer with alleged links to al-Qaeda slip out the back door. George W. Bush should cancel tomorrow's scheduled meeting with President Obasanjo." He warned of serious sanctions by Congress against any country giving sanctuary to Taylor.[16]

The following day, Taylor was arrested near the Cameroon border, in northeastern Nigeria. He was driving a vehicle with diplomatic plates, accompanied by a woman and suitcases full of cash. He was immediately handcuffed and shipped to Freetown, Sierra Leone wearing a bullet-proof vest and reportedly appeared cowed and defeated upon his arrival. "There was absolute euphoria when the helicopter arrived," said chief prosecutor Desmond da Silva. Security concerns led Court officials to request that the trial be moved to The Hague, Netherlands. A UN Security Council draft resolution reported that Taylor's presence in West Africa was a threat to regional and international peace and security. Some feared a rescue mission on Taylor's behalf involving foreign mercenaries. Nigerian officials hoped that his capture would enhance president Obasanjo's status with the US, particularly since his government had recently persuaded insurgents in the Delta to release two American hostages.

Taylor was the principal architect of a 14-year regional conflict in which an estimated 300,000 people were killed. The eleven-count indictment was amalgamated from the seventeen original counts as a way of accelerating both the trial and pre-trial. "We could try him probably this year,' said chief prosecutor da Silva. On April 3, 2005, he went from his cell in Freetown, Sierra Leone to face the UN court, where he was indicted on eleven charges of crimes against humanity including killings, rapes, mutilations, and recruiting child soldiers by backing Sierra Leonean rebels who fought to control the diamond fields.

Transferring Taylor to ICC in The Hague, posed several logistical problems despite plans for witnesses to appear from Sierra Leone via video link. Some questioned the strength of the prosecution's case and how Taylor's trial and those of nine other suspected rebel war criminals in Sierra Leone would affect regional stability. Critics of the prosecution said the sweeping indictments against Taylor might make it difficult to corroborate allegations of how much "effective control" and influence he really exercised over the rebels. There was no recourse to witnesses, who themselves had committed similar crimes. Prosecutors said their mandate was to try only those who were most responsible for the crimes thus, some key witnesses were guaranteed immunity from prosecution.

Most citizens of both Liberia and Sierra Leone were glad to see Taylor taken from the region but worried that his former associates would re-ignite conflict if their interests were threatened by the trial. Many of them remain active in politics and could destabilize the region which is awash with a generation of hungry, disillusioned and restless professional fighters with guns. Some of Taylor's most loyal associates, including his most recent wife, Jewel Howard Taylor, who is an elected senator, have forged alliances with President Sirleaf-Johnson. Some of Taylor's other associates have been arrested, including his son, who ran Liberia's anti-terrorist squad and was arrested on a charge of passport fraud in Miami.

A serious concern, was the threat to stability posed by the trial of Hinga Norman, a former deputy defense minister who had organized the pro-government militia. "Taylor has a negative image but Norman has a patriotic and nationalistic image for some people here," said J. Victor Angelo, the UN representative in Sierra Leone. One of Norman's co-defendants requested that Sierra Leonean president, Ahmad Tejan Kabbah, be called to testify about his role in the war. Norman's supporters called the government traitors and left the ruling party.

With 15,000 UN troops and strong US diplomatic backing, Liberia is unlikely to see a return to civil war. The former fighters probably understand that fighting for Taylor is not even going to be in their short term interests;" said Mike McGovern, West Africa director of the *International Crisis Group*. Those more likely to cause trouble are the high level commanders who could be going down with Taylor."[17] According to ICC prosecutor Stephen Rapp, the indictments against Taylor are stronger than those brought against Serbian war criminal Slobodan Milosevic, who faced more than 60 charges. There are more than 100 witnesses and the trial was predicted to last 12-18 months.[18] The UK offered to incarcerate Taylor, if he were convicted.

The devastating war and economic mismanagement left Liberia with a $3.7 billion dollar foreign debt. President Sirleaf-Johnson addressed the World Bank and the IMF requesting debt relief and long-term developmental assistance. Liberia emerged from the war as a test case for the international community's ability to intervene effectively and support post-conflict states. Liberian officials believe that if external intervention to boost the government's capacity to govern were delayed, the political institutions could fall prey to corrupt officials with war-lord connections who likely would drain state resources for personal gain. Luigi Giovanni, the World Bank's country director, estimated Liberia's overlapping financial requirements in the "hundreds of millions of dollars" per year.[19] As long as its debts remain unpaid, Liberia cannot normalize its relations with either institution or draw on development funds. Humanitarian aid could decline before development aid began to flow. Liberia was in such dire straits that state donors never set aside money to cover its debts when they designed debt relief packages for other heavily indebted poor countries. "The international community has got to decide whether it is serious about helping Liberia," noted an IMF official.

"It has got to dip into its pockets." Despite the psychological trauma of being left to politically disintegrate by the nation to which they felt the strongest attachment, Liberians, natives and descendants of former slave settlers, have begun to rebuild their nation.

---

1. Wayne Edge, *Africa: Liberia Country Report,* Global Studies with Annual Editions (Dubuque: McGraw-Hill/Dushkin 200), 229.

2. Ibid .

3. *The Financial Times, Coverage of Liberian election campaign.*

4. Dino, Mahtani, 'Twenty years on, Taylor again faces court prosecutors,' *The Financial Times*, April 3, 2006 p. 4.

5. Dino, Mahtani, 'Liberians face challenge of rebuilding a nation left in ruins by years of abuse,' *The Financial Times,* September 16, 2003.

5. Dino Mahtani, 'UN urges US to act as Monrovia fighting intensifies,' *The Financial Times*, October 22. 2003.

7. Dino Mahtani, 'Liberia does not fit the doctrine,' *The Financial Times*, July 25. 2003.

8. PIPA/Knowledge Networks poll "US Attitudes toward Liberia," (2000).

9. Dino Mahtani, 'Liberia weapons funded by maritime revenue,' *The Financial Times,* October 24, 2003.

10. Dino, Mahtani, 'Wrangle for minerals casts' pall over Liberia's economic revival,' *The Financial Times.*

11 Dino, Mahtani. "Nigeria pressed to hand Charles Taylor to war crimes court,' *The Financial Times*, May 5, 2005.

12. Guy Dinmore and Mark Turner, "UN war crimes prosecutor seeks Taylor handover,' *The Financial Times*, October 12, 2005.

13. Reuters Wire Report, "Liberians vote in first polls since civil war," *The Financial Times*, October 12, 2005.

14. Dino, Mahtani, 'Football star fights 'iron lady' for the chance to heal Liberia's wounds,' *The Financial Times*, November 9, 2005.

15. Dino, Mahtani, 'Liberians seek nation-building president,' *The Financial Times*, October 4, 2005.

16. Dino Mahtani and Guy Dinmore, 'US raps Nigeria as Liberian warlord vanishes,' *The Financial Times*, March 29, 2006. p. 8.

17. Dino, Mahtani, 'Charles Taylor on course for war crimes trial,' *The Financial Times,* March 2, 2006 p.4.

18. Nikki Tait, 'War crimes trial tests international justice,' *The Financial Times*, June, 4, 2007 p. 5.

19. Guha, Krishna and Dino, Mahtani, 'Pressure increases to write off Liberia's $1.2 debt,' *The Financial Times*, February 13, 2007. p. 4.

11: Nigeria: Administrative Sclerosis

Nigeria is Africa's most populated country. With a per capita income of less than $300 a year, Nigerians simultaneously enjoy the unique distinction being citizens one of the world's largest oil producing and one of the world's poorest countries. International donors provide only $2 a year in aid per capita, compared with an average of $21 per person for the rest of sub-Saharan Africa. The World Bank estimates that about 20 percent of Nigeria's children die before their fifth birthday. In 1995, the UN Center for Human Settlements (Habitat) estimated that there were 25 million people living in the capital, Lagos. A 2002 UN Development Program human development report on Nigeria, said the proportion of the population living in poverty rose from 48.5 per cent in 1998 to between 66 and 70 percent in 2005. The average life expectancy for Nigerian males and females is 51 years. Seventy-three out of every one-thousand infants dies at birth. The adult HIV/Aids infection rate is 5 % and there is one doctor for every 4, 496 people. Dysentery, measles, pneumonia, gonorrhea, whooping cough, schistosomiasis, meningitis and leprosy are also common.

In the over 100 years since the British imperialist, Sir Frederick "Lord" Lugard, amalgamated two protectorates to form a single territory called Nigeria; that state has struggled against centrifugal political forces. The name "Nigeria" was coined by Flora Shaw, one of Lugard's wives. Independent Nigeria has had six constitutions, many years when none of them was in force, a two and a half year civil war and seven military coups. The system was created not by amalgamating existing territories, but on the US model, a process of politically expedient sub-division. At independence, Nigeria had three regions, which were later increased to four. In 1967, in an effort to break regional power bases in the run up to the Biafran civil war, these were replaced by 12 states. Later, seven more states were added, then another two, then nine more and in the last expansion in 1996 an extra six, bringing the total to 36, plus the Federal Capital Territory of Abuja. Some states sought to establish their own police forces. A third of them institutionalized the Islamic Code of *Sharia* to adjudicate criminal cases. This added a volatile third layer to the legal system alongside English-style common law and "customary" or traditional courts.

Olesegun Obasanjo

Under the leadership of Olesegun Obasanjo, Nigeria emerged from over sixteen years of military dictatorship. As president, Obasanjo sought to accomplish what had not been done since independence in 1960: hold two successive elections without a military takeover. He was elected in 1999 after the death of the dictator, Sani Abacha. Twice postponed, the 2002 elections were hailed as a major step for Nigeria given the high levels of corruption and ethnic hostility. Obasanjo served as an army commander during the 1967-70 Nigerian civil-war. He rose through the military-controlled political hierarchy, to become head of state, in 1976, after the coup and assassination of his Murtala Muhammad. Known as a unifier, in 1979, Obasanjo received international praise after handing power over to an elected civilian government. Nicknamed "OBJ" or "Uncle Shege," Obasanjo is known as a gruff and stubborn man. A born-again Christian, from the southwestern Yoruba heartland, he was never captive to any elite constituency and his political base merged religious with ethnic groups. Obasanjo justified the lack of economic achievement during his first four- year term, as the need to first secure political stability. In 1999 he mandated the retirement of all senior "political officers" in the military and began a program of ethnic distribution in the ranks.[1]

Speaking about the 2002 scheduled elections, Obasanjo stated; "What worries me...as we approach the coming elections is the pervasive pessimism in the land. There seems to be a general feeling that we, as a free people, are incapable of holding elections that can be judged as free, fair and successful." Salim Ahmed Salim, the former secretary-general of the OAU, told participants in a Democracy Day event, that the elections would have a pan-continental impact. "Africa and the whole world are watching you," he stated. "Your successful accomplishment of this feat is Africa's success." Concern that the election returns would be manipulated by military and civilian oligarchs fueled this skepticism.[2] The skeptics were not disappointed; electoral fraud at the local polls was rampant. There were stories from the northern city of Kaduna, of Peoples Democratic Party ballot boxes being opened and votes tossed into the streets. Nana Ismail, a student member of the Alliance for Democracy, complained; "We are not happy at all. They refused to allow the voting to take place."

This political instability was exacerbated by a constitutional dispute between the federal government and the country's powerful local government councils. The councils tried to overturn a Supreme Court ruling that their terms of office had expired, even though elections were not scheduled until August 2002. Tafa Balogun, the country's most senior law enforcement officer, threatened to use force against local politicians who failed to vacate their seats. This dispute, reflected longstanding tensions between the national government and politicians representing the 36 states of Nigeria. The 36 governors decided, by consensus, that it would be impossible to hold the elections scheduled for August 10th. Obasanjo postponed elections due to lack of voter's lists, and set no date for a new vote.[3]

Obasanjo's People's Democratic Party, one of six registered to contest the local and national elections, was torn by a series of violent feuds among its local leaders. The Court of Appeals added to the confusion by annulling the rules of the Independent National Electoral Commission, the regulator of political parties. The court upheld an action brought by five union leaders, who argued that their exclusion from the elections was unconstitutional and designed to guarantee that only organizations backed by wealthy and powerful individuals could compete. The Nigerian Senate threw out a bill tabling a constitutional amendment which paved the way for a Obasanjo's third term. This act was greeted by shouts of approval from the Senate floor in Abuja.[4] Obasanjo accepted the decision, which should have eased tensions. Despite the president's acquiescence, Nigeria faced pre-election turbulence and politicians competed by exploiting ethnic and religious cleavages. Obasanjo's opponents expected him to take advantage of civil unrest as a pretext to maintain to his rule by declaring an emergency.[5]

Since Obasanjo's 1999 election Nigeria has experienced several outbreaks of religious conflict between Muslims and Christians and ethnic conflict between majority-minority groups, seeking the economic spoils of political power. In 2001, an estimated two thousand people died in Muslim-Christian clashes. During the 2002 campaign for national elections, Muslims were warned that the government would attempt to entrench civilian rule. In November 2002, riots swept the northern Nigerian city of Kaduna, leaving more than 200 people dead. As elections approached, these events underscored the myriad ethnic, religious and political tensions plaguing Africa's most populous state. This pattern of elite and communal instability is a legacy of British colonialism and nation-building which fused the northern and southern regions of empire, and created the nation-state called Nigeria. The political violence multiplied across the continent as Africa's 360,000,000 Christians, spread their faith to resist to the spread of Islamic *Sharia* law in Nigeria, Sudan, Chad and other states.[6]

More religious riots were triggered by a newspaper article in *ThisDay,* which suggested, that the Prophet Muhammad would have approved of the winner of the Miss World beauty pageant. The pageant was immediately moved to Paris. The Red Cross reported that 1450 persons were hospitalized and 13,000 were displaced during the rioting.[7] The local offices of *ThisDay* newspaper were burned. Christians launched reprisal attacks, after Muslim rioter's reportedly chanted anti-Miss World and Anti-American slogans, burned churches and vandalized vehicles with pro-*Sharia* graffiti. In Kaduna which has a large Christian population the Deeper Life Bible Church and the Redeemed Christian Church of God, typify a Christian fundamentalism that is ascendant in Nigerian social life. In February 2006, twenty people died in the south-eastern city of Onitsha, during an outbreak of religious conflict. The attacks were blamed on Christian mobs, after anti-Christian violence killed dozens and left thousands homeless, in the largely mainly Muslim populated north. This time, the violence, which accelerating the "clash of cultures," was linked to the publication of a Danish cartoon depicting the Prophet Mohammed. In 2002, the main market of the city of Jos was destroyed by fire and explosives following a religio-ethnic blood-bath between minority Hausa Muslims and Christians. According to both government officials and independent observers, over 3,000 people were killed in Jos and the outlying villages. The instability was heightened by President Obasanjo's defiant bid for an unconstitutional third term, which could possibly have resulted in more political violence, secessionist movement's, major refugee flows, a spillover of instability into neighboring states and, most importantly from the perspective of US intelligence chief, John Negroponte, a disruption in the US oil supply.

Given Nigeria's ethnic diversity, the status of women varies considerably. Among the Igbo, Yoruba and other southern Nigerian groups, women enjoy considerable control over their own affairs and exert considerable economic independence. In the Islamic north, Hausa women have considerably more freedom than their counterparts in the Middle East, but were not allowed to participate in politics until 1979. Nigerian women vote in equal numbers to men in most parts of the country.[8]

Several of Nigeria's northern states have introduced severe forms of *Sharia* law, involving punishment such as amputation for stealing and stoning for adultery. Islamic law is winning support from Muslim religious leaders and ordinary people, who see in Islam, an answer to their poverty and to crime. In Kaduna, the federal high court shares offices with the *Sharia* appeal court, reflecting the fragile coexistence of secular and Islamic law. *Sharia* provides an alternative to Nigeria's lack of law and order, the judicial void, deepening poverty and the state's failure to share the benefits of oil wealth with the people. Thus, the conflict between Islamist and secular politics finds its most virulent expression in cities with large populations of Muslims and Christians, such as Kaduna.

For many in Kaduna, the local elections reinforced their perceptions of a flawed political system. After years of military rule, voter turnout was low. Disillusioned voters complained of the widespread fraud and ballot-rigging during both the presidential elections and the gubernatorial elections held the previous year. European Union election monitors, reported that the polling was seriously flawed in Kaduna.

The controversy over local polls and political appointments is part of the fundamental paradox of Nigeria's attempt to adopt western-style civilian government. The relaxation of centralized military repression, facilitates state and local corruption and federal disintegration. Dozens were killed before and during local elections. Voting was delayed in three states and cancelled in others for fear of violence, shortages of ballots or other security problems.

Local elections are critical because of their economic significance and the potential for power that they represent. Under a 2002 Supreme Court ruling,

45 percent of oil revenues go directly to the 36 state governments and 774 local authorities. In 2003, the IMF estimated that Nigeria's national oil revenues would exceed $100 billion over the next five years.

Administrative Sclerosis

Jos, the sprawling capital city of Plateau state, is located in Nigeria's central zone. Famous for its rocky landscape, the city was once a popular tourist site. Plateau state was a major producer of groundnuts and cocoa. It is home has one of the Nigeria's most oversized bureaucracies. Jos, is known as the "civil service" state. Its largest employer is the state administration, which depends on its share of the revenues allocated by the federal government in Abuja. In Abuja, the streets indiscriminately bear the names of Nigeria's democrats and despots and the routines and habits of military rule are embedded in the bureaucracy. The federal allocation to Plateau state barely covers the bureaucratic costs and little if anything is left for health, education or for developing the infrastructure, which is so necessary to attract investment. With a population of only 3 million people, Jos has 18,000 civil servants. When state governor and accountant, Joshua Dariye, tried to reduce the size of state bureaucracy, he was forced to back off. Some blame unemployment for both the huge bureaucracy and for the outbreak of ethnic violence. "We haven't advanced at the pace we thought we would;" stated Andrew Gwaivangmin, manager of Rurcon, a rural services organization working with Christian churches. "Jos has grown through constant migration from the countryside. There are not a lot of jobs in rural areas. Either you're a teacher, or health personnel, or you work for the ministry of works."

Nigeria's fissiparous style of federalism has resulted in the exponential growth of administrative structures. "Initially this was quite manageable because quite a number of states were able to break even. But the increased demand for the creation of states became a more of a problem;" observed Silas Janfa, a former Plateau state senator. "Criteria were thrown to the dogs. Many state governments are incapacitated by foreign debt, charges for which are deducted from their federal allocations. Some of the states will end up only being able to pay salaries." At the time, civil servants in Plateau had not been paid. Former Aviation minister, Samuel Mafuyai observed that: "The public is aware that exclusive dependence on government will not bail us out." Mafuyai, who held several post in Plateau's state administration, noted that opportunities for generating income locally had been ignored because of over-dependence on revenues from the oil produced in the south.

Federalism was supposed to provide a solution to regional diversity, by striking a balance between federal and state power. Some argued, that without its federal structure, Nigeria would not have avoided another war and likely could have disintegrated politically. Instead, federalism gave license to steal to high-handed state governments living off federal handouts. States have a guaranteed share of influential jobs. Presidential cabinets must have at least one member from each state.[9] Even Ambassadorial nominations are based on state quotas. Thus, governors, taking precedence over federal ministers are very powerful and many are adept at self-promotion. For example, when Queen Elizabeth II paid a state visit to Nigeria in December 2004, although it was not on her itinerary, she visited the governor of the Delta state. Governors are less accountable to their tame elected state assemblies than Nigerian presidents are to the senate and national assembly. In some state assemblies, there is no opposition party. David Tukura, a University of Jos sociologist, compared Nigeria's governorships to African chieftaincies, relying on the on traditional "patron-client" relationships, but without all the traditional obligations of a chief. State politics often becomes bizarre as in July 2003, when the governor of the southeastern state of Anambra, was kidnapped in an attempted "civilian coup."

In 2002, some parliamentarians backed by a vote in the House of Representatives accused Obasanjo of "monumental inadequacies," and gave him two weeks to resign or face removal. Obasanjo, who had survived numerous attempts to impeach him, ignored the threat. This event raised fresh concerns about the country's political stability and the fate of landmark presidential and parliamentary elections scheduled for 2003.[10] The House motion accused him of ineptitude and a "persistent disrespect" for the rule of law. While admitting that efforts to improve financial transparency had failed, the government announced another widespread inquiry into official corruption. Farouk Lawan chairman of the House information committee, called the probe into the president's office by parliament and the judiciary as an "exercise in futility."

Soldiers have ruled Nigeria for most of its history. At the end of military rule in 1999, the dominant political actors were former soldiers or officials from the military era. President Obasanjo systematically purged the military leaving the country with an apolitical and loyal senior class of officers. This was quite an achievement, considering that none of Nigeria's successful coups were led exclusively by junior class officers. Better training and more officers' benefits reinforced the president's standing. This was particularly true of the Brigade of Guards, which is located behind the presidential village near, Abuja. "We are faring much better than when we were in government ourselves. The president understands soldiers. He was one himself;" said Brigadier Ganiyu Adewale, a member of the national military planning committee." Obasanjo's control of the military, like that of his political counterparts across the continent, was maintained through a network of agents who helped keep him one step ahead of coup plotters.

Analysts point to deeper institutional problems within Nigeria's estimated 70,000 strong military that may pose threats. There is inadequate funding to keep regular units in operational condition, and problems within the political system that threaten stability. "The political establishment is not aware or as aware as it should be of the level of decay in living conditions, lack of equipment and poor maintenance for soldiers;" said Nowa Omoigui, a lecturer at Abuja's elite Officers National War College.

Nigerian security sources admit that China has become one of their primary sources of military hardware. Vice-president, Atiku Abubakar, stated that the US had been too slow in helping to protect the oil-rich Niger Delta from the growing insurgency. He complained that talks with the US over security plans for the region did not "appear to be moving as fast as the situation is unfolding;" and that Nigeria was instead sourcing military equipment elsewhere. A Naval official said that Nigeria had; "felt let down" by the reluctance of the US military to offer more support and that dozens of patrol-boats to secure the swamps had been purchased from China. In addition, Nigeria made a $250 million deal with China to supply 12 fighter aircraft. Analyst reported that Nigeria wanted an additional 200 boats to patrol the Delta. According to a senior Nigerian security analyst, the US offered the Nigeria technical assistance and training, but only provided four old coastal patrol boats. Nigeria placed an order for 35 smaller high-speed patrol boats from a US company, but fewer than half were received.

Nigeria is one of nine African nations participating in the US-led, Trans-Sahara Counter-Terrorism Initiative. The TSCTI project is a $500 million seven-year initiative to help African countries ensure that radical extremist groups do not take root in the expansive uncontrolled areas of the Sahara and sub-Saharan Africa. In Tunisia, Algeria and Morocco, former Secretary of Defense, Donald Rumsfeld sought to establish counter-terrorism and military cooperation in the "war on terror." Other states, including Nigeria, Chad, Mali, Mauritius, Niger, and Senegal have joined this counter-terrorism initiative.

The US provides military financing to Tunisia and Morocco, but not to Algeria. Algeria refused to sign end-user agreements, designed to ensure the recipient does not provide the equipment to another country, as required by US law. US diplomats said that concerns over the level of corruption within the Nigerian security forces and the record of human rights violations, made them reluctant to supply more equipment. Walter Carrington, US ambassador to Nigeria from 1993 to 1997, said Chinese military sales to Nigeria reflected Beijing's desire to establish a greater economic foothold in Nigeria, and were not a threat to the US. "The Chinese moves in Nigeria are motivated more by their desire to have a secure source of oil than almost anything else;" Carrington observed. China insists that it did not use arms sales for diplomatic or political ends, but analysts note that Beijing has been willing to approve weapons shipments to almost any willing state buyer.[11] China sold the thousands of ten cent machetes to the Hutu who plotted genocide in Rwanda.

In May 2006, the Movement for the Emancipation of the Niger Delta (MEND), warned Chinese companies to "stay well clear" of the Niger Delta, or risk attack. The threat to Chinese companies and employees came a few days after China agreed to a $4 billion infrastructure investment, in exchange for preferential rights on four blocks, in an oil-field acreage auction.[12] It thus came as no surprise when, *Royal Dutch Shell* admitted that it had subcontracted work to companies run by MEND activists involved in the insurrection of 2003, that shut down 40 percent of the country's oil production. Industry analysts noted that sub-contracting work to local strong-men was but one method some oil companies used to buy off militants threatening attacks on oil facilities in the Delta. *Shell International* spokesperson, Caroline Wittgen, confirmed signing clandestine contracts with two firms, *Shad-Ro* services, which is run by Shadrack Otuaro, half-brother to Kingsley Otuaro, secretary-general of the Federated Niger Delta Ijaw Community (FNDIC), a group that targeted *Chevron* in 2003. The other company, IPPS is run by Messio German, an associate of Kingsley Otuaro and other FNDIC members. These contracts were worth as much as $100,000. *Chevron* abandoned its corporate policies on community relations because it had led to or added to the "causes of conflict among Delta state communities".[13]

The Oputa Panel, commissioned to model South Africa's Truth and Reconciliation Commission; recommended barring military rulers from contesting elections, but the Obasanjo government failed to implement any Oputa panel recommendations. Retired generals continued to meddle in politics, sometimes inflaming religious and ethnic tensions to maintain their footholds in national politics. What authorities called a security breach in 2003, turned out to be an alleged assassination plot, masterminded by Sani Abacha's former security chief, who had once incarcerated Obasanjo on charges of plotting a coup. The accused had gone to the Cote d'Ivoire and Togo to procure a Stinger missile, to shoot down the president's helicopter. Obasanjo had political enemies but according to Kayode Fayemi, who advised the government on security, the most likely threat was an assassination attempt not a regime changing coup d'état.

The labyrinth of bureaucracy, from the legislature to the ministry of defense, cut back on spending and on rehabilitating the armed forces. The decayed during the era of military rule. Recurrent costs represent more than 80 percent of the $400-500 million annual defense budget leaving little for investment in equipment. However, the Nigerian military's participation in peacekeeping missions in Liberia, Sierra Leone, and Sudan, helped to instill professionalism, within 4,000 officers corps performing markedly better than during Nigeria's earlier chaotic attempts at peacekeeping during the 1990s.[14]

'Come and Eat' Politics

Many prominent Nigerians point to the violence created by those with political protection. The acclaimed writer, Chinua Achebe, turned down a national honor in 2005 in protest of the Nigerian government's, "silence, if not connivance" regarding the problems in his home state. In a letter to Obasanjo, Achebe stated that Nigeria was "too dangerous for silence." In both *No Longer at Ease* and *A Man of the People*, Achebe examined corruption as an internal political conflict between norms of using power to help friends and relatives as opposed to playing the role of the attached bureaucrat and following colonial government regulations.

In October 2003, the Nigerian Senate Ethics Committee, held hearings on parliamentary corruption. Nasir el-Rufai, minister for the federal capital territory, was asked to explain why he had accused two unnamed senators of asking him to pay a N54 million (Naira) bribe, to ensure his confirmation. He made a detailed statement naming Ibrahim Mantu, deputy senate president, and Jonathan Zwingina, deputy leader of the ruling People's Democratic Party group in the senate. Both men denied the charges and a few days later the full senate voted unanimously to sweep the allegations 'under the carpet'. The accusations against public officials proliferated and numerous investigations were launched, but few cases made it to court and none resulted in conviction.

The government has announced a few high-profile prosecutions and launched initiatives on improved financial transparency, but most Nigerians do not believe that the political elite are serious about reducing the endemic graft of public and corporate life. Many Nigerians expressed dismay at how little President Obasanjo's first government did to change the culture of institutionalized corruption, which had built up over two decades of military-rule. Nigeria's political and social dilemma was succinctly described by Ishola Williams, vice-president of the Nigerian Transparency International: "We have a lot of people who are skeptical. Society itself must have a change of mentality to believe that corruption is bad."

President Obasanjo helped to found Nigeria's branch of Transparency International and established the Independent Corrupt Practices Commission, the flagship public-sector anti graft organization. In a 2003 TI survey on perceptions of corruption of more than 100 countries, Nigeria ranked second worst. The Independent Corrupt Practices Commission failed to secure a single conviction after investigating several state governors and parliamentarians. Its legal authority has been challenged by the judicial branch and there is the perception that senior officials, appointed by the president, only pursue cases which the president deemed politically expedient.

Senior officials pointed to the role that foreign governments and corporations played in perpetuating the corruption through financial regulation or direct involvement in bribery. In December 2003, three former ministers stood trial on charges of taking bribes from an agent of *Sagem*, the French electronics company. *Sagem* was alleged to have secured a $214 million contract as a result of bribery. *Sagem* officials refused to comment on the case, except to describe the detailed allegations as "rumors."

Nigerian government institutions are notorious for bribery. According to a widely-used shorthand, many unelected officials use their political positions as an opportunity to "come and eat." A commonly expressed concern is that corruption worsened after the 2002 elections. The end of centralized and authoritarian military government provided greater incentives to state and local officials to create personal fiefdoms. State and local governments now received 45 percent of national oil revenues, corporate taxes and customs duties. In other words, the opportunities for graft and corruption have been democratized. The creation of more states provides extra opportunities for contracts, corruption and patronage. Newspapers frequently publish full page advertisements congratulating governors on their good deeds. The deputy governor of Lagos state merited four pages of birthday wishes from his business friends, including fellow golfers. "May your life be showered with many holes-in-one," read one greeting. [15]

Obasanjo fired his minister of labor after he was arrested, along with two former internal affairs ministers, on bribery charges linked to an identity card contract. One former official observed: "If you're not corrupt people think you're from another planet. It might not be as brazen as it used to be but that does not mean corruption has been reduced."

Bequeathed a legacy of corruption at independence, both Nigeria's civilian and military leaders have used government as a means of personal enrichment. Cleintelism was a feature of almost all of Nigeria's pre-colonial traditions. It was based on a series of patron-client relations in which an individual of higher socio-economic status (patron) to protected one of lower status (client), who reciprocated by offering support and services to the patron. Nigerian popular culture is replete with stories of high-level misconduct. But, there is little empirical evidence on the degree to which market corruption has become an accepted part of Nigerian culture, but political corruption is widely condemned.

The scent of public corruption is palpable despite governmental promises to tackle the problem. Former finance minister, Ngozi Okonjo Iweala, said that Nigeria's attempts to tackle corruption in public life should be accompanied by greater efforts by wealthy nations to return stolen money. According to Iweala, limited governmental attempts to increase accountability at state and local levels met with resistance. Her decision to publish the government oil revenues proved popular with the Nigerian people, but unpopular with the political class, who faced awkward questions. Iweala is part of a small group of ministers and advisors who led Obasanjo's anti-corruption program. She announced plans to oversee audits of the notoriously opaque Nigerian National Petroleum Corporation (NNPC) and to publish more details on payments made to multinational oil companies and to the government. The plan was supported by the major oil companies. She claimed that the government was making progress on transparency through policies such as vetting public works contracts to ensure they were not inflated and that they offered value for money.

Some questioned how much scandalous revelation the political system could tolerate without internal backlash. Others, said Nigeria's battle against corruption had already been lost and that the government was only paying lip service to transparency. They pointed to the recently fired education minister, the ex-senate president and five legislators, who resigned over the alleged payment of $400,000 in bribes in order to win committee approval for an inflated departmental budget, as examples.

A March 2006 audit of Nigeria's oil industry, revealed a $325 million gap between what oil companies claimed to have paid the government and receipts acknowledged by the Nigerian Central Bank. Asked whether the graft was for the unaccounted millions, central bank governor, Charles Soludo, stated that he had no basis to reach that conclusion, and that all discrepancies would be fully investigated. "I believe that they are essentially accounting discrepancies and the reconciliation will show this."[16]

Such rampant corruption does not occur in a vacuum and could not flourish without international cooperation. *Halliburton*, the Houston-based oil services multinational, formerly run by Dick Cheney, disclosed that the Department of Justice had requested documents in the investigation into whether *TSKJ*-a construction consortium owned by *Technip, Halliburton,* and two other companies, paid bribes to win a huge construction project in Nigeria. *Halliburton* fired senior executive Albert 'Jack' Stanley and a consultant for receiving "improper personal benefits," in relation to the Nigerian project. The Securities and Exchange Commission launched a parallel investigation into *Technip* because the French company lists its shares on the New York and Paris Stock Exchanges. Former *Technip* executive, Georges Krammer, reportedly told French magistrate, Renaud Van Ruymbeke, that *TSKJ* operated a $180m slush fund to pay commissions to various officials and company executives involved in the Nigerian gas project. France's best known investigating magistrate, Judge Ruymbeke, had stumbled across the allegations while working on a series of corruption scandals involving the French oil company *Elf*. A former *TSKJ* executive, told him that the consortium operated a multi-million dollar offshore slush fund, to win a building contract on Nigeria's Bonny Island.

Halliburton acquired *TSKJ* in a 1998 takeover of *Dresser Industries*. Vice-president Cheney's office declined to comment on the investigation, referring the questions back to *Halliburton*. Under US law, Dick Cheney could have been forced to answer, whether or not, he knew, or should have known of the payoffs. In October 2005, the Securities and Exchange Commission subpoenaed documents from *Royal Dutch Shell*. This time, investigators had evidence in the form of hand written notes, discovered by *Halliburton,* which the company claimed, showed *TSKJ* had "considered payments" to Nigerian officials. According to the *Financial Times*, the language used in the notes strongly suggested that *TSKJ* officials were eager to conceal their plans.

The minutes of a December 1994 meeting of *TSKJ* executives, made explicit a concern that, companies based in Madeira, the offshore, remote-control headquarters where *TSKJ* is registered, "must be audited and creates difficulties concerning cultural agreements," they also describe, "significant financial action." The notes states that "all services" will cost the consortium $180 million with a further $60 million allocated to culture. An apparent

reference to a payment made to the consortium's London-based agent, Jeffrey Tesler, who the consortium had agreed to pay $60 million to finance his work toward winning the crucial first gas plant. Tesler, later won three more contracts worth $111.5 million to help the consortium win expansion projects. He denied using the money to pay bribes. However, in the notes, *TSKJ* partners, *KBR*, *Technip* of France, *Snamprogetti* an Italian company and *JGC* of Japan, discussed a series of possible "secret" and "open" agency payments. One proposal was rejected because it might leave the consortium open to blackmail. Another because it "sets up a wrong" paper trail". A paper trail leading to a December, 1993 "cultural meeting," listed seven people to "cover directly." Among the names listed as "already covered" were those of the gas plant directors Victoria Ihonde, Olutoyin Olakuri and Hamman Tukur. Below the note reads" "M" requested approval and commitment for $30 million for Sani Abacha, extra for Etiebet." The note does not say whether the proposals were agreed to or implemented. [17]
One can only speculate as to whom the mysterious "M" refers.

The British Exports Credits Guarantee Department (ECGD), investigated the bribes claims by asking four companies accused of paying $172 million in bribes, whether the allegations were true. According to ECGD memos, some of *Halliburton's* responses were misleading, or omitted crucial details. The documents raised questions about whether *MW Kellogg Ltd*, *Halliburton's* 55 percent owned subsidiary, was truthful in an application for more than $200 million worth of insurance funded by British taxpayers. The records reveal an unusual degree of coordination between ECGD and *Halliburton* over their responses to the bribery allegations. In confidential discussions, *Halliburton* claimed it would supply the ECGD with the "bare minimum" of information on the case in order to avoid the risk of the disclosures being "misconstrued by a third party." The ECGD accepted *Halliburton's* position, with the proviso, that it had an obligation to answer questions from the parliament.

In December 2002, the ECGD provided $215 million worth of trade insurance to *MW Kellogg* to expand a massive gas liquefaction plant in Nigeria. The project, which is partly funded by the Nigerian government, will cost more than $10 billion. About half the money has gone to a multinational building consortium owned by *Halliburton* and partners from Japan, France and Italy. In January 2005, authorities in the US, Nigeria and France began investigating allegations that the contracts were won with the help of bribes funneled through *LNG Servicios*, a Madeira-registered company, which is half owned by *MW Kellogg*.[18] *KBR*, the *Halliburton* subsidiary was investigated by the Britain's Serious Fraud Office (SFO) over its role in an alleged plot to pay more than $170 million in bribes in order to win billions of dollars of contracts, at a Nigerian gas plant.[19]

As in most countries with long records of governmental corruption and deceit, Nigerians increasingly question their moral obligation to pay taxes, which they feel, will be squandered or stolen by government officials. President Obasanjo fired housing minister Mobolaii Osomo for scheming to "surreptitiously" sell 207 prime properties in Lagos, valued at $100 million, to other senior government officials." Lower level officials, reportedly placed spiked studded planks or metal bars on the roads to block vehicles and levy duties on cars and their contents. Over the years, too many such stories have led many Nigerians to conclude that their taxation system is illegitimate.

In cities such as Lagos, Johannesburg and Nairobi, citizens are increasingly paying the price for their bad habits and for the lack of basic infrastructure. Around Nairobi gangs of men caught littering or urinating in public, are sentenced to labor on road gangs clearing litter and debris. Ironically, their punishment takes food out of the mouths of those who collect litter as a means of subsistence. In 1993, the Lagos state governor introduced a campaign known as the "Kick Against Indiscipline." The campaign uses mobile courtrooms and marshals in lime-green shirts to dispense instant justice to citizens who block drains, litter, or relieve themselves in public. "We are saving Lagosians from their own bad habits;" proclaimed Babatunde Ogungbamila, a government advisor. [20]

On the potholed streets of central Lagos, a building displays a poster of Governor Bola Tinubu, urging citizens of the city to pay their taxes. "Lagos has been kind to you. What do you give her in return?," it reads." This, was part of a five-year fiscal crackdown by state authorities and *Alpha-Beta Consulting*, a private company. Tax collection and fiscal policy are fundamental to the issue of African political and economic development. However, in Kenya, Nigeria as in other states, taxation has become the tool of freelance extortionists. Since the return to civilian rule in 1999, *Alpha-Beta* purports to have helped increase Lagos' state tax base from 600 million naira, to more than 3 billion Naira per month. This is only a fraction of taxes due. Almost half a million, of the five million Lagosians, pay no taxes at all. Of the 300,000 companies in Lagos, only 25,000 make pay as you earn tax payments on behalf of their employees, and only 5000 pay their taxes in full. Corrupt tax collectors present taxpayers checks to bank workers who cash them. A popular trick is to get taxpayers to make tax payments to accounts that had similar sounding names to those of the Lagos State Board of Internal Revenue. These accounts are controlled by con men. To prevent fraudulent collusion between tax officials from the Nigeria's collapsing bureaucracy; *Alpha-Beta* instituted more sophisticated collection methods, such as an online reporting system between tax authorities and the banks. There are plans for a system of individual electronic smartcards to store taxpayer information.

From Abidjan to Nairobi, few urban dwelling Africans see evidence of public spending on the city's open sewers, garbage dumps, potholed roads, collapsing schools, waterless hospitals or collapsed rail lines. "The citizen is to be kind to Lagos by paying tax," says David Apara, deputy managing director of *Alpha-Beta*. Lagos state's finance commissioner, Adebayo Adewusi, claimed conditions were improving and dismissed the idea that people are justified in not paying their taxes. "Is it the egg or the chicken?"

he asked. "In my own understanding, nobody could legitimately claim the time when you see the benefits from the government is time when you honor your tax."

In August 2002, the Nigerian press launched a series of full-page advertisements on the behalf of the victims of an alleged $190 million international fraud and money laundering operation in Brazil. *Peters & Peters*, an international law firm acting for the plaintiffs, said its clients arranged to have the advertisement appear in the Nigerian newspapers in order to serve notice on defendants who refused to comply with court demands This well known *modus operandi,* is familiar to international entrepreneurs who are the target of similar "419" scams, named after the sections of Nigerian criminal code that deals with this type of fraud. They involve e-mail messages promising large fiscal returns, in exchange for providing seed money to either invest in a corrupt deal, or to help transfer stolen of money out of Nigeria.[21] Former shareholders of *Banco Noroeste*, a Brazilian bank, had used the newspapers to publicize a British court judgment that they should be paid $150 million over a deception allegedly perpetrated by a Nigerian businessman and his wife.

Responding to investor litigation after Spain's *Santander Group* purchased *Banco Noroeste,* and the alleged misappropriation of $242 million; Nigerian judge, Jacob outlined how the most of the stolen money was allegedly removed from *Banco Noroeste* via payments from the bank's Cayman Island branch. Nelson Sakaguchi, a former official of the bank, now imprisoned in Switzerland, authorized the transfer. The shareholders presented into evidence a series of letters sent to Sakaguchi between 1995 and 1998, that he falsely claimed to be from the Central Bank of Nigeria and other government ministries. They claimed the letters, which offered a series of investment opportunities in projects such as airport construction, were part of an "advance fee" offering large returns in exchange for low down payments. The Sakaguchi case was just the tip of an iceberg of fraud perpetrated by a type of notorious con artist that has damaged Nigeria's reputation and image. "No one can doubt, looking at the detailed documents here, of the existence of a sophisticated money laundering operation;" wrote Justice Jacob. "Every individual who received that money must have known that their receipt was illegitimate."[22]

The Nigerian House of Representatives debate focused on a devastating report prepared by the public accounts committee, which scrutinized the nations budgeting and public spending since the 1999 election. The committee claimed government spending had breached constitutional rules and contributed to a "virtual slide into financial anarchy." A specific discrepancy between N40.7 billion ($340 million), stolen by Sani Abacha, and officially recovered, and the N29 billion recorded in the budget as revenue. It painted a gloomy prospect for the country's ability to develop its human resources and infrastructure and makes it equally impossible to plan for investment in Nigeria. In June 2002, the Obasanjo government asked the

Blair government to help track down up to $5 billion thought to been stolen by Sani Abacha. It sought bank statements and other evidence to trace the funds laundered through British banks. Three years later, the UK had not provided the documents, claiming that further clarification was required on technical guidelines that were ruled irrelevant by courts in Britain, Switzerland, Luxembourg, Liechtenstein and New Jersey.

In June 2004, the Nigerian senate voted to debate in secret, allegations that the government mismanaged finances, including $100 million in stolen money recovered from the family of Sani Abacha. Nigeria had threatened legal action against the UK unless it returned with interest, £3 million ($5 million), allegedly stolen from the central bank. This was a small fraction of the billions of dollars thought to have been plundered by Abacha. The money was seized in 1998 from Nigerian businessman, Alhaji Dauran at Heathrow airport. The UK Treasury seized the money after the customs service argued it was probably the proceeds of drug trafficking. However, the Nigerian government contended that Daura, who arrived at Heathrow on a private jet carrying three suitcases full of cash, was a self-confessed courier for President Abacha, who had transferred $110 million from the Central Bank of Nigeria into British banks.

The Nigerian government requested urgent talk's with UK Minister of Exchequer Gordon Brown, to discuss the return of the money with interest. The *Financial Times* obtained a copy of the letter to Brown which read: "If a solution is not found by October 2003, I very much regret to say I am instructed to commence court proceedings." The UK Treasury declined to comment, but the threat of legal action strained Nigerian-UK relations. Tony Blair's government pressed African nations to tackle corruption and boasted of the UK's "leading role" in efforts to stop the laundering of stolen money through western banks. But Nigerian officials complained of little help from Britain in their efforts to retrieve the money. British lawyers representing for the Nigerian government are also trying to trace $2.1 billion that passed through British banks, of which $50 million remains frozen in the UK, and the larger amount believed to be held in the Channel Islands.

The British government was harshly criticized for its "lack of political will at the highest levels to take a lead in fighting global corruption." A March 2006 report, by the Africa all-party parliamentary group, found that UK government action fell short of the goals set by Prime Minister Blair's Commission for Africa, which emphasized the need for greater transparency to fight corruption. "It is disappointing that we are failing to take the lead on some anti-corruption commitments," the report stated. According to the Commission's report, about $150 billion leaves Africa annually in illicit proceeds. This is equivalent to almost a quarter of the continent's gross domestic product. It is many times more than the amount Africa receives in aid and debt relief. The report recommended that Blair appoint an "anti-corruption champion," and urged the UK to update current laws, which date to 1916. It also called for sanctions barring convicted companies from procuring public of contracts, if there is overwhelming evidence of corruption. The World Bank's list of 213 companies that have been disqualified for breaching procurement and guidelines includes 39 from England.[23]

Frustrated by Britain's apparent refusal to cooperate, Enrico Monfrini, a Swiss lawyer acting on behalf of Nigeria, said: "The British authorities have not yet complied with their undertaking to grant assistance to Nigeria." Eager to rehabilitate their image in wake of their legal conflicts with holocaust survivors, Swiss Bankers and officials are eager to demonstrate determination to tackle money laundering and illegal transfers. Laws have been implemented requiring banks to determine the origins of large deposits. One Nigerian Federal Office of Justice official remarked: "Switzerland will be the first country in which Abacha funds were deposited to return these assets to Nigeria on an official decision."

Nigeria continued to seek restitution of the estimated $50 million in stolen in UK banks through civil courts. "In terms of mutual assistance in criminal matters we decided not to waste any more time and money." Obasanjo's advisor, Oby Ezekwesili explained; "We hope the likes of Britain and other countries look at the Swiss as an example of what they ought to be doing. They have seen how quickly some of the red tape can be dismissed in order to bring this thing into resolution." Discouraged but undeterred, the Nigerian government now seeks to repatriate funds held in more cooperative countries. The value of Swiss investment linked to the Abacha regime is about $550 million. Investigators estimate that as much as $800 million passed through UK-based banks, "the fate of which no one knows;" said Monfrini.

After rejecting an appeal by the Abacha family in February 2005, The Swiss Supreme Court removed the last obstacle to unfreeze and return most of the stolen assets. The court ruled that $458 million could be transferred to the Nigerian government without the latter having to go through the bureaucracy of a confiscation order. A further $40 million would remain frozen in Switzerland. The court believes that the funds were "probably of criminal origin," leaving it up to the Abacha family to prove differently. Failure by the family to prove differently would result in the return of the money to Nigeria. According to the court, a remaining $7 million which was "only probably" of criminal origin, would be transferred to an escrow account in Nigeria. The government announced that it had reached an agreement with the Abacha family to return $40 million and allowing them to keep $100 million of disputed funds.

Anti-corruption activists feared that despite strong rhetoric from government officials, transparency efforts were being undermined as senior politicians built their campaign war chests for the forthcoming national elections. Reflecting Obasanjo's efforts to improve transparency in the hydrocarbons sector, in October 2006, Nigeria's senior anti-corruption minister, Nuhu Ribadu, announced an investigation into the sale of oil acreage offered in open auction, but sold under the table. Petroleum ministry officials failed to explain how the block was awarded to *Starcrest*, a company with no proven track record in the oil industry, but with strong political connections. *Starcrest* privately negotiated control of the block after the bidding was closed in May, 2006. [24]

Another glaring example of mismanagement, was the $13 million interest-free loan made to the police force of Ghana; while Nigeria's police went on strike over unpaid entitlements. Oby Ezekwesili, special advisor to the president, called the public accounts committee a product of "grandstanding" by political opponents and that the anti-corruption drive resulted in setting up a team that vetted all large expenditures to ensure they were legitimate. Obasanjo clashed with parliament after it voted to add N250 billion of spending to the budget, bringing the total to N1065. The dispute between the committee and president reflected tension over the balance of power between the executive and legislative branches of government. Dome Duo Dome, chairman of the senate appropriations committee and the presidents People's Democratic Party, publicly criticized Obasanjo for portraying the senate as 'irresponsible and spendthrift'. The much criticized anti-corruption campaign became even more surreal when it was revealed that President Obasanjo grew giant rats to supplement his income. Obasanjo's rat farming came to epitomize corruption of Nigeria's political elite.

In September 2004, Joshua Dariye, Governor of the Plateau state, was arrested in a London hotel carrying more than $175,000). The Dariye episode began with the release of a dossier the day before he resumed power in Plateau. The accusations followed investigations by Nigerian and British law enforcement for money laundering. Despite evidence that members of his family lived there, Dariye told British police that the £395,000 London apartment he was accused of owning, belonged to a friend. But, he turned up at the apartment during the raid. According to the dossier, the stalled investigation of Dariye, was part of a clumsy cover-up, emblematic of the civilian government's failure to implement anti-graft measures. Koyode Fayemi, director of the Centre for Democracy and Development, explained: "This is what you get when you undergo transition without transformation. You had a pact between a departing military that didn't want to be disgraced and incoming political elite that wasn't interested in change."

The negative publicity forced President Obasanjo's advisor to declare his N30 million ($230,000) income a month, earned from a farm raising ostriches and the giant rodents known as "grass cutters." In December 2005, Governor Diepreye Alamaieyeseigha, of Nigeria's oil-producing Baylesa state, was arrested on money-laundering charges after his immunity was removed and he was impeached. The central government was forced to deploy hundreds of troops to prevent violent protests.

A few days before Queen Elizabeth opened the Commonwealth Heads of Government Summit in Nigeria, Human Rights Watch issued a scathing report detailing a series of attacks on activists and journalists by government security services. Presidential spokesman, Remi Oyo, responded angrily and dismissed the document as an attempt to "precipitate discord within the distinguished gathering and to cast undeserved aspersion on the integrity of the Nigerian government and its people." The meeting of former British colonies underscored Nigeria's precarious status in the community. On one hand, the country's diplomatic status and its record on human rights had improved since the brutal era of Sani Abacha. On the other hand, Human Rights Watch alleged abuses such as the shooting of at least 12 people, during July 2004 fuel price protests, and the torture of activists protesting the visit of George W. Bush that same month. "African and western governments alike have a responsibility to use their political and economic alliances with Nigeria to push for improvements. Their message should be clear: end impunity for human rights abuses and initiate reforms that will ensure genuine and long-lasting democracy in Nigeria;" wrote Carina Tertsakian, author of the Human Rights Report.

Professionalism among the Nigerian security forces is also controversial. Under Obasanjo, the size of the police force doubled within three years. According to a 2005 report by the US Department of State; "National police, army, and other security forces committed extra-judicial killings or used excessive force to apprehend criminals and disperse protestors." The army is accused of killing hundreds of civilians in the states of Bayelsa and Benue. Many ordinary Nigerians report instances of police brutality daily. Shehu Sani, a leading activist imprisoned by General Abacha, said that there had been "significant improvement" of human rights and he accused western countries of failing to ensure that the government's emphasis on increasing security was matched with safeguards against the abuse of power. Western nations are focused on Nigeria's strategic importance as Africa's largest oil producer. "That's why they are not really clamping down on the Nigerian government on human rights;" he observed. The military is not a cohesive interest, but it plays a major role in national politics. Many ranking officers enriched themselves during military rule, but lower ranking officers saw no direct benefit. The country's ethnic divisions are reflected in the military, although competition is based upon well ingrained-professionalism.

Abubakar Siddique Mohammed, a political scientist at Ahmadu Bello University, stated that the human rights situation in the country in areas such as political freedom, is "far far better" than under the military and that Nigeria's critics sometimes exaggerate the problems. He noted that the most problematic issue is the breakdown of law and order in the south, where aspiring politicians have gangs of thugs to enforce their claims to office.[25]

Security analysts report that the Nigerian military is riddled with corruption and not sufficiently disciplined to protect the petroleum industry or the local communities. Police employed by the Nigerian state to protect the oil facilities, often receive their salaries and perks from the oil companies. "They take on the character of mercenaries who are protecting companies that are seen as despoiling the environment," explained Nowa Omoigui, a lecturer at the National War College.

Petro–Politics

Nigeria has 160,000 billion cubic feet of natural gas reserves, the equivalent of about 27 billion barrels of oil, making it the world's seventh largest oil exporter and the source of 10 percent of all US crude oil imports. Moreover, much of the country has not been geologically explored. "If you actually began exploring for gas you would find a hell of a lot more;" stated Andrew Jamieson, the managing director of Nigeria Liquefied Natural Gas. However, unlike other oil producing states, the per capita income of Nigeria has declined by an average of 1.5 percent per year over the past 25 years. A decade ago, at least $3 billion of oil revenue windfalls reportedly disappeared from state reserves. Anti-graft campaigners argued that the corrupt ruling class enjoys enjoy near criminal impunity. Oil prices ensure an income of about $2 billion of petrodollars per month. Outside of the oil sector, the Nigerian economy remains poorly developed and is heavily dependent on imports. Thus, spending by both business and consumers creates a demand for hard currency, the dollar. In November 2003, the Nigerian Central Bank sold $729 million in foreign exchange at auction, while holding $7.36 billion in reserves. This was just enough to cover about six months worth of imports.

In November 2003, the head of the Nigerian National Petroleum Corporation, Funsho Kupolokun, announced an aggressive policy of market deregulation and improved transparency. A former special assistant to Obasanjo, Kupolokun said he expected OPEC to offer Nigeria a higher quota reflecting the expected increase in the country's production capacity from the 2.75 million barrels per day (bpd) to 4.1 million bpd by 2007. This was part of a bid to attract greater foreign and domestic investment and to alleviate concerns about corruption. However, the government's deregulation attempt generated political controversy that only served to deter interest in the country's decrepit refineries. Kupolokun announced the government would try to sell a 51 percent stake in the country's first four refineries within a year. He denied that the country's finances were opaque and admitted there was an "information gap" and promised that publication of improved NNPC accounts would appear by the spring of 2004.

That October, Nigerian workers began a four-day strike over rising fuel prices alarming global petroleum markets and accenting the challenge to the government's economic reform program. Fuel prices in Nigeria have risen at regular intervals since government deregulation and the removal of state subsidies. Impoverished Nigerians see petroleum subsidies as the only social benefit offered to them in a country where most social services and the infrastructure have collapsed. The October strike was triggered by a petroleum price increase of about 25 cent to N55 (42 cents) per liter. Many businesses capital, Abuja and Lagos, the main commercial center, were closed in response to a call from the umbrella Nigeria Labour Congress Union Movement.

Obasanjo invited labor several leaders to join a 33-member committee, established to mitigate the impact of rising petroleum prices. The committee of ministers, officials and union leaders was to "bring about short-term relief and medium-term positive impact, on the effects of high oil prices." It was a key part of Obasanjo's economic policy put to together a small group of technocrats led by Ngozi Okonjo Iweala, the finance member and a former vice president of the World Bank. The International Monetary Fund, The Paris Club and western governments greeted the news with enthusiasm.

Under pressure from The Paris Club creditors to increase payments on the country's $34 billion foreign debt, Nigeria was scheduled to pay $1 billion of the $2.2 billion due for debt servicing. With amounts overdue, the amount due increased to $5 billion in 2005. "How can we pay that?" finance minister Iweala inquired; while arguing that lenders should extend HIPC debt relief to Nigeria. The Paris Club, is comprised of western creditor nations and held more than 80 percent of Nigeria's debt. This provides it with great deal of input into Nigerian oil policy. "Now they want to get the little money we have and take it also for themselves;" Iweala complained.

Despite projected windfall revenues, in October 2004, Iweala announced a decline in oil prices. She said the government was not happy about high crude oil prices because the country had to import most of its refined oil products. "Right now the government is not very popular. They're hitting us from all angles. We'd like to see the price of oil come down: It's not in our interest over a long period of time to have these prices because people will start looking for alternative sources, and that has ramifications for us," she said the government was doing all it could to settle the conflict with the "thugs" in the Niger Delta, and warned against overreacting to strikes over the governments oil policy, which she called "part of a functioning democracy." Iweala vehemently insisted that windfall oil revenues would be used to build essential infrastructure, rather than to accelerate debt payment to the IMF and the Paris Club.

The Central Bank warned that the fall of the Naira against the US dollar signaled that heavy government spending threatened to further destabilize the economy. In November 2003, on the *Reuters* inter-bank exchange, the Naira rate fell to 149:1 against the dollar. The Naira also fell on Nigeria's black market. Analysts blamed the strong demand for dollars on federal, state and local government spending. Also blamed were the special funds allocated to supplementary budgets for international events such as the All Africa games, and the Commonwealth heads of state meeting.

In October 2005, international creditors agreed to write off $18 billion in Nigerian debt. The debt relief deal between Nigeria and The Paris Club committed Nigeria to repay the remaining $31 billion in bilateral debts to rich countries from that years soaring oil revenues. Drawing on windfall profits from crude oil exports, Nigeria agreed to immediately contribute $12.4 billion in arrears to the UK. The agreement freed Nigeria from a staggering debt burden and from $1 billion in debt service payments. The Paris Club's debt relief plan for Nigeria was separate from that agreed to by leaders at the G8 meeting in Scotland that July.[26] Iweala argued that Nigeria might not have another such a debt-relief opportunity stating; "We think it's a good use of the money. Nigeria saved almost $12 billion from higher than expected oil prices." She said the additional resources would go towards poverty reduction and enable Nigeria to increase the number of children attending school by 3.5 million. It would reduce Nigeria's risk premium, encourage investors and improve the country's international image.

Determined to privatize many state industries by 2007, vice president, Atiku Abubakar, told the *Financial Times* that the government had the commitment and the political will to press ahead with privatization in the power, oil, gas, telecommunications and petrochemical industries. He stated his intentions to play a "very central" role in the economic reform program, aimed at stimulating the private sector, diversifying the oil-dependent economy, and improving governance standards. Extra oil revenues would not be used to finance the deficit which was projected at two percent of gross domestic product. Nigeria's decision to raise government spending by a quarter in 2004 exemplified how much the impact of high oil prices confounds international plans to cut poverty in Africa. The draft budget, introduced as part of an economic program, was supported by domestic economists and western governments but opposed by corrupt interests and by some unions.

War in the Delta

The man who began 2005 serving as Nigeria's chief law enforcement officer, appeared handcuffed in court four months later, on a 70-count charge of theft and money laundering. In that same two week period, two cabinet ministers and the president of the senate were fired over similar allegations. Ironically, petroleum riches were fueling the Nigerian elite conflict that threatened to disrupt the oil industry. Nigerian militia leader and bush warlord, Alhaji Mujahadid Dokubo-Asari, unnerved international oil markets with threats and military strike activities.

In the fall of 2005, more than 100 armed Nigerians stormed a *Chevron* oil production platform in the Niger Delta. *Chevron* was forced to close the facility. It was but one episode in the political crisis brewing in the world's eighth largest oil exporting state. In January 2006, the Movement for the Emancipation of the Niger Delta (MEND) kidnapped four *Shell* contract workers (American, British, Bulgarian and Honduran), from an offshore oilfield and held them for 19 days. A MEND spokesman said the hostages were released on "humanitarian grounds." An e-mail believed to be from a MEND representative, said the group would ensure a "February target of a 30 percent reduction in Nigeria's oil capacity."

Dokubo-Asari and his militia, siphon off hundreds of pipeline barrels of crude, refine and sell it cheaply to the local people. "As far as we are concerned, it's the Nigerian state that is stealing oil... Most of the villages in my area have been devastated, it makes me concerned that my people have suffered so much pain because of me," Dokubu-Asari explained. He warned foreigners to leave the oil producing Niger Delta and threatened to start an offensive known as "Operation Locust Feast." He responded series military attacks by the government by issuing a statement condemning the government, threatening that action would start the following day. He further warned that he could not be held responsible for the safety of foreigners in the Delta after the launch of "Operation Locust Feast," and that he would not attack oil installations because of the pollution risks. A former supporter of the Obasanjo regime, Dokubo-Asari added to his populist credentials by presenting himself as an enemy of the state. He claims to have excellent political connections and he articulates widespread and popular grievances. His rhetoric reminds his listeners of their humiliation and of the arrogance of the 1914 British colonialists, who deviously fused together north and south and created Nigeria. Like leaders in other regions, Dokubo-Asari wants a "sovereign national conference" to determine whether Nigeria should remain a single nation, or split up. "Our fathers signed a treaty of protection with Britain. We never bargained for Nigeria;" he once declared.

A convert to Islam, Dokubo-Asari purportedly trained in Libya with Charles Taylor, Liberia's former warlord-president. His campaign is for the self-determination and control over regional resources for the fourteen million impoverished Ijaw people, the Delta's largest ethnic group. Opinions vary over whether Dokubo-Asari is an opportunistic gangster or an idealistic freedom fighter. His political visibility illuminates serious flaws in the Niger-Delta's governance and Nigerian system civilian rule. Minister of Information, Magnus Abe, said the events were part of a long dispute between former criminal allies. Dokubo-Asari is wanted over the gangland killings that resulted in the death of Ateke Tom. Dokubo-Asari claims that Ateke Tom, another political outlaw, hired the government to hunt him down and kill him. The information minister declined to say whether he echoed the accusations by other observers, but that both men profited from oil theft. Some saw Magnus Abe's resistance, as symptomatic of a multi-layered saga of mass poverty resulting from the inevitable mixture of economics, crime and politics.

The unfolding war in the Delta has its roots in the linkages and previous relationships between the various political parties involved; including the government of River state and Ateke Tom, Dokubo-Asari's rival warlord. Local activists believe the militias were armed with guns and machetes by ambitious politicians prior to elections; which Peter Odili, state governor, and President Obasanjo won with 90 per cent of the vote. Dokubo-Asari claimed to have at least 2000 fighters and wide popular support in networks of militia camps and communities around the Delta's creeks. Dokubo-Asari was an ally of Peter Odili, but clashed with him over ballot-rigging during the elections. Given the remoteness of the terrain, these claims were difficult to verify. In response to the escalating violence, the government established a military taskforce known as "Operation Flush Out Tree." Amnesty International reported that possibly, as many as 500 people were killed in the region during September of 2003. *Royal Dutch Shell* commissioned consultants to compare the Delta's level of violence to that in Chechnya and Colombia. Fighting broke out in Warri, a major city in the Niger Delta, between the Ijaw and Itsekiri ethnic groups. Dozens were killed and 4,000 people were internally displaced.

Royal Dutch Shell is involved in a reputation damaging conflict in the Ogoni region of southern Nigeria. The wellheads of the oil conglomerate continue to leak, emitting an ominous hissing sound from the branching pipes and valves. The local population calls the imposing tall metal structures Christmas trees. They complain that a 1993 spill destroyed their crops. *Shell* stopped production output from the Ogoni region amid protest over pollution and the absence of benefits to the local population from the oil wealth. The corporate ethical and economic challenge was reflected in an internally-commissioned *Shell* report which concluded that the conflict could force it to abandon onshore production in Nigeria by 2008. *Shell* resisted providing essential maintenance for the trans-Niger pipeline, which carries 185,000 barrels of crude per day. After problems with tampering, the company stationed members of Nigeria's paramilitary mobile police known as the "kill and go" to guard its facilities.

Royal Dutch Shell, the first and the largest oil company in Nigeria, is accused of decades of environmental degradation in the Niger Delta. Diepreye Alamieyei-Seigha, the governor of Bayelsa state, blamed environmental damage for the violence and unrest among local youth and accused *Shell* and the other oil companies of insensitivity. In a critical indictment of *Shell,* two Nigerian environmental activists, Ike Okonta and Oronto Douglas, charged the company with "negligence and cynical indifference," and they called for a boycott of Nigerian oil. In their book, *Where Vultures Feast*, they write that the producing oil communities saw *Shell* as "the number one culprit in the economic war currently being waged against them." "The general complaint," the authors note; "is one of broken promises, development assistance programs that are abandoned halfway, and poor quality facilities, that break down and simply rust away as soon as they are installed." They accused the company of playing a "key role" in the trial of writer, Nobel Prize winner and the leader of the Movement for the Survival of the Ogoni People, Ken Saro-Wiwa who, along with eight others, was hanged by Sani Abacha in 1995 after they mobilized protests among the Ogoni people of Rivers state.

These executions led to Nigeria's suspension from the British Commonwealth in 1999. *Royal Dutch Shell* pointed to its commitment to mitigating the environmental impact of its operations and offered to support the 1500 communities affected. Its local support programs includes infrastructural projects such as: health centers, schools, roads, electricity, drinking water as well as occupational training in plumbing, bee keeping, hairdressing and snail farming. However, *Shell Petroleum Development Company* (SPDC), the joint venture in which *Shell* is the leading multinational partner, insisted that it could not perform the functions of government in the region.

Because of the spread of its onshore operations, with more than 1,000 oil wells and 6,200 kilometers of pipeline, *SPDC* is more exposed than the other five Nigerian oil production ventures to what it calls "community incidents." According to *SPDC's* 2002 business review, there were 282 such incidents, primarily disturbances at new construction projects. The damage in terms of deferred production was estimated at 40 million barrels. There were an estimated thirty-four cases of organized theft of another 6 million barrels. There were 24 hostage takings and 18 gunshot victims were treated in *SPCD* hospitals. The company complained that its community development programs were "obstructed by certain negative attitudinal challenges of the host communities, which threatened the operational environment." In addition, frequent demands for cash payments by young militants not only instigated general communal strike, but provided an easy source of funds for recurring armed conflicts.

A 2004 Human Rights Watch report dealing with inter-ethnic conflict in the Delta state, identified competition for government funds as one of the causes of violence. The report found the violence was driven by disputes over the control of oil theft, which it described as "effectively Nigeria's most profitable private business." Moreover, the practice of clandestine oil siphoning, known as "illegal bunkering," involves "significant criminal syndicates." So called "harvesters" use sophisticated engineering equipment to tap into pipelines and some lay their own buried pipelines. In addition to oil thieves, "flowline harvesters" dig up pipelines and sell them for scrap. The siphoned oil is transported by barges and transferred to coastal tankers. "Revenues are then recycled into arms in the Delta to fan local conflicts;" said Chris Finlayson, *SPDC* chairman and managing director. The theft can be tracked by aerial surveillance and by monitoring pipeline pressure. But it is harder to detect when thieves siphon the oil off at a slow rate.[27] Hundreds were killed in a fuel pipeline explosion in May 2006. In December that same year, over 500 Lagosians were burned to death as they were scooping spilled fuel, after a vandalized fuel pipeline exploded. Fuel pipeline explosions are relatively common, and the nation's oil riches are frequently a deadly curse for its impoverished masses. President Obasanjo, who doubled as oil minister, admitted that his government had done little to improve the daily lives of his people.[28]

The aggressive government reaction to MEND, angered local people linked to the Movement for the Survival of the Ogoni People (MOSOP). They accused the paramilitary police of brutality and said that *Shell's* pipeline cleaning was likely to cause more pollution of the surrounding land. There are complaints about the clean up efforts of *Casella,* the UK contractor employed by *Shell* to clean a spill in K-Dere village, of the Ogoni region.

Reportedly, the earth and reeds in the area remain blackened and a large pools glint with the iridescence of petroleum. Many MOSOP supporters claim to have been assaulted by members of a gang organized by Chief Fabian Gberesu, K-Dere's hereditary ruler.

Casella abandoned the clean up project in January 2004, following a dispute with Chief Fabian Gberesu. MOSOP president, Ledum Mitee, claimed that *Shell* made inappropriate payments to Chief Fabian that are which contributed to conflict between Fabian and members of the community opposed to *Shell's and Casella's* plans. Accusations against *Shell* have resonance and include allegations of oil spills, security police brutality, improper payments to local leaders, and charges that foreign oil companies are failing to respond to criticism of their activities in Nigeria and elsewhere in Africa. Jerry Ellison, technical manager of *Casella's* Nigerian subsidiary, stated that the company paid 450, 000 Naira ($3,360) for a car given as a gift to Chief Fabian and money for wider local development programs in education and health. Chief Fabian's car was firebombed and several MOSOP supporters were charged and arrested. Fabian claimed he was being persecuted by MOSOP and suggested that the reporters should replace his burned vehicle, which he also claimed to have purchased with his own money.

Casella reportedly gave Fabian a further 100, 000 Naira while bidding for community approval of the clean-up contract, which Ellison claimed, was below the 150, 000 Naira "homage payment" that it routinely makes to local leaders and much less than others pay. The company gave N100, 000 to refurbish toilets at the chief's palace that Ellison said are community property and now have "the deepest septic tanks in the world." Chief Fabian also asked for a helicopter but "not in such a way as we took him seriously." Ellison noted that *Casella's* payments should be seen as public relations and part of the contract deal rather than as bribes. "If you want to stay in business you have got to pay." *Shell* admits that it told *Casella* to stay out of K-Dere, after it saw signs of trouble in the community, but gave the company a job elsewhere. *Casella* said it wanted to complete the project and that it would be a welcomed provider of needed equipment and trade in a community that has had few opportunities since *Shell's* departure. In an interview with the *Financial Times,* Chief Fabian declined to answer questions about his dealings with *Casella* until he was provided with alcohol and N100, 000 which he described as a "palace fee" for his community.

In October 2005, the oil companies were forced to pay attention after MEND threatened to attack oil facilities in response to the arrest of Dokubu-Asari on charges of treason. Boatloads of insurgents forced the closure of *Chevron* operations, costing the company an estimated 28,000 barrels per day, about one percent of national output. The company closed a flow station as a precaution and *Shell* evacuated part of its staff from flow stations and at a gas plant as a precautionary measure.

Dokubu-Asari's arrest reignited violence in the Delta, where many believe they have been cheated out of their share of the national wealth. The Niger Delta People's Volunteer Force (NDPVF) issued a statement threatening to "kill every iota of oil operations in the Niger Delta if Mujahid Dokubu-Asari was not released within 48 hours." His Ijaw troops, who battled government forces from bases along the river, eventually agreed to disarm in return for amnesty. Although previous NDPVF threats had not been executed, some feared that Dokubu-Asari's militia could splinter into uncontrolled groups if he were detained too long. "The arrest doesn't look like a stabilizing act, and has got the company quite worried;" observed a western diplomat.[29]

In November 2004, the Nigerian House of Assembly was firebombed in the eastern state of Anambra. Sessions were resumed in the ruins of bare walls and a caved in roof. "It is now a lawless country. We are now in a state of anarchy;" bewailed Anambra assembly speaker, Chike Balonwu. The Anambra legislature was destroyed during three days of targeted violence in Akwa, the state capitol. The attackers ransacked several government buildings including the Government House, the judicial headquarters and the headquarters of the Independent Peoples Democratic Party governor. Anambrans inside and outside the government blamed the violence on supporters of Chris Uba, a powerful businessman and backer turned enemy of Chris Ngige, the state's governor. Chris Ngige's supporters claimed he was being punished for resisting Chris Uba's attempt to control political appointments.

As in other Nigerian conflicts, the Anambra situation underscored the absence of national political legitimacy stemming from the 2003 elections. In Anambra, and at least another 26 states, European Union observers said the polls were seriously undermined by ballot fraud and intimidation. Ngige's critics accused him of failing to respond to accusations of deal-making to secure Uba's backing. Obasanjo distanced himself by refusing to support governor Ngige. Obansanjo wrote that he was "horrified" when the Anambra governor admitted privately that the poll was fixed and that the governor and his two rivals were like two armed robbers who conspired to loot a house and then disagreed. Some of his own party members pointed to the hypocrisy noting that Obasanjo benefited from the election fraud which resulted in a government landslide. For many, the election was symptomatic of a gangster political culture that had grown stronger since the end of military rule by granting local leaders unchecked political power and control over half the country's inert resources. As elsewhere in Africa, sudden and frequent orgies of ethnic violence are often stoked by politicians to further their personal interests.

In another somewhat predictable turn of events, President Obasanjo found himself in dispute with Audu Ogbeh, the chairman of his own President's Democratic Party. Ogbeh had written the president that Nigeria could be drifting toward another military coup against an unpopular government. Ogbeh wrote: "In life perception is reality and today, we are perceived in the worst light by an angry scornful Nigerian public for reasons which are absolutely unnecessary."

According to Amnesty International, a conflict between armed militias and government authorities around Port Harcourt, Nigeria's main oil city, resulted in over 500 deaths. Amnesty expressed concern that the deployment of extra security forces would lead to human right abuses in Port Harcourt, as they had in Bayelsa in 1999 and Benue in 2001, when hundreds of civilians were killed by the army. The Port Harcourt violence illustrated the nexus of political rivalry, theft and the flow of arms. In an open letter to Peter Odili, governor of Rivers state, of which Port Harcourt is the capital, *Amnesty International* said the civilians were thought to have been killed in a series of incidents over several months by gangs armed with submachine guns and dynamite. Predictably, Magnus Abe, information commissioner for Rivers state, said the reports of violence were overblown and he denied local allegations that violent gangs were armed by Odili supporters. "As governor, he can tell the police to lock someone up for 24 hours. He doesn't need guns to fight them;" he stated.

In the commercial city of Onitsha, there is increasing demand for the illegal currency of the breakaway Republic of Biafra, the Biafran £ note, which was minted during the 1967-70 civil-war. Biafran pound note was reintroduced by activists of Massob, a banned group advocating peaceful Biafran secession. For the Obasanjo regime, this represented a threatening rejection of the central government. Many Igbo say the government has imposed ruling party governors through flawed elections. But the mere hint of secession is sufficient to prompt crackdowns by the military and police. Massob activists were arrested for using Biafran currency and for fielding "Biafran" players during an amateur football tournament. Stay-at-home protests organized by Massob in August 2004 and December 2005 brought most major cities in eastern Nigeria to a standstill, demonstrating the movement's popularity.

The wounds from Nigeria's civil-war remain open. Biafra declared itself an independent state in the wake of political turbulence, coups and pogroms against Nigeria's third largest ethnic group, the Igbo, in 1967. Over 1 million people died from violence and starvation before Obasanjo, then a military commander, received the surrender of rebel Biafran forces. While some officials, such as the finance minister, come from the eastern part of the country, many Igbo complain that the government eschews them when appointing top security personnel and that the two main ethnic groups, the Hausa and Yoruba, monopolize the presidency. "We are aware that we are now part of Nigeria, but under a glass ceiling," said Emeka Odumegwu Ojukwu, the former political and military leader of secessionist Biafra.

The impeachment of a Delta-state governor prompted accusations of selective attacks on corruption; the governor was a key proponent of increasing the share of Nigeria's oil revenue to Delta-state. The government also cracked down on the influential Yoruba militia. "We have many people, regional groups, and even militia who will tell you they don't believe in Nigeria. We tolerate them. But what are they start doing something about it the government must react," said Femi-Fani-Kadoye, a presidential spokesman.

In October 2006, the government declared a state of emergency in the state of Ekiti, following unrest over the impeachment of Governor Ayadele Fayose after he was indicted on corruption charges. The suspension of civil administration heightened fear that Obasanjo would extend his emergency powers to other parts of the country. Obasanjo said that Ekiti had been plagued by violent politics and gangster-like rule and that the situation there had become "sad and ridiculous". Two other governors faced possible impeachment proceedings. "This is a clear trend. It has been known the president has had plans to remove a number of governors for some time;" observed Jibran Ibrahim, director of the Center for Democracy and Development. After failing to win a constitutional extension of his two four-year terms, Obasanjo became engaged in bitter political conflict with his rivals and former allies.[30] To galvanize its power, the ruling People's Democratic Party (PDP) forged alliances through an elaborate system of patronage networks. The majority of state governors and law makers are from the PDP. One eastern PDP governor, fell out of favor with Obasanjo and his electoral victory was annulled by an election tribunal.[31]

Days before a Commonwealth summit on Zimbabwe, Human Rights Watch reported that the Nigerian government was responsible for killings, torture and harassment of its citizens. The report documented 20 police shootings and cases of official targeting of protestors, journalists and other civilians during a protest against increased fuel prices. Ijaw community leaders and militants agree that the Nigerian state has marginalized their people in spite of the huge oil wealth pumped from their tribal lands.[32] One day after being repelled in an attack on the Italian oil multinational oil platform, gunmen in the Delta wearing combat fatigues and berets, attacked the offices of *Agip*, and shot nine people dead.

The Nigerian military has had limited success tracking down the MEND, guerillas whose well coordinated attacks worry security analysts. Petroleum industry officials question whether Nigeria's military has the resources and capability to control the situation and fear heightened political tension. MEND claims it has the capability and is "determined to destroy the ability of Nigeria to export oil." Oil companies usually make a quick cash settlement to kidnappers but doubt they are dealing with such. "These people have a clear political agenda. It is clear that kidnapping for money is not their agenda;" said Dimieari Von Kemedi, a Niger Delta peace and security strategist.[33] Brigadier General Elias Zamani, commander of Nigeria's military operation in the Niger Delta, warned of more unrest as national elections approached but stated the government had no plans to increase its troop presence in the Delta.

"We are not terrorists we are freedom fighters;" declared a member of the MEND militia. The secretive movement then released six of the nine oil workers taken hostage twelve days earlier. Negotiating their release involved the use of former militants as intermediaries. They, were rewarded state appointments in exchange for bringing their minions under control after the pre-2003 election campaign insurgency. Many of the former militants, acting as intermediaries, remain critical of government authorities for breaking promises to empower more Ijaw leaders in local government as authorities responsible for handling cash payments. "Until there is fair play, there will be more trouble," said a former militant known as "Duty Calls." In an e-mail, MEND's favored means of communication, the group said that: "Without any doubt the Nigerian military cannot provide security for anyone in the Niger Delta."[34] Three hostage oil workers (two Americans and a Briton), were released in late March 2006, and MEND threatened the oil industry with more destruction. MEND said that they had released the hostages to free up hundreds of its fighters used for guarding them. The e-mail stated: "We are not in negotiations with the Nigerian government so oil companies and their workers should not be deceived into a false sense of relief." Government officials said the hostage release was brokered by member of another militant group, the FNDIC, This group has operated in the Delta for years and was central to an Ijaw insurgency that shut down 40 percent of Nigeria's oil production in 2003. According to Delta-state human rights activists, FNDIC has a close relationship with MEND.

FNDIC threatened to cut another 1 million barrels per day in addition to the existing reduction of more than 630,000 per day or 26 percent of Nigeria's production. FNDIC's relationship with MEND is very complicated. Some of its leaders and loyalists claim to have registered companies with *Royal Dutch Shell* to solicit jobs such as pipeline clamping, surveillance, oil spill clearances and waste disposal. FNDIC secretary-general, Kingsley Otuaro, claims he and his half-brother have registered contracting companies to work in the area where the militant attacks and abductions occurred. He complained that *Shell* had not honored many of its promises to provide work. "*Shell* has a cumbersome bureaucracy and often relies on their local syndicate. We feel cheated;" Otuaro complained. *Shell* confirmed that Kingsley Otuaro's half brother does own a company that is a *Shell* sub-contractor.[35]

Dressed in slick combat gear and carrying sub-machine guns and rocket launchers, MEND's level of operational mobility, coordination and discipline is visibly superior to that of other militias. "The way they hold their guns, with the finger outside the trigger, is just one sign that they are well trained," said one diplomatic observer referring to the sophisticated weaponry MEND which includes American M-16 rifles. Although MEND may have had strong connections to a fragmented group, responsible for the 2004 uprising. Security analysts doubt it can reach out to militant groups in the east, who are involved in their own strategic battles. Moreover, the command structure is unclear. "Our movement is fluid and therefore capable of flowing with ease between states of the Niger Delta;" MEND claims.

Many armed groups in the Niger Delta built sophisticated arsenals from the illegal trade in stolen crude. In late February 2006, residents of the settlement of Okerenkoko, a once peaceful Niger Delta village, people waited in fear of arriving military. "Helicopters have been flying over us, and there have been navy boats shooting warning shots in the air. Some people have fled and are not come back;" lamented Talbort Babanimi, a frightened village elder. Okerenkoko lies in the middle of the Niger Delta's labyrinth of swamps and creeks which from which attacks on *Shell's* facilities are launched. "It's easy to avoid the navy and soldier's;" said a boatman in the area. According to MEND, the attacks were sparked by operations of the military near Okerenkoko that bombed oil barges suspected of being used for stealing crude. They also claimed the army randomly strafed nearby villages. While stolen crude helps purchase militia arms; army and navy personnel as well as some political figures are also involved in the theft of wells and pipelines.[37]

By January 2006, *Shell* had cut 10 percent of Nigeria's 2.6 million barrels per day of production. *Shell* announced plans to pull out of the Niger Delta and evacuated 330 staff from four oil flow stations after the attacks. Oil futures fluctuated forcing traders to look for alternative sources from other African suppliers. The unrest compounded fears of supply shortages from the Organization of Petroleum Countries (OPEC). The Western European and US stand-off with Iran, the world's third largest oil exporter, shook the market with further worries of supply shortages resulting from sanctions and strikes, and Iran's possible use of petroleum as geostrategic weapon. By May 2007, *Shell* announced that it had been forced to cut 170,000 barrels per day, after villagers occupied a pipeline and demanded money. Attacks on oil facilities escalated and MEND announced the beginning of a month of 'mayhem' on the oil industry.[38]

"The Niger Delta is pregnant and what it will deliver I don't know;" remarked Niger Delta political activist, Oronto Douglas. Delta militias increased their strength and numbers during 2006. Many, backed by political figures, served as strong-men in the run-up in the 2003 national elections which were marred by voter fraud. Using hostage-taking, protection rackets and the theft of crude from wells and pipelines, the militias use their political, military and industrial collaborators to build their arsenals. The diversity of the militias poses a hydra-like security threat to the oil companies. A fresh wave of hostage-taking in August 2006, raised fears of renewed attacks on oil facilities. More than a dozen expatriate workers were abducted in several on-shore and off-shore attacks. Analysts said the spike in abductions demonstrated a wider breakdown in law and order that threatened multinational oil facilities. Nigerian security forces arrested over 100 people and later released 50, in operations in the Port Harcourt area. A military spokesman said the operation, was the "start of something bigger" in response to President Obasanjo's order to use force.

The death of one of seven the British oil workers taken hostage, shattered confidence in Nigeria's counter-insurgency strategy. Security analysts said the death of David Hunt, the first foreign oil worker killed by a hostage-takers in Nigeria, demonstrated that attempts to counter the attacks on the oil industry put foreign workers at risk. Obasanjo responded by asking the military to meet militant activity with "force for force".[39]

In January 2006, *Shell* announced that it was cutting 106,000 barrels per day of production feeding its Forcados export terminal, after an explosion damaged a large export pipeline. Production at *Shell's* 115,000 bpd EA field, where the hostages were taken was resumed. *Shell* withdrew 500 workers from facilities in the Delta and oil workers unions threatened to withdraw their staff if security did not improve. Industry and security officials say the government lacks the capacity to guarantee the capability to guarantee the complete safety of the network of pipelines, oilfields and several hundred oilfields and several hundred oil wells dotted around the swamps and creeks of the Niger Delta, where most of Nigeria's oil is produced.

There is growing concern that armed militias will attack one another as politicians begin to manipulate them in the struggle for power. The worst scenario envisioned by western analysts was that major unrest in the Delta would force the government to declare a state of emergency and suspend elections, causing critical damage to Nigeria's oil industry and western supply.[40] "If it turns into a major military operation, we can expect more attacks on facilities. The oil industry is the Achilles' heel for the government;" observed one analyst. Violence in the Delta pushed up operating costs for companies such as *Halliburton* and *Schlumberger* and for smaller specialist companies as well. Higher costs means slower access to oil and gas reserves. The industry is turning toward deep water operations and ultimately more expensive oil.[41] A security report submitted to Obasanjo, recommended that the Delta states should control 50 percent of their resources, as opposed to the 13 percent they currently control.[42]

When the US Congress threatened to cut tens of millions of dollars in assistance to Nigeria; unless it extradited Charles Taylor to stand trial for war crimes in Liberia, Nigerian-US tensions heightened. In November 2003, Congress approved a $2 million bounty for Taylor's capture and delivery to trial. Congress also approved an offer of $2m for the capture of those indicted by the UN backed court in Sierra Leone. The Nigerian government voiced concern about the implications of US bounty hunters violating its national sovereignty. Femi Fani Kayode, advisor to President Obasanjo, threatened that: "If you take Mr. Taylor out in any way, harass him or remove him from here, you jeopardize the peace process. This is the light in which we would like the international community to view this situation." The US Embassy said that not all of Nigeria's $75 million in US Aid would be affected. Nigeria then contributed the first two battalions of peacekeepers to Liberia, which stabilized the capital, Monrovia.

In October 2002, the governments of Nigeria and Cameroon were braced for an International Court of Justice ruling on a border dispute which threatened to further destabilize the oil-rich region of the Gulf of Guinea. Irredentist tensions, the residue of colonialism, have flared in the region since 1964 when border skirmishes led both nations to deploy troops. Because the region is a potential bulwark against interruptions in Middle East oil supplies, the US took an interest. According to the US government figures, the Gulf of Guinea provides 15 percent of total US crude oil imports.[43] The Hague-based tribunal ruled on Cameroon's 1994 ownership claim of a 1,000 sq. kilometer strip of swampland known as the Bakassi Peninsula. Bakassi controls the seaway leading to Calabar, the nearest major Nigerian seaport and export processing zone. The government of Cameroon posited that a 1975 agreement between the two states, gave it the right to the territory; which offers access to offshore waters thought to hold large petroleum reserves. Nigerian officials expected the ICJ to rule in Cameroon's favor, but hoped for a mutually beneficial ruling. Both president Obasanjo and Paul Biya, his Cameroon counterpart, agreed to respect the ICJ's decision to work toward eventual demilitarization of the peninsula and to avoid inflammatory rhetoric. The ICJ ruled in favor of Cameroon, but Nigeria emerged as the long-term economic winner. The UN urged both states to honor their pledge to abide by ICJ decisions made at a meeting in Paris and called for the immediate withdrawal of Nigerian forces from the Guinea peninsula. "The result is better than expected;" said Paul Biya, "Taken in its totality, it is actually a no-loser no-winner situation." The court awarded the Bakassi peninsula and areas around Lake Chad to Cameroon, but gave a series of other territories near the border to Nigeria. The ruling meant that Nigeria could exploit a series of large and deep offshore fields and could proceed with oil field division agreements reached with Equatorial Guinea and the archipelago state of Sao Tòme and Principe.[44]

The Gulf of Guinea is expected to increase African oil supply to the US from 15 to 25 percent by 2015. A Nigerian oil official said the loss of Bokassi was important symbolically because proven oil reserves in the peninsula are small but that the judgment gave Nigeria "rights over waters where there is serious oil." "Cameroon won the political things; Nigeria won the economic side of it. Nobody should feel bad about it;" he stated. The loss of Bokassi stirred up political tensions in the run up to the 2003 elections, when both the government officials and military officers in the peninsula expressed their reluctance to withdraw their forces. Advisors to Obasanjo urged him to hold on to the territory and seek a negotiated solution.

Much of Nigeria's potential oil revenue is wasted in the environmental damaging practice of burning off unused natural gas known as "gas flaring." The government announced a commitment to end the practice by 2008. This is part of an attempt to find commercial solutions for gas produced in conjunction with oil pumped from the Niger Delta. Environmental groups estimate that Nigeria burns off almost half of the 5 billion cubic feet produced daily because of a lack of gas gathering networks. Levels of gas flaring in Nigeria are among the highest in the world. Friends of the Earth, an environmental group, estimates that Nigerian gas flaring causes more greenhouse gases than all of sub-Saharan Africa combined. The giant orange flares cause respiratory diseases, premature deaths and pollute the croplands close to the villages of the Delta's vast network of swamps and creeks.

After four decades of failure, Nigeria's Liquefied Natural Gas (LNG) project almost collapsed in the mid-1990s. In response the government agreed to relinquish its majority share in the international petroleum companies involved: *Shell*, *Elf* (now *Total* of France) and Italy's *Agip*. In 2004, there was more than $ 9 billion invested in the project and it was projected to reach $11-12 billion by 2006. Andrew Jamieson of Nigerian Liquefied Natural Gas stated: "We could not grow faster; we are the fastest growing, LNG project in history. We will go from nothing to 22 million tons a year, the equivalent of about one-third of the UK's usage, in eight years." According to *Shell's* program technical advisor, it is the largest program of internal investment made by private sector investors in Africa.

One LNG project's under are consideration by Nigeria's National Petroleum Company (NNPC), *Chevron, Texaco*, *ConocoPhillips* (the US's second and third largest energy groups) and *ENI,* the *Agip* parent company. Jackson Gaius Obaseki, NNPC's former managing director predicted: "This will be a world-class LNG facility and an important and strategic opportunity for the co-venturers to reduce gas-flaring in Nigeria. Furthermore, it will be an additional opportunity for Nigeria to monetize part of its vast natural gas reserves." The consumer base has grown along with the project. Thirty-five percent of the expected gas will be exported to the US and 40 percent to the Iberian Peninsula and other destinations in Europe. [45]

Royal Dutch Shell reported that absolute levels of associated Nigerian gas flaring increased from 570 million cubic feet in 2002 to 728 million cubic feet daily in 2004. The increase, prompted by higher oil production, represented a lost opportunity for Nigeria to process its gas reserves into LNG for international shipment. Billions of dollars invested by multinationals in gas-gathering networks have decreased gas-flaring from increasing as quickly as oil production. Billions more, were earmarked for LNG gas export plants, a regional gas pipeline, gas-powered electricity plants and gas re-injection projects, which should theoretically reduce flaring levels within the next few years. *Shell's* latest flaring measures show a reduction from 2004 levels to an average of 614 million cubic feet of associated gas flared daily for 2005. But environmentalists maintain these figure remain too high. *Shell* said progress toward reduction is slowed by shortfalls in funding from the Nigerian government, which is a silent partner in onshore joint ventures with *Shell, ExxonMobil, Chevron, Elf* and *Agip*. The government is required to contribute to a yearly "cash call" that would be used to speed the construction of gas-sharing networks. According to the multinational oil companies, the government shortfall for 2005 was estimated at $1 billion.[46]

The Nigerian government and *Shell* agreed that the latter would no longer drill for oil without having a solution for gas flaring. One alternative involves re-injecting the gas into oil fields, a plan popular with *ExxonMobil* and *Chevron/Texaco.* But, the most attractive plan to the oil companies is to convert it into LNG through super-cooling, load it onto tankers and export it to Europe and the US. Global demand for LNG is growing as the indigenous gas reserves in the North Sea and the continental US diminish. By 2020, LNG is expected to make up 25 percent of overall gas demand in the US, making current levels of US petroleum consumption miniscule.

Contrasting Nigeria's position as Africa's largest oil producer is its large population estimated at 140 million. Nigeria's population has been growing at an annual rate of 6 percent, but the country needs a more diversified economy to help create jobs and combat poverty. Relative to its size, Nigeria is under-aided. Its population has tripled since 1960. Only China and India have more poor and destitute people. By 2015, the target date set by the United Nations to meet its Millennium Goals for poverty reduction, Nigeria's population is expected to be reach 180 million.

Oil revenue per capita is less than any of the other top exporting countries. In 2004, after the deduction of the shares of corporate production costs, each Nigerian received only $0.53 per day. There is little to show for the tripling of oil revenues that took place in the seven years following the end of military rule. Bismarck Rewane, managing director of *Financial Derivatives*, an economic consultant, noted that whatever growth occurred cannot be attributable to any real policy change. The nation's oil wealth is therefore, is the object of illusory, but constant political demands. In reality, if all the proceeds from current Nigerian oil production were equally shared, Nigerians would only be 50 US cents a day richer per capita. There are indicators an increase in Nigeria's capacity utilization, but this primarily reflects the extent to which that capacity has been degraded. New fixed investment is quite limited. The private sector showed little appetite for risk, Bismarck Rewane noted. Bunmi Oni, Nigeria chief executive of the candy producer *Cadbury*, put the cost of disadvantage for operating in Nigeria at 20 to 25 percent, including; red tape, customs delays and the need to ensure independent power supplies. The former, finance minister, Okonjo Iweala, noted that although there had been some private sector investment: "We are so far behind that we massively need more to come in." She placed the priority on employment generating projects in agriculture, solid materials and manufacturing.

The IMF approved Nigeria's 2004 performance as "commendable" and forecasted 7 percent economic growth for the following year. With the help of increased gas and oil production and rising prices some analysts said the growth rate could be even higher. The remaining question is why given such a steep rise in export revenues, Nigeria is unable to achieve dramatic growth. "Because we do not have the infrastructure to drive it;" Okonjo Iweala contends. "Even if you were to drive out all of the corruption in the world and make the place as clean as a white handkerchief, the business sector would have to cooperate."

The windfall to Nigeria from 2004 oil price increases brought savings of $5.9 billion. Half of this was earmarked for priority spending in education, health and vital infrastructure facilities. The remainder was earmarked as a buffer against future oil price volatility. However, the government's plans for building a solid base for economic growth provoked vitriolic reactions from the press. The cost of living rose steeply in May and official figures reflected a doubling of the 12-month inflation rate between January and November when it passed 21 percent. State television station commercials on cheerfully invoked the merits of public service with the slogan: "Today's pain will pave the way for tomorrow's joy." The policies were attacked as "anti-people" by the trade union federation, which was pressing the grievances of urban workers. In a nation where people feel entitled to their share of the benefits of oil abundance, unions charged that rising fuel prices would lead to the "pauperization of the populace."

A road to effective Nigerian economic management was mapped out in a document titled the National Economic Empowerment and Development Strategy (NEEDS). A four-year program announced in September 2004, NEEDS is a home-grown Poverty Reduction Strategy Paper. A document used by low-income countries as a basis for soliciting support from the IMF and the World Bank, which outlines the government's financial needs and its approach to meeting them. NEEDS is based on macroeconomic stability, a prudent budgetary process, improved productivity, administrative reform, a smaller state role, better delivery of public services, greater accountability and a more "favorable climate" for private sector investment. Analysts saw the NEEDS plan as a race against time to produce positive results before the battle to succeed President Obasanjo began. The share of public spending taken up by payments on foreign loans and rising debt more than doubled from 15 percent in 2001 to 32 percent in 2004. Privatization fell behind and shifted from relatively straightforward sectors such as reinsurance and hotels, to more complex investments such as the state electricity utility, which was be broken up into 18 companies. The government also announced plans to privatize the refineries and ports.

After a bitter disagreement with the IMF in 2002 over government spending, Nigeria broke away from an IMF-monitored program. In 2004, Nigeria did not seek IMF funding; but rather only its stamp of approval, enabling it to seek debt relief from the Paris Club, which held more than 80 percent of Nigeria's $31 billion foreign debt. The NEEDS plan was to raise economic growth to 7 percent a year from 2007 onward, the rate considered necessary to achieve a significant reduction in poverty. In 2003, Nigeria's economic growth, projected at 5 percent, reached only 3.5 percent. The government planned to keep its fiscal deficit down to 2 percent of gross domestic product that year compared with an average of over 4.5 percent between 2001 and 2006.

Nigeria's protective trade policy, contradicted its new agenda of economic orthodoxy. Import restrictions announced in January 2004 clashed with the economic interests of regional and global trading partners. The government imposed trade barriers on imports ranging from textiles, plastics, meat and fresh fruit men's shoes, bicycles, ballpoint pens, cutlery, toothpaste, detergents, buckets, pickaxes and wheelbarrows. This was in response to pressure from industrial sectors and underscored the absence of competitiveness resulting from poor infrastructure, high manufacturing costs and expensive borrowing. Nigerian and foreign critics agreed that the trade ban would merely increase smuggling, deprive the government of import tariff revenues and raise the level of financial risk and uncertainty.[47]

Nigeria attracted the attention of global fund managers for being one of the few emerging markets insulated from the global sell-off. After clearing more than $30 billion in external debt, the nation's stock capitalization doubled between 2006 and 2007, rising to about $45 billion in domestic and foreign investment. Nigeria alongside countries such as Vietnam, Indonesia and Mexico is classified by some international financial houses as an emerging market. However, it remains relatively marginalized from international markets and is thus, unable to avoid global economic shocks. Most stocks are undervalued according to the assistant director-general of the Nigerian Stock Exchange. Many Nigerian executives feared political violence would discredit the elections and deter investment. "All bets are off if a political crisis coincides with market concerns. The political turbulence, or a change in the character of the regime, could also upset the deal flow and patronage networks that sustain the present situation;" cautioned director of *Financial Derivatives,* Bismarck Rewayne,.[48]

Agriculture is another potential source of nutrition and revenue for Nigerian development. President Obasanjo told parliament that the agricultural sector had grown 7 percent in 2003. In reality, even with good rains and supportive policies, it was closer to 4.5 percent. Once a leading producer of cash crops such as palm oil, Nigeria has been surpassed by south-east Asian countries such as Malaysia, in terms of both size and yields per hectare. Only the country's innate fertility has helped it avoid economic devastation. As the world's fourth-largest cocoa producer, the country is somewhat food self-sufficient. The International Institute of Tropical Agriculture (IITA) estimated that Nigeria is just one of five African countries where the per capita daily caloric intake is more than 2,529. But experts warn of shortages of foods rich in critical nutrients such as iron, zinc and certain types of amino acids. The issue of subsistence is likely to become more acute with increased rural-to-urban migration. Many farmers were left with unsold stock during the latest cassava glut, because they lacked the processing equipment to dry their crops, which would have made then easier to transport and less likely to rot.

The government's agricultural policy focused on subsidizing fertilizers and grain prices, and launching "presidential initiatives" to promote the growth of crops such as cassava, rice and sugar. The draft budget for 2004 proposed spending 9 billion Naira on agriculture; comprising 4 billon Naira on fertilizers, 2 billion Naira on a national food security initiative and N3 billion on a buyers of last resort program and funds to refurbish crop silos and various presidential programs. The most common criticism of the government's agricultural policy was that it focused too narrowly on increasing production, without taking into account the investments required to support the infrastructure.

Low agricultural technology constrains economic growth. The ministry of agriculture claimed that Nigeria was on the path toward genuine economic revival. But to the farmers of Osegere, a village in the south west, this claim is premature. They said they had heard about programs offering assistance to farmers on the radio, but had been unable to find out any further information. "We are not being encouraged and we are not very proud to be called farmers because we lack basic implements and equipment;" said a member of the local farmers association. But we are rooted to our future because we can't work in offices, we can't get any other employment and we need to stay with what we are doing."[49]

Election Allergies

When the 1993 national election was voided by the Babangida government, all political party activity was banned. Nigeria's military governments have always abolished and banned political parties. Parties largely based along ethnic and regional divisions are incompatible with political cohesion. Parties were briefly reconstituted before the Second Republic (1979-1983); in the Third Republic; in 1996 when the National Election Commission (NECON), created by Abacha, registered five new parties to contest local, state and national elections. Parties were allowed again under Abubakar in 1999 and under Obasanjo.

Nigeria's political tensions exploded in March 2006 when the government began taking the census. In a country where political representation and access to petroleum revenue are determined by population figures, the process is considered a political exercise. The 1991 census was annulled in order to avert national riots. Militant attacks in the Niger Delta cost Nigeria $1 billion in oil revenues during the first three months of the year. This loss of revenue increased political tensions between politicians hungry for money to launch projects in their constituencies. "Census is a hot topic. There is strong competition for numerical superiority;" said Samuila Makama, head of Nigeria's national population commission. Over 30 people were killed in religious conflicts during the previous month. Current estimates put Nigeria's population between 120 and 150 million people, evenly divided between Christians and Muslims. As a precaution, the government deployed an additional 60,000 national police. Nigerian census forms ask for details pertaining to ethnicity, race and religious affiliation. Government officials say that by using new satellite imagery and fingerprint recognition technology, methods of counting and avoiding manipulation of the count, have improved.

Obasanjo urged his countrymen not to perceive the census as a battle for "political supremacy." But there were too many reports of communities not being surveyed by census takers, poor delivery of census materials to some areas, and slow payment of census officials. "The exercise is going to be contested by some groups. Nobody is going to be satisfied;" observed a western diplomat.[50] The following month, Nigeria's political stability was threatened by a leadership crisis, when the president and vice president called for one another's resignation. Vice-president, Atiku Abubakar, issued a statement calling on President Obasanjo to resign for pursuing an attempt to amend the constitution and remain in power for a third term. President Obasanjo had called for the vice president's resignation, after Abubakar attended a high-profile meeting in Abuja of legislators and political figures opposed to his possible third term. Legislators said the president did not have the two-thirds majority in the national assembly to change the constitution.[51] Anther leading presidential candidate and former military ruler, Muhammadu Buhari stated that both local and international pressure were imperative to ensure the credibility of the 2007 elections. Fair elections were also a prerequisite to quelling the violence by Ijaw youth militias in the Niger Delta. "Nigeria will face a crisis of very serious proportions, if forthcoming elections are marred by rigging;" Buhari warned.[52]

The final candidate for the presidency, Umaru Yar'Adua, emerged from relative obscurity. Yar' Adua served as Obasanjo's personal secretary for eight years and was groomed and placed in power for his service. Many in the ruling Peoples Democratic Party (PDP) feared that, should he win the elections, Yar' Adua would "seek to be his own man". However, the reclusive soft-spoken 55 year-old governor of the mainly Muslim of state of Katsina, promised to follow the path "charted out" by Obasanjo. Yar' Adua claimed that his opponents would set Nigeria back by seeking to reverse: "the current policies of deregulation, privatization, getting the Nigerian economy right...getting the conditions for foreign investment." His call for dialogue between "stakeholders, ourselves, the state governments, the Niger Delta leaders," echoed Obasanjo.[53] On March 16, 2007, Nigeria's electoral commission blocked Abubakar's candidacy, because he had been indicted for corruption by a panel of Obasanjo's minister's. All indications pointed to an intensified political climate that "might erupt in the kind of political violence we only hope Nigeria can avoid;" said Dapo Oywwole, director of the Center for African Policy and Peace Strategy.[54] The federal appeals court ruled that the electoral commission had the authority to remove candidates from the official electoral list. Abubakar's appeal was rejected, but he won another legal action compelling the elections commission to include him on the ballot. Election analysts predicted that Abubakar's inclusion would complicate the PDP's attempt to secure a first-round victory Yar' Adua.[55]

In southeastern Nigeria, former state governor, Chris Ngige, campaigned from a bulletproof four wheel drive vehicle as policemen fired their weapons in the air and his driver distributed cash to supporters. "They are not asking for money, but we have to make them happy," said Ngige. Chudi Offodile, a former PDP lawmaker who was also expelled by Obasanjo, ran a grass-roots campaign for his old Senate seat as an opposition candidate. He rushed around Anambra's poor areas accompanied by musicians and dancers who handed out money to local constituents, party leaders and the police. "Elections are not a popularity contest. You need the right structures and organization to win otherwise you will be rigged out;" said Chudi Offodile. Criminal gangs with names such as the Vikings, Black Axes, Pirates and Buccaneers offered their services, attacking their rivals, to political candidates. Chudi Offodile paid street gangs to protect and escort his convoys. He said he might be not be able to hand out bags of rice, sewing machines and even cars like other politicians, but he felt motivated by his supporters.[56]

In the Niger Delta, the presidential elections were viewed with greater skepticism by the both Nigerians and the oil companies. "None of us see anything getting better...after elections...What we need is a government of businessmen backed by a mercenary army;" said one contractor to a multinational oil company. In state elections that were marred by fraud and intimidation, the PDP won control of the Delta. Presidential candidate Yar'Adua had promised a Nigerian "Marshall Plan" to develop the impoverished region just Obasanjo had done eight years earlier.[57]

In the largely Islamic north, fear of election violence ran high in Kano state, a stronghold of the opposition. Brutalized by decades of military rule and economic hardship, under eight years of civilian rule much of the population turned to Islam as a social safety-net. Many Imams escalated their critical condemnation of the Obasanjo regime. Ordinary Muslims realized that the politicians who backed *Sharia* law for political expedience, have failed to deliver on the other tenets of Islam, such as social justice and caring for the poor. "*Sharia* prohibits many vices, but many of our political leaders have been stealing with impunity;" complained twenty-five year old Islamic student, Salisu Mohammed. The politically orchestrated religious conflicts with Christians over the past several years, left many Muslims feeling used, bitter and betrayed. In Sabon Gari, a neighborhood of Kano largely inhabited by Christian settlers, many people fearing flawed elections would ignite a pogrom and looting, fled. Many families left the area, although Muslim partisans of rival political parties, were expected to fight each other. Institutional anti-terrorism regulations had already thwarted the terrorist activities of many Islamic charities operating in northern Nigeria.[58]

The politics of greed, suspicion and poverty in Nigeria were further underscored with the resignation of finance minister Iweala, who led the economic reform effort, successfully negotiated the cancellation of the country's $18 billion external debt and presided over a healthy increase in

Nigeria's foreign reserves to an estimated $50 billion. Her departure was perceived as the result of a personality clash with Obasanjo, who resented the international prominence and adulation that accompanied her accomplishments. Her departure seemed to occur at a critical political juncture, eight months before schedule presidential elections. Perhaps the international community, multilateral agencies, private and public creditors and the media reportedly exaggerated Ngozi-Iweala's personal role, causing a fatal political rift between she and the president. As Obasanjo prepared to stepped down, he did as much as possible to maintain the overwhelming dominance of his party. This included using of legal means and corruption indictments against Yar' Adua's rivals. Of his legacy of tough economic reforms and the heavy-handed rule, Obasanjo told reporters; "Jesus Christ was even crucified, Prophet Mohammed was driven out of his home town. Churchill was called a warmonger but he won the war. Look, this is a job not a popularity contest." Obasanjo insisted that he would hand power over to the winner, even to his estranged vice-president. "It's not by any means a perfect election, but there is no human arrangement you can describe as perfect until we get to God and eternity."[59],

The PDP claimed victory in the state elections, but again the process was marred by widespread allegations of fraud, violence and twenty-one deaths. Human Rights activists and election monitors reported cases of ballot stuffing, under-age voting, intimidation, confusion over voter lists and interference by security agencies. In some areas there were no ballots cast because they did not arrive. Some politicians warned that another questionable election would undermine national stability. Early results gave the PDP eight of ten declared states. In Rivers State, in the richest oil producing part of the country, the PDP retained power but election day began with the bombing of two police stations.[60] Western journalist and local monitors were unable to verify the official results. A report by Human Rights Watch cited "gross interference in the state electoral process" to date.[61] In some areas, the electoral commission had to reschedule the polls.

In many areas, voter turnout was high and voting took place peacefully. "We did not anticipate a 100 percent hitch free election. One or two infractions would not make the election and its results unacceptable;" said Maurice Iwu, chairman of the Independent Electoral Commission. Of the flawed process, Obansanjo remarked; "I won't say I am absolutely unconcerned, but I'm not to the point that I would say that we haven't won. The way the elections have been conducted to date has not lived up to the hopes of Nigerians;" Remarked John Munis, a 26-year old who reflects the cynicism of many Nigerians; "These elections are not for the people. They are for the politicians. They send their children to school in Britain and America but look at us here. There is no better future for us, we are just roaming the streets...The president's children don't look like us. We are suffering and smiling. This election will change nothing. The politicians will still be going abroad and stashing our money there."[62]

The elections were followed by recriminations and opposition party accusations of unprecedented electoral fraud. The government responded with allegations of a coup plot. The Transition Monitoring Group, the largest domestic observer organization, said that the elections were so flawed they should be held again. Some of the fiercest controversy was in the northern state of Katsina, home of Umaru Yar'Adua and of former General, Muhammadu Buhari. In the presence of foreign observers, unsealed ballot boxes and election materials were snatched from several polling stations by thugs. Journalists witnessed similar and worse civil abuses in other parts of the country. In many areas, residents complained that there were fewer ballots than voters. Delays and the failure to distribute some 60 million ballots meant that only half the country was able to vote. Max van den Berg, head of the EU observer mission, stated there was less violence then there had been during the April state elections, in which an estimated 50 people were killed. Both Obasanjo and Maurice Iwu defended the overall process, but other senior political officials warned of the dangers of wholesale condemnation of the election. "We would be inciting a revolution or a military intervention;" said a senior PDP senator. Ken Nnamani, president of the Senate, called for a reconvening the body a week early, leading to speculation the Senate would try to annul the polls and impeach Obasanjo's information minister, Frank Nweke. Nweke accused Nnamani of plotting to form and interim national government and suggested that there was an attempt to blow up election headquarters in Abuja, after a truck-bomb loaded with petrol and gas cylinders hit a lamp-post but failed to detonate.[63]

Umaru Yar'Adua was declared the victor of the election, which the US government described as deeply flawed. Moreover, the results seriously undermined the possibility of a peaceful political transition, as opposition leaders called for the election to be annulled. In a press conference EU election monitors denounced the conduct of the elections, but the Nigeria Elections Commission declared that Umaru Yar' Adua had won 24.6 million votes, or roughly 70 percent of the poll.[64] His supporters claim he is better equipped to build consensus than Obasanjo. His detractors say he lacks the strength of character to steer Nigeria through its imminent political crisis. Yar' Adua was sworn into office on May 29th, 2007. He swore the oath of office in front of Obasanjo and promised to be a "servant leader.' He was immediately confronted with the issue of political corruption. Earlier that month, Obasanjo had authorized, what opponents called a "fire sale" of state assets to some of his favored cronies. This included the auction of 1,000 mining licenses and the sale of two large state-owned oil refineries. During his campaign Yar' Adua promised that Nigeria would be one among the top 20 global economies by 2020. However, according to finance ministry officials, the planned annual 20 percent spending increase was already undermining economic stability. Finance ministry officials fear that a government account established to hold billions of dollars of oil revenue savings does not have sufficient protection to safeguard the money from corrupt governors.[65] From the presidential palace to the lean-to shanties of the countryside, in Nigeria, the politics of greed and personal insecurity are pandemic.[66]

---

1. Aborisade, Oladimeji and Robert J. Mundt. *Politics In Nigeria*. New York, Longman 2002 and David White and Michael Peel, 'A crucial year for credibility,' *The Financial Times*, February 24, 2004.

2. David White, 'Nigerian leader campaigns to consolidate democracy,' *The Financial Times*, May 11, 2002.

3. David White, 'Nigeria delays local poll again,' *The Financial Times*, August 8, 2002.

4. Dino Mahtani, 'Nigerian Senate rules out third term for leader,' *The Financial Times* May 17, 2006.

5. Dino, Mahtani, 'Obasanjo accepts decision to bar third term,' *The Financial Times* May 19, 2006.

6. Dino, Mahtani, 'Wider world ratchets up Kaduna's local tension,' *The Financial Times*, November 11, 2003.

7. Dino Mahtani, 'Miss World riots expose high tension,' *The Financial Times*, November 28, 2002.

8. Kole Ahmed Shettima, "Engendering Nigeria's Third Republic," *African Studies Review* 38:3, (December, 1995)p. 85. and Dino, Mahtani, 'Religious violence spreads in Nigeria,' *The Financial Times* February 23, 2006. p 5.

9. Tom Forrest. *Politics and Economic Development in Nigeria*. Boulder, CO. Westview 1995. pp 83-84. and David White, 'The trouble with federalism,' *The Financial Times*, February 24, 2004.

10. David White, 'Nigeria's president shrugs off legislators' impeachment threat,' *The Financial Times*, August 16, 2002.

11. Dino Mahtani, 'Nigeria shifts to China arms,' *The Financial Times* February 28, 2006. p.1

12. Dino Mahtani, 'Stay away from the Delta, Nigerian rebels tell China,' *The Financial Times*, May 5, 2006 p. 3

13. Dino Mahtani, 'Shell signs up Nigerian companies linked to violent 2004 insurrection,' *The Financial Times*, April 27, 2006 p. 8.

14. Samuel P. Huntington, *The Clash of Civilizations and the Remaking of World Order* (New York: Simon and Schuster, 1966) pp 255-256. and Dino Mahtani. 'A system in which failings are evident,' Nigeria Special Report, *The Financial Times,* April 26, 2004. 3.

15. Michael Peel, 'Plenty of opportunity to 'come and eat,' *The Financial Times,* February 24, 2004. p.3.

16. Daniel Balint-Kurti, 'Millions missing in Nigeria's oil accounts,' *The Financial Times*, March 15, 2006 p.4.

17. Peel Michael and Thomas Catan, 'SEC widens Nigeria bribery probe with Shell subpoena,' *The Financial Times*, October 13, 2005.

18. Peel Michael and Thomas Catan, "UK agency failed to tackle Nigerian bribes claim,' *The Financial Times,* June 22. 2005.

19.Peel Michael, 'Probe into KBR role in Nigeria bribe case,' *The Financial Times*, August 8, 2006. p1.

20. Michal Peel, 'Lagos citizens pay the price for their bad habits,' *The Financial Times,* October 21-22, 2005.

21. Michael Peel, 'Victims pursue alleged fraudsters in Nigeria,' *The Financial Times*, August 30, 2002.

22. William Reno classified Abacha as a "warlord," because he focused on short-term personal goals , not the patron-client system. See: Reno, William. *Warlord Politics and African States*. Boulder, Co.: Lynne Reinner 1998. pp. 194-204: and Michael Peel, 'Nigerians 'misused' Abacha's stolen money,' *The Financial Times*.

23. David White, 'Britain accused of failing to combat African corruption,' *The Financial Times,* March 28, 2006 p. 6.

24. Dino Mahtani. 'Nigeria vows to investigate $90 million oil deal,' *The Financial Times* October 31, 2006 p.4.

25. Aborisade, Oladimeji and Robert J. Mundt op. Cit. p. 152 and Michael Peel, 'Bid to end pariah state image,' Nigeria: Special Report *The Financial Times,* February 24, 2004. p.2

26. David White, 'Nigeria agrees deal to cancel $18 billion owed to lenders.' *The Financial Times*, October 21, 2005.

27. David White, Shell tries to repair troubled Delta relation,' Nigeria: Special Report, *The Financial Times* February 24, 2004. p.5.

28. Dino Mahtani, 'Hundreds die in Nigerian oil pipeline explosion,'

The Financial Times, December, 27, 2006, p.4.

29. Dino Mahtani, 'Attacks feared on Nigerian oil facilities.' *The Financial Times*, September, 25, 2005.

30. Dino Mahtani, 'Nigeria suspends civil rule in Ekiti,' *The Financial Times*, October 20, 2006 p.8.

31. Dino Mahtani, 'Biafran voices of dissent grow even louder,' *The Financial Times*, January 5, 2006. p5.

32. Dino Mahtani, 'Nigerian militants free kidnapped oil workers,' *The Financial Times*, January 31, 2006. p.4.

33. Dino Mahtani, 'Nigeria security alert after Shell attacks,' *The Financial Times*, January 17, 2006 p.4.

34. Dino Mahtani, 'Nigerian attacks show oil group's vulnerability,' *The Financial Times*, February 20, 2006. p. 3.

35. Dino, Mahtani. 'Delta militants release hostages but threat to oil supply not over,' *The Financial Times*, March 28, 2006. p .6.

37. Dino, Mahtani, 'Nigerian oil industry helpless as militants declare war on Obasanjo,' *The Financial Times*, February 21, 2006. p 4.

38. Dino Mahtani, 'Nigeria unrest forces Shell to cut capacity,' *The Financial Times*, May 16, 2007 p.6.

39. Dino Mahtani, Niger Delta oil hostage's death sparks alarm at navy strategy,' *The Financial Times*, November 11, 2006.

40. Dino, Mahtani, 'Nigeria hostage-taking raises fears over fresh attacks on oil facilities,' *The Financial Times*, August 15, 2006 p. 5.

41. Dino, Mahtani, 'Security costs mount for oil industry in Nigeria,' *The Financial Times*, September 16-17, 2006, p. 3.

42. Dino, Mahtani, 'Nigeria's oil delta crackdown heightens fear of attacks,' *The Financial Times*, August 22, 2006, p.2.

43. Dino Mahtani, 'Court to rule on Nigeria and Cameroon border dispute,' *The Financial Times*, October 10, 2002.

44. Dino, Mahtani, 'Nigerians see material gains in UN defeat,' *The Financial Times*, October 17, 2002.

45. Carola Hoyos, 'Betting on a global thirst for LNG' Nigeria: Special Report,'

The Financial Times February 24, 2004 p.6.

46. Dino, Mahtani, 'Giant orange gas flare mean lost opportunities for Nigeria,' *The Financial Times*, December 28, 2005 p.4.

47. David White, 'Fuel price rises first plank of reform plan,' Nigeria: Special Report, *The Financial Times*, February 14, 2004. p .2.

48. Dino, Mahtani, 'Nigeria's stable market wary of political shock,' *The Financial Times*, March 21, 2007 p. 4.

49. Michal Peel, 'Blighted by low morale and suspicion: The farming sector has been identified as a main driver of growth outside the oil industry,' Nigeria: Special Report, *The Financial Times* February 24, 2005 p.7.

50. Dino, Mahtani, 'Nigeria on alert as census takers begin mammoth task,' *The Financial Times,* March 22, 2006, p.7.

51. Dino, Mahtani. 'Stability fears in Nigeria as leaders fall out.' *The Financial Times,* April 8-9, 2006, p. 4.

52. Dudley, Billy. *An Introduction to Nigerian Government. and Politics*, Bloomington, Indiana University Press 1982, pp. 18-178

Wallis, William and Michal Peel, 'Nigeria will face serious crisis if voting is rigged.' *The Financial Times*, January 22, 2007 p. 6.

53. Mahtani, Dino, 'Presidential hopeful vows to follow Obasanjo path.' *The Financial Times*, February 21, 2007. p. 2.

54.Dino Mahtani, 'Threat to Nigeria poll as candidate barred.' *The Financial Times*, March 16, 2007. p. 6.

55. Dino, Mahtani and Wallace, William. 'Nigeria court allows Abubakar to stand,' *The Financial Times,* April 17, 2007 p.4.

56. Dino Mahtani, 'Guns, money and dancers oil up the electioneering process in Nigeria," *The Financial Times,* April 3, 2007, p.8.

57. Dino Mahtani, 'Besieged oil industry has little hope Nigerian elections will bring relief,' *The Financial Times*, April 20, 2007.

58. Dino Mahtani, 'Election breeds fear in Nigeria's Muslim north,' *The Financial Times*, April 13, 2007. p. 6.

59. William Wallis and Dino Mahtani, 'Mission accomplished? Why a messianic Obasanjo is pleased by Nigeria's progress,' Comment and Analysis: *The Financial Times*, April 18, 2007.

60. Dino Mahtani and Wallace, William. 'Nigeria' s ruling party ahead amid violence at polls.' *The Financial Times*, April 16, 2007, p.4.

61. Dino Mahtani, 'Abubakar candidacy in legal limbo,' *The Financial Times*, April 4, 2007 p.6.

62. Wallis, William and Dino Mahtani, 'Cynicism rife as Nigerians go to the polls,' *The Financial Times*, April 21/22, 2007 p.2.

63. Dino, Mahtani and William Wallis, 'Claims of coup plot and fraud cloud Nigerian polls,' *The Financial Times*, April 23, 2007, p. 6.

64. Dino Mahtani, Yar' Adua declared winner by landslide,' *The Financial Times,* April 24, 2007 p.6.

65. Dino Mahtani, 'Nigeria's new leader must fight old ways,' *The Financial Times*, May 29, 2004. p.2.

66. William Wallis William and Dino Mahtani, 'Devout Muslim faces unenviable task,' *The Financial Times,* April 24, 2007, p. 6.

12: Rwanda: Mass Psychosis & Genocide

Colonial mapmakers crammed 8 million people into an area smaller than the state of Maryland and called it Rwanda. It is one of the world's most densely settled agrarian countries. In many parts of the country, nearly every patch of reddish earth is cultivated into a patchwork of fields that stretches up and often over boundless beautiful rolling hills. The country was bequeathed a system of ethnic-dominance which cultivated fratricidal ethnic hostility, making conflict inevitable. When the Europeans arrived in the late 19th century, Rwanda was a relatively stable kingdom ruled by a Tutsi aristocracy that, given its mountainous topography, managed to remain isolated from the incursions of the coastal-based slave traders. The colonial powers fabricated, reinforced and perpetuated distictions and animosities between Tutsis and Hutus. Most historians agree that the first inhabitants of Rwanda were the hunter-gatherers known as the Twa who today comprise only 1% of the population. The country was then settled in succession by those known as Hutus, then Tutsis although the accuracy of these ethnic labels is the subject of vigorous debate. The roots of Hutu-Tutsi animosity run deep.

The Hutus, who make up 84% of the population, were considered by early colonizers to be a Bantu people, while the Tutsis were considered a Nilotic or Hamitic people who arrived as conquerors in the 15th century. The Hutus were believed to be primarily agriculturalists and the Tutsis pastoral.[1] There is no evidence of pre-colonial ethnic violence between Hutus and Tutsis. In fact, they traditionally lived together and fought in the same armies, shared the same culture and speak the same language, Kinyarwanda. They sang praises to the same heroes and danced the same dances. Prior to the arrival of German and Belgian colonizers, Hutus became Tutsis and exchanged ethnicity based upon economic fortune. They intermarried and it was not uncommon for families and clans to include members of both groups.[2]

The complexity of their traditional hierarchical political systems was misunderstood by the colonizers who governed by imposing their own ethnocentric biases and exacerbating existing social conflicts. The European concocted history of Rwanda is the source of much confusion and resulted in genocide. The German and Belgian colonizers demonstrated a bias favoring the less "Negroid" appearing Tutsis. These efforts included propagating the theory that the Tutsis were a "separate race" of foreign invaders who had conquered and subjugated the Hutu masses.[3] The Europeans identified the Tutsi as Hamites i.e., caucasians in black skin. A pseudo-history of Tutsi migration from the Somalia, a land of Hamites, was created to facilitate this divide and conquer strategy. The Hamitic thesis was reinforced throughout the colonial era. The Tutsi were considered the segment of Rwandan society with whom the Europeans could easily work.

When the Belgians replaced the Germans as the colonial power, they adopted the Hamitic thesis and continued the policy of indirect rule via the Tutsi minority. However, the Belgians added a system of slavery in which groups of Tutsi supervised the Hutu, thereby exacerbating the enmity between them.[4] The predominantly Catholic educational system openly favoured the Tutsis and the colonial government, in alliance with Catholic missionaries, helped exacerabte Hutu and Tutsi enmity. The colonial privileges extended to the Tutsis enabled their aristocracy to control the allocation of land and to act as agents through which the Belgians could extract taxes in the form of force labour from the Hutus.[5] Thus, the Belgians felt "betrayed" when, in 1959, Tutsi political leaders began agitating for political independence. The Belgian response to Tutsi nationalism was to conspire with extremist Hutu nationalists in order to usurp Tutsi political dominance.

The legal system bequeathed to Rwanda at the end of colonial rule was nothing more than a corrupt mimicry of a judicial systeme.[6] Between 1959 and 1994, the political gap created by the politics of decolonization grew wider. They continued to live in close proximity to one another, there were no Hutu or Tutsi areas in the countryside and the people lived in relative peace. Rwanda is one of the world's most densely populated countries. The scarcity of land and other social ills lie at the core of Rwanda's political turmoil. When Rwanda achieved independence in 1962, the new rulers implemented policies designed to permanently deny Tutsi political participation. Anti-Tutsi discrimination was institutionalized. State sanctioned pogroms killed thousands and drove hundreds of thousands into exile in neighboring Uganda, Burundi and the DRC. Rwanda's health system collapsed and there is one doctor for every 50,000 people. The average life expectancy for males is 38 years and for females 39 years. One hundred and eighteen out every thousand infants dies at birth and the adult HIV/Aids infection rate is 11.12 percent.

Post independence hostilities between Hutus and Tutsis began with the formation of a Tutsi guerrilla organization called the *Inyezi*, or Cockroach, with bases in Burundi where the Tutsis were in power. In December 1963, the *Inyezi* invaded Rwanda from bases in Burundi with the objective of toppling the government. Many Tutsis in Rwanda openly supported the invasion, but in the ensuing battle the *Inyezi* were defeated. In 1972, thousands of Hutus were massacred by the predominantly Tutsi army in Burundi when they resisted the purge by the army, police and civil service of Tutsi supremacist, Colonel Michel Micombero.

Genocide is never a sudden or unplanned act. Like war, it is a deliberate, pre-meditated and carefully orchestrated orgy of mass murder for political purposes. In this well organized campaign of carnage, the participants followed instructions from the highest levels of the political, military and civil establishments.[7] For 100 days in 1994 genocide was committed in Rwanda. Between the 6th day of April and the 15th day of July, over 800,000 people were hunted down, rounded up and murdered.

The evidence of genocide includes dossiers documenting the training and arming of radical Hutu militias, minutes of the meetings in which an extermination campaign was planned and tapes of broadcasts inciting Hutus "to fill the half-empty graves once the killing began".[8] The killers took numerous lives in a flash using relatively primitive methods and weapons because the civilian population was forced to participate in the slaughter. Tutsis were killed for being Tutsis. Hutus were killed for opposing the violence, or simply for hiding the intended victims from the rampaging psychotic murderers. Some were killed in error because they were thought to be Tutsi. Murder became a cottage industry, a collective social activity. The killing was indiscriminate, men, women and children, all were victims. Other men, women and children were the killers. Neighbor killed neighbor. Friends killed friends. In some cases, family members killed family members. Politicians, civil administrators, judges, police officers, lawyers, journalists, teachers, priests, nuns, businessmen, students, peasants and NGO staff members, were both victims of and zombie-like participants in the genocide.[9]

There were no sanctuaries; the killers invaded homes, places of business, schools, hospitals and churches in search of victims. The dead and dying were stripped of their clothing, jewelry and anything else of value. Some were shot, others killed with grenades. Most were chopped to death with machetes, knives or farm hoes. Their bodies were thrown down pit latrines or wells. Some were bound and tossed into rivers, others down ravines or buried alive. Some victims bribed their killers, begging to be shot rather than endure the pain of being hacked or beaten to death. Women were forced to kill their husbands or their children. Children were forced to kill other children. Women and young girls were gang-raped, tortured and sexually mutilated. As Gerard Prunier incisively observed: "The national trauma that has resulted from this carnage is so great that it is difficult to discuss, painful to document, and impossible to forget."[10] Many of the killings were committed as ethnic

Hutu militias rampaged through steep hillside villages in search of Tutsis, or those trying to defend them. In Shyorongi, a roadside market town about 12 miles north of the capital of Kigali, Hutu militias killed an estimated 6,000 people, more people than reside there today.

The Rwandan Hutu extremists and their sympathizers fled to Congo after the genocide. There were an estimated 15,000 Hutu rebels at large in Congo. These are disaffected young Rwandans and remnants of the former Rwandan army and the Interahamwe militia that carried out the 1994 genocide of the Tutsi's. In November 2003, hundreds of Hutu militiamen gathered in the eastern section of the Democratic Republic of Congo. They waited in anticipation for a return to Rwanda, precipitated by the surrender of their commander to UN and Rwandan officials. General Paul Rwarakabije crossed into Rwanda with some of his men who were said to include several other military commanders of the (Democratic Forces for the Democratic Liberation of Rwanda (FDLR), who were allied with government troops during Congo's five year war. Generals Rwarakabije's surrender raised hopes that the guerrilla war against the government of Paul Kagame and his allies in the DRC, might soon end. Rwanda officially withdrew its soldiers from Congo in 2002. In exchange, the DRC agreed to stop supplying the Hutu rebels who had fought on their side. Hans Rokema, a Dutch peace activist who helped arrange the cease-fire, said that Paul Kagame's controversial yet comprehensive election victory, had weakened the rebels resolve. Kagame offered that, if they surrendered, most rebels would be allowed rejoin their families, but some would be prosecuted for their role in the genocide.[11]

The disarmament process was one of the major issues facing the international community and DRC president, Joseph Kabila. The rebels used DRC territory to steal inert resources and as a base from which to launch strikes into Rwanda. In response, Rwanda has twice invaded the DRC in pursuit of the rebels Kabila had failed to disarm. Paul Kagame threatened a third intervention if the rebels were not disbanded. In January 2005, UN peacekeepers adopted a proactive stance in the DRC and began launching several raids against Congolese militias in the Ituri district north of Kivu. The Kivu crisis, is a continuing threat to the shaky peace-process that ended the DRC's civil war.

Under the Tree Justice

By 1999 genocide was the most common charge made by the International Community Tribunal Rwanda (ICTR), but only 21 indictments had been were issued. Moreover by 2002, 25 convictions and $1 billion later, only 36% of Rwandans believed that the ICTR had promoted reconciliation. An estimated 1 million Rwandans (one-eighth of the population) were expected to be tried in traditional "Gacaca" village courts for alleged participation in the genocide. Gacaca courts were traditionally used by village communities who would gather on a patch of grass to resolve conflicts between two families, employing the heads of each household as judges.

Domitilla Mukantaganzwa, executive secretary of the National Service of Gacaca (grass roots or under the tree) Jurisdictions, announced that some trials would start in February 2005, with proceedings beginning in the rest of the country in 2006. "Drawing from the experience and figures accruing from the pilot trials, we estimate a figure slightly above 1 million people that are supposed to be tried under the Gacaca courts;" she told *Reuters*. Her comment illustrated the immense task awaiting the courts, preparing to hear accusations against hundreds of thousands of people, presently at large, and often in the company of neighbors whose relatives they are suspected of killing.

Gacaca courts cannot impose the death penalty, but they can sentence the convicted to lengthy prison terms, community service and order restitution be paid to the victims. They can refer cases of rape and murder to the criminal justice system, if clear evidence is found. Thousands of suspects were questioned by 751 village courts, sitting as investigative panels, listening to allegations and determining issues of jurisdiction. Another 8,262 trials and investigative hearings were scheduled. "We hope all this should be over by years end to have full trials commence in 2006. Ringleaders of the killings, however, will be tried by conventional courts," prosecutor, Mukantaganzwa stated. Focusing on confessions and apologies,, the Gacaca courts are intended to ease the way to national reconciliation. Under Gacaca, those who confess and plead guilty by a certain date have their sentences reduced.

The Gacaca courts, were initiated on an exploratory basis to accelerate the trials of suspects charged in conventional courts, with taking part in the genocide. Eleven years after the massacres, the backlog of suspects awaiting trial in conventional courts was enormous. There were 80,000 people behind bars and many were likely die before their cases could be heard. Many would eventually be transferred to Gacaca courts for trial. With investigations nearly complete, 717,000 people were due to face trial in 12,100 courts. By September 2006, 34,000 people had been tried, and most of them confessed. Many of the prisoners were released in exchange for a guilty plea which implicated others in their testimony. [12]

Critics noted that the investigative panels appeared to lack order and *Amnesty International* stated that: "Gacaca may become a vehicle for summary and arbitrary justice that fails defendants and genocide survivors alike." Rwandan officials admitted that Gacaca justice has flaws but that there is no alternative and that the international donor community, which is funding Gacaca courts, seemed to agree. Gacaca courts are a world away from the robed lawyers and air-conditioned hallways of the International Criminal Tribunal for Rwanda which is located in the northern Tanzanian town of Arusha, There, those accused of murder, rape and of organizing and inciting the genocide are tried in proceedings carried out behind bullet-proof glass. The ICTR had so far completed 26 cases. Cases involving 27 others were ongoing and 15 were awaiting trial. In the 10 years since it was established to try the architects of the genocide, the ICTR had indicted 81 people for genocide-related crimes. By January 2005, had been convicted 20 and three were acquitted. [13]

In the years since the genocide, 39 year-old Innocent Mulinda, started a family, took care of his red-earth farm and won a local election for a government job. Rumors that he participated in a murderous militia in his hillside town seemed to be behind him. But witnesses said a confessed militia member told a Gacaca court that Mulinda was not merely a fellow militiaman, but a leader who carried an AK-47, manned roadblocks and exhorted others to kill. Hours after the testimony, when darkness had fallen across his neighborhood of mud-walled homes, Mulinda drank a bottle of pesticide. He left behind a grieving wife, two young sons and much confusion among in neighbors who had hoped for justice in the form of a full confession and punishment befitting his crimes. According to his wife, Mulinda's agonizing death, took more than two days. His was one among many suicides and attempted suicides of Rwandan officials recorded in one year among genocide suspects, as Gacaca courts began to hear cases. Between March and December 2006, 69 suspects killed themselves and 44 others attempted to do so. Many others attempted or committed suicide in the several months before genocide victim record-keeping began.

It is unclear exactly what motivated the suicides: belated guilt, shame, fear of prison, or fear of exposing friends who also participated in the 100-day rampage of ethnic slaughter. The man who accused Mulinda of participating in the genocide, Canisous Munyeraraba, was a fellow militia member, implicated for more than a dozen killings. For confessing to illegal possession of a gun and looting, Munyeraraba was temporarily released from jail and will eventually receive a reduced sentence. Munyeraraba said the torment of confronting their own horrendous crimes is more than some men can bear. He said Mulinda had been a gentle, honorable man, both before and after his alleged crimes. "Many people changed during the genocide Mulinda was not a violent person. He just found himself in the atrocities, like many others;" Munyeraraba explained.

Others were less ready to excuse Mulinda's actions. Beatrice Mukamusoni, a 41 year-old Tutsi, said she did not see Mulinda commit any crimes, because she fled Shyorongi in the early days of the killing. But her husband, parents, sister and eldest child were killed in the genocide and she had long heard rumors that Mulinda was a leader within his neighborhood militia. Without a trace of remorse, she said: "All these people who had a role, they should resolve their cases by committing suicide." But her emotions concerning Mulinda's death are more complex. She respected his work as a government official and said they enjoyed an amicable relationship. Upon hearing the news of Mulinda's suicide, she said, she felt only sadness. "If he's not innocent, that means many other people around us are not innocent, so shall we live in this country alone."

Whatever their alleged crimes during the genocide, those who committed suicide, have ripped an hole in the lives of the friends and family left behind. In the village, thirty one year-old Jeanviere Nzamwitakuze, married Mulinda one year after the genocide. She had heard rumors of his involvement but said she believed his account of being only a low-ranking militia member who never killed anybody. Now she must tend to the family's crop of beans, corn and peas by herself, as well as raise their sons. His decision to leave them behind has caused her great sadness and turmoil, she said, though she maintained it was the pain of a boil on his leg that caused him to kill himself, not anguish over the accusations. "There are so many people accused of the same thing, and they are still living," she wept, averting her teary eyes.[14]

Such feelings are not uncommon in post-genocide Rwanda, where killers and survivors returned to the same villages, often living side by side Although survivors express little sympathy for the participants who committed suicide a decade later, some say their hopes for closure, a full public accounting of crimes and accomplices, as well as details about the victims' final hours, have been dashed. "No person has the right to punish themselves;" said Benoit Kaboyi, executive secretary of Rwanda's largest association of genocide survivors. "They have to suffer for what they have done."

Gacaca officials, who began tracking suicides in January and February of 2003, documented these deaths: An elderly man drowned himself in Lake Kivu, on Rwanda's western border, on the day he was accused of killing several of his grandchildren. A 28-year-old man, the last surviving member of his family, killed himself after being accused of raping his Tutsi mother. "Sometimes we discover a situation we cannot understand ourselves;" said the court's executive secretary, Domitilla Mukantaganzwa. "We are praying for our nation."

In Gashora, about 30 miles east of Kigali, 56 year-old Sylvester Ngiriyambonye, returned home after spending years in Rwanda's notoriously grim and crowded prisons, for his role in the death of a Tutsi woman and her teenage daughter. Two years later, a government official visited Gashora to begin organizing the Gacaca court where, under the rules of Ngiriyambonye's guilty plea, he would have been forced to testify against other militia members. Instead, his widow said, he hanged himself from a tree.

In nearby Lirima, 67 year-old Charles Rubuga, was accused of killing a man at a roadblock. He denied the charge during three days of Gacaca hearings, his family members said. "He came back a changed man;" said his widow, Angelina Ntibanoga, who had been married to Rubuga for 45 years. "All these years we've lived together, I have never assaulted anybody," she recalled him saying despondently. "I have never killed anybody. And now they have accused me of killing." The next morning, Rubuga walked several miles to the crocodile-infested Nyabarongo River, removed his clothes, laid down his machete and hurled himself in.

In July 2005, Former US Ambassador Robert Flatten defended the late Rwandan President Juvenal Habyarimana government's record at the ICTR trials in Arusha, Tanzania. Flatten's testimony was requested by defense attorney Peter Erlinder, on behalf of Major Aloys Ntabakuze, the former commander of the Kanombe paramilitary battalion in Kigali. Flatten served as the US envoy between December 1990 and November 1993. He left Rwanda five months before the genocide began. Upon returning to Washington, he worked as a consultant on the Rwandan crisis at the State Department. Flatten testified at the "military trial" of four former army officers, including that of Hutu leader Theoneste Bagosora and he told the court that the late president Habyarimana talked of peace and democracy, and asked the US "to help build democracy in Rwanda." He considered that the late president was genuinely committed to a peaceful resolution of the ethnic animosity between Hutu and Tutsi.

The prosecution charged that the genocide was planned by Theoneste Bagosora, Major Ntabakuze, Brigadier Gratien Kabiligi (former head of army operations) and Lieutenant Anatole Nsengiyumva (former army commander of Gisenyi in northwest Rwanda). Although all four plead not guilty, the prosecution also alleged the genocide was planned and implemented immediately following the April 6, 1994 plane crash, which killed president Habyarimana as he returned from regional power-sharing peace talks in Dar es Salaam. The Tribunal expected to complete its task by 2010. Seventeen more trials were scheduled by the end of 2005. The shortest sentence of six-years was to Vincent Rutaganira, a former councilor.[15]

After tracking Calixte Mbarushimana to France, the ICTR requested the French government either his prosecute or extradite him. Mbarushimana, (a former UNDP employee, suspected of directing or participating in the killing of 32 people), who was granted French refugee status in 2003, repeatedly denied the allegations, which include killing a colleague. However, his accusers (survivors and UNDP staff) stood by their claims. Among his victims was Florence Ngirumpatse, the UNDP administrator in Kigali, who was hacked to death along with schoolgirls she was protecting. Witnesses testified that Mbarushimana manned roadblocks where people were killed. They told investigators that the suspect was seen collaborating with Hutu death squads fingering Tutsis. While the UN collected evidence, he continued working in Angola and Kosovo, until charges against him became public and he was dismissed. In 2002, ICTR prosecutor, Carla Del Ponte, refused to prosecute Mbarushimana for lack of evidence. In September 2005, an independent UN administrative tribunal awarded him 13 months back pay, because he had not been found guilty of genocide charges. The panels overruled arguments from UNDP and from Secretary-General, Kofi Annan. Other suspects have been tried in Belgium, where investigations began in early 2005. In July 2005 the Rwandan government began releasing more than

36,000 prisoners from the country's overcrowded prisons. Those who confessed to their behavior and roles during the genocide would be gradually reintegrated into society.

In December 2005, a French military tribunal opened an investigation into allegations that French peacekeepers facilitated attacks on ethnic minority Tutsis during the genocide. A French judge visited Rwanda, interviewed six survivors and filed a lawsuit accusing French troops of "complicity in genocide" and "crimes against humanity." President Kagame became involved in the dispute when he blamed some of the continent's problems on French involvement in Africa. Kagame severed diplomatic ties with France after French judge, Jean-Louis Bruguiere, called for charges against him in the downing of former President Habyarimana's aircraft. There is deep enmity between French authorities and Kagame over their alleged roles leading up to the genocide. Kagame accuses France of supporting the old regime. Allison Des Forges, a Rwandan specialist at Human Rights Watch said: "While justice has to be served, there was growing willingness on the part of some Hutus to diminish the importance of the genocide before the Bruguiere issue. Unfortunately, this judgment could have the consequence of increasing that kind of rhetoric."[16] A few weeks later, the Paris prosecutor approved the issue of arrest warrants against President Kagame and nine of his associates. French law grants immunity to sitting heads of state, thus a warrant can not be issued against Kagame while he remains in office. Rwandan minister of justice, Tharcisse Karagurama, angrily responded saying: "It is very absurd for a foreign judge in a foreign country to issue indictments against authorities in a sovereign state for alleged crimes committed in that sovereign state… We view this as political intimidation by a big power using judicial power to enhance a political program"[17]

In April 2006, German authorities arrested Hutu leader, Ignace Murwanashyaka on immigration violations and held him in pre-extradition custody. He was under UN investigation, but no international warrant had been issued. German Police spokesman, Martin Boll, said Murwanashyaka was being held because he was the commander of 8,000 fighters of the Democratic Liberation Forces of Rwanda based in the eastern DRC.

Tanzania was asked to assume the responsibility of prosecuting Rwandan genocide suspects. Tanzanian Minister of Justice, Dr. Mary Nagu, said her ministry would look into the matter after receiving a formal request; because extensive preparations were necessary before accommodating such an international obligation. She said preparations might include resources like manpower, financial support from the international community and an examination of whether Tanzanian law allows the prosecution of someone who has committed a crime in another country. Her remarks followed a meeting with the top officials of the ICTR including its President, Judge Erik Mose (Norway), the Chief Prosecutor Hassan Bubacar Jallow (Gambia) and the Registrar, Adama Dieng (Senegal). The UN Security Council directed the

ICTR to complete trials within two years and to complete appellate cases by 2010.[18]

Despite their support for the ICC, Africans are concerned that their continent is being used as a laboratory for the new court. This is not the fault of the ICC prosecutor: the first four referrals were the DRC, Uganda, The Central African Republic and Sudan (Darfur). Three of those referrals came from the countries themselves and one from the Security Council. "The prosecutor has to draw on the moral authority of his office to make clear his impartiality and independence in complex highly divisive political situations;" said Director of Human Rights Watch, Richard Dicker. "At the moment he is failing to address concerns that he is being used by one side or another. In eastern Congo, he needs to look at all parties, with responsibility for horrific crimes and injury including political leaders in Kinshasa, Kigali and Kampala." Dicker further acknowledged that: "the prosecutor is in a tough spot: he is dependent on the cooperation of states to assist him in his investigation. It is in some cases mission impossible." In his report, Prosecutor, Moreno-Ocampo, defended the selection of the DRC and Uganda because "they were the gravest admissible situations" within his jurisdiction. He emphasized the difficulty of conducting investigations into areas of ongoing violence and executing arrest warrants. To operate in Uganda, Darfur and Congo required three to four languages and in some cases, 90 percent of the ICC's investigators returned with illnesses.

According to Zachary Lomo, former director of the Refugee Law Project at Kampala's Makrere University: "The fundamental issue is whether international law is international and capable of accommodating other rules and values systems or maintains it biased western model and cultural roots. Can we only punish crime with one specific model or can we use other models that allow communities and countries to get to the causes of the crime?"

Daniel Osabu Kle argued that the IMF and the World bank might well be considered among the hidden killers in the Rwandan genocide and elsewhere in the Third World. Despite the complete failure of their prescriptions to cure economic maladies, those financial institutions were not held accountable. Shielded from any accountability, the IMF and the World Bankwere encouraged in their irresponsibility. While others were being brought to justice for the part they played in the Rwanda genocide, the complicity of the IMF and the World Bank's "structural adjustment" crimes against humanity went ignored. The IMF and World Bank were insensitive to the sufferings of the Rwandan people or the evident signs of a bloody confrontation developing out of the harsh economic policies imposed on Rwanda.

---

1. Robert F. Van Lierop, *Report on the International Criminal Tribunal for Rwanda*. (Hempstead, N. J.: Hofstra University Press 1998) 207.

2. Ibid. 208.

3. Gerard Prunier, "The Rwanda Crisis: A History of A Genocide." 39 and Philip Gourevitch,

4. "Letter from Rwanda: After the Genocide," *The New Yorker*, December 18, 1995. p.78.

5. Daniel Osabu-Kle, *Compatible Cultural Democracy: The Key To African Development.* (Ontario: Broadview Press, 2000) 217.

6. William Schabas, "Justice Democracy and Impunity in Post-Genocide Rwanda:Searching for Solutions to Impossible Problems." 7 *Criminal L. F.* 523,531, 1998.

7. Ibid.

8. Tom Masland, "Will It Be Peace or Punishment?" *Newsweek* (crediting the Rwandan ethnic cleansing to the group officially responsible-the radical Hutu militia) August 1, 1994.

9. Van Licrop, Op. Cit. p.209.

10. Ibid

11. *See* Prunier, Op. Cit. *see also African Rights*, "Rwanda: Death, Despair and Defiance", (1995); *African Rights*, "Rwanda Not So Innocent: When Women Become Killers" (1995);

12. *Human Rights Watch*, "Playing the 'Communal Card: Communal Violence and Human Rights." (1995); *Genocide in Rwanda: A Collective Memory*, John A. Berry, et. al. translated, 1995.

13. 'Hutu rebels seek return to Rwanda after surrender.' *The Financial Times*, November 19, 2003.

14. Arthur Asiimwe, 'Rwanda Estimates 1 Million Face Genocide Charges,' *Reuters* January 14, 2005.

15. Craig Timberg, 'In Rwanda, Suicides Haunt Search for Justice and Closure,' *The Washington Post,* February 17, 2006.

16. Andrew England, 'Warrants prompt Rwanda to recall envoy,' *The Financial Times,* November 25-26, 2006, p3.

17. Andrew England, 'Rwanda president faces arrest warrant,' *The Financial Times*, November 22, 2006. p. 6.

18. Hirondelle News Agency. Rwanda: 'Tanzania Asked to Prosecute Genocide Suspects After ICTR Mandate,' (Lausanne, March 27, 2006) Posted to the web March 27, 2006

13: Sierra Leone: Compromised Auto-Immunity

Sierra Leone is a mountainous country with fertile soil, abundant mineral wealth and warm beaches. However, overpopulation, migration, environmental degradation, economic instability and the breakdown of social cohesion have made Sierra Leone case study in national lawlessness. A product of British colonialism before the end of their slave trade, the capital of Freetown, was founded by former-slaves, repatriated by the British. The first to arrive were the so-called "Black Poor," a group of 400 people sent from England in 1787. Shortly thereafter, former slaves from Nova Scotia and Jamaica, who had gained their freedom by fighting with the British against their American masters arrived. About 40,000 Africans were liberated by the British and others from slave ships captured along the West African coast and they also settled in Freetown and the surrounding areas in during first half of the nineteenth century.

The descendants of Sierra Leone's repatriated African settlers blended African and British culture and lifestyles into a distinctive Krio or Creole, culture. They developed their own language, Krio, which became the nation's national language. The politically dominant Krio make up only 5 percent of Sierra Leone's multi-ethnic population. The people of Sierra Leone take pride in their society where Muslims and Christians coexist peacefully and tribal and religious boundaries are nominal. The once renowned education system, Freetown's Fourah Bay College, is the oldest university south of the Sahara,.

Since independence in 1961, Sierra Leone's rulers have struggled to unify a nation of more than a dozen ethnic groups by purchasing the loyalty of ethnically diverse warlords and strongmen who control natural resources, command local authority and, whose allegiances are requisite for effective exercise and control of power. Fearing that these strongmen could use state institutions to threaten the state, Sierra Leone's rulers weakened the state bureaucracies and manipulated access to natural resources in order to neutralize any would be challengers.[1] Journalists who criticize the governmental policy face jail and possible torture.

Krio political dominance declined during the 1950s, as more Sierra Leonean's were given the right to vote. The first party to win widespread national support was the Sierra Leone People's Party (SLPP), led by Milton Margai which led the country to independence. The SLPP was narrowly defeated in 1967 by Siaka Stevens and the All People's Congress (APC).

Siaka Stevens ruled form 1967 to 1985 and turned the country's diamond industry over to his associates, whom he exempted from taxation. Sierra Leone's diamond industry once provided nearly 70 percent of the country's export earnings and a quarter of its GNP. In the 1985 staged election, the retiring president chose an associate Joseph Momoh as his successor. Momoh lacked the strong personal base of political and following of economic sycophants that Stevens commanded, rendering him incapable of ending private control of the country's natural wealth enjoyed by the warlords. He promised to improve producer market prices as part of a "Green Revolution," but the promise rang hollow. Like its inert resources, and precious mineral wealth, much of Sierra Leone's agricultural produce had been smuggled out of the country.

The loss of official revenues impoverished most state institutions. Momoh's inability to supply essential services, or to act effectively as a personal patron, prompted many young men, to seek their fortunes in the diamond-mining areas under the control of various regional strongmen.

. Sierra Leone's descent into hell, was the result of the collapse of a patron-client political system that characterizes many neo-colonial states including neighboring Liberia. The war left tens of thousands dead and many more mutilated and destroyed much of the country's infrastructure.

The war began with a 1991 insurgency launched from neighboring Liberia, which fed off of Sierra Leone's diamond fields. It was a brutal, confusing conflict in which fighters frequently switched allegiances. Paradoxically, despite over a decade of war, in which atrocities by the rebels include looting villages, recruiting (kidnapping) child soldiers as young as 10 year of age, and hacking off of noses, breasts and limbs, the people, reportedly, remain among the friendliest in Africa

Momoh was not prepared to counter the rebel threat from Liberia. Charles Taylor, using dissidents and the Revolutionary Unity Front (RUF) guerilla army as a proxy, invaded and exploited the economically lucrative, mineral-rich regions of the country in order to purchase arms and pay off his own supporters. The RUF quickly became a domestic insurgency under the leadership of Foday Sankoh, whom Charles Taylor had met in Libya and who had spent six years in prison for his role in an alleged 1971 coup plot. In response to the RUF invasion, Momoh increased the army's strength from 3,000 to 14,000 soldiers. The expansion was made just as creditors such as the World Bank and the IMF demanded that Momoh reduce the country's deficit. Cut off from further loans until he accomplished this, Momoh was unable to finance his expanded army. Soldiers went unpaid and commanders "led" from the rear, leaving young non-commissioned officers in charge of actual battle operations. Inevitably, on April 29, 1992, Valentine Strasser and several other dissident officers marched on Freetown, and overthrew Momoh.[2]

President Strasser faced even more problems than Momoh. He tried to use his youth and military origins to appeal to his countrymen by wearing wrap-around sunglasses and billing himself as the "Redeemer." He encouraged the expression of national pride by sponsoring political murals around Freetown. The war continued to take its toll Strasser postponed elections and by early 1995 the country's finance minister estimated that fighting rebels had consumed 75 percent of government expenditures. Strasser found that he could hardly finance a loyal and efficient military; much less deliver on his many popular promises to provide state services, so he turned to short-term solutions. One strategy, included executing prisoners in Freetown's Pademba Road Prison for allegedly plotting a coup from behind bars. This event drew international condemnation and further weakened the country's financial situation.

Eventually, the rebels severed the Strasser's regime's ties to its major domestic source of revenue. RUF guerillas attacked foreign workers at *Sierra Rutile's* titanium oxide mine and *SIEROMCO*, a Swiss-owned bauxite mine. The attacks ended production at both mines, which accounted for 15 percent of GNP, and in 1994, supplied 57 percent of the country's official export earnings. A combination of RUF soldiers turned rebels (sobels), rogue military commanders and warlords controlled the clandestine diamond and agricultural trade valued at over $200 million, while in 1994 and 1995, government domestic revenues totaled only $60 million.

Outsourcing Security

When South Africa elected a government of national unity in 1994, it faced the dilemma of how to dismantle the apartheid-era security establishment. Many former South Africa's Defense Force personnel, found commercial mercenary opportunities with *Executive Outcomes* (EO). Headed by Eeban Barlow, *EO* recruited soldiers from the 32nd Buffalo Battalion, the unit once charged with aiding Angola's (UNITA) rebels. The Angolan civil war provided them in marketable counterinsurgency skills. Barlow had previously worked with South Africa's Civil Cooperation Bureau, which was designed to counter anti-apartheid movement and identify sanctions busting commercial contacts. This put him in contact with a global network of mercenaries for hire and rapacious arms merchants.

In April 1995, Strasser requested the services of *EO*. Within two weeks, *EO* suppressed all rebel activity in Freetown, and by August had conquered the main diamond-mining areas, removing all and rebels and rogue military units. The firm's military offenses against the RUF were instrumental in bringing rebels Foday Sankoh and Ahmed Tejan Kabbah to the negotiating table in Abidjan Cote d'Ivoire where they signed a peace treaty in April 2006.[3]

Executive Outcomes trained local self-defense units called Kamajors, to replace the undisciplined army of Sierra Leone. *EO's* competitive advantage in Sierra Leone was due in part to its close ties to the UK-based firm, *British Mining*. Because the government of Sierra Leone was perennially on the brink of bankruptcy, *EO* found it extremely useful to have a relationship with a mining firm which produces precious gems. *British Mining's* $80 million commitment to develop a kimberlite diamond mine in the heart of the contested areas of the country required an ally that would pay for mutually beneficial security and solve the regime's serious revenue crunch, a new "dual mandate." *EO's* successful military offensives brought enough political stability to permit the national elections in 1996, and eventually bring Ahmed Tejan Kabbah to power. As a former UN official, Kabbah generated considerable global goodwill and his political legitimacy translated into a threefold increase in bilateral aid. Subsequent official revenue and debt payments improved relations with international donors and creditors, who granted a 20 percent reduction in the country's foreign debt in 1995 and 1996.[4]

President Kabbah studied economics in Wales, qualified as a barrister in London and served almost 20 years with the United Nations Development Program (UNDP) in New York and Africa before joining the Strasser administration. He retired at the age of 60, was elected president in 1996, ousted by military coup the following year and reinstated a year later. Kabbah and his Sierra Leone People's Party won a 70 percent landslide victory in 2002, and his vice-president, Solomon Birwa, was chosen to replace him in the next election. Although the Kabbah government had begun post-war reconstruction, the political and economic causes of the war remain unaddressed. Bishop Joseph Humper, chaired Sierra Leone's Truth and Reconciliation Commission, which investigated war atrocities. He identified factors common to all African governments including bad governance, endemic corruption, marginalization, social and economic inequalities, nepotism and tribalism. For Bishop Humper offered his prescription which reflected this widespread frustration; "A chronic sore requires a chronic treatment." For the first in local elections for three decades, the SLPP A resounding defeat .

The price Sierra Leone paid for centralized government was estimated between $3 and $4 million a month, plus the cost of weapons that *EO* and *Life Guard*, a firm closely associated with *EO*, for providing the security services. The Kabbah government mortgaged valuable natural resources it would otherwise not control to pay for the mercenaries, thus, making the services of *EO* quite a bargain. Some endorse the use of private militaries like *Executive Outcomes* to replace risky, strings-attached military aid from foreign states. William Reno asserts that the case of Sierra Leone, underscored the costs of outsourcing essential state military and revenue tasks to foreign firms. First, *EO* played an autonomous role in Sierra Leonean politics, at the expense of government individuals who originally contracted the firm's services. Second, *EO* did not support Strasser when he appeared to renege on holding a scheduled election. Instead, *EO's* presence gave Kabbah sufficient security to force his opponent Julius Maada Bindo and twenty senior level officers to take "educational leave" in exile.[5]

The merging of interests between *EO* executives and advocates of civilian rule obscures an important aspect of the firm's ominous presence. *EO* and its partners rely on political instability as a market force. *EO*'s presence made it possible to establish a corporate web of allied mining, engineering, medical, transport, and even tourist firms made up of the former South African security forces merged with carrion seeking entrepreneurs. Under *EO*'s protection, can do business where others merchants fear to tread. The government's dependence on *EO* allowed these investors to demand favorable deals, while excluding all serious competition. Therefore, *EO's* presence was pivotal in creating and maintaining a political-commercial network that replaced an indigenous state bureaucracy and compromised its auto-immune system. This begs the question; who are the real bosses of the commercial networks that have become deeply insinuated in the economic and political life of a country that hires a private military? They are foreign shareholders, who expect operations to turn a profit. Profit, not the promotion of democracy, is the real business of *EO*. Ultimately, conflict resolution is not *EO's* interest because this would open economies to competition from larger, more efficient firms.[6]

While employing a mercenary officer corps under the *EO* security umbrella may provide short-term security in Sierra Leone, it creates a long term, if not unending dependency on a profit driven entity to defend, if not to define its national security interests. Moreover, thousands of armed men were left idle to constitute a new, non-state army. Thus, in September and October of 1996, the Kamajors clashed with regular army soldiers caught looting near the provincial capital of Kenema. They also battled Jombolas, a rival irregular militia in the diamond fields that protects freelance illicit mining by local residents. At best *EO's* intervention established a holding pattern that only worsened the situation and further compromised the nation's auto-immune system. Under IMF pressure to cut expenses, Kabbah dismissed *Executive Outcomes* in 1997. However, he did not repatriate the Nigerians who had intervened to protect their own interests.

Nigeria inserted itself into Sierra Leone through the Economic Community Monitoring Group (ECOMOG). Nigeria used the peacekeeping operation as an instrument of foreign policy to cover its unilateral objective in Sierra Leone, to restore Kabbah to power. ECOMOG was created in August 1990 as a mechanism to stop the bloody Liberian civil war, and was hailed as a promising model for regional peacekeeping. Nigeria formed ECOMOG to prevent Charles Taylor from toppling an ally, Samuel K. Doe. Taylor's indiscriminate use of violence, allowed Nigeria to tacitly enlist ECOWAS, in its pursuit of Nigerian foreign policy interests, maintaining a friendly regime in an Anglophone enclave, Liberia and Sierra Leone, which are surrounded by francophone states. It soon became apparent that regional peacekeepers in Africa faced the universal dilemma encountered by peacekeepers, when their interests are at stake. In Liberia, ECOMOG became a party to the struggle for power among the warlords. This was because Nigeria, always the dominant power within ECOMOG, had strong preferences about who should rule Liberia. Nigeria had two stakes in the Kabbah regime. On the one hand, supporting "democracy" in Sierra Leone, if only to improve the country's image and to erase image of the Abacha regime and to isolate Charles Taylor from the Revolutionary Unity Front (RUF), whose formation he had encouraged. [7]

Throughout ECOMOG's operation in Liberia, Freetown served as a rear base for the Nigerian military command. Nigeria sent troops and supplies to the capital, after the National Patriotic Front of Liberia (NPFL) made incursions into the country. Some Nigerian officers commanding ECOMOG units used their positions for economic gain. As Francis Picard reported in *Le Monde:* "ECOMOG had often been accused of engaging the same racketeering and pillaging activities as the Liberian militias."[8]

Owing his restored presidency to Nigeria, Kabbah was in no position to dismiss Nigerian forces. Thus, Nigeria retained the capacity to project its power in the sub region and was well positioned to assist other regional allies, such as the government of Guinea, which was also concerned about subversion by Charles Taylor. Nigerian commanders accused Taylor of sending NPFL troops across the border to assist the military junta in Sierra Leone. Taylor became irate when ECOMOG planes forced down two helicopters carrying junta officials over Liberian airspace and when a Nigerian alpha-jet buzzed the presidential residence in an obvious act of intimidation. Taylor's continued presence also precluded the need for Nigeria to repatriate some 7,000 battle-hardened, frustrated and somewhat dissatisfied troops.[9]

Sierra Leone became a test case for the rehabilitation of failed African states. A country rich in resources, with a population of manageable size, it is one of the most devastated places on the planet. Britain, acting as the country's guardian and mentor, spent £100 million per year on aid, training and security support for this nation of five million. The UN Development Program's Human Development Index (HDI), ranks Sierra Leone last of all countries for which data are available, with life expectancy of 34 years, and an adult literacy of 36 percent The country has international communities highest levels of infant and pregnancy related deaths. Freetown's population overflows with young rural economic refugees seeking a better life. Most lack basic skills and live in the squalor of the streets. Three-quarters of these are between the ages of 18 and 35 and are unemployed. Many among them are ex-combatants, child soldiers who are of particular concern.

Years after the disarmament, demobilization and reintegration program, unemployed youth feel the government ignores their needs. Sierra Leone is divided between the western area around Freetown and the "provinces," where the traditional system of land-ownership by chiefdom remains. There are a few large, mechanized farms but the country has some of the worst roads in Africa. The railway system, which collapsed long before the war, requires a massive infusion of capital to function. Most towns lack telephone service and clean water and many only receive electricity on alternate days. The government hopes to reduce its crippling energy deficit by completing the long delayed, Bumbuna dam project in the south.

There are little, if any, domestic savings in a subsistence economy. Seventy-five percent of Sierra Leone's 5 million people are farmers and there are vast tracts of arable land. What is needed are the roads and technological infrastructure to meet domestic food needs. The country exported rice until the 1980s but now imports it. In 2004, economists estimated it would take three or four years before growth in economic income was sufficient to overtake consumption. Sierra Leone's per capita income stagnated in the 1970s, declined in the 1980s and dropped by 40 percent during the 1990s. The legal monthly minimum wage is about $14, less than twice the hourly minimum wage for adults in the UK. Seventy per cent of the population is lives below the poverty line on about $0.75 a day. The people suffer from diseases such as bacterial diarrhea, e-coli infections and river blindness. Sixty-nine out of every one thousand infants dies at birth, and the adult HIV/Aids infection rate is 5.98 percent and there is only one doctor for every 11,270 people.

Among Africa's low wage economies, Sierra Leone's public sector faces a capacity shortage that is more acute than the investment shortage. The IMF complains of "substantial difficulties in tracking financial transactions of the public and private sectors that circumvent the central bank." A public expenditure tracking survey found, that only a fraction of the drugs passing through the country's public health system were accounted for.

Despite steep increases of officially registered diamond exports, the country is far from realizing its export potential and maintains a large trade deficit. The informal sector, which includes most domestic business, extends to external trade through diamond smuggling and the opaque fisheries industry. Since 1995, the country's currency has been devalued against the dollar by 95%. It would take nothing short of a miracle for Sierra Leone to meet the first of the UN's Millennium Development Goals, to cut the poverty rate in half by 2015. Some estimates of the economic growth indicated a real-term increase of 6 or 7 per cent in 2003-2004. A new statistical series, utilized by the IMF, recorded the country's economic growth at 9.3 percent in 2003 and 7.4 percent in 2004. Absent the recovery process is significant private sector investment, although there are some ventures in mobile telephone services and small-scale mining. Chinese companies have moved in to fill the investment vacuum establishing a growing and diverse economic foothold and exploiting Sierra Leone's vast supply of strategic materials.

After eleven ears of war, the worst damaged is the eastern part of Freetown. Years after the war, burned out and bullet ridden houses reflect the intensity of the violence. But, new churches, hospitals and administrative buildings, decked in scaffolding, demonstrate the determination to rebuild. Roads, clinics and schools are also being rebuilt. Exports are on the rise and the nation has declared its readiness to "wean itself off UN military support." Despite the many improvements since the end of the war, government officials fear the international community will fail to deliver the volume of assistance required to secure the peace.

The United Nations Mission in Sierra Leone (UNAMSIL) reduced its peacekeeping force from 17,500 to about 3,000. Despite an extensive military training program, international officials detect potential problems in Sierra Leone's over-sized and under-funded army. Internal tensions among the newly-incorporated rebels of RUF are festering over unemployment, barracks conditions and equipment. The 2,000 peacemaking British intervention force, which played a decisive role in ending the war, continues to provide training and is committed to deploy forces within 48 hours, if needed. The UK offered to donate a fleet of new police vehicles, until it was discovered that their maintenance would consume most of the law enforcement budget.

In June 2004, Global Witness, a UK based group, claimed that classified briefings given to congressional members by the FBI's terrorist finance team, confirmed that al-Qaeda operatives had visited Liberia and Sierra Leone in order to gain access to the diamond trade. Although the FBI declined to comment on the investigation, the smuggling of "conflict diamonds" grew as an international issue in the wake of the human rights abuses supported by the trade. During the 1991-2002 civil war, the Revolutionary United Front was notorious for chopping off civilian limbs and abducting children to serve as fighters. In response to the governments campaign slogan to encourage voting "the future is in your hands," the RUF chopped off civilian hands. The RUF took over the country's main diamond mining areas and proceeds from the trade, enhanced their power. Reacting to international condemnation for its atrocities against civilians, The RUF signed a cease-fire, clearing the way for elections in 1999 as the UN deployed 17,500 peacekeepers and the UK sent troops to support the Kabbah administration. Foday Sankoh, who was imprisoned for war crimes, died of natural causes in July 2003. The Post-war elections were orderly, Ahmad Tejan Kabbah was re-elected. President Kabbah testified to the Truth and Reconciliation Commission that he had no say over the operations of pre-government militias during the civil war. In March 2004, the UN-backed International Criminal Court (ICC), began preparing for the trials of senior militia leaders from both sides of the civil war.

In June 2004, a Special Court was convened in Freetown to prosecute war crimes. The court was an innovative hybrid, a joint venture between the UN and the government of Sierra Leone. Other than the Nuremberg and Tokyo tribunals, it was the first of its kind to be established within the country concerned. Based on the theory that a local court backed by international authority would be more efficient in dispensing justice than an external tribunal, this is justice on the cheap. The court seeks to avoid the costs and delays associated with the International Court of former Yugoslavian (ICTY) war criminals, in The Hague and the ICTR Rwanda genocide tribunal, in Tanzania. This is not a full-scale UN court; it relies on contributions from 33 individual members, led by the US, UK and the Netherlands. Though free of bureaucratic constraints, it lacks the mandated support of courts established under Chapter 7 of the UN Charter, which obliges other countries to cooperate. Three years of $81 million in voluntary funding ended in 2005, but the UN funded the gap.

Government officials warned of potential trouble by some of the factions involved in the conflict. There are three groups of defendants; the Civil Defense Forces, the RUF and the Armed Forces Revolutionary Council, (the junta that seized power between May 1997 and March 1998). The court was less than successful because of the sparsity of accused in the dock, and the absence of Charles Taylor. The Liberian-backed RUF is responsible for initiating the conflict and inflicting terror and horror by cutting off hands, arms, feet, legs, lips or ears. In the opening stages of the trial, many were shocked to discover that the number one defendant was not a rebel, but a government official. Former defense minister, Sam Hinga Norman, was indicted as the coordinator of the tribal militias in the pro-government Civil Defense Forces and commander of the notorious cult-based Kamajors.

This Sierra Leone court's mandate is restricted to those alleged to bear "the greatest responsibility" for organizing atrocities and to crimes committed through November 1996. It was to involve between 20 and 30 indictments, but only 13 were issued. RUF leader Sam "Mosquito" Bockarie was killed in Liberia. Military junta leader, Johnny Paul Koroma was missing and believed dead, while Charles Taylor was on trial in the Hague.

Also controversial, was the decision to simultaneously hold a South-African-style Truth and Reconciliation Commission, gathering testimony from victims and perpetrators of the atrocities. Some were reluctant to testify even though prosecutors promised to use only evidence from their own investigations. Like war ICTR, Sierra Leone's' Reconciliations Council was under-funded. The four Sierra Leonean's on the seven-member commission were widely criticized for being too sympathetic to the government. When the court's four-volume report was written, only ten copies were published.

Blood Diamonds

Sierra Leone's became synonymous with "blood" or "conflict" diamonds. Diamonds are cited as one of the prime causes of the eleven year civil war.

The RUF was, in part, made up of itinerant diamond diggers. Rebels control of the diamond fields, helped finance and sustain the conflict.

The significance of diamonds in Sierra Leone is demonstrated by the fact that it is much more difficult to get an appointment with an official of the department of mineral resources, than with the president. The government reported that official diamond revenues doubled between 2000 and 2004 to $126 million. Alimany Wuri, the director of mines, stated: "We're trying to convince people to stop smuggling but it's not easy. We lack the logistics. There are simply not enough officers to monitor it. Alluvial diamonds are scattered all over the country. We've been overstretched."

There is persistent industrial speculation about a $70,000 diamond that went "missing". Sierra Leone's diamond fields are dominated by small-scale miners of alluvial deposits. The only industrial scale mining operation is conducted by *Koido Holdings* of China. In 2004, the official figure for extracted diamonds was estimated at 643,000 carats. This compares with 2 million carats mined annually during the peak years of the late 1960s. The government is seeking the elusive large scale investment of a big name corporations such as *DeBeers*. In May 2004, *Mano River Resources*, a British-Canadian prospecting group announced a $3.4 million joint venture with *BHP Billiton*, to explore of a9700 square miles in the south-east of the country. *Mano River Resources* planned to start production of a $3 million, hard rock kimberlite joint venture mine in the Kono district.

The US government never officially confirmed its claims that al-Qaeda earned $20 million selling African conflict diamonds; the connection is possible. One intelligence official stated that it was easy to point to plausible financial links between al-Qaeda and West Africa, but much more difficult to find any evidence. In an interview with *the Financial Times*, US prosecutor, David Crane, stated that there was a terrorist presence in the region but declined to go into detail because: "There are all sorts of things going on that are outside our mandate and we do not pursue." On November 5, 2002, forty-five nations met in Interlaken, Switzerland, to finalize an agreement preventing the international marketing of conflict diamonds. The implementation of UN-backed measures to certify the source of diamonds, known as the Kimberly Process, began the following year.

Threats of a consumer boycott forced the industry to begin self-regulation. According to Jonathan Oppenheimer, the head of production relations at *DeBeers* (the South African diamond mining group): "Conflict diamonds are a tangible risk whether around the corner or already upon us. Public opinion is a fickle beast. It either doesn't care or it cares a lot.... The challenge is to preserve the unique honor system that exists within the diamond trading system without putting bureaucratic burdens on it." The British Foreign Office established the Customs and Excise diamonds department, to ensure UK compliance with the Kimberly Process.[10]

Tougher measures to curb the conflict diamond trade were threatened by the New-York based *World Diamond Council* (WDC). More self-regulation and an international monitoring body are required to screen out conflict diamonds. Some *WDC* members complained that African governments did not have the resources to upgrade their diamond export systems. Matthew Run, a *WDC* executive, stated: "We are persuaded that to attempt any changes now, on the brink of implementation, would serve to delay implementation perhaps indefinitely."

De Beers, which stood to lose the most from negative publicity and a boycott of diamonds, led the industry to the Kimberly Process, which Oppenheimer compared to "herding cats." The number of diamonds that originate in the conflict zones of countries such as; Angola, Sierra Leone, the Democratic Republic of the Congo and Sierra Leone is disputed. The industry estimates that only about 2 per cent of the world's supply comes from these areas and warns that overemphasizing the dangers of these illegal markets could jeopardize legitimate production in Botswana, South Africa and Namibia. *Global Witness* estimated that as much as 20 per cent of diamonds are illicitly traded. They claim that diamond traders, many of them based in Europe and Israel, are slow in screening out the diamonds that fund civil conflict in Africa and finance terrorist organizations. The *Sierra Rutile* mine in southwest Sierra Leone, yields titanium dioxide which is used in pigments and high-tech alloys. The mine was once a primary source of government revenue, and scheduled to restart production with US and EU backing in 2005. Controls on the diamond trade have resulted in a steep rise in production costs.

The Chinese Prescription

China leads the way in assisting Sierra Leone in business investment and development. Beginning in the 1970s, Chinese investment grew until forced by the war to withdraw. Convinced in 2002 by the Kabbah government to resume operations, Chinese investors have regained their momentum. The Chinese have numerous construction projects, including the 60,000-capacity national stadium in Freetown, the Youyi building, which houses most government ministries and the army headquarters. *The Beijing Urban Construction Group,* which has a 25-year lease on the facility with the government, rehabilitated the prominent Bintumani Hotel and planned to upgrade the site to include a Casino. China re-invested in the Megabass Sugar Complex, the country's only sugar production enterprise, which it helped to establish in the 1980s. The facility consists of a sugar-cane farm and mill which produces 6000 tons of sugar per year. In January 2003, a lease contract was signed between the *Chinese National Complete Plant Import and Export Corporation,* and Sierra Leone to begin production in 2005. Over fifteen Chinese companies planned to occupy the site. They will be engaged in diverse production activities including; the manufacture of building materials, pharmaceuticals, mattress-making and garage diagnostics. A tractor assembly plant will be built at a former bricks works in Freetown.

The Chinese firm, *Henan Guoji,* plans a $266 million project to revitalize the ocean-front of Freetown's Lumley beach area. An agreement signed with the Sierra Leone's national tourist board in 2004; includes plans to build a 250-bed luxury hotel complex and conference center, holiday apartments, townhouses and a promenade. There are long-term plans for a mini-sport stadium in the southern provincial capital of Bo. Another Chinese interest in Sierra Leone is rice production and the country is almost meeting Chinese food production targets. China has long-term interests in Sierra Leone's fisheries and two Chinese companies signed joint-venture contracts during the 1980s.

The government of China indicates many reasons for investing in Sierra Leone. Central among these are the long-standing ties between the two governments. Sierra Leone helped China enter the diplomatic community three decades ago. "Bilateral relations are very good;" said China's UK embassy economic and commercial counselor, Zhao Zhongqui. "Sierra Leone helped China re-enter the international community in the 1970's and the Chinese people will never forget friends like these. They have supported us on many important issues." A closer look reveals shared historic reasons for renewed Sino-African cooperation. Mr. Zhongqui went onto state that: "Both countries have been developing countries, and now we are helping Sierra Leone to develop quickly to maximize prosperity." While Chinese investment is welcomed, there remain concerns about the special incentives awarded Chinese companies, the limited training of African workers, and the degree to which Chinese companies (like US companies), might be using the country as a dumping ground for cheap goods. These concerns were expressed by Chris Jasabe, managing director of the *Sierra Leone Export Development and Investment Corporation:* "All investors should be treated the same. The problem is that investors come in and take risks and demand concessions that might not be applicable. Then everyone else starts asking for them. We are trying to put a stop to this."

The greatest drawback to Sierra Leone's reliance on Chinese investment is the possibility of renewed instability, which could prompt another withdrawal. Sierra Leone remains vulnerable to regional instability with possible spill-over effects from the conflict in the Cote d'Ivoire and the instability in Guinea, which surround Sierra Leone geographically. An ongoing border dispute near the geographic juncture with Liberia and Guinea, remains unresolved. A contingent of Guinean soldiers continues to occupy what Sierra Leone considers to be its side of the river.

The UN blueprint for Sierra Leone's transition voiced concern over "the slow pace of reforms in critical areas," particularly in the justice system which it described as largely ineffective. While the UK and other donor nations have pressed the Kabbah government to tackle official corruption, they were reluctant to protest as vehemently as they would against for example, Kenyan corruption. While sympathetic to investors need for reassurance about security, concerns about corruption were a sore point with

President Kabbah, as he told the *Financial Times*: "Frankly, I have always viewed corruption as two-way traffic. Say you want to invest in something here and then you go and see an official and the official demands something from you then you blow the whistle and come to me and we will take immediate steps. But to go to the corner and start talking about it, that is not quite helpful."

Sierra Leone's short-term economic fate rested partially with the outcome of the World Bank's Paris meeting in May 2005, where donors made their aid pledges for the next three years. The World Bank and the UN estimated the country's financial needs at between $800 million and $1 billion. To enhance government revenues, President Kabbah announced a 3 percent export tax and a tax increase on diamond sales. "Because of this new system, the Kimberly process, it is no longer attractive for people who were doing the smuggling. So this is the time for us to increase our export duty on diamonds so we can raise more funds for our development projects;" said Kabbah. However, director of mines, Alimany Wuri, announced the rate would remain at 3 percent stating: "We don't want to destroy the momentum." In order to preclude unrest, the government seemed to shift its focus to the workers. A quarter of diamond export taxes are reinvested in local communities in the form of development grants. There is nascent infrastructural development such as school, roads, assistance to diggers and other artisanal workers to set up mining cooperatives and to educate the workers to negotiate better prices for their finds. USAID and the Peace Diamond Alliance are involved in these efforts.

The system of agreed controls designed to end the illicit trade in "conflict diamonds," brought a much larger share of the rough gem exports into government accounts, increasing 2003 revenues by two-thirds, to $126 million. However, this was estimated to be only between a quarter and a half of the total, and some of those registered exports may be diamonds from other countries laundered through Sierra Leone. Because of the informal nature of the diamond industry, potential investors lack sufficient market data on which to base their decisions. The IMF, highlight concerns over "special agreements" between the government and investors that may deviate from industry norms and the need to weigh diamond tax revenues against investor incentives.

President Kabbah announced plans to levy higher taxes on the diamond sector. Higher taxation on diamond exports had been ruled out, because it would encourage the smuggling of gems to other countries and export from there. But the enforcement controls of the Kimberly certification scheme make unnecessary to keep the export tax at 3 percent. Therein lies the promise for an increase in development funds. "And that's the way we are going to move;" promised Kabbah. In the end, Sierra Leone's compromised auto immune system also compromised national control over the nations most valuable inert resources.

---

1. William Reno, (1997) 'Privatizing War in Sierra Leone,' *Current History*, Vol. 96 # 610 p. 227.

2. Ibid. 228.

3. Ibid. 229.

4. Ibid. 229.

5. Ibid.

6. Ibid. 30.

7. Robert Mortimer, "From ECOMOG to ECOMOG II: Intervention in Sierra Leone," in John Harbeson and Donald Rothchild, editors, *Africa in World Politics: The African State System in Flux*. (Oxford Press: London, 2000), 188-195.

8. Quoted in *Le Monde*, January 14-15 1996. During the looting of Monrovia in April 1996, a UN worker asserted that "the best cars, the best video players, the best air conditioners went to ECOMOG officers." *New York Times*, April 30, 1996.

9. Ibid. pp. 198-199.

10. *The Financial Times*, 'Diamond division to aid UK customs,' November 26, 2002.

14: South Africa's Mixed Prognosis

The history of the South Africa began in 1652, when the *Dutch India Company* established a way station known as Cape Town. The inhabitants of Cape Town raised livestock and food crops, selling them at company prices to European ships traveling to and from Asia. The sixty original European settlers, led by Jan van Riebeck, waged war against the local Khoisan people between and gradually expanded their settlements thereafter. Further wars of conquest led to expanded settlements by Dutch, German and French Protestants.

With the arrival of European women, the initial practice of marrying local women or imported slave (usually Malaysian women) was abandoned. But the children of these early interracial marriages became the first of what became the increasing mixed race (colored) population. Interracial liaisons (between white men and black women) continued and many coloreds learned to think, speak and act as their fathers. They attended the services of the Dutch Reformed Church, worked loyally and fought for Boer farmers against the Khoisan people. The Khoisan continued to resist settlement, but as the colony expanded, their cattle were killed or stolen. In the 1700s, the Khoisan were decimated by smallpox epidemics. Some kingdoms continued to resist, but the Boers continued their expansion, at least until 1779, when they encountered the Xhosa.[1]

During the 1770s, the Xhosa kingdoms created a loose confederacy which split into two major coalitions, following Gcaleka in the east and Rharhabe in the west. They united to fight Boer expansion in (1779-1781, 1793, and 1799-1803). Other Xhosa alliances were formed under Hintsa (1804-1835) from the senior Gcaleka branch of the Xhosa royal family. The Rharhabe Xhosa, split into two large confederacies (headed by Ndlambe and Qqika) that fought the British colonizing armies. In the 1800s, chiefdoms and confederacies were formed among the Nguni people, north of the Xhosa. They began forming permanent political alliances in order to promote regional security and trade. After many years of famine (c. 1800-1810), fierce competition for grazing lands among the Nguni prompted a young Zulu officer named Shaka in the army of Dingiswayo's Mtethwa confederation, to refine existing military tactics and introduce superior standards of efficiency and professionalism in warfare.

Shaka was born in 1787, and within his forty-year life span he made colonialism costly. At one point it seemed as though Shaka might unite under is rule the whole of the region that is now Natal, Lesotho and Swaziland. He grew up during the era when questions of unity and of effective armies were being considered for the first time among the Ama-Ngoni people. Previously the clans were based on smaller segments or units. As the eldest son of a clan head, at adulthood Shaka went to settle his own Kraal; and a new junior clan was born. His father's clan remained senior and the headship of his clan went to the eldest son of the "great wife." This pattern of segmentation was only possible so long as population density remained low and land for farming and grazing was plentiful. Early in the 19th century, demographic political pressures changed Zulu life. Population growth meant less grazing land and room for junior members of the clan to start their own Kraals. As they began to fight among themselves, they realized the necessity to learn to fight more efficiently and effectively.

Shaka became a chief of the Zulu after defeating his father in 1816 and the larger Mtethwa confederation in 1818. Shaka studied the political military problems of Zululand. He reasoned, that the center of political power should demonstrate military power. This would eventually result in the peaceful acceptance of a greater political state. All who resisted were crushed. He instituted more rigorous warrior training and armed his fighters with improved weaponry, the assegai spear, for in-close fighting. The weapon proved devastating in hand to hand combat. He discarded the loose sandals in order achieve more speed in closing with the enemy and more dexterity at close quarters.

Shaka introduced a new battlefield tactic, the "horns of the bull" attack formation, a method of encircling and terrifying his enemies. He incorporated defeated warriors into his national army and restructured and expanded the Mtethwa confederation of chiefdoms into a powerful new Zulu federation. With increased centralized authority, his armies waged relentless warfare against neighboring groups, killing, absorbing or scattering them, confiscating their cattle, and burning their villages.[2] When Zulus warriors surrounded and attacked their adversaries, they gave them the choice "to become Zulu or die," a scorched earth policy. The Zulu army was more than a fighting force. It was an educational institution for the young, and an instrument of building loyalties that went beyond clan lines that could be considered national.

In the process of building the Zulu nation, Shaka and his successor half brother, Dingane (1828-1838), devastated so many surrounding communities and chiefdoms that vast tracts of land to the south and east of Zululand were deserted as no man's land. When Shaka died in 1828, the Zulu federation was organized almost entirely along military lines, emphasizing national loyalty. Element's of Shaka's polices were adopted by other states throughout central Africa. European travelers left written accounts of Zululand describing its cleanliness, the social order, the absence of theft and sense of security. In reality, these conditions existed in Zululand long before Shaka's rule. A European biographer wrote of Shaka:

> Napoleon, Julius Caesar, Hannibal, Charlemagne such men as these have arisen periodically throughout history of the world to blaze a trail of glory that has raised them above the common level. Such a man was Shaka, perhaps the greatest of them all.[3]

Shaka was a herdsman and a warrior who invested his talents and creative energies not on fighting slave traders or reselling manufactured European goods, but on developing the Zulu nation. Despite his genius, because the scientific basis and the experimental preconditions were absent, Shaka could not have devised a firearm. But he got his people to forge better weapons and utilizing their vast empirical knowledge of cattle, engage in improved e breeding practices. It was a tribute to Zulu organizational and agricultural capacity a whole that they could feed and maintain a standing army of thirty-thousand men, re-equip them with iron weapons, and issue each soldier a full length Zulu shield made from cattle hide[4]

The discovery of diamonds in 1870 near the Orange and Vaal Rivers brought another wave of European settlers and more British military to protect them. By 1872, prospectors from as far away as Australia and North America had joined the 30,000 inhabitants of a boom town, called Kimberley, near the expanding diamond mines. By 1880, England's preeminent imperialist, Cecil Rhodes, together with some partners managed to purchase and consolidate the claims of the independent prospectors. They introduced the use of steam-driven mining machinery and founded the *DeBeers Mining Company,* South Africa's first modern industry. Labor policy in the diamond mines at Kimberley became the model for future South African labor policy. Africans were recruited to dig mines under six-month contracts and to work for very long hours for very low wages. They were housed and fed in closed barracks, where they were confined for the duration of their contracts.

Even under these adverse working conditions, Vincent Khapoya notes, that during the 1870s tens of thousands of African men migrated to Kimberley. Drawn by the opportunity to earn cash to pay British "head" and "hut" taxes, in newly industrialized towns like Kimberley, Johannesburg, Port Elizabeth, Cape Town and Durban. Many Africans joined new independent African churches. Some were affiliated with the African Methodist Episcopal (AME) Church of the US (then under the leadership of Bishop Henry McNeal Turner, a pan-African nationalist). This affiliation broadened their political perspective, shifting their political orientation from ethnic nationalism to pan-Africanism. Mission educated South Africans such as Jon Tengo Javubu, Solomon Plaatje, and Reverend John Dube established newspapers written in

Xhosa, Tswana, and Zulu. These papers advocated pan-Africanism as a solution to the development of a broader multi-ethnic African nationalism (rather than Xhosa, Tswana, Sotho, or Zulu ethnic-nationalisms) in South Africa. They earned just enough to purchase such imported commodities as clothes, tools, cooking utensils, guns and ammunition. With these guns, African leaders mobilized their respective confederacies and nations to resist British colonial expansion and defend their sovereignty. [5]

Apartheid South Africa

The policy of racial dominance, began to crystallize when England annexed and temporarily ruled, the Republic of Transvaal between 1877 and 1881. After the two month, First Boer War, the British surrendered political authority to the Boers in the Transvaal. The Boers used the "people's war" victory, as an occasion to develop a distinct identity as Afrikaners. This new political and cultural identity was known as the Broederbond or Afrikaner Bond. Afrikaans, their common language was standardized. They created a folk history and legends about the "Great Trek" and the Battle of Blood River, which were embellished and celebrated in Boer communities in much the same fashion as the American western genre mythologizes the cowboy and pioneer in the "taming" of the west.

Determined to annex the Transvaal and its abundant resources, the British Colonial Office under Lord Milner, deployed imperial troops to the Cape and Natal in preparation for a full-scale assault on the territory. In response, Afrikaners from all over South Africa rallied some 85,000 troops to their defense. Between 1899 and 1902, they engaged over 500,000 British soldiers in a bitter conflict known as the Second Boer War. The Boers waged a guerilla war using commando hit and run tactics, while the British burned homes, farms and forced Afrikaner wives, children and servants into concentration camps, where many thousands died. A treaty, the Union Agreement of 1909 was eventually negotiated recognizing British colonial authority over the Transvaal and Orange Free State, but allowing the Afrikaners in these territories to determine their own domestic policies. The Afrikaners, led by General Jan Smuts, Louis Botha and J.B.M. Hertzog assumed national leadership in the newest independent dominion of Britain's Commonwealth of Nations. [6]

By 1910, the British had transferred power to the Afrikaners and the Anglo-dominated government began to develop a racial dominance system. Colonial officials in South Africa sought the advice of Booker T. Washington, who was contacted by South African Commissioner of Education, E.B. Sergeant, to help devise and education plan for the Orange Free State and Transvaal. Washington's responses to Sergeant's questions revealed the latter's belief that there was 'no very great difference between the native problem and the Negro problem in America. Since missions did not always teach respect and acquiescence to governmental authority,

Washington supported those conservative South Africans who considered missionaries, particularly Negro American missionaries as subversives.[7] The first act of Afrikaner racial domination the *Natives Land Act*, was enacted in 1913. This law divided the country into African and European zones. Africans (87 % of the population) were allocated 13 percent of the land. Certain areas known as "Reserves" (as in American Indian Reservation), were established for Africans. Africans could not own or acquire land outside these areas. The law was refined in 1936, when the *Bantu Trust and Land Act* was passed. Anticipating the passage of the *Natives Land Act*, African leaders from primarily Christian denominations met to form the precursor organization to the Africa National Congress.

They sent a delegation to London requesting UK intervention on their behalf but the Crown ignored them. The South Africans courts ruled in favor of Afrikanerdom and Africans were stripped of all rights pertaining to movement and property. The government provided protection for white workers, or, as in the language of Minister of labor to; "safeguard against interracial competition," by passing the *Mines and Works Act of 1911*. Renewed in 1926 and 1956, the *Mines and Work Act* limited skilled mining jobs to whites and coloreds only. The law was later extended to include the building industry, in which skilled labor was broadly defined to include virtually everything: "bricklaying, plastering, masonry, carpentry, painting, sign writing, plumbing and electrical fitting."[8]

The National Party (NP) of the Afrikaners came to power in 1948 and proclaimed the new government to be based on a policy of *apartheid* or separate development. The assumptions behind this policy were, of course, racist. The first assumption was that South Africa consisted of many nations at differing levels of development so variant that political and social stability could only be preserved if maximum social and political distance was maintained between them. The Afrikaners believed that human ability is determined by race and that of all the races of South Africa, the whites or Europeans were superior to Africans. Africans were divided into many nations based on language. *The Population Registration Act of 1950* was passed to ensure that every South African was classified as a member of a specified group. All rights and privileges of South Africans flowed from these artificial distinctions. A large bureaucracy was created to register people accordingly and to hear appeals by those who believed they had been misclassified and could provide evidence to support their contention.[9]

The *apartheid* policy humiliated Africans and Europeans alike. Occasionally, a white couple bore a child whose complexion was a little too dark to qualify for white status and they had to endure the anguish and indignity of re-classification. In such cases, the stakes were high; (family and friends, a way of life, church, educational opportunities etc...) In a case made the subject of a television documentary, the daughter of an Afrikaner couple named Sandra Laing, who attended an all-white school, was expelled because the principal and other children regarded her skin too dark to be a white person. She was re-classified as colored. The family was ordered out of the neighborhood. The father, a staunch supporter of *apartheid*, disowned his daughter. She met and married a African and as a black person, applied in order to live in the tribal homeland.[10]

To prevent the blurring of these socially constructed categories, the *Prohibition of Mixed Marriages Act* was passed in 1949. However, sexual liaisons between persons in different racial categories continued. So the *Immorality Act of 1957* was enacted making sexual intercourse between whites and non-whites a criminal offense. The police were given wide discretionary powers of enforcement and most violators, contrary to racial myth and expectation, were white males. *The Natives Land Act* was refined in 1959 and enacted to create the façade African of self-governance. A new law, entitled the *Promotion of Bantu Self-Government Act of 1959*, was enacted to formalize the idea that African people were a highly heterogeneous group composed of eight distinct ethnic-nations. Traditional chiefs were now conveniently recognized as the legitimate authorities of the African people. Parliamentary representation for blacks could be denied, since they now had symbolic self-rule in the homelands or Bantustans. Reservations were established for each African ethnic group.

South Africa's Homelands

Homeland	Group
Bophuthatswana	Tswana
Ciskei	Xhosa
Gazankulu	Tsonga
KaNgwane	Swazi
KwaNdebele	Ndebele
KwaZulu	Zulu
Lebowa	North Sotho
QwaQwa	South Sotho
Venda	

When Hendrick Verwoerd, a major theoretician of apartheid, became Prime Minister in 1958, he declared that under apartheid white people were entrusted with a "sacred responsibility" of looking after the Africans and with guiding them to their own reserves for self-government. In his election manifesto, Verwoerd stated: "We not only seek and fight for a solution which will mean our survival as a white race, but we will also seek a solution which will ensure survival and full development-political and economic-to each of the other racial group...In the transition stage the guardian must teach and guide his ward".[11] In essence, the Africans were stripped of South African citizenship.

The Group Areas Act passed in 1957 and amended in 1966, created separate residential areas in cities and towns based on racial classification. The implementation of this law resulted in the forced relocation of Africans, Asians and Coloreds from areas they had lived in for several generations.

These areas were declared white areas. For example, a subdivision of Cape Town occupied by 61,000 Coloreds and 800 whites, called District Six, was declared a white area. The Coloreds, who had lived there since 1834, were relocated to a dusty, windy and desolate hilly patch of land located ten miles from the center of Cape Town.[12] Over time, several million non-whites were forcefully relocated to make way for white families or merely so that the government could eliminate the so called "black spots" in areas considered to be or declared white.

The next brick in the edifice of *apartheid* was legislation to control and restrict the movement of Africans throughout the country. These so-called pass laws predated Afrikanerdom, dating to 1809 in the Cape Province, where free blacks had to obtain permits from magistrates in order to travel in that province. In 1952, all pass laws were consolidated under the *Bantu* (Abolition of Passes and Coordination of Developments) *Act*, which required all Africans to carry an internal passport. Every African was fingerprinted and required to carry a reference book containing all personal information. This included birth date, place of birth and tribal grouping, as well as tax information, travel permits, work permits and anything else the law might require to identify them. The pass laws were the most humiliating and despised of all apartheid legislation. An average 500,000 Africans were arrested each year for violations related to internal passport laws. As in all racial dominance systems, Africans faced police harassment and brutality on a daily basis. The police had wide discretionary powers to stop any African and ask for their pass book.

It was impossible for an African to go about life unless this internal passport was in order. The African was subject to arrest for as little as missing an information stamp that verified their racial domination. *The Bantu* (Urban Areas) *Consolidation Act of 1945*, and amended in 1952, was drafted to regulate the movement of Africans into urban areas and control their behavior while there. Africans were required to obtain a permit, (which was indicated in the internal passport) allowing them to remain in the city for more than 72 hours. The right to reside in the city was earned by continuous employment with the same employer for ten years, or by being a dependent a person with this right. White employers, determined to deny African legal residence in white areas, often terminated an Africans employment in order to break the "continuous term of service" clause, only to rehire them. Even after earning legal residence, Africans were subject to curfew or prohibited "from attending churches, schools, clubs, hospitals or places of entertainment;" if, in the opinion of government officials, the African's presence at these facilities caused a nuisance to white people in the area.[13]

The Bantu Education Act and the Extension *of University Education Act* segregated all educational facilities from nursery schools to universities. *The Reservation of Separate Amenities Act of 1953* segregated all social facilities such as clubs and hospitals, buses and libraries. *The Bantu Labor Relations Regulations Act of 1953* and the *Industrial Conciliation Act of 1953* banned all African trade unions, even though many continued to exist during the height of the apartheid era. *The Publication and Entertainment Act of 1953* made certain that the books and film challenging the racist orthodoxy of the apartheid regime, or offensive to the pseudo-moral sensibilities of the puritanical Afrikaners, were banned fro the country. The strict penalties for violators, irrespective of their racial classification, were rigidly adhered to. There were draconian security laws that empowered the police to declare organizations subversive, ban them and forbid the gathering of people during times of unrest. Three people conversing on the street constituted an illegal assembly and were subject to arrest. There was no due process for Africans. These human rights atrocities went ignored by many leaders in the West, justified as part of the fight against global communism.

The African National Congress formed in 1912, predates the National Association for the Advancement of Colored People (NAACP) and the Bolshevik Revolution. The ANC was not the first political organization formed in South Africa. That distinction belongs to the *Imbumba Yama Afrika*, the 1886 Union of Africans in the Eastern Cape. The ANC was essentially a reformist, elite-led association for the improvement of African economic, social and political conditions, within a non-violent, legal framework. The ANC leadership regarded their primary task to more to speak for the people rather than to speak to them.[14]

The ANC's founders were moderates desperate to petition the British government to intervene and stop the proposed *Natives Land Act,* which would inevitably dispossess them of their land. Their petition was ignored and for the next forty years, the ANC used every non-violent means available to grieve the rights of the African people. Mohandas K. Gandhi successfully introduced the strategy of *Satyaghraha* (passive resistance) on behalf of the Indian population and pass laws in 1893. His ideas found utility among people conditioned by Christianity and a British education. One such person, was Albert Luthuli, the president of the ANC who during most of the 1950s, led a non-violent nationalist struggle and in 1960 was awarded the Nobel Peace Prize.

In 1944, Nelson Mandela, Walter Sisulu and Oliver Tambo founded the ANC Youth League. The Youth League's Manifesto asserted that the struggles and sacrifices of their fathers had not been in vain and they vowed to take up the struggle. However, the Youth League introduced a Program of Action, marking the transition from passive resistance to political education, political organization, meetings and delegations, strikes and demonstrations and other forms of civil disobedience. Soon, thereafter, a nation-wide series of strikes, protests and boycotts was planned. There was a Freedom of Speech convention, interracial May Day demonstrations against apartheid and protests against all of the laws supporting the racial dominance system. The ANC coordinated joint actions with Indian and colored people, culminating in a massive civil disobedience campaign in June 1952.

Afrikaner reaction was swift and severe. Participants were charged under the pass laws and the leaders charged under the *Suppression of Communism Act.*

The Suppression of Communism Act of July 1950 enhanced the influence of the South African Communist Party (SACP) within the ANC. This legislation was written around a ludicrous definition of communism which permitted the Afrikaner regime to 'name' and organization or individual who "aims at bringing about any political, industrial, social or economic change within the Union." The SACP dissolved itself before the bill became law and SACP members shifted their political focus to building the ANC.[15] In fact, by 1953 the ex-communists had successfully pushed through their proposal for a broad alliance. To the Indian Congress were added the European Congress of Democrats, the Coloureds People's Organization (later Coloureds People's Congress) and the non-racial South African Congress of Trade Unions, all theoretically, under the leadership of the ANC. Through equal representation of each Congress on coordinating committees, the thousand or so Indians and the few hundred Coloreds and white 'progressives' were, in effect, able to wield disproportionate influence over the larger ANC. To many in the ANC, the white tail was wagging the black dog.[16]

Additional laws were passed granting the police even more draconian powers. This brutal response had two consequences. First, the ANC became much more visible, attracting thousands of new members and gaining political legitimacy as the vanguard liberation movement. Secondly, white liberals were now motivated to form two new political parties, the Congress of Democrats and the South African Liberal Party. Despite his obscure chieftainship, Albert Lithuli; who had many white friends, was a pacifist democrat and far from a nationalist, assumed leadership of the ANC.[17]

The Defiance Campaign of 1952 was directed at six specific laws; the *Pass Laws*, the *Group Areas Act*, the *Separate Representation of Voters Act*, the *Suppression of Communism Act*, the *Bantu Authorities Act*, and *Compulsory Cattle Culling Policy*. Using strategies and tactics adapted from the burgeoning US Civil Rights Movement; such as sit-ins and strikes, the Defiance Campaign, which began on the June 26th with prayers and massive work stoppages, was responded to quickly with mass arrests. By October, thousands of ANC members were behind bars only to be replaced by new volunteers and membership grew to over 100,000. Some ANC youth opposed the inclusive nationalism enshrined in the *Freedom Charter*. These Africanists felt that including whites, coloreds, and Indians in the ANC; diluted the movement and allowed others to influence the ANC's strategy, tactics, philosophy and timing. Some embraced Chairman Mao Tse Tung's maxim that "political power comes from the barrel of a gun;" choosing to abandon non-violence and take up armed struggle.

Another major campaign was launched in 1955 with the cooperation of the Indians and the Coloureds, resulting in the adoption of the *Freedom Charter* by the ANC Executive Council and the 3000 members of the Congress of African People. There were invariably fissures in the liberation movement.

These campaigns were coordinated despite political and economic tensions between African and Indians. African resentment of economic exploitation by Indian shopkeepers and merchants continues. Historically, the Africans believed that the Indians were also racially prejudiced.[19] There were tensions between Africans and Coloureds, based on the long-standing feeling that Coloureds were not subject to apartheid restrictions with the same severity (e.g., they did not have to carry internal passports) and somehow thought themselves superior to the Africans.

Strong armed tactics and arbitrary expulsions of members at the 1958 Transvaal Congress of the ANC resulted in a final walk-out by the Africanists. In April 1959, they formed the Pan-Africanist Congress (PAC). At its first annual conference, Robert Sobukwe and the PAC decided upon a plan of militant action: a non-violent campaign against the pass laws. Calling for a massive campaign of civil disobedience and mass arrests, the PAC planned to disrupt the entire life of the country under the slogan; 'no bail, no defense, no fine." Not to be outdone, The ANC announced its own anti-pass day on March 30, 1960. PAC leader, Robert Sobukwe therefore chose March 21 as the start of the anti-pass campaign.

There were demonstrations in Cape Town and Johannesburg and the government responded with the usual brutality. At Sharpeville, the police panicked at the size of the crowds and opened fire on unarmed civilians, killing 69 people and wounding over 200. At Langa, 60 police clubbed and shot at a crowd of African protestors, killing 5 and wounding 59. On April 8, 1960, the Verwoerd government declared the ANC and the PAC 'unlawful organizations' and called them a 'serious threat to the safety of the public.' The ban was ratified by the overwhelming racist all-white parliament, by 128 votes to 16.

ANC leader, Oliver Tambo left the country prior to the ban, while most of the other leaders awaited arrest or went underground. At an all-African Conference in Pietermariztburg in 1961, Nelson Mandela, who had recently been released from successive bans, proposed a three-day work strike. The strike was opposed by the PAC and response was poor, except among the Colored workers in Cape Town and some Indians in Durban. Nelson Mandela, who was in hiding, conceded failure and even the Congress Alliance began doubting the utility of non-violence. Mandela met with a few leaders and in June 1961, reluctantly agreed to limited violence. A sabotage campaign that would be directed against property, not persons. There would be no efforts to seize power, or attack South African Defense Forces or police, or assassinations of Europeans. They also feared that any 'indiscriminate violence' might provoke a racial blood bath. African fear of white retaliation, the indiscriminate killing of Africans and other non-whites and mass destruction moderated their response.[20]

Mandela left the country and went on a speaking tour of independent African countries. He addressed the Pan African Freedom Conference in Addis Ababa and visited the Moroccan headquarters of Algerian Colonel,

Houari Boumedienne's National Liberation Army, where he observed the concrete results of a protracted armed struggle against French minority rule. In July 1962, the Algerian army, under the political leadership of the National Liberation Front (NLF), defeated France after 132 years of colonial rule, winning Algerian independence.

ANC militants, led by Nelson Mandela, formed a military wing known as *Umkhonto we Sizwe* (the Spear of the Nation). This new wing would engage in violence, sabotage and disruption to underscore the African determination for democratic self-rule. Again the emphasis was placed on multiracialism, as an ANC policy statement announcing the new underground organization declared:

> This is a new, independent body formed by Africans. It includes in its ranks South Africans of all races...We believe our actions to be a blow against Nationalist preparation for civil war and military rule. In these actions we are working in the best interests of all people of this country, Black, Brown and White, whose future happiness and well-being cannot be attained without the overthrow of the Nationalists.[21]

Umkhonto we Sizwe did not strike the first military blow to the apartheid regime. The first sabotage was initiated in October 1961 by a group of white liberals called the National Committee of Resistance; later renamed the National Resistance Movement (ARM). *Umkhonto we Sizwe* exploded its first bombs on December 16th, Dingaan's Day, the day celebrating the Dutch victory over Zulu Chief Dingaan at the Battle of Blood River. Ten bombs in Johannesburg and five in Port Elizabeth exploded damaging electric pylons and government offices. One inexperienced saboteur blew himself up. In 1961 and 1962 Afrikaner repression grew so intense, that hundreds of South Africans began leaving the country. The first and largest groups to go into exile were European communists and liberals. They were followed by prominent PAC and ANC leaders, believed to be wanted by the police, who went into exile in the British Protectorates of Basutoland (Lesotho), Bechuanaland, and Swaziland. In each of these countries, the leading nationalist parties were more sympathetic to the Africanism of the PAC than to the multiracialism of the ANC.[22]

The economic boom of the 1960s and 1970s was accompanied by a net emigration of white professionals and people with much-needed industrial and managerial experience. At the same time, the African population increased far more rapidly with demographers forecasting a rapid decline in the white population, which had already dropped from a peak of 21 to 16 percent. The illusion of a "decolonization" process, which the Afrikaner's hoped would assuage international condemnation and blunt hostilities, failed. No foreign government recognized the independence of Transkei or Bophuthatswana. The corrupt, inefficient and authoritarian rulers of the

Homelands, became an embarrassment. Their obvious dependence on Pretoria for subsidies and protection belayed their illegitimacy. Their territories were impoverished and their inhabitants struggled to survive by sending migrant family members to work in white cities and on white farms.

In 1977, the UN passed a mandatory embargo on the sale of arms to South Africa. This perfunctory diplomatic isolation, broke Afrikaner solidarity which was the key to the electoral strength of the National Party. People, who a decade earlier placed ethnic issues above class issues, now examined their class interests more conscientiously. Eighty percent of Afrikaners were urban, 70 percent of those held white-collar jobs. Prosperous professionals, business people, and absentee landlords replaced the old rural and cultural elites in control of the National Party. On the right, Afrikaner urban workers and marginal farmers, who relied on apartheid to defend them from black competition; and bureaucrats, and those who earned their living implementing apartheid, feared black political empowerment. [23]

In 1978, Prime Minister Vorster resigned after National Party members misappropriated public funds for secret propaganda purposes. He was replaced by Pieter Willem Botha, who as defense minister had made the South African Army the most formidable in Africa. Botha claimed the international community was waging a "total onslaught" against his country and gave the military a key policy making role in his government. The Botha administration was fortunate; administrative changes in London and Washington brought Margaret Thatcher and Ronald Reagan to power, both of whom were sympathetic to minority rule and racial dominance. Accepting Pretoria's propaganda at face value, Reagan remained ignorant about the situation in South Africa and prejudiced in favor of the white population. South Africa, he said in 1985, has "eliminated the segregation we once had in our own country." US cities, universities and foreign investors began to divesting and disinvesting of their interests in South African companies.

In July, 1985 *Chase Manhattan* bank created a financial crisis in South Africa when it refused to roll over the country's short-term loans, other banks followed suit. The Vorster government stopped journalists from reporting on these international developments. Thatcher rejected demands by other Commonwealth members that the UK should join them in taking strong economic measures against apartheid. She tried to prevent the Commonwealth from taking collective action against apartheid. In 1986, a delegation of former Australian Prime Minister, Malcolm Fraser and senior Commonwealth politicians from Barbados, Canada, India and Tanzania visited South Africa. They agreed to "promote a political dialogue aimed at replacing apartheid by popular government." After meeting with a wide range of South African society, including President Botha and Nelson Mandela, the delegation made a proposal to the South African government. The government should remove the military from the townships, provide for freedom of assembly and discussion, suspend detention without trial, release Nelson Mandela and other political prisoners, sanction the ANC and the Pan

African Congress and permit normal political activity. For its part, the ANC was to enter negotiations with the government and suspend all insurgent violence, conditions to which Mandela had already agreed.

The Civil Rights Movement in the US which sought to eliminate *de jure* and *de facto* legal forms of institutional racism, linked US racial domestic politics to US foreign policy toward South Africa. In the US, Randall Robinson, the executive director of *TransAfrica*, built a coalition of clergy, students, trade unions and civil rights leaders. Between November 1984 and 1986, six thousand Americans, including eighteen members of Congress were arrested for picketing the South African embassy. The Reagan administration opposed sanctions and ignored the domestic anti-apartheid movement just as they had ignored the civil rights leaders and members of the Congressional Black Caucus. Ronald Reagan's assistant secretary for African Affairs, Chester Crocker, focused most of his time and energy on a prolonged diplomatic effort to protect the invading South African forces from Cuban troops defending Angola, in exchange for implementation of a UN security plan for the liberation of Namibia from South African invasion and control.[24] Crocker sold Reagan on the policy of "constructive engagement" as opposed to what he had characterized as the "Tar Baby Option," i.e., of becoming politically stuck to the racist minority regime. He appointed, Alan Keyes as ambassador to the UN to articulate and promote this policy. Reagan issued an Executive Order imposing limited sanctions, but anti-apartheid momentum grew and Congress passed The Anti-Apartheid Act of 1986 over his veto.

Between July 20, 1985 and March 7, 1986, the South African government declared a state of emergency over much of the country. On June 12, 1986 it declared an indefinite, nationwide state of emergency and arrested hundreds of anti-apartheid activists. The emergency regulations gave every police officer broad powers of arrest, detention, and unwarranted interrogation; they empowered the police commissioner to ban any meeting; and they prohibited all coverage of unrest by television and radio reporters and severely curtailed newspaper coverage. This news blackout demonstrated that the Botha government had resorted to legal tyranny.[25] In 1984, the apartheid regime fell.

The New South Africa

Against widespread expectations, post-*apartheid* South Africa, avoided a bloody inter-racial conflict and remains Africa's most economically prosperous and politically stable state. However, South Africa has not been spared the political pressure to reduce poverty, combat disease, prevent violence and deter corruption. People respond to what to what their leaders tell them they are entitled to expect. Unrealistic expectations are created and governments often set themselves up for failure. The UN praised South Africa in a 2006 report for its "consistent political commitment" to upgrading slums and providing for the urban poor. Under Nelson Mandela, the African

National Congress created illusory and unrealistic expectations of social benefits. A survey conducted in 2001 by the South African Institute of Race Relations (SAIRR), indicated that South Africans had been made more aware of the difficulties they face since the end of apartheid and minority-rule. In 1991, only 1 percent of South African blacks thought the water supply as a "serious problem," by 2001, 25 percent thought so. Four percent viewed health service as a problem in 1991 compared to 15 percent a decade later. In 2002, South Africa male and female life expectancy was 45 and 46 years of age respectively. Sixty- one out of every thousand infants died at birth and the adult HIV/Aids infection rate is 21.5 percent. There is one physician for every 1,529 people. ANC leaders promised better service delivery without emphasizing the economic price tag that would be attached. Unemployment has increased and a generation of young, uneducated, apartheid-era South Africans is growing impatient. A Survey of 2,144 South African residents over the age of 16, across all racial groups, the one successful policy area identified is housing where over 2 million houses were delivered. Under pressure from the leftist wing of the party, the Congress of South African Trade Unions (COSATU), the ANC promised to spend more on the provision of basic services and increase the budget deficit; President Mbeki warned that a relaxation of fiscal and monetary control would weaken the economy.

In contrast to the United States, from which the model of apartheid was adopted, popular concerns about race have subsided in South Africa since 1991. Only 5 percent of black Africans viewed racial issues as an unresolved problem in their society. In fact, since 1997, political leadership has tried to put racism back on the political agenda by labeling more and more of whatever it does not like as 'racist' the SAIRR report stated.[26] However, like the United States, South Africa, amazingly under the ANC has returned to racial categorization. Anti-apartheid leader, Allan Boesak was critical of the policy stating; "We have deliberately allowed the ANC to bring back the language of racial categorization. In the 1990s we were told again, you are colored, you are Indians, you are white."[27] This policy, however is instrumental to South Africa's policy of Black Economic Empowerment.

In an attempt to redress the racially skewed patterns of ownership bequeathed by apartheid and minority-rule, the ANC launched the policy of Black Economic Empowerment (BEE). Most South Africans, other than the political extremists, support BEE as a historical necessity in a country that so recently aggressively disenfranchised blacks. But BEE policy is yielding some unintended consequences. BEE is a series of guidelines drawn up by the Mbeki government in consultation with business. The rules require white-controlled companies to do more business with blacks, notably through the sale of equity stakes to black-controlled consortia. At best, BEE represents a pragmatic compromise between white capital and black political power that will promote economic prosperity and political stability. Middle class blacks with new jobs in business or the public sector, are an important force behind

South Africa's 5 percent GDP growth and its longest period of economic expansion in years.

Some South Africa's larger companies such as *Old Mutual Insurance,* have used BEE to recruit talented black investors and generate new business. BEE guidelines require companies to favor black subcontractors thereby helping to nurture a new crop of small and mid-sized companies. However, as with Affirmative Action in the United States, BEE has been the object of cynical political manipulation and outright abuse.

Many white companies, following the path of least resistance, choose partners largely on the basis of their ANC connections rather than for any demonstrable business acumen. Some white businesses don't even understand the policy. "Access to parties and decision-makers is denied, so they rely on BEE partners to access them on their behalf;" said one businessman with an intimate knowledge of the program. There is growing frustration over the very limited progress of BEE. The message to Mbeki was unequivocal. "The process of drawing black people into the mainstream economy is going much too slowly. "We have been spectators up to now. We need to be participants. "You can't trust the white man any more;" said South African businessman, Peter Vundla. "They've been behaving badly for years. This is why the country needs a set of rules that tells white business, "This is how you behave." We have this very thin band of very rich people and a very thick band of very poor people, this isn't sustainable;" Vundla observed. He believes the objectives of economic growth and BEE are a virtuous circle. "You can't have strong growth if the majority of the people in the country are excluded from the economy. We have been part of it only as laborers and consumers. We need a bigger stake."[28]

Attempts to influence government policy are driven by other political factors; such as growing unease about the implementation of BEE and who the policy benefits. The government is aware that there is danger of alienating the poor who are its largest constituency. "We need to move away from the narrow-based black economic empowerment. There has to be a meaningful transfer of wealth into black hands;" said Polo Radebe, director in charge of empowering policy in the Department of Trade and Industry. Many argued, that too much emphasis was placed on selling equity to black business people, which resulted in a small group becoming wealthy while the majority of black South Africans remain poor. "In the past it was all about selling an equity stake. But government has realized that the only people who can play in that space are the explained;" said Jimmy Manyi, president of the Black Management Forum.

South Africa's new political elite is an extremely narrow and incestuous economic group. This increases the potential for political infighting. A small group of ANC activists rose to power, many of whom became acquainted while in exile. Several members of President Mbeki's cabinet are married to each other or to other prominent business figures. Power corrupts, and the accumulation of power by the elite of the ANC provides several examples.

Miambo-Ngcuka was harshly criticized by the media when it was revealed that she had flown on holiday to the United Arab Emirates for Christmas at taxpayer expense and stayed as a guest of the Emir in Abu Dhabi. Although her visit was originally described as private, it was later revealed that her entourage included a businesswoman with interests in oil and mineral markets, who was also the wife of the minister of social development. Her husband, who also traveled with her, runs a prominent BEE real estate company .

Some BEE deals may less serve public than private interests. In a widely criticized transaction, the black-controlled *Elephant Consortium* bought 6.7 percent of *Telkom*, South Africa's dominant fixed-line telecommunications provider and one of the country's largest companies. *Elephant* is headed by Andile Ngcaba, a former director of the department of communications, a job which provided him insight into and oversight of *Telkom*. Defending his role in the deal, ANC spokesman, Smuts Ngonyama was quoted saying he had not joined the anti-apartheid struggle "to stay poor." This attitude indicates the danger that the next generation of South Africans may come to view politics and government service as merely a path to riches. The ANC Youth League, while rhetorically radical, now accounts among its members those with expensive cars and business investments.[30]

The final set of BEE codes was a compromise intended to expand the programs impact by rewarding companies that assist the development of black enterprises, the promotion of black managers, the hiring of black staff and spending on social projects. Other changes, designed to stake the sting out of the debate, exempt small and foreign businesses from compliance with having to sell a stake in local subsidiaries to black partners. Many believed the Mbeki government had embarked on a complex system that will burden companies with red tape and stifle competitiveness. "We have been given a much simpler code to what we saw 18 months ago. But there are more hoops and loops and I don't' think we are out of the woods yet in creating an environment to attract foreign investors;" commented a foreign businessman.

South Africa's trade minister, Trevor Manuel, called for a reform of the BEE regulations and suggested the flawed policy was rife with abuses. "There were all kinds of things that businesses have done good and bad cynical and genuine. There will have to be a review;" he told reporters. Opponents of the policy warned that BEE was nurturing a dependency culture by encouraging the nation's small, educated black elite to pursue lucrative BEE deals rather than build careers.[31]

There is conspicuous evidence of a growing black market and middle class in South Africa. A combination of relatively low borrowing rates, cheap imported goods and a demand for durable goods fueled a consumer boom that pushed growth to rates to near unprecedented levels. A survey by Professor Johns Simpson of Unilever Institute in Cape Town, reported that in 2006 Johannesburg's fledgling middle class, known as "Black Diamonds," rose by 30 percent. The findings helped the government to prove to its critics that its handling of the economy and BEE policies were benefiting more than the ANC elite. Professor Simpson cautioned that the "Black Diamonds" were spending their wealth on items of conspicuous consumption rather than on traditional middle class concerns such as life insurance and healthcare and education which might entrench their new class status.[32]

Despite this progress, relations between the ANC and COSATU intensified after Johannesburg police fired stun grenades and rubber bullets at striking nurses and teachers. The unions, who represent 1 million public service workers, were striking for a 12 percent pay increase while the government only offered a six percent.[33] In the most significant industrial action since the end of apartheid, the strike force hospitals to rely on skeleton staffs and many schools were closed. Striking teachers threatened colleagues who showed up for work and one Johannesburg teacher was reportedly whipped in her classroom. The Minister of Enterprises, Alec Erwin, stated that the unions were doing what they should be expected to do, given South Africa's successful growth. The 280,000-strong National Union of Mineworkers, threatened to join the strike. "Where you've got a vibrant union movement, where you have a period of economic growth, you'd be surprised if this was not the moment the unions chose to make demands;" he explained.[34]

Finance minister, Trevor Manuel announced that the government's Accelerated Growth Initiative intended to keep growth at or above 4.5-4.6 percent until 2011. The recognition of the need to bring in qualified people to help develop power and transport infrastructure had paid off, but there is a shortage of black engineers. The finance minister was critical of the quality and training for both management and mid-tier personnel and wanted the private sector to intervene and upgrade it. "If, black people were going to be cheap labor in the mines and on farms with not much else to do, then, the old system served them quite adequately. But in this environment where those two big sectors have shed employment over the past two decades, we haven't been able to-do enough in respect of skills," Manuel observed. South Africa weathered the impact of oil shock for expensive imports with its exports of platinum, gold and other commodities. But the demand for commodities masked problems for companies involved in marketing other tradable goods and services, which could lead to a wider deficit in South Africa's balance of payments. [35]

Of course, far too many South Africans remain impoverished. Not far from Johannesburg's new Brickfield's inner-city housing development, a showpiece of three and four-story walk-ups and nine-story tower blocks; sits the Hillbrow district is a sink-hole of dilapidated high-rise tenements filled with impoverished immigrants from other African countries. The overcrowding and crime in Hillbrow is endemic. Many of these buildings have been without running water or sewage for years. Criminal gangs hi-jack properties extorting rents from 10 or more tenants crowded into in a single apartment. The immigrant's of Hillbrow come from as far away as Sierra Leone, an 8,000 kilometer journey in the back of a truck.

During the apartheid era, South Africa was a major source of refugees. But since the first democratic elections, the tide has reversed, bringing asylum seekers and other migrants from the rest of the continent and from Asia, seeking security and opportunity. The urban inflow provoked anti-immigrant sentiment and prejudice against other Africans, which fits uncomfortably with South Africa's reputation for racial reconciliation. Forty-two refugees were killed and 25,000 were made homeless during anti-immigrant riots in April and May of 2008. Reminicent of of ANC-Zulu clashes of the Vortser era, two people were "necklaced," i.e., set ablaze with tires filled with petrol and two others were lynched. Frustration over rising prices and poor living conditions have led to increased xenophobia towards other Africans. The government was strongly condemned for its failure to predict the arrival of 1.5 people fleeing Zimbabwe.

Experts from the University of Witwatersrand and Lawyers for Human Rights, a South African NGO, say their research uncovered "widespread administrative irregularities, illegalities and exploitation" as well as "outright discrimination." They cited the lack of facilities at border posts, entrenched networks of corruption and violence by "civilian commandos," authorized to assist the government in controlling the border with Zimbabwe. "You need money to get into South Africa;" said Loren Landau, who runs a graduate program in forced migration studies at Johannesburg's University of Witwatersrand. Migrants complain of "inhumane living conditions, extortion and physical abuse." South African officials reportedly deport 160,000 people a year, most are Zimbabweans and Mozambicans. Human Rights Watch activists argue the policy is costly and does not solve the problem of clandestine migration. A Draft Protocol on the Free Movement of Refugees by the 13-nation Southern African Development Community has yet to be signed by either South Africa or Botswana, the two major recipients of immigrant flows.[36] Nigerian foreign minister, Ojo Maduekwe reminded South Africans of their debt to African countries for their part in the struggle against apartheid. "When you have embarked on great acts of solidarity like that and you don't teach your children what you did and how you worked together, they will come out on the streets killing foreigners from the very countrie that fought for their freedom. Xenophobia is a sign that conversations that ought to be taking place have not been taking place;" he stated.

In order to keep its pledge to eliminate shacks and other sub-standard housing by 2014, the government must build 48,000 units a year. "Government has not been able to come to terms with the level of funding required;" observed Taffy Adler, CEO of Johannesburg Housing Company, the non-profit community development fund behind Brickfields.[37] Across South Africa, unemployment is officially estimated at 40 percent. Many job seekers and the poor seeking to be nearer to their jobs, are pushed into shacks or subsidized houses on the city's periphery. The result is an unmanageable urban sprawl and the reinforcement of the racially segregated urban geography of the apartheid era. "The city doesn't have an urban design framework and it desperately needs one;" said Niel Fraser, director of *Urban Inc.,* a planning and development consultant. Unmotivated and unskilled urban planners are partly to blame. Middle class housing developments are sprouting north of the city with little evidence of planning for housing the poor. "We have been patient. They promised a better life for all. But we don't see changes. Their policy does not help poor people; it only helps the wealthy;" complained 54 year-old veteran, Sam Makgoka, who oversees a self-help recycling project near Johannesburg.

Despite these problems, South Africa remains an increasingly attractive tourist destination. Tourism's contribution to South Africa's economic growth has doubled since the transition to democracy. South Africa's tourist industry dominates the tourist market in Southern Africa, either directly or indirectly employing 1 million people. Tourism has become South Africa's "new gold," since overtaking metal as the major source of foreign exchange. The industry launched a second phase of growth that could increase its share of GDP from 8 to 12 percent.[38]

In Durban, a popular attraction is the Tourist Junction Pietermaritzberg railway station, where Mohandas Gandhi confronted racial discrimination. The favorable climate makes KwaZulu-Natal (KZN) a premiere destination for internal tourism. There are plans to increase tourist-related jobs from 140,000 to almost 200,000. There are also plans for a new international airport named Shaka north of the city. There are campaigns in KwaZulu-Natal to increase foreign tourism by emphasizing not just safari hunting, but the province's array of attractions: beaches, sports facilities, mountains, nature parks and battlefields of the Zulu and Boer wars.[39]

Gross social and economic inequities make South Africa one of the world's most violent societies and the security forces are often criticized for their brutality. South Africa has the highest murder rate in the world. Four South African policemen were convicted of assault after admittedly setting their Alsatian dogs on three black illegal immigrants in what they called a "training exercise." A video showed the policemen laughing while their dogs viciously attacked the men who screamed for help and mercy. After the video was screened, six pòlicemen were suspended without pay and some were reassigned. The four plead guilty to three counts of assault with intent to do grievous bodily harm. They admitted hitting the men, inciting their dogs to bite them and neglecting to intervene to stop the attacks. A charge of corruption for admittedly asking the immigrants for money in exchange for setting them free was dropped.[40]

In September 2006, President Mbeki asked the departments of justice, security, home affairs and corrections to cooperate with "Business Against Crime," a business-funded crime-fighting group, to address the worsening crime rate. "Business Against Crime", which compiles it own data, cites a rise in some categories including aggravated robbery. Strangely enough, the Mbeki government and business groups were unable to explain the rising crime rate. The country's unemployment rates, poverty and impoverishment evidently provided few clues. The chairman of *Richemont*, a luxury goods company warned that if aggressive crime-fighting measures were not taken, South Africa could go the way of Colombia.[41]

Obviously, corruption is not limited to African governments and politicians. European and American multinationals often take the initiative to exploit the laws of their own states as well as the weak political economies of the impoverished. Neither are Africans alone in decrying the blurred lines between politics and business as the examples of former German chancellor Gerhard Schröder and US vice president Dick Cheney illustrate. In October 2001, the "Scorpions," South Africa's elite investigative unit, raided the business offices of *Thales International, Thomson-CSF, African Defence Systems* (ADS) and *Futuristic Business Solutions,* searching for documents that would shed light on an alleged corrupt arms deal worth $4.6 million. Later that month, the court began proceedings against Michael Woerfel, the local managing director of the *European Aeronautic Defence and Space Company* (formerly called *Daimler-Chrysler Aerospace*, which was partly owned by *Daimler-Chrysler)*.

Transparency International's 2005 Corruption Perceptions Index (CPI), ranked South Africa 46th out of 158 corrupt countries, just ahead of the Czech Republic and Greece. In response, the South African government reversed its plan to bar foreign investment in the private security industry. After a meeting with *Securicor*, *Chubb, Group 4* and *ADT Fire and Security*, South African minister of safety and security, Steve Tshwete, announced draft legislation to remove restrictions on foreign ownership of security companies and to provide for foreign buy outs.[42] The Mbeki government was dealt another blow when auditors uncovered extensive evidence of financial ties between mining magnate, Brett Kebble and prominent members of the ANC youth league. Kebble was noted for his role in deals that increased black ownership of the economy. His murder sent shocks through a business community that prided itself on rectitude and respect for the rule of law and the murder remains unsolved. Forensic auditors discovered that Kebble defrauded the two mining houses he headed, *Randgold Exploration* and *JCL*. A list of names found on Kebble's desk, headed "Loan Account," included the names of several prominent ANC officials. The ANC, disavowed any knowledge of loans to any of its members by Kebble or his mining companies. But Kebble apparently made no secret of his ties to top ANC officials; he hosted lavish parties annually for ANC officials and was an open supporter of Jacob Zuma, the party's deputy president who was charged with rape and corruption. When the Kebble economic empire collapsed, none of his BEE deals survived.

The scandal fueled a growing outcry over crony capitalism in Africa's largest economy and coincided with the publication of a report by South Africa's auditor-general verifying that eleven ministers and deputy ministers in the Mbeki government, failed to declare their directorships of companies. Among about 6,000 lower-level government employees, auditors found 1,678 cases of undeclared business interests. Auditor-general, Shauket Fakie, said that the audit revealed; "that there's some scope of conflict of interest" among government representatives, including through ties to companies doing business with government, which he vowed to examine in a separate report.

President Mbeki sounded the party alarm on the issue warning about "the abuse of membership of our movement to gain positions of state power in order to use these positions of state power for personal enrichment and benefit". The ANC's smaller partner in government, COSATU, claimed there was a "massive crisis in our public service" and that politician's business conflicts represent "a dangerous cancer eating into the body of our democracy". The ANC tasked a team to draft new guidelines for members with corporate interests. "There's a danger that politics becomes a proxy of competition for resources. That's something the ANC wants to nip in the bud;" said a member of the ANC's National Executive Committee.

In March, 2006 President Mbeki fired Billy Masethla, the chief of the National Intelligence Agency (NIA), following a "breakdown of trust" related to e-mail. Although apparently fake, the e-mails fanned conspiracy theories and revived memories of abuses under minority rule and apartheid. Masethla, appealed his dismissal. The following month, South African police prepared to make arrests in an intelligence scandal that led to the dismissal of its chief spy. This scandal centered on a series of hoax e-mails, allegedly intercepted by intelligence officials that purported to expose a plot to kill ANC deputy vice-president, Jacob Zuma. Zuma, who was slated to succeed Mbeki, was dismissed as deputy vice-president after being charged with rape. Zuma's arraignment on rape and corruption charges split the ANC. Many were skeptical of a report by the Inspector-General of Intelligence that found the e-mails to be "patently fraudulent," forcing the ANC to launch its own investigation.

Mbeki's intelligence minister, Ronnie Kasrils, ordered the initial audit after a prominent businessman and senior ANC official complained that he had been subject to harassment by the NIA. The audit uncovered the existence of "Project Avanti," a secret intelligence probe "to identify any threat or potential threat posed by the succession debate." The NIA claimed to have intercepted communications demonstrating a conspiracy by ethnic Xhosas against Zulu-speaking Jacob Zuma, Billy Masethla, and Kgalema Motlan the, the ANC' s general–secretary. The hoax e-mails used the pejorative term "Zuluboy" to describe Zuma and spoke of "nailing the Zulu bastard." President Mbeki is a Xhosa and the increased tension between South Africa's two largest linguistic groups has long been an undercurrent of national politics waters. Zuma supporters, convinced that he is a victim of political conspiracy, converged on the Johannesburg High Court wearing T-shirts reading "100% Zuluboy." They seized on the fact that the former prosecutor who uncovered Zuma's alleged corruption, was married to

Phumzile Mlambo-Ngcuka, whom Mbeki had named to replace Zuma as ANC deputy secretary.[43]

A second group of e-mails purportedly to involved opposition politicians, media officials and members of the ethnic white minority. The group, operating under the banner "Whiteman's Struggle," also targeted the three accused. The auditor's report ruled that the purported exchanges, which were full of spelling and factual errors, "were in fact mock-ups". A computer scientist found inconsistencies in the e-mails by using timestop formats, angled brackets, and other cyberspace details.

Unchecked, corruption could foment a populist backlash, threatening ANC political dominance and the country's macroeconomic and political stability. However, unlike many more poorly governed African countries, South Africa has a strong independent media and vigorous oversight institutions. It also has a well-entrenched, autonomous private sector, which minimizes the potential for conflict over resources and gives ambitious politicians something to do once they leave government service. But too many South Africans remain impoverished and they demand their say on issues of national wealth and political health.

Jacob Zuma

In a ruling that had repercussions throughout politics and society, Jacob Zuma was found not guilty of raping a 31-year old HIV positive, family friend in his home. The accuser was placed under witness protection and her name kept confidential. The victim, the daughter of a late ANC prisoner formally interned on Robben Island, had been counseled for psychological problems. She had made several accusations of rape before and was described as "a sick person who needs help." The judge, paraphrasing Rudyard Kipling's "If," castigated Zuma stating: "If you can control your body and your sexual urges, then you are a man my son." Zuma's power base among the ethnic Zulu's, disgruntled many of his governing allies. Supporters clad in traditional Zulu skins and bearing shields, sat behind him in court. "He has suffered damage to his image and damage politically. But it unclear whether he suffered damage where it matters most-in the ANC's rank and file;" observed political analyst, Aubrey Matshiqi. The ANC was expected to lift its ban on Zuma's exercise of political functions as deputy president and the verdict fueled the belief among his supporter's of a plot to preclude his chance of becoming president. Some compared Zuma's rape trial to the impeachment of former president Clinton. He faced separate corruption charges in a Pietermariztburg court stemming from an arms deal and was accused of accepting bribes from a local unit of the defense group *Thales*. Zuma plead not guilty and *Thales* denied any wrong doing.[44]

Some speculated that the twice postponed trial would be dismissed because the prosecutions case was weak. Zuma's lawyers argued that another postponement would harm his career. The prosecution argued that the "very serious charges against him" had to be tested in court. The trial also threatened to ensnarl President Mbeki. A fax from Schabir Shaik, Zuma's former financial advisor, was admitted as evidence at Shaik's trial claiming that *Thales*, was seeking a meeting with Mbeki. Mbeki claimed that he remembered no such meeting. Schabir Shaik was found guilty of fraud and corruption by a judge who concluded that he and Mr. Zuma had "a generally corrupt relationship."[45] One week later, Zuma escalated his opposition presidential campaign by criticizing Mbeki's policies of privatization, workforce casualization, and the "unilateral restructuring" of Transnet, the state-owned freight and logistics company. "The ANC is a broad church, thus we cannot be apologetic about wanting it to have the interests of the poor who form its largest majority at heart;" said Zuma. The absence of any serious rivals allowed Zuma to dominate the succession debate.[46]

In the battle for succession, delegates to the ANC's five-year conference were reminded of Zuma's links to his former financial advisor, who is serving a 15-year sentence for corruption. The populist deputy president became an early contender for the presidency by stirring an angry debate about policy, personalities and leadership style which highlighted fissures within the ANC.[47] Branches of the ANC adopted positions behind their favorite presidential candidates and their votes reflected the results of local lobbying efforts. Zuma was the favored presidential candidate and on paper, the succession was seamless. But in reality, the practice was more complicated than expected. In 1997, former president Mandela's favorite candidate, businessman and former COSATU director, Cyril Ramaphosa was defeated by Thabo Mbeki; who won the support of the ANC's youth and women leagues. Although Ramaphosa had wide appeal, president Mbeki proved more astute at using the ANC's decision making apparatus. The 55 year-old Ramaphosa disavowed any further notion that he would stand as a presidential candidate, thus averting another political crisis. However, by May 2007, the list of candidates seeking ANC leadership included deputy vice-president Jacob Zuma, one of South Africa's richest men, Tokyo Sexwale, Cyril Ramaphosa and Kgalema Mothlane.[48] In October 2007, ANC centrists began agitating for both Mbeki and Zuma step down in favor of the compromise candidate, Ramaphosa's was nominated by Kadae Asmal, an ANC intellectual and Sue van der Merwe, the deputy minister of foreign affairs. Ramaphosa, an urbane union leader turned businessman, responded to speculation of his candidacy stating that; "I'm planting mealies" (corn on the cob). [49] Meanwhile, Jacob Zuma's aids emphasized his reputation for reconciliation. They pointed to his record in helping to bring peace to the his region of KwaZulu-Natal; which was embroiled in conflict between the ANC and the Zulu-based Inkatha Freedom party during the late 1980s, and his attempts to broker a peace deal in Burundi. "We are not naïve," said Che Matlhako, a senior official in the South African Communist Party. "We are not expecting socialism overnight;" What Zuma's allies expected was a new national debate over economic policy.

By November 2007, Zuma winning five of four provinces in the party elections and he emerged the undisputed favorite to become the next leader of the ANC. He attracted the support of the investment bankers, communist party members, rural peasants and Freedom Front; the white rightwing Afrikaner party. Even Zuma's former comrade in exile, the billionaire businessman Tokyo Sexwale, endorsed him. Zuma announced that he was "fit to govern and ready to rule" and immediately sought to reassure the private sector that he would not threaten South Africa's growth by presiding over the reversal of the country's liberal market policies. The business community saw the contest as a redefining moment because of Zuma's ties to the unions which agitated to abandon liberal trade policies. His hard-line supporters announced their intentions to prematurely force Mbeki to stand for a no-confidence vote, but required either a majority of all 400 parliamentarians or the dissolution of parliament, which would trigger national elections. President Mbeki cautioned against party purges and revenge after the succession battle. "The people who might be opposing one another in these contests must not see themselves as enemies;" he stated during a radio interview. One of Mbeki's senior aides, Frank Chikane, noted that he believed Jacob Zuma "was smart enough not to create a situation of instability, because he knew the people would turn against him."[50] Zuma astutely took care not to make bold wealth distribution pledges. In fact he went out of his way to court the business community. Desmond Tutu appealed to the ANC to reject both Mbeki and Zuma.[51] Mbeki's leadership was dealt a further blow when the ANC Women's League, which helped propel him to power, came out against him due to his position on HIV and aids. Zuma's leadership was also threatened by state prosecutors who continued preparing to bring new corruption charges. A high-ranking ANC member and chairman of *Liberty Group* and *Stanlib*, the financial services group, warned that; "Most of the government officials favored by the West, most importantly finance minister Trevor Manuel, would not serve under Zuma. It would not be "Armageddon" for South Africa, but the pronouncements and personalities of Zuma's allies are cause for concern in the business community." Trevor Manuel, (the manager of GEAR South Africa's business friendly macro-economic program which led to the nations annual 5.2 economic growth), became a lightning rod for Zuma's allies, when he was heckled by Zuma supporters while he was voting.

In the worst intra-party conflict in ANC history, Zuma defeated Mbeki by winning more than 60 percent of the 4,000 delegate votes. His supporters celebrated by singing Zuma's trademark liberation song "Bring Me My Machine Gun."[52] While international investors and fund managers widely accept that Zuma is by tradition a centrist, rather than a socialist, many remained wary of his political debts and promises to trade unions and to the South African Communist Party (SACP), whose support fueled his comeback. Implicit in Zuma's victory is the message that is time for a change from Xhosa rule. His immersion in Zulu traditions reflects his comfort in his cultural skin. "Behind the technocracy... people want to see socio-cultural life acknowledged;" noted Pearl Sithole, who studies rural issues at the Human Sciences Research Council in Durban. "To some people Zuma offers an acknowledgment that there are social values on the ground that can be local and positive and that still empower the community."[53] An unintended consequence of Zuma's victory was the political resurrection of Winnie Madikizela-Mandela. She, along with Cyril Ramaphosa and Tokyo Sexwale also won seats on the ANC's 80-member, national executive. Trevor Manuel, was reelected to the national executive with the largest margin of victory (57 percent). One week after his election, the National Prosecuting Authority served Jacob Zuma with papers charging him with racketeering, tax evasion, and corruption. [54]

Myriad Challenges

After years of under investment, South Africa's infrastructure is deteriorating under the pressure of a growing population and expanding economy. The Ben Schoeman highway stretches from Pretoria to Johannesburg, exemplifying this growth. However congested and difficult to navigate, increased traffic is a healthy economic sign. High commodity prices, a sustained period of solid economic growth and low interest rates have contributed to an annual 10 percent growth in vehicle ownership. As more Africans purchase vehicles, highway racial demographics reflect the emergence of the Black middle class. In May 2006, ground was broken on the *Gautrain*, a European-style rapid rail network linking Pretoria and Johannesburg the airport. The project is scheduled for completion by mid-2010 for the World Cup in football. The project is criticized for catering to the elite while ignoring the transportation needs of the poor. At present the public transportation system of matatus and ramshackle trains is under great strain. Poor people pay disproportionately for travel from work to home and back. Forty-six percent of households in Johannesburg spend more than 10 percent of their disposable income on public transportation.

President Mbeki's government responded to the challenge with the Accelerated and Shared Growth Initiative-South Africa (Asgisa), a plan to pursue promising economic opportunities and remove bottlenecks and obstacles. The objective is to achieve sustained economic growth of 6 percent, which is necessary to create new jobs and reinforce social stability. South Africa's economic constraints go beyond the need for mass public transit however. The country's cheap and abundant power supply is being squeezed by accelerating GDP growth. Power cuts in Cape Town, leaves tourists sitting in dark cafes and restaurants, costing businesses billions of Rand. In the suburbs of Johannesburg, consumers suffer power blackouts as *Eskom*, the state-owned power utility, struggles to meet demand.

South Africa's economy remains heavily commodity-reliant, as was made evident when world market corrections sent the rand and Johannesburg Stock Exchange listed stocks tumbling. With many of its mining assets maturing, the government wants to promote service sectors such as business process outsourcing (BPO) and tourism. While the country cannot compete on price for BPO business with India or the Philippines, investors say it offers excellent value and service and a good source of suitable labor. According to *Asgisa* director, Phumzile Mlambo Ngcuka, what the country lacks across all industries, are enough skilled people. The apartheid system deprived most Africans opportunities at a decent education or skilled employment. But, with the advent of majority-rule, many skilled whites in public-service jobs were forced into retirement. *Eskom*, for example has been recruiting expatriate and local whites to mentor younger black workers and help with its expansion.

Some companies complain that a new immigration law makes it difficult or impossible to obtain and extend work permits for their skilled foreign employees. Other obstacles threaten South Africa's economic progress. Chief among these is increased political risk. After years of fearing South Africa would become "another Zimbabwe" for foreign investors, and being lulled by a benign economic picture and some underestimate the potential for volatility. Democracy *per se* may not be under threat, but the long dominant ANC is showing signs of strain. In February 2007, fiscal discipline and tax collection resulted in the country's first budget surplus. The surplus was 0.3 percent in 2006-07 and expected to rise to 0.6 percent in 2007-08. Finance minister Manuel conceded that ironically, a lack of governmental skills and infrastructure had hindered the government's ability to spend this windfall revenue. He noted that it was not possible to distribute some money due to shortcomings in local government, which had contributed to the surplus. More money was pledged for social services, crime fighting, infrastructure and a proposed social security system is scheduled to begin in 2010. The director of the South African Revenue Service, Pravin Gordhan is known as an "activist" tax collector. In seven years he managed an astonishing turn around collection performance that led to an average annual increase of 10 percent in tax revenues.

A former communist party activist, Gordhan, said; "In the end the proof is in the pudding. Is the money in the Bank or not?" When he took over in 1999, he faced two major challenges. The first was to coax, cajole and ultimately threaten companies that had become accustomed to the passive tax collection system of the apartheid era. "For South African business to thrive during the sanctions era of apartheid it had to scheme its way around and develop its own creative mindsets;" notes Gordhan. The other challenge was to try to overturn the ethos of the old days when the ANC urged non-compliance with tax authorities to hasten the end of white rule. "There was a black population that had disengaged economically," he explained. Between March 1996 and 2006, the tax base doubled from 1.9 million individuals to about 5 million. In the same period, corporate registrations increased from

518,000 to 1.9 million. Optimistic in his diagnosis, Gordhan stated: "We have turned a major corner to what may become a normal situation".[55]

South Africa's global status was enhanced in March 2007 when it took a seat on the UN Security Council. South Africa flexed this new political muscle by joining China and Russia in opposing a US resolution to censure Burma (Myanmar) over its repressive human rights record. South Africa aspires to a permanent seat and sees the Security Council term as a trial run. "South Africa being very vocal about being a leader of the developing world rather than the patsy of the developed world;" said a European diplomat. Elizabeth Sideropolous, the director of South Africa's Institute of International Affairs, said Mbeki's government felt a need to prove its credentials to the other countries of Africa. South Africa is ready to be seen as the leader of sub-Saharan Africa, but faces skepticism from more influential African states. Thus, South Africa resisted western demands for a stronger denunciation of Robert Mugabe's rule because it did not want to be seen to be working with the West against another African state.[56]

In Soweto's Jubalani Mall, rows of late model automobiles are parked opposite a phalanx of electronic tellers. Thousands of Sowetans flock to the Jubalani mall daily to enjoy the experience of shopping and saving at *Shoprite* supermarket. Of course this new economic freedom comes at a price. A price well known in the developed world, where the local green grocer and the butcher have given way to *Wal-Mart* and other monopolistic chains. An unforeseen consequence of South Africa's economic boom, is the devastating impact on the country's desperately poor townships. In the past, these townships were the focus of economic and community life. Sixty-five year old veteran and Soweto shopkeeper, Balfour Maketha, recalls that in the latter years of apartheid and the early years of democracy after 1994, he was something of a shopkeeper. "I wouldn't have had time to talk to you then, we were so busy;" he recalled. "We would make a pile of mealie meal (the staple carbohydrate) in the morning and it would be gone in the evening. But now I am sitting crossing my fingers and toes. They have come to take our money and leave us impoverished. The end of apartheid was meant to be the leveling of the playing field. But now the white man, white capital, white stores and businesses are here and we cannot compete."[57] If allowed to rule, president elect Zuma's most daunting challenge would be to keep his "coalition of the disaffected" unified. The inevitable conflict between white capital and black impoverishment does not bode well for such a desperate alliance.

---

1. Vincent B. Khapoya, *The African Experience: An Introduction*. (New Jersey: Prentice-Hall, 1998) p. 222.

2. Ibid. 223.

3 Rodney, Walter, *How Europe Underdeveloped Africa*. (Washington, D.C., 1982, Howard University Press) p. 129.

4. Ibid. p. 132.

5. Ibid. 228-229.

6. Ibid. 230.

7. George Shepperson, and Thomas Price, *Independent African: John Chilembwe and the Origins, Setting and Significance of the Nyasaland Native Uprising of 1915*. (Edinburgh Press, 1958).

8. John Dugard, *Human Rights and the South African Legal Order* (Princeton: Princeton University Press, 1978) 87.

9. Khapoya, Op. Cit. 236.

10. Ibid.

11. Leonard, Thompson. *The Political Mythology of Apartheid*. Quoted in Vincent Khapoya: *The African Experience: An Introduction*. (New Jersey: Prentice Hall, 1998) 27.
p. 237.

12. Dugard Op. Cit. 82-83.

13. Ibid.

14. Richard Gibson, *African Liberation Movements: Contemporary Struggles Against White Minority Rule* (London, Oxford University Press, 1972) 38-39.

15. Ibid. p. 49.

16. Ibid. p. 51.

17. Ibid. p. 50.

18. Kuper, Hilda. "Strangers in Plural Societies: Asians in South Africa and Uganda," in Leo Kuper and M.G. Smith, ed., *Pluralism in Africa Berkeley*: University of California Press. pp. 257-258.

19. Gibson, Op. Cit. pp 56-57. 1972.

20. Quoted in Bunting, Brian. *The Rise of the South African Reich* (Hammondsworth Penguin Books 1969) 216.

21. Gibson, Op. Cit. 59.

22. Thompson, Leonard. *A History of South Africa* (New Haven and London: Yale University Press, 1990) 221-223.

23 .Ibid. 232-233.

24. South African Institute of Race Relations, *Survey of Race Relations in South Africa 1978*. Johannesburg, 1979.

25. James Lamont, 'South Africans' expectations at odds with reality,' *The Financial Times*, December 12, 2001.

26. *The Financial Times* 'S. 'Africa returning' to racial categories,' July 25, 2006, p.4.

27. Caroline Southey, 'Black South Africans frustrated by paltry progress,' *The Financial Times*, January 6-7, 2006.

28. *The Financial Times,* 'Open to abuse? Why cronyism threatens to sour the South African dream,' May 18, 2006 Comment & Analysis. p. 11.

29. Alec Russell and Lionel Barber, 'Concern on SA law to empower blacks,' *The Financial Times*, April 10, 2007, p.1.

30. Alec Russell, 'Rise in S. African black middle class.' *The Financial Times*, May 24, 2007, p. 7.

31. Alec Russell, 'Brutal Durban clash raises union tensions," *The Financial Times*, June 5, 2007 p.8.

32. Alec Russell, 'Public sector strike shakes old alliance in South Africa, *The Financial Times,*' June, 7, 2007, p.6.

33. David White, 'Black middle class helps fuel spending spree' Special Report: South Africa, *The Financial Times*, June 6, 2006, p.2.

34. David White, 'Migrants represent shadow side of the rainbow nation.' *The Financial Times*, May 25, 2005. p.18. ; Alec Russell, 'Anti-foreigner attacks mount in South Africa,' *The Financial Times*, May 20, 2008.; Alec Russell, 'Ugly side of the Rainbow Nation,' *The Financial Times*, May 24-25 2008 p.3 and William Wallis and Matthew Green, 'Nigeria reminds South Africa of Shared history,' *The Financial Times*, June 2, 2008, p.6.

35. John Reed, 'Johannesburg's poor find little for their comfort.' August 9, 2006, p. 7.

36. David White, "Search is on for a much broader appeal.' Special Report, South Africa, *The Financial Times*, June 10, 2006, p.8.

35. David White "Zulu kingdom builds its empire.' Special Report: South Africa, *The Financial Times* June 6, 2006, p.8.

37. Nicol S. Degli, 'African police guilty of dog attacks on immigrants,' *The Financial Times*, October 11, 2001.

38. John Reed, 'S. Africa to tackle rise in crime.' *The Financial Times,* September 2-3, 2006. p.4.

39. James Lamont, 'Probe into South Africa arms deals,' *The Financial Times,* October 11, 2001.

40. John Reed, 'Zuluboy' scandal shakes ANC leaders,' *The Financial Times*, April 1-2, 2006, p. 4.

41. Reed, John. 'South Africa reacts with delight and dismay after Zuma is cleared of rape,' *The Financial Times*, May 9, 2006 p. 4.

42. John Reed, 'ANC chief's corruption trial to hear claims of corporate bribery,' *The Financial Times,* September 5, 2006. p.4.

43. John Reed, 'Aspirant president Zuma moves to left,' *The Financial Times.* September, 16-17, 2006. p.3.

44. John Reed, 'Good times put system under strain.' *The Financial Times,* FT South Africa, Special Report June 6, 2006. p.1.

45. 'Alec Russell, 'ANC leadership race heats up.' *The Financial Times,* May 15, 2007, p.8. 'Ramaphosa nomination shakes up the ANC contest' October 30, 2007. p. 3.

46. Alec Russell, "Ramaphosa awaits the call.' *The Financial Times* November 1, 2007, p.5.

47. Alec Russell, 'South Africa records the first fiscal surplus in its history,' *The Financial Times,* February 2, 2007 p. 4.

48. Alec Rusell, 'Zuma gains lead over Mbeki in race that threatens to split ANC' and 'Zuma 'ready to rule' after leadership boost.' *The Financial Times November 26, 2007*, p.4.

49. William MacNamara 'Tycoon gives boot to Zuma campaign.' p. 8.; Alec Russell, 'Gloves come off in the fight to halt Zuma' *The Financial Times* December 12, 2007. p.2; and 'Mbeki pressed to quit ANC leadership race.' *The Financial Times*, November 29, 2007 p.2; and 'Zuma's aides are prepared to oust president early,' *The Financial Times,* December 7, 2007 p.8.

50. Alec Russell, 'Townships grow restless for ANC to deliver,' *The Financial Times*, December 16, 2007 p.5.

51. Alec Russell, 'Zuma beats Mbeki to become ANC leader,' *The Financial Times*, December 19, 2007 p.3. William MacNamara, 'Winnie Mandela tops ANC poll,' *The Financial Times*, December 22-23, 2007 p. 5.

52. Alec Russell, "Post apartheid phase two," and William MacNamara and William Wallis, 'He is ready to say what does not work,' *The Financial Times*, December 20, 2007 p.7.

53. Alec Russell, 'ANC leader Zuma charged with corruption, *The Financial Times*, December 30, 2007, p. 3.

54. Alec Russell, 'Tax activist fills South Africa's coffers.' *The Financial Times*, February 24-25, 2007 p.3.

55. Alec Russell, 'South Africa shrugs off criticism over Burma stance,' *The Financial Times*, March 1, 2007 p. 5.

56. Alec Russell, 'Soweto's gleaming malls lure customers from township's small shops,' *The Financial Times*, March 13, 2007.

15: Uganda: Psychotic Leadership

The nation called Uganda, consists of two major zones: the plains of the northeast and the southern highlands. A legend claims that, you can drop anything into Uganda's well-watered rich volcanic soils of the south, and it will grow. Traditionally, the area was divided into four kingdoms: The Buganda, the Buyoro, the Ankole and the Toro. European explorers traversing the area in the nineteenth century were impressed by the sophisticated social orders they encountered and equated them with the feudal monarchies of medieval Europe. British colonialists integrated the ruling class of the southern highlands into their system of "indirect rule". Missionaries converted many southern Ugandans to Christianity, which led to a civil war within Buganda between Protestants, Catholics and Muslims, which the British used as a pretext to overthrow the Bugandan King. The British united the two regions as the Uganda Protectorate during the 1890s.[1]

While the term "Buganda" now refers to the larger ethnic group, the two zones were developed separately under colonialism. Cash crop farming, especially of cotton by local peasants, spurred an economic boom in the south and the Bugandan ruling class were the beneficiaries. Increasing levels of education and wealth led to stereotypes of the progressive "Europeanized" Bugandan's as the "Japanese" of Africa. The Bugandan elite were accompanied by a growing class of Asian entrepreneurs who controlled the local economies, although both groups were subordinate to resident British. The south's economic growth stood in stark contrast to the poverty of the northeast. Many from that region were forced to become migrant workers in the south in order to earn sufficient money to pay taxes and they were recruited, almost exclusively, to serve in the colonial security forces.[2]

Many Buganda feared that the other ethnic groups would compromise their interests in an independent Uganda. Under the leadership of King Mutesa II, they tried to maintain their separate status. The other ethnic groups feared that Bugandan wealth and educational levels would lead to Bugandan political and economic dominance. The new federal state structure was based on a compromise. At independence, the southern kingdoms retained their autonomy within the "United Kingdom of Uganda." The first government was made up of Mutesa's royalist party and the United People's Congress (UPC), a largely non-Bugandan coalition, led by Milton Obote, a Langi. Mutesa was elected president and Milton Obote became prime minister.[3]

Uganda's fragile balance of power was upset in 1966 when Obote used the army, which was dominated by northerners and easterners, to overthrow Mutesa and shred the constitution. During his first term in office, Obote using an autocratic ruling style, pursued a socialist agenda. He claimed these actions were necessary to abolish "tribalism." He established a one-party state and ruled as a dictator. In 1971, Obote was overthrown in a coup by his army chief, Idi Amin. Obote was distinguished for re-winning leadership at the ballot box in 1980 after being deposed in a coup nine years earlier by Idi Amin. When he was overthrown by Idi Amin, there was little sympathy from UK Prime Minister, Edward Heath with whom Obote was clashing over UK arms supply to South Africa. The British and North American media welcomed Amin as an honest soldier, but a buffoon. However, many believed there was British complicity in the coup.

Throughout the world Idi Amin's name became synonymous with despotic rule. But as former head of the "King's African Rifles," Amin began his regime with widespread international and domestic support. He quickly alienated himself by showing favor to fellow Muslims and members of the Kakwa ethnic group. He then expelled the 40,000-member Asian community and distributed their property among his associates. Langi, suspected of being pro-Obote, were targeted for political persecution but these attacks quickly spread to other members of the Christian community, which at the time was about 80 percent of Uganda's population. The educated class was purged and many of Uganda's best and brightest went into exile.

Amin's regime was described as "a state of blood." He committed genocide against minority ethnic groups, assisted Palestinian hijackers, expelled much of the merchant-class Indian population and threatened to lock Englishmen in cages. The true number of victims of Idi Amin's death squads is unknown; the most commonly cited figure is 300,000, but estimates range from 50,000 to 1 million. The 1979 military incursion by Amin's' forces into Tanzania led to a war in which many Ugandans supported the Tanzanian army is defeating Amin and his Libyan allies and driving him into exile. The regional instability caused by Amin, motivated President Nyerere to invade and expel the Ugandan leader.

With the Support of Tanzanian President Nyerere, Obote regained office. Although Commonwealth observers declared the 1980 election was flawed, at a rally celebrating his return from exile in Tanzania staged by the Uganda's People Party, Obote was greeted by a police band playing the party song: "Oh Uganda, We Are Moving Forward." Obote's political comeback was greeted with skepticism. Upon returning to power, he moved to reverse the economic policies he had introduced a decade earlier by vigorously adopting IMF and World Bank reforms. But his economic reforms were overshadowed by human right violations. The second regime mirrored that of Amin and the violence continued. Much of the killing took place in the previously remote Bugandan area known as the Luwero triangle where Obote's security forces murdered estimated 300,000 people. Another 300,000 southerners became refugees.

After elections failed in 1985, the resistance led by Yoweri Museveni and the National Resistance Movement (NRM) guerillas, took to the bush. A conflict between Ancholi and Langi military officers led to Milton Obote's overthrow and another round of ethnic violence ensued. In 1986, the NRM emerged victorious and a new political system based on Museveni's vision of a "no-party government" was advanced. The March 1994 Constituent Assembly elections, resulted in Museveni's supporters capturing more than two thirds of the parliamentary seats. In another controversial initiative, Museveni allowed the restoration of the traditional Bugandan kingship.[4]

Northern Uganda includes the towns of Kitgum, Pader, Gulu, Adjumani, Moyo, Nebbi, Mashindi, Lira, Kotido and Katakwi. Due to attacks by the Lords Resistance Army (LRA), virtually all of the inhabitants of these villages were internally displaced. Both of Obote's terms in office proved disastrous and the country is recovering from the legacy of his rule. Northern Uganda experienced one of the world's worst humanitarian crises because of the extensive and prolonged displacement of a very high proportion of its inhabitants, into large refugee camps where the conditions are appalling and there was little prospect of work, health care, education, or the possibility of returning home. The refugee crisis was exacerbated by widespread human rights abuses on both sides. For years, Ugandans suffered some of the worse war crimes and atrocities imaginable. The conflict between the government of Yoweri Museveni and the LRA sent 1.5 million people into refugee camps. The LRA was accused of killing two charity workers and two members of a UN de-mining team contracted to the World Food Program in neighboring Sudan, which the rebels use as a base of support.

War Crimes

For 18 years the LRA engaged in serial murder, beatings, large-scale abductions, forced recruitment of adults and children, sexual violence against girls (whom it assigned as "wives" or sex slaves to commanders), large-scale looting and the destruction of civilian property. The LRA is responsible for displacing hundreds of thousands of people and was a prime factor in destroying the economy of northern Uganda and the resulting impoverishment. The cult-like LRA terrorized civilian populations in a brutal campaign of child-abduction where young boys were forced to bear arms. The guerillas left a trail of corpses and mutilated people in their wake; chopping of the hands, feet and lips and ears of civilians. Although many Ugandan's longed for peace at any price, they abandoned any hope of justice; but they have not abandoned thoughts of personal revenge.

Under international humanitarian law (the laws of war), the armed conflict in northern Uganda was considered non-international i.e., a civil conflict. Applicable law includes Article 3 common to the four *Geneva Conventions of 1949*, the *Second Additional Protocol of 1977* to the *Geneva Conventions*,[5] and customary international humanitarian law. International humanitarian law applies to both government forces and rebel groups and prohibits direct or indiscriminate attacks against civilians and civilian property and requires the humane treatment of all persons in custody. The Ugandan government is bound by international and regional human rights law under provisions found in the *International Covenant on Civil and Political Rights and the African Charter on Human and Peoples' Rights* (The Banjul Charter).[6] Human rights law requires states not only to prevent abuses by government officials and personnel, but too also prosecute those responsible for serious violations.[7]

In each camp they visited, *Human Rights Watch* found cases of abuse by both the LRA and by UPDF soldiers. UPDF-administered beatings of civilians were common, but the killing of civilians, sometimes inside the camps, was also documented. In some camps, civilians faced UPDF abuse on a daily basis. The scale of UPDF abuse continues at an unacceptable level and the governmental protection and accountability structures that would put a stop to such abuse are not in place. The following accounts were reported by Human Rights Watch.

The LRA brutalizes all abductees to deter escape attempts. Those attempting to escape are either killed or seriously wounded as an example to others. A woman, abducted by the LRA in August 2004, told Human Rights Watch how a girl, a fellow abductee, tried to escape. When she was captured the rebels "beat her until she died. They used traditional tools, used to make sculpture, to beat her—they hit her on her neck, her hands and her legs until she died."[8]

On February 24, 2005, The LRA abducted a group of women going to get water on. Several eyewitnesses told Human Rights Watch, that one of the women had a crying baby. Five LRA fighters told the woman they wanted the baby and that they were going to kill it. The woman threw the baby down and ran. The rebels grabbed the woman and beat her with a gun. When the woman was dead one of the rebels got a stick and pierced the two weeks old child's head. [9]

The LRA does not hesitate to execute those who do not obey orders to perform certain tasks, even if the person is physically incapable of doing so. A woman described how the rebels beat to death Malone Okwir, a man of about sixty years-old, after he threw down the heavy load of food he was carrying on his back. He was unable to transport it further than the three miles he had already traveled," so they beat him to death with a hoe and cut him with a *panga* (a farming implement with a long blade)."[10]

Local officials were commonly targeted by the LRA. A relative of a parish-level local councilor, recalled how Okello Saul was killed May 20,

2004 while performing his duties. He went from Paicho camp to Cwero, to supervise the building of the hospital. Upon his return, he was ambushed by the LRA, while his motorcycle. They shot him eight times, burned his motorcycle, undressed him and took his belongings; leaving him in his underwear. He left behind a wife and four children.[11]

Table 15.1 Violence against Refugees in the Adjumani District of Northern Uganda

Incident Type	2002	2003	2004
LRA killing of refugee	9	11	25
LRA looting of refugee home	173	81	41
LRA abductions of refugees	19	114	99
UPDF killing of refugee	1	2	2
UPDF looting of refugee home	0	15	0
Unidentified killing of a refugee	4	9	0
Unidentified looting of refugee home	8	5	0
SPLA recruitment of refugee	4	3	0
Relief workers/convoy employees killed	3	21	0
Relief/commercial convoys ambushed	2	16	0
Total number of refugees killed	14	22	27
Firearm Homicide rates per 100,000	23	36	44

Several LRA killings were committed under duress by the abductees, often children. A twelve-year-old boy interviewed by Human Rights Watch, killed a civilian by beating him with a stick. This occurred one week after the child was abducted by the LRA in a village outside the camp. At first he refused the order to kill the civilian, but LRA guerillas beat him until he agreed. He escaped two months later. A similar case involving a twenty-four-year-old farmer occurred in 2003. During the two months he was a prisoner of the LRA, he witnessed and under duress participated, in the deliberate killings of nine civilians.[12] A thirty-eight-year-old man was riding his bicycle in January 2005, when he saw five LRA fighters coming toward him on the road. He threw down his bicycle and ran. They caught him and shot him through the cheek from a distance of less than two meters. He lost consciousness. When he awoke hours later, he found they had stolen his bicycle and the clothes he was wearing. He was hospitalized for three weeks.[13] Some people were killed, or left for dead, because the LRA fighters simply wanted to rob them.

One woman was abducted by a group of LRA rebels who were interested in surrendering to the UPDF. The commander of the rebels asked her to ensure that the soldiers would not attack them if they went to surrender. When she failed to sufficiently comply, they beat her unconscious and left her for dead. According to the woman:

> When I tried to answer the questions they got four young boys to go and get sticks." They returned with many sticks. They began to

> beat me seriously. I tried to cry and reached a position where I kept quiet. While they beat me they told me I would be beaten to death because I was tricking them. They said, "You women like to make false statements in order that we release you."[14] When they left me I was unaware. It was dark. I tried to wake up. I looked around and didn't see rebels. I couldn't walk. I was very thirsty, very hungry and very very weak. I started to crawl following the way back. I crawled looking for water at the river. I crawled into the water and got water. I tried to cry but I couldn't.[15] When I came out of the water I tried to walk with grass as a support. I was dizzy, fell down, rested a bit. I began to crawl and heard vehicles. I tried to crawl in their direction and came abruptly to the road. The road was too hard to crawl on and I fell to the roadside. I met a man coming from Namkara and he took me to Kitgum Matidi, to the barracks. The Intelligence officer took a brief statement then they took me to the hospital.[16]

Another woman described her temporary abduction in January 2004 by a unit of the LRA under the command of Lagony Otti. She was pregnant at the time, and had gone with a group of ten women to harvest their fields. The rebels intercepted the women, who were beaten for two days. "The rebels kept hitting my chest and waist. They hit my chest with the butt of a gun while at the same time using tree branches to hit me." The baby survived but was born very weak, which she attributed to the beating. "Up to now I feel chest pain. I was beaten until I was unconscious. I don't know how they set me free-I was rescued by friends."[17]

A nineteen-year-old woman said that she lived in fear of the LRA. In 2003, her father and two brothers were abducted from their camp and beaten to death with sticks by the LRA rebels. Her sister was abducted one week later by the LRA and killed. She reported: "I stopped school in 2003 when I was in P.6. My father died and I was heartbroken and stopped going. There was no one paying the school fees. I live with my mother and one brother and two sisters." In December 2004, she went with another woman to a garden five miles from the camp, where seven LRA fighters found them at 10 a.m. "The rebels ordered us to go with them to the bush. They beat us. One of the rebels said they should kill me, but another said let her go back home. They were boys and men. I was undressed, they took everything, I was naked. They told me to hurry back home. None of them defiled me."[18]

In February 2005 there was a surge in attacks, in which the LRA brutally employed mutilation and torture to disfigure civilians. They first began mutilating civilians in the early 1990s in response to the government's attempts to form local militias in northern Uganda. Victims' hands, feet, noses, ears, lips and breasts were cut off, often as punishment, causing widespread panic amongst the population. These brutal tactics proved extremely effective for spreading fear and deterring cooperation with the government. According to what the LRA fighters tell the victims, these mutilations symbolically cut off the allegedly offending part, i.e., the ears that hear, the lips that kiss.[19] As with other methods, surge mutilations were the LRA's method of responding to adverse government policy pronouncements.

President Museveni declared peace on February 17, 2005 following the surrender of LRA leader and peace negotiator Sam Kolo's announcement that the military conflict in northern Uganda was; "finished those remaining fugitive commanders can't fight anymore." Just a few days after the publication of Kolo's statements, eleven women were abducted by the LRA near Ngomoromo, Kitgum. One of the women was beaten to death with her baby because the baby was making too much noise. The other women were herded into an abandoned hut, made to strip naked, and were mutilated.

One witness told Human Rights Watch: "After discussing with his colleagues he came in and started chopping off our lips. When he was cutting he ordered us not to make any noise otherwise he would kill us, so we persevered. The rebels cut our lips because they said we "loved the soldiers at Ngomoromo barracks." In the following weeks the LRA conducted several more brutal attacks on civilians. Thirty women who went to collect firewood were attacked by the LRA in Agoro, Kitgum. The rebels cut the lips and ears off one woman and the breasts off another. They left, abducting others among the group of thirty women and leaving the disfigured victims to find a way home. One man's four children were abducted by the LRA on May 24, 2004 and his finger was cut off as punishment for farming. He stated: It was at eight in the night. A group of LRA came to my house. I was living there with my wife and children. The rebels looted my household.... They beat me with pangas on my back and rear three times. They burned all of our huts. Then they put my hand down. They cut off my finger with a panga. The rebel who cut off my finger was a young boy in his early teens. I pleaded with them not to hurt my hand, but they said since they found me farming at home they would have to kill me.... Then they left with my children.[20]

Human Rights Watch did not document cases of rape by the LRA in the camps, or when rebels encountered women or girls in the fields. Rape, on many occasions gang rape, was committed after the young women and adolescent girls were taken back to the LRA camp. The absence of rape in the field and the gang rape after returning to base, suggests that these crimes are sanctioned if committed according to orders. A woman told *Human Rights Watch* how she was abducted with her sister in January 2004 by a group of one hundred rebels near Agoro camp in Kitgum. They were taken back to a rebel encampment and distributed to the top commanders who raped them

A community leader told *Human Rights Watch* that the reason the LRA fighters did not rape captured women and girls before taking them to the LRA base was Kony's hold over his combatants: "They are superstitious that Kony knows everything they do. Kony doesn't want them to 'contaminate' women because Kony picks the women and then shares the rest among the others." The LRA abducted thousands of women and girls who are still being held and give birth to children in captivity. Others have escaped, with or without their children. Over the years, many caretakers and community leaders surmise that this behavior is due to their perverse understanding of HIV/Aids. LRA fighters have accused older married women they have captured and then released, of being wives of UPDF soldiers; and therefore of being infected with the HIV virus. The LRA abducts younger girls who are more likely to be virgins and therefore are less likely to be exposed to the HIV virus.[21]

UNICEF estimates that approximately 20,000 Ugandan children were abducted during the nineteen years of war. The level of abductions surged after the LRA returned from Sudan following the UPDF Operation "Iron Fist" launched inside Sudan in mid-2002. Abductions appeared to be declining during the second half of 2004, but reports in February and March 2005 indicated that the LRA was again abducting children to increase its ranks.[23]

The LRA often engaged in large-scale attacks on refugee camps or villages committing *en masse* abductions. At other times, farmers and others were abducted in small groups when went to their fields in search of food to supplement the small emergency food rations. Although they were forced outside the camps to look for the necessities supplies the camps lacked, the displaced rarely were given protection by the UPDF when they ventured outside the camps.[24]

Children are intimidated and brutalized to such an extent that often they are too frightened to return home. Extreme violence is a way for the LRA to psychologically remove the abductees from their previous lives. The LRA forced the children and adults to commit atrocities as part of an indoctrination process. A twelve-year old abductee from Agoro camp told Human Rights Watch how, after he was abducted in July, 2004, he was beaten until he agreed to kill a civilian with a stick.[25] Although they claimed to have been fighting against the perceived marginalization of the northern Acholi people, the cruelty was extremely inhumane. Thousands of children known as the "night commuters," fled their rural homes to safer confines each evening to avoid LRA abduction.

According to surgeons working in the Gulu district hospital, which treats refugee victims from all over northern Uganda; between 6 and 7 per cent of all traumatized admissions are gun shot related. While landmine injuries appeared to have declined since 2000, small-arms-related wounds remain far too common.[26]

Table 15.2 Injuries Treated Lacor Hospital Gulu, Uganda 2001

Cause	Frequency	Percentage	Cumulative Percentage
Traffic	476	41.6	41.6
Falls	277	24.2	65.8
Burns	38	3.3	69.1
Gunshot	76	6.6	75.7

Stabbing	95	8.3	84.0
Blunt Injury	118	10.3	94.3
Poisoning	1	0.1	94.4
Animal Bite	8	0.7	95.1
Other	56		100

Source: Kobusingye, et al. (2003); Small Arms Survey 2004. Source: Robert Muggah's Interviews and archival records from UNHCR sub-offices.

Peace or Justice?

In the ancestral tradition, many tribal elders and local human rights activists announced that in the name of peace they were prepared to forgive. To his followers, Joseph Kony, leader of the Lord's Resistance Army (LRA), is a God-like, leader with mystical powers rendering him immortal. To president Museveni, of Uganda, Kony is a mass murderer who terrorized the population of the northern Uganda for two decades. To the kidnapped children that constitute the rank and file of Kony's army, he is a serial rapist and murderer. And to the US State Department, he is the leader of a terrorist group. Kony's newest designation, however, could provide his most durable; as the world's first fugitive-at-large from the International Criminal Court (ICC). The ICC was established by treaty in 1998 to try the world's worst war criminals when local courts have neither the competence nor the will to do so. It first opened its doors in The Hague, Netherlands in the summer of 2002. "People think the ICC is the spoiler;" said James Otto, director of Human Rights Focus a monitoring group in the northern town of Gulu. Should we have peace and justice at the same time, do we have the capacity to do both? [27]

At the request of President Museveni, the ICC issued an indictment against the LRA rebel leader Joseph Kony in November, 2005. He was charged with 21 war crimes and 12 charges of crimes against humanity including sexual enslavement. Ugandan officials report that LRA forces, weakened by defections in exchange for amnesty had been reduced to a few hundred armed men In February 2005, the LRA chief negotiator surrendered. Local, international non-governmental organizations and church leaders involved in promoting dialogue, urged delaying in issue of ICC warrants. The ICC indictments dealt a blow to the mediation efforts of Betty Bigombe, a former Ugandan government minister backed by the UK, the Netherlands and Norway. But Richard Dicker, head of Human Rights Watch's international justice program stated that: "I don't think the leadership of the LRA was ever genuinely interested in a peace deal." "We see justice as an absolutely crucial component of a meaningful and durable peace."

The indictments re-focused attention on the Bush administration's troublesome policy toward the ICC and many hoped it would perhaps convince the Bush administration to release the executive branch from prohibitions against cooperating with the court. Kony's crimes in northern Uganda became the target of ICC investigations in January 2004, and although it had not yet been made official by the ICC; UN Under-Secretary General for Political Affairs, Ibrahim Gambari, told reporters that Kony indictment was sealed. Once unsealed, that indictment would detail Kony's role in a rebellion that devastated the civilian population of northern Uganda for over a decade. Although the ICC is legally permitted to prosecute only the crimes that occurred after 2002, prosecutor, Luis Moreno Ocampo has plenty of material evidence to work with.

For these reasons, and the fact that Yoweri Museveni, voluntarily ceded national jurisdiction over these crimes to the ICC, Kony became the ideal first target of an ICC indictment. Meanwhile, the politically savvy Ocampo, thought that he had found an ally in the Bush administration. Museveni is an ally in Bush's "war on terror" and the LRA consistently appears in State Department reports on foreign terrorist organizations. The Kony indictment exposed a major contradiction in US foreign policy. Now that an international pariah has been indicted by the ICC, US law makes it illegal for the United States to aid in his apprehension. The American Service Members Protection Act (ASPA), which was passed under the watchful eye of the late Senator Jesse Helms,' prohibits any agency of the US government from aiding the ICC. For the moment, it is illegal for the US government to help the only court that is seeking the apprehension of a man the United States considers the leader of a terrorist group. This policy is at odds with the promotion of international cooperation in the capture of al Qaeda members.

It was the logic of Senator Helms that led to this absurd policy and is mirrored in the Bush administration's policy toward the court. In May 2002, fearing the prospect that Americans would be the target of politically motivated indictments; Bush took the highly unusual step of "unsigning" President Clinton's name to the Rome Statute that created the ICC. The Bush administration subsequently went on an unrelenting campaign to limit the court's jurisdiction throughout the world by coercing countries into signing bilateral immunity agreements with the United States. When those countries (which are often close allies) refuse to grant Americans inmunity from the ICC in their territory, the United States suspends military or economic assistance earmarked for combating more urgent transnational threats such as arms, human being and drug trafficking.

The ICC is not above criticism. There is genuine concern that some ICC indictments may be detrimental to local efforts for peace and reconciliation, which have borne fruitful results. The Kony indictment highlights something about the court that its prosecutor would prefer unsaid: namely that the ICC is likely to only prosecute Africans, since the ICC, only asserts its jurisdiction when national courts are unwilling or unable to effectively prosecute their own war criminals. Moreover, it is much easier to generate international political will to prosecute warlords in isolated or failed states, than it is to take on sitting governments in developed countries. Thus, the only ongoing ICC investigations, aside from Uganda are in the Democratic Republic of Congo and Sudan.

Once the ICC issued an indictment for Kony, the United States was constrained with respect to how to deal with him. Even if US agencies come across intelligence concerning his location, they would be prohibited from passing that information on to the ICC. Furthermore, the State Department cannot even include Kony in its "Rewards for Justice" program, which was used to some success in apprehending war criminals in former Yugoslavia for trial at the International Criminal Court (ICTY). Bush could have helped by signing a waiver releasing US agencies from their prohibition from helping in the apprehension of Kony. It would mark the second time that his administration tacitly endorsed the work of the ICC (if not the court itself). In February 2005, after a bitter dispute between the United States and the rest of the UN Security Council over the venue in which war crimes in Sudan ought to be tried, the United States relented on its opposition to the ICC and abstained from a vote that granted the ICC jurisdiction in Sudan.[28] The ICC is largely a European experiment and the LRA provides a soft political test case. For the European Union it was a better bet than the hard issues of Afghanistan, Iraq or anywhere in the Middle East where war crimes and crimes against humanity are committed daily.

Although the indictments against Kony and four others (one who is reported dead) were welcomed by human rights organizations and those seeking justice; aid agencies were concerned that the indictments would make a lasting peace even more remote now that the rebel leaders have arrest warrants hanging over their heads.

Under heavy Ugandan military convoy including armored personnel carriers, the World Food Program continued its operations, but LRA commanders reacted by obstructing their operations to deliver food and medicine to affected civilian populations. According to WFP director in Uganda, Ken Davies, in 2005 the situation improved and people began leaving the camps to plant their crops. "[29]

In the all too familiar pattern of African political leadership, Yoweri Museveni, who was once quite critical of African leaders clinging to power; announced his plans to do exactly that. Since seizing power in 1986, Museveni is one of the continent's longest serving presidents. He earned praise for Uganda's effective fight against the HIV/Aids virus and for the economic reforms that pulled the country out of the devastation of the brutal regimes of Idi Amin and Milton Obote. However, there is concern that Museveni, like his predecessors, is falling into Africa's "Big Man" syndrome or psychosis of leadership i.e., someone who convinced he is the only person capable of leading his country and is unwilling to step aside. "I am ready, as in the past to lead you," he told delegates after accepting the National Resistance Movement's (NRM) 2006 presidential election endorsement.

In October 2005, Uganda's parliament voted to remove presidential term limits amid allegations that many legislators were bribed 5 million shillings ($2700) to support the legislation. At an NRM conference, Museveni told delegates that the term-limit provision "was not wise at all, because the problems Africa faces are not always time-bound." At a campaign closing rally, Museveni lashed out at "foreign meddlers who sought to dictate Uganda's development projects and political affairs." His remarks targeted the World Bank, upon which the country relies for help in financing vital power projects. He also singled out the UK and other bilateral donors, which have restricted aid to Uganda over military spending and the slow pace of political liberalization. "Henceforth we will not listen to anybody when it comes to vital matters like defense, like energy, like roads, like politics;" Museveni told thousands of supporters in Kampala. He declared that Uganda would not continue to beg from the World Bank and blamed a serious electrical shortage on Ugandan parliamentarians, local and foreign environmentalists and foreign partners for preventing the construction of more hydroelectric dams.

Kampala is subject to regular power outages in 12 or 24 hour cycles, the country is moving along with a long-delayed plan to build a 250 megawatt dam at Bujagali Falls on the Nile. These projects are ambitious given that the average life expectancy for Ugandan males is 39 years and for females 40. Eighty-nine out of every 1,000 infants dies at birth, the HIV/Aids rate is 6.1 percent and there is but 1 doctor for every 20,700 people.

The Bujagali Falls dam construction project was delayed in 2003 after an environmentalist protest, the suspension of World Bank funds, a corruption probe and a decision by the US contractor, *AES* to abandon the project. Museveni said that "foreign meddlers" had insisted on building dams one at a time, when Uganda needed several at once to make up for the shortfall in the power supply. Power output has been hurt by the drastically low level of Lake Victoria, which feeds the Nile River. Drought stalks the region. Ugandan officials deny that Uganda's draining off water for power generation is the cause of declining lake levels. However, a report by the International Rivers Network Organization, claimed the drainage process resulted in a 3 percent drop of the lakes volume within three years.[30]

The 2006 first multi-party elections in more than 20 years, challenged Uganda's "no-party" system. Museveni argued that it was party politics that fueled the country's bloody past. Under the "no-party" system, political parties were restricted and candidates were to be elected on "merit" rather than party affiliation. In November 2005, three weeks after returning from exile, Kizza Besigye, Museveni's former doctor, became a rival candidate in the 2006 elections. He was immediately arrested and charged with treason. Government prosecutors claimed the charges linked Besigye to two rebel groups and charged him with rape one week later. Besigye's arrest ignited two days of rioting in Kampala. Museveni's opponents saw these charges against Besigye as another example of his lack of democratic values and argued that he was unwilling to accept democracy. "He no longer cares what he said about democracy when he came. Everything he is doing now is contradicting what he said;" charged Mugisha Muntu, a member of the opposition Forum for Democratic Change (FDC).[31] The FDC, created in

2005, appeared to have supplanted Uganda's traditionalist parties, attracting support among the young who only had known rule under Museveni. Despite widespread fear of a Museveni victory and post-ballot violence, on February 23, 2006, Ugandans went to the polls.

Closing his campaign, Museveni warned opponents not to cause trouble. "The state is ready to deal with whoever will try violence;" he warned. This was the first partisan presidential and parliamentary election since 1980 and the contest between President Museveni and Kizza Besigye, was expected to be close. Three other presidential candidates included the widow of Milton Obote. If Museveni received less than 50 percent of the vote, there would be an unprecedented second election. In such a case, Besigye would receive the backing of the Ugandan Peoples Congress. There was concern that an upset victory might provoke a response from the army, whose senior officers were hand-picked by Museveni. Besigye's candidacy tested the Ugandan judicial system. The move to try him by court martial on charges of terrorism was blocked, and the Attorney General failed to disqualify him on the grounds that he was in jail at the time of his nomination. Asked if he would challenge the outcome through a legal appeal or by calling on his Forum for Democratic Change to take to the streets; Besigye told journalists: "All options are open." However, he urged supporters to remain calm while the FDC decided the next step. Some FDC officials voiced concern over post-election violence and the governmental crackdown on the opposition. Riot police used tear gas to disperse FDC supporter's at the Kampala party headquarters. Chief of Police, Kale Kayihura claimed the FDC was mobilizing countrywide to prepare for violent disruptions.[32]

Diplomats reported that voter intimidation was much less widespread than in the 2001 election, when Museveni won what was supposed to have been his final term. The balloting was monitored by 600 foreign and 20,000 Ugandan observers. "It will be very difficult to cheat without the international community knowing about it;" one observer remarked. There were also 284 parliamentary seats open for election, 16 of which Museveni's party contested unopposed.[33] Delays in opening the political process hurt relations with foreign donors despite Uganda's applauded policy of economic reform and recovery. The day before the election, riot police fired tear gas into a crowd and shot and killed three people who were waiting for Besigye at a Kampala rugby match. "This is part of the rigging process," said the FDC's local parliamentary candidate. "You don't get power on a silver plate." [34]

A 200-member EU team monitoring the election, criticized the Museveni government for the "lack of a level playing field" during the elections. With 60 percent of the votes counted, the results gave Museveni a clear lead. The EU team reported that both presidential and parliamentary elections were generally well-run and transparent. However, they also noted that Museveni's National Resistance Movement Party used government resources, staff and biased coverage on state broadcasting networks to bolster its position against the opposition parties. State television devoted almost 80 percent of its coverage to Museveni. Max Van den Berg, head of the EU mission, pointed to "serious technical short-comings" in the election and called on the electoral commission to investigate why many voters were turned away from the polling stations. He said observers had not declared systematic patterns of irregularities that would skew the results and urged opposition parties to take their complaints to the courts rather than "go to the streets." The Forum for Democratic Change accused the authorities of announcing selective results in order to prepare the country for a pre-ordained victory for Museveni. The Democracy Monitoring Group, an umbrella Organization for poll observers, said the election fell short of its expectations for a free and fair contest, but called on Ugandans to accept the results or use the courts to appeal.

On August 29, 2006, an agreement between the Museveni government and the LRA became effective. Under the terms of the agreement, within three weeks hundreds of LRA fighters were to march in from hideouts in the DRC and northern Uganda into designated areas in southern Sudan. Museveni pledged an amnesty to the LRA if a comprehensive cease-fire was reached. However, he referred the prosecution of the LRA leadership to the ICC. As a member of the Hague-based court, Uganda, the DRC and Sudan are legally obliged to arrest and extradite those accused of war crimes, genocide and crimes against humanity. Too often, a lamentable dilemma of African-conflict resolution and healing the trauma; is the unfair choice between the pursuit of peace and the pursuit of justice.

---

1. Wayne Edge, (2002) *Africa, Uganda: Country Report*, Global Studies with Annual Editions (Dubuque: McGraw-Hill-Dushkin, 2000) 100.

2. Ibid.

3. Ibid.

4. Ibid.

5. *Additional Protocol to the Geneva Conventions of 12 August 1949*, and *Relating to the Protection of Victims of Non-International Armed Conflicts* (Protocol II), June 8, 1977. Uganda ratified Protocol II in 1991. Protocol II prohibits, among other things, murder, torture and other cruel treatment, rape, acts of terrorism, and pillage. Article 4.

6. African [Banjul] Charter on Human and Peoples' Rights, adopted June 27, 1981, OAU Doc. CAB/LEG/67/3 rev. 5, 21 I.L.M. 58 (1982), entered into force October 21, 1986. Uganda ratified in charter in 1995.

7.*International Covenant on Civil and Political Rights,* G.A. res. 2200A, (XXI), 21 UN GAOR Supp. (No. 16) at 52, UN Doc. A/6316 (1966), 999 U.N.T.S. 171, *entered into force* March 23, 1976. Uganda ratified the ICCPR in 1995

8. http://www.hrw.org/reports/uganda09095.htm
9. http://www.hrw.org/reports/uganda09095.htm
10. http://www.hrw.org/reports/uganda09095.htm
11. http://www.hrw.org/reports/uganda09095.htm
12. http://www.hrw.org/reports/uganda09095.htm
13. http://www.hrw.org/reports/uganda09095.htm
14. http://www.hrw.org/reports/uganda09095.htm
15. http://www.hrw.org/reports/uganda09095.htm
16. http://www.hrw.org/reports/uganda09095.htm
17. http://www.hrw.org/reports/uganda09095.htm
18. http://www.hrw.org/reports/uganda09095.htm
19. http://www.hrw.org/reports/uganda09095.htm
20.http://www.hrw.org/reports/uganda09095.htm
21. http://www.hrw.org/reports/uganda09095.htm

22. http://www.hrw.org/reports/uganda09095.htm

23. http://www.hrw.org/reports/uganda09095.htm

24. http://www.hrw.org/reports/uganda09095.htm

25. http://www.hrw.org/reports/uganda09095.htm

26. Robert Muggah, 'Protection Failures: Outward and inward militarization of refugee settlements and IDP camps in Uganda," in Robert Muggah ed. *No Refuge: The Crisis of Refugee Militarization in Africa.* London and New York: Zed Books, 2006). p.105.

27. Andrew England, 'First steps to peace, but no justice, for Ugandans,' *The Financial Times*, August 30, 2006.

28. *American Prospect* , Hunting Kony will the ICC's First Indictment Inspire Détente between the Bush Administration and the World Court? October 7, 2005.

29. David White, "ICC indictments 'hinder' relief agency efforts in northern Uganda,' *The Financial Times,* November 7, 2005.

30. David White "Ugandan president seeks votes with attack on foreign meddlers' *The Financial Times,* February 22, 2006. p.7.

31. Andrew England, 'Museveni to stand for third term in Uganda,' *The Financial Times*, November 21, 2005.

32. David White, 'Fears of violence over results mar Uganda's presidential elections,' *The Financial Times*, February 27, 2006.

33. David White, 'Ugandan army prepares for poll protests,' *The Financial Times*, February 23, 2006 p.5.

34. David White, 'Dirty tricks surround Ugandan election campaigns,' *The Financial Times*, February 21, 2006 p.5.

16: Zimbabwe: Starving to Vote

Zimbabwe (formerly known as Rhodesia after England's most infamous imperialist Cecil Rhodes) was a British colony until Ian Smith announced a Universal Declaration of Independence (UDI) in 1965. The government ran an apartheid-like regime established under Smith and the white minority ruled until 1980. After 14 years of armed struggle by the Zimbabwe African Peoples Union (ZAPU) and the Zimbabwe African National Union (ZANU), these Africans won their independence. For the black majority, Rhodesia's name was symbolic of their subordination to a small minority of privileged white settlers and the racial dominance system. They renamed the nation Zimbabwe, which is symbolic of the greatness of their pre-colonial history. Robert Mugabe the ZAPU-Patriotic Front (PF) formed a one-party government that inherited the economic legacy not only of colonialism but also of apartheid. Mugabe and ZANU-PF, have governed the country since independence from Britain. The party campaigns on its record of bringing freedom and sovereignty to the country. It claimed to represent non-racial democracy, improved social conditions and health and education for all.

Zimbabwe's pre-colonial history is very rich one. One of the great brick constructions from the 14th century, the stone ruins of Great Zimbabwe, are among the world's architectural wonders and were described in the writings of 14th century Portuguese explorers Barbosa and DeBarros. However, Basil Davidson notes that there is nothing to show that they or any other early Europeans explorers actually reached Great Zimbabwe; and if they did, these records were lost or not unpublished. The ruins of Great Zimbabwe may have had their beginnings much longer than a thousand years ago. Though simpler structures have vanished these simpler structures may have foundations on the debris of older structures of straw and mud. In fact, these earliest dwellings may have risen as long ago as the fifth or sixth century.[1] As their architectural legacy, these civilizations left the remains of stone settlements known as *Zimbabwe's*. The term "Zimbabwe" is used to designate the flourishing Zambezi-Limpopo cultures existing three centuries before European arrival.

The largest of the structures, the "Great Zimbabwe" is located near the modern town of Masvingo. Within its massive walls are distinctively carved birds whose likeness became the symbol of the modern state. They were built of granite rock and flaked granite, on granite hills. One of the principal structures was 300 feet long and 200 feet wide, with walls 30 feet high and 20 feet thick. A European archaeologist reportedly observed that there was a much labor expended on Zimbabwe as on the Egyptian pyramids. When Cecil Rhodes sent his mercenary army to loot Zimbabwe, they marveled at the surviving ruins and assumed they had been built by Europeans or some other "white people".[2] Early European fortune seekers and archaeologists looted and destroyed much of the archaeological evidence of this site, but what survives confirms that the state had trading contacts with people as far away as China.[3]

By the fifteenth century, Zimbabwe was the center of a group of states that prospered through the trade of gold and other products with wayfaring Indian Ocean merchants. Through their understanding of the material environment, the people of Zimbabwe produced hydrologists who diverted streams and made water flow around hills, in a manner indicating a mastery of the scientific principles governing the motion of water. They also produced geologists who knew where to look for gold and copper in the subsoil. When the colonialists arrived in the 19th century, they found virtually all gold-bearing and copper-bearing strata had been previously mined by Africans, though not on the same scale achievable with steam powered drilling equipment.

By the 16th century, the Zimbabwean civilizations were on the decline, the result of the disruption of their trade by the Portuguese. These states survived well into the 19th century and their cultural legacy exists in seventy-one percent of Zimbabwe's population who speak Shona. The country's other major ethno-linguistic group are the Ndebele-speakers who are an estimated 16 percent of the population. This group traces its local origin to the mid-nineteenth century conquest of much of modern Zimbabwe by invaders from the south under the leadership of Umzilagazi; who established a militarily strong Ndebele kingdom, which was subsequently ruled by his son.[4]

The famed Dr. David Livingstone, arrived in 1851 and by 1855 reached what he had deemed to be Victoria Falls. By 1861 the London Missionary Society was active among the Ndebele. But imported religions failed to meet the needs of Africa's impoverished masses and messianic nativist religious movements began to develop. One of these, the Kitawala cult, was founded by Romo Nyirenda of Nyasaland, who proclaimed himself *Muana Lesa*, the Son of God. This cult was an 'Africanized' version of the *American Watch Tower* movement (Jehovah's Witnesses). Romo Nyirenda traveled widely preaching his doctrine condemning colonial exploitation and repression of the Congolese by the Belgians. In 1926 he was accused of killing whites and hanged.[5]

Zimbabwe is unique in that it was never under the direct rule of any single European power. In the 1890s the lands of the Ndebele and Shona were invaded by the Cecil Rhode's mercenary army and agents of the British South African Company (BASCO). In the 1890s, both groups strongly resisted the encroachment of BASCO settlers, but eventually succumbed to the invaders. In 1924, the BASCO administration was dissolved and Southern Rhodesia became a self-governing British crown colony. This "self-government" was confined to the white-settler community, which grew rapidly, but never numbered more than 5 percent of the total population. By 1900, Britain had crushed all African tribal resistance to colonialism.

In 1953, Southern Rhodesia was federated with the British colonial territories of Northern Rhodesia (Zambia) and Nyasaland (Malawi). This Central African Federation was supposed to evolve into a "multiracial" dominion, but was perceived by the black majority as vehicle for extended white dominance. In 1962, white voters responded by electing the Rhodesian Front (RF), a party committed to maintaining a regime based on "white supremacy." In 1963, the Central African Federation collapsed under pressure of the local resistance. Black nationalists established the independent "nonracial" states of Malawi and Zambia and there was concern that white minority rule would be extended to Southern Rhodesia. The new government enacted emergency powers to suppress nationalist organizations and liberation movements such as the Zimbabwe African National Union (ZANU, led by Ndabaningi Sithole), and the Zimbabwe African People's Union (ZAPU, led by Joshua Nkomo).[6] The underground movements ZANU and ZAPU began their armed struggle in 1966. The initial success of these attacks was limited, but after 1973 the Rhodesian Security Forces were besieged by the guerilla campaign. Testifying before the UN Committee on Colonialism on May 12, 1969, George Silundika, Secretary for Publicity and Information of ZAPU, defended his organization's choice of armed struggle as the only way to liberate Zimbabwe. He reminded the committee that under the apartheid-style land act, for every acre held by an African a European settler owned 500 acres, whose soil was on the average four times as fertile as an Africans' land.[7]

In 1958, Joshua Nkomo traveled across Africa to represent the African National Congress at the first All-African Peoples' Conference. He remained abroad for two-years, operating from exile in London. He returned to Rhodesia in 1960 as President of the National Democratic Party (NDP), which was formed to replace the banned ANC.[8] Shortly after ZAPU was formed; Nkomo and his associates agreed that, if it too were banned, they would not try to form another party, but would go underground at home and operate from offices in exile. ZAPU was outlawed in September 1962, after fewer than nine months in existence. Nkomo flew to Tanganyika (Tanzania) where he proposed establishing a government in exile. He remained under government restriction until 1963, but despite surveillance, managed to keep contact with his colleagues. The creation of a new party, The People's

Caretaker Council (PCC), forced Nkomo to acknowledge the emergence of a new splinter group. However, the PCC, ZAPU and ZANU were all outlawed by the Ian Smith regime in 1964.

In a 1965 move to consolidate a white power base resembling that of the neighboring apartheid regime of the Afrikaners, the Rhodesian Front made a Unilaterally Declared of Independence (UDI) from the British Crown. The UK and the UN both refused to recognize the RF's independent status and in 1967, the UN imposed mandatory but ineffective economic sanctions against the illegal regime. The sanctions were ignored by South Africa and the Portugal who controlled Mozambique and Angola. The United States ignored the sanctions and continued to purchase Rhodesian chrome, but many other states and individuals engaged in covert forms of sanctions-busting. Initially, the Rhodesian economy benefited from blockade, which encouraged the development of many import-substitution-industries. The limited impact of the sanctions and the failure of the international community to act, put the burden of treating this particular case of racial dominance, on the ZANU, ZAPU and the local population.

Unable to deter the military advance of the ZANU/ZAPU Patriotic Front, in 1978-1979 the Rhodesian Front government offered to forge a power-sharing arrangement which would preserve most white settler privilege. This "internal settlement" was rejected by ZANU and ZAPU, but was implemented nonetheless. A puppet black government was installed but the insurgent uprising only intensified. Finally, in 1979, all belligerent parties met at Lancaster House in London, and agreed to a peace agreement leading to majority rule and Robert Mugabe became Zimbabwe's first prime minister.

The Mugabe Regime

Mugabe inherited a wounded nation with formidable political, economic and social challenges, but he too became the archetype of the African leader who cannot surrender power. Segregation prevailed in virtually all sectors of life and the facilities provided for the Africans were vastly inferior to those provided for whites. Approximately 4,000 white farmers owned more than one-third of the land. The best land was reserved for whites and large commercial farms prospered growing corn, tobacco, and other crops for domestic consumption. In contrast, in the black areas, formally known as Tribal Trust Lands, the farmers struggled with inferior and infertile soil, poor rainfall, overcrowding and a dilapidated infrastructure. Most black adults were forced to obtain seasonal work in the white areas. Even black "unskilled" workers on white plantations, like the numerous domestic servants, were impoverished. During the apartheid era there were few opportunities for blacks with higher skills, because as in all racial dominance systems, the *dejure* color bar reserved the best jobs for whites. Mugabe's commitment to improving Zimbabwe's schools for all is widely known. As a former school teacher he took personal time as president, to give lessons to his staff at State House, teaching some whom have since become government ministers.

Despite rhetorically pursuing a revolutionary and socialist agenda, Mugabe took an evolutionary and pragmatic approach to dismantling Rhodesia's racial-dominance regime. He promoted racial reconciliation, although the reserved seats for whites were abolished in 1987. The white minority makes up less than 2 percent of the population but were well represented in business. By regional standards the economy was prosperous and the economy relatively self-sufficient. Mugabe's new government was constrained by the Lancaster House Accords, which provided that private property, including large settler estates, could not be confiscated without compensation. In the early years, the government made impressive progress in improving the livelihoods of the majority by redistributing some of the surplus land still dominated by the white private sector. In fact, some speculated that Zimbabwe had the food production capacity to feed the rest of the continent. Mugabe hoped that foreign investment and aid would finance an ambitious scheme to buy-out of many white farmers and re-settle black peasants and veterans of the anti-colonial war on their land.

Exports of minerals, corn and tobacco rose rapidly and a minimum wage, which notably covered agricultural workers, was introduced. Rising consumer purchasing power initially benefited local manufacturers. Health and sanitation facilities were expanded and an increasing number of Africans black began to move into managerial positions in the civil service and to a lesser degree, into business. In 1992, the government passed a bill that allowed for the involuntary purchase of up to fifty percent of the land at an officially set price. The policy enjoyed overwhelming domestic support, but came under a great deal of international criticism for violating the private property and judicial rights of Zimbabwe's white large-scale farmers. Others pointed out that, besides producing large surpluses of food in non-drought years, many jobs were tied to the commercial estates. Revelations in 1993-1994 that some confiscated property had been turned over to leading ZANU politicians gave rise to further controversy.[9]

In September 2001, a land re-distribution agreement was signed in Abuja, Nigeria. Zimbabwe's ties to the Commonwealth functioned well until Mugabe, under pressure from the "war veterans" who led the campaigns to occupy white-owned farmland and the council of chiefs representing the small-scale black farmers, demanded the implementation of land reforms. A low-key Commonwealth delegation of former British territories comprised of junior ministers and officials from Australia, Britain, Canada, Jamaica, Kenya and South Africa; met to discuss the implementation of a land reform agreement the following month. Delegation officials promised that government ministers would meet with opposition groups, including Morgan Tsvangirai, of the Movement for Democratic Change (MDC), and human rights organizations. After agreeing to cooperate with the electoral system, the MDC threatened to boycott parliamentary elections after the banning of the independent *Daily News,* which opposed the Mugabe regime. Morgan Tsvangirai called upon Mugabe to run the polls "in accordance with universally accepted norms."

The United States extended a thorny olive branch to Mugabe's ZANU-PF government, by condescendingly insisting the country had time to bring itself back to a "democratic course" before the 2002 elections. On the eve of a ruling by the ZANU-PF party conference, US assistant secretary for African affairs, Walter Kansteiner, announced that the requirement of a free and fair election in had become a priority. "The Zimbabwean government does not have time to put the election process on the road to be a free and fair one. There is time for Zimbabwe to start making the right moves. It could start signaling that any day. The international community would be very receptive to that;" Kansteiner stated in a veiled threatened after an extensive four-day visit to the country. Kansteiner then warned that continued intimidation of the opposition, state-sponsored violence and an arbitrary application of the rule of law, indicated that leaders Harare were paying little heed to international dialogue. "This is not going well. It's not going in the right direction;" he told *Financial Times.*[10]

Although his 2002 victory was not recognized as free and fair by the Commonwealth's electoral observer mission, the Mugabe government warned that challenges to its post-election record could sink reconciliation talks between ZANU and the MDC. ZANU-PF also said the MDC's legal challenge to Mugabe's victory undermined reconciliation. Following Mugabe's re-election, the leader of the MDC leader, Morgan Tsvangirai and Welshman Ncube, the MDC's secretary-general, were charged with treason for allegedly conspiring to assassinate Mugabe.[11] According to a statement by *Amani Trust*, which assists victims of political violence, levels of state-sponsored political violence, intimidation, forced displacement and systematic torture increased. About 30,000 people were estimated to have been displaced from their homes by political violence. The Harare-based Human Rights Forum, reported that between January and April 2002, 55 people were killed by politically motivated violence. But ZANU-PF opinions hardened against any political compromise that would reverse the unfolding economic and humanitarian crisis.

Backed by a majority of African governments ZANU-PF, ruled out new elections with a two-pronged strategy. The first prong involved the simmering inter-party talks undertaken to reassure South Africa and Nigeria, whose presidents feared a disruptive Zimbabwe delegation at the June 2002 G8 summit in Canada, where funding for NEPAD would be considered. ZANU-PF participation at G8 might help to persuade some donors to contribute food aid.[12] The second prong of the strategy was to strike a tough political pose by proceeding with the prosecution of Tsvangirai and two of his senior party colleagues on charges of treason. Several journalists were detained under new draconian press laws. Fast-track land resettlement accelerated and human rights organizations reported increased violence against opposition groups.

Both Zimbabwe's government and national media celebrated what was considered a victory over colonialism. The Commercial Farmers Union (CFU) said that in a country already facing food shortages, Mugabe's order threatened Zimbabwe's crucial winter wheat crop. Other analysts blamed the fast-track land redistribution program. "We have 22,567 hectares of wheat in the ground which will only be harvested in September/October. Who is going to after the crop if the farmers stop working?" A CFU spokeswoman asked.[13]

The August deadline passed without incident and under the controversial land redistribution policy, white farms became the property of landless Zimbabweans. After the deadline to vacate, 2,900 white farmers faced growing uncertainty as to how and when the government would actually carry out its threat to evict them. The Commercial Farmers Union said that most farmers would stay put and wait to see how the government would enforce the order. Police spokesman, Wayne Bvudzijena, insisted: "The law is very clear that eviction starts today." Under the law, white farmers faced fines and two years imprisonment for doing farm-related work. However, after an earlier ruling by the High Court; that the eviction order was 'null and void' because the government had not properly informed the financial institutions holding the title deed of a previously owned white farm as collateral, the law was not quite clear. Some farmers believed they were covered by the court's ruling that properties with loans from financial institutions could not be taken over by the state without advising the banks. They were wrong. The state-owned *Herald* newspaper described the legal judgment against the government as a technicality, adding that most of the white farmers who had left their farms "wore sullen faces as if it finally dawned upon them that the 1890 invasion of the country by white colonialists had been reversed."

Mugabe's first official eviction was of six white farmers in Matabeleland in the south-west. A spokeswoman for the Justice for Agriculture Group (JAG), a white farmer's organization, said officials visited farmers in the north-east and threatened to prosecute them if they remained on the land. Across Zimbabwe incidents of violence were reported as the new settlers and their war-veteran allies moved against farmers who refused to leave.

The CFU charged that the restrictions placed more than $350 million (22 percent), of potential tobacco exports at risk adversely affecting 90 percent of tobacco farmers. Early tobacco planting indicators suggested that unless the government changed course, the 2003 crop would drop by 66 percent, to around 55 million hectares. Some farmers, who were supposed to stop producing, received private 'advice-and pleas' from government ministers, to carry on as normal because they were strategic producers of food. "But we are getting nothing in writing and risk going to prison for two years if we continue farming;" said one white farmer. Some farmers took heart from Mugabe's Heroes' Day speech in which he said he would allow "loyal" white farmers to remain on their land. The JAG said that incidents had been reported on white-owned farms, most of which had not been served with "Section-Eight" orders requiring them to vacate. Four farms in the wheat producing area of Middle Sabiwere were visited by an armed group that included soldiers and policemen and their occupants were told to vacate the next morning, although they had not been served with "Section Eight" orders.

In May 2002, the CFU reported that 85 percent of the 6,000 white-owned farms had been listed for compulsory acquisition, meaning that 10 of 11 million hectares of commercial area farmland was being confiscated by the state. CFU president, Colin Cloete stated that 250 white farmers had already been illegally evicted from their farms and that others had left of their own accord. Cloete said that many were being forced off their lands "with little more than the clothes they were wearing." He stressed that the evictions were illegal, since the Land Acquisition Act required the issuance of a court order. Many farmers lost moveable assets such as tractors and other vehicles and farm implements which under law remained their property. "Farmers have had their trucks with equipment seized at police roadblocks;" Cloete told journalist Tony Hawkins. Mugabe's undeclared Pan-Africanist vision of an 'Africa for Africans' would bring much hunger pain.[14]

The Oppenheimer's, founders of *Anglo-American* and owners of the diamond group *DeBeers*, were one of the largest landowners in Zimbabwe. The family farms cattle on a 140,000 acre *DeBeers*-Shangani farm in Matabeleland Southern Zimbabwe. Its 21,000 head of cattle are bred for beef exports to Europe. The government called upon the Oppenheimer family to provide up 65,000 hectares of farmland for the resettlement program within two months. Part of the farm was occupied by about 1,000 settlers who moved onto the land during a country-wide wave of illegal occupations that led to the evacuations and the deaths of white farmers. The ranch is one of about 5,000 white-owned commercial farms identified for resettlement under the land reform program. Vice-president, Joseph Msika, was quoted in the country's independent *Daily News* as saying the ruling ZANU-PF government wanted the Oppenheimer land by the end of 2001 and that it was sending a team of officials to demarcate the land for expropriation.

The Oppenheimer family offered to cooperate with the government's land program and to remove some cattle, but refused to hand over any land. "Our interpretation is that we haven't handed over any land permanently. Maybe our interpretation is not that of the politicians;" reasoned Clifford Elphick, director of *DB Investments*, a shareholder for *DeBeers*. He described the land-sharing proposal as "phase-one" of a long-running discussion about Oppenheimer's contribution to land reform. There was a constant dialogue between *DeBeers* chairman, Nicky Oppenheimer who wanted to keep his farm and the Zimbabwean government. The family proposed a trust fund which would extend loans to help settle African farmers. However, the government insisted that the Oppenheimer's surrender almost half of the cattle ranch, after an agreement was reached by farmers to implement the sale of 1.3m hectares to the government. Thus, under the Zimbabwe Joint Resettlement Initiative, the first of 562 farms was sold to the government.

Lina Mohohlo, governor of the Central Bank of Botswana, invited Zimbabwe's estimated 4500 fugitive white farmers to come to Botswana, if they could use their technological expertise to contribute to the countries diamond-dependent economy. The Botswanan Ministry of Agriculture told the white Zimbabweans that the country did not have enough fertile land to accommodate them, but that: "If anyone wants to come and help turn desert into productive farmland, they are welcome. Skilled people are welcomed if we have jobs they can occupy;" said Lina Mohohlo. Botswana's economy is growing at about 5 per cent and soaking up human capital from the collapsing Zimbabwean economy, which was projected to shrink by 11 per cent.[15]

In a 51-page report entitled *Not Eligible: The Politicization of Food in Zimbabwe*, Human Rights Watch accused the Mugabe government of using food as a weapon. The report claimed that food was denied to suspected supporters of the main opposition party and to residents of former commercial farms, resettled under the land reform program. Human Rights Watch also accused the ZANU-PF of systematically manipulating the supply and the distribution of food aid. Donor agencies were accused of tacit complicity in preventing food from reaching farm areas resettled under land reform. Hundreds of millions of dollars in food assistance flowed to Zimbabwe where thousands faced hunger and malnourishment. Estimates are that 5.5 million people (45 percent of the population) would require food aid within nine months. Peter Takirambudde, of Human Rights Watch accused the Mugabe government of manipulating food relief while the international community "played along."

According to Famine Early Warning Systems Network (FEWSNET), a non-governmental organization that monitors food problems, food imports to close the cereal deficit Africa 2002 were estimated at 28 percent. FEWSNET warned that while rainfall prospects were "fair to good," there were signs that Zimbabwe would not produce two thirds of its annual maize requirements, unless steps were taken to overcome shortages of fuel, fertilizer, foreign currency and maize seed. Despite repeated warnings of a poor harvest for 2003-04, the government insisted that its land resettlement program was working, and Zimbabwe would produce double its consumption of maize (3.5 billion tons). In 2003, tobacco sales totaled about 80 million kilograms, less than half of the 166 million kilograms produced the previous year and the 2004 crop was forecast to be only 40 million kilograms.

In August 2002, the European Union agreed to step up its "smart sanctions" and further isolate Mugabe's government. That February the travel ban on government officials and the freeze on assets was extended to include 52 more people. This included all remaining cabinet members, politburo secretaries, deputy ministers and assistant secretaries of the politburo including Grace Mugabe, the president's wife. Britain and Germany warned Zimbabwe of pushing itself into a corner of ever-increasing isolation by ruthlessly crushing the opposition and destroying a rich and fertile country stating: "The measures we have taken create a sense of isolation for those responsible for the dire situation in Zimbabwe."[16] The decision was based on graphic accounts of intimidation by the ZANU-PF which began linking the distribution of food to political support for the Mugabe government. Zimbabwe's deputy foreign minister, Abednico Ncube, told the residents of Matabeleland that they would not starve, "as long as you value your government of the day....We do not want people who vote for colonialists and then come to us when they want food. You cannot vote for the Movement for Democratic Change and expect ZANU-PF to help you." "Our quarrel is not with the people of Zimbabwe but with the regime responsible for this man-made disaster;" said British foreign secretary, Jack Straw. Jürgen Chrobog of the German foreign ministry, stated that no would should accept "that people responsible for the crisis, who suppress the opposition and falsify elections should go on shopping trips." This was in reference to Mugabe and some of his colleagues who had recently gone shopping in Paris while en route to UN headquarters in New York. The European Union foreign ministers said that they had for the moment gone as far as they could with the imposition of sanctions and they did not want to alienate the SADC, the group of southern African countries whose support the EU had disappointedly sought in pressuring the Mugabe regime.

Although the West imposed "smart sanctions" on his government, the possibility of mass starvation posed a greater threat. While western governments refused to play the "food card" in order to destabilize his regime, it became increasingly clear that a serious humanitarian crisis was inevitable. Three interrelated factors precipitated the crisis: the severe drought of 2001-2002; President Mugabe's chaotic land resettlement program, which resulted in a 500,000 ton reduction in commercial maize production; and the HIV/Aids pandemic. According to the UN, there is a direct link between malnutrition and the estimated 2.3 million Zimbabweans living with HIV/Aids. Zimbabwe has the world's third-largest prevalence of HIV/Aids. Health care consumes 12 percent of recurrent spending, education accounts for another 30 percent. In August 2002, the most authoritative assessment, the UN's Consolidated Inter-Agency Appeal, estimated the country's urgent food needs at 1.8 million tons. That year the UN sought $236.5 million in direct food assistance and a further $50 million in back up support. [17]

According to the UN, "macroeconomic instability" was a fundamental cause of the Zimbabwe crisis. It called on the Mugabe government to abolish the state monopoly on grain imports, lift price controls, devalue the currency and tackle the 116 percent rate of inflation. The UN also called for government restoration of the rule of law in rural areas and the removal of illegal squatters from commercial farm lands.

Mugabe rejected offers of conditional food aid in exchange for economic and human rights reforms blaming "British machinations" and drought for

Zimbabwe's worsening economic crisis.[18] Opposition members of parliament walked out on his opening parliamentary session speech, in which he described his land resettlement program as an "unparalleled success story." Mugabe said that he rejected attempts to use the drought relief effort to "smuggle in failed and inappropriate IMF policies which we know have exacerbated our vulnerability." In a thinly veiled attack on his finance minister and the central bank governor; both advocates of devaluating Zimbabwe's dollar, Mugabe stated: "Devaluation is dead and can only be advocated by saboteurs and enemies;" He argued that UN demands for reforms as a condition for food aid were designed "to get the soul of our sovereignty" and that his government would ensure that "no one takes advantage of our stomachs to get to our souls." He promised tough measures to clamp down on the foreign parallel foreign exchange market where Zimbabwe's currency traded at Z$700 to one US dollar, nearly 14 times the official exchange rate.[19]

The WFP feeds about 2.6 million people in southern Africa annually. Emergency WFP operations regularly feed 300,000 people in Malawi and 1.3 million people in Zambia. In April 2002, the World Food Program warned that the number of Zimbabweans requiring food aid would rise dramatically by years end. Critical of the effects of Mugabe's land reform policy, the WFP report said Zimbabwe, Malawi and Zambia faced "an unprecedented food catastrophe, which will ripple throughout the region." In February 2002, the WFP launched an emergency food relief operation to feed 560,000 rural Zimbabweans. According to SADC, overall food production fell by 40 percent and crop estimates and production by the commercial farming sector fell by 25 percent.

The WFP blamed Zimbabwe's food shortages on poor rainfall and a deliberate reduction of planting by commercial farming enterprises in reaction to Mugabe's land reform program. According to WFP regional director Judith Lewis, "Land acquisitions in Zimbabwe have had a dramatic effect on the amount of food that should have been produced in the country; there are no staple foods available at all. Sugar and vegetable oil are beginning to disappear." Among the worst hit crops were maize and wheat. Maize production fell by 70 percent and the wheat crop was similarly affected. Lack of foreign currency and the implementation of government price controls to make more food available only aggravated the shortages.

Britain voiced concern over the government's diversion of scarce food supplies to political supporters at a time when 6 million faced starvation. Baroness Valerie Amos, Britain's minister for Africa, said half of Zimbabwe's population was suffering needlessly because of the policies of the Mugabe government. "There is water in the dams in Zimbabwe that could be used for irrigation. It is essential we work together to find a solution which puts the needs of the people of Zimbabwe first;" the Baroness added. She pointed out that Zimbabwe had cast a shadow over the New Partnership for African Development (NEPAD). FEWSNET warned that the emergency response had been complicated by the "politicization of food aid" and by Mugabe's refusal to accept genetically modified cereals, a market policy which US farmers would like to impose on Africans. Africans fear that genetically modified foods will compromise Zimbabwe's beef exports to the EU. The role of the private sector has been constrained by the government's insistence that cereals be imported by the state-owned Grain Marketing Board. When the state monopoly was revived in 2001, prices surged by more than 40 percent as food manufacturers were allowed to buy directly from farmers. However, even where subsidized food is available, millions are unable to afford it.

By the end of 2002, per capita income had fallen by 30 percent and 200,000 workers had lost their jobs, as a consequence of the land resettlement policy. Finance Minister, Simba Makoni stated the government was committed and striving to ensure that no citizen died of starvation. In his 2002 supplementary budget, he estimated that 7.8 million Zimbabweans would need food assistance before May of 2003. Mr. Makoni's estimate was 2.2m people greater than that of the *Famine Early Warning Systems Network*. In July 2002, Makoni devalued the nation's currency 48 hours after President Mugabe pronounced devaluation a "dead" policy. Makoni responded by devaluing the Zimbabwe dollar by more than 80 percent in respect of import tariffs on luxury goods and 37.5 percent for tobacco exporters. After describing his newly formed cabinet as a "fully-fledged war council established to fight economic problems and counter actions taken by Britain and its allies against Zimbabwe, Mugabe fired Simba Makoni. Market analysts feared that the combination of Mugabe's hard-line cabinet and Mr. Makoni's departure would have an adverse impact on the South Africa's currency.

Absent from the 54-member 2003 Commonwealth meeting in Abuja Nigeria. This was the second Commonwealth leaders meeting to be held in Nigeria. The first also concerned Zimbabwe and the minority regime of Ian Smith's unilateral declaration of independence. A commonwealth panel ordered Zimbabwe's 12 month suspension from the ministerial council after Mugabe's disputed 2002 re-election. His presence would have precluded Tony Blair's attendance and created an embarrassing problem for Queen Elizabeth II, titular head of the organization. Mugabe threatened leaving the Commonwealth and tried to rally other African states to stay away from the conference.

The Commercial Farmers Union (CFU) was the only overtly critical organization heard from by the Commonwealth, leaving ZANU-PF officials in the position of having to deny that the two-day talks had been "hijacked" to exclude government opponents. CFU officials complained of having no input into the selection of farms visited by the Commonwealth delegates. Agriculture minister, Joseph Made accused the CFU of posting misleading and "negative" information on its website and of falsely claiming that 688 farms had been occupied since the deal had been signed. The agreement was supposed to stop militants from seizing white-owned farms while Britain financed a land reform program. The CFU said that 104,000 settlers had moved on to commercial farms and over 800 hostile incidents had been reported. It warned that commercial farm output could fall as much as 35 percent and that 20 percent of the commercial cattle herds had been destroyed. Government officials dismissed these figures and insisting there would be a "massive" maize crop in 2002, but that Zimbabwe would have to import wheat and maize over the next four months.

African Commonwealth states were less critical of the elections than their European counterparts. The issue drove a wedge between Zimbabwe's African neighbors and the "old" or "white" Commonwealth (Britain, Australia, Canada and New Zealand). The rift threatens to undermine the role that the Commonwealth (a voluntary, non-treaty organization comprised of former colonies), seeks to play in managing future north-south conflict. In his state to the nation address, Mugabe railed against "the Anglo-Saxon unholy alliance." The three-member panel responsible for looking into Zimbabwe's case included Australian Prime Minister, John Howard, who was already involved in a lengthy stand-off with South African president Mbeki and Nigerian president Obasanjo. South African officials argued that the attempts to isolate Mugabe would fail and many African states spoke of Commonwealth double standards pointing to the lifting of Pakistan's Commonwealth suspension after General Pervez Musharraf's 1999 coup. In a December 2003 television interview, Tony Blair appeared to accuse southern African countries of being apologists for Mugabe's regime, which he described as "a bit like some people on the left used to apologize for the excesses of the dictatorships of Eastern Europe."

In November 2003, Mugabe pledged to restructure Zimbabwe's reserve bank, by making it "much more of a development institution that protects the national interest." The announcement followed the appointment of a "whistleblowers" task force of nine-cabinet ministers to resolve the country's foreign currency crisis and report on those who were "starving the country of foreign currency." This was seen as merely replacing seasoned professionals with party functionaries who would impose artificially low interest rates while maintaining overvalued exchange rates. Zimbabwe's balance of payments predictions for 2003 were for a $1.5 billion deficit; 25 percent of the domestic GDP.

Following land redistribution, government policy shifted to the effective use of the land. The value of farm production fell sharply following the resettlement of 400,000 small-scale farmers. In November 2004, acting finance minister Herbert Murerwa, forecasted an end to the five-year economic decline. He reported that in the first nine months of 2004, the deficit of Z$1,346 billion n (US $234 million) was only 62 percent of the budget forecast for that period. It was also little more than half of the IMF projection because government spending was 5% below target, which the IMF estimated at $2.5 billion in arrears on Zimbabwe's 2004 foreign debt.

Zimbabwe's mining sector is also failing. Around the town of Gwanda, hundreds of men women and children using picks, shovels and paraffin lamps made of broken bottles, disfigure the earth panning for gold. Though the yield is meager, these people are not driven by dreams of quick wealth but by desperation, the result of Mugabe's economic policies. There are no health or safety regulations and the environmental damage done by panning excavation is of little concern. The Chairman of Mines of Zimbabwe, Ian Saunders, noted that: "There is no concern for the chemical waste done by excavation by the first white-miners showed a century ago." *Financial Times* Journalist, David White, wrote that Mugabe's land takeover and redistribution program engendered Zimbabwe people with a new sense of ownership. "People in the last year have been illegally mining wherever they find a deposit." For many families working outside the mine is better than working it. A panner digging for ore in shallow veins of quartz can count on a gram in a day or two and sell it to a middleman for Z$40,000, enough to minimally survive for up to three weeks. In defiance of a crackdown on contraband gold exports, the government offered premium prices to small producers. Industry experts believe large quantities are continually smuggled out and there is continued speculation about gold smuggling by ZANU-PF officials.

Zimbabwe produced only 12 tons of gold in 2004, less than half the output of 1999. The country's economic recovery is largely dependent on the productivity of its mining industry. Platinum, gold and chromium are its best foreign exchange earning products. Gold mining provides the quickest, easiest cash flow for the government According to Ian Saunders, legal production has been overtaken by 18 tons of illegal gold mining worth about $230 million on the world market. In an effort to curb contraband mining, mining authorities purchase gold from small claim-holders finds at Z$60,000 a gram, more than the world market price and three times the local currency prices available to larger companies. The money is paid in temporary, high-denomination bearer checks; tender the government began issuing in 2003 when banknotes were in short supply.

Unlike other African inert resource mining countries, Zimbabwe's gold industry involves dozens of mid-sized companies which have thus far proven sufficiently cost-effective in the production of low grade ore. Now, even this sector of the industrial fabric is at risk. "We are trying to operate in a hyperinflationary environment;" explained mines manager Clive Costs. "Not only is there zero development and infrastructure investment. There hasn't been a new gold project for at least five years."

One mining company in Gwanda reports that between 15-20 percent of its workers are absent at a time either as a result of HIV/Aids or because they have gone panning. The Aids epidemic has decimated the extended family system which traditionally served as an economic cushion.

Gold companies battled Zimbabwe's soaring 600 percent inflation rate and the Mugabe government's crippling trade policies. All gold in Zimbabwe is supposed to go through the Zimbabwe's Central Bank. Its banknote-printing arm, *Fidelity Printing and Refiners*, acts as the sole buyer of gold and processes it for export. Large producers are entitled to half the value of their gold in foreign currency. This is to pay for immediate expenses such as supplies, fuel and electricity. Another 25 percent is converted into Zimbabwe dollars at the official exchange rate. Some of the larger mining companies have moved out of Zimbabwe. *Lonmin*, formerly *Lonrho*, sold its five gold mines in 2002 to Mzi Khumalo, a black South African entrepreneur at a discount price of $15.5 million. *Falcon Gold*, Zimbabwe's former top gold producer threatened to close its entire operation, warning that it would not survive the year under the current gold revenue regime. Mining companies complained that, in addition to a January 2004, 3 percent tax by using the official rate the government was taking part of their revenues. *Falcon Gold* managing director "AB" Beattie said Mugabe's policies had stopped all development at its mines and a fifth of its work force was put on compulsory leave after seeing all its cash resources eaten by inflation. *Falcon Gold's* troubles were multiplied when the company and Mr. Beattie were arraigned on charges of illegal exchange dealings.

The dilemma facing mining company stockholders is whether to continue investing in exploration and development for new ore reserves, or the easier alternative of "killing" their mines, by removing their accessible deposits and closing them. Richard Dollar, a third generation small-scale miner and geologist, describes a mining industry in the throes of revolution. While the formal mining sector breaks down, informal mining "is ripping the place apart." The damage done to Zimbabwe's mining and agricultural sectors and an economy that was once among the strongest in Africa may seem permanent. The world awaits conciliation, or a post-Mugabe government that would open the way for a large foreign aid program and a new economic strategy.

In his 2005 budget report to parliament, Murerwa projected that Zimbabwe would enjoy 3.5 percent economic growth. This was highly optimistic given the government's international political and economic problems. With a projected deficit of $532 million, an increase of $335m since 2003, the people of Zimbabwe had little to celebrate. Murerwa predicted a 28 percent growth in the agricultural sector and a 7.5 percent growth in mining. However, other economists pointed to the absence of budgetary figures indicating the huge losses incurred by parastatals (state-owned enterprises) and the discrepancy between official projections of inflation slowing from 150 percent at the end of 2004 to about 50 percent by December 2005. The security budget, military and police combined consume about 10 percent. Savings only accounted for 2 percent of the GNP.

The EU renewed sanctions against Zimbabwe in February 2005, but said the decision would be reviewed following March's parliamentary elections. The sanctions, which include a ban on arms sales, military assistance and on the supply of equipment used for internal repression, were extended until February 2006. The 2005 UN Human Development Index showed was

Zimbabwe worse off than at independence, and reported that both GDP and per capita incomes were lower than when Zanu-PF took power in 1980. Seizing upon this news for use as political capital, Morgan Tsvangirai launched a campaign promising a fresh start and a new Zimbabwe. "Our families are desperate for food and jobs, with a worthless currency, a huge budget deficit, a shocking external debt, a runaway unemployment rate and a devastating HIV pandemic... We are confident of victory. We shall win the popular vote as we did in 2000 and 2002;" he declared.

In 2007, life expectancy in Zimbabwe was about 36 years for both men and women. To stave off starvation, people were desperately eating mice. Sixty-four out of every thousand infants die at birth. The HIV/Aids infection rate among adults is 25.06 percent and there is one physician for every 6,909 people. There are about 9,000 trained nurses (72:1000) and about 1800 public and environmental health workers.

The MDC claimed it won both the 2002 presidential and the 2000 primary elections but was reluctant to participate in the March 2005 contest because the electoral field was tilted against it. The voters' roll was dated and independent election groups claimed it still listed thousands of dead voters, while Zimbabweans living abroad were banned from voting. State media was effectively closed to opposition advertising and opposition candidates were told they would only have access to radio and TV if they were prepared to pay, a perennial problem of cash poor parties like the MDC. Even if he were to win the popular vote, Morgan Tsvangirai would lose the count. Mugabe banned all observers from western nations although he did invite observers from Africa, Russia and a few Asian and Latin American countries. But only two of the six foreign groups that observed the 2002 presidential election judged it fair.

Morgan Tsvangirai

In October 2004, a judge in Harare prepared to hand down a verdict in the closely watched trail of Morgan Tsvangirai, If found guilt, he faced the death penalty. The state's case rested on three meetings Tsvangirai held in 2001 with representatives of *Dickens & Madson*, a Canadian political consulting and lobbying firm with offices in London and Montreal. Ari Ben Menashe, the firm's director and the state's key witness, testified that Tsvangirai asked for his help in the plot. Given the pressure Mugabe's government put on the judiciary, MDC leaders were prepared for a guilty verdict. "If there's an acquittal, it will vindicate our position that this has been a political trial since day one. If there's a conviction this will be a confirmation in the minds of sensible people that the justice system has been subverted;" David Coltart told the *Financial Times*. Independent-minded members of the judiciary faced intimidation and attacks by the Mugabe government.

Morgan Tsvangirai admitted having met Menashe, but insisted that Menashe had approached MDC and denied any meetings had to do with such plotting. A clandestine video recording of the third meeting showed the lobbyist, not Tsvangirai speaking about the "elimination" of Mugabe. Under cross-examination, Menashe, who earlier denied receiving any money from Zimbabwe's government, admitted he had received $615,000. The Zimbabwe Defense and Aid Fund UK, whose patrons include Noble Laureate Desmond Tutu, called the trial a "legal circus." George Bizos, the veteran South African Lawyer who defended Nelson Mandela, served as Tsvangirai's counsel. In his closing argument he claimed there was no evidence of an assassination or a coup plot and that "Menashe had lied from start to finish." Coltart said that if Morgan was convicted they would appeal to the Supreme Court. Tsvangirai was acquitted on the rape charge.

Morgan Tsvangirai and Pius Ncube, the Roman Catholic Archbishop of Bulawayo, warned of an angry public response to perceived voter fraud. MDC secretary-general Welshman Ncube only said: "What we can say is we won't go to court, that strategy proved futile and useless. These are political issues that could only be solved through mass mobilization of people." The MDC accused Thabo Mbeki of "aiding and abetting" Robert Mugabe by expressing confidence that the March 31 of 2005, parliamentary elections would be free and fair. The MDC claimed that Zanu-PF was preparing to rig the poll. Ncube said that Thabo Mbeki had made upbeat comments about the Harare government's compliance with regional election standards. He argued that Mbeki was "not only misinformed", but that he was also "dangerously premature" in expressing optimism about the vote. "To the people of Zimbabwe, the optimism expressed by the South African government is increasingly viewed as misplaced solidarity and a deliberate attempt to frustrate the new beginning they so desperately desire;" Ncube stated. Separate observer teams from the Southern African Development Community (SADC) and Mbeki's ANC, which arrived a few days later, were prevented from observing the vote. *Amnesty International* warned that the elections would not be credible because of the government's persistent, long-term and systemic violation of human rights."

By November, disagreement over whether to contest one of President Mugabe's several constitutional amendments creating a Senate, divided the MDC. The election split the MDC into two hostile camps when the party's National Council voted 33-31 to contest the election. Morgan Tsvangirai defied the result by holding a series of rallies to persuade MDC members to boycott the vote. The MDC party split revealed ominous overtones of ethnic conflict. Tsvangirai is a member of the Shona majority. Most of the rival MDC camp including Welshman Ncube, are members of the Ndebele minority; thousands of whom were massacred by Mugabe's troops in the 1980s.

At some rallies Morgan Tsvangirai stood by as youthful supporters sang songs and chanted slogans urging violence against rival faction members. In

Harare, youth drawing fingers across their own throats chanting "Welshman Ncube needs to have his throat slit." Tsvangirai angered other party members when he reinstated two aides, who allegedly coordinated violent assaults on some national and provincial party executives. "He's turning into a mini-Mugabe;" said an anonymous MDC member. It's no longer about the Senate; it's about this guy not playing by the rules of the democratic regime."[20]

But Tsvangirai's spokesman, William Bango, said; "Tsvangirai himself has never uttered a word to the effect that violence is promoted in the party. If there are individuals doing so they are doing so without his sanction." In response to the conflict, Welshman Ncube replied: It's self-evident that we have parallel parties now. The issue is, which of the two groups is the lawful and legal MDC?" A senior advisor to Tsvangirai dismissed Ncube's remarks, and pointed out that the so-called Pro-Democracy faction knew it had nowhere to go unless it joined ZANU-PF.[21]

The MDC implosion exemplifies how the pitfalls of western-style partisan politics continue to arrest the development of culturally compatible democratic systems in Africa. Minority parties or ethnic groups are forced ally themselves with major parties in order to gain access to government. However, once in office, the ruling or governing party abandons, ignores or persecutes the smaller coalition parties or ethnic groups which helped it come to power.

Innovative and marginally more subtle fraudulent tactics were used by Mugabe's Zanu-PF in the elections. Opposition activists, human rights groups and nongovernmental organizations all reported a significant decrease in the level of violence between the 2002 and 2004 elections. However, Zanu-PF continued to use the weapon of political intimidation. After threatening to boycott the elections, the MDC caught Zanu-PF off guard by waging an efficient and vigorous campaign and extending its reach deep into traditional Zanu-PF constituencies. Two rallies in Chegutu, a small town about 70 miles from Harare, reflecting how much the political landscape had changed within five-years. The MDC's rally was much better attended than Zanu-PF's. An enthusiastic crowd filled the stadium shouting *chinja* (change) and calling for the end to 25 years of Zanu-PF rule. Twenty-four hours later, schools were closed, schoolchildren were forced to attend the rally and farmers were told to bring their workers, to that same stadium, which was only half-full for the Zanu-PF rally. The MDC drew crowds in excess of 20,000 compared to the fewer than 5,000 that attended Mugabe's ZANU-PF rallies.

In previous elections, white farmers were in the forefront of the MDC campaigns. Many believed this was to the MDC's detriment. Mugabe referred to the MDC as a stooge of the British and the whites. In this election, the few remaining white farmers backed Zanu-PF hoping their support would help them to remain on their farms. Although, they were more likely to take their workers to listen to President Mugabe than to Morgan Tsvangirai. Most observers detected a substantial swing against the Mugabe government in rural constituencies across the country.

Under pressure from the MDC and neighboring countries, Mugabe implemented some of the reforms agreed to at the regional 2004 meeting of the Southern African Development Community, including translucent ballot boxes and one day voting. Political parties, including the MDC, were allowed to post agents at more than 8200 polling stations on election day. Again, history intervened in Mugabe's political favor. The death of Pope John Paul II diverted world attention from Zimbabwe's controversial elections. Accusations of electoral fraud aside, the election also exposed serious weaknesses in Morgan Tsvangirai's Movement for Democratic Change, which saw the number of its MP's fall from 50 to 41 in the 150 seat parliament. Again, only two African observer delegations endorsed the vote. Observer teams from the South African government and the Southern African Development Community concluded separately that the vote "reflected the will of the Zimbabwean people." The Zimbabwe Election Support Network, a group of 35 human-rights organizations, echoed the MDC's misgivings about alleged discrepancies in results in some constituencies. Seventeen thousand observers monitored the 2004 Ukrainian-style election, which allowed foreign diplomats to raise immediate international political fury. Zimbabwe accredited only 400 observers, primarily from other African countries.

Questions emerged after the final results were announced exposing large discrepancies with the number of votes cast earlier. For example, in the Gormonzi constituency, the number of votes announced by the electoral commission rose 62 percent between the closing of the polls and the announcement of the results. The nongovernmental Zimbabwe Election Support Network urged the Zimbabwe Election Commission (ZEC) to investigate" the matter as a matter of extreme urgency." The ZEC acknowledged that an average of 10 percent of the voters had been turned away. The twenty-five US diplomats observing the vote reported seeing uniformed police counting the ballots rather than election officials, as stipulated by law.

The Crisis in Zimbabwe Coalition, reported isolated events of voter intimidation and coercion. They also reported seeing fifteen buses heading from Gweru towards Bulawayo, which raised concerns of recriminations against MDC supporters if Zanu-PF lost the elections there. In Mashonaland province near Harare, an MDC official claimed that Zanu-PF youth militias intimidated voters. In the Zvimba province, election manager John Kituli told the *Financial Times* that; Zanu-PF youth were conducting "forced registration" outside the polling stations, asking voters to give their names and ID numbers. Two British journalists traveling with an opposition candidate, were arrested on charges of covering the election without credentials. A member of the nominally independent Zimbabwe Electoral Commission, charged with organizing the vote, sent home 800 election agents from the Mudzi East constituency east of Harare because they were supposedly MDC sympathizers or supporters.

The MDC lost by a landslide but said it was studying questionable results in 76 of Zimbabwe's 120 electoral districts. Final results gave Zanu-PF 78 seats in parliament and Mugabe the right to appoint another 30 MPs. Zanu-PF now enjoyed a majority, giving them power to amend the constitution without or with little opposition support. Mugabe confirmed that the Zanu-PF would consider various constitutional amendments, including the introduction of a Senate or House of Lords. Analysts speculated that this body might be the given power to appoint a president, smoothing the way for Mugabe's successor. Mugabe planned to retire in 2008. Upon victory, he congratulated Zimbabweans "for having voted correctly." He said his party "remained ready to interact with the MDC", but warned the opposition against keeping its vow to mobilize supporters to protest voter fraud. "We can also raise mass action against their mass action to protest alleged voter fraud;" Mugabe threatened. The Bush administration was in no position to criticize the flawed election, and therefore remained silent. The MDC provided few and conflicting details of its post-election strategy. Nevertheless, on April 4, the MDC lodged a formal complaint about irregularities and fraud in vote counting and demanded a repeat of the election. The MDC asked the Electoral Commission to respond to its claim of widespread discrepancies between votes counted at polling stations and the final results reported.

Economic Hypertension

In fiscal year February 2003-2004, Zimbabwe's real exchange rate appreciated by about 50 percent, reflecting one of the world's highest inflation rates of 127 percent. An exchange rate of between $Z6, 080 to Z$ 3,500 to one $US reflected the gap in US-Zimbabwean economic conditions. The Reserve Bank of Zimbabwe (RBZ) could meet only 8 percent of companies' bids for foreign currency. The RBZ managed the auction as part of its anti-inflationary policy. Bids for foreign currency ran from $140 million (at the twice weekly currency auction), but the RBZ could provide only $11 million per auction. Analysts expected Zimbabwe to devalue its currency between Z$8,500 and Z$10,000 to 1 US dollar by June, 2007. Economist also predicted that the country's prolonged decline in inflation, from 622 percent at the start of 2004 to 127 by March 2005, was finally ending. The devaluation of the Zimbabwean dollar meant steep rises in the price of food, fuel and electricity, all held down by the government before the election. The Zimbabwe Central Bank's interest rate and borrowing policies began unraveling and within the month domestic debt surged by 140 percent.

The government began trying to raise Z$10,000 billion to finance an ambitious restructuring program for state-controlled companies and local government. The first local bond issue to raise Z$500 billion raised only

Z$124 billion. Many market analysts said the target was out of reach. With a budget deficit target of Z$4.5,00 billion (7 percent of the GDP) and off-budget subsidies estimated at Z$3,000 billion, the states total borrowing requirements, including the reinvestment plan for state-owned companies was 30 percent of Zimbabwe's forecast GDP. The vote rigging allegations made Zimbabwe's return to the international financial community and the lifting of European Union sanctions highly unlikely.

In July 2006, Zimbabwe again devalued its currency by 39 percent against the dollar and Mugabe began an urban eviction program called "Operation Restore Order" and "Operation Clear Out the Trash" to reform the slums. The military-style urban resettlement program immediately made 700,000 poor people homeless. Most of the people evicted were squatters and many claimed to have government or city permits allowing them to build shanties. The UN called the slum clearances a "catastrophic injustice." The Zimbabwe police announced plans to "deal severely" with any illegal demonstrations against the program. A Broad Alliance, a group comprised of civic organizations, trade unions and the parliamentary opposition for the MDC called for a strike. Morgan Tsvangirai said people had reached "the upper levels of tolerance against an insensitive regime." Miloon Kothari, the UN special rapporteur on the Right Adequate Housing, accused the Mugabe government of hundreds of thousands of mass evictions which were "a clear violation of human rights".[22] The story of Christopher Ncube exemplifies the plight of the victims of "Operation Clear Out the Trash". The police set fire to his shack and he, his wife and five children were transferred to a five hectare plot outside of Bulawayo to begin life as peasant farmers. "I have never farmed before. The land was not cleared. We don't have cattle or farming implements...the government has given us nothing:" Ncube lamented. His was quite a common experience. Edward Sibanda, a former security guard, was moved to an 11 acre plot, a few chickens and a vegetable patch outside Bulawayo, on what used to be a very profitable white farm but he lacks the tools and the knowledge to feed his family.

In August 2006, Zimbabweans were again forced to queue outside the banks of Harare and exchange their banknotes before they were drawn from circulation. With just three weeks notice the government announced a currency revaluation which would wipe three zeroes off their face value. Independent journalist, Trevor Ncube stated that: "Lopping off three zeroes is semantics" not unlike "rearranging deck chairs on the Titanic." This time dubbed the "Sunrise Project," the revaluation replaced the Z$100,000 with the Z$100 note. By the fall of 2007, the largest new Z$200,000 note traded 13:1 against the US dollar. This was supposed to be a fresh drive against inflation which was running at 1000 percent with black market trading. The Central Bank was unable to report how many new notes had been issued or what volume of old notes had been exchanged. The "Sunrise Project" was criticized for over-zealous police and central bank officials confiscating so-called "excess currency," and because the authorities used the project to crack down on illegal trading in parallel markets for foreign exchange, food and fuel. Retailers and manufacturers took advantage of the changeover to engage in profiteering, although they claimed to be merely passing cost increases on to consumer. This "redenomination non-event" was dismissed by economist John Robertson because; "It doesn't address the underlying causes of the economic problems in Zimbabwe. In other parts of the world where re-denomination has worked, they have been preceded by major policy overhauls."[23]

Impervious to UN criticism, Mugabe traveled to China, where he was named an honorary professor by Beijing's College of Foreign Affairs for his "brilliant contribution" to diplomacy and international relations. While noting his early work as an educator and an anti-colonial freedom fighter, Chinese media avoided Mugabe's domestic problems. President, Hu Jintao's, embrace of African leaders who are shunned by the West, is seen as part of a strategy to build Chinese influence in Africa while ensuring access to strategic resources. China's expansion of economic ties with Sudan and the Chinese Eximbank's $2 billion line of credit for Angola in 2004 are examples of this strategy. Angola, like Zimbabwe, has a poor human rights record but is Africa's second largest petroleum producer. After the US, China is the main customer. During their talks, Hu Jintao told Mugabe that China and Zimbabwe were "sincere friends and trustworthy partners." Beijing announced plans to expand diplomatic cooperation with Mugabe's government. It is possible that China is financing Zimbabwe in exchange for concessions to mine reserves of strategic materials. In November 2005, Zimbabwe announced the discovery of uranium on its territory. The government announced that it would mine it only to generate electricity. "We have found uranium...but we would not want it to be used for bomb-making...We would use it to give us electricity;" Mugabe announced on state television.[24]

The Ministry of Mines unveiled a plan to "indigenize" the mining sector by nationalizing 51 percent of ownership, almost half of which would go straight into government coffers. The timing of this nationalization proposal was ironic given the upcoming IMF meeting. Minister of Mines, Amos Midzi, warned that potential foreign investors had been identified to take over the mines should existing owners refuse to cooperate. These foreign investors are most likely Indian and Chinese companies. The adversely affected mining companies include; *Mettalon Gold* of South Africa, *Aquarius Mining* (Platinum), *Anglo-American* and *Rio Tinto*, which already have gold, diamonds and nickel operations in the country.

In March 2006, with a 700 percent inflation rate and a worsening economic crisis, Zimbabwe approached the IMF for technical and financial assistance. The nation was already $119 million in debt to the IMF under the poverty reduction and growth facility. This debt and the government's refusal to adopt the comprehensive package of reforms repeatedly advocated by IMF missions, made further IMF assistance highly unlikely. "We know this assistance will not be automatically restored but this is something we hope to negotiate;" said finance minister Herbert Murerwa before leaving Harare for meetings in Washington. [25]

By January 2007, Zimbabwe's inflation rate reached had 1594 percent and was forecast by some private sector analysts to reach 5,000 percent by years end. Meanwhile, Mugabe, by now somewhat delusional, celebrated his 83 rd birthday by imposing a three month ban on all political rallies; suggesting that senior ZANU-PF party members might be plotting against him. The three-month ban followed clashes between the police and supporters of the MDC who were protesting the announced four month price and income freeze. The price freeze, part of a "social contract" between business, trade unions and the government, was rejected by labor unions and divided the business community. Many said their businesses would be ruined if they could not pass on the rise in costs to consumers. Some business executives feared Mugabe's retribution should they oppose the freeze.

Mugabe exemplifies Africa's modern-day dictator. However, continues to work until late in the evening and his mind is sharper than perhaps many of his opponent's. He sports a Hitleresque moustache, waves his fists at campaign rallies and runs into crowds punching the air and spitting personal abuse at his opponents. His rivals and enemies underestimate him; and in doing so, have made it harder to get him out of office. He has a gift for making people do as he wishes. His secret police, the much feared Central Intelligence Organization, spreads terror in the cities, especially in the poorer townships after dark. Young men are regularly beaten with truncheons known as knobkerries, a weapon long synonymous with repression in Africa. In the parks of Harare, groups of men armed with shotguns, rifles and riot gear, are seen lurking in the bushes. According to Chris Maroleng of the Institute for Security Studies, a South African concern Robert Mugabe "has emptied out the state and filled it with the military."[26] A report published in May, 2007, by *Human Rights Watch* entitled; *Bashing Dissent: Escalating Violence and Repression in Zimbabwe*, documents widespread and systematic abuses of both supporters of the opposition MDC and of other Zimbabweans. Some of the worst abuses occurred in the suburbs of Harare, where witnesses and victims of police security forces said the security forces randomly beat passers by in the streets, shopping malls and people in bars.[27]

In a rambling interview on state television Mugabe denied that plans to harmonize presidential and parliamentary elections in 2010 were a clandestine way of extending his term in office. He accused senior members of trying to "push President Mugabe out now". "Every individual in the upper echelons is now looking at himself, positioning themselves;" he said, adding: "Those who think they are most immediate are resorting to all kinds of nonsense;" he stated.[28]

In February 2007, Zimbabwe's central bank governor, Gideon Gono, admitted that it was "practically impossible" to satisfy the country's foreign currency demands. He blamed the country's "new farmers" for the shortage of foreign currency. He said that "some people, including senior politicians" who had been allocated land expropriated from white commercial farmers since 2000, were not fully utilizing it." Gono accused some people of being "professional land occupiers, vandalizing equipment and moving from one farm to another." He admitted that the country was also losing $40 million to $50 million monthly to those smuggling precious metals. Moreover, he described how during a typical day he was deluged with appeals from parastatals, including *Air Zimbabwe* and the railways pleading for injections of foreign exchange so that they could maintain operations.[29] Gono called on local industry to build 100,000 ploughs, harrows and ox carts stating: Its time now we stop importing maize and even wheat, wasting the little foreign currency we have. We have to produce." The equipment was to be distributed to small farmers, however even if the ploughs were produced and distributed there are not enough oxen to pull them.[30]

In 1997, the Zimbabwe dollar traded against the US dollar at a ratio of 2:1. By March 2007, the Zimbabwe dollar was trading 200,000:1[31]. Rocked by hyperinflation, many wealthy Zimbabweans turned to the stock market, generating volatile share prices and exacerbating the crisis. By December 2007, each brick of $Z500 notes was only worth about 20 US cents on Zimbabwe's parallel exchange market. The Zimbabwe Stock Exchange's industrials index rose 569,000 points in a single day. In real money, Zimbabwe's stock market is small; its entire market capitalization is approximately $3.6 billion. Small investors flocked to the exchange causing share prices in Zimbabwe to outpace inflation and the country's collapsing currency.[32] By April the inflation rate had grown to 2200 percent and the currency was devalued by 95 percent or (Z$15,000 to the US dollar).

Mugabe's decision to stand for another six-year term infuriated both his supporters and his opponents. A senior party official said the announcement shocked the party and could have the effect of uniting the deeply divided factions of the ruling ZANU-PF.[33] Opposition activists believed that they had the government on the ropes. "We are not going to stop: we do believe that we have a legitimate right to demand democratic change to end this tyranny;" said Jacob Mafume of the *Save Zimbabwe Campaign.* [34]

Mugabe's determination to cling to power was demonstrated when Morgan Tsvangirai and 14 other political activists were beaten and hospitalized by the police and security forces after being accused of organizing an illegal political protest. An MDC spokesman stated that Tsvangirai had been "brutally assaulted and his face badly swollen and in bandages." Just two days before Tsvangirai was arrested when he delivered a trenchant ultimatum to the regions leader's over their policy of "quiet diplomacy" toward the Mugabe regime. "When your house is on fire, you depend on your neighbors to put it out. We cannot afford to have a failed state;" he told reporters. The brutal attacks prompted the South African government to call on Mugabe to respect the rule of law and the rights of opposition leaders. In South Africa there was fear over the prospect of Zimbabwe's implosion. Facing its own succession battle among ANC leaders, the Mbeki government was fearful of provoking a debate on foreign policy by changing its stance toward Zimbabwe. The governments' failed "softly softly" policy came under attack by both the opposition and the media, but officials responded that condemning Mugabe would only force him to dig in and become more defiant. Morgan Tsvangirai was rearrested and released just as fourteen SADC countries were meeting in Tanzania to discuss the crisis. His arrest prompted South Africa's trade minister, Trevor Manuel to question Mugabe's good faith asking;" Why would you behave in such a silly fashion if you want to resolve the issues?" [35].

The attacks reinvigorated the MDC, providing the party an opportunity to increase pressure on Mugabe's government, which had no strategy for coping with the political and economic crisis. MDC reunification was averted when David Coltart, an influential opposition and human rights lawyer, who left the MDC following a disagreement over whether or not to contest the 2005 Senate elections, failed to reached an agreement with Tsvangirai. "The idea of a coalition is not officially a dead letter, but it's not going to happen;" said one MDC supporter. "The two groups will fight the election independently;" said Arthur Mutambara, a leader of the splinter group. The two sides agreed that Morgan Tsvangirai should be the MDC's presidential candidate, but disagreed over how many parliamentary races should be allocated to each faction.[36]

There were reports that Mugabe had convened his security advisers to consider declaring a state of emergency. However, fearing the adverse international reaction, decided against it. The US threatened unspecified sanctions and US ambassador, Christopher Dell, complained about what he called the "passivity" of Zimbabwe's neighbors.[37] The ZANU-PF central committee endorsed Mugabe as their candidate for the March 2008 elections.

Meanwhile, African heads of state, long derided in the West for their political immaturity, worked through their regional and continental institutions and used careful diplomacy, to find a durable solution to the protracted crisis. African leaders acknowledged that Mugabe had broken promises in the past and that he must be kept under pressure. Behind the scenes, South Africa supported Tanzania, Lesotho and Namibia in finding a solution, respecting the structures of the main inter-governmental bodies the Southern African Development Community (SADC) and the African Union. South Africa, long reluctant to criticize Mugabe the "old man" of anti-colonial struggle, had failed to recognize the risk of anarchy and of a failed state on its border.

The African National Congress proposed a motion in parliament urging an investigation into police brutality and demanding that the Zimbabwean government respect the rule of law. [38] SADC leaders mandated Thabo Mbeki to mediate between ZANU-PF and the MDC. But some opposition leaders saw Mugabe as: "the author of the violence". And as such: "He can't be part of any dialogue. He is part of the past. Even if you have a dialogue tomorrow how does that reduce inflation from 1730 percent to say 2 percent?" asked MDC secretary- general Tendai Biti.[39]

Zambia indicated that it would take a more direct approach to addressing the Mugabe regime when it became chair of the SADC in August, 2007. Zambian president, Levy Mwanawasa, broke ranks with other regional leaders and called for a new approach to Zimbabwe, which he compared to a "sinking Titanic." President Mwanawasa, said the region's "Quiet diplomacy" had failed to solve the political meltdown and that: "As I speak one SADC country has sunk into such economic difficulties that it may be likened to a sinking a sinking Titanic whose passengers are jumping out to save their lives." This was a reference to the several million Zimbabweans who had fled to neighboring countries in search of work. While he stopped short of repudiating quiet diplomacy, he Mwanawasa made it clear it was time to take a jab at South Africa, the regional power house. However, Thabo Mbeki ruled out regime change choosing to put his confidence in free and fair elections. Asked if he believed Mugabe would ever peacefully renounce power, Mbeki said: "I think so. Yes. President Mugabe and the leadership of ZANU-PF believe they are running a democratic country." Mbeki drew an analogy between his role and that of the British government in the Northern Ireland peace talks, although London enjoyed greater political and economic leverage due to its constitutional responsibilities in the colonial outpost. "We don't have a big stick;" he said, ruling out regime change through military intervention or drastic action such as cutting off South Africa's electricity supplies to Zimbabwe.[40]

Mbeki reminded reporters how Mugabe had been educated in the Eastern Cape at Fort Hare University, the intellectual incubator of many African liberation leaders such as Nelson Mandela. He also remembered how the ANC was inspired by Mugabe's post-independence gestures of national reconciliation including retention of white Rhodesian incumbents as heads of the army and intelligence agency. "It encourages the adoption of a similar position. So we have this history in common;" he noted. "When things go wrong in Zimbabwe, we feel that I am not talking about refugees coming in here. I am talking about marching in step."[41] More than 3 out of 15 million Zimbabwe's refugees live in South Africa and the residents of Johannesburg have become used to employing highly qualified Zimbabweans as gardeners and waiters.[42]

Angola signed a security cooperation agreement with Zimbabwe providing paramilitary forces and sending a powerful message of support for Mugabe. The Angolan government denied reports that the accord would lead to the deployment of several thousand military police to Zimbabwe. The Mugabe government said the Angolans were coming merely on a "training exchange program." Angola's minister of interior, General Roberto Leal issued a clear signal of defiance to the West over Zimbabwean state radio stating: "Angola will do everything in its power to help the Zimbabwe police force and will not allow western imperialism to take over Zimbabwe. President Mugabe and

I have agreed on a law and order maintenance agreement that will see Angolan police helping with the situation in the country."

Responding to reports that 2500 "Ninja" paramilitaries were to be sent, with the first thousand arriving on April 1, 2007, the Angolan embassy in Harare issued the following statement: "It is not the custom of the Angolan government to interfere in the internal matters of other governments."[43] The *International Crisis Group* added impetus to the regional debate, by urging South Africa as chair of the SADC, to adopt a joint strategy with the US and the EU. This was highly improbable given the strained nature of US-South African relations and the US disagreement with the EU over how to confront Mugabe.[44]

As many anticipated, SADC leaders avoided chastising President Mugabe and instead called for easing Western sanctions and for renewed dialogue with his opponents. The following day at the ZANU-PF politburo meeting, Mugabe's supporters reached an agreement on the timing of elections. Nine Zimbabwean opposition activists were charged in connection with a series of fire bombings and with weapons violations, which the MDC denied.[45] The nation's main labor organization, The Zimbabwe Congress of Trade Unions, announced a mobilized strike in protest of the government's failure to address the economic meltdown. However analysts said that the threat would probably fail because of government intimidation and workers fear of losing their jobs in a country with an 80 percent unemployment rate. The strike was broken after two days of government intimidation. "Time and time again there are random beatings and a suppression of anyone found walking the streets of Harare accused of being an opposition member;" said Human Rights Watch researcher, Tiseke Kasambala, who had just compiled a report on the country. Even regional leaders denounced their formal hero whose the regime many believed was near the end. "Zimbabwe is facing a "tipping point;" said Immanuel Hlabangana, of the Crisis in Zimbabwe Coalition. "But how long this will take is a different matter. It seems more likely that this crisis will last a couple of years."

The country's inflation rate was expected to reach 2,000 percent and the Reserve Bank of Zimbabwe published figures showing that gross domestic debt rose Z$ 1 trillion (10 percent of estimated GDP) in only four weeks. At the end of March 2007, domestic debt was $4 billion ($Z 1.2 trillion) or close to 75 percent of Zimbabwe's GDP. By May 2007, Zimbabwe's official inflation rate reached 4,000 percent. In an acknowledgment that 'quiet diplomacy' had failed, South Africa convened a meeting in Pretoria between the ZANU-PF minister of justice, Patrick Chinamasa, ZANU-PF labor minister, Nicholas Goche and members of the opposition MDC. Each faction of the MDC sent two delegates to the talks and both agreed to participate in the forthcoming parliamentary and presidential elections. Diplomats described the meeting in Pretoria as only "talks about talks,' a phrase used with respect to the initial negotiations over the end of white rule in South Africa.[46]

The World Food Program estimated that the country would need to import at least 900,000 tons of grain in 2007. Government officials admitted Zimbabwe did not have the foreign currency to pay for it.[47] In the midst of this economic catastrophe, African governments nominated Francis Nhema, Zimbabwe's environment minister, to head the UN Commission for Sustainable Development. It was Africa's turn in the rotating chairmanship the organization. The nomination was politically tainted because many African leaders, who were trying to reform Africa's image, were frustrated with the negative media attention that Mugabe attracts. Francis Nhema's nomination also sent a negative message to donor states meeting to recapitalize the African Development Bank. By December 2007, inflation had reached over 26,000 percent and there were severe shortages of food, fuel and electricity. 97 percent of the newly issued Z67,000 billion ($13.3 million) was held by speculators, hoarders and so called "cash barons".[48] The March 2008 elections resulted in yet another political crisis with both Morgan Tsvangirai and Robert Mugabe claiming victory. Tsvangirai was again detained, beaten and released. By May 2008 inflation reached 400,000 percent and the starvation rate in Zimbabwe accelerated. International aid agencies requested humanitarian relief for Zimabawe's 2 million most vulnerable, the children. US ambassador to Zimbabwe, James McGee observed that to get any food aid MDC supporters were being forced to surrender their identity or voting cards. "The only way you can access food is to give up your right to vote." [49]

---

1. Basil Davidson, *The Lost Cities of Africa*, (Boston: Little Brown, 1987) 244-245.

2. Rodney, Walter, *How Europe Underdeveloped Africa*. (Washington, D.C., 1982, Howard University Press). p. 65.

3. Wayne Edge, *Africa: Zimbabwe Country Report* Global Studies with Annual Editions, (Dubuque,: McGraw-Hill-Dushkin, 2002) p. 192.

4. Ibid.

5. Gibson, Richard (1972) *African Liberation Movements: Contemporary Struggles Against White Minority Rule* London, Oxford University Press pp. 151-152.

6. Ibid.

7. Gibson, Richard , Op. Cit. 149-150.

8. Ibid. 159.

9. Edge, Wayne (2002) Africa, Global Studies with Annual Editions *Zimbabwe: Country Report*, Dubuque, IA: McGraw-Hill-Dushkin. p. 193.

10. *The Financial Times,* 'Zimbabwe's white farms evacuated as unrest widens,' *August* 10, 2001.

11. *The Financial Times,* 'Zimbabwe's defiant farmers served court orders to evacuate property,' October 12, 2005.

12. *The Financial Times*, 'Mugabe hopes donors will help dig him out of 'disaster,' May 3, 2002.

13. *The Financial Times*, 'White farmers confused by Mugabe order,' June 25, 2002.

14. *The Financial Times*, 'Zimbabwe's farmers uncertain over eviction Police break up opposition rally,' August 10-11, 2002.

15. James Lamont, 'Botswana offers glimmer of hope to farmer,' *The Financial Times,* August 30, 2002.

16. *The Financial Times,* 'EU to step up smart sanctions on Zimbabwe,' July 23, 2002.

17. *The Financial Times*, 'UN warns Zimbabwe faces food disaster, April 26, 2002.

18. *The Financial Times*, 'Mugabe rejects aid in return for reforms,' July 24, 2002.

19. *The Financial Times*, 'Food crisis threatens Mugabe's grip on power,' August 1, 2002.

20. John Reed, 'Split opens in Zimbabwe MDC,' *The Financial Times*, November 3. 2005.

21. Tony Hawkins and John Reed, 'Zimbabwe's opposition party splits,' *The Financial Times*, January 13, 2006. p.3

22. Tony Hawkins, "Harare warns against strike as urban clean-up leaves thousands homeless,' *The Financial Times,* June, 7 2005 p.6.

23. Tony Hawkins, 'Fears of gridlock at banks as Zimbabwe revalues currency,' *The Financial Times* August 19-20, 2006 p.3.

24. 'Mugabe pledge on Zimbabwe uranium' *The Financial Times* November 21, 2005.

25. Tony Hawkins, 'Harare in IMF appeal to fend off crisis' *The Financial Times* March 8, 2006 p. 4.

26. *The Economist,* "The Man behind the fist" Briefing Robert Mugabe, March 31st-April 6th 2007. pp 27-28.

27. Alec, Russell, 'Hundreds hit in crackdown by Mugabe,' *The Financial Times,* May 7, 2007, p.4.

28. Tony Hawkins, 'Mugabe bans all political rallies,' *The Financial Times,* February 22, 2007, p. 4.

29. Tony Hawkins, 'Zimbabwe bank chief warns on foreign currency,' *The Financial Times,* March 1, 2007, p 5.

30. Alec Russell, 'Framers struggling to survive without tools or training,' *The Financial Times,* May 25, 2007, p.4.

31. BBC World Service March 30, 2007.

32. Tony Hawkins, 'Investors flock to Harare exchange,' *The Financial Times,* March 23, 2007 p. 4.

33. Tony Hawkins, "Mugabe sets sights on another six years,' *The Financial Times,* March 3, 2005 p. 3.

34. Tony Hawkins, "Mugabe sets sights on another six years,' *The Financial Times,* March 3, 2005.

35. Tony Hawkins and Lionel Barber, "Re-arrest of MDC leader sparks criticism," *The Financial Times,* March, 29, 2007.

36. Alec Russell, 'Opposition feud aids Mugabe in poll fight.' *The Financial Times,* May 23, 2007, p.4.

37. Tony Hawkins, 'Zimbabwe opposition steps up pressure on Mugabe,' *The Financial Times,* March 17, 2007 p. 8.

38. Trevor Ncube 'Africa's moment to take on the old man of Harare,' Editorial *The Financial Times,* March 23, 2007.

39. Alec Russell and Tony Hawkins, 'Mugabe endorsed by party as poll candidate,' *The Financial Times,* March 31/April 1 2007, p.5.

40. Lionel Barber and Russell, Alec, 'Mbeki rejects Harare regime change,' *The Financial Times,* April 3, 2007 p.8.

41. Lionel Barber and Alec Russell, 'Softly, softly: Mbeki seeks ways to limit chaos to the north and tension within,' Interview with Thabo Mbeki, Comment and Analysis *The Financial Times*, April 3, 2007. p. 13.

42. Alec Russell, 'At 17, a goodbye note and then over the wire from Zimbabwe's shambles,' *The Financial Times*, March 24-25, 2007 p. 4.

43. Alec Russell, 'Zimbabwe signs deal with Angola on security,' *The Financial Times*, March 23, 2007 p.5.

44. Alec Russell, "Arrest fails to rouse Harare's neighbours," *The Financial Times*, March 13, 2007 p.3.

45. Tony Hawkins and Alec Russell, 'African leaders duck showdown with Mugabe,' *The Financial Times*, March, 30, 2007, p.3.

46. Alec Russell, 'Pretoria hosts secret Zimbabwe talks,' *The Financial Times*, May 22, 2007 p.6.

47. Alec Russell and Tony Hawkins, 'Opposition licks wounds as Mugabe staves off tipping point,' *The Financial Times,* April 7-8, 2007 p. 2.

48. Tony Hawkins, 'Zimbabweans have little to celebrate this festive season," *The Financial Times*, December 26, 2007, p.3.

49 Tony Hawkins and Daniel Dombey, 'Warning of Zimbabwe's mass hunger,' *The Financial Times* June 7-8, 2008, p.3.

17: Death Merchants

Guns play a long and historic role in the enslavement, decimation, occupation, colonization, segregation and political liberation of Africans. They are also instruments of ethnic violence, crime and the tools many of the continuing conflagrations Africans suffer daily.

Arms transfers and trafficking are one of sub-Saharan Africa's most serious security problems. Since Africa has more ongoing conflicts than any other continent, they are, in effect, weapons of mass destruction. According to some estimates, there are at least 8 million small arms in West Africa. More than half are in the hands of insurgents and criminals. Criminals in Ghana reportedly possess some 40,000 small arms. In 2001, latent or open hostilities affected Angola, Burundi, Chad, Cote d'Ivoire, the Democratic Republic of Congo, Djibouti, Eritrea, Ethiopia, Guinea, Guinea-Bissau, Kenya, Liberia, Nigeria, Cameroon, Republic of Congo, Rwanda, Senegal, Sierra Leone, Somalia, Sudan, Tanzania, Zanzibar, Uganda, and Zimbabwe.

The influx of light weapons financed by cash, timber, petroleum and diamonds or other commodities, does not cause Africa's wars, but prolongs them, thereby, making them more lethal. Given the number of conflicts in sub-Saharan Africa, it is not surprising that cumulatively small arms have claimed at 7 to 8 million lives. By 2001, more than 3.5 million of the more than 14 million refugees and asylum seekers in the world were in Africa. Of the approximately 21 million internally displaced people in the world, more than 10 million are Africans.[1]

A study conducted by the *Coalition to Stop the Use of Child Soldiers* claims that 120,000 minors, out of a worldwide total of 300,000, are participating in various African wars. Angola, Burundi, the Democratic Republic of Congo, Ethiopia, Liberia, Rwanda, Sierra Leone, Sudan and Uganda are reported to have some of the largest numbers of under-aged soldiers. Nation-states and arms manufacturers eager to dispose of arsenals of arms made superfluous by post-Cold War political developments and technological innovations, continue to exploit Africa as an attractive and lucrative market. The international community's inability to control arms transfers and arms trafficking contributes to the persistence of these devastating conflicts. African leaders acknowledge that their porous borders are ineffective. National legal codes governing the profitable arms trade play a critical role in the continent's vulnerability to predatory arms merchants.

In addition to undermining the processes of democratization and development, armed conflicts facilitate state collapse, human rights abuses, create refugees flows and internally displaced persons and exacerbates famine conditions. These conflicts divert scarce resources from social services, disrupt trade, discourage tourism, and contribute to the breakdown of family structures. The pervasiveness and persistence of conflict has grave psychological consequences as children are traumatized or become accustomed to a culture of violence.

International efforts to control the exchange of natural resources such as diamonds and other precious stones, coltan, timber, and other commodities for weapons, have done little more than drive much of the illicit trade deeper into the shadows. On the positive side, insurgents in Sierra Leone, the Democratic Republic of the Congo and Angola may not be smuggling out as many diamonds as previously and the cost of the guns has risen. Lamentably, this has not been sufficient to diminish the illicit trade.[2]

Arms transfers and trafficking continue to spiral because the international community has not effectively enforced UN sanctions against criminalized embargo violations, or penalized financial institutions that act as conduits for weapons purchases. The UN has failed to promote indigenous controls over African arms production and sales to countries under UN arms embargoes. Nor has the UN taken action against countries that serve as arms trans-shipment points. Numerous international and regional programs seek to reduce the flow of weapons into sub Saharan Africa. These initiatives have succeeded only in documenting the devastating impact that arms transfers have on Africa.

International legal and relations international scholars examining international refugee issues. Their conflict models focus on the political and military implications of refugee flows. Refugees are an unintended or unfortunate consequence or collateral damage not an independent variable.[3] Realist theory in particular, has focused on traditional security threats and conflicts between nation-states (whether political or resource related), and before the "war on terror" assigned to a lesser degree the role of non-state actors such as refugee populations.[4]

The militarization of refugee camps in Africa is threat to continental peace and security. This is particularly true in Guinea, Uganda, Rwanda and Tanzania. For example, during the 1970s and the 1980s, camps for South African refugees in Mozambique and Tanzania were controlled by members of the military wing of the African National Congress, *Umkhoto We Sizwe.* During that same period, in Angola, Namibian refugee camps administered by the Southwest African People's Organization (SWAPO), were attacked by the South African air force. In Zambia and Mozambique, refugee camps, controlled by the Zimbabwe African National Union, were repeatedly attacked by Rhodesian military forces.[5]

The problems of Internationally Displaced Persons (IDP's) and refugee camp militarization intensified during the post-colonial era and continues unabated into the 21st century. This is particularly true for western, central and northeastern Africa. Throughout West Africa, refugee camps are frequently a source for recruiting experienced fighters. The movement of heavily armed militia between Sierra Leone, Liberia, Guinea, Côte d'Ivoire and other countries in the region, exacerbated political tensions between these states undermining the physical security and safety of both refugees and hosting populations.

Although many are unsubstantiated, several reports describe refugee camps as conduits for smuggling small arms. It is often assumed that refugees, particularly young unemployed males, perpetuate and maintain the lucrative arms trade in cooperation with criminal gangs, corrupt police officials and former combatants. The UN High Commission for Refugees (UNHCR), the Small Arms Survey and the Bonn International Center for Conversion (BICC) called for comparative research on the issue and for a systemic empirical investigation in Africa.[6] Their research was guided by five core questions:

- What is the nature and extent of refugee and IDP camp militarization?
- What are the pre-conditions for IDP camp militarization?
- What is the scale and distribution of arms availability in refugee camps?
- What is the impact of militarization on refugees and host community security?
- What are UNHCR, host state and regional responses?

The term 'refugee militarization' refers to the 'the involvement of individual (or groups of refugees) and of exiles (diasporas) in militaristic activities within and outside refugee camps'. These activities include political violence, military training, explicit or tacit support for combatants and armed resistance. 'Refugee camp militarization' refers to the combination of military and armed attacks on refugees within camps; the storage and diffusion of munitions, weapons, military training and recruitment; the presence of armed elements, political activism and criminal violence within camps; and the exploitative use of development relief resources by non-refugee residents and their dependents.[7]

Research reveals that refugees are the instruments of warfare. Their misery is often manipulated by warring parties to advance specific political and strategic interests. Examples of this manipulation vary from the siphoning-off of humanitarian assistance and efforts to establish international legitimacy by elites in and outside the camps; to the prevention of (voluntary) refugee repatriation.[8] Since the logistical demands of initiating small-scale armed conflicts in Africa are modest, even poor states can facilitate the emergence of an insurgent movement to harass their neighbors. African refugees are frequently manipulated by host states and 'third parties' for these reasons.

Governments in the Horn of Africa, particularly Ethiopia, Somalia and Sudan use asylum and assistance to so-called "refugee warriors" as a surrogate form of support to rebel movements in neighboring states.[9]

African Refugees are both the agents and victims of militarization. In some cases they are forced to inhabit politically established 'settlements' led by armed leaders engaged in warfare for irredentist purposes including: recapturing a homeland, destabilizing an existing regime or securing a separate and independent state.[10] Moreover, humanitarian aid is widely used both by weak and strong states to serve their strategic and military goals.[11]

The UN has imposed arms embargoes on Liberia and Somalia and against various insurgent groups, including the Revolutionary United Front (Sierra Leone), the National Union for the Total Independence of Angola (UNITA), and Hutu far right extremists in Burundi and Rwanda. The UN made its greatest effort to enforce its arms embargo against UNITA by essentially freezing its bank accounts, restricting the travel of UNITA officials, and limiting UNITA's ability to market diamonds. Despite these measures, UNITA continued to wage a fierce guerrilla war. None of the embargoes was effectively enforced; despite repeated violations acknowledged by the UN and revealed by non-governmental organizations such as *Amnesty International* and *Human Rights Watch*. Similarly, the one-year (2000-2001) arms embargo against Eritrea and Ethiopia failed to deter deliveries of heavy and light weapons to either party. Neither the UN, nor any of its member states has focused on Africa's role in arms trafficking. In particular, there has been no UN action against countries like Burkina-Faso, Kenya, Tanzania and Uganda; each is a major transshipment point for arms shipments to west, central, and eastern Africa. The UN Register of Conventional Arms, which has been in operation since 1993, received data about weapons sales from 153 nations and the response by African states was the lowest.

Beyond arms embargoes, the UN and some member states, notably Canada and Great Britain, advocated a "name and shame" policy. According to former UN Secretary General Kofi Annan, the "public identification of international arms merchants" is the single most important tool in combating the arms trafficking problem. On September 24, 1999, the UN Security Council held its first ministerial meeting on small arms. This led to a Security Council presidential statement urging member states to curb arms trafficking. Lamentably, the UN's "name and shame" strategy had no impact on weapons flows.

In July 1999, the Organization of African Unity (OAU) issued a Declaration on the *Illicit Proliferation, Circulation and Trafficking of Small Arms and Light Weapons*. The Declaration called for a coordinated African solution to the problem of arms trafficking. In collaboration with the Pretoria-based Institute for Security Studies, the OAU devised the *Initiative on Small Arms Proliferation and Africa*, to raise awareness of the small arms proliferation problem and to facilitate an in-depth discussion of the menace that the arms merchants pose in Africa.[12]

There are several sub-regional initiatives designed to control arms trafficking, but they lack the investigative capabilities and the legal authority to enforce strictures against the traffic. Working through the Economic Community of West African States (ECOWAS), Mali, Benin, Burkina-Faso, Cape Verde, Cote d'Ivoire, Gambia, Ghana, Guinea, Guinea-Bissau, Liberia, Mali, Mauritania, Niger, Nigeria, Senegal, Sierra Leone, and Togo devised the West African Small Arms Moratorium that imposed a renewable three-year (1998-2001) voluntary ban on the manufacture, import, and export of weapons throughout member states. However, lacking an enforcement mechanism, the moratorium failed to significantly impact arms trafficking activities in Liberia and Sierra Leone. Weapons sales to other West African countries also continued unimpeded. With the exception of the more conventional warfare of the Eritrean-Ethiopian conflict (1998-2000), efforts to end Africa's conflicts have yielded no lasting gains. A major obstacle is war-profiteering by both soldiers and guerrillas. The arms market continues to offer many opportunities to those who possess assets other than hard currency to finance weapons purchases. Diamonds, other gemstones and minerals enable cash poor governments and insurgents the means to purchase arms. In the DRC, for example, soldiers from Rwanda, Uganda, and Zimbabwe enriched themselves by plundering natural resources such as diamonds, columbite-tantalite (coltan) and ivory. Insurgent groups, such as the Congolese Liberation Front (FLC) and the Mai Mai, engage in similar practices. In West Africa, the sale of conflict diamonds smuggled out of Sierra Leone fueled the Revolutionary United Front (RUF) insurgency and enriched the guerrillas' regional patrons. Diamond smuggling and arms trafficking funded by oil revenues, yielded substantial profits to arms merchants willing to sell to one or both parties during Angola's sixteen- year civil war.

The Southern African Development Community (SADC) Committee on Small Arms seeks to control weapons flows to Africa by encouraging all states to observe and enforce UN arms embargoes and to criminalize their violations. SADC has yet to persuade its members (Angola, Botswana, Lesotho, Malawi, Mauritius, Mozambique, Namibia, South Africa Swaziland, Tanzania, Zambia, and Zimbabwe) to undertake such actions.

Arms' trafficking is a complex, convoluted and mercenary business. A single weapons sale involves an array of brokers, banks, transportation companies, and transshipment points. The availability of false end-user certificates enables traffickers and their clients to circumvent UN arms embargoes. Victor Butt, a Russian national based in United Arab Emirates, came to symbolize the arms trafficking problem in sub Saharan Africa. His story illustrates the multi-faceted nature of the arms trafficking problem and its deleterious impact on African society. Butt owned at least five airlines that fly 60-aircraft and employ some 300 people. Over the past several years, Butt has repeatedly demonstrated his ability to deliver weapons and other military supplies to clients throughout Africa. Currently, he operates in Angola,

Cameroon DRC, Kenya, Libya, Republic of Congo, Rwanda, Sierra Leone, Sudan, and Uganda. International efforts to arrest Butt or curtail his operations have thus far proven unsuccessful. He and other arms traffickers transport weapons and other military supplies through Africa using a variety of routes, sometimes directly, often through one or more trans-shipment points. These nodes comprise an elaborate network of options for arms dealers who wish to keep their activities undetected. [13]

Some of the more frequently used African airfields transited by Butt and his cohorts include; Entebbe, Goma, Kigali, and Luanda. African seaports used by arms traffickers include; Aseb, Beira, Conakry, Dar-es-Salaam, Djibouti, Durban, Luanda, Merca, Mombasa, Monrovia, and Nacala. Upon arrival, the arms are forwarded to their destinations by road, rail, air, or ferry. For example, shipments through Dar-es-Salaam are normally sent by rail to Mwanza, a port on Lake Victoria, and then loaded onto a ferry for Port Bell in southern Uganda or other regional destinations. In March 2008, Victor Butt was eventually arrested in Thailand.

Many of Africa's pastoral groups are threatened by the proliferation of small arms, making conflicts with their neighbors more lethal. A typical example concerns the Karimajong of northeast Uganda, who for centuries relied on traditional weapons when engaged in cattle-rustling and clan warfare. Such fighting claimed relatively few lives and was traditionally settled by elders. By the late 1990s, there were an estimated 30,000-40,000 AK-47s in the hands of Karimojong and neighboring pastoral communities. Ownership of such a weapon conferred political, social, and economic status. Often, an AK-47 is part of a bride price. Not surprisingly, cattle rustling and clan warfare became more lethal. Efforts by the Uganda People's Defense Force (UPDF) to disarm the Karimojong led to occasional clashes. The proliferation of AK-47s not only intensified conflict, but undermined the authority of the elders. As a result, Karimojong society is not only less cohesive, their conflict has become part of the contagion of conflict that stretches from the Horn of Africa to east, central, and southern Africa.

Years of work by two non-governmental organizations, *Humanitarian Aid* in Guinea-Bissau and *Let's Fight Against Mines* have cleared the capital of more than 73,000 land mines and other explosive devices. The mines, laid during the anti-colonial war that ended in 1974 and the civil war of 1998 and 1999, are still maiming and killing people.[14]

In Kenya, the proliferation of illegal firearms reached crisis proportions. A study by South Africa's Institute for Security Studies indicates that black marketers sell some 11,000 guns annually, most of which enter Kenya from Ethiopia, Somalia, Sudan and Uganda. According to Kenya's chief licensing firearms officer, seventy-five percent of the country is awash with illicit arms. As a result, in 1995, gun-related incidents rose 200% over the previous year. The situation in Nairobi, a city of some 2.8 million people, is particularly morbid. Guns are increasingly used in car-jackings, kidnappings, rapes, muggings, and robberies. Police suspect that organized crime syndicates, retired or serving military personnel, even some of the police are responsible for these incidents. Reportedly, Somali gun dealers in the Eastleigh section of Nairobi regularly rent weapons for an afternoon to anyone who can pay their fee. When these weapons are rented the client must pay for the ammunition. In mid-2000, the Kenya Police reported recovering between 1,800 and 2,000 unlicensed guns per month in Nairobi. One year later, there still were an estimated 5,000 illegal firearms circulating in the city, or one illegal weapon for every 560 Nairobi residents. This figure does not include unrecorded sales that are undoubtedly much higher. Gun-related crimes will probably continue to escalate as long as the police and other security forces lack the resources to stem the flow of weapons into Nairobi.[15]

The Small Arms Survey, an independent Geneva-based research group; estimates that about 25 percent of the $4 billion in small arms sales are not recorded. Kenya was scheduled to present draft guidelines; including an innocuous commitment by states not to authorize the transfer of small arms "which are likely to be used to commit grave or persistent violations of human rights."[16]

Nigeria is both a significant producer and consumer of weapons. Press reports indicate South African and Russian arms manufacturers visited Nigeria in early 2001 with proposals to rehabilitate and expand Nigeria's Defense Industries Corporation (DICON). Press reports suggested an eagerness to acquire weapons that may have been involved in at least one unorthodox and politically suspect transaction. In late May 2001, Nigerian police seized a shipment of weapons at the port of Apapa that allegedly originated in Pakistan and were purchased, with the assistance of unnamed Indian agents, by several retired Nigerian generals with links to the late Sani Abacha.

The intensification of hostilities along the Guinean-Liberian-Sierra Leone border heightened the demand for arms in that weapons saturated area. In 2001, Liberian dissidents operating across the Guinean border, allegedly received arms and ammunition delivered to the port of Conakry. Several reports suggested that Liberian timber exports were increasingly used to finance and smuggle weapons, further facilitating Charles Taylor's ability to evade UN sanctions and exchange conflict diamonds for arms.

The United Nations High Commissioner for Refugees (UNHCR) was slow to recognize the relationship between enhancing security and controlling the spread of small arms. Partly in response to failures to appropriately manage the aftermath of the 1994 Rwandan genocide, the UNHCR introduced a 'ladder' of options in 1999 to identify, prepare for and respond to militarized situations as they occur. The UNHCR advanced a three pronged approach to improving the physical security of refugee camps which included locating camps a suitable distance from international borders and ensuring they did not exceed a certain population size.[17]

Europe, Latin America, Africa and a coalition of NGO's, recently moved to draft a UN commitment to keep light weapons from any group that might use them in human rights atrocities. African diplomats have been quite active on the issue of small arms control. In West Africa, members of ECOWAS signed the *Bamako Memorandum on the Importation, Exportation and Manufacture of Light Weapons in West Africa*, which covers both legal and illicit transfers. In southern Africa, members of the Southern Africa Development Community (SADC), endorsed the Southern African Regional Action Program, which has taken several initiatives against small arms dealers. The East African Community (EAC) launched the Nairobi Declaration in 2000, which seeks to increase cooperation and control arms trafficking and transfers between virtually all the countries of the Great Lakes, Horn and EAC regions. In the final analysis, neither Africa nor the international community has been willing to implement any political, economic or legal penalties against individuals or countries sufficient to dissuade them from selling arms to or within Africa, making it unlikely that the marketing of death in Africa will end anytime soon.[18]

---

1. Bureau of Intelligence and Research, *Fact Sheet* US Department of State Washington, DC July 1, 2001

2. Ibid.

3. M. Weiner, "Security, Stability and international migration", in M. Weiner (ed.), *International Migration and Security*, 17(3) (1991) pp. 91-126.

4. E. Ferris, *Beyond Borders: Refugees, Migrants and Human Rights in the Post Cold-War Era,* (Geneva: WCC Publications, 1993).

5. Muggah, Robert and Edward Mogire "Arms availability and refugee militarization in Africa: conceptualizing the issues" in Robert Muggah (ed.), No Refuge: *The Crisis of Refugee Militarization in Africa.* (London: Zed Books, 2006) 4.

6. Ibid. 6.

7. Ibid 7.

8. S. J. Stedman, and F. Tanner, 'Refugees as resources in war,' *Refugee Manipulation: War, Politics and the Abuse of Human Suffering*, Washington, DC: Brookings Institution Press, 2003).

9. Y. Sayigh, *Confronting the 1990s: Security in the Developing Countries*, Adelphi Paper no. 251, (London: Brassey's for the International Institute for Strategic Studies, 1990).

10. G. Loescher, *Beyond Charity: International Cooperation and the Global Crisis*, New York and (Oxford: Oxford University Press, 1993).

11. G. Loescher, *Refugee Movements and International Security*, (London: Brassey's for the International Institute for Strategic Studies, 1992).

12. Ibid.

13. Ibid.

14. Peter Wise, 'Faltering steps on path to democracy,' *The Financial Times*, Special Report: Guinea-Bissau, October 31, 2006, p. 3.

15. Ibid.

16. Mark Turner, 'UK leads move to curb spread of small arms,' *The Financial Times,* June 26, 2006 p.2.

17. Muggah and Mogire, Op. Cit.

18. Ibid.

18: The HEENT Examination

Anyone fortunate enough to have visited a physician knows that in addition to taking ones blood pressure, blood and urine samples, the physical examination includes a quick diagnosis of the Head including the Eyes, Ears, Nose and Throat (HEENT). Traditional and modern medicine both utilize the same basic approaches to determine the origins of malady. What has been consumed by the patient through the sight and hearing senses? Mass media increasingly determines much of what human eyes and ears consume. Thus, for many the media determines what is important, and marketing firms determine what is of value. In Africa, as elsewhere, the media often distorts social, economic and political reality. Assessing the role of the press on the image of Africa and Africans, Stephen Ellis poses two central sets of questions. How and by whom is certain information identified as news, especially with regard to Africa? And what roles do the African media play in determining what foreign journalist regard as news and in providing information for the African Public?

Much of what Africans and westerners read of Africa emanates from western media. The relevant British and American newspapers extensively covering African affairs include; *The Daily Telegraph, The Times, The Guardian, The Financial Times, The Independent, Le Monde, Le Figaro, The New York Times, The Washington Post* and *The Los Angeles Times*. All these newspapers carry regular dispatches on Africa and have a relative tradition of appointing their own correspondents to report on African affairs. These correspondents play a critical role in informing European and American readers of events in Africa.[1] In some respects, they enjoyed a great degree of freedom to determine what made a "good story" until many of the continent's one-party states were dismantled and replaced by multi-party states in the early 1990s.

Stephen Ellis notes that the relationship between foreign correspondents and African journalists is changing with the greater freedom of the African press. During the era of one-party states, with the exception of the South African press, European and American correspondents association with the local press was strained or nonexistent. Many considered local reporters poor sources of reliable information. Under one-party rule, the balance of power between the African press and politicians rested with the latter, who could expect substantial or total loyalty from a national press and full of front-page headline such as the following: "Minister Meets Taiwanese Trade Delegation" or "Minister Urges Framers to Work Harder." Foreign correspondents considered such as "non-news", which is one reason they did not regard most of the local African press as sources of "hard" stories.

Fundamentally, news is an attempt to represent a reality perceived by those employed by interests and organizations of mass communication. The editors and journalist are themselves influenced by a wider circle of people with a professional interest in the subject matter. The latter include politicians and their aides, who are often both the subjects and sources of news and who attempt to influence reality created by journalists according to their interests or points of view (spinning of spin-doctoring). The epitome of this is the presidential press conference, a ministerial briefing or a governmental press release or terror update.

Eyes and Ears: The Media

For decades, independent Africa was notorious for the paucity and thinness of its newspapers. According to a United Nations survey, Africa and its offshore islands had 220 daily newspapers in 1964, of which 169 were sub-Saharan. By 1997 the number of dailies was estimated to have fallen to 156 of which north African accounted for 35, Rhodesia (Zimbabwe and South Africa 24 and Madagascar and Mauritius 30. The remaining 36 states with had only 67 daily newspapers between them. The majority of these were owned by governments or ruling political parties and virtually all were subject to censorship. However, most Africans do not read newspapers and like Americans are far more likely to derive their information about current events from radio (domestic or international), by television or by word of mouth. The latter, also known in French as *radio trottoir* (literally translated, "pavement radio") remains an important source of news.[2] By 1997, there were 157 daily newspapers in sub-Saharan Africa and by 2000, most African states had dozens of newspapers including the old government and party owned papers. In addition, several small newspapers such as *The East African* are published irregularly appearing and disappearing with such speed that it is often difficult for foreigners to follow their progress.

The emerging press freedoms in Africa should not be exaggerated. Government officials continue to use various legal processes to intimidate the press. Journalists who anger or embarrass a government are subject to unlawful physical intimidation or worse. The number of reporters murdered or physically intimidated in Sub-Saharan Africa grows with increased press freedoms. According to the US-based Committee to Protect Journalists, 13 journalists were murdered in 1999. After the Movement for Multiparty Democracy was elected to in 1991 in what was interpreted as an exemplary transition to democracy, the Zambian government tried to intimidate *The Post* the country's leading independent newspaper. Between 1991 and 1996, *The Post* faced more than 100 actions for civil libel, many initiated by government officials. The paper was subjected to the most legal action since the colonial era. In the case, *The People v. Bright Mapwe and Fred M'membe*, senior editors of *The Post* were charged with insulting President Frederick Chiluba by reporting that a deputy minister had referred to him as a "twit." In 1996, the same two defendants and columnist Lucy Banda Sichone were found guilty of contempt of parliament by the Standing Orders Committee of the Zambian National Assembly, which is not a court of law, for publishing articles critical of a parliamentary speech made by the vice president. The Speaker of the National Assembly then directed the inspector-general of police to arrest the three journalists.[3]

A Sierra Leonean journalist, Amadu Wurie Khan, described a phenomenon known as "blackmail journalism," whereby journalists threaten to write derogatory and false accounts of people unless they are paid off. Other evidence suggests that this and comparable forms of media corruption are widespread in African. Freedom of expression reforms introduced between 1989 and 1992 do not guarantee democracy, quality of information or a reasoned discussion of public policy.

As with the European and American press, analysts can easily distinguish which newspapers in Africa are the most authoritative, even if those newspapers occasionally make factual errors.[4] Nevertheless, even the best African newspapers often contain stories that to the western reader appear shockingly grotesque, bizarre or inexplicable. For Example, in 1998, the Nairobi-based *Kenya Times*, reported and described the appearance of Jesus Christ in Kawangware, a poor section of Nairobi. Jesus was said to be dressed in white robes and wearing a turban, and was immediately recognized by onlookers. "I am convinced this was a miracle," said Job Mutungi, editor of the Swahili edition of the *Kenya Times*. "I saw a bright star in daytime thrice. This person appeared mysteriously in the crowd, had a light around his head and sparks flying from his bare feet." According to witnesses, Jesus pronounced a blessing in Swahili before leaving in a car driven by a man named Gurnam Singh. Jesus then descended at a bus terminal and vanished into thin air.[5]

It is usual for Kenya's *Daily Nation* to publish the photos of the deceased with the obituary. On any given day there may be as many as 100 photos of the deceased. Stories about the lives of celebrities are seemingly ubiquitous A story on down in the dumps" pop stars describes the drug abuse problems of Whitney Houston, the child molestation trial of Michael Jackson and the problems of Hugh Masakela and Brenda Fassie the South African vocalist.

Another story, laments the tribulations of pop star Shakira's latest US tour. Almost all other stories cover politics and crime.

One series of sensationalist stories concerned an illegal alcoholic brew which killed its consumers: The following stories covered the front pages for weeks: "Man dies after taking brew;" "Killer brew: Kibaki orders probe as toll now hits 50;" "Kibaki orders investigations as killer brew claims more victims;" "Deadly moonshine attacks central nervous system;" "Angry residents raid outlets of brew;" "Anger over denial of drinks source;" "Blind man vows to quit drinking;" "Nine deny causing 50 deaths through sale of brew;" "Michuki shuts down bars close to homes;" "Police step up hunt for suspect in killer brew;" "Police link to woman in deadly drink saga;" "Government launches crackdown on illicit brew dens countrywide;" "Family loses three people to illicit brew;" "Young man's death shakes quiet town;" "Police linked to liquor saga;" "200 arrested in crackdown on drink dens." In this respect African newspapers are not unlike the tabloid counterparts in America; feeding their readers with fear and anxiety.

The *Daily Nation* exemplifies some of Africa's editorial page press freedoms. The following editorial topics are representative of Africa's emerging fourth estate: "Keep Politicians out of Development funds;" "Parliament in dire need of urgent reforms;" "Global Court: US critics evade issues;" "Debt relief no solution to Africa's woes;" "Draft laws on environment faulty;" " "Managing risk to save the poor;" Why Bush is wrong on Debt relief;" "Kenyans must step up fight against graft;" "Is our health sector in terminal decline;" "Keep MP's out of local authorities funds."

African newspapers are well represented on the World Wide Web. The African studies department of Columbia University in New York identified over 120 African newspapers and news magazines on the internet. The best represented countries are those with more advanced telecommunications sectors: Egypt, Ghana, Cote d'Ivoire, Kenya, Senegal, South Africa, Tanzania, Zambia, and Zimbabwe. *AllAfrica.com* and the *Africa Online* host daily newspapers and the latter has offices in six countries. Two major continent wide African news agencies extensively use electronic media: *Inter Press Service* and the *Pan-African News Agency.*[6]

Turning on the television in any major sub-Saharan African city exposes the viewer to western lifestyles, images and values. *BBC Africa* is a major source of international news. In addition to the *BBC*, *CNN* and the *Cartoon Network* there is a great deal of local programming in local languages. There is also ubiquitous televangelist exploitation of faith and fear by numerous faith merchants such as Robert Tilton, John Hagee, Benny Hinn and Robert Tilton, Creflo Dollar, Eddie Long and T.D. Jakes. African television channels are replete with British and American programming such as *The Cosby Show, The Bold and The Beautiful, Joan of Arcadia, Bernie Mac, Boston Public, Little House on the Prairie, Malcolm in the Middle, Walker Texas Ranger, Days of Our Lives, The Pretender, Sex and the City, The Apprentice, Who wants to be a Millionaire* and of course, *Oprah*. The African airwaves are full of the sounds of vibrant local music, hip hop reggae, and American pop artists. Religious programming and call in talk shows offering all sorts of practical and impractical advice are common.

As one story goes, Michael Jackson stepped from the plane in Nairobi, took one whiff of the air and got right back on the plane. The distinct smell poverty is discernable anywhere. It is the pungent aroma of disease, death and hopelessness that lingers in the nasal passages and sticks to the mind. In most poor countries, the smell of poverty usually emanates from the mountains of garbage and the open sewers that are common throughout the cities. Families often live in these mountains of refuse and it is not uncommon to see a person sleeping on a pile of rotting waste. The morgues filled are with unclaimed rotting corpses, which adds to the smell of death and decay that permeates the central city. As if attracted to and waiting to feast on human carrion, rows of vultures patiently perch in the treetops. Like their human counterparts, they can smell and are quite prepared to take advantage of the death all around them and they often do. The smell of poverty is ubiquitous it is in the orphanages, the hospitals and the schools. Impoverished Africans are often chased away from the upscale churches, for their smell often reminds the middle-class parishioners of their own tenable economic status.

---

1. Stephen Ellis, "Reporting Africa," *Current History*, (May 2000) 223

2. Ibid. 224

3. Ibid.

4. Ibid. 225

5. Ibid.

6. Mike Jensen, "Making the Connection: Africa and the Internet," *Current History*, (May, 2000). 217.

19: Education: The Cardiovascular System

The Lungs are the essential organs of respiration. They are separated from each other by the heart. The weight of both lungs together is about forty-two ounces, the right lung being two ounces heavier than the left; but much variation is found according to the amount of blood or serous fluid they may contain.[1] On its passage through the capillaries of the body the blood gives the tissues materials necessary for growth and nourishment while receiving their waste products from the tissues, a product of their metabolism.

Similarly, educational systems, from primary to university levels, provide the respiration necessary for the development and growth of national economies. Working people, particularly the educated class of physicians, artists, teachers, professors, engineers, and business leaders, are the equivalent of national blood supply. Thus, the retention and circulation of educated people is critical to national survival, well-being and growth. They supply the skills and services requisite for innovation, the diffusion of information and knowledge, economic growth and political stability. The circulation among and access to the "blood cells" by people in both the urban and rural areas is critical to peace, economic growth and political stability. Too many of thee people leave Africa. Thus, there are more Ethiopian physicians practicing in Washington D.C., than there are in all of Ethiopia, a country of 70 million people. The loss of these highly-skilled educated people to the West represents more than a brain drain. For a surgeon, the proportional loss of blood in a patient would constitute a hemorrhage.

Colonial Education

In sharp contrast to the systems of education introduced by the colonizers, pre-colonial African education was relevant to Africans. Indigenous education was closely linked to social, material and spiritual life. It was collective in nature with progressive development in conformity with the successive stages of physical, emotional and mental development of the child. The teaching programs were restricted to certain periods in the life of every individual, notably the period of initiation or "coming of age." Many African societies had circumcision ceremonies for males or for both sexes, and for some time before the ceremonies a teaching program was arranged.[2] Colonization destroyed these educational systems.

The role of the Christian church deserves special attention. Christian missionaries were critical to the colonization process. They served a explorers, traders and soldiers. There is room for the chicken vs. egg argument over whether in a given colony the missionaries brought the colonialist forces or vice-versa, but there is no doubt that missionaries were agents of colonialism. The imperialist adventurer, Sir Henry Johnston is said to have disliked missionaries but conceded in praise of them that "each mission station is an exercise in colonization." The church taught docility, humility, acceptance and to turn the other cheek in the face of brutality and exploitation in exchange for paradise in the next world. However, in its hostility toward African cultural and religious manifestations, the church did perform certain progressive functions. Practices such as killing twins and trial by ordeal were held in disdain by the missionaries, and those were reflections of suppositious ideas rooted in an early stage of African development. The birth of twins could not be scientifically explained, and therefore gave rise to religious fear.[3]

In his work, *How Europe Underdeveloped Africa*, Walter Rodney, mission schools in Africa had three goal.: First; to provide the basic literacy that would enable Africans to absorb religious indoctrination and training and help spread the Christian gospel. Second; to impart the values of Western society and Third; to raise the level of productivity of African clerical and staff workers without empowering them sufficiently to challenge colonial rule. The adage was that, if you teach a man how to go, you must not teach him to decide where to go. Hence, Africans learned the mechanics of administration and planning without the decision making powers to implement those plans. This socialization involved the church, whose role was to tame the African societies by teaching that colonialism was ordained by God and that it was a sin to question colonial authority. The church also served to preserve disintegrating African communities, without challenging the reasons for their disintegration. Mission schools had similar goals. First; to provide the basic literacy that would enable Africans to absorb religious indoctrination and training and help spread the Gospel. Second; to impart the values of Western society. Third; to raise the level of productivity of African clerical and staff workers without empowering them sufficiently to challenge colonial rule.[4] Missionary education was sorely inadequate, especially with its emphasis on a religious education that Western societies were already challenging. The intense desire and demand for education among both African children and adults was of little or no interest to the colonizers. Thus, one of the most damning legacies of colonialism is the absence of a trained body of African technicians and administrators.

In *Africa Must Unite*, Kwame Nkrumah provided a glimpse of colonial educational initiatives.[5] In 1960 Northern Rhodesia, he found that only 43 percent of African children of school age attended school. The 1954 report for Southern Rhodesia revealed that only 16.5 percent of school age children were attendance. In Kenya the government provided minimal education until 1930.[6] In central Kenya, the Kikuyu people though motivated by the possibilities offered by a western education, were so dissatisfied with the missionary education provided by Anglican and Scottish missions that they established their own school. These African wanted an education for their children that would take them beyond reading the Bible and writing in their indigenous languages. They wanted their children to acquire the sufficient intellectual and linguistic formidability to fight for the land that had been taken from their fathers by the European settlers. Missionary education thus had dual consequences for the Africans: it provided them skills with which to articulate their demands and question the legitimacy of colonial authorities; and it turned out to be a powerful medium of African acculturation of Western Christian and political values.

Ali Mazrui notes that missionary education was perhaps far more successful at producing a culturally hybrid African than a consistent Christian. The impact of the Christian church is evident all over the continent. The majority of the first generation of African leaders were products of missionary education.[7] However, while Africans were exploring the use of colonial educational systems, they were learning the vocabulary of the modern political economy world via national planning plans, foreign investors and IMF rules and regulations. This information and knowledge fueled the desire for self-rule and independence.

Colonial education involved selecting some Africans over others and compelling them by their own survival needs to participate in the domination and exploitation of their continent and fellow Africans. This education was not intended to make Africans proud of their cultures and societies. It was designed to re-shape the minds, volition and personalities of the recipients and to make them acquiesce to subordination and exploitation. The curriculum and syllabi focused on European history, culture and geography at the expense of African history, language and geography. For example, students in a British colony were taught of Sir John Hawkins that "we defeated the Spanish Armada in 1588". They were not taught that in 1588, Hawkins was stealing Africans. Hawkins made three trips to West Africa in the 1560s and made such huge profits Queen Elizabeth invested in his next venture. She provided with a ship named *The Jesus*. *The Jesus* returned with such a profit in human cargo that John Hawkins was knighted. As his coat of arms, he chose the representation of an African in chains. Students in a French Colony were learning that "the Gaul's our ancestors had blue eyes," and that "Napoleon was our greatest general." Napoleon, who had reinstituted slavery in the Caribbean island of Guadaloupe, was prevented from doing the same in Haiti because his army had been defeated by an even greater African strategist and tactician, Toussaint L'Overture. This fact, they would not be taught. As late as 1949 in Tanzania, the colonial education officer carefully outlined that the Africans should be bombarded in primary school with propaganda about the British royal family. "The theme of the British king as father should be stressed throughout the syllabus and mentioned in every lesson," he wrote. He demanded that African children be shown numerous pictures of English princesses and their ponies at Sandringham and Windsor Castle.[8]

Those few schools and medical institutions of the colonial infrastructure were located in the large towns. Most rural Africans relied on traditional methods of healing with limited access if any to colonial education or medical treatment. This resulted in structural spatial inequalities between schools in urban and rural areas and among regions.

Colonial education policy was to assimilate African students into the value systems of the colonialists. The consequence was to make the recipients aliens in their own societies.[9] In order to be accepted into the position of training, one had to adopt a Western name, style of dress and even consume certain kinds of food. However, the African was always a shadow of the 'white man' and a ghost of his own past. Neither of these phantoms could operate the functions of a state or its enterprises. The recipients of this education were trained to disdain African values, denounce African culture and to emulate the lifestyle, dress and speech of the Europeans. Some, like Blaise Diagne of Senegal became so estranged from African conditions and culture that they boasted that they were and would always be "European." Frantz Fanon describes this process:

> The settler makes history; his life is an epoch, an Odyssey. He is the absolute beginning: This land was created by us; he is the unceasing cause: If we leave, all is lost, and the country will go back to the "Middle Ages." The history that the settler writes is not the history of the country which he plunders but the history of his own nation in regard to all that she skims off, all that she violates and starves.[10]

The pursuit by Africans of a European education began even before the colonial period. The mulatto sons of white traders and sons of African rulers made the greatest effort to "Europeanize" themselves. Africans conducting trade on behalf of Europeans were not merely commercial agents, but also cultural agents since invariably they were heavily influenced by European thoughts and values. A European education would help them to learn to conduct business more efficiently. One" 18th century Sierra Leone ruler explained that he wished to learn book to be rogue as good as white man"; and there were many others who realized the practical advantages of literacy.

As Walter Rodney observed, European type school systems were rare during the first forty years of colonialism. In that era, missionaries provided schooling in order to proselytize and pacify the Africans.[11] The colonizing governments and their African administrations claimed there was not enough money for education. That is because most of Africa's surplus was exported; and of the little which remained behind as government revenue, very little was budgeted for educating Africans. For example, in 1935 of the total revenue collected from taxing Africans in French West Africa, only 4.03 percent was spent on education. In the British colony of Nigeria it was 3.4 percent. In Kenya, as late as 1946 only 2.6 percent was spent on African education. in 1938, all of French West Africa, with a population of at least 15 million, France provided education for only 77,000 pupils. British colonial education policy was a little better that that of France, because of missionary initiatives rather than government policy. Ghana, Nigeria and Uganda were had better colonial African education systems than most. Sierra Leone was better off educationally that French West Africa with 7 out of every 100 going to school compared with 5 out of every 100 in French West Africa.[12]

With respect to offering educational opportunities at all levels, African colonies without a large settler population had more racist structures. In Senegal in 1946, the high school had 723 pupils, of whom 174 were Africans. Later, a university was established in Dakar to serve the whole of French West Africa. However, on the eve of Senegalese independence, over half of the university students were French. Long unavailable, records of Portuguese colonial policy, when published, contained inflated figures. What is certain is that African children growing up in Portuguese territories had one chance in one-hundred of being educated beyond the third grade. The people of the Belgian Congo and Rwanda-Urundi had access to primary education, but secondary education was almost impossible to obtain. This was the consequence of a deliberate policy pursued by the Belgian government and the Catholic church. The African "native" was to be gradually civilized. To give him an education was like asking a child to chew meat when he should be eating porridge. Moreover, the Belgians argued, no highly educated African would be able to serve his own people.

The Belgians insisted that primary education would be in just one of the five main African languages of the territory. This allowed Belgium to seal off one Congolese ethnic group from another and to isolate educated off from a wider world of knowledge. The missionaries translated into the local languages only what they wanted the Africans to know. The French established *Alliance Française* in 1884, as an instrument of educational and cultural imperialism. The reports of *Alliance Française* clearly show that these "educators" thought of themselves as tools of the French empire. One report stated: "They have to combat the redoubtable influence of the English Schools of Sierra Leone in this region. The struggle between the two languages becomes more intense as one moves south, invaded by English natives and Methodist pastors."[13] Only in Tanganyika, under German rule, was there a positive reaction to the potential of Swahili as a teaching language, so that it could be used to expand African trade, political relations and personal contacts. Educators often referred to "the educational pyramid," comprising primary education at the base rising through secondary education, teacher training, higher technical education and university at the tip. Only a few British colonies provided this pyramid. West Africa had Achimota, and Yaba Colleges and Fourah Bay University. Ibadan and the University of Ghana came into existence only a few years before colonialism ended. In the Sudan there was Gordon College which evolved into the University of Khartoum, and in East Africa, there is Makrere University.

A Hunger For Learning

Educating African females has profound social implications. In addition to empowering women, it presupposes that society will usefully employ them. Walter Rodney noted that capitalist-colonial society had little interest in providing education to females. Access to and the right to an education, is almost universally considered a fundamental human right. In sub-Saharan Africa, many children report to the fields and mines rather than to school. Girls in sub-Saharan Africa face discrimination with respect to access to schools. Researchers monitoring progress towards the Education for All targets set at the Dakar summit in April 2000, projected that several countries would fail to achieve gender parity by the 2005 target date. Chad, Benin Burkina-Faso, Guinea-Bissau, Mali and Niger had the poorest access for girls. In addition to being an established human right, educating females is a sound economic and social investment. Great inequality correlates strongly with poverty, fertility rates, household and child health and opportunities for the rest of the family. In some parts of Africa, early marriage precludes female education. Females are more adversely affected by HIV/Aids, 4-7 per cent more likely to contract the disease and more likely to be pulled out of school to care for sick relatives.[14]

In January 2006, Oprah Winfrey opened her 52-acre Leadership Academy in South Africa, admitting 152 poverty-stricken young women. In addition to classrooms and laboratories, the school features indoor and outdoor theatres, a yoga studio and a beauty salon. Oprah Winfrey believes that she can groom them to become leaders who will one day eradicate the nation's impoverishment. She began working on the $40 million project in 2001 after a conversation with her friend Nelson Mandela and she monitored every detail from the architectural to curriculum design. Camfed International, a non-governmental group is also encouraging investment in African female education. Working in Ghana, Tanzania, Zambia and Zimbabwe, provides oversight of funds for education projects. Camfed money follows a student from one school to another school and has integrated financial resources with a database tracking how much is allocated per student. Camfed's involvement of local volunteers to monitor the schools helps reduce corruption in an environment where public sector salaries are low and teachers are often not paid on time.[15]

In both urban and rural Africa one sees throngs uniformed children on their way to and from school. These schools have dirt floors, are often windowless, without desks and the young students are often without books, paper or writing utensils. They have dedicated, but poorly trained teachers since many of the best teachers have emigrated to Europe or the US. There are many private academies, religious and missionary schools for those who are able to afford them. The many orphanages, in addition to keeping the children alive, struggle to provide them with a basic education. In "Mama Tunza's" orphanage in the Kenyan slum of Kibera, over 50 children live and learn in a small space not much larger than a small one-bedroom American apartment. Volunteers from the local universities hospitals donate their time and their medical skills to provide the orphans rudimentary education and health care. Many more orphans roam the streets carrying their younger siblings on their backs and begging for spare change to maintain their existence; they may never see the inside of a schoolroom.

In Zimbabwe, three quarters of the population earns less than US $1 a day. One could starve on a teacher's salary, so many teachers work as cross-border traders, forced to spend their weekends and holidays traveling to and from South Africa or Botswana to supplement their meager wages. In 1997, more than 15,000 teaches migrated to South Africa and Botswana in search of work, however menial. Many teachers could not afford the bus fares to work; forcing them to improvise informal work share arrangements whereby they work only two or three days a week.

Cecelia Shiri earns more as a part-time gardener in neighboring Botswana, than she does as a teacher in Zimbabwe. For one day's work she earns fifty Botswanan pula (Z$75,000), which is less than half the monthly salary offered to Zimbabwe's striking teachers in February 2007. "I can't survive on my salary," she just laments; "When I weed in the fields, I don't think about the plight of my children but how the black market can help us survive these never-ending hardships."[16] Raymond Majongwe, Secretary-General of Zimbabwe's Progressive Teachers' Union, estimated that graduate teachers were earning the equivalent of "four and a half bananas a day". One of Zimbabwe's most prestigious schools is located in Bulawayo. The secretary's office has no printer paper, ink or typewriter ribbons. The school has 1600 children and only 75 staff. The secretary and a quarter of the staff left in search of a living wage. Following independence in 1980, President Mugabe's invested heavily in education. Years of under-funding and economic mismanagement is rapidly destroying Zimbabwe's reputation for having the highest standard of education on the continent. Tens of thousands of state school teachers went on strike to protest their meager wages of about $10 dollars per month. Many state schools now employ secondary school dropouts as teachers. The qualifying level pass rate is less than 20 percent. In the rural areas, one-third of the schools have a zero percent pass rate.[17]

In Nigeria, primary education is provided by the Federal Primary School Commission, which regulates school programs. Children enter elementary school at the age of six and follow a six year curriculum, finishing with a Primary School Leaving Certificate. Secondary education is primarily the responsibility of the states. It consists of three years of junior and three years of secondary school. Graduates go on to university education enter the job market. In 1970, the states took control over private (church-related) schools which are now the sole providers of primary and secondary education.

A new phenomenon of increasing popularity is the mixed curriculum Islamic school. These schools reflect the desire for meaningful social change among ordinary Muslims. Muslim leaders such as the Emir of Kano, are backing plans by the US and the UK to fund hundreds of Islamic schools where modern subjects are taught and Islamic teachings respected. Those supporting the schools report that many parents are slowly beginning to realize that a technical, modern education is the only hope of reversing the economic decline in the north. Many northerners complain that much of the skilled work in their region is monopolized by the better educated and mostly Christian southerners. Bela Muhammed, director of a state Kano government body known as "Straighten Your Rows," stated that he had been tasked with "social reorientation," and charged with enforcing hard work, honesty and love for state among public servants and the public. The shift in attitudes is perceptible but the presence of "radicalism" persists along with some old suspicions. "We are being Christianized;" said Abdulkadir Orire, secretary-general of Jama'atu Nasril Islam, Nigeria's top pan-Islamic representative group, in reference to the mixed schools.[18]

Timbuktu, located near the Niger River in Mali, was once the world's center of learning.[19] Colonialism disrupted and supplanted the traditional African educational systems which were designed towards training Africans to provide goods and services for themselves and their societies. Traditional education was integrated with productive activity and was age-graded to endure and to measure progressive development in successive stages. The ancient Ghana, Mali, Songhai, Ashanti, Ovimbundu and Zulu empires could not have survived for long without a system transferring knowledge from one generation to another.

Perhaps one the most daunting and yet rewarding challenges confronting Africans is to invest in human resources. This begins with literacy. Illiteracy rates across the continent remain much too high. As Tom Mboya pointed out over thirty years ago, adult illiteracy is not simply a social and cultural problem. It must be eradicated in order to promote national unity and to create the foundation for an effective labor force. In the 1970s, there was much talk of the pressing need for technical education. But those with the requisite training and skills needed to carry out such an economic and social transformation were not as forthcoming as some African leaders wished.[20]

Recognizing that education is a source of human capital that enhances productivity in many ways, Daniel Osabu-Kle recommends that the majority of Africans living in rural areas, suburbs and cities be the target of mass education programs integrating education productivity and culture. Such a program might be organized on a voluntary basis and offered in local languages before the introduction of any other language. This might facilitate more effective communication between the state and the masses in local languages. Those who received education would be encouraged to spread knowledge to others (creating more healthy blood cells), including extended family members thereby creating more literate and educated people.

The lack of human resources is the fundamental dilemma of African education. In addition, African educators face issues of the viability of their product given the political economic realities. Education is seen as a ladder; you climb one rung to gain access to the next. Therefore, the purpose of elementary school is to prepare for exams that facilitate access to the next rung, secondary school. Throughout the educational system, credentialism drives purveyors and consumers of counterfeit diplomas. Curricula are planned around conditioning students to answer exam questions correctly. Thus, a student of public works may have no intention of making his career in the sewers and pipes of Lagos or Nairobi, his ultimate objective is to wear expensive suits, drive an expensive vehicle, sit behind a large desk in the ministry of water and then, perhaps, move on to a more lucrative position in the light and power parastatal.

Compared with universities of Europe or Japan, most contemporary African universities were hastily created. University costs per African student remain relatively high compared to tuition costs the West. At independence, governments seeking to promote equity granted free tuition as well as ample living allowances to those making it to the university. Today, the cost per student precludes such government investment in human potential. Obviously, elementary schools should receive priority. There is an educational the resource crunch in Africa. The continent's many educational dilemmas raises questions about the usefulness and universality of elementary and secondary education and are deeply rooted in local and bureaucratic culture. If Africa's schools and universities are to acquire the tradition of high-level study and research needed to support self reliant intellectual development, they will need technical, financial and moral support." Given Africa's myriad maladies, the state must make universal elementary and secondary education a priority. This Education must be controlled by the state. Only then, will Africa's human resources ensure the development of natural resources and culture.

Table: 19.0 Illiteracy Rates 1990-2000 and Primary & Secondary School Enrollment 1990

Country	Illiteracy rate adult female (% of females ages 15 and above)		Illiteracy rate adult male (% of males ages 15 and above)	
	1990	2000	1990	2000

Benin	84.51	76.42	61.93	47.88
Botswana	29.74	20.22	34.24	25.48
Burkina-Faso	92.04	85.92	74.97	66.07
Burundi	73.39	59.58	51.48	43.8
Cameroon	46.84	30.54	27.8	17.62
Cape Verde	45.66	34.28	23.74	15.45
Central African Republic	79.32	65.09	52.78	40.27
Chad	81.16	65.97	63.01	48.43
Comoros	53.62	51.29	38.61	36.81
Congo Dem. Rep.	65.63	49.79	38.55	26.9
Congo Rep.	42.08	25.56	22.86	12.54
Cote d'Ivoire	76.62	61.37	57.37	45.5
Equatorial Guinea	38.93	25.55	14.18	7.46
Eritrea	65.22	55.49	41.51	32.65
Ethiopia	80.16	69.05	62.48	52.8
Gambia The	80.41	70.58	68.16	55.98
Ghana	53.02	37.07	29.85	19.65
Guinea-Bissau	87.14	76.67	57.48	45.61
Kenya	39.21	23.97	19.03	11.11
Lesotho	10.52	6.42	34.63	27.5
Liberia	76.85	62.31	44.65	29.88
Madagascar	50.17	40.32	33.55	26.44
Malawi	63.76	53.49	31.2	25.53
Mali	81.28	65.6	67.09	51.09
Mauritania	76.09	69.92	53.67	49.25
Mauritius	24.99	18.72	15.2	12.16
Mozambique	81.57	71.31	50.65	39.91
Namibia	27.55	18.84	22.55	17.17
Niger	94.88	91.56	81.99	76.23
Nigeria	61.93	44.27	40.44	27.57
Rwanda	56.07	39.77	37.02	26.34
Senegal	81.41	72.36	61.77	52.69
South Africa	19.73	15.42	17.75	14.02
Sudan	68.37	53.71	39.7	30.54
Swaziland	30.11	21.36	26.33	19.24
Tanzania	48.96	33.45	24.36	16.05
Togo	71.3	57.51	39.45	27.61
Uganda	56.58	43.16	30.7	22.45
Zambia	41.3	28.51	21.44	14.79
Zimbabwe	25.04	15.33	13.38	7.2

The World Bank 2002: Note: Most indicators do not have data for all countries or for every year. A blank field mean there is no data for that year/indicator/country.

Henry Gray, T. Pickering Pick and Robert Howden *Gray's Anatomy: Descriptive and Surgical* (New York: Bounty Books, 1977) 973-975.

2. Rodney, Walter, *How Europe Underdeveloped Africa*. (Washington, D.C., 1982, Howard University Press) 252-253.

3. Ibid. p. 239.

4. Vincent Khapoya, *The African Experience: An Introduction*, (Saddle River, NJ: Prentice Hall, 1998), 153.

5. Nkrumah, Kwame *Africa Must Unite*, (New York: International Publishers, 1963), p. 42.

6. Surendra J. Patel, "Economic Transition in Africa," Reprinted in the *Journal of Modern African Studies*, Vol. 2. No. 1., in Irving Leonard Markovitz *African Politics and Society*, (New York Free Press, 1964) 329-349

7. Ali, A. Mazrui, *Political Values and the Educated Class* (Englewood Cliffs, NJ: Johns Hopkins Press, 1978) 23-24.

8. Rodney, Op. Cit. 247.

9. Surendra J. Patel, Op. Cit. 50.

10. Frantz Fanon, *The Wretched of the Earth* (New York: Grove Press, 1963) 51.

11. Rodney, Op. Cit. 142.

12. Ibid. 242-243.

13. Ibid. 245-257.

14. Miranda Green, "Poorest nations miss targets for girl's schooling," *The Financial Times*, November 6, 2005.

15. Caroline Daniel and Michael Peel, 'Camfed rides to aid of girl's schooling,' *The Financial Times*, December, 17, 2007, p.2.

16. Tony Hawkins, 'Zimbabwe teachers 'earn' 4½ bananas a day,' *The Financial Times*, March 17, 2007 p. 2.

17. Alec Russell, ' Zimbabwean teachers quit their schools in search of a living wage,' *The Financial Times*, December 14, 2007, p. 8.

18. Izervbuwa, Osayimwese and Sunday Iyare, "The Economics of Nigerian Federalism: Selected Issues in Economic Management." *Publius: The Journal of Federalism* 21 (4) (fall) 1991 pp. 89-101. and Dino Mahtani, 'Election breeds fear in Nigeria's Muslim north, *The Financial Times*, April 13, 2007. p. 6.

19. Daniel Osabu Kle, *Compatible Cultural Democracy: The Key to Development in Africa* (Broadview Press: Petersborough, Ontario 2000), 48.

20. Tom Mboya, "An Escape From Stagnation," Reprinted from *Africa Report* Vol. 12. no. 3 in Irving Leonard Markovitz African Politics and Society,(New York ; Free Press, 1967), pp. 14-39.

20: Nutrition: The Gastrointestinal System:

That dull listless look: is it a protein deficit or chronic and acute pain?

Resources are as vital to the health of a nation as food (nutrition) is essential to health of the body. Why then is there sufficient nutrition for export but not enough to meet minimum caloric domestic requirements? When protein leaves Africa, what is left behind are food shortages, protein deficits, malnutrition, hunger and starvation; which provide a breeding ground for disease. In Africa's case, the gastrointestinal system, lacks sufficient nutrition to function and is failing due to malnutrition.

Some serious questions deserve attention. To what degree does the presence of the American and European food and agricultural industries play a parasitic role on African agricultural production and policies? What is the impact of US genetically modified food export policy and subsidies to US farmers? What do complex land reform issues play in African nutritional deficits and African hunger? Where are the hungry? How is the pattern of hunger worsening; and what are the causes?

Africa is one of five areas where food production developed along with the domestication of animals and indigenous crops (and in some cases animals and crops from other areas). The others include Southwest Asia, also known as the Near East or Fertile Crescent; China; Mesoamerica (the term applied to central and southern Mexico and adjacent areas of Central America); the Andes of South America, and possibly the adjacent Amazon Basin; New Guinea and the eastern United States. In the Sahelian zone, tropical West Africa and Ethiopia were probably the most productive. Indigenous wild plants were domesticated in Africa's Sahel zone where cattle herding may have preceded agriculture. The arrival of crops from the Sahel triggered the local domestication of wild plants throughout tropical West Africa and in Ethiopia.[1]

When Europeans reached sub-Saharan Africa in the 1400s, Africans were growing five sets of crops, each with historical significance. The first set was grown only in North Africa, extending to the highlands of Ethiopia which enjoys a Mediterranean climate, characterized by rainfall concentrated in the winter months. Thus, North Africa's original crops adapted to germinating and growing with winter rains, and as known from archaeological evidence; to have been first domesticated in the Fertile Crescent around 10,000 years ago. They include such familiar crops as wheat, barley, peas, beans and grapes. These are familiar because they spread into climatically similar adjacent areas of Europe, then to America and Australia and became staple crops of temperate–zone agriculture around the planet.[2]

South of the Sahara are two sets of crops adapted to summer rains and less seasonal variation. The first are plants whose ancestors are widely distributed across the Sahel zone and which were probably domesticated there. These include sorghum, and pearl millet, the staple cereal of much of much-sub-Saharan Africa. Sorghum is now grown in area with hot dry climates on all continents, including the United States. The third set of plants wild ancestors grow in Ethiopia and are unfamiliar to Americans. These include the narcotic chat, which is used to brew Ethiopia's national beer. Ethiopian farmers first domesticated the coffee plant, which remained confined to Ethiopia until it became popular in Arabia and immediately went global. The fourth set of crops come from the wet tropical climate of West Africa. Some, remained in Africa; others such as African yams spread throughout sub-Saharan Africa; and two, the palm and kola nut, reached other continents and helped to build Western candy and pharmaceutical industries.[3] West Africans chewed the caffeine and cola nuts, the latter served as a narcotic. The last set of crops also adapted to wet climates. Bananas, Asian yams and taro were widespread in sub-Saharan Africa in the 1400s, and Asian rice was established on the coast of East Africa. But those crops originated in tropical Southeast Asia. Jared Diamond asks; "Did Austronesian's sailing from Borneo, land on the East African coast, bestow their crops on grateful African farmers, pick up African fishermen, and sail off into the sunrise to colonize Madagascar, leaving no other trace in Africa? [4]

Africa's domesticated animal species are fewer more easily summarized. The only known animal domesticated in Africa, because its wild ancestor is confined there, is a turkey-like bird called the guinea fowl. Wild ancestors of domestic cattle, donkeys, pigs, dogs and house cats were native to North Africa and Southwest Asia. Wild ancestors of domestic cattle, donkeys, pigs, dogs, and house cats were native to North Africa, Southwest Asia and India all of these stocks have contributed to modern African cattle breeds. According to Diamond, all the other domestic mammals must have been domesticated elsewhere and introduced to Africa, because their wild ancestors occur only in Eurasia. Africa's sheep and goats were domesticated in Southwest Asia, its chickens in Southeast Asia, its horses in southern Russia, and its camels probably in Arabia.[5] The most unexpected feature of this list of African domestic animals is that it excludes the abundant big wild mammal species for which Africa is renowned such as; zebras, elephants, wildebeests, rhinoceros, giraffes, buffalo and hippopotamus. The absence of these, like the absence of native domestic plants, had dire consequences on sub-equatorial African history.[6]

Food Insecurity

Nutrition is essential to survival, health and productivity and thus, essential to the foundation of human economic development. Therefore, any discussion of food insecurity must consider the devastating historic impact of colonialism on the African diet and its stunting effect on Africans as a physical species. Colonialism created conditions which led not just to periodic famine but to chronic undernourishment, malnutrition and deterioration in the physique of the Africans. When westerners see African children with a distended belly or transparent ribcage, protruding eyes and twig-like arms and legs, they are led to believe that malnutrition and hunger are endemic to the nature of things in Africa. NGOs such as *Save The Children* and *Oxfam* do not tell their contributors that capitalism and colonialism created and help to sustain the conditions for starvation and chronic malnutrition.

Josue de Castro, a Brazilian scientist, examined the food and health conditions among pre-colonial Africans societies and found that the African diet was more diverse because it was based on a more diversified agriculture than was possible under colonialism. One study in Kenya could find not a single case of tooth decay among six ethnic groups. But once those same people were put on the "civilized" diet available under colonialism, their tooth decay began. Kwashiorkor became noticeable wherever African contact with Europeans was prolonged. A Committee on Nutrition in the Colonial Empire found a noticeable absence of animal fat and protein in the Gambia. Studies in Equatorial Africa revealed frequent signs of dietary deficiencies caused by the absence of fresh foods among those entering the service of the colonizers. The Gambia grew not only a variety of food in the pre-colonial era, but was a cattle raising society where meat was consumed regularly. Throughout the 17th and 18th centuries, each year cattle hides were sold to the Europeans by the thousands and the local population ate the meat.[7]

Other maladies borne of malnutrition and the absence of fresh foods among the Africans include; beri-beri, rickets and scurvy. Rickets, a temperate climate disease is caused by lack of vitamin-C. After colonialism destroyed the pattern of cautious food consumption, these diseases appeared. Scurvy broke out among the workers in the gold fields of Tanganyika because their wages and labor conditions did not permit them access to fresh citrus and other nourishment. In South Africa, white settlement and capitalism malformed the African diet from meat and cereal to dependence on mealy-meal (maize). The result was an outbreak of *pellegra*, or "rough skin." There are examples of groups of Africans who, until globalization, managed to maintain their own patterns of existence with respect to food and nutrition. In short, colonialism had a deleterious effect on the Africans as a physical (and hence mental) well-being.

Southern Africa suffers severe food shortages. The UN's *World Food Program* (WFP) estimates that about 10 million people in four countries in the region require emergency relief as a result of poor rainfall. Currently, the most acute shortages are in Ethiopia, Zimbabwe, Zambia and Malawi. The shortage in Zimbabwe is worsened by economic mismanagement and disruptions in farming operations stemming from Zimbabwe's controversial land reform policy. In southern Zambia, NGO's gave hungry families a week's supply of maize to last them for more than a month. "People are already starving. They've just harvested but stacks are already depleted; said Joanne Mute, a field worker with the Evangelical Fellowship of Zimbabwe told the *Financial Times*.

Nigerian President, Obasanjo, warned those attending a WFP meeting in Durban, South Africa that state subsidies to African farmers undermined food security. "Most of us in Africa produce from agriculture. If subsidies are allowed to continue, there can be no market access for Africa. Without any subsidies on our side we can't break into that market;" said Obasanjo. He noted that food security in Africa depended on the ability to produce food for sale on the international market, as well as the capacity to provide local populations with adequate food stocks. Food shortages in southern Africa are chronic and the impact of hunger ripples throughout the continent. Food aid to Africa dropped by half between 2000 and 2005. In addition to drought, earthquake and a tsunami; politics played a key role in the failure.

The most flexible aid comes without political preconditions. Most food aid donated to the UN's World Food Program (WFP) is "tied" to recipient country purchases from donor countries. The issue of African hunger is further complicated by trade disputes between the European Union and the United States. These disputes threaten to lead to further cutbacks in donations to the WFP. The WFP receives no core funding from the UN budget and each year must raise every cent for its humanitarian and development work.

Agriculture is a potential source of nutrition and revenue for Nigerian economic development. President Obasanjo told parliament that the agricultural sector had grown 7 percent in 2003. In reality, even with good rains and supportive policies, it was closer to 4.5 percent. Once a leading producer of cash crops such as palm oil, Nigeria has been surpassed by Southeast Asian countries such as Malaysia, in terms of both size and yields per hectare. Only Nigeria's innate fertility has helped it avoid more economic devastation. As the world's fourth-largest cocoa producer, the country is somewhat food self-sufficient. The International Institute of Tropical Agriculture (IITA) estimates that Nigeria is just one of five African countries where the per capita intake is more than 2,529 calories per day. But, experts warn of shortages of foods rich in critical nutrients such as iron, zinc and certain types of amino acids. The issue of subsistence will likely become more acute with increased rural-to-urban migration. Many farmers were left with unsold stock during a recent cassava glut because they lacked the processing equipment to dry their crops; which would make then easier to transport and less prone to rot. [9]

WFP policy is intended to ensure food distribution without undermining farming. The United States and the European Union are the WFP's largest donors. Donor fatigue from reacting to humanitarian disasters such as the tsunami in Asia, the earthquake in Kashmir and hurricane Katrina, made raising increased food aid difficult. A survey by WFP and *Helen Keller International* indicated a malnutrition rate of 13.4 per cent in the worst affected provinces of Niger. This rate is comparable with those seen only in conflict zones and in areas devastated by natural disaster.

Recent food crises forced the WFP to respond in North Korea, Burma and Afghanistan. WFP director, James Morris, noted that: "I think my job is to work very hard at separating the humanitarian from the political. Nobody wants the small child in North Korea to starve no matter what the political differences might be. There are 113 million people around the world facing immediate starvation. They are primarily women and children. If you keep your focus on the beneficiaries, that poor child in Niger, Mali, Malawi or Lesotho-they really don't care where the food came from."

To supplement the WFP's food aid program, Morris launched a private sector initiative. He wanted 10-15 per cent of the WFP's budget to come from business and business expertise. "Much of the revenue we give back to NGOs. NGOs do much of the work that we make possible on the ground. It's to their advantage for us to be more aggressive in getting the private sector engaged with the issue of world hunger. The humanitarian agenda needs a growth mentality;" he observed.

In addition to increasing its transparency, the WFP decentralized responsibility to its 12,000 employees around the world, strengthened its logistics and improved nutrition by adding micronutrients such as iron to food aid. Morris forged partnerships with donor countries and companies including *TNT*, the Dutch logistics group, *Citigroup*, *International Paper*. *The Japan Advertising Council*. This private-sector initiative encountered strong opposition from some development charities. The European Food Security Group, a non-governmental organization network, argued that it was unacceptable for the WFP, with it's predominantly government funding, to compete with them for private donations. Morris noted that "*TNT* has helped us become better risk managers. They've helped us do a better job of our internal audit. *The Boston Consulting Group* has helped us think through how we use aid commitments in the future today, and rethink how the UN works as a team in southern Africa." Of course, private initiative food aid to Africa also serves to strengthen marketing to recipient nations. [10]

In Malawi, the WFP provides half the daily caloric intake required for human survival. Emergency dietary supplements include water-lily roots, which the Chichewa speaking people of the Shire River valley call Nyika. Digging for Nyika is dangerous business because numerous crocodiles prowl the river banks. The women of Chichewa cook these roots for hours until they become an edible porridge. This simple meal requires massive amounts of firewood stripped from the surrounding heavily cut forests.

Due to high transportation costs and tariff barriers, Malawi cannot compete with its coastal neighbors in the production of manufactured goods. Relief workers are searching for long-term solutions to Malawi's crisis. Pressured by donors, the government of Malawi began drafting an economic growth strategy aimed at mapping an economic future for the landlocked country.

Malawi's population has nearly doubled since the 1970s, but farm production growth remains stagnant. Prices for tobacco, the country's main crop, dropped with western tobacco consumption, while fertilizer prices continue to rise with petroleum prices. Following the advice of foreign donors, Malawi partially dismantled *Admarc*; an agricultural marketing board, that formerly sold bought and sold crops at guaranteed prices and exposed Malawi's farmers to new market risks. The UK's Department for International Development (Dfid) drafted a paper supporting the governments' strategy suggesting agriculture as a future "engine of growth." However, the government continued to subsidize fertilizer for maize crops. Advocates of free trade in Africa criticized the government for creating market distortions which compounded the effects of the drought and the food crisis. According to one western diplomatic observer; "The fundamental problem is that there are too many people on too little land, farming very badly."[11]

Malawi's poverty is exacerbated by political instability. The government went through four ministers of agriculture within two years. Ever since President, Bigu wa Mutharika took office in 2004, the parliament has passed no significant legislation, other than a few budgetary bills.. President Mutharika was threatened with impeachment by angry parliamentarians of the United Democratic Front, the party with which he had broken. After standing as his party's candidate, he declared a policy of "zero tolerance for corruption," and presided over the arrest of several allegedly corrupt UDF officials. He was supported by international donors led by the UK, who wrote to the MPs warning them that an impeachment would imperil future aid to Malawi. This led to the usual counter-accusations by the opposition that the president and his associates were themselves corrupt.

Malawi's hunger crisis due to persistent drought and the worsening HIV/Aids pandemic seems perennial. The pandemic compounds the chronic hunger problem by killing off the breadwinners and fracturing their families. Oxfam officials urged donors to use southern Africa's crisis as "a window of opportunity" to address the root problem of poverty and HIV/Aids rather than to dole out emergency funds, which only facilitate the impoverishment process.[12]

Malawi's bitter harvest of 2005 brought the hunger season three months early; prompting aid agencies and the WFP to launch emergency appeals. Twelve million people are "food insecure" in Malawi, Zambia, Zimbabwe, Mozambique, Lesotho and Swaziland. James Morris called the unfolding problem "the worst humanitarian crisis in the world." The shortfall of food aid forced the UN to cutback on its feeding projects and intensified calls for a new fund designed to facilitate a rapid response to food emergencies. Unfortunately, donors in the United States and European Union typically pledge only after being inundated with pictures of starving people on their television screens. This guilt-ridden aid usually reaches the stricken areas long after the emaciated have been televised. This, too little too late guilt aid, is then spent on cash intensive emergency efforts rather than on long-term programs that would mitigate hunger and starvation. In January 2006, the WFP warned of another impending food crisis in eastern Africa. According to the WFP, 2.5 million Kenyans, 1.4 million Somalis, 1.5 million Ethiopians and 60,000 Djiboutian's faced starvation. The WFP to expanded its operations in all four countries.

Niger is one of the poorest of the 18 countries whose debt was written off in 2005 by G8 ministers. However, this did little to alleviate starvation. With food stocks depleted every year, the country relies on food imports. The government's system of selling cereals at subsidized prices failed to alleviate the scarcity and hold down food prices. This was due in part, to the unwillingness of neighboring states, which were also facing food shortages, to export food to Niger. Amazingly, Niger's 2005 crop shortfall took both the government and the World Food Program by surprise. The policy of blanket food distribution, raised the cost of large-scale supplies, which were needed quickly to avert the sudden spread of malnutrition and hunger. The WFP pursued a targeted policy as opposed to blanket food distribution. *Médecins Sans Frontiéres* fed 1,800 severely malnourished children under the age of five at its feeding centers in Maradi province every week. A millet farmer in the province stated that; "I had to sell off many animals last year to buy food. I have virtually no savings left. We will run out of food in six months, so we are at the mercy of the aid agencies now."[13]

Per usual, in response to African crisis situations, the WFP received only 60 percent of the $57 million pledged by the international community. Analysts observed that anti-locust programs and assistance by the World Bank were insufficient to stem the deepening regional hunger crisis. Millions of people are also affected by food shortages in Burkina-Faso, Mali and Mauritania. The *International Crisis Group* pointed out that development assistance to Sahelian states was being sidelined in favor of expensive plans to support a regional counter-terrorism plan, where US spending on military assistance to Saharan states could reach $500 million by 2010.

Somalia has not had effective government since 1991. Lawlessness and clan-based violence have prohibited aid workers reaching affected areas and state relief is non-existent. Kenya by contrast has the regions most developed economy and infrastructure. However, the drought-affected northern and eastern parts of Kenya suffer from decades of economic neglect and impoverishment. The Kenyan economy has been crippled by decades of mismanagement and corruption resulting in glaring gaps in wealth and well-being. According to the *Society for International Development*, millions of Kenyans go hungry while the country's richest 10 per cent control and consume 42 percent of the national income. Food aid to Kenya is routinely misused or sold illegally.[14] Malnutrition has two faces, one is obesity. The WHO warns of a staggering increase in obesity within ten years in the Middle East and Africa.[15]

Comparative methods of measuring food insecurity in Africa suffer are limited, but are the only feasible methods, because of a lack of sufficient food data collected at the household or individual level of analysis. For purposes of food security policy decision-making, methodology based on aggregate food availabilities and incomes suffer three specific limitations: (1) they cannot be used for determining the location of food insecurity within countries; (2) They have limited use for understanding the causes of food insecurity; and (3) They focus only on diet quantity excluding other aspects of food security, such as diet quality and vulnerability.[16]

The International Food Policy Research Institute (IFPRI) measures food insecurity based on food data collected directly from households as part of National Household Expenditure surveys (HES's), to provide household information on the quantities of, or expenditure on foods over the past two weeks. Participants are asked about their food purchases, the food they consume from their own fields or gardens, and usually food received in trade. The data, when complemented by metric tons, weights of food reported in local units and measure or metric food prices, allow an estimation of quantities of food acquired by households. These data can then be used to calculate measures of food security and insecurity at national and sub national levels.

The IFPRI defines food security thusly: "Food security is achieved when all people, at all times, have physical and economic access to sufficient, safe and nutritious food preferences for an active and healthy life" (Adopted at the 1996 World Food Summit).[17] The IFPRI utilizes four indicators of food insecurity. The first two are indicators of diet quantity, the amount of food consumed. The first HES indicator is the data collected from households in HES's are either (1) expenditures on each food or (2) Quantities reported in non-metric or "local" units of measure, such as bunches or cans. The first essential step in calculating this measure is to convert the data to metric quantities (grams or kilograms). The second diet quantity indicator is the percentage of people in a population group who do not consume sufficient dietary energy. This is measured by determining whether or not a person lives in a household that acquires sufficient food over the survey reference period to meet the dietary requirements for all its members. The requirements employed are for basal metabolic function (a state of complete rest) and light activity such as sitting or standing.

The next two HES indicators, Household Diet Diversity and percentage of households with "low diet diversity," indicators of diet quality. Diet diversity indicates how much variety of food a household consumes. The percentage of households with low diet diversity is measured by determining whether a household fails to acquire at least one food from four of the seven food groups over the reference period. The seven food groups: 1) cereals, roots and tubers; 2) pulses and legumes; 3) dairy products; 4) meats, fish, seafood and eggs; 5) oils and fats; 6) fruits and 7) vegetables.[18]

The percentage of people who are food energy deficient varies from 36.8 percent in Uganda to over 75 percent in Burundi and Ethiopia. Food insecurity is a problem in twelve countries. At least one-third and in most countries a much higher percentage of the population is not consuming enough food to meet requirements for basal metabolic function and light activity. The Spearman correlation coefficient between energy availability per capita and the prevalence of food deficiency is -0.96 (P=0.000), a strong correlation between national-level food availabilities and food energy deficiency.

Data on food security for urban and rural areas within countries, reveal that for seven of the countries examined by IFPRI, energy availability per capita is higher in rural than in urban areas, despite the fact that urban areas have lower poverty rates. In fact, urban Africans may have lower energy consumption than rural dwellers because they are more dependent on purchased foods that have higher prices than in rural areas. Moreover, rural Africans are more physically active and consume more energy-dense foods (starchy staples) in order to meet their higher energy requirement.[19]

Table 22.0 Estimates of Household Food Security & Diet Diversity

		Food Energy Availability		Diet Quality		
Country	**Year**	Energy Availability Per Capita	% of People food energy deficient	% of households food energy deficient	Household Diet Diversity	% of Hh deficient Diet/div.
Burundi	1998	1,592	74.8	68.2	4.5	44.0
Ethiopia	1999	1,648	76.4	72.0	4.8	36.4
Ghana	1998	2,328	51.4	43.6	5.8	8.0
Guinea	1994	2,510	45.1	37.3	6.0	7.7
Kenya	1997	2,579	43.9	35.1	5.4	25.0
Malawi	1997	1,614	73.3	66.9	4.4	49.8
Mozambique	1996	2,059	60.3	53.6	4.2	62.6
Rwanda	2000	1,860	65.3	60.6	4.5	49.2
Senegal	2001	1,967	60.2	52.8	5.9	8.1
Tanzania	2000	2,454	43.9	37.5	5.9	9.7
Uganda	1999	2,636	36.8	31.9	4.4	50.9
Zambia	1996	1,764	71.1	63.1	4.6	43.0

Source: International Food Policy Research Institute Research Report 146, 2006.

Because the IFPRI study uses an energy requirement for basal metabolic function and light activity, a minimum normative requirement, below which a person is defined to be food energy deficient regardless of his or her actual activity level, urban-rural differences in the prevalence of food energy deficiency are variable. Four of the eight countries have substantial urban-rural differences in food energy deficiency (Burundi, Kenya, Mozambique and Rwanda). The difference is particularly high for Burundi where the percentage of energy deficient rural dwellers is 76 percent, while the percent of urban dwellers is 41 percent. For the other four countries (Ethiopia, Guinea, Senegal and Tanzania), the opposite is true.

HES data revealed expected differences in the food security measures between male and female-headed households. Female headed households are often considered more vulnerable to food insecurity than male-headed households because of tighter time and income constraints.[20] Other studies find that when women have the power to make decisions over the allocation of resources, they tend to allocate their scarce resources toward goods that benefit the entire household, such as food rather than only themselves.[21] The analysis of HES data shows that it is not the FAO method itself that underlies divergences in the estimates of food energy deficiency, but differences in the underlying parameters used. One way to determine whether HES data can be used to improve the accuracy of FAO estimates of food deficiency is to investigate how both compare to other indicators that are related to food security and that are widely believed to be accurately measured.

Table 20.1 Urban-rural differences in estimates of food Security/Insecurity for Selected Countries

		Food Energy Availability				Diet Quality		% of households	
		Energy		food energy		% of people	Household with low diet	Availability	
				deficit		Diet diversity	diversity	per capita	
Country	Year	Rural	Urban	Rural	Urban	Rural	Urban	Rural	Urban
Burundi	1998	1,539	2,674	76.2	41.3	4.4	5.9	46.0	6.5
Ethiopia	1999	1,680	1,444	74.4	89.2	4.7	5.5	40.0	15.2
Ghana	1998	2,538	2,269	50.5	53.1	5.7	6.0	7.6	8.6
Guinea	1994	2,645	2,234	40.6	54.3	5.8	6.6	9.7	3.5
Kenya	1997	2,473	3,168	46.3	30.2	5.2	5.9	28.2	12.0
Malawi	1997	1,621	1,533	73.0	76.3	4.2	5.7	53.6	16.8
Mozambique	1996	1,935	2,524	62.9	50.7	4.0	5.1	70.1	29.3
Rwanda	2000	2,065	1,827	54.3	68.5	5.6	6.3	11.0	4.3
Tanzania	2000	2,487	2,314	41.8	52.7	5.8	6.2	11.0	5.1
Uganda	1996	2,658	2,493	36.3	40.7	4.2	5.3	56.5	21.1
Zambia	1996	1,750	1,788	71.2	70.9	4.1	5.6	60.9	11.8
Mean		2,091	2,203	58.1	57.1	4.8	5.9	37.4	11.6

Source: International Food Policy Research Institute Research Report 146, 2006.

Table 20.2 Estimates of food insecurity for Male/Female households

Food Energy Availability		Diet Quality	
Energy Availability	% of People Food	Household Diet	% of Households

Per Capita		Energy Deficit				with Low Diversity Diet			
			Diversity						
Country	Year	Male	Female	Male	Female	Male	Female	Male	Female
Burundi	1998	1,654	1,395	73.4	78.3	4.7	4.0	39.2	57.6
Ethiopia	1999	1,653	1,628	76.4	76.2	4.9	4.7	4.6	41.5
Ghana	1998	2,237	2,333	52.4	48.7	5.8	5.9	8.5	6.9
Guinea	1994	2,496	2,625	45.6	40.7	6.0	5.2	6.9	12.0
Kenya	1997	2,581	2,572	45.2	39.7	5.4	4.2	23.4	29.0
Malawi	1997	1,631	1,546	73.1	74.2	4.5	4.2	47.3	57.6
Mozam.	1996	2,045	2,124	60.8	58.2	4.2	4.2	62.6	62.4
Rwanda	2000	1,903	1,746	64.1	68.6	5.9	4.3	45.2	57.9
Senegal	2001	1,986	1,868	59.5	63.7	5.9	6.1	8.2	7.4
Tanzania	2000	2,460	2,247	44.2	42.8	4.5	5.9	9.6	10.1
Uganda	1999	2,687	2,460	34.7	44.4	4.5	4.2	8.6	57.2
Zambia	1996	1,762	1,774	71.5	69.2	4.7	4.3	40.8	53.1
Mean		2,103	2,045	58.7	59.0	5.1	4.9	31.2	37.0

Source: International Food Policy Research Institute Research Report 146, 2006

Table 20.3 Percentage of Starving or Malnourished Africans 2000

Angola	
Benin	
Botswana	12.5
Burkina-Faso	
Burundi	45.1
Cameroon	
Cape Verde	
Central African Republic	24.3
Chad	28.0
Congo, Dem. Rep.	
Cote d'Ivoire	
Equatorial Guinea	18.6
Ethiopia	47.2
Gabon	12.0
Gambia, The	17.2
Ghana	
Guinea	32.7
Guinea-Bissau	25.0
Kenya	21.2
Lesotho	18.0
Liberia	26.5
Mozambique	26.0

Niger	40.1
Nigeria	
Rwanda	24.3
Senegal	22.7
Sierra Leone	27.2
Somalia	25.8
South Africa	
Togo	
Zambia	
Zimbabwe	

Source: World Bank Economic Indicators 2000

Throughout the 1980s and 1990s, African farm production failed to keep pace with population growth. Africa's agricultural research capability received little attention as governments were forced to cut back on basic science. Thirty years after the first "green revolution" transformed Asia and Latin America, African farmers are trying to follow their lead. But African policy-makers disagree over whether they should follow an agribusiness model based on large commercial farms or concentrate on millions of small farmers. The Alliance for a Green Revolution in Africa (Agra), is an association of farmers, agricultural businesses, scientists and research institutions, founded in 2006 with $150 million from the Rockefeller Foundation and the Gates Foundation. Namanga Ngongi, president of Agra, notes that Asian farmeing systems are dominated by smaller varieties of wheat, Africa has a much wider variety of crops. Agra is spending $40.5 million to establish a network of 10,000 dealers to sell fertilizer and other agricultural products to farmers in "market-smart" countries such as Malawi where subsidies are designed to stimulate rather than replace private sector farming. The Nairobi-based African Agricultural Technology Foundation (AATF), is trying to develop a "water-efficient maize" that will tolerate longer periods of drought. The project is funded by *Monsanto*, the US-based agribusiness. Africa's green revolution includes addressing the controversial issue of genetically modified crops (GM). Except for South Africa, African countries have resisted adopting GM crops. Acording to AATF executive director, Mpoko Bokanga; "It is not true that all African governments are opposed to GM. You have a lot of opponents of biotech who make a lot of noise and capture local media and then the outside media thinks that farmers are opposed. Most farmers don't know anything about GM. Advocates of large-scale export-oriented farming argue that small and medium sized enterprises rotating around massive farms will plug small farmers into the global economy. Many agronomists, such as a Glen Denning, of Millennium

Development Goals Centre in Kenya, disagree. They argue that the first is to improve the output and condition of the small farmers, who need food security before they can diversify. Raj Patel, a fellow at the US Institute for Food and Development Policy, told a US congressional committee that projects such as AGRA are models of unaccountable and unsustainable technological investment. He called for "programs that further the adoption and research into locally appropriate and democratically controlled agro-ecological methods.

Water and Climate Change

What is the impact of lack of access to clean water, the privatization of water on African health? Why do water access and usage and disease from water borne parasites continue to plague Africans? How effective is and what impact does digging wells, have on water access and infrastructural development? Lack of water is a basic constraint to agricultural production.

As the forces of globalization fought over the spoils of PPI investment in water privatization, the Tanzanian people suffered. A contract dispute between *Biwater,* a British water company and the Dar es Salaam Water and Sewage Authority (Dawasa) illustrated the dilemma of privatization aid for African countries. The dispute highlighted the politically charged issue surrounding the privatization of Africa's public utilities. Eighty-seven percent of *Biwater*'s $164 million lease contract was to upgrade water services to some 3 million people in Dar es Salaam, where only one in five homes is connected to a water main. The joint-venture was financed by the African Development Bank and the European Investment Bank.

Two years after operations under began, a 10-year lease with Tanzanian city water services the joint venture collapsed. *Biwater* and its German partner *Gauff Ingenieure*, withdrew in response to what *Biwater* referred to as the "unlawful" termination of a joint venture management contract and the deportation of three British expatriate executives. *Biwater* attacked the government's management of a project, covering water and sewage services in and around Dar es Salaam. The government placed an advertisement critical of *Biwater* in weekly African publications reading: "When aid flows through political pipes, it sometimes leaks." A Tanzanian official said the lease-contract to manage technical and commercial operations, awarded after a competitive bid in 2003, "looked pretty sensible," but many complained the water supply had worsened not improved. *Biwater* chief executive, Larry Magor, threatened to consult lawyers about the means to recover its investment after what he called "a repudiatory breach of contract." He said the lease-contract model is regarded as an "enlightened" solution for public water supply. However, most multilateral agency experts agreed that the UK-German-Tanzanian joint venture performed poorly. They also agreed that Tanzania had abided by the contract. The point is that PPI investment in such critical infrastructure as water and sanitation are primarily based on profit margins not on the delivery of quality services. In addition to natural disaster such as drought, Tanzanian taxpayers were subject to an additional market disaster.

When drought and famine revisited Kenya in 2005-2006, there was plenty of food in Nairobi, while people in the north faced starvation. Dr. Michael Johnson provides a distressing three step description of the famine preparation process:

Step One: Gathering: Climb up high in a banana tree that has some remaining leaves throwing down some of the largest while saving the smallest and the most tender for tomorrow. Then walk two or three hours to the nearest puddle of water or stream to fill any container available with water. One must be careful to stir up the water or you will get only mud and silt. One must avoid places where animals may have deposited body waste for fecal material adds an undesirable color, taste, texture and fragrance to the water which leads to death by diarrhea. One must also avoid the crocodiles and other wild animals that swallow children easily. They will kill to be first in line for water. Half of this water is spilled on the return walk home. Next one must gather some dried grass or dung to place on the charcoals remaining from yesterday's fire.

Step Two: Preparation: Place the banana leaves and water in a pan (recycled from discarded oil drums) on the fire of dried grass, charcoal and dung. Watch the children, for if they get burned, and they often do, there is no place to receive treatment and they will most likely die of their injuries. The smoke inhalation predisposes them to pneumonia, asthma and damages their eyes.

Step Three: These are the ingredients available that comprise the staple diet for millions of Africans, if they can find leaves and water. If you can find no banana leaves, substitute sawdust as many in sub-Saharan Africa must do. Sawdust requires no special sauces and is eaten by the handful. They will also try to fill their bellies with rocks and soil which are very slow to pass through the digestive system thereby providing a prolonged sense of fullness. Of course, there are also roots and tree bark seasoned with natural silt. As you pound these roots, some of the sap exudes adding a pliable consistency and making them easier to swallow. Taste is not a factor when you are eating to survive. After all, remember you are starving. One of the best things about these modern African recipes is that they never spoil and can be eaten again and again. The alternative is death.[22]

In February 2005, at the peak of Africa's rainy season, the rains stopped, bringing renewed drought. Perennial drought is a familiar story from Africa. From the Horn of Africa to the western Sahel region and southern African countries such as Malawi, cycles of water shortage recur with devastating impact. *Sterns Review*, a UK publication, which reports on the economics of climate change, warned that Africa will come under "severe pressure" as one of the most vulnerable regions. In many areas Africa has falling lake levels and persistent declines in rainfall. Lake Victoria, Africa's largest lake shared by Uganda, Tanzania and Kenya is three meters below normal. Lake Chad, between Niger, Chad, Nigeria and Cameroon is one-tenth of its size of forty years ago. Over a wide belt south of the Sahara, water is at the center of tension and a source of conflict between nomadic pastoralists and settled farmers. According to the African Development Bank (AfDB), about 3 percent of renewable water resources in Africa are under managed conditions, less than 6 percent of the cultivated land is under irrigation and nearly 40 percent of people are without access to clean water or sanitation. At the same time, Africa exploits only a fraction of its hydro power potential.

The United Nations Development Program reported that forty percent of the world's population will suffer water shortages by 2050 due to global warming. According to the 2006 United Nations Human Development Report, $23.5 billion a year would be saved by providing basic access in sub-Saharan Africa (5 percent of the regions gross domestic product). In most African countries there has been "an absence of consciousness about the reality of the problem;" observed Kordjé Bedoumra, director of AfDB's water and sanitation department. "The first thing we have to do in Africa is to store water. These issues are complicated by the fact that different countries rely on the same river basins and underground aquifers. There's practically no country that doesn't share water with its neighbors."[23]

Drought afflicts several parts of the world, but serious drought-related food crisis seem to be concentrated in sub-Saharan Africa. *Nature* Magazine reported that agriculture in Botswana, Namibia, Angola, Zimbabwe, and Zambia could be destroyed by sand dunes shifts caused by global warming. A team of scientists used computer simulations on the likely movement of sand dunes in southern Africa as influenced by predicted changes in the global climate. When the wind picks up sand and deposits it elsewhere, these vast dunes shift and move. Agricultural land can thus be turned into desert within a few years. Science suggests that the southern dune fields of Botswana and Namibia could become "activated" i.e., start to move by 2040. By the end of the 21st century, all dune fields from South Africa to Angola are likely to be activated.

The severe drought of 2002-03 was the last time the UN launched a UN feeding center in Niger. Irrigation is rare and most farmers rely on rainfall to water their crops. About 3,000 patiently waited in line for a 50 kilogram bags of maize, which supplies on average five people per month with 1,100 calories a day. This is half the recommended amount for subsistence. Peasants queuing for UN food spoke of the heat wave that had withered their maize crops. Maize is always available for sale from traders who sell at prices few of the supplicants can afford. After the starving populace of Niger lost world attention in 2005, pledges dropped to about 60 percent of what the WFP had requested for southern Africa. The UN raised $229 million. Many of Niger's farmers had to mortgage their 2005 harvests or migrate from their fields to help raise money to meet escalating food prices.

In Malawi, political turmoil contributes to the food crisis. Infighting between President Binguwa Mutharika and members of parliament seeking to impeach him distracted the government from the crisis at hand. Experts agree that drought is a trigger for the crisis, but not the cause. They point to the marginalization and underdevelopment of the arid and semi-arid pastoralist areas, which is due to poor land management, degradation and poor governance. In some arid and semi-arid areas some 65 percent of the population lives in poverty. Critics of the repeated cycle of crisis appeal and of aid without the required levels of development, say it perpetuates the situation and allows governments to shirk responsibility.

As in most countries, the economic gap between rich and poor, urban and rural, is expanding exponentially. Kenyan President, Mwai Kibaki declared a "national disaster," and appealed for international assistance to help millions of his countrymen, 3.5 million people, mainly pastoralists whose lives depend on cattle. They face starvation or "food insecurity" because of recurrent drought. Kenya has suffered poor rain seasons every year but one since 1999. In the northern, eastern and southern parts of the country cattle symbolize wealth, are a source of milk, used to trade and to pay dowries. If the cattle die, the herdsmen have nothing. Masai herdsmen have been forced to move to the capital with their livestock in search of grazing land by grassy roadsides. After visiting Masai lands, Kjell Magne Bondevik, a UN humanitarian envoy, warned that "it was very serious and a big crisis;" and asked the world community to wake up. Ironically, there was no national food shortage. There was a bumper harvest of maize, the staple food in 2005. "In many countries the cost of ignoring investment and addressing the underlying chronic vulnerability of pastoralists is borne by foreigners so, in effect, they reward governments for not investing in long-term projects;" said Eric Patrick, a policy expert at the UN Drylands Development Center. "If governments were held responsible, then money would have to come out of funds they want to spend in areas where there's high political reward."[24]

Tanzania experienced short rainfalls for several years preceding the IFPRI survey, including the drought of 1996-97 and the floods of "El Niño" in 1997-98. Guinea experienced the destabilizing effects of the influx of refugees fleeing civil wars in Liberia and Sierra Leone. And despite fifteen years of economic reform and democratization in Ghana, the collapse of cocoa prices in the early 1980s, left the country with a weak economy and slow growth in the agricultural sector. Although falling real food prices during the 1980s and 1990s may have improved the food security situation, the IFPRI study found that over half of the population was food energy deficient.[25] Ethiopia experienced recurrent droughts for decades, including that of 1984, which was followed by a devastating famine. Over one million people perished, despite world galvanizing media attention.

At the time of their surveys, Rwanda and Burundi were recovering from ethnically motivated civil wars accompanied by population displacements that severely disrupted food production and devastated people's livelihoods. Economic embargoes against Burundi by neighboring countries exacerbated the situation there. Malawi, Zambia and Mozambique were also recovering from effects of severe droughts. The food security situation in these countries is compounded by the high prevalence of HIV/Aids,[26] Malawi and Zambia with food energy deficiency prevalence's of 73 percent and 71 percent respectively, share a similar story of endemic poverty exacerbated by economic crisis associated with 1980s agricultural liberalization and drought. The drought led to food shortages, credit defaulting and a depletion of household assets that had the effect of exacerbating impoverishment. With the exception of Senegal, all of the countries with aggregate food deficits experienced adverse climatic shocks or severe conflict-induced instability in the years preceding the surveys.

While the question has not been conclusively examined, there is evidence that Africa underutilizes rural resources. First, there is clear evidence of seasonal sagging periods in rural areas covering much of the year, combined with varying degrees of underutilized land resources in Burkina-Faso, Niger and Zambia. Second, there are other constraints on farm exports than the supplies of land and labor that constrain non-tradable foods in much of Africa that can allow food production to expand without causing the export crop production to contract. Farm exports in Africa have been highly-dependent on commodity-specific organizations and resources, such as specialized export infrastructure and a reliable supply in rural areas of imported pesticides and fertilizers.[27] The UN Food and Agriculture Organization reports that the global cost of imported food reached $1,035 billion in 2008. The price increase was most severe in sub-Saharan Africa, where food prices increased 40 percent to $169 billion.[28] These external agricultural mechanisms and controls have a devastating affect on African nutrition, and negatively impact physical and mental development.

---

1. Jared Diamond, Jared *Guns Germs and Steel: The Fates of Human Societies* (New York, W.W.) Norton, 2005) 98.

2 Ibid. 386.

3. Ibid. 388.

4. Ibid. 389.

5. Ibid.

7. Rodney, Walter, *How Europe Underdeveloped Africa*. (Washington, D.C., 1982, Howard University Press) 236-238.

8. Ibid.

9. Michael Peel, 'Blighted by low morale and suspicion: The farming sector has been identified as a main driver of growth outside the oil industry,' Nigeria: Special Report, *The Financial Times* February 24, 2005 p.7.

10. Allison Maitland, "The struggle against the injustice of hunger," *The Financial Times,* October 13, 2005.

11. John Reed, 'Instability and bad advice worsen Malawi food crisis,' *The Financial Times*, December 28, 2005.

12. John Reed, "UN struggles to feed Africa's hungry people" *The Financial Times,* October 8-9, 2005.

13. Dino Mahtani, 'Aid workers warn of another bitter harvest for Niger after season of drought and locusts,' *The Financial Times,* October 4, 2005.

14. Andrew England, 'UN warns of food crisis in eastern Africa,' *The Financial Times,* January 17, 2006 p. 7.

15. Francis Williams, 'WHO warns of 'staggering' increase in obesity problem,' *The Financial Times,*

16. L.C. Smith, The use of household expenditure surveys for the assessment of food insecurity. In *Measurement and assessment of food deprivation and undernutrition*, 57-88. Rome: FAO, (2003).

17. Lisa C. Smith, Harold Alderman and Dede Aduayom, *Food Insecurity in Africa New Estimates from Household Expenditure Surveys,* International Food Policy Research Institute Research Report 146.(2006) p.5.

18. Ibid.

19. P. A Higgins and H. Alderman, Labour and women's nutrition: The impact of work effort and fertility on nutritional status in Ghana. *Journal of Human Resources* 32 (3): 577-595. (1997).

20. R. M. Caldwell, C. Seroussi, J. Hagens, C. Huddle, Mbizule, and Kay Uny, "Malawi baseline survey: Report of findings," Prepared for C-SAFE. Tucson, AZ TANGO International. http:''www.c-safe.org/dwnloads/Mal-baseline%Fin-Report.doc. (2003).

21. Haddad, L. J. Hoddinott, and H. Alderman, eds (1997) Intra-household resource allocation in developing countries; Models, methods and policy. Baltimore, MD and London: Johns Hopkins University Press for the International Food Policy Research Institute.

22. Michael Johnson, M.D., 'How to Prepare for Famine in Three Easy Steps,' *Call To Prayer* Magazine (July/August 2006) pp. 12-13.

23. David White, 'Uneven distribution,' *The Financial Times* Special Report, African Infrastructure November 21, 2006, p. 5. ; and 'Tanzanian spat puts focus on aid dilemma' *The Financial Times,* June, 29, 2005.

24. Andrew England, Kenya pushed into cycle of crisis, appeal and aid, ' *The Financial Times,* March 8, 2006 p.6.

25. V. K. Nyanteng, and S. Asuming-Brempong, The role of Agriculture in food security in Ghana. Paper prepared for the Role of Agriculture International Conference, Rome 20-22, 2006, FAO.

26. Zhang, X. Johnson, D. Resnick and S. Robinson, *Cross-country typologies and development strategies to end hunger in Africa,* Development Strategy and Governance Division Discussion Paper 8. Washington, D. C.: International Food Policy Research Institute, (2004).

27. Christopher Delgado, Jane Hopkins and Valery A. Kelly *Agricultural Growth Linkages in Sub-Saharan Africa,* International Food Policy Research Institute, Research Report 107 (1998), 20.

28. Javier Blas, "Import bill for food tops $1,000 billion" *The Financial Times* May 23, 2008. p.2.

21: The Respiratory System: Inert Resource Usage

The respiratory system provides more than just the passive exchange of gases. Molecules of gas must be inhaled into the lungs and absorbed into the blood stream as liquids, which requires a complete reconfiguration of their properties. For a gas to become a liquid, it must undergo changes in temperature and pressure. For it to be consumed by the cells as a source of energy, it must be further denatured as sub-electronic particles are changed and exchanged from living matter and inert substances. This living matter must again 'excrete' the toxins back into the blood stream delivery system for it to, again, be changed from liquid to gas and exhaled.

The issue of Africa's internal *vs.* external usage of these resources (timber, uranium, diamonds, petroleum, tin, cobalt, coltan, gold, platinum and rubber), is a critical factor to short and long-term individual and national health. To what degree do Africans effectively utilize or waste these resources? What are the measurable environmental costs of e.g., deforestation for beef production, oil drilling, industrial and peasant mining? Where are the profits from Africa's inert resources realized? Are these resources effectively utilized to provide the accelerated economic growth needed for the eradication of African impoverishment? Is the reconfiguration of these properties and the exchange with the environment hurting the patient, or actually providing it with life and energy?

Diamonds

During the long-wars of African liberation, South African diamonds provided much of the South African government's revenue to terrorize neighboring states and fight the African National Congress (ANC), the Southwest African Peoples Organization (SWAPO) in Namibia, the Popular Movement for the Liberation of Angola (MPLA), The Mozambique Liberation Front (FRELIMO) and other liberation movements. When the diamond industry was financing counter-liberation and national resistance movements, the West made no issue of "conflict diamonds" unless, the diamonds in question were in the hands of a fictional African liberation movement, such as portrayed by Sidney Poitier and the "Black Congress" in the film *The Wilby Conspiracy*. The diamonds in questions supported the maintenance of both intranational and the international racial dominance systems.

During the Cold War, 007 in *Diamonds Are Forever*, fought those who would utilize "blood or conflict diamonds" for nefarious purposes, even if his government did not. "I think James Bond did more for consumer awareness of conflict diamonds than anything else;" said Michael Einhorn, chief executive of *Cooldiamonds.com*, an online retailer. In *Die Another Day*, 007 intercepts conflict diamonds from Sierra Leone. Consumers rarely inquire into the origin of their diamonds. According to Luke Marriott, owner of *Wint & Kidd*, a chic jewelry shop in the Notting Hill section of London: "It is less of an issue than a few years ago, we contribute to a small school in Angola but we don't tell our customers because they are not interested." [1] To address potential marketing problems, the Kimberley Process, a means of certifying the origins of commercial diamonds was introduced.

The issue is often far from the minds of American consumers. "Customers are not really aware of the conflict diamonds issue. Their awareness has been actually diminished in the last few years;" stated Ernie Blom, Chairman of the *Jewelry Council of South Africa.* Although the civil wars in Angola, Sierra Leone and Liberia have officially ended; supposedly informed and socially aware think the problem ended with overt political hostilities. Jennifer Lopez, Jessica Simpson, the David Beckhams' and every Hip Hop performer wears diamonds. Thus, diamonds are forever marketed.

The success of the Kimberley Process (KP) stemmed the trade in conflict diamonds in Dubai, Democratic Republic of Congo, Israel, Botswana, South Africa, Lesotho, Zimbabwe and Mauritius. Canada, the European Union, Switzerland, Sierra Leone, Guinea, India and Sri Lanka were scheduled to follow. An alliance of industry, NGO's and governments has persuaded diamond producing, politically unstable countries, like the Democratic Republic of the Congo to accept inspections.

The focus on conflict diamonds shifted in 2004 and fear of loss of momentum increased when Russia took over leadership of the Kimberly Process. Although the Russians repeatedly reaffirmed their commitment to KP, there were fears the initiative could lose credibility if Russia did not comply. Russia has proven reluctant to agree to measures implementing the process domestically. In 1994, the Kimberly voluntary peer review process expelled the Democratic Republic Congo for diamond smuggling.

Illegal production in the northern, rebel held areas of Cote d'Ivoire, is estimated at 300,000 carats a year. The government of Laurent Gbagbo is seen as the "victim" in this scenario because it has no control over the country's diamond-producing areas. The government banned all exports of rough diamonds in November 2002. In November 2005, diamond producing countries and the diamond industry took an unprecedented step to stem the flow of conflict gems from West Africa and a resolution on Cote d'Ivoire's diamonds was unanimously approved at the Moscow plenary meeting of the Kimberley Process.

Cote d'Ivoire was the first *de facto* conflict situation the Kimberley Process confronted. Realizing that millions of dollars worth of conflict diamonds were being smuggled out of rebel held territory, Kimberley Process member countries agreed to establish practical measures to stop the flow. "Intervention on the trade side will impose specific controls for diamonds in the whole West Africa region and will require significant effort and cooperation from all participants;" said Kim Eling, chairman of the working group. Under the terms of the resolution, all diamond production from West Africa will be monitored and all exports from the region will be profiled. The peer review process is a success story according to Eling. "Diamond profiling means that more detailed information about the technical specifications of diamonds will have to be included in each shipment. It makes it easier to detect anomalies and will send alarm bells ringing;" Eling explained.

Global Witness, a UK-based group, released a report criticizing the Kimberley Process for it's "lack of action" and welcomed this long overdue breakthrough. According to *Global Witness*, Cote d'Ivoire's diamonds are smuggled to Mali, which has applied to join the Kimberley Process and to Guinea, which is a participant. "This is the ultimate test for the Kimberley Process, if they get this conflict diamond situation right, they will be able to get everything right;" said an NGO spokesman.[2]

Africa's people are the least beneficiaries of their continents' natural resources, particularly diamonds. The rapidly changing diamond trade in southern Africa is almost monopolized by foreign investors. An Israeli industrialist, Lev Leviev, has long monopolized the export of Angola's diamonds. In 2002, pressure from the *DeBeers* Group and the Angolan government's desire to improve its economic performance, resulted in the restructuring of Angola's diamond sales policy, which required four licenses. "There is a feeling within the Angolan government that Mr. Leviev has not delivered all he was expected to deliver;" said an Angolan mining executive. According to *Financial Times* journalist, James Lamont, *The Leviev Group'*s, multinational, private, offshore company, saved the Namibian Minerals Company (Namco) from liquidation with an initial investment of $15 million. Namco's diamond production for 2002 was 220,000 carats, double the output of 2001.

Lev Leviev emerged as one of *DeBeers* main competitors and forged a close relationship with Namibian president, Sam Nujoma. With help from the Nujoma government he expanded his presence with a diamond polishing facility on the Namibian coast. According to John Rogers, the general manager of the Namibian Chamber of Mines, senior managers at *DeBeers* were threatened by the *Leviev Group's* plan to build a huge diamond processing plant and its search for a supply of diamonds to produce. Leviev also enjoys strong political and business muscle with Russia and Israel: he is a close associate of both President Vladimir Putin and former Prime Minister

Ariel Sharon. He also owns one of Israel's largest companies, *African-Israel Investment;* which controls property, transport, infrastructure, development, metals, chemicals, hotels and oil information technology.

The *Leviev Group* replaced *DeBeers* in Angola in February 2002, when it was awarded the $400 million export contract for Angolan diamonds.[3] It now has a foothold in Namibia, one of *DeBeers* most secure source nations and is a contender for Russian sales due to Leviev's connections. Christian Dietrich, an international analyst with the International Peace Information Service in Antwerp, observed that: "Leviev holds considerable power in Russia, particularly through his influence in the Federation of Jewish Communities. He is reportedly protected by the highest Israeli authorities and has cultivated close relations with Russian oligarchs through his position as the president of the Russian-Israeli chamber of commerce." *The Leviev Group* has diamond polishing plats in Russia, India, China, South Africa, Ukraine and Armenia, and is seeking mining rights in Botswana and Canada.[4] *The Leviev Group* has eight global marketing agencies and its turnover in diamonds is estimated at over $2 billion annually. Leviev applauds the independence of diamond dealers and is critical of the price control regime imposed by *DeBeers*' marketing arm, the *Diamond Trading Company*.

In 2004, diamond retailers in the England and the US were largely ignoring the issue of conflict diamonds, putting at risk and undermining UN efforts to legitimatize the industry. A survey conducted by *Amnesty International* and *Global Witness*, titled *Déjà vu* looked into the implementation of diamond retailers of the Kimberley Process rules. They found that despite making a voluntary pledge to provide guarantees on the origin of all diamonds traded or sold, "the retail sector is largely unable to provide consumers with meaningful assurances that diamonds are conflict free."

The report further stated that the World Diamond Council, the industry established to combat the trade in "conflict diamonds," is falling short on adequately monitoring self-regulation. Forty-eight companies including *Asprey, Boodle & Duthorne, Debenhams*, and *Theo Fennell* in the United Kingdom and *Friedman's, Kmart* and *T.J. Maxx* in the United States failed to cooperate. The majority of companies polled requesting information on their conflict diamond policy failed to provide details on how the policy is implemented. Diamonds are forever a source of war, hunger, starvation and refugee flows.

Diamond merchants were not required, nor was it in the stockholder's interest to inform the consumer of the human cost of these shiny rocks. Random visits to 579 stores in the US and UK revealed that fewer than half have a policy on conflict diamonds and a tiny minority provide a warranty certificate for customers confirming the diamonds sold come from legitimate sources. The World Diamond Council could not be reached to comment on these findings. *Wal-Mart* offered a single diamond pendant valued at $1 million for $560,000 and a 27-carat diamond ring for $61,000 on its website.

In response to discount store competitors such as *Sam's Club* and *Wal-Mart* *Amazon*.com announced it would begin selling diamonds on-line. A new search tool allows customers to sort diamonds by multiple attributes, including color, carat, shape and price. Only two companies, *Tiffany & Co*. and *Signet*, have taken stronger measures by commissioning rigorous internal and third-party auditing procedures to ensure the source of their diamonds.

In Botswana, one of Africa's best-governed countries, ethnic differences are a threat to *DeBeers* corporate profits. Botswana's diamonds bring significant revenues to the small country of 1.7 million people. The San Bushmen and *Survival International* won a land mark victory in November 2006 when Botswana's High Court ruled they had been unlawfully removed from their ancestral homelands.[5] As part of a policy of consolidating remote areas and relocating the Basarwa people to areas where they could receive public services, the government began moving residents from the Kalahari reserve. While most of the residents accepted financial incentives to relocate, about 200 remained. Botswana is the size of Switzerland and the government claims the presence of the Basarwa is incompatible its wildlife preservation policy. The government also claims, that unlike their hunter-gatherer ancestors, these modern Bushmen use guns and dogs to hunt. Hoping to encourage and accelerate their departure, the government refused to renew the Basarwa's radio licenses. Jumanda Gakelebone of the "First People of the Kalahari," a group allied with *Survival International,* a UK pressure group said; "I think its pressure for people to give up so they leave the reserve."

In September 2005, twenty-one Basarwa tribesmen, were arrested while attempting to enter the Central Kalahari Game Reserve. They were charged with rioting and attacking the police "with an assortment of weapons." This incident is part of a long-running conflict between the government of Botswana and *Survival International* that supports those seeking to occupy the reserves. Caught in the middle is *DeBeers*, the government's partner in mining the world's richest diamond deposits. *Survival International* initially claimed the government wanted to clear the game reserve of human residents to make way for diamond mining interests, but could not establish a causal nexus between current diamond prospecting and the relocation of the Basarwa people. *Survival International's* director, Stephen Corry announced that he would call for a boycott of *DeBeers* and of Botswana's lucrative tourism industry; and enlisted actress Julie Christie to address a rally at a *DeBeers* exhibition. *DeBeers* rejected the diamond-relocation link as "a deliberate deception" describing *Survival International's* campaigns on behalf of indigenous people worldwide as "patronizing and deluded." Botswana's government branded *Survival International* as "racist", accusing it of distorting facts to raise funds. Stephen Corry dismisses such criticism saying: "We've been asked by Africa's most indigenous and least powerful people to help them. They are powerless without an outside voice."

A compromise plan allowing managed settlement on the reserve exacerbated the acrimony between the government and *Survival*

International. Although modestly funded, *Survival International is* a well organized campaign putting both *DeBeers* and the diamond industry on the defensive. *Survival International* is the major financier of the most costly court case in Botswanan history. Most of its $1.8 million annual budget comes from individual donors. According to *Survival International* and its local allies, police and game wardens intimidate and harass the remaining Bushmen. The government refuted *Survival International's* claims of "genocide" and two groups that represent the majority of Bushmen living outside the reserve, distanced themselves from *Survival International*'s efforts. The conflict inflamed hostile ethnic attitudes between the Botswana majority and the Basarwa minority groups. In September 2005, the Basarwa won an adjournment of the trial until February 2006 in order to raise additional funding, but the rights of indigenous populations in Africa remains a perennial source of political conflict.[6]

After years of growing consumer demand and rising prices, *DeBeers* was forced to cut prices in June 2006. The slowdown was attributed to cutters and polishers having built up stockpiles. But industry experts feared that rising interest rates and negative publicity played a role. US consumers account for half of the diamond jewelry market, and half of all diamond sales are made between Thanksgiving and Christmas. *DeBeers* feared Hollywood's influence on the market with the release of the film *Blood Diamond,* which focused on conflict diamond smuggling in war-torn Sierra-Leone. The people of Angola, Liberia and the DRC and Cote d'Ivoire have somehow been cursed by their inert resources. Liberia and Cote d'Ivoire have yet to qualify for the Kimberley Process. Shmuel Schnitzer, president of the World Federation of Diamond Resources, told the World Diamond Congress in Tel Aviv that the film would lead the public to think the industry had done nothing to solve the problem of conflict diamonds. The organization claims that more than 99 percent of diamonds are from conflict-free sources," and that diamond revenues enable every child in Botswana to receive free education up to the age of thirteen. Pressure groups point to wider problems of African diamond mining such as child labor, organized crime and terrorist financing.[7] The film prompted the diamond industry to launce an information campaign to educate retailers and to prepare them to answer consumers' questions about the true cost of blood diamonds.

According to an October 2006 UN report, diamonds from rebel-controlled areas of the Cote d'Ivoire are smuggled into Ghana in violation of the Kimberley Process. Experts estimate Cote d'Ivoire's production at 300,000 carats or between $9-23 million per year. Ghanaian officials say their export figures have increased because they have managed to control the smuggling of Ghanaian diamonds. Ghana was one of the first participants to join in the Kimberley Process in 2003, but was criticized in the UN report for failing to respond to the reports of its own diamond evaluators about suspicious diamond shipments. The report said diamond authorities in the United Arab Emirates intercepted a Kimberley certified diamond parcel from Ghana and concluded the goods were not of Ghanaian origin. The report identified two Belgian dealers specializing in the Ivorian diamonds trade who relocated to Ghana after the outbreak of war in the Cote d'Ivoire in 2002. They became the dominant exporters of rough diamonds from Ghana and were under judicial investigation in Brussels for possibly violating the UN import ban on Ivorian diamonds. Two well known local diamond merchants, one Ghanaian and one Ivorian, with assets in the rebel-held town of Segueala, conducted business with the Belgians regularly. Conflict diamonds specialists say other West African countries continue to import Ivorian diamonds. [8]

The alarming report on Ghana's diamond activity prompted the diamond industry, governments and NGO's to agree to new measures in the Kimberley Process to arrest the trade. Governments pledged to strengthen the supervision of the industry's self-regulation, including spot checks and random verification of records and all production statistics and to publish all trade data. The KP plenary session act to restore the scheme's credibility was declared a success: "Every issue we were worried about was agreed on;" said Ian Smilie of *Partnership Africa-Canada*, a KP supporting NGO. The most serious issue on the table was Ghana, which according to the evidence gathered by UN and KP experts had exported millions in illegal gems. Ghana has agreed to the new action plan and committed itself to a system of rigorous internal controls.[9]

Amnesty International and *Global Witness* conducted a survey of 42 of the most prominent jewelry stores in the UK. The eleven retailers that failed to provide any information on their diamond policy included: *Cartier, Graff Diamonds*, and *The House of Fraser*. According to Kimberley Process accounts, the percentage of conflict diamonds dropped from 4 percent to 0.2 percent. However, conflict diamonds still reach the international market from Zimbabwe and Venezuela.[10]

The diamond industry is entering a new relationship with African diamond producing states. This has much to do with the *DeBeers* loosing its stranglehold on the market. A new political imperative by African states called "benefication" means that they are demanding larger shares of their natural wealth. In Botswana, the benefication program has resulted in $83 million building, funded by *DeBeers,* to handle future diamond sorting operations which are now handled in its London *Charterhouse Street* office. For *DeBeers*, this centralization of sorting operations is also matter of production-chain efficiency. However, the decision to "Africanize" the *Charterhouse Street* functions was made by the government of Botswana.[11]

Gold & Platinum

Europeans often justified their presence in Africa as a mission for "God, Gold and Glory." Perhaps the greatest of these three justifications was gold. For the Africans, gold was a stimulus to external trade. It was external demand which accelerating large-scale mining. Gold is required in large quantities only in societies which produce a very large economic surplus and can afford to transform part of that surplus into gold for purposes of prestige and status (as in India) or into coinage and money to promote capitalism. However, pre-feudal African societies had so such surpluses nor did they practice social relations which made it necessary for gold to circulate internally.[12]

The Kilo-Moto mines are fabled for their mineral wealth. In 1903, two Australians on an expedition in King Leopold's Congo Free State found gold in the Kilo-Moto hills. By the end of Belgian colonial rule in 1960, the area was estimated to have produced 10 million ounces of gold, or more than 300 tons valued at over $4 billion in current dollars. Mobutu's nationalization of the mines led to a decline in output and when war broke out in 1996, mining operations were all but paralyzed. *AngloGold-Ashanti,* the world's second largest gold producer, has a 10,000 kilometer exploration concession surrounding the original mine and a mining license covering 2,000 additional square kilometers of the area. The region is covered by dense rainforests where downpours of rain produce vaporous clouds of mist. "I think God has an inherent sense of justice and humor so that he puts gold in interesting places;" *AngloGold-Ashanti* CEO, Bobby Goodsell, told stockholders. Howard Fall, the exploration manager describes it as; "one of the last greenstone belts unexplored by modern methods." [13]

The roads, built in the colonial era have, not been maintained. The 100 kilometer drive from Bunia, the main town, to the Ituri mining center of Mongbwalu can take days. Ituri, a province which is three percent of the total area of the Democratic Republic of the Congo, but twice the size of Belgium, has been the scene of ongoing tension and violence since the war ended and a transitional government was established in Kinshasa in 2003. *AngloGold-Ashanti's* Mongbwalu camp is protected by a team of unarmed former Gurka soldiers from the British Army, guard dogs and a razor-wire fence. The area has no official police force and depends on 150 Pakistani UN peacekeepers for additional protection. Before the arrival of the UN force, law was dictated by the tribal militia of Mongbwalu's majority Lendu population, the Nationalist and Integrationist Front (FNI). Floribert Njabu, the FNI president, took over an unoccupied company house outside the camp using it as a base of operations. UN officials in Bunia became concerned about tensions between *AngloGold-Ashanti* and the militias. A UN arms embargo imposed in 2003 and reinforced in 2005, banned any assistance to armed groups other than the DRC's new national army and police forces.

AngloGold-Ashanti is unable to exploit all the area over which it has mining rights because part of the south is under the control of a rival militia group the Union of Congolese Patriots (UPC). In 2005, the company began a confined search for a new mining territory within a 150 hectare tract around Mongbwalu. Almost immediately it faced demands from the FNI for goods and services and for several months it complied, with a levy of 6 US cents per kilogram on freight arriving at the local airstrip. When company officials discovered the practice: It was immediately stopped, according to an

AngloGold-Ashanti official. In December 2004, the FNI asked for $8,000 to fly a delegation to Kinshasa. The company refused. In January, the FNI issued an ultimatum to pay up. The freight landing fees paid by the company were made "under protest and duress and without executive management approval." The $8,000 payment was purportedly made to protect employee safety. Another company spokesman stated that such payments were "technically in contravention" of the UN arms embargo, but denied intentionally violating the ban or having a "working or any relationship" with the militia or providing other assistance.[14]

The Gold industry in the DRC came under closer scrutiny following a *Human Rights Watch* report critical of *Anglo-Gold Ashanti* for operating in conflict zones. *Metalor Technologies*, a Swiss precious metals company announced that it would stop buying gold from Uganda due to concerns that gold bought in the country could have originated in the DRC. Human Rights Watch reported that: "Continued fighting in the mining areas of eastern DRC threatens the country's fragile peace and adds daily to the 3.3 million deaths in the world's most devastating conflict since World War II.[15]

The company claimed it only paid after being advised to do so by Ituri district commissioner, Petronille Vaweka, who stated; "I told them, it's your responsibility." A leading and respected figure in local pacification efforts, she denied giving such advice and advocates renegotiating *AngloGold-Ashanti's* license and said the company should not have been given the whole area but instead kept part "for the future."

In February 2005, the FNI demanded more money, but according to Howard Fall; "There was no way we were going to put ourselves in that position again." *AngloGold-Ashanti's* twenty staff left the country and did not return for a month.

South African high grade mine deposits are diminishing making them less profitable. Therefore, *AngloGold-Ashanti* is seeking new reserves in high-risk countries such as Congo and Colombia. A company spokesman said one of the risks of investing in the DRC was that of "offending human rights sensibilities."

In August 2005, *Metalor Technologies*, a leading Swiss precious metals company, announced that it was suspending gold imports from Uganda because of the controversy over the origin of the supplies. The decision followed investigations by UN experts and human rights groups into the armed militia's involvement in the gold trade in the DRC's volatile eastern provinces bordering Uganda. The UN report identified *Metalor* as one of the refiners to which gold was sold by Ugandan companies. "We intend not to do business in Uganda any more;" said Scott Morrison, *Metalor's* CEO. He claimed that all its Ugandan imports came from domestic production, and that the company suspended purchases once current deliveries were completed because of the risk to its corporate reputation.

Human Rights Watch issued a report timed to coincide with the World Economic Forum's 2005 African economic summit. The report raised serious questions concerning the impact of companies moving into conflict zones and the effectiveness of voluntary rules governing their operations. *Metalor* spokesman, Bobby Goodsell said the company was "indeed in error" in two specific instances of payments to a militia group accused of atrocities in the north-eastern district of Ituri. Internecine conflict killed tens of thousands between 1998 and 2005. He told the *Financial Times* that the $8,000 payment was "unambiguously" wrong. The Payments ceased in September, were "equally wrong" he said, "but there are now management systems to ensure our economic activities give no support to any armed group." In 2004, *AngloGold Ashanti* merged with *Anglo American* which ironically prides itself on social responsibility, community involvement, good stewardship and ethical behavior. *Human Rights Watch* reported that *AngloGold Ashanti* failed to uphold its own stated principles and to follow international norms in the DRC.

Banks in Hong Kong, Brussels and London reap the profits of the DRC's illegal gold trade. Transfers are made on behalf of cross border traders and used to purchase goods that are then imported to the DRC. J.V. Lodia, owner of *Uganda Commercial Impex*, a gold import business in Kampala Uganda, states that suppliers bring consignments of unprocessed gold dust and nuggets or crude bricks, without any export or import documents. "How do you expect them to come with papers?" he asks; "It is smuggled."

The gold is smelted into Kampala and exported to primarily Swiss refiners. *Uganda Commercial Impex* operates a discrete but legitimate business, which includes a hotel and a rose farm, but is also one of three Ugandan companies involved in the export of gold. Such trade makes a major contribution to Uganda's balance of payments. J.V. Lodia has been called in "two or three times" for consultations with government mining officials. According to Lodia: "They support us, but at the same time they are not happy." [16]

While Ugandan officials admit that small quantities of gold are easily concealed, they deny the existence of large smuggling operations and that export data reflects growing domestic gold production. J.V. Lodia claims that almost all his gold originated in the DRC. However, figures form the Ugandan Bureau of Statistics show that gold exports averaged about $45 million a year between 1998-2003; accounting for about 10 percent of total exports and making gold exports second only to coffee exports during this period. However, these data do not match the official figures either for gold imports which averaged $800,000 a year for the same period, or for domestic gold production. According to the ministry of energy and mineral development, Uganda produced just 40 kilograms in 2003, worth less than $500,000 but exported more than four tons. In 2004, registered gold production was 2.6 kilograms while reported exports were 7.6 tons. Thus, Uganda came under scrutiny and pressure to tighten border controls, after reports from two UN panels highlighted illegal flows of extracted resources and weapons.

Floribert Kanda, a representative of the Office des Mines d'Or de Kilo-Moto (Okimo), the state company in charge of concessions areas, described the deal with *Anglo-Ashanti* as a diktat and complained that Okimo had no say in the deal with *AngloGold-Ashanti*, which was negotiated under the regime Joseph Kabila. Under the contract, Okimo received only 13 percent of profit share. *AngloGold-Ashanti*, which pays Okimo fees, is "both landlord and tenant," Kanda explained. Okimo is trying to restore its regulatory power over the scattered small-scale mining concessions. Miners are supposed to send 30 percent of their production to Okimo and sell the rest through official trading houses. This system fails because gold diggers have to pay protection fees to the militias. The FNI has supplanted Okimo in the control of artisanal miners. The result is that over 70 percent of all gold mined in the area is exported illegally.

Manufacturers and commodity traders came under pressure to stop importing metals from the DRC, after *Global Witness* charged that the country's natural resources were fueling persistent conflict in the eastern provinces bordering Rwanda. On June 6, 2005, *BBC 4* news broadcasted the story of a reporter who was arrested after trying to question a little known British company called *Afrimex*, about its role in exporting casserite (tin ore) from the DRC. *Afrimex* issued a report describing the problems and poor working conditions of those engaged in "conflict tin" mining. Tin mined in the DRC, sold to traders in Southern Africa and Europe, soon finds it way onto international markets and the production lines of the world's largest corporations. *Global Witness* says the pro-Rwandan groups in the DRC mine tin and smuggle it over the border into Rwanda, where it is labeled as domestic product. *Human Rights Watch* asked the G8 at its 2005 meeting in Gleneagles, to pressure Rwanda to end its part in the illegal tin trade to the DRC. Rwanda was one of the countries scheduled for debt relief from the G8.[17]

In July, 2005 President Mugabe visited China, a key political ally to his diplomatically isolated regime. After South Africa's Bushveld complex, Zimbabwe has the world's second-largest known reserves of platinum. *Anglo Platinum,* which is controlled by *Anglo American,* is expanding its operations in Zimbabwe by increasing the scope of a long running venture still in the development stage. *Anglo American's* farm at Hippo Valley Sugar Estates, was occupied by the settlers and another farm was issued a preliminary notice of the state's intent to acquire it. If the company reaches clarification on specific guarantees from the Mugabe government, Zimbabwe's resources could help to reduce African impoverishment. The company plans to increase its ore extraction goals from 85,000 to 120,000 tons of ore per month although these goals are preliminary and conditional. Both *Anglo American* and *Anglo Platinum* are eager to reap profits from the price of Zimbabwe's platinum wealth. Chinese demand for platinum is increasing and the metal is used by the automobile industry for the production of catalytic converters. There is pressure from western producers to secure a new supply. President

Mugabe signed legislation removing the right of landowners to appeal expropriation decisions.

Anglo Platinum has invested in the infrastructure; building roads and a 35 kilometer power line to serve its facility at Unki. *Impala Platinum*, the world second largest producer, and its partner, *Aquarius Platinum* announced plans for a $14 million expansion of their Mimosa mine. Depending on similar assurances from the Mugabe government, *Impala Platinum* prepared to invest $700 million- $1 billion in the major platinum producer *Zimplats*, of which it is the majority owner. David Brown, *Impala Platinum's* financial director, said the company "security of tenure" after the media reported that Mugabe might award resource-hungry Chinese investors lucrative and unspecified mining concessions. *Impala Platinum* expressed hope of signing a bilateral investment protection accord between South Africa and Zimbabwe.[18]

The guarantees sought by platinum mining corporations include assurances that they will be able to keep their profits off shore. *Anglo Platinum* wants to pay taxes and report its financial statements in US dollars. The companies' budgets will be affected by South Africa's Black Economic Empowerment (BEE) provisions of draft mining legislation which is similar to that legislated in South Africa. These provisions require companies to sell 20 percent stakes to local African investors within two years and 30 percent within 10 ten years. The companies are seeking clarification on how the transactions would be underwritten and financed.

Both *Anglo-Platinum* and *Impala Platinum* are based in South Africa where they enjoy lower production costs than their competitors. Both also face difficult operating conditions and eroding profit margins in Zimbabwe with its soaring rate of inflation and state-managed foreign exchange regime. Although it accounts for only a small proportion of world production, Zimbabwe's platinum is less exploited and therefore nearer the surface than in South Africa, making for lower production costs. Few Zimbabwean opposition leaders support the international sanctions or disinvestment. Morgan Tsvangirai, president of the Movement for Democratic Change, criticized *Anglo Platinum* and *Impala Platinum* for "still negotiating while the country is imploding." Both companies involvement in Zimbabwe predate the current political crisis and both *Anglo Platinum* and *Impala Platinum* declare their political neutrality and commitment to local staff. Evidently confused about who employed him, Godfrey Gomwe, chief operating officer of *Anglo-American* South Africa, told the *Financial Times*; "We're politicians, not business people...We are working on the finalization of our plans at a time when the political environment is difficult...That's why it's important to make sure the investment regime is clear."

Uranium

Africa accounts for 20 percent of global uranium production. Namibia, Niger, South Africa and Gabon are the main sources of the strategic mineral. Before the Invasion of Iraq George Bush falsely stated as did Tony Blair; that Iraq was suspected of acquiring significant quantities of weapons-grade uranium from nuclear stockpiles in Africa. Some speculated that the Democratic Republic of Congo was the likely source of the smuggled uranium. In an investigation of the story, *Financial Times* journalists James Lamont, Nicole Degli and Mark Hubbard reported on the Congo's largest uranium mine in southern Shinkolobwe province of Katanga, where the flooded mine and the area is under the control of Zimbabwean military forces.

South Africa is the only sub-Saharan state to have an advanced uranium producing program. The Pelinda Plant near Pretoria produced 500 kg of enriched uranium during the 1970s and 1980s. The Apartheid regime of South Africa produced highly enriched uranium, gathered a pool of nuclear and military scientists and built ballistic missile delivery systems to protect the minority regime. In 1989, South Africa had six deliverable nuclear weapons. Former president, F.W. DeKlerk dismantled the country's weapons capability in 1991, but analysts suspect this act sparked an underground trade in expertise and materiel. South Africa, uranium is also produced by the mining company *Anglo-Gold*, as a by-product of gold production.

Among Africa's main uranium producing states, production is strictly monitored and sales to power stations are made under exclusive contract. Experts say it is highly unlikely that any uranium could be smuggled out. In the former French colonies of Niger and Gabon, production is controlled by *Cogema*, a French company which specializes in the nuclear fuel cycle. In Namibia, production is controlled by *Rio Tinto*, the global mining giant and then sold to the French electricity supplier *Elf* under a long-term supply agreement. Exemplifying Africa's marginalization from its own inert resources, was the recent agreement by the French nuclear company, *Areva*, to supply China with African uranium for the next 14 years. According to the agreement, the Chinese company CGNPC will purchase 35 percent of the uranium produced by *Uramin*, a Canadian mining company with uranium deposits in South Africa, Namibia and the Central African Republic, which *Areva* purchased for $2.5 billion.[19] Africa has little economic breath, its gold, diamonds, tin, platinum coltan, copper, tin, rubber and chromium and petroleum are extracted to bring growth to the US, Chinese and European economies, while marginalized African economies continue to slowly suffocate. Until the corruption that accompanies weak political institutions is adequately addressed, Africa's respiratory system will weaken as the patient's blood pressure slips to life-threatening levels.

---

1. 'Nicole Diamond, 'Nations try to restore industry's sparkle'

The Financial Times, November 25, 2002.

2. Nicol Degli, 'Accord on conflict diamond smuggling,' *The Financial Times*, November 16, 2005.

3. Rebecca Bream, 'Stage set for competition,' *The Financial Times,* June 14, 2006.

4. Rebecca Bream, 'Africa promising prospects emerge,' *The Financial Times,* July 14, 2006.

5. Caroline Southey, 'Botswana's court rules San Bushmen evicted illegally,' *The Financial Times*, October 7-8, 2006 p. 9.

6. John Reed 'Protest of Botswana's Bushmen kick up dust' *The Financial Times*, September 28, 2005.

7. Rebecca Bream, ' Gem trade,' *The Financial Times.*

8.Dino Mahtani, Conflict diamonds 'smuggled into Ghana,' *The Financial Times* October 7-8, 2006 p.2.

9. Nicol Degli and Andrew Jack. 'Conflict diamond curbs agreed,' *The Financial Times*, November 10, 2006.

10. Nicol Degli , 'UK retailers fail to curb conflict gems,' *The Financial Times*, May 29, 2007, p.7.

11. William MacNamara, 'DeBeers cedes diamond grip to African states," *The Financial Times*, November 29, 2007 p.2.

12. Rodney, Walter, *How Europe Underdeveloped Africa.* (Washington, D.C., 1982, Howard University Press) 66.

13. David White, 'Curse of Africa's precious metal haunts miners,' *The Financial Times*, June, 2, 2005.

14. David White, 'Gold Group admits militia cash 'error,' *The Financial Times,* June 2, 2005.

15. David White, "Swiss group to suspend Ugandan gold imports," *The Financial Times, August 22, 2005.*

16. David White, 'Banks handling smuggled gold proceeds,' *The Financial Times,* June 2, 2005.

17. Rebecca Bream, 'Traders urged to stop Congo metal imports," *The Financial Times*, June 30, 2005.

18. John Reed, 'Platinum groups seek Harare guarantees before expanding,' *The Financial Times*.

19. Jamil Anderlini, ' China seals $12 billion deal for Areva's African uranium,' *The Financial Times*, November 11, 2007 p.2.

22: Auto-Immune Systems: The Military and Police

In response to human viral infection the immune is mobilized. White blood cells and other cells actively seek out and destroy foreign microbes. Once cured, the specific antibodies that human beings gradually build up against particular microbes; making them less likely to be re-infected. Of course, there are some illnesses, such as influenza and the common cold, to which resistance is only temporary; we eventually contract the illness again. Against others, including; measles, mumps, rubella, pertussis and smallpox, human antibodies, stimulated by one infection, confer life-long immunity. This is the principle of vaccination: to stimulate our antibody production without having to suffer the actual experience of the disease, by inoculating us with a dead or weakened strain of the microbe. However, some clever microbes don't acquiesce to our immune defenses. Some change their molecular structures (so called antigens) making them difficult for our antibodies to recognize. Among the most adaptative is the HIV virus, which evolves new antigens as it sits within an individual patient and eventually overwhelms the immune system.[1]

The other challenge to the immune system occurs when the it actually attacks the body it is meant to defend. This is known as an 'auto-immune disease' and implies that the defense mechanism actually goes on the offense and seeks to kill the organism it is designed to protect. Common forms of this disease in the human are 'connective tissue disorders' such as rheumatoid arthritis and thromobocytopenia, where the body destroys platelets which are meant to promote homeostasis and prevent bleeding. There are myriad of other illnesses of this variety. For almost any disease, some people prove to be more genetically resistant than others.

Similarly, some political and military systems are more resistant to infections of elite instability and corruption. As a result, over the course of African and human history, populations repeatedly exposed to a particular pathogen have come to consist of a higher proportion of individuals with genes for resistance. Unfortunate individuals without those resistant-genes for this are less likely to survive to pass their genes on to their offspring.[2]

Just as white blood cells, the anti-bodies serve to provide immunity against biological and bacteriological threats to the body, the military and police exist to provide internal security and national defense i.e., political homeostasis. The questions concerning the role of the military in Africa, include: Can the African the military adapt to serve as protector of African life and sovereignty, or will it remain a recurring cancer of violence on the political-economies of the continent? What are the future prospects for African Union peacekeeping, peacemaking and peace-building, i.e., what is the level of efficacy to the disease of political instability? Africa's military and police are analogous to antibodies. In many African states the antibodies and auto-immune system have failed or turned upon the body politic.

From The OAU to the African Union

International and domestic political conflict constrain the creation of wealth and perpetuate poverty in Africa while simultaneously creating large refugee populations. Africa's complex and protracted security problems were accelerated after the Cold–War, linking poverty alleviation with peacekeeping. In 1991 and 1993, the total number of refugees and internally displaced persons (IDP's) in Africa reached 5 million and 6 million respectively. The figure rose to 7 million in 1994, dropped to 4 million and 3 million in respectively 1996 and 1998. In 1998, Africans accounted for 25 percent of the world's refugees. Since independence Sudan and Angola have experienced some form of domestic conflict, which accounted for 4 million and Internally Displaced Person's (IDP's). The other countries that accounted for Africa's 10 million IDP's in 1998 included among others: the DRC (960,000); Burundi (800,000); Liberia (725,000); Sierra Leone (700,000); Uganda (622,000); Mozambique (500,000); Nigeria (470,000); Somalia (350,000) and Kenya (300,000). According to the 2000 US Committee for Refugees report, these figures varied depending on the annual levels of inter-state and intra-state conflict.

In 1997, the OAU Chiefs of Defense Staff underscored the importance of encouraging cooperation between the UN and the OAU's regional organizations involved in training, staff exchanges and logistical and financial support in order to more effectively manage inter-state and intra-state conflict. To that end, African states, regional and sub regional organizations embarked upon numerous bilateral and multilateral initiatives.

During the Cold War, Africa was a geo-political chessboard for US-Soviet confrontation. The continent's wars of liberation and the subsequent counter-revolutionary conflicts terrorized the people and arrested African economic and political development. The war on terror will be largely fought in Africa, where centuries of conflict between Christianity and Islam also underscores much communal and elite instability.

The ubiquitous US presence in Africa dates from slavery to the colonial-era and to the New World Order. Historically, the impact of that presence has largely been negative. The legacy historically underscores Africa's current political-economic crisis and remains ripe for exploitation by myriad state and non-state actors. Under the guise of revolutionaries, developers, investors, consultants and elected officials, many are prepared to exploit African conflict. Some utilize violence to maintain or challenge corrupt state regimes in order to reposition and restructure their status in the international economic and political systems. A report by a UN appointed panel warned that West Africa risked succumbing to "a vicious cycle of violence" prosecuted by armed youth wandering freely between countries.

At the 1963 Conference in Addis Ababa, Emperor Haile Selassie encouraged the establishment of the OAU stating that the destiny of Africa depended on its political union. Created to support African de-colonization, the OAU focused upon maintaining the sovereignty of African states at the expense of protecting human rights and advancing economic development. Described by one African president as a "trade union" of dictators, the OAU ignored most inter-national and intra-national African conflicts, and turned a blind eye to autocratic rule, corruption and human rights abuses. However, the OAU was the first forum where African leaders could discuss problems.

One of the purposes of the OAU, as enshrined in the Charter, was to "promote the unity and solidarity of African states." In this context, unity meant not territorial integration, but the dissolution of externally imposed ideological blocs by the dominant international political powers. The collective entity known as the OAU would speak for the interests of the African continent only on global and regional issues. Any dissenting African state could be censured by the organization but, the Charter failed to provide for the imposition of sanctions or any type of punishment against those acting against the position of the organization.

African leaders took irrational advantage of the loopholes and weaknesses in the OAU Charter. This fact is reflected in the policy positions they adopted on issues that violated the policies of the organization. Although they all rhetorically condemned apartheid, many violated OAU declarations and collaborated with the Afrikaner regime. Malawi's president, Hastings Banda, opposed the African National Congress and established trade and diplomatic relations with South Africa's minority government. Banda opposed the South West African Peoples Organization's struggle against South African colonization of Namibia and he ignored OAU member pleas to boycott the racist regime. The OAU failed to censure illegal attempts to cling to power by such leaders as Zimbabwe's Robert Mugabe and Didier Ratsiraka, the former president of Madagascar. Most of these leaders merely enriched themselves via mismanaged state kleptocracies, their greed pushing the continent further into poverty.

The OAU was further constrained by its need to mediate increased tensions between Pan-Arabism and Pan-Africanism. In an expression of solidarity with the Palestinians, many African states broke diplomatic relations with Israel. The Charter did not provide for the eventuality of peacekeeping missions and therefore for no peacekeeping structure. It was thus too weak an organization to resolve the myriad conflicts in Africa. Two of the principles enshrined in the Charter are that of "non-interference" in the "internal affairs of states," and that of "respect for the sovereignty and territorial integrity of each state" and its "inalienable right to independent existence."

In addition to these structural weaknesses, the OAU lacked the funding to function effectively. Many members were delinquent in their financial responsibilities and there was no debt collection clause in the OAU Charter. The low level of demonstrable financial and therefore, political support for the OAU, contributed to the communal and elite political instability that plagued the continent. In addition to the OAU's structural and functional constraints, serious irredentist conflicts and external power machinations plagued the organization. First; the creation of the sovereign state of Mauritania from territory claimed by Morocco, divided the OAU. Morocco boycotted the OAU's 1963 founding conference. Second; following the assassination of Congolese Prime Minister Patrice Lumumba. Lumumba's deputy in mineral-rich Stanleyville, Antoine Gizenga, claimed to be head of state. The pro-western states recognized Kasavubu's government; while states undergoing radical transformation of their political and economic systems recognized the Gizenga government. The third division and setback to African unity was the simultaneous independence of the thirteen French colonies. The great degree of French synchophantic xenophilia shared among the political leadership in these colonies made them politically suspect among other African leaders.

The first proposal to create African peacekeeping and peacemaking institutions was made by Kwame Nkrumah of Ghana, who envisaged an African High Command as part of his program of Pan-Africanism. However, the African High Command and other Pan-African ideals were abandoned and the Westphalian, state-centric model of political organization and the legitimization of the power politics of *Realpolitik* were embedded in the Charter. Although the concept of peacekeeping was not inscribed in the OAU Charter; Article XIX provided for a Commission on Mediation, Conciliation and Arbitration. Unfortunately, Article XIX never became operational. Articles XIII (2), XIV and XX of the Protocol establishing the Commission on Mediation was concluded in Cairo in 1964, did not provide for a system of compulsory jurisdiction, but rather was based on the consent of the parties.[3]

The first African involvement in postcolonial peacekeeping and peace-enforcement operations occurred in Tanganyika in 1961, to protect the political leadership from mutinous soldiers. In 1964, the UK helped Kenya, Tanzania and Uganda in peacekeeping operations against threats from mutinous soldiers. In 1980, at the seventeenth summit of the OAU in Freetown, Sierra Leone proposed the formation of an African Political Security Council (APSC) in response to the civil war in Chad. The 4,800

OAU Neutral Forces in Chad, deployed from Nigeria, Senegal and Zaire (1981-82) is the only time that an African peacekeeping force was deployed within the continent during the entire Cold-War era.

Although The OAU was unable to resolve many of Africa's political problems, it did project a common identity among people of diverse ethnic backgrounds, thereby keeping the sprit of African unity alive. It also provided a forum for conflict resolution among leaders who where not prepared to negotiate with their opponents. To its credit, the OAU successfully mediated disputes and resolved conflicts between: Morocco and Algeria in 1963; between Chad and Sudan in 1966; the Ghana-Guinea dispute of 1966 and recurring conflicts between Rwanda and Burundi.

Most African conflicts are intra-national with regional and global dimensions and thus, have the potential to become internationalized. Despite increased emphasis on conflict resolution by state and non-state actors alike, Africans had not found the political will to establish a standing peacekeeping force. "Peacemaking" refers to UN sanctioned efforts under Chapter VI of the United Nations Charter. "Peacekeeping" is based on the premise that the belligerent parties have accepted international assistance to help re-establish stability and the *status quo ante*. It refers to forces positioned with the belligerent parties' consent to monitor a peace agreement not specified in the Charter. "Peace enforcement" refers to the deployment of UN military personnel to bring belligerents under control as provided for under Chapter VII of the UN Charter. "Peace-building" is the establishment of structures which function to prevent recurring violence.[4]

At the UN, the African bloc of the OAU successfully sponsored and co-sponsored numerous resolutions adopted by the world body. The African bloc facilitated important amendment changes to the UN Charter, particularly Articles 23, 27, and 61 resulting in increased Security Council membership from eleven to fifteen states and that of the Economic and Social Council (ECOSOC) from eighteen to twenty-seven.

In 1992, a peacekeeping observer mission, code named Neutral Military Observer Group (NMOG I) and the *Group d'Observations Militaires Neutres* (GOMN), made up of fifty personnel from Egypt, Nigeria, Senegal and Zimbabwe, was deployed to Rwanda to secure a cease fire between government forces and the Rwandan Patriotic Front (RPF). The United States provided the funding for deploying and maintaining the observer force. The mandate for NMOG I was extended in August 1993 becoming NMOG II with a peacekeeping mission of 180 soldiers from African countries. In November 1993, NMOG II soldiers were merged with those attached to the UN Mission in Rwanda (UNAMIR), with an expanded mandate to secure peace in the country. Although, the UNAMIR force of 2,217 soldiers, 331 military observers and 60 civilian police had a greater impact on the conflict than the NMOG forces, it did little to prevent the subsequent genocide which claimed over 900,000 lives in Rwanda and 100,000 lives in Burundi. After the genocide, the United Nations set up Human Rights field Operations in Rwanda (MFROR) and Burundi (HRFOB).[5]

Following the assassination of President Melchier Ndadaye of Burundi in October 1993, an African peacekeeping force called for a Military Observation Mission in Burundi *(Mission d'Observations au Burundi)* (MOBU), which was deployed to the country. Although the MOBU force was comprised of 67 military personnel from Burkina-Faso, Cameroon, Mali, Niger and Tunisia, the new leadership of Burundi rejected the mission. Therefore, under Resolution S/RES/1049 of March 5, 1996; the United Nations requested that the OAU expand its peacekeeping mission in Burundi. Unfortunately, financial constraints and the size of the force limited the effectiveness of the mission. Because of their limited scope, capability and strictly observer functions, NMOG and MOBU are not considered full-fledged African peacekeeping operations.

During the July 1992 OAU summit meeting in Dakar, Senegal, African heads of state agreed, in principle, to establish a mechanism for conflict prevention, management and resolution. What emerged was a clear consensus on a new paradigm based upon the concept of African solutions to African problems. The following year at the Cairo summit, the OAU adopted a Mechanism for Conflict Prevention, Management and Resolution (MCPMR). At the summit's closing declaration, the heads of state and government stated, *inter alia*, that; "in circumstances where conflicts have occurred, it will be its responsibility to undertake peacemaking and peace building functions...In this respect, civilian and military missions of observation and monitoring of limited scope and duration may be mounted and deployed." (OAU 1993, Article 15) The Cairo Declaration laid the foundation for a proactive African conflict resolution and peacekeeping initiative. More importantly, MCPMR redefined African diplomatic norms and international relations with respect to issues of sovereignty, security and intervention.

MCPMR decisions are made by the nine-member Central Organ which is primarily responsible for sanctioning the deployment of African military observers and peacekeepers (OAU 1993, Articles 18-21). The Central Organ is headed by the country chairing the OAU proceedings. The chairman has the right to convene the body at any time. While the heads of state and government meet once and twice a year respectively, the ambassadors meet once a month. All Central Organ decisions are made on the basis of a consensus. (OAU, 1993 Article 20).

Following the unilateral of declaration of independence of the Anjouna Islands from the Comoros, an African military force; the Observer Mission in Comoros, with military observers from Egypt, Niger, Senegal and Tunisia, was deployed to the Capitol of Moroni and the island of Moheli to maintain stability and to establish a more conducive negotiating environment. The NMOG, MOBU and Comoros observer operations provided confidence in peace-building measures and signified a paradigm shift with respect to African conflict-resolution. The concept of absolute sovereignty, held sacrosanct during the Cold War, is eroding as Africa's military leaders explore means of providing peace and a peaceful and more stable environment for economic growth.

Much of the credit for restructuring and better equipping the OAU is credited to Muammar al-Qadhafi, who in September 1999, proposed the idea to the Africans heads of state at the Fourth Extraordinary Session of the OAU Assembly in Sirte, Libya. Two days later, the delegates adopted the so-called *Sirte Declaration* which emphasized the "imperative need and high sense of urgency to rekindle the aspirations of our peoples for stronger unity, solidarity and cohesion in a larger community of peoples transcending cultural, ideological, ethnic and national differences." Like Nkrumah a generation earlier, Qadhafi envisioned a conceptual framework for unity culminating in a United States of Africa. Delegates at the Sirte Conference ultimately rejected Qadhafi's call the formation of the United States of Africa, but agreed to begin the transformation of sovereignty via policy cooperation and coordination, a rudimentary step and toward regional integration.

Responding to a call from South African President Thabo Mbeki, 53 African heads of state and government met in Lusaka to adopt a *Millennium Action Plan*. Mbeki worked closely with Algerian president, Boutiflika and Nigerian president, Obasanjo to designate an all-African team to draft the plan. On July 8, 2002, the leaders of fifty-three African states met in Durban to create the African Union (AU) and terminate the dysfunctional and discredited Organization of African Unity.

In July 2005, Burundi held its first elections since 1993. The peaceful transition was hailed as a major accomplishment for a country destroyed by ethnic violence between Hutu and Tutsi. The conflict pitted rebels from the Hutu majority against the Tutsi-dominated army. Tutsis dominated Burundi's government, economy and military despite being estimated to account for only 14 percent of the population of 7 million. A small hard-line Hutu group, the National Liberation Forces (FNL), remains outside the peace process and continues operations in the hills surrounding Bujumbura, the capital.[6]

The Burundi operation cost $300 million per year and in April 2006, MOBU special representative Carolyn McAskie, announced plans to withdraw peacekeepers from the country. Forty percent of the force began preparing to leave and the remaining 3500 were scheduled to leave by August. Their departure came as the UN faced continuing difficulties in the neighboring DRC where the largest peacekeeping force was stationed. Ambassador McAskie acknowledged the FNL was a "major worry" as long as it was outside the political process, but that $300 million a year spent on the peacekeeping mission would be better spent on revitalizing the nations shattered economy. If we put this in the perspective of say, US spending on the Super Bowl, as the President and CEO of the American Advertising Federation said: "This is the biggest day for advertising in America. Last year (2005) there was a $140 million dollars spent to buy the advertising time on the Super Bowl. I suspect that will go up this year because the cost of a 30 second commercial has gone up to about two and a half million dollars."

The Millennium Action Plan does not claim aid from rich countries as compensation for slavery, colonialism and exploitation, nor does it demand huge aid flows. However, it does ask that new aid practices be streamlined, transparent and that both donor and recipient be held accountable for how the money is spent. This will avert the repeat of past crimes where both sides share complicity in the looting of African wealth. There is a need for monitoring not just by governments, but by groups outside government. "That is important because our governments have not shown a good record of monitoring themselves;" observed Muhtari Aminu-Kano, executive director of the Nigerian Conservative Foundation, a nongovernmental body.

Modeled after the European Union, the African Union set the ambitious goal of making this the African Century of "Peace, Prosperity and Development," signifying that it seeks to promote democracy, good governance and economic prosperity. The African Union promises to be much more active than its predecessor in promoting economic cooperation, internal free trade and improving Africa's transportation infrastructure. The OAU's overriding principle of non-interference is replaced by an explicit mandate to intervene in other countries when necessary to preserve peace and the rule of law. The AU is structured with a series of powerful, supranational institutions including a pan-African parliament, a Court of Justice, an African Bank and a Peace and Security Council modeled on that of the UN. Skeptics and pessimists assert that the O has merely been dropped from OAU and that beyond the name change, there will be little difference. Africa has witnessed a number of failed reform initiatives and renaissances, including the ambitious 1980's "Lagos Plan of Action" to accelerate African economic development and numerous declarations from a series of UN conferences. But the best intentions of political and economic reform consistently come into conflict with the realities and temptations of power and the realities of international political economy.

The reliance on mercenary security firms such as *Executive Outcomes,* blurs the boundaries between state and corporate interests in Africa. Firms like *Executive Outcomes* not only undermine the ability of international organizations to regulate trade, they create another external dependency. Other firms, such as; *Panasec, Strategic Concepts, Stuart Mills, Bridge Resources, Corporate Training International* and *Omega Support, Ltd.,* plus an estimated 90 private armies have descended on the continent to exploit African political instability, misery and violence. Some are linked to *Executive Outcomes*, while others like the American company *Military Professional Resources*, are fierce competitors in places like Angola. The African Union will have to address the presence of such firms in the post-Cold War era of minimal government and globalized commerce.[7]

The Constitutive Act of the African Union is much more elaborate than that outlined in the OAU Charter. Where the OAU Charter provided four organs and "institutions" (Article VII), the African Union provides for nine functional "organs": (1) the Assembly of the Union, (2) the Executive Council, (3) the Pan-African Parliament, (4) the Court of Justice, (5) the Commission, (6) the Permanent Representatives Committee, (7) the Special Technical Committees, (8) The Economic and Social Council, and (9) the financial institutions. The Council of Ministers of the OAU is now the AU Executive Council and it is charged with coordinating member state policy. The Constitutive Act provides for seven specialized technical committees: (1) foreign trade; (2) energy and industry and mineral resources; (3) food agricultural, and animal resources, livestock production and forestry; (4) water resources and irrigation; (5) environmental protection, humanitarian action, disaster relief and response; (6) transportation and communications; and (7) insurance.

Respect for human rights, political democracy and efficient governance are the criteria for attracting investment and provide the basic framework for development. In the past, African leaders rejected external criticism and external donors abandoned or shied away from their promises of development assistance. African leaders are often castigated for failing to invest in their people by combating disease, providing nutrition, education and housing. Dictatorial regimes and corrupt governments in Africa cling to power by resisting change. According to South African foreign minister, Nkosazana Dlamini-Zuma: "These Afro-skeptics clearly misunderstand and misread the mood in our continent." The African Union initiative underscores the realization of the role that African states have in their own survival by recognizing the need for domestic reform.

Since the end of the Cold War, one source of optimism is the spread of political democracy in Africa. Between 1960 and 1990, only one sub-Saharan leader was peacefully voted out of power; in the 1990's there were twelve. Some of the new leaders continue to ignore and subvert the democratic process, but the principal of political secession, has been established. Political democracy has brought change to South Africa, which has Africa's largest economy and accounts for 30 per cent of the continent's gross national product. In Nigeria, the most populous African state, president Obasanjo vowed to keep his promise to root out the corruption that keeps the state dysfunctional.

During the launch of the African Union in July 2002, business organization, civil organizations, human rights activists and anti-corruption campaigners, requested the G-8 industrialized nations to undertake more multilateral initiatives for African development and to check the abuse of power. The G8 announced it's "Africa Action Plan" during a Canadian summit on the New Partnership for African Development (NEPAD) advocated by South Africa, Nigeria, Senegal, and Algeria.

The G8 announced that it could direct half of the 2002 international aid and budget increase to Africa which would amount to $12 billion a year by 2006. This was viewed as a paltry sum given the continent's economic difficulties and the history of exploitation by Britain and France. "The amount looks like a pittance to everybody considering the serious financial situations of most of these countries," observed Beko-Ransome-Kuti director of the Nigerian NGO, the Center for Constitutional Governance. "The G8 should have committed itself more," according to Sabelo Macinwane, chief executive of the National Federated Chamber of Commerce and Industry (Nafcoc), South Africa's main black business movement. "But we must look at it positively and do everything we can to make it work." There was concern that economic tensions between the G8 and Africa would deteriorate into a patchwork series of bilateral trade deals between the responsible NEPAD governments and the G8, which has left decisions on aid to its individual member states. A common complaint is that NEPAD is the creation of a handful of high-profile leaders and their political advisors and has little input from outside government i.e., unions or the private sector. "We are in favor of an African plan;" said Patrick Craven, spokesman for the Congress of South African Trade Unions (COSATU). "But that means all Africans, and not just heads of state."[8]

The AU plans to answer the regional security question by decades end. A July 2004 meeting in Addis Ababa proceeded with plans to create a permanent peacekeeping force and to seek backing the UN. The idea had it roots in the AU's failure to prevent the Rwandan genocide and would enable the AU to act when the UN is unable or unwilling to do so. Military missions will be undertaken in agreement with host countries. The AU could intercede without UN authorization to prevent genocide or war crimes. But, the AU's peacekeeping initiatives rest on the question of how to finance such operations? Also undetermined, are the shape and roles of the standby forces, their means of deployment, and the cost of preparing and equipping them. AU Commissioner, Oumar Konare, wants member states to fund a $200 million a year peace fund, almost five times its current annual budget. The AU's plans found rhetorical favor in Washington and the Bush administration proposed $660 million for regional peacekeeping through 2009.

On May 2, 2004, UN officials from various African conflict zones met in Senegal to discuss an approach to ending Africa's civil wars. While adapting to fiscal constraints, the UN explored ways to increase coordination between its African peacekeeping units which faced increasing international and transnational crises. There were proposals for sharing facilities, such as trucks and aircraft, and moving troops from one conflict zone to another as needed. The lack of urgency placed on the resolution of these conflicts was perhaps best described by one Security Council official at the Lagos meeting who said: "We are examining how to improve our capacity to interlink quickly. We've been talking for six or seven months now about a regional approach." The US, which pays about 25 percent of UN peacekeeping costs, opposed these proposals because they posed the problematic prospect of a permanent, standing African military force. USUN ambassador, John

Negroponte, expressed skepticism but was "hopeful" the US would "be in a position" to support the proposal for UN troops, despite earlier skepticism about the plan.

The EU set aside $300 million to support an African peacekeeping command (AFRICOM). A July 2004 meeting in Addis Ababa, proceeded with plans to create a permanent peacekeeping force and to seek backing from donors and the UN. Returning to traditional African forms of security and conflict resolution, AFRICOM plans include five regional brigades of 3,000 troops each; made up of national battalions based in their home countries but trained together. Headquarters at the AU and in each of the regions were scheduled for completion by 2005 and the fully operational battalions deployed by 2010. The short-term plausibility of AFRICOM is best suited for West Africa, where ECOWAS has had peacekeeping experience since the early 1990s, specifically in Liberia and the Cote d'Ivoire and in the southern region, where it benefits from South Africa's defense capability.

In June, 2001 the US summit of the G8 nations pledged to provide training for 75,000 African peacekeepers by 2010. The UN has the bulk of its international peacekeeping troops engaged in Africa, including it three largest operations in Liberia, Sierra Leone and the Democratic Republic of Congo. The AU operated one mission in Burundi in 2003 and AU members contributed only $1.2 million to the mission's $120 million budget, and it took almost a year to deploy troops.[9]

Painted in UN blue and facing the sea on the outskirts of Ghana is the Kofi Annan International Peacekeeping Training Center. Part of the African Union's attempt to build peacekeeping autonomy, the center opened in January 2004 and has hosted participants from forty-five countries. Annan Training Center director, Colonel John Kane, believes the facility to be unique it its field. The center provides services for the 15 member nations of ECOWAS, which conducted the peacekeeping operations in Liberia, Sierra Leone and the Cote d'Ivoire. African peacekeepers have been trained by the US, Britain and France, but these troops will learn more about traditional "blue helmet" operations. Additional courses cover training in to how to behave as an observer, how to handle unexploded bombs and the disarmament, demobilization and reintegration of combatants, for which there are few adaptable successful models.

Despite the title, the Annan Training Center is a Ghanaian, not a UN institution. It is almost entirely government and private donor funded. Ghana's original plan for a training facility went unfulfilled until events in Zimbabwe led to sanctions on the Mugabe regime. The Dutch-based Zimbabwe project, which was to be a regional training center for southern Africa, was shifted to Ghana. The UK, Canada, Italy and the Netherlands provided the additional funding.

The only analogous facility Reinforcement of African Peacekeeping Capabilities (Recamp) is currently located in Mali. Recamp, established in

1999, caters to the armies of French-speaking countries. The French peacekeeping facility was based in Cote d'Ivoire, but was displaced by conflict there. The Accra training facility seeks to a instill wider scope of operational training and to create an integrated regional approach, bringing together the kind of instruction provided at the Mali facility and the higher-level courses of the National War College in Nigeria. The Annan center has six UK, German and French military staff with additional support offered by the US and the EU was to train 6500 troops by December 2004. Colonel Kane says; "what we're in danger of running out of is trained and capable individuals, not so much military, although that's also a problem, but police and civil components."

The challenge to AFRICOM is to both demonstrate its effectiveness and to realize its limitations. Thus far, it has deployed 400 South African soldiers to Burundi to protect politicians taking part in the peace process there. Burundi and Darfur are just two of nine African "conflict situations" from Comoros-to Togo where the AU is involved. On April 26, 2005 AU leaders met in Addis Ababa with Kofi Annan, NATO secretary-general Jaap de Hoop Scheffer, and EU foreign affairs chief, Javier Solana; to solicit financial and logistical support to increase the size of the AU force in Darfur to 7,700. The expanded mission would cost about $467 million but the AU expected only negligible contributions from African states.[10] The peace and security department has only six full-time desk officers and the "peace fund" relies largely on contributions from Europe. In fact the AU contributed only $2.67 million of its 2005 budget, and there have only been $5 million in voluntary contributions from African states since 1993. Their parsimony underscores a questionable commitment to the organization. "We are overstretched; we need more resources, more people. We are aware of these constraints and that is why we have to manage expectations;" said El Ghassim Wane, the AU division chief in Burundi. The AU is obligated to take action in places such as Somalia and Congo and assume tasks non-African bodies would refuse to consider. "The important thing is we do not want the AU to feel in a position of too much credibility, where it is trying to do too much and setting itself up for a fall." El Ghassim Wane described the AU as " a glass half-empty, half-full. The peace and security department should have more than 50 staff but recruitment is hurt by bureaucratic lethargy and the politicization of the personnel hiring process.[11]

The African Union must resume the work of the OAU and provide an environment for increased continental cooperation and policy coordination. Suresh Chandra Saxena suggests: "the most appropriate structure for this is a commonwealth that is democratic and provides the structures for all relevant stakeholder groups to maximize their values," i.e. some form of constitutional federalism must inform the establishment of a continental government.[12]

Protecting Human Rights

The Eighteenth Ordinary Assembly of the Heads of State and Government of the Organization of African Unity (OAU), met in Nairobi Kenya between June 24 and 28, 1981, to adopt an "African Charter on Human and People Rights." The delegates created conditions for a regional mechanism to promote and protect the fundamental rights of over 400 million people in Africa. In the preamble to the Charter of the OAU, the framers clearly stated that they were "conscious of the fact that freedom, equality, justice and dignity are essential objectives for the achievement of the legitimate aspirations of the African peoples." They also invoked the Charter of the United Nations and the Universal Declaration of Human Rights, as "to the principles of which we reaffirm our adherence."

In the eighteen year interim, between the founding of the Organization of African Unity and the 1981 Summit Conference, the organization was confronted with several serious political calamaties, many resulting in gross human rights violations. With each crisis, as Kwame Nkrumah had envisioned, the OAU became the proper forum for handling African problems. Therefore, it was quite natural for African leaders to look to the OAU as the proper agency to create a mechanism for the regional protection and promotion of human rights.

Tanzania played the catalytic role in promoting the creation of an OAU mechanism for monitoring human rights. Following the deposing and arrest of Emperor, Haile Selassie in 1974, and the execution of some fifty-seven former officials of the Ethiopian Imperial Regime, there were reports of impending further executions. The African Groups at the United Nations made a public appeal to the new Ethiopian government to spare the Emperors life and those of other detainees. In a statement to the General Assembly, Salim Ahmed Salim, Tanzania's chief delegate and Chairman of the African Group, pointed out that action was being taken "in conformity with our collective concern for human life and fundamental freedom" and emphasized that we have no desire to intervene in the domestic affairs of another state."

The Banjul Charter laid the foundation for a human rights system in Africa. As a declaration, the document imposes no binding obligation upon states but merely constitutes a promotional...statement of goals for States to achieve progressively. It differed dramatically from other regional conventions for the protection of human rights. Richard Gittleman observes that in keeping with its peculiarly African inspiration, the Banjul Charter relied upon "historical tradition and values of African inspiration," and reminds member states of their duty to "eliminate colonialism, neocolonialism, apartheid, Zionism and to dismantle aggressive foreign military bases.[13]

The Banjul Charter is divided into three parts. Part I established rights and duties under the Charter. Part II elaborated the measures to safeguard the rights articulated in part I; and Part III established general provisions concerning the commencement of the African Commission on Human and People Rights. The sixth clause of the Preamble illustrates that the Charter embodies a concept of duty different from those contained in the European and American Conventions. It provides that the "enjoyment of rights and freedoms also implies the performance of duties on the part of everyone." The notion of individual responsibility to the community is firmly ingrained in African traditions and values of African culture. Socialist states such as Mozambique and Ethiopia had a difficult time reconciling traditional human rights conventions with socialist philosophy which emphasizes the community not the individual. The notion of the individual in a socialist state differs markedly from that notion in a capitalist state. As a result, to ensure the adoption of the Charter by all states, the drafters stated that if the individual is to have rights recognized by the state, he must also have obligations flowing back to the state.

The recognition of rights without a guarantee of their implementation could allow one to interpret the Charter as merely a set of rights to be promoted but not protected. As the language of the AU Charter reveals, there is no express guarantee of rights:

> States, parties to the present Charter shall have the duty to Promote and ensure through education and publication, the respect of the rights and freedoms contained in the present Charter, to see to it that these freedoms and rights as well as corresponding obligations and duties are understood.

The African Charter contained no specific provisions entitling a state to derogate from its obligations i.e., to temporarily suspend a right guaranteed under the Charter. Many of the provisions contained "clawback" clauses entitling the state to restrict the granted rights permitted to the extent permitted by domestic law. Western analysts found such protection substantively questionable.[14] However, they often overlooked the fact that in socialist states such as Angola, Mozambique or Ethiopia, western attempts to destabilize and overthrow the regime necessitated the violation of some individual rights in order to protect the state. African political elites reserved the right to declare states by exception-of emergency, states of siege, or martial law and thereby to close down the legitimate struggle for human rights by suspending freedom of association.

War Crimes

In the war against the Lord's Resistance Army, the Ugandan military has killed many civilians in northern Uganda. *Human Rights watch* documented atrocities committed by both the LRA and UPDF forces by interviewing people in the refugee camps. People found outside the camps are commonly assumed by the army to be rebels or "rebel collaborators" and are frequently killed by the army. But several victims have been shot inside the camps. Many shootings occur at night at close range, are deliberate and not merely cases of mistaken identity as the army often asserts in its defense.[15] Other deaths were the result of severe beatings.

David Nyeko was killed around by 11th Battalion foot patrol soldiers. He had a military background and served in various armies respectively; UNLA, UPDA and later in the LDU at Awach. He later deserted as an LDU and was living at Obade village. Inquiries indicated he had ambushed the foot patrol soldiers; he aimed and threw a spear at them. This took place at Gwengdia village in Awach in Gulu district.[16] After his death he was buried by the locals of Awach Internally Displaced Persons Camp.

Human Rights Watch found witnesses whose account sharply contradicted the Ugandan government version of events. *Human Rights Watch* was told that the shooting was witnessed by several people who were present with the victim in his house and one witness said: "We were in our house with some friends conversing, but not drinking.... One LDU soldier came to the house and ordered all of the men to lie down. But they protested, saying they would not lie down. The LDU then fired three shots, without saying anything. Two shots went into the wall, and one hit Nyeko in the stomach. He died instantly. In this case, the LDU soldier, ran away and was arrested. A postmortem autopsy of Nyenko was conducted. The LDU, whose identity is known to community members, apparently remained on duty in the same barracks at the time of the *Human Rights Watch* interview six months later.[17]

The killings often seem to be for no discernible reason, other because the soldiers can do as they wish and later claim the civilians injured or killed were "rebel collaborators." For example, a man identified as Charles B left his wife and fifteen-year-old daughter in Pabbo camp, Gulu overnight to go to work his small plot of land. When he returned to the camp the next day, he found his wife and daughter dead. His neighbors told him that ten UPDF soldiers had surrounded the house of a nearby prostitute and knocked repeatedly on her door. When she did not answer they fired into her hut. These neighbors saw one of the soldiers enter Charles' hut. A short time later they heard gunshots from inside the hut. After the soldiers left, the neighbors went to look inside Charles' home and found his wife and daughter dead. He reported the case to the local barracks and a few days later soldiers arrived and removed some discarded bullet casings, presumably evidence. A military report about the incident, which Charles B read, said that the soldiers had been looking for rebel collaborators at the house of the prostitute, and they saw two men in black approach Charles B's hut nearby, so they started shooting into it. His neighbors who witnessed the shootings told *Human Rights Watch* that this story was false. The official investigation apparently ended there.[18]

Regardless of the presence of possible rebels or rebel collaborators inside displaced persons' homes inside the camps, the UPDF has the duty to take all feasible precautions to protect the civilian population under its control against the effects of attacks. Soldiers carrying out an attack must be able to distinguish between legitimate military targets and civilians. Shooting into huts inside displaced persons camps, where there was no apparent rebel activity, is an indiscriminate use of force in violation of the laws of war. The summary execution of any person is a war crime.

The abuses in the Cwero and Awach displaced persons camps stand out among the ten camps that *Human Rights Watch* visited in February and March 2005. The refugees were "protected" by the 11th Battalion of the UPDF, which had generated many more complaints of abuse than other military units in northern Uganda at that time. These two camps, situated next to each other some ten to fifteen kilometers northeast of Gulu, had experienced the same pattern of general UPDF abuses noted in other camps until the 11th battalion was deployed to the area at the end of 2004. In the few months that the 11th Battalion was stationed near those camps, UPDF abuses of displaced persons increased dramatically.

The abuses were not the acts of just a few undisciplined soldiers. People going out to the fields to harvest or gather firewood and water invariably found themselves confronted by the UPDF, whose soldiers who beat or tortured people almost every day during the first two months of 2005. In February 2005 alone, *Human Rights Watch* documented four negligent or willful killings of civilians by the UPDF. Beatings of civilians occurred almost daily after the 11th battalion arrived. This does not include one person suspected of being summarily executed by the army and two people who reported being shot at and wounded. The government of Uganda provided the following information to *Human Rights Watch* about the cases of Vincent Ayeila and Richard Kidega: The two were killed during across-fire between UPDF and LRA enemies. On February 19, 2005 their dead bodies were identified in the battle areas together with those of LRA by a Willy Obina Willy who later informed government forces that the two had been abducted by LRA at Pukanyo village.[19] One witness, a farmer living in Awach camp, told a different story, however. He left the camp on February 18 with Vincent Ayeila and Richard Kudega to fetch poles to build a hut. Soldiers found them in the bush and shouted at them to stop and fired at them. The witness managed to escape but the other two were arrested by the soldiers. The following day, a friend went to the barracks to ask for the two men. Both nearby barracks denied arresting the two. At 4:00 p.m. that day, their bodies were found. "Both had been shot in the head and chest, and both had been cut with bayonets on their hands and arms. One of the dead was still wearing gumboots and if the LRA finds these, they take them, so we suspected it was the army;" said a friend.[20]

The 11th battalion treated civilians, whom they are supposed to protect, callously and brutally. In Cwero camp, an old man was beaten to death by 11th battalion soldiers. The man was out late at night attending a funeral. A witness narrated how soldiers ordered a group of people to disperse, and then beat the elderly man as he emerged from the latrine: The soldiers began to beat him with the butt of his rifle several times in the chest until the old man fell to the ground. The soldiers then turned back to the group which was now dispersing and threatened them, telling them to leave. My mother went to the old man and tried to help him get up, but he couldn't move. Then one of the soldiers went over and started talking to the old man, but he wouldn't respond. After lying incapacitated in his hut for two days, the man died.[21]

The 11th battalion also brutally punished breaches of the camp curfew. The curfew hours were irregular, depending on the mood of the soldiers. According to a local leader at Awach; "The soldiers are not cooperative at all, they don't listen to the leadership of the camp. They normally accept people to leave the camp between 9-5. Even if they have set the time for curfew, sometimes they open the roadblock at 11, depending on their mood. Sometimes you enter return to the camp five minutes late and you get beaten and taken to the barracks."[22]

At a UPDF roadblock outside Cwero camp during February, 2005, a local council official found soldiers arresting civilians for violating the curfew. He protested that the curfew did not begin until 5 p.m., and it was only 4 p.m. The soldiers said they had changed the law. The council official (referred to as an "LC" throughout Uganda) continued to protest, and, according to him, the soldiers said they would "cane me also. They gave me sixteen strokes." At the same time they beat the civilians at the roadblock. When the LC went to the barracks to complain he saw other civilians being beaten at the barracks in front of a lieutenant. When he asked why the people were being beaten the lieutenant asked him, "Do you know the rebels?" The elected official went away without registering a complaint, fearful of the repercussions.[23]

Soldiers of the 11th battalion were also committed torture. A forty-year-old farmer from Cwero was accosted by soldiers when he was found making a fire break around his cultivation five kilometers outside the camp. The soldiers claimed that he was working for the rebels and then tortured him, he said: "They made me lie down and started caning me and kicking me so many times. Then they tied a rope around my testicles and pulled on it. They took me unconscious to Cwero barracks where I stayed one night. Because I was very sick they released me."[24]

The LC lodged a complaint with the police who sent a letter to the UPDF Public Relations Officer and the 11th Battalion. The UPDF 11th Battalion commander in Awach claimed that the other three men who were in the victim's home "should find the soldier who shot..., otherwise they were the ones with the gun." One of the three men was detained for two days at the barracks then released with orders to report daily as to whether he had found the soldier, which orders were not enforced. "It is a way to intimidate us," the victim said. A case was also filed with the Uganda Human Rights Commission, the government human rights monitoring body that has the power to hear and decide human rights cases.[25]

Such gross mistreatment was a routine at Cwero and Awach camps. One woman who was beaten by soldiers who pulled her out of her shop. "I did not complain. I thought soldiers were on their work so I didn't take it to the LC local councilor, she recounted."[26] Government soldiers routinely abuse civilians in the displaced persons camps of northern Uganda. Civilians alleged to be "rebel collaborators" are commonly detained and sometimes tortured or severely beaten with sticks as part of the interrogation process. Some of the detainees reported being held in pits with other prisoners for several days. Very few of those detained ever received a trial.

One twenty-three year old farmer was beaten by UPDF soldiers near Cwero camp on the morning of January 23, 2005. The soldiers, apparently as punishment, beat the hands of nine men captured that day with a large stick until they bled, then the soldiers left. The man said: "That morning my friend and I went to cut sorghum in a garden near the camp. While we were working a group of soldiers approached us. They had with them seven other civilians from the camp who they had stopped along the path to the camp. They must have been coming to the fields to work as well. Anyway, they forced all of us on the ground. One by one, we were taken to a tree stump and told to put our hands across it. Then they beat our hands with a large stick until they bled. When they had beaten everyone they left. I took my friend to a nearby river and washed his hands because they were bleeding so badly.... The soldiers also destroyed my identity papers."[27]

A relative of LRA commander Vincent Otti, was arrested by soldiers near Pabbo camp in Gulu on February 20, 2005. They alleged that he was a rebel collaborator and took him back to the barracks. At the barracks he was taken into a "small hut, a torture house, where they kill people. Four big wooden logs were hanging in the hut. The soldiers tried to hit me with the logs but I dodged them." The soldiers then took him out of the barracks; they "beat me with sticks, hitting my head and chest with the butts of their guns. When they beat me they said I had no energy to move." The soldiers forced him to walk on further until they reached a place called Guru and stopped. The man said: "The soldiers were hitting me with sticks and the butts of their guns. I was suffering from in my legs and chest. When I was hit on the head I was spinning around. I couldn't move anymore. The men put a rope around my neck and started strangling me. Four soldiers were sitting on my chest and the fifth was pulling the rope around my neck. They told me they were going to kill me because I was the relative of Otti. I fainted; I don't know what happened after."[28]

Many UPDF beatings occurred where the soldiers believed the victims were breaking the army-imposed local curfew, which restricts the times that civilians are allowed to be outside the camps. They even impose a curfew on how late the displaced can be outside their homes at night-although the homes are small huts in the middle of a displaced persons camp. Soldiers in Paicor camp beat Patrick F outside his home in August, 2004. "Two soldiers came when I was sitting in front of my house. They started beating me. They were drunk and said. Get inside, nobody should be outside by now, and just started beating me. They hit me with their sticks and told me to lie down inside the hut. As I was lying down they hit me and wounded me badly."[29]

The situation became so serious that some civilians seemed to view such abuse at the hands of the soldiers as normal. As one man related after being beaten by LDU's for returning late to the camp, "We did not complain to anyone about this. It is a normal thing when you come late and no one follows it up. We were late because we had gone far."[30] The soldiers stole what the men had hunted, leaving them with one small animal each. Many more than one-third of the 170 people at displaced persons camps interviewed by *Human Rights Watch* said that they had experienced or witnessed a beating by the UPDF between 2004 and 2005.

Rape and other sexual violence are also frequent occurrences in and around the camps. Rape is highly stigmatizing in Ugandan society and women often are ashamed to report it; many women *Human Rights Watch* spoke to had never described their experiences to anyone. These women were fearful that the community would shun or reject them. A June 15, 2005 report by UNICEF concluded that rape was the most common form of violence in the sprawling Pabbo internally displaced persons camp of Gulu district.[31] Rape was not limited to one camp or town. The lack of discipline within the army and the almost complete lack of accountability contributed to an environment and atmosphere in which women are extremely vulnerable to abuse, both from the UPDF and within the community. Women in a number of camps told *Human Rights Watch* how they had been raped by soldiers from the Ugandan army. Women are particularly exposed at night if they are found outside of their huts. One woman from Amida camp in Kitgum went out at night to use the latrine. A soldier forced her at gunpoint to the edge of the camp and raped her, threatening to kill her if she refused him. She said: "He said to me if I rejected him he would kill me. He began to squeeze me, he forced me on the ground and raped me. When he finished he left me he knocked me down on the legs with his knee so I didn't know where he was going."[32]

Young girls are too often the victims. On the morning of January 26, 2005, a man from Bobi camp, Gulu discovered that his sixteen-year-old daughter was missing. He learned from a nephew that she had been taken by UPDF soldiers and that one of the soldiers was raping her in a hut on the other side of the camp. He said, "When I arrived at the hut the soldier had gone and my daughter was inside the hut crying." At the hospital the next day doctors confirmed she had been raped." [33]

In Kitgum's Matidi camp, the UPDF beefed up its presence due to increased LRA activity in the area. The supposed "extra protection" turned out to be a nightmare for the residents of the camp. One woman described how "a lot of women were raped at that time." Two women told *Human Rights Watch* about similar incidents of soldiers barging into their huts and raping them. In the same month at Kitgum Matidi camp, a soldier raped a grandmother, according to her adult son, whose hut was also invaded by soldiers. He said: "Afterwards they went to my mother—perhaps the soldiers organized themselves before going to abuse the civilians. They beat my mother. They raped my mother. At night I didn't know but in the morning we organized as a group of fifteen households to find out what had happened. My mother explained that she had been raped. She was raped by one soldier...I did not report the incident." The chairman of the household took the report to the army barracks but there were no repercussions.[34]

Soldiers prey upon women and girls they find traveling outside the camps out of necessity—to collect firewood or water or to sow, tend or harvest crops. In such situations they are risking not only an attack and abduction by the LRA but also rape and physical abuse by the army. In August 2004 case, a sixteen-year-old girl was raped by a soldier while she was in the fields picking millet; her mother had left her alone briefly to go to another garden. The mother took her daughter to the doctor and then complained to the Pabbo police post. The police asked the UPDF to investigate, according to the victim, and the rapist and his commanding officer came to the hut of the girl and her mother in Pabbo camp. The rapist then returned to the hut when the mother was out, kidnapped the victim and made her his third wife. She lived in his hut in another camp for two months with the two other co-wives, became pregnant and returned to her mother after the "husband" mistreated her. At the time of the interview was conducted, the rapist was still in the barracks and had not been punished.

In Jengare camp a married woman with two children was raped when she left the camp. She told *Human Rights Watch*: "It was around 9 pm. I wanted to boil some groundnuts for my son and went to look for some firewood. Out in the bush I ran into one soldier. He got me and took me behind the camp and raped me. He threatened me with the gun. I told him that I didn't want to and he replied that if I refused he would shoot me. I stopped fighting and he raped me."[35] After the rape, he told her to get up and start running without looking back. She fled, hid and slept in the bush. When she did not return that night, her husband reported her missing. She identified the soldier the next day and he was taken to Pabbo barracks; both were tested for the HIV virus. Although the soldier was positive she tested negative. After two days the family took the matter to the police, but no action was taken and the soldier, a private, was been seen moving freely about the barracks.[36] It is extremely difficult for women to find protection from sexual abuse by soldiers.

Among other factors, the impoverishment of displaced persons, has undermined many social values. As one community leader put it, "Soldiers are often the only ones in the camps with money. They can entice young girls, even married women, into sex."[37] Soldiers are often the "richest" people in area because they receive regular income. Parents sometimes complain that soldiers have "defiled" their children, many younger than sixteen. They complain that soldiers have tried to marry girls without the parental consent and sometimes in the face of the parental opposition. Overcrowded camp conditions have contributed to the occurrence of sexual violence and rape, which are reported to occur at a higher rate than when people lived in rural outposts.

Fear of authorities and reluctance to report abuses inflicted by the UPDF on the part of victims is often a function of fear of retaliation. Victims fear beatings, torture and perhaps death, inflicted in the barracks or elsewhere. UPDF officers have suggested that protests against UPDF abuses may be false propaganda designed to "make the government look bad," particularly when the complaints are made to international organizations.[38] Military intelligence suspicions may be raised against those complaining on the grounds that they may be "rebel supporters." The complainant may be detained for military interrogation. The UPDF's practice of detaining suspects for prolonged periods in barracks is not only used against people complaining of army abuses but also against others suspected of rebel activity. It is in the barracks where torture and other forms of ill treatment most often occur.[39] Those held are denied their right to be free from arbitrary arrest and detention under international human rights law.[40]

While the Ugandan army is entitled to capture LRA fighters on the battlefield as a matter of international humanitarian law, the military must turn such persons over to the civilian justice authorities for possible prosecution. Under international law, LRA fighters may be prosecuted by the Ugandan government for taking up arms or for specific criminal acts, although the government has chosen to grant amnesty to most LRA fighters. There is no basis under Ugandan law for the military to detain persons beyond an immediate battlefield situation.

Most of those interviewed by *Human Rights Watch* were held in military detention, often for weeks or months; and were not captured on the battlefield. They rarely had the opportunity to challenge their detention or evidence against them in a court of law. If charged with a capital crime such as treason or terrorism, they usually had to wait the constitutional period of 360 days on remand in prison, while the public prosecutor investigates the case.[41] The remand period starts when the UPDF turns the suspects over to the police and they are brought to the Magistrates' Court. Without however, credit for the time already spent in military detention.

Furthermore, the military does not investigate cases in the manner required by the criminal law. The superintendent of police in Gulu district complained to *Human Rights Watch* that the UPDF would sometimes arrest suspects, usually civilians, and then dump them on the police without obtaining sufficient evidence to allow for a conviction. "The police are not involved in the preliminary investigation in these cases, and as a result we almost always lose them."[42] Most of these cases, however, are never brought to trial.[43]

The Chieftaincy of Military Intelligence (CMI) of the UPDF sometimes intrudes into on-going police investigations. While *Human Rights Watch* was visiting northern Uganda, two men were in the Gulu police station under police investigation for a complaint of assault filed by a local political rival. UPDF agents arrived and removed the men from police custody to the UPDF barracks. They were held several weeks for investigation by CMI, before they were returned to the police and charged with another, earlier crime; a murder not related to combat. *Human Rights Watch* asked to interview them in private while they were in UPDF custody of 4th Brigade headquarters, but was refused a private meeting.[44] According to *Human Rights Watch*, such violations of criminal procedure and civil rights law by the UPDF have not been investigated nor punished. The atrocities committed by Rwandan government forces exemplify the dangers and threats that such compromised auto-immune systems present to African nation-states.

As part of an long overdue process of UN political reform, Africa will receive two new permanent seats in the United Nations Security Council. Not surprisingly, the current five permanent members are unwilling to give Africa veto power along with the seats. The George W. Bush administration considers any reform of the Security Council detrimental to status-quo national interests and pledged to vigorously oppose political reform. Why should the strong share power with the weak? A high-level panel on reforming the United Nations has proposed adding six new permanent members without veto power, including two from Africa, plus three new non-permanent members for a two-year term. The demand for veto power, raised during a summit of African leaders in Nigeria, presented a challenge to the victors of WWII which had unveiled plans to raise the number of seats, but leave veto powers in the hands of the existing five permanent members: the United States, Britain, France, Russia and China. Speaking on behalf of the 53-member African Union, South African President Thabo Mbeki expressed the AU's disappointment with the second-class Security Council membership offered Africa. "The AU is saying you should not have two degrees of permanent members, some with a veto right and others not,'' Thabo Mbeki stated. He said a 15-member committee of African Union foreign ministers would draw up detailed proposals to present to the United Nations before former secretary-general, Kofi Annan was expected to present his report on the reform. AU members were deadlocked over which nations should hold the two new U.N. seats. The candidates were Nigeria, South Africa and Egypt. However, Egypt warily keeps its distance from the African Union, leading some to suspect if got one of the seats, it might seek to appease concerns of Islamic states. Observers at a February summit in Swaziland, said Nigeria and South Africa were the primary contenders for a seat on an expanded Security Council. Prospects for peace and security in Africa would certainly be enhanced with an African voice on the Security Council.

In October 2008, AFRICOM, took effective control of African conflict resolution. the UN-backed five brigade military command is headquartered in Stuttgart, Germany. The five brigades are scheduled for deployment in East, West, North, South and Central Africa. These five professional brigades will be made up of African troops trained by western and African advisors in peacekeeping operations.

---

1. Jared Diamond, *Guns Germs and Steel: The Fates of Human Societies* (New York W.W. Norton, 2005). p. 200.

2. Ibid.

3. Korwa G. Adar, "Beyond Rhetoric: Peacekeeping in the new Millennium" in *Africa at the Crossroads: Between Regionalism and Globalism* Edited by John Mukum Mbaku and Suresh Chandra Saxena. (Praeger Press, Westport Connecticut, 2004) 269-285.

4. A. James, Problems *of internal peacekeeping. Diplomacy and Statecraft* (5 (1) 1994), pp. 21-46.

5. Korwa G. Adar, Op. Cit . 273.

6. Turner, Mark, and Andrew England, 'UN to withdraw Burundi troops by end of year,' *The Financial Times*, April 4, 2006, p.6.

7. Reno, William, Privatizing War in Sierra Leone, *Current History,* Vol. 96. No 610. (1997) p. 230.

8. Andrew England, 'African groups urge support for G8 development plan' *The Financial Times*, July, 13, 2002.

9. *The International Herald Tribune,* 'US Reviews it's training of African Peacekeepers,' October 9, 20.

10. Andrew England, 'Donors to give boost to aid mission in Darfur,' *The Financial Times* May 27, 2005.

11. Andrew England, 'African Peacekeepers battle to win better funding,' *The Financial Times*, May 27, 2005

12. Saxena, Suresh, Chandra "The African Union: Africa's Giant Step Toward Continental Unity' in *Africa at the Crossroads: Between Regionalism and Globalism* Edited by John Mukum Mbaku and Suresh Chandra Saxena. (Westport: Praeger Press, 2004) p. 170.

13. Gittleman, Richard "The Banjul Charter On Human and Peoples Rights: A Legal Analysis" in Claude E. Welch, Jr., and Robert Meltzer, (1984) (eds.), Human Rights and Development in Africa (Albany: State University of New York p. 318.

14. Higgins, Rosalynn "Derogations Under Human Rights Treaties." *British Yearbook of International Law* 48, (1978) 281. Rosalynn Higgins defines the term "clawback" as a clause that permits in normal circumstances, breach of an obligation for a specified number of public reasons. She distinguishes the clawback clause from derogations in a strict sense which allow suspension or breach of certain obligations in circumstances of war or emergency.

15. http://www.hrw.org/reports/uganda09095.htm
16. http://www.hrw.org/reports/uganda09095.htm
17. http://www.hrw.org/reports/uganda09095.htm
18. http://www.hrw.org/reports/uganda09095.htm
19. http://www.hrw.org/reports/uganda09095.htm
20. http://www.hrw.org/reports/uganda09095.htm
21.http://www.hrw.org/reports/uganda09095.htm
22. http://www.hrw.org/reports/uganda09095.htm
23. http://www.hrw.org/reports/uganda09095.htm
24. http://www.hrw.org/reports/uganda09095.htm
25. http://www.hrw.org/reports/uganda09095.htm
26. http://www.hrw.org/reports/uganda09095.htm
27. http://www.hrw.org/reports/uganda09095.htm
28. http://www.hrw.org/reports/uganda09095.htm
29. http://www.hrw.org/reports/uganda09095.htm
30. http://www.hrw.org/reports/uganda09095.htm
31. http://www.hrw.org/reports/uganda09095.htm
32. http://www.hrw.org/reports/uganda09095.htm
33.http://www.hrw.org/reports/uganda09095.htm
34. http://www.hrw.org/reports/uganda09095.htm
35. http://www.hrw.org/reports/uganda09095.htm
36. http://www.hrw.org/reports/uganda09095.htm
37. http://www.hrw.org/reports/uganda09095.htm
38.http://www.hrw.org/reports/uganda09095.htm
39. http://www.hrw.org/reports/uganda09095.htm
40. http://www.hrw.org/reports/uganda09095.htm
41. http://www.hrw.org/reports/uganda09095.htm
42. http://www.hrw.org/reports/uganda09095.htm
43. http://www.hrw.org/reports/uganda09095.htm
44. http://www.hrw.org/reports/uganda09095.htm

23: The Skeletal System: Infrastructure

The infrastructure of the adult human consists of 206 distinct bones. These are: the Spine or vertebral column 26, Cranium 8, Face 14, Hyoid bone, sternum and ribs, 26, upper extremities 64, lower extremities 62. They are divisible into four classes: long, short, flat and irregular. These bones facilitate human physical development. The infrastructure of African states were created to facilitate European leisure and comfort and to export African resources. Facilitating African economic development or providing social services to the Africans were not priorities.

During the colonial era, many Africans migrated to the cities in search of employment opportunities and the other benefits of urban life. Modern sanitation, electricity, piped water, paved road, hospitals and clinics and schools were as unfamiliar at the end of the colonial era as they were at the beginning. Julius Nyerere's Arusha Declaration simply and powerfully expressed one of most profound truths of Africa's colonial experience when it stated: "We have been oppressed a great deal, we have been exploited a great deal, we have been disregarded a great deal." The combination of being oppressed, exploited, and disregarded is illustrated by the pattern of the economic infrastructure of colonial African: notably, their roads and railways. These were geographically distributed according to which particular regions needed to be opened to import-export activities. Where export where not available infrastructure had no place. There were of course exceptions, certain roads and railways were built to move troops and to make conquest and oppression more efficient[1]

All colonial roads and railways led to the sea. They were built to extract huge quantities of cotton, copper, gold or manganese, not to make it easier for one African to visit another. They were constructed with African labor to make business possible for timber companies, trading companies and agricultural concession firms, and for the white settlers, most of whom came from European poverty. With minimal investment of capital, the colonial powers were able mobilize thousands of workers. That capital invested in African infrastructure was derived from the previous robbery of workers and peasants in Europe, Africa and the world at large.

A Pathological Fracture

A trickle of water runs down the polluted contributory to the Nairobi River. The river bank and the river overflow with trash and plastic bags; the water is polluted with human and animal fecal waste. Many families live along the bank of the river in crudely constructed huts. Some live in the heaps of trash. These impoverished people are part of the nation's human infrastructure, but almost peripheral to the Kenyan economy. People sell pirated CD's and videos, telephones and telephone adapters, photographs of the president, photographs of the Pope, postcards, assorted toys, cooked corn, souvenirs, clothing, key chains, belts, watches, magazines, newspapers, women selling flowers and fruit, each struggling to make enough money to survive that day or that year. Most of their products are mass produced in Asia or Eastern Europe. A few years ago, while shopping for traditional Masai patterned cloth, finding fabric woven in Kenya proved quite a quest, because most vendors we approached only sold Masai patterned cloth woven in Eastern Europe.

One of Africa's first and greatest challenges is the development of basic infrastructure. The continent's vast distances and low population density make the provision of roads and rail travel too costly. The Berlin Conference of 1885, which divided sub-Saharan Africa into forty-eight states, many of them land locked, created barriers which continue to inhibit the provision of goods and services because small national markets limit economies of scale, reduce competition, and increased investment risk. In the late 19th century, Cecil Rhodes envisioned a railway from the Cape to Cairo through British controlled territory. The infrastructure built by the colonialists facilitated the extraction of African resources not the connection of colonial states. The result, less than ten percent of Africa's international trade is conducted between African countries.

A pathological fracture is the result of bone disease, cancer or some other horrible type of infection. Such fractures are both debilitating and painful. Africans must often walk around for weeks in pain with broken limbs. Most can only afford to seek treatment when the pain becomes unbearable and many die of their injuries. They are too often the victims of Africa's infrastructure, or lack thereof. In this respect, the absence of roads and their lack of maintenance constitutes a medical problem. Geographical handicaps are compounded by war, misgovernment, corruption and failed aid policies.

Africa trails the rest of the world on almost every dimension of infrastructure development: quantity, quality, cost, and equality of access. The continent's population has tripled since the wars of independence in the

1960s. The cities, which are to house a majority of the next generation of Africans, are struggling to provide basic amenities.

According to a 1999-2000 World Bank report, the infrastructure gap between African and the rest of the world increased during the 1990s. The value of infrastructure for African growth and development is a singularly important. Infrastructure is critical to all modes of modern production. A majority of Africans lack access to education, health care, clean and accessible water and electricity. Consequently, they pay a heavy price for the continent's poor infrastructure in lost opportunities for physical growth, poverty reduction, and access to services that could improve their lives. In fact, the African infrastructure kills. All indicators show that poor infrastructure is a major cause of Africa's low competitiveness, weak market integration, slower growth, poor health, poverty and inequality.

The demand for infrastructure in African is rapidly accelerating in part due to the rapid growth in both urban and rural population and the demands for increased well-being and productivity. A well-functioning infrastructure is a prerequisite for productive investment and economic development. Most African countries lack the fiscal resources to meet the demands and, or arrangements for such investment. Such investment requires government planning and development cooperation from international agencies. Africa must build physical and institutional infrastructure, invest in its human resources and break its dependence on unprocessed exports. International investors, eager to realize quick and large profits margins are inappropriate for long-term objectives, but carefully selected investment can help raise revenue to finance some public efforts.

Public investment in the health infrastructure is urgently needed. Education and the advancement of women are equally critical to ending aid as "welfare." Drastic cuts in African government budgets, such as reductions in free public health services, impose a collective suffering that further debilitates the development of human and social capital, i.e., the foundation of a productive workforce. Africa's poor infrastructure deters foreign investment. The poor quality of telecommunications, public utilities and road network raises the cost of doing business in such areas as manufacturing where there is high growth potential. Many African governments have chosen to decentralize their infrastructures. The result is a "devolution of power" to sub national governments (SNGs) which are given responsibility for determining the level of quality and manner in which those services will be provided. Multilateral and bilateral aid donors have supported these decentralization initiatives throughout the developing world toward the objective of linking gains in service and infrastructure efficiency with promotion of democratic processes and improved governance.

A combination of natural causes, poor planning, growing demand, erratic investment and high petroleum prices causes energy disruptions across the continent. Places accustomed to regular power cuts have been caught up in the wave of so-called "load-shedding". Power cuts have even affected South

Africa. Even oil-producing countries have not been spared. Nigeria the continent's top exporter of crude had to import most of its fuel. "What we are seeing is basically an "energy crisis," says Jamal Saghir, World Bank director for energy and water. Low water levels at hydroelectric plants and delays in getting new generating capacity have aggravated Africa's disadvantages compared with other developing regions. "Not only is Africa lagging behind other regions, but in recent years the access gap has been widening;" he notes. Average electricity access stands at about 25 percent, much less in some rural areas. While Asia and Latin America are moving towards universal access, by contrast 60 percent of sub-Saharan Africans will still lack electricity by 2030.[2]

Part of the Africa's infrastructure decentralization effort involves addressing the allocation and mobilization of public fiscal resources. Total reliance on public ownership and finance of infrastructure creates inefficiencies of management, encourages corruption and places undue fiscal and managerial burdens on the young impoverished states. Public resources are clearly not enough, significant private financing is required to meet the growing demand. In the view of some, Africa is not attracting significant private investment in infrastructure (especially electricity, urban water, and solid waste). However, the resurgence of private infrastructure during the last decade promises spillover benefits for all African countries while cutting costs and improving business services.

In an examination of Private sector Participation in African Infrastructural development (PPI) Wangi and Wilson found that with the proper incentives and regulations, the private sector and other non-state institutions can deliver services that satisfy the socioeconomic objective of public goods, often more efficiently than the state. Their study revealed that privatizing the infrastructure establishes distances between what they provide and short-term political pressures. The spillover benefits of PPI include increased efficiency in investment, management and operations resulting from the commitment to cost-covering tariffs; improved incentives for operational efficiency; competitive discipline and access to management expertise and technology.[3]

Surface Transportation

The joke goes, 'how many people can you fit into a matatu? The answer: One more!' If you've never been to Africa or a non-industrialized country, this picture may be hard to grasp. But try anyway. A matatu (pronounced mu as in mud, ta as in tot, tu as in too) is any vehicle designed to carry a limited load of people or things which exceeds that limit by a multiple of three to four. They are named after the three penny fare they charged in the 1960s.

If you were to take a typical minivan designed for 6-8 passengers in the US and put 18 to 20 people in it. Then, load the top of the van with their belongings, baskets and boxes of clothes, crates of live chickens, a bicycle and maybe someone's new piece of furniture. You are now a Matatu operator. This vehicle is often times nothing more than a 'bucket of bolts' held together with rust. The fenders and body are beaten and misshapen by several accidents. The doors are fitted with a variety of devices serving as handles, often a rope or knobs from other vehicle makes and models. These kinds of vehicles and their larger counterparts, the buses commonly traverse the roads of Kenya, creating what Missionaries, Kay and Michael Johnson describe as "Matatu Hell."

Matatu Hell is a bus station. There is a Matatu Hell in most of the major towns of Africa. Their similarity is ubiquitous, dozens of dilapidated vehicles spewing diesel fumes, racing their motors, incessantly honking their horns and yelling at the passengers to board as they desperately compete for fares. Crowds of people are in these places, carrying their loads on their backs, heads and arms. Men, women, boys and girls climb aboard praying that they will reach their destination alive with all their body parts intact and with their personal property.

Usually, the matatu has not been inspected since it was pressed into service. The brakes are checked only when needed, usually while moving at an uncontrollable speed and slowing down is necessary to avoid running over the policeman waiting for a bribe at the bottom of the hill. This would be considered bad form since policemen are an integral part of Kenya's vast underground economy.

The passengers are arranged in a variety of positions, some sitting, some standing, and some crouching. Many are forced to place their less flattering body parts in the faces of their fellow travelers. The conductor or 'turn-boy' squeezes people into and off the vehicle at each of its frequent stops and collects the fares. The 'turn boy' must also keep an eye out for competing matatu's and prospective passengers while holding on to his own space out of fear of death along the road with its treacherous curves and bumps. Those who cannot fit inside the van must cling to the outside railings or to the vehicles open doors. They get the added benefit of the wind in their faces and the rain over their bodies. This comes at no change of rider fees and if they hit a bump and are lost on the road with a broken limb or an open skull fracture, there is no refund. Over the years, the matatu driver has earned a reputation for his wrecks and recklessness. Of an estimated 3,000 annual road accident deaths in Kenya, over than half are caused by matatu's weaving through traffic, racing along pot-holed highways and running red lights.

Although it is a visually breathtaking trip, many of these passengers have been traveling for several hours, sometimes days, without the benefit of water or other essentials of personal body hygiene. They are tired and hungry peasants who travel this way because there is no alternative. Personal belongings are sometimes shared with strangers who pick their pockets, bags and luggage.

The fatality rates on Kenyan roads are incredible with as many as 12,000 to 13,000 thousand deaths annually, according to a 1999 newsletter published in by Kenyatta National Hospital. These statistics were supported in a

December, 1999 article published in the *East and Central Africa Journal of Surgery*. The article reported mortality and morbidity rates from road traffic accidents that were incomparable to such nations as Britain, Canada, Japan, and Nigeria. In Britain, for instance, there were 6 deaths and 311 injuries for every 10,000 vehicles on the road. In Kenya, there were 55 deaths and 500 injuries for every 10,000 vehicles and Nigeria 125 deaths and 1,750 injuries for every 10,000 vehicles. During the month of April of 2000, there were two major bus accidents in Kenya which death toll killed more than 140 people, not counting those who survived and had to be admitted to hospitals or later died from their injuries.

On the desolate roads of Kenya, there are no service stations, only the overworked driver with the drugged like buzz and his often inebriated assistant. They may or may not have a spare tire and it may or may not have air or treads. A breakdown on the road subjects the passengers to winds of fate. Murderers, robbers, rapists and thieves work the roads. People allow themselves to be degraded to a state lower than animals and to gamble their very lives and limbs, hoping they will arrive at a given destination at some point in time. On this journey, there are no accommodations, there may be no food, there are no restrooms with functioning toilets. The only things that separates Matatu Hell from the Old Testament Hell is that you pay for this experience in Kenya shillings and people pray harder to get out of Matatu Hell.

All over Africa the collapse of the infrastructure has given rise to such uncontrolled transportation alternatives. Former president, Daniel Arap Moi, attempted to introduce safety controls but failed due to corruption. The matatu business is estimated to be worth hundreds of millions of dollars each year. No African government has succeeded in arresting this economic energy. However, in 2004 transport minister John Michuki confronted the cartel of thugs that control a fleet of 40,000 battered matatu's. New regulations brought threats of strikes and violence.

Today Kenyan matatu's have seat belts and carry no more than 14 people. The government regulated matatu's to travel no faster than 80 kilometers per hour. Journalist, William Wallis observed that the matatu culture, which is associated with Nairobi's urban unrelenting blend of Swahili and lyrically violent African-American hip-hop, has given way to a less menacing Swahili hip hop. Prior to governmental regulation, local criminals' extorted money from the drivers at each stop in return for cramming in more passengers. When matatu's doubled their fares to recover the cost of the new regulations, they forced thousands of people to walk to work and many more to choose between transportation and a meal. After dozens were arrested under the new regulations, such banditry began to decrease. Matatu drivers now earn more and are encouraged to pay taxes.

Rail Travel

In most of Africa, railways are non-existent or in great disrepair. The Chinese have recently engaged in rebuilding and restoring rail line in many sub-Saharan countries. In South Africa, the trip from Soweto to Johannesburg can take as long as two hours and usually involves changing taxis. Transport costs constitute a hidden tax on poor South Africans who have longer commutes and pay a larger share of their salaries for transportation than do the minority whites. Traffic on the crowded Ben Schoeman highway has risen 7 percent per year. As a partial solution, construction began on a massive and ambitious public transport project, called the *Gautrain*, a high-speed European-style rail link. Built with the help of the company that runs commuter train in Paris, the *Gautrain* will travel between Johannesburg and Pretoria in just over half an hour. A network of color-coded buses will shuttle commuters from a 10 kilometer radius to each of the *Gautrain* stations. The first segment of the two phase development, linking Sandton to Pretoria, will be ready to take passengers to the football world cup. "We intend to cut the ribbon in June 2010," said project lead engineer Jack Van der Merwe. He is confident the 18 Rand one-way fare is cheap enough to lure commuters out of cars, but not cheap enough to draw people out of existing public transport. The project came under attack from COSATU, the union federation that governs in alliance with the African National Congress for targeting a small minority of affluent passengers, while failing to tackle larger transportation problems. Van der Merwe denied such claims saying: "Stand by the road at Ben Schoeman and see who is going by. They range from the lower middle-class and there are lots of people of color."[4]

Table 23.1 Percentage of Paved Roads in African Countries

Angola	10.4
Ethiopia	12.0
Gabon	9.9
Kenya	12.1
Senegal	29.3
South Africa	20.3

Source: World Bank Economic Indicators

Air Travel

Air travel to and within Africa is largely determined by demand; and demand is determined by access to African resources including Africa's wildlife. In

1953 Nairobi, several thousand Mau Mau suspects labored under armed guards on a million ton excavation project, filling in craters, laying a half million tons of stone using nothing but shovels, stone hammers and their bare hands. The construction of Embakasi's airport was financed with US loans. Embakasi airport initially covered seven square miles and had four runways and was described as "the world's first hand-made international airport."

Each year 130,000 passengers fly to Lagos from the New York area, and another 80,000 fly to Ghana. There are very few non-stop flights between the United States and Africa and most are operated by non-US carriers. Despite the high-margin of traffic created by rising oil and gas production in West Africa and trade boosting initiatives such as the US-African Growth and Opportunity Act (AGOA); West Africa remains one of the most underserved and the most dangerous air traffic regions in the world. West African petroleum reserves have raised the regions status as a promising source for the US consumers, resulting in a boost in regional business air travel. The end of the civil wars in Liberia and Sierra Leone accelerated travel to the region. Now, PPI development promises to bring efficient, affordable intra-state air travel to the continent. Air travel from West Africa to Europe has long been relatively easy. As air hubs to the rest of the world, the European metropoles benefit immensely from travel to the neocolonial infrastructure by en-route passenger spending and taxes. However, at Lagos's airport, passenger jets once flown by the bankrupt national airline, *Nigerian Airways* sit rusting in their hangers a testament to the failure to revive the West African airline infrastructure.

The liquidation of *Nigerian Airways* in 2003 mirrored the decline of other regional state sponsored carriers. Airline operators say that West Africa remains underserved given the escalating demand. In August 2002, the Ministry of Aviation agreed to sell 49 percent of the troubled state-owned airline without consulting the agency in charge of the nation's privatization program. This dealt a blow to President Obasanjo's attempts to portray Nigeria as a transparent, investor-friendly environment in which to do business. Idris Ibrahim Kuta, chairman of the senate subcommittee on aviation called for an investigation into aviation minister Kema Chikwe's decision to bypass the Parliament and the Bureau of Public Enterprises. "It was a surprise;" said remarked Senator Kuta. "When you are privatizing or doing whatever the minister is doing we believe opportunities should be open to other companies to submit their proposals...The Ministry should have given us a lead on what they intended to do. We don't know yet if it's a good deal or not-that's what we want the minister to come and tell us." The agreement included a plan to transfer the assets of *Nigerian Airways* to a separate company called *Air Nigeria*.

Airwing Aerospace, a British company specializing in aircraft sales would own 49 per cent of *Air Nigeria*, provide aircraft and manage the joint venture for five years. The UK-based company which is described on its website as experienced in buying and selling aircraft with an ability to "satisfy the most unusual of requirements for even the most obscure parts of the world;" ignored media inquiries into the deal. Officials at the Bureau of Public Enterprises became concerned that the agreement would undermine its attempts to transparently sell assets such as the auction of the Abuja *Hilton* and other prestigious real estate. The aviation ministry said Ms. Chikwe signed the agreement only after receiving the approval of President Obasanjo, whose office also declined to comment. This level of corruption usually involves foreign parties seeking market advantage or control. "She did not unilaterally sign the agreement;" an aviation ministry official said. "Everything she has done is for the benefit of the country." Another sweeping probe into industry corruption was announced.

West African air travel safety was dealt a blow when a *Bellview* plane crashed about 20 miles north of Lagos en route Abuja. The aircraft sent a distress signal shortly after take off during a heavy storm. Nigerian Red Cross officials investigated the crash site only to find a destroyed aircraft with no survivors. Nigerian authorities confirmed the presence of government and ECOWAS officials were aboard the crashed airliner. *Bellview* built a reputation for safety and reliability gradually becoming the preferred carrier for diplomats and businessmen in the region. The company operates routes within Nigeria and pioneered the connection of many West African countries.

Air travel has increased over the past few years due to carriers such as *Bellview* and *Virgin Niagara*.[6] The result is an emerging patchwork of intra-regional networks that has provided an incentive for long-haul carriers to increase service to West African hubs and take advantage of the market. Many African companies seek cooperative agreements with more established long-haul carriers, but the success of these ventures depends largely on the implementation of safety regulations. In all of West Africa there exists not one single hanger suitable to perform the most stringent international safety and industry servicing requirements, so airlines must fly their aircraft to Europe for such diagnostics. Roland Iyayi, director of Nigeria's airspace management agency said that the two 2005 plane crashes which killed more than 220, people highlighted the "systemic failures" in Nigerian aviation.[7]

Nigerian civil industry experts say urgent aviation reforms commissioned by the government in the wake of recent airline crashes are not likely to succeed without airline industry transparency. The government grounded several airlines for inspection, began recertifying national aviation staff and requested the assistance of international crash experts and regulatory agencies. President Obasanjo fired several senior aviation officials after the crashes were blamed on corruption stating; "The greatest bane of the aircraft industry is corruption. Corruption leads to death and we're not having any more of it. There's a lot of corner cutting, at the expense of precious lives of Nigerians." However, the government appeared unwilling to prosecute senior government officials indicted by a judicial committee set up by the president to investigate the events that led to the failure of *Nigerian Airways*. Obasanjo committed $150 million to upgrade the safety equipment and standards of the country's four main airports. In an effort to consolidate the industry, the Nigerian aviation ministry proposed new legislation increasing the minimum capital base of airlines between 25 and 100 percent to just under $4 million for local airlines and $15 million for international carriers.

The death of 10 Nigerian generals in a September 2006, *Dornier 228* crash, prompted Obasanjo to return from an IMF meeting in Singapore and call for an investigation into what he described as a "monumental national tragedy". The eight dead major generals, and two brigadier generals included three of four future army chiefs said a senior military analyst. The loss came at a challenging time for the armed forces which was reorganizing its taskforce in the Niger Delta.[8] The following month an aircraft carrying 105 passengers crashed shortly after taking off from Abuja. Among the victims was the Sultan of Sokoto, Mohammed Maccido, whose death sent a shockwave through the Islamic community. The influential Sultan was expected to play a role in the endorsement and selection of a Muslim presidential candidate for the 2007 elections. These crashes also hurt Nigerian efforts to persuade international aviation agencies that it had done enough to warrant a clean bill of health in its aviation sector. That November, the airline industry was scheduled to be audited by the International Civil Aviation Organization (ICAO).[9]

These patchwork efforts were criticized by Captain Dung Pam, chairman of the Nigerian Aviation Safety Initiative (NASI), who said; "some of the policies are chasing shadows, are myopic and not thought through." The grounding of aircraft could not have led to rigorous safety checks given the quality of repair facilities and staff on the ground. Other critics said that half-baked government policy-making persists because of a lack of accountability in decision making and because politics and policy are often mixed.[10] In 2004, the government revoked the license of *Slok Air*, a local airline owned by a state governor who was too vocal in his dislike for Obasanjo. Moreover, the government failed to make public the findings of a report on a 2002 airline crash which killed more than 150 people. Military air crashes are common in Nigeria. A crash in 1992 killed over 160 military personnel.[11]

There is other evidence that West Africa has awakened to the economic potential of intra-regional air travel. In June 2005, Richard Branson launched *Virgin Nigeria*, a joint venture with 51 per cent held by Nigerian institutional investors and 49 percent by Branson's *Virgin Atlantic*. In December 2005, the *Virgin Atlantic* began offering low cost flights on the lucrative Lagos to London route. From Nigeria, the airline plans to open several new routes within Africa and other international destinations. Anticipating intensified regional competition from *Virgin Nigeria*, and other well capitalized airlines have improved their services, gradually filling the vacuum left by the collapse of debt-ridden carriers such as *Air-Afrique*, which was once sponsored by 11 Francophone states to provide air travel to the region. Airlines such as *AeroContractors*, a Dutch owned carrier that enjoys a reputation for punctuality and safety has operated in Nigeria for 45 years, and *Bellview*, which is registered between Sierra Leone and Nigeria, are on the cutting edge of providing regional routes and travel to their destinations. *British Airways* initiated a loose arrangement with *AeroContractors*. Through code-sharing agreements, PPI partnerships are likely to raise regional safety standards, which are critical to establishing confidence in air travel in a region which suffers disproportionate air disasters.[12]

The mélange of flight networks emerging in West Africa is another reason why international airlines from Europe to the Middle East are increasing their frequencies to regional hubs such as Lagos. Their strategy is to siphon off some of the increased passenger traffic on the long haul routes to other continents. Critical to the sustainability of the increased demand for West African air travel is the ability of African governments to regulate the industry. Solomon Quaynor, of the International Finance Corporation (IFC), the private finance arm of the World Bank, admitted that an agreement signed in 1999 to facilitate more air travel between African countries, has a basic flaw. "The framework for the agreement gives governments the right to designate flights. If governments want to frustrate, they will not designate. What is needed is a move to a regional regulatory institution to remove states exercising vested interests through their national carriers;" said Quaynor. A regional regulatory institutional network would help other African airlines follow successful precedents such as *Air Senegal International*, a joint venture between Senegal's national carrier and *Air Maroc*. The airline feeds its passengers to *South African Airways* for onward travel from Senegal to the United States. Revenues of *Air Senegal International* increased from $18 million between 2001 and 2003 to more than $100 million in 2005, according to Nick Fadugba of the consultant group *African Aviation Services*, who noted that this reflects an opportunity to capitalize on burgeoning passenger demand.

Realizing the potential profitability of traffic from the West African market, *Ethiopian Airlines* and *Kenyan Airways* offered services between West African cities, Addis Ababa and Nairobi. *Ethiopian Airlines* is considering starting a private Ghanaian carrier in conjunction with a US investor, to replace the bankrupt *Ghana Airways*. Increased direct air traffic between the US and West Africa is on the horizon. A dispute between US and UK authorities over airspace for British and American carriers delayed *Virgin Nigeria's* plans to fly directly to the US. The Nigerian government countered by stalling plans for US carrier, *Continental Airlines*, to fly into Nigeria. *Virgin Nigeria* officials said that US authorities were slowly accepting the idea that it is an African airline and should be exempt from trade disputes between the UK and the US. Increased African business access to intra-African markets is a precondition to African economic growth and economic interdependence. It is another small step in Africa's economic integration and participation in the global economy.

Africa-US travel is growing much faster than US travel to Asia according to Glen Hauenstein, the executive vice-president in charge of network development for *Delta Air Lines*, which planned to start service from Atlanta to Johannesburg *via* Dakar, Senegal. This would make *Delta* the first US carrier to serve Africa since the demise of *Pan-Am* and *TWA* over a decade ago. According to Robert Binns, chief marketing officer of *World Airways*, the largest commercial operator for the US military, "West Africa is the most underserved." *World Airways* acquired *North American Airlines* when it discovered commercial opportunities in Africa. The airline started scheduling flights to Accra, Ghana in 2005. Binns says the reluctance of US carriers to serve the market reflects perceptions that Africa is a more difficult, high-risk operating environment, but one which his carrier, which flies to Iraq and Afghanistan, is well equipped to do. "It's not just Houston," says Hauenstein, referring to the traffic generated by the petroleum business. "It's the United Nations, aid relief, visiting friends and relatives and Africa is the next frontier of tourism, US airlines have lost their imagination."[13]

The Ports

Known to tourists as the gateway to Kenya's most popular beach resorts, Mombasa has been a trading center since the 12th century. Today, Kenya's Port of Mombasa is besieged by persistent delays and congestion. Cargo logjams deprive East African industry of raw materials and delay exports. The transport links to Mombasa, Nairobi and beyond are a long-running source of misery and despair. The roads are dilapidated and too dangerous to travel at night. Rail transport is incredibly slow and there are too few wagons to meet rail transport demand. Overwhelming paperwork and administrivia exacerbate the slow down because there are multiple organizations within and affiliated with the Kenyan Port Authority, including the Bureau of Standards, and Kenya Plant Health Inspectorate Services. But there is no centralized authority. To some, the largest impediment to improving East Africa's ports is politics. Self-aggrandizing political infighting between ministries and ministers and jostling for comparative advantage between competing industry groups slows progress.

The Port of Mombasa is a critical component of Kenya's infrastructure and thereby its economic system. Mombasa is Kenya's lifeline to the world; exporting tea and coffee and importing food, steel, sugar, paper and other goods. The intense activity on the docks is an indicator of Kenya's strong 6.1 percent economic growth. There are so many stoppages that shipments remain in port for ten days. The port therefore can be an economic depressant if it is not able to keep up with demand. To compete with rival ports in Dar es Salaam, and Maputo, Kenya began investing in cranes, forklifts, terminal tractors, a control tower and process automation systems. Mombasa is also vital to Kenya's neighbors, most notably to landlocked, Uganda. Seventy-two percent of Ugandan exports pass through Mombasa. Transit cargo makes up just 27 percent of the total tonnage passing through Mombasa, but that will rise if the port keeps pace with regional economic growth. The port of

Mombassa remains a state enterprise. There are plans for an extra berth and eventually a new terminal and Kenyan Port Authority plans to drain a main channel to attract larger vessels. Richard Bridges, a transport consultant who advised Mombasa on container shipping in the 1980's, and who is critical of Kenyan ministers observed: "When you look around the world, where you see port concessions have come in, there has been a significant improvement in performance. For some reason, they're not convinced." [14]

Telecommunications: Crossing the Digital Divide

During the colonial era, in order to make a telephone call from Accra in the British colony of the Gold Coast, to Abidjan in the neighboring French colony of the Cote d'Ivoire; it was necessary to be connected first with an operator in London, then with an operator in Paris, who would could provide a line to Abidjan. In Kenya, electricity is unreliable, particularly in rural areas where less than 3 percent of all homes have telephones. However, at Mbita Point primary school on Lake Victoria, in a pilot study to see whether they could replace textbooks in the impoverished world, pupils use handheld computers known as E-slates. In 2004, a class of 53 students tested the computers which use satellite technology and wireless communications to transmit digital textbooks to handheld computers in the classroom. According to Matthew Herren, co-founder of *EduVision*, the NGO responsible for the project: "The students around here come from fishing and farming families, but they jumped at the chance to use these E-Slates. Kids are sharp, and in a day they mastered them." This one of the latest examples of technology leapfrogging in Africa, where dial up internet connections are slow, unreliable and prohibitively expensive to all but a few in areas accessible via mobile telephone. "Our satellite and radio system covers the whole of Africa-there are no blackspots. If you want to convince to use this system it really has to work in all schools. Once the network is set up it costs the same to do one school or the whole of Africa-and that's about $24,000 to send out a years textbooks;" says Herren.

The E-Slates use a Linux-based operating system distributed freely by Debian, not-for-profit community of programmers in conjunction with a content reader based on *Mozilla's* Gecko engine. Textbooks are converted into digital files and sent via an internet connection to the *WorldSpace* radio satellite, which bounces the signal across the whole of Africa. A base station at the school which is nothing more than an antenna, hard disc and a wireless connection, collects and stores the data. When the students turn on their E-Slates each morning the base station automatically sends updates. At present, E-Slates cost about $300, but the objective is to reduce the price to $100, the annual cost of textbooks.

At the Kenyan Agricultural Commodity Exchange, which provides farmers with market information, planters receive the latest market prices via text messages. The country's largest mobile telephone network *Safaricom* participates in a job advertising service that sends job advertisements to the subscriber's handsets. Similarly, those without bank accounts can establish them by using their mobile phones to make deposits.

Calestous Juma, professor of the practice of international development at Harvard's Kennedy School of Government, observes that rural Africa is ripe for the adoption this kind of technology. "We are finding it easier to do that in areas where you do not have prior commitment to older technologies;" he explained. "Such projects could go straight to the emerging technologies sector, but such change may be difficult in areas where there are more vested interests." *EduVision* believes the system can be tailored for health workers, civil servants and farmers and negotiated with Kenya Technical Teachers College to adapt it for its teacher training program.

The African entrepreneurial spirit is indefatigable. *GSM* services arrived in Africa in the late 1990s. The streets of urban Africa are now filled with "umbrella people" selling air time by the minute from makeshift phone booths fashioned of plastic chairs, tables, umbrellas and a mobile hand set. They represent the revolution in African telecommunications. Mobile telephony has radically transformed the way many Africans live their lives. Mobile phones are an essential tool for farmers, taxi drivers, mechanics, prostitutes, politicians, newspaper vendors and merchants of used items. In Cameroon, municipal authorities in Yaoundé and Douala are trying to stop the proliferation of these improvised phone kiosks. In Nigeria, selling phone card minutes is a favored occupation of school drop-outs. Tuberculosis sufferers receive text messages reminding them to take their medication. As in the west, small businesses compete with cell phone numbers emblazoned on billboards. Cell phones reached Africa's rural populations before land lines, electricity grids and drinkable water. The network stretches from Liberia to Somalia and the Democratic Republic of Congo.

According to the Geneva-based International Telecommunications Union (ITU), since 1998 mobile telephony has grown faster in Africa than in any other region of the world at an average of 78 percent. Because it started from nothing, the telephony penetration rate in Africa remains lower than any other region. Only 4.5 percent of the African population used mobile phones in 2002 compared with 30 % in the America's and more than 50% in Europe. The impact of mobile phone services has been so dynamic because there were so few land lines in Africa to begin with. Their instant popularity reflects the frustration with inefficient public monopolies. Africa now adds about 11 million new mobile phone subscribers each year. Land line installation has doubled in an effort to keep up, but there are now twice as many mobile than land-line or fixed telephone connections. In 17 African countries more consumers use mobile phones than land line networks. These include some of Africa's strongest economies: Uganda, Cote d'Ivoire, Morocco, South Africa, Botswana and Tanzania. Only three countries, the Democratic Republic of Congo, Uganda and Ghana, have more than one fixed-line supplier. Many African countries have three or more mobile operators. People in Kinshasa and Brazzaville, who are divided by the Congo River, can now speak directly without their calls being relayed through Europe. Market experts predict the number of mobile users across the continent will grow to over 90 million within five years.

Ninety percent African cellular phone users are pre-paid cash customers, because pre-payment is the only option requiring no credit history or permanent address. The cash and call business is also less risky for the "umbrella people." An opaque trade has developed in the sale second-hand mobile handsets. Much of the business is pre-paid, "bundled" packages offering discounted or free handsets. Asian manufacturers such as *Nokia*, even offer a scaled-down model for the African market.

The growing African telecommunications industry is driven by African-led multinational corporations. *Orascom*, an Egyptian corporation, once operated in 17 northern Africa countries. In 2000, *Orascom* purchased and subsequently resold, *Telecel*, a pan-African telecommunications group based in the Congo. *MSI Cellular,* a company registered in the Netherlands and is headed Sudanese-born, Mohamed Ibrahim. The company is better known in a dozen African countries as *Celtel.* In Zimbabwe, *Econet,* the creation of entrepreneur Strive Masiyiwa, is the only technology company traded on the Harare Stock Exchange. *Econet* has interests in Kenya and a *GSM* mobile service in New Zealand. In southern Africa mobile groups such as *Vodacom* and *Telkom* are ascendant. *Vodacom* is a minority partner in the partially state-owned *Telkom* group. Their rival for new African markets, *MTN*, spent $600 million looking for markets outside the continent. "There are still a number of attractive African countries;" said *MTN*s' chief executive, Phuthuma Nhleko. *MTN* reported that after two or three years in operation its existing foreign businesses were all profitable.

Investor's ignored *MTN* when it spent $258 million on a Nigerian license in 2001. But Nigeria was a prime market for growth. Frequent complaints about high costs and poor service provoked a one-day consumer boycott in October 2003. The accelerated demand for service surprisingly outstripped *MTN*s' production capability. In two years, Nigeria's *GSM* phone market grew from zero to 2 million, four times the total number of land lines installed since 1975.[15] Mobile phones network are more reliable than the antiquated land line networks which have only one connected line for every 250 Nigerians. "We found the market somewhat deeper than we anticipated;" Nhleko stated. Between February and May of 2003 the company took "a short break" and suspended sales of prepaid starter packs in Nigeria while erecting more antenna based stations and switching centers to handle the traffic.

The growth of Africa's telecommunication's industry is linked to developments in other sectors of the infrastructure such as transportation, shipping, rails, roads and airports. "We're always amazed at the pace at which things have progressed;" said Guy Zibi, an expert at Boston-based

Pyramid Research, who speculates that market penetration in Africa will hit a limit of $8-10 million. Beyond that he predicts new clients will not spend enough to make the business profitable. Call costs now consume a large part of household budgets. There is anecdotal evidence of a cutback on items such as soft drinks to pay phone bills. Despite the gloomy market forecast, competition in the region is growing more fierce.

In June 2007, the International Finance Corporation unveiled a $320 million package to finance expanded mobile telephone networks in sub-Saharan Africa, The IFC will loan the money to five subsidiaries of *Celtel*. Ibrahim sold *Celtel* to the Kuwaiti Group *MTC* for $3.4 billion According to Mohsen Khalil, director of the World Bank's global information and communications technologies department; "Africa is now the fastest growing cellular market, leading the world with truly innovative service offerings such as *Celtel's* borderless free roaming across six countries."[16]

Internet Access

Approximately two out of every three people in the US have direct access to a computer. In sub-Saharan Africa, fewer than two in every 100 have such access.[17] In 1996, 11 of Africa's 54 countries had internet access. By January 2000, all African capital cities, a total of 25,000 computers; were permanently connected to the World Wide Web. With a population of 750 million people, Africa has about as many internet-connected computers as Latvia, which has a population of 2 million. The Economic Commission for Africa (ECA), estimates the number of African internet users at between 1.5 and 2 million people. Most are South Africans, leaving only about 500,000 among the remaining 750 million on the continent. African Internet Service Providers (ISPs) showed that in 2000 Africa had 500,000 subscribers. Each computer with an internet or e-mail connection supports an average of three users.[18]

In 2000 there were over 26 countries with 1,000 or more dial up subscribers, but only 9 countries with 5,000 or more (Egypt, Morocco, Kenya, Ghana, Mozambique, South Africa, Tunisia, Uganda and Zimbabwe). The average cost of using a local dial-up internet account for five hours a month in an African country is about $60 (usage fees and telephone time included, but not telephone line rental). Contrast this to the United States, where, according to the Organization for Economic Cooperation and Development (OECD), twenty hours of internet access costs $29 a month, including telephone charges. Moreover, ISP charges in Africa range from $10 and $100 a month, largely reflecting the level of market maturity, the varying tariff policies of the different public telecommunications operators (PTOs) and the different national policies on access to international telecommunications bandwidth. In some countries, the PTOs provide local call internet access facilities for ISPs across the entire country by establishing a special area code for internet access that is charged as a local call. Almost all the PC equipment uses *Intel* or *Intel* compatible processors (the exception is the publishing industry which uses *Apple Macintosh PCs*). Poor maintenance and insufficient system diagnostic skills, leave many machines that could easily be reactivated out of commission. Underutilization of existing computer resources is common therefore the preponderance of stand alone PCs in the same office, remain unconnected to Local Area Networks (LANs). Often, an office will have many machines, but only one with a modem connecting to the Internet. This usually means there is much competition for the machine and a shared e-mail account. [19]

A survey conducted by the ECA found the greatest number of users belonged to nongovernmental organizations, private companies and universities. Most users were male: 86 percent in Ethiopia, 83 percent in Senegal, and 64 percent in Zambia. The majority of users were well educated: 89 percent in Zambia and 98 percent in Ethiopia had college degrees. Universities were initially on the cutting edge of internet development in Africa. In 1999, only 20 counties had universities with full internet connectivity.[20]

A new scramble for Africa is under way as multinationals from all over the world take interest in acquiring telecommunications companies on the continent. The political climate for fresh deals has improved for a number of companies seeking to shape new regional and international economic strategies. A rapid succession of deals and announcements of acquisition strategies means that even if only half of what is announced happens, the landscape of the African communications sector will be very different within the next several years.

The largest global player with an interest in Africa is *Vodafone*. Under an agreement, it only operated as *Vodafone* above the Sub-Sahara; leaving its minority partner *Vodacom* a free hand across the territory in the south. In late 2005, in a deal worth $2.4 billion *Vodafone* increased its stake in *Vodacom* from 35% to 50%. However, getting complete market control is not easy because *Telkom South Africa* has the remaining half of the shares. *Vodacom's* relationship with *Telkom South Africa* is troubled. Originally both bid for the Nigerian incumbent *Nitel* but *Vodacom* dropped out of the deal. *Vodafone* then failed it its attempt to buy control of the larger of Kenya's two mobile operators, *Safaricom*. It was unable to agree a price for the shares with the Kenyan Government. The latter needed the money to fund a redundancy (compensation) package at the incumbent *Telkom Kenya*.

The other large multinational with an interest in the Africa is *France Telecom* and its mobile subsidiary *Orange*. *France Telecom* is the preferred buyer for incumbent telecoms in francophone Africa, acquiring majority or controlling interests in Senegal's (*Sonatel)*, Mali's (the *SNO Ikatel*), Cote d'Ivoire's (Cote d'Ivoire Telecom) and Mauritius' (*Mauritius Telecom*). However, *France Telecom* lost out in Niger to a consortium that combined Libyan money with the state-owned Chinese equipment manufacturer *ZTE*. Through its *Orange* subsidiary, *ZTE* has operations in Botswana, Cote d'Ivoire, Cameroon and Madagascar. It wanted *Sonatel's* mobile operation (currently branded *Alize*) to take on the *Orange* brand (and pay for the privilege), but this was fiercely resisted by *Sonatel's* own workforce and the plan was dropped. One of the big issues for *France Telecom* is language. It has only really managed to venture out of the francophone area in one country (Botswana) and in two other countries where it has a presence; French is as widely used as English. Unfortunately for French businesses like *France Telecom,* Jacques Chirac took a dim view of facilitating English speakers. They will need them if they are to become global businesses outside of their former colonial possessions.

The other French player is *Vivendi*; a dot.com created conglomerate that describes itself as a leader in media and telecommunications with activities in music, interactive games, television, film and fixed and mobile telecommunications. It claims to be a major player in each of these sectors but has only two operations: a 56% interest in France's number two mobile operators, *SFR* and a 51% stake in *Maroc Telecom*, Morocco's former provider.

Among of recent investors are the Gulf-based, *ArabTelecoms* and *MTC Kuwait,* which acquired *Celtel* for US$ 3.4 billion and announced plans to spend a further US $1 billion plus to gain control of the contested *V-Mobile* in Nigeria. In December 2004, *Celtel* added to its 13 existing country operations by buying a controlling share in Madagascar's *Madacom* from the *Distacom Group*. On a buying spree, it set its sight on acquiring a third mobile operator's license in Egypt. The other Arab company that has entered the ring is the UAE's *Etisalat*. In April 2005, it bought *Atlantique Telecom* and acquired mobile operations in six countries: Benin, Burkina-Faso, Cote d'Ivoire, Gabon, Niger and Togo. The local owner of the Ivorian operation had pre-emption rights. *Etisalat* is behind the new Sudanese *SNO Canartel* in which it has taken a 40% stake. Finally the Dubai-based company *SNO Telecom* won the bidding for a 35% stake in *Tunisie Telecom* in a US $2.27 billion deal. It was to be expected that Arab companies would seek to expand their markets to North Africa but the wide range of purchases made shows they too are seriously interested in making money in sub-Saharan Africa.

Investment in infrastructure involves a major risk because the investment is often large and the cost is only slowly. Two factors are dissuasive: (1) the investments are tied up; the assets cannot be used elsewhere except at great cost; and (2) the infrastructure projects often provide services that are considered essential and provided by monopolies. As a result, essential services become highly politicized making the investors vulnerable to opportunistic government action. Governments may promise to treat foreign investors fairly, but once the investment is made, governments have an incentive to renege on their promises. Governments may satisfy political demands by reducing prices which in turn reduce the investor's profit margin. African leadership reaction to these political-economic pressures largely determine investor incentives.

The London-based *Control Risk Group* (CRG), is an international business risk consulting firm that provides assessments of countries and regions for political and security risks. *CRG* investigates fraud, conducts detailed due-diligence studies, traces and recovers misappropriated assets and provides litigation support. *CRG* identifies four main risks for investors in Africa: 1) contract frustrations and government corruption; 2) conflict and instability from regional and ethnic tensions; 3) poorly managed economic programs and; 4) risks to assets and personnel posed by crime. *CRG* analysts' project relatively optimistic prospects for investment in Africa, forecasting continued gradual political and economic reforms accompanied by periods of instability and renewed conflict. The countries to monitor are Liberia, the Central African Republic, Chad, Kenya, Zimbabwe, Guinea-Conakry and Equatorial Guinea. Mozambique, Tanzania and Zambia are singled out as examples of low-risk opportunities.[21]

In an attempt to increase European visibility and credibility in Africa, the EU recently announced the creation of a fund for infrastructure projects in Africa. The €60 million in EU grants and up to €260 million in European Investment Bank (EIB) loans would challenge the World Bank's hegemony over high-profile projects. The money would be used to develop water, electricity, communications and transportation projects. The announcement came one day after the EIB was criticized in a report commissioned by the European parliament for its African projects. The report attacked the EIB for inadequate supervision of projects, accused it of lack of transparency and failure to meet EU standards on poverty reduction, social sustainability and the environment. Luisa Morgantini, chair of the European parliament's development committee said: "The global credibility of the EU is at stake if the EIB, the largest public bank in the world, undermines key European development goals and strategies on lending operations to Africa."

EU officials urged the EIB's critics to "give the bank a chance" to show the EIB could play a more important role in Africa's development.[22] However, the primary advantage of the new fund was that it would allow the EIB to become a competitive lender by tapping into EU subsidized loans, thereby circumventing its own restrictions. The EIB normally grants 20 year loans at an interest rate of 4 percent in order to cover its costs. It would be able to use the fund to lower that lending rate in Africa to as low as 2 percent. EU development commissioner, Louis Michel, denied any direct competition between leading institutions in Africa; but admitted the fund was important as a means of boosting the European corporate presence in African aid projects at a time when companies from countries such as China were rapidly increasing their presence in the region. "This is clearly beneficial for the Africans but it also represents an economic challenge for the Europeans. I have no reason to hide that;" Michel observed.

Africa's infrastructure deficit gained priority status in the development planning of the World Bank. According to John Page, the chief Africa economist of the World Bank, during the 1990s, the institution held to the belief that the private sector could be counted on to fill the infrastructure gap. By the time they realized that private enterprise would not meet the requirements in key sectors, Africa had fallen further behind. According to the World Bank, infrastructures' share of development assistance by rich countries shrank from 30 percent in 1973 to 10 percent in 2003. However, the World Bank is not blameless for Africa's weak skeletal system. A poignant example is water, which the World Bank pushed many municipal governments to privatize. But the public benefits of water supply were not factored into the World Bank designed South African national infrastructural policy. In August 2000, South Africa suffered an outbreak of cholera that led to many deaths, tens of thousands of infections, and cost tens of millions in Rand. Poor people were unable to pay full cost-recovery for water systems that either broke down or suffered cut-offs by municipal officials. At the same time, the World Bank circulated a document entitled *Sourcebook on Community Driven Development in the African Region*, which warned other World Bank staff that; "work is still needed with political leaders in some national governments to move away from the concept of free water for all."[23]

Behind the "big push" in infrastructure investment is the hope that it will help kick-start the kind of growth poor African countries need to become self-reliant. Over $500 billion has been granted in aid to post-colonial Africa, but the development benefits are negligible. At best this aid has treated symptoms of underdevelopment not the underlying malady. Health and education programs remain priorities, but the greatest improvement to health would be if people could drink clean water and get to clinics. The cost of doing business in Africa is twice as high as in East Asia and 30 percent higher than any other region. For Africa's 16 land-locked nations, transportation costs are on average 50 percent higher than for coastal countries. Poor planning and poor maintenance make matters worse. Africa's infrastructure was designed to enrich Europe while exploiting Africa's human and natural resources. Road, rails and harbors were constructed to extract and export the continents wealth, not to stimulate trade and communications between Africans. The impact of such development on Africa's infrastructure is a crippling pathological fracture.

Table 23.2 Investment Security Risk in Africa

Security Risk	Exemplary Countries
Insignificant:	Botswana, Burkina-Faso, Ghana, Sao Tome & Principe
Low	Egypt, Mali, Mauritania, Namibia, Senegal, Tanzania, Uganda & Zambia
Medium:	Algeria, Cote d'Ivoire, Kenya, Nigeria, South Africa & N. Sudan
High:	Angola, Democratic Republic of Congo, Liberia
Extreme	Central African Republic, Sierra Leone, Somalia and S. Sudan
Political Risk	
Insignificant:	Sao Tome & Principe
Low:	Botswana, Ghana, Madagascar, Namibia, South Africa, Tanzania and Uganda

Medium	Chad, Cote d'Ivoire, Ethiopia, Kenya, Liberia, Rwanda, Mozambique Nigeria,
High	Angola, Burundi, Democratic Republic of Congo, Somalia & Zimbabwe
Extreme	Central African Republic & Sierra Leone

Source: Kimenyi and Wasike created this table to illustrate the CRG's "Risk Map."

---

1. Rodney, Walter, *How Europe Underdeveloped Africa*. (Washington, D.C., 1982, Howard University Press) 209.

2. David White, 'Sixty percent of sub-Sahara will still lack power in 2030,' *The Financial Times*, Special Report, *African Infrastructure,* November 26, 2006. p. 4.

3. Kimenyi, Mwangi S. and Wilson S. K. Wasike (2004) Decentralization and Privatization of Infrastructure. In *Africa at the Crossroads*: *Between Regionalism and Globalism* John Mukum Mbaku and Suresh Chandra Saxena eds. (Westport: Praeger Press, 2004) 234-244.

4. John Reed, "Rail link set to break the mould,' Special Report, *South Africa*, *The Financial Times*, June 6, 2006 p.4.

5. Dino Mahtani, "Doubts over air travel after Nigerian crash" *The Financial Times*, October 24, 2005.

6. Nigeria in state of mourning after air crash *The Financial Times* May 6, 2002

7. Dino, Mahtani, 'National tragedy' for Nigeria as 10 generals die in air crash,' *The Financial Times*, September 19, 2006 p. 9

8. Dino, Mahtani. 'Muslim leader and senators die in Nigeria air crash,' *The Financial Times*, October 30, 2006.

9. Dino Mahtani and Daniel Balint-Kurti "Nigeria's aviation reforms need more transparency, experts warn" *The Financial Times,* July, 3, 2006. p.6.

10. Dino, Mahtani, 'National Tragedy for Nigeria as 10 generals die in air crash,' *The Financial Times* September 19, 2006.

11. Dino, Mahtani, 'Air Travel in West Africa prepares for take-off,' *The Financial Times* June, 28 2005.

12. Doug Cameron, 'Business set to gain from US to Africa direct flights,' *The Financial Times,* August 30, 2006, p. 5.

13. Barney Jopson, Mombasa Port: A frantic game of catch-up with rivals, Kenya: Special Report, *The Financial Times*, June 13, 2007. p. 4.

14. 'Mobile phone networks open in Nigeria' *The Financial Times,'* *The Financial Times*, August 10, 2001.

15. Alec Russell, 'World Bank to finance African phone networks,' *The Financial Times*, June 13, 2007 p. 7.

16. Michael Dell, 'The digital sector can make poor nations prosper,' Editorial in *The Financial Times,* May 4, 2006 p. 13.

17. Mike Jensen (2000) "Making the Connection: Africa and the Internet" *Current History*,(May, 2000) . 215.

18. Ibid. 216.

19. Ibid.

20. Kimenyi, Mwangi and Wilson S. K., Wasike (2004), Decentralization and Privatization of Infrastructure. In *Africa at the Crossroads: Between Regionalism and Globalism* John Mukum Mbaku and Suresh Chandra Saxena eds. (Westport: Praeger Press, 20040 240.

21. Raphael Minder, 'Fund set to raise EU's profile as biggest African donor,' *The Financial Times*, February 11-12, 2006.

22. Patrick Bond, *Against Global Apartheid: South Africa meets World Bank, IMF and International Finance*, (Capetown: London and New York: Zed Books. 2004) p. 23.

23. Kimenyi and Wasike, Op. Cit.

24: The Central Nervous System: Political Leadership

The Nervous system is composed of: 1) A series of large centers nerve matter, called collectively, the *cerebro-spinal* centers or *cerebro-spinal cortex*; 2) Of smaller centers, called *ganglia;* 3) Of centers connected either with the *cerebro-spinal cortex* or *ganglia*, and; 4) Of certain modifications of the peripheral terminations of the nerves forming the organs of the external senses.[1] In many respects, its structure and function is reflected in the structure and function of the classic political system. The leadership sends signals to the body politic that sustains and promotes political survival and economic growth.

The effectiveness of traditional leadership patterns *vs.* adapted western political systems remains a critical issue. There are some who call for the return to the traditional "Chief" system and other forms of ancestral governance. However, some questions face most African states as they seek political stability and economic growth including: 1. What level of Training and Experience (TE) does the leadership possess and how does this provide the ability to deal with current political and economic crisis? 2. What is the role and impact of foreign support *vs.* internal support and pressure? 3. How effective are leaders and their political systems at policy implementation? 4. What is the impact of leadership decentralization on political stability? How much do ethno-national politics influence leadership or vice- versa?

The death of Milton Obote, in October 2005, marked the next to last death of the first generation of African political leaders. Obote was the last of a group of eastern and southern African politicians who led their countries to independence from Britain. This diverse and elite group included; Hastings Banda of Malawi, Julius Nyerere of Tanzania, Jomo Kenyatta of Kenya and the only survivor, Kenneth Kaunda of Zambia. Most of these rulers linked the mystique and rewards of the presidency to their own personality. Thus, as Napoleon stated: L'etat c'est moi' (I am the state), these men were the state.

At the dawn of the twenty-first century, an important question, posed by writer Ayi Kwei Armah, remains unanswered. "How long will Africa be cursed by its leaders?" The first generation African political leaders came to power coveting and mimicking the kleptocratic power behavior of the colonialists. In almost every case, those who took power emptied the public coffers into their own and their supporter's pockets. For example, president Moi of Kenya routinely sent his personal agents to take the taxes collected at Nairobi international airport. However, the corruption nutured under colonization does not explain postcolonial political malaise, corruption and the ethnic conflict.

On July 26 2005, King Mswati III of Swaziland signed a new constitution for his tiny kingdom banning all opposition political parties and cementing his power as sub-Saharan Africa's last absolute monarch. From a continental level of analysis, it seems as though the African people's greatest enemies are their own political leaders. As Francis Nyamjoh observes, over the past 50 years, many leaders have promoted perverse economic policies that enriched themselves and impoverished their people. Guided by a mercenary ethos or kleptocratic instincts they cannot afford to commit themselves to popular rule. Neither are they likely to adopt democratic checks on the abuse of power, or concede power when defeated in elections. Only eight heads of state, Kerekou and Soglo of Benin, Kaunda of Zambia, Sassou-Nguesso of Congo, Ratsiraka of Madagascar, Pereira of Cape Verde, Da Costa of Sao Tome, and De Klerk of South Africa, have conceded power more or less gracefully as a result of defeat in democratic elections.[2] Only Kenya, Ghana, Benin, Senegal, Zambia and more recently, Sierra Leone have successfully transferred executive power from one political leadership to another. Even Kenya, long lauded as exemplary of stable western-style democracy in Africa, is less stable and democratic. Kenya's 2007 post-presidential election conflict re-exposed the country's ethnic divisions and confirmed that Africans, like many Americans often vote for who they are, not what they believe in.

Most of the first generation of African leaders wrapped themselves in the banner of democracy and the public interest while pursuing personal economic goals with capitalist impunity. Some purchased personal shares and stocks in foreign companies with the intention of ownership of these companies. President Omar Bongo of Gabon is Africa's longest serving ruler. He has ruled since 1967 and is widely expected to win another new seven-year term. One African ruler helped to finance the construction of free hostels for European school children, while the illiterate children of his impoverished country languished villages and urban slums. Another ruler lavishly contributed money to French politicians seeking re-election, while civil servants in his own country went unpaid and his nations poor died for lack of medicine. Félix Houphouët-Boigny, the first president of the independent Côte d'Ivoire, built a replica of the St. Peters Basilica in Yamoussoukro and sponsored the construction of Rosicrucian lodges in France with his personal fortune. Thus Francis Nyamnjoh appropriately asks: "How can such externally pious and ambitious political behavior be rationalized while, the toiling peasants and slum dwellers of Africa die of hunger and thirst in the darkness and illusion of prayer?"[3] He speculates that perhaps most would abandon their political ambition if after stealing an election or taking power by coup there was nothing more to steal, sell or embezzle.

One sees the rotting fruit of political corruption in the ornate empty mansions that ring the district of Karen and similar outlying districts of Nairobi and other African capitals. These "leaders" are popularly ridiculed for leaving Africa only to perform two B's, to beg and to bank. They only beg and bank in US dollars and Euros. Aid which never leaves the donor countries finds its way into various private accounts in Zurich, New York, Paris, Brussels, Panama, San Francisco or somewhere else in the west. Educated in the west, these leaders are often knowledgeable of American and European history, or of European history in Africa. Of the history of their own people and nations, they have little knowledge. The intellectual elite among them received western educations as children and later assumed leadership of their countries. As Nyamnjoh laments:

> They excel in the classics, Greek philosophy, and Elizabethan literature, uphold Victorian values and remember with nostalgia and native emotion the good old days when they could recite all volumes from Shakespeare, chuckle at Chaucer's tongue-in-cheek humor, praise the psychology of genius of Dickens's plume, criticize Racine's sentimentalism and agree with Cornville's heartlessness or fanatical commitment to "La Patria." Their superficial understanding of their mission, of Africa and of the world, leaves most callous to their subjects/citizens because they know little of them. They only think of their grandparents while acknowledging their foresightedness to have purged them from primitive savagery by providing them with a colonial education...Apart from that passing reference, which often takes the form of a footnote, they know little else about their people or "tribes, and don't really care to, except, of course, when it comes to manipulating these for political ends. [4]

Diaspora scholars justified their flight to and enslavement by western intellectual traditions with the rhetoric of:

> "We must defeat westerners at their own game!" If defeating them at their own game is measured by being more ignorant of Africa than Europeans, there is no contest. As Nyamnjoh observes; "The paradox of the African elite or political leadership is that they know what they need do not need and need what they do not know...When there is a natural disaster, that is when they send around for information to be made available about the populations affected, they ask the location of the village or "tribe" concerned, the number of elites from the area, and whether or not the afflicted are party affiliates, peace loving and respectful of their sacralized leadership." They are unable to identify the major traditional kings and chiefs of their own countries (whom they often publicly derogate and undermine), but they can name British, French, Belgian or American kings, queens or presidents with facility.[5]

In short, they have little training or experience for the, challenges and responsibilities of national leadership.

What quality of leadership and citizenry is required to devolve power to the African people? Although quality national leadership may be in short supply in Africa, Akin Mabogunje of Ogun State University (Nigeria) warns that: "Africa cannot afford to continue with ill prepared and unassisted leaders...if they are to meet the challenges that will face them." African societies must invest tremendous resources in inculcating, nurturing and promoting the right leadership qualities so that future leaders will fully comprehend their duties and obligations; he argues. They cannot afford to be "lackadaisical and indifferent to the type of qualities evinced by those who seek to lead them if they are to avoid the agonies of purposelessness, deprivation and insecurity." Mabogunje maintains that Africa needs leaders who are "knowledgeable, dedicated to some ideals, visionary, selfless in commitment to the aspirations of the populace, astute, critical of cant, rigorously honest and tolerant of alternative opinions." [6]

The Problem With Parties

In Senegal, computer technology is successfully utilized to win elections. President Abdoulaye Wade used calculations drawn from lists of voters to predict he would win 56 percent of the vote. He is celebrated abroad as one of Africa's most progressive leaders but criticized at home for his autocratic style. His databases includes details such as phone number, party identification, party member seniority, religious affiliation, ties to local witch doctors and political "godfathers." If the voter is sufficiently influential, a long personal history is contained in the notes. The detailed personal profiles of voters are invaluable in Senegal's mostly fishing and farming economy, where political loyalties depend on local issues. The database is translated into a map of Senegal and color coded to show the president's popularity ratings from one area to another. The president targeted key swing constituencies, identifying who were the political figures with the most supporters. He would meet them directly knowing their personal histories and political demands in advance.[7]"All the information compiled from different areas goes into crafting an appropriate political speech;" explained Thierno Ousamane Sy, President Wade's advisor.

In Guinea, President Lansana Conté responded to a general-strike and calls for him to stand down by declaring martial law. He convinced the top military leaders to back him, but this so narrowed the window for political dialogue that a political crisis in Guinea seems inevitable. Soldiers rioted at a key army barracks complaining that they were not as well paid as the presidential guard, which includes foreign mercenaries.[8]

Samir Amin described the role autocratic that leaders' play in the process of facilitating global capitalism's inequitable penetration of the African periphery. He explained how the polarization of power and wealth produced by global capitalism makes democratic rule in Africa virtually impossible. Economic life in Africa becomes "little more than an appendage to the exercise of state functions. Amin observed that for any meaningful revolution (whether agrarian or technological) to take place in Africa, there must be another form of political governance in which the African people are no longer passive spectators of decision-making, but organized social forces with contributions to make.[9]

Any examination of western-style political leadership must scrutinize the role and function of political parties as a mode of political representation. The fact that most African politicians are unable to articulate any original or critical view of political economy in part reflects the poverty of ideological choices provided by their political parties. Although political parties in Africa seemingly compete for the same social constituencies, they find it difficult to identify with or represent any social or economic group interest group which has been previously under-represented, unless that group is ethnically defined.[10] Some suggest that it is time to look beyond political parties as the *modus operandi* of political organization and government in Africa. They have come to recognize that there is nothing inherently authoritarian about the one-party state and nothing inherently democratic about the multi-party state.[11]

The suggestion that Africans experiment with the consensual democracy is based on the consent without consensus system of the Ashanti, which preceded the imposition and embrace of western "majoritarian democracy." Some argue that this was a true democracy because government was by consent, and subject to the control, of the people as expressed through their representatives.[12] Others seek a better understanding of popular responses to African state delinquency and elite consumer capitalism by examining the growing volume of literature on Pentecostal movements and healing charismatic churches.[13] There is an increased focus on the need to understand the role and practice of witchcraft and zombification.[14] Many arguments were advanced by first generation African leaders as to why a one-party system was more suitable to their needs than a multiparty system. They pointed to the danger that permitting more than one party encouraged people to form parties based along "tribal" or micro-national and ethnic interests rather than based on national issues. Claude Ake suggested that such regional and ethnic differences emerged in societies where "blood ties" are the basis of social organization. In these societies, status is ascribed not achieved, primary groups dominate social interaction; and the development of secondary groups is at best rudimentary. Social structures, inherited from the past make the social and political integration of members of secondary groups into society both complicated and deliberate.[15] In too many of Africa's elections these micro-national partisan dramas play a violently dysfunctional role. In short, the nerves of government in Africa have yet to develop to the degree that the central nervous system effectively sends signals to and control the other systems of the body politic.

---

1. Henry Gray, T. Pickering Pick and Robert Howden (1977) *Gray's Anatomy: Descriptive and Surgical, New* York: Bounty Books p. 640.

2. S. Ellis, "Democracy and human Rights in Africa," in R. Van den Berg and U. Bosma. eds. *Poverty and development; Historical Dimensions of Development Change and Conflict in the South* (The Hague: Ministry of Foreign Affairs, 1994).

3. Francis B. Nyamnjoh, "Globalization and Popular Disenchantment in Africa" in *Africa at the Crossroads: Between Regionalism and Globalism* Edited by John Mukum Mbaku and Suresh Chandra Saxena. (Westport: Praeger Press, 2004) 66-76.

4. Ibid.

5. Ibid. 68

6. Nyamnjoh, F. B. *The Disillusioned African* (Limbe, Cameroon: Nooremac, 1995).

7. Dino, Mahtani. 'Computer wizardry that swung Senegal election,' *The Financial Times*, March 3, 2007 p.4.

8. Dino Mahtani, 'Martial law in Guinea may worsen crisis,' *The Financial Times*, February 14, 2007. p.2

9. Amin, Samir, "Reflections the international system" In *Beyond Cultural Imperialism: Globalization, Communication & the New International Order*, edited by P. Goulding and P. Harris. (London: Sage. 1997).

10. Francis B. Nyamnjoh, Op. Cit. 80.

11. Neocosmos, M. "From People's politics to state politics: Aspects of the National liberation in South Africa." in, *The Politics of opposition in contemporary Africa.* Edited by, A. Olukoshi (Uppsala: Noordiska Afrikanininstitutet, 1998).

12. Wiredu, K. "Democracy and consensus in African traditional politics; A plea for a nonparty polity". In *Postcolonial African Philosophy: A critical reader*, edited by E. C. Eze. (Oxford: Blackwell, 1997).

13. B. Meyer, "Make a complete break with the past": Memory and Postcolonial Modernity in Ghanaian Pentecostalist Discourse," *Journal of Religion of Africa* 28 (3): 316-349. (1998).

14. Van Dijk, R. and P. Pels, "Contested authorities and politics of perception," Deconstructing the study of religion in Africa. *In Postcolonial identities in Africa*, edited by R Werbner and T. Ranger. (London: Zed Books, 1996).

15. Ake, Claude "Explaining Political Instability in New States," *Journal of Modern African Studies*. Vol. 11. No. 3. p. 354. (1973).

25: The Psychological State

Five hundred years of white-supremacist programming has resulted in the mental enslavement of many Africans. In the perceptions of far too many, all that is western is superior. For example, as a parting gift for our work with World Gospel Mission, each volunteer was given a clay sculpture depicting a scene from the New Testament such as the tomb of Lazarus, or the Good Samaritan. A local African artisan was commissioned to create these works of art. One piece depicted the last supper of the Christ and his disciples. However, in this rendition, Jesus alone was white. The piece was returned and the artisan was asked why only Jesus was white? Like many Africans in the diaspora, he could not or would not offer an explanation of why his God did not look like him. During the, era of European colonization, inhuman atrocities were committed against the African. Educational and religious institutions presented Jesus, the prophets, the saints, and the angels to the African mind as Europeans, while Satan, the demons and devils were depicted as black. In other words, the xenophobia and racism of the European imagination has infected the self-image, personality and self-value of the African. as Frantz Fanon noted: "If there is an inferiority complex, it is the outcome of a double process: primarily economic; subsequently, the internalization or, better, the epidermilization- of this inferiority." [1] Pride in anything African was supplanted for an insatiable desire for European culture and products which inflated the trade deficits and perverted the markets of all African economies. For example, many economically enabled Africans prefer fast foods, pizza, *McDonalds* and chicken chains proliferate in Lagos, Nairobi, Johannesburg and other cities, in preference to the fresh, nutritious meat of the antelope, deer, gazelle or the sweet meat of the ostrich and crocodile.[2]

In *Toward a Psychology of Being* (1970), Abraham Maslow identified what he termed a hierarchy of human needs. One of the many interesting things Maslow noticed was that among primates some needs take precedence over others. For example, if you are hungry and thirsty, you will first seek to quench your thirst. Humans can do without food for weeks, but you can only do without water for a few days! Thirst is a stronger need than hunger.

Similarly, if you are quite thirsty, but someone is choking you, breathing, the need for air, takes precedence.

Maslow developed this now famous hierarchy of needs. Beyond the need for air, water, food, and sex, he identified five broader levels: the physiological needs, the needs for safety and security, the needs for love and belonging, the needs for esteem, and the need to actualize the self, in that order.

1. The physiological needs include the needs we have for oxygen, water, protein, salt, sugar, calcium, and other minerals and vitamins. They also include the need to maintain a pH balance (getting too acidic or base will kill you) and temperature (98.6 or near to it). There are also the needs to be active, to rest, to sleep, to get rid of wastes (CO2, sweat, urine, and feces), to avoid pain, and to have sex. Maslow theorized, and research supports him, that these are in fact individual needs, and that a lack of, vitamin C for example will lead to a very specific hunger for things which have in the past provided that vitamin C, for example orange juice.

2. The safety and security needs. Once the physiological needs are satisfied this second layer of needs comes into play. One becomes increasingly concerned with finding safe circumstances, stability and protection. One might develop a need for structure, for order, some limits. From a negative perspective, one becomes concerned, not with needs like hunger and thirst, but with your fears and anxieties. In the ordinary American adult, this set of needs manifest themselves in the form of our urges to have a home in a safe neighborhood, job security and a nest egg, a good retirement plan and a bit of insurance, and so on. Few adult Africans feel safe or secure.

3. The love and belonging needs. Once physiological needs and safety needs are satisfied, a third layer becomes manifest. One feels the need for friends, intimacy, children, and filial relationships in general. One aspires to develop a sense of community. From a negative perspective, one becomes increasing susceptible to loneliness and social anxieties. In our daily lives, we exhibit these needs in our desires to marry, have a family, be a part of a community, a member of a church, a brother in the fraternity, a part of a gang or a bowling club. It is also a part of what we look for in a career.

4. The next is need is for a sense of self-esteem. Maslow noted two versions of esteem needs, a lower one and a higher one. The lower one is the need for the respect of others, the need for status, fame, glory, recognition, attention, reputation, appreciation, dignity, even dominance. The higher form involves the need for self-respect; including such feelings as confidence, competence, achievement, mastery, independence, and freedom. Note that this is the higher form because, unlike the respect of others, once you have self-respect, it is much harder to lose. The negative aspect related to these needs is low self-esteem and inferiority complexes. Maslow thought that these were at the roots of many, if not most, of our psychological problems. In modern countries, most of us have what we need in regard to our physiological and safety needs. The preceding four levels are what Maslow

called deficit needs (D-needs). If one does not have enough of something, attention, money, self-esteem, respect they have a deficit. Once these needs are fulfilled they cease to be motivating.

Metaneeds & Metapathologies: The Locus of Control

Another way Maslow approached the problem of self-actualization was to describe the special, driving needs (B-needs) of the self-actualizers. These utopic individuals must fulfill the metaneeds in their lives in order to be happy: truth, rather than dishonesty; goodness, rather than evil; beauty, not ugliness or vulgarity; unity and wholeness; and the transcendence of opposites, not arbitrariness or forced choices; the non-mechanization of life; uniqueness, not bland uniformity; excellence not sloppiness and inconsistency or accident; justice and order, not injustice and lawlessness; simplicity not unnecessary complexity; well-being, but not environmental impoverishment; effortlessness, not strain; playfulness not humorless, drudgery; self-sufficiency, rather than dependency.

At first consideration, it may seem obvious that everyone values these metaneeds. But imagine that you are an impoverished African living through an economic depression or a war, or a refugee living in a desert camp or in a urban ghetto or rural poverty. Do you worry about these metaneeds or do you worry about getting enough food to eat, water to drink, a roof over your head and health and education for your children,? Are you concerned about your human needs or your human wants? Are you concerned with civil and political rights or economic and social justice? Should your government pursue political democracy with political parties and elections or economic democracy with the provision of basic needs? Which is the meta priority?

Maslow theorized that much of what is wrong with the world comes down to the fact that very few people really are interested in these values—not because they are bad people, but because they have not had their basic needs taken care of. When a self-actualizer does not get these needs fulfilled, they respond with Metapathologies, i.e., problems as long as the list of Metaneeds. When forced to live without these values, the self-actualizer develops depression, despair, disgust, alienation, and a degree of cynicism. This is the psychological state of the impoverished and suffering patient.[3]

The further one travels from Nairobi, the greater the potential for violence. On the road to Masai Mara a policeman and a civilian stand by the body of man hanging from a tree. We are cautioned not to take photographs. Was this a lynching or a suicide? Was the man a refugee, a poacher, a criminal, a stranger? Such murders are often reported in print media. Sam Mowoe is a friend of the family, successful Kenyan artist and farmer who has traveled to the United States to sell his art. His work hangs in my home. In honor of our visit, he brought a goat to roast. He recounted the story of how his brother was murdered with a machete by his sister-in-law, and of how his body was placed in a burlap sack and thrown into a river by her accomplices. Under police interrogation, the men confessed and the sister in-law was imprisoned for life. She said that wanted her husband dead so that she would inherit his land. Still obviously struggling with his pain, Sam a Christian, said he had spoken to her and offered his forgiveness. One driven by greed and the other by the need to heal it is not easy to judge which one felt self-actualized.

In an essay entitled, *Globalization and Popular Disenchantment in Africa*, Francis Nyamnjoh argues that the causes of Africa's problems are neither simply external nor exclusively internal. Africans remain both dependent and autonomous agents in relation to the historical and contemporary forces which impinge on them and their continent. However, he cautions against the simplistic perception of Africans as zombies who are overwhelmed by external forces as well as against crediting them with utopic agency..[4] Nyamnjoh suggests that we imagine a cow in a valley being milked by a herdsman under instructions from a distant patron. Africa is best seen, as being milked by external forces with the active collaboration of internal counterparts conditioned to act like zombies.

Following the July 7, 2005 bombings of London's Underground and buses, Prime Minister Tony Blair alerted commuters to be on the look out for people with a zombie like countenance. They were informed that such people would have the appearance of a zombie, staring straight ahead, not making eye contact and moving as if in some sort of a trance. When does the pain of being a zombie grow so acute, that one willingly decides to share that pain and become a suicide bomber? Suicide bombers too are offered as victims. Suicide bomber's have committed their lives and evidently appear this to be in such a trance before offering their lives to destroy the lives of other. Just as in traditional accounts of sorcery where one becomes a victim only after being offered by one's own relative to be "eaten," Africans cannot be exploited by external forces such as multinationals and western states, if they are not first sacrificed by their own "brothers and sisters" with political and economic power.[5]

For Nyamjoh, Africans have embraced western modernity at the cost of their own spiritual and cultural estrangement. If the consumer cultural empire represented by the *Coca-colonization* of the world is a sign of development, then Africans have developed. In the process, they have devalued their institutions and their cultures and replaced them with the institutionalized consumerism and dependency. Africans have embraced modernity at the cost of self-denial, self-humiliation and the adulation of all things western. They have been invited to devalue themselves, their institutions and their cultures by cultivating an uncritical empathy for western economic, cultural, and political values. The poorest decorate their walls with the labels of the western goods they have rummaged or purchased. You find walls adorned with empty *Kelloggs's* cornflake boxes and *Campbell's* soup labels.

Frantz Fanon identified this as the result of the myth of the inferior native, created to justify colonization and estrange Africans from their cultures. The enduring psychological damage of colonization and the western ideal of modernization are evidenced in the plethora skin lightening products, which are primarily manufactured in the US and the UK and marketed and sold in Africa. Consequently, today in every country south of the Sahara, thousands of African men and women attempt to lighten their complexions with various skin poisoning, cancer causing, mercury-and hydroquinone-ridden toners and soaps. Colonialism created in Africans "a pathological case of xenophilia" by teaching Africans to value things Western "not for their efficacy but simply because of their foreignness." For the colonized mind, being human is also measured by a patchwork of "whiteness" one has accomplished through conspicuous consumption and the physical transformation of skin and hair.[6]

If development means to emulate the media perception of western consumption, then as Nobel Laureate Wole Soyinka has observed; "Africans are encouraged to develop an incurable dependency syndrome and consume themselves to death."[7] In South Africa and Kenya, the black elite wallow in conspicuous consumption with large houses, large cars, Jacuzzi's and the latest electronic gadgetry, the majority of their fellow citizens wallow in the hopelessness of their poverty in shantytowns and marveling at how the former come to their riches so easily and with so little work.[8]

This inequality created and nurtures a belief system "that it is only through magical means, by consuming others, that people may enrich themselves in these perplexing times," and consequently, to a resurgence in accusations of witchcraft and zombification and scape-goating of immigrants (*makwererkwere*), whose readiness to provide devalued labor, like zombies, compounds the disenchantment of South Africa's poor.[9] Western culture has been forced on Africans as the "culmination of human progress," a model to be followed without equivocation or reservation. Supposedly, universal achievement oriented western-oriented cultures were expected to penetrate "backward-looking" African cultures through a linear process of intercultural communications. Social change is advocated in everything from blue jeans, cell phones, beer, and chewing gum and sex. The use of profanity is diffused and stereotypically reinforced by Hollywood and western tourist's in search of the three s': sun, sea and sex.

Development to the Africans therefore involves self-denial, self-evacuation, or self-devaluation and the glorification of all that is western.[10] Africans are induced to devalue themselves, their institutions and their cultures by cultivating an uncritical imitation of Western economic, cultural and political values.[11] In essence, for many Africans modernity represents cultural superiority. The persistent impulse to be western or to go to the west attests to an exogenously induced self-hatred and inferiority-complex. Ali Mazrui explains that "Africa's culture of tolerance" or its "short memory of hate" can be explained by this western devaluation of African cultural identities that has made the Africans a "people more sinned against than sinning," and people keener to forgive and forget than to exact restitution and rehabilitation.[12] A people conditioned to suffer and smile. The patient has been beaten, raped, traumatized and betrayed. The pain is both acute and chronic. To cope with the pain the patient uses various methods of distraction that are part of the socialization process, i.e., endurance. Issues of daily survival and subsistence such as joblessness, homelessness, fear of violence, disease, hunger and family responsibility supersede personal suffering.

The Psychology of Corruption

In a candid admission about corrupt business practices in oil-rich West Africa, Teodorin Nguema Obiang, the 37 year-old son of and likely successor of the president, stated that; companies owned by ministers often bid for government contracts with foreign groups and if successful, received a percentage of the total contract. He made this sworn affidavit to Cape Town's High Court, where his lawyers were opposing the seizure of his two luxury houses. *Maseve Investments*, a South African company, sought damages from Equatorial Guinea in connection with a commercial property dispute. The company claimed that Obiang could not have afforded the houses, for which he paid $7 million, on his salary as minister of forestry in his father's government. "We maintain that if his salary is $4,000 a month, where did he get the money? The Only answer is that the government stole it from the people;" said *Maseve's* director, Errol Eldson.

Obiang's sworn statement confirmed widespread concerns about a rampant culture of corruption in Equatorial Guinea and other African countries including; Angola, Congo-Brazzaville and other oil rich West African states. The statement led Sarah Wykes, a campaigner with the London-based *Global Witness* to ask: "Which US or other foreign companies are doing these kinds of deals?"[13] The answer is that there are myriad western investors who are involved in and benefit from these corrupt practices. US congressional representative and chair of the House subcommittee on Africa and Global Health, Donald Payne, turned the spotlight on what are referred to as 'vulture funds' operating in Africa. He singled out *Donegal International*, run by US businessman Michael Sheehan from his *Debt Advisory International* company in Washington, D.C. Operating through shell companies in the Caribbean, vulture funds prey on the weakest countries by purchasing cheap debt obligations at a fraction of their face value on secondary markets and then taking court action to get full payment plus interest. Congressman Payne said the funds were "feeding upon financially distressed nations" and that the court cases filed by those feeding off Africa's economic weakness were "morally reprehensible and exploitative." Several African states are forced to hire costly defense attorneys in the US, the UK and France. Danny Glover, the actor/activist and chairman of *TransAfrica Forum*, urged congress to move against these vulture funds.[14]

There is a growing body of literature which seeks to describe the habits, procedures and justifications involved in corrupt practices. Most of this research is based on quantitative surveys, which are not designed to provide an explanation of the phenomenon. The study of corruption involves dealing with allegations, accusations, suspicions that are aired in the press or in private conversations.[15] The Corruption Perception Index (CPI) is compiled by German economist Johann Graf Lambsdorff on behalf of *Transparency International* (TI). The TI index is presented as the 'survey of surveys' and is compiled on the basis of sixteen different sources.[16] While some of the bias of which TI has been accused, particularly of focusing on the perspective of the business community and international experts, has been eliminated, it analytical weaknesses lie in other areas. For example, there is the question as to whether it is possible to compare surveys carried out among elites with those carried out among the general population, or perceptions of expatriates with those of economic functionaries and national civil servants.

The other main type of quantitative research on corruption consists of survey research conducted at the national level. The use of extensive surveys based on highly standardized questionnaires poses numerous problems. For example, the 1994 CLARION study, which sought to provide an accurate image of the spread of corruption in Kenya, used a sample composed of an urban and educated population and was based on the assumption that corruption is a phenomenon most widespread among urban elites. Informants were requested to estimate the extent of corrupt practices in a given service, to specify the sums involved, and to select between different options in the context of one typical situation. Blundo and de Sardan argue that such studies are necessary because they offer they only approach that makes it possible to demonstrate the 'action logics' of the actors involved, the description of corrupt processes and the associated techniques, the analysis of the popular representations and the forms of justification and the condemnation associated with corruption. They posit that it is not possible to dissociate corruption analytically from a regime of 'favors', 'preferential treatment', 'recommendations', 'string-pulling', nepotism and the various and myriad advantages bestowed in the name of family, neighborly relations, friendship, school, university and professional relationships and professional protectionism, all topics that have been examined by cultural anthropologists.[17]

The comparative study of corruption is primarily an examination of the similarities and differences between countries and concerns the relationships corruption maintains within economic and political arenas, the public debates it triggers, the measures taken to combat it and its international linkages. The first anthropological studies of corruption were conducted in the late 1960s by S. Ottenberg and M.G. Smith. Ottenberg examined the phenomenon in the local governments of southern Nigeria. He found that corruption occurred in societies undergoing rapid change, in which the coexistence of different styles of political action exacerbated the gap between legal norms and realistic political behavior. He observed that borrowing from traditional forms of gift exchange and reciprocity current in spheres of family relationships; corrupt exchange practices made it possible to secure and regulate relations between unrelated partners.[18] M.G. Smith conducted ethnographic fieldwork and historical research in northern Nigeria between 1949 and 1951 and described the evolution of corruption among the Hausa. He initiated the first systematic observation of corruption: in order to test the veracity of local allegations concerning the practices of the 'cotton mallams' who were responsible for the purchase of cotton on behalf of the Native Administration.[19]

Many explanations for the absence of interest shown by anthropologists in the study of corrupt practices refer to African 'miserabilist' or populist tendencies. Others admit the people under scrutiny are often so poor and marginalized that anthropologists do not want to add to their problems. Since the study of African politics is usually approached from a 'top-down' perspective, drawing analogies with western states; the research is heavily influenced by the theoretical frameworks of political science. Over the past two decades, 'neo-patrimonialism' and the 'politics of the belly' have been the main concepts around which the debates on the nature of the state in Africa have been structured. Jean-Francois Médard used the concept of neo-patrimonialism, which is less normative than that of corruption and more comparative than that of "politics of the belly," to characterize the contradictory nature of African states, in which the process of bureaucratization coexisted with the patrimonial management of public resources.[20] According to Médard, while the constitutions of African states acknowledge the formal differentiation between the public and private sectors, this distinction is not respected or is ignored in the actual practices of African leaders.

Rejecting the western diagnosis of corruption, 'externalist' or dependency theorists provide alternative explanations. For example, economist Mamadou Diouf explored the heuristic virtues of the concept of corruption which incorporate the dangers of 'very unsuccessfully imitating and reproducing' the paradigms of failed Bretton-Woods institutions.

There is of course much speculation and debate concerning the relationship between culture and corruption. In a review of the literature, Giorgio Blundo notes that none of the documents examined in his research confirmed that corruption is an exclusively African pathology and that the cause of this pathology should be sought in an improbable 'culture' specific to the continent.[21]

Culturalist explanations have been widely used to diagnose the phenomenon of corruption in Africa. There are those who study the genealogy of corrupt practices, and those who consider the emergence of corruption in African traditions and ancestral values the result of the historic rupture that coincided with the importation of the colonial state. While the former, 'continuists' claim that corrupt behavior is endogenous in nature, the 'purists' confirm the external origin of these practices, which they identify as modern.[22] John Mbaku refers to 'defective cultural norms," while others castigate the 'pressures of tradition,' which make the political leader the victim of the ethnic group'.[23] Still others stigmatize the 'weight' of traditional social structures, conveying a conception of the family based on parasitism and tribalism in a socio-cultural context immersed in superstitious belief systems that encourage extravagant spending.[24] Thus, in this debate, African culture is either the source of corruption or African political culture has been infected by an external entity which had grossly perverted or destroyed it. Either the modern state is corrupted by traditional culture, or traditional culture is corrupted by the modern state. Giorgio Blundo notes that trapped in this unproductive dichotomy between endogeneity and exogeneity, the controversy loses sight of the fact that culture itself is a social construct that can be used at any point in history to legitimatize predatory regimes and mask the social inequities they foment.[25]

One thing is certain; corruption is an international and transnational cancer that could not metastasize in Africa without the support of IGO's, foreign corporations and foreign governments. Anti-corruption campaigners celebrated a significant victory when the European Bank for Reconstruction and Development (EBRD) announced that it had blacklisted *Lahmeyer*, a German engineering consulting firm found guilty of bribery on a World Bank project in Lesotho. The sanction followed court proceedings in Lesotho in 2003 and 2004, which convicted *Lahmeyer* of bribing a government official responsible for awarding contracts related to the Lesotho Highlands Water Project; a multi-billion dollar hydro-electric and water transfer project partly funded by the World Bank. Other European companies were also found guilty of corrupt activities relating to the Lesotho project.[26] The case underscored the need to focus on the international system of corruption and to increase the cost to businesses caught in such practices. Corruption has undermined the everyday sense efficacy of the African people debilitating both the individual and the state.

African Perceptions of Globalization

What do Africans think of the New World Order and globalization? According to a *GlobeScan* poll of 19 nations, Africa is the region of the world most positive about globalization. Two out of three Africans have a positive view of the effect of globalization on their lives. In all countries this was a strong majority, reaching as high as 82 percent in Ghana and 79 percent in Kenya. Support was more muted in Tanzania (53%), and Zimbabwe only 35% felt this way. A majority of Africans in all demographic categories were positive toward globalization, with especially positive views among those with higher education and higher income, and the young.

Positive views of globalization were more common among those who saw their lives, their country and the world going in a positive direction; and who saw US influence as something positive. This suggests that those who are optimistic have pinned their hopes on integration into the world economy. Consistent with their support for globalization Africans have a positive view of global corporations. A large majority (73%) favored large foreign countries coming into their country and setting up operations there. This was true of nearly all countries, ranging from 70 percent of respondents in South Africa to 90 percent in the Cote d'Ivoire and Ghana. The one exception was Tanzania, where opinion was divided and only 56 percent said they trusted global corporations operating in their country to act in the best interests of the country.

While showing considerable enthusiasm for globalization, a majority of Africans (60% overall) believe that rich countries are not playing fair in trade negotiations with poor countries. Such views ranged from being very widespread in the Cote d'Ivoire (88%) and Zimbabwe (72%), to being divided in Nigeria and South Africa. A clear majority (57% overall) also rejected the idea that poor countries benefit from trade as much as rich countries. Those who feel that rich countries are not playing fair were less likely to support globalization. But even among those with a positive view of globalization, 60 percent felt that rich countries are not playing fair. Those with a negative view of how poor countries are being treated also had a diminished view of the influence of the US and the EU and less trust of global corporations. However, they were not less supportive of corporations establishing operations in their country. Steven Kull, director of Program on International Policy Attitudes (PIPA), comments: "These findings suggest that Africans are eager and willing to join the game of world economic integration even as they have resentments that they are being treated unfairly by the wealthy countries." Interestingly, dissatisfaction with the trading policies of rich countries is more common at the highest levels of income and education. Though these groups arguably are benefiting more from globalization, they are also more aware of the actions of rich countries which could be regarded as unfair.

African Views of the US

Many Africans do not appear to be make a distinction between Europe and the US, thus positive views of Europe are correlated with positive views of the US. Despite their exploitation, marginalization and impoverishment, a majority of Africans (55%) said that the US has a positive influence in the world. Countries differ significantly, with majorities in Ghana, Kenya, the Cote d'Ivoire, and Nigeria sharing a positive view, while other nations had more mixed views. In the *GlobeScan* poll, Africa stands out as the only region, other than North America, where majorities have a positive view of the influence of the US. A clear majority of African Christians have a positive view of America. African Muslims are more divided. Those with higher incomes had a more negative view of the US. Forty-nine percent viewed Europe as having a positive influence in the world.

Eighty-three 83% (overall) agreed with the proposition that: "Democracy may have its problems, but it is the best system of government for my country." This majority was at 80 percent for every country except Tanzania, where only 54 percent agreed. However, a majority (56%) do not believe that their country is being run by the will of the people. Large majorities felt this way in Nigeria (85%) and Zimbabwe (73%). Only in Ghana did a clear majority of the population (61%) affirm that their government was representative. In Kenya and the Cote d'Ivoire, opinion is particularly divided on this question. Large percentages of the public in many wealthy democracies are also not very confident that their governments are truly representative.

According to PIPA poll results, 86 percent of the respondents thought the US government should not get involved in trying to stop poor countries from producing generic HIV/Aids drugs. Only 32 percent approved of US foreign policy behavior.

With respect to development, 75 percent thought it was important to help poor countries develop their economies so they might become more self-sufficient. Twenty-two percent thought that helping poor countries was too complicated and could not tell if it was doing much good. On average, the respondents thought that between 20 and 25 percent of all foreign humanitarian and economic aid should go to Africa.

Overall, only 40 percent believed that corruption had diminished in their country over the last year. Corruption, is a cancerous disease on African political economy. A strong majority in Zimbabwe, Nigeria, South Africa and the Cote d'Ivoire said that corruption had not improved. Only in Kenya and Ghana did a majority say levels of corruption had improved. One in four Africans stated that they or someone in their family has been personally affected by an act of corruption by government officials within the past 12 months. This ranged from ten percent in South Africa and Ghana, to forty percent in ten in the Cote d'Ivoire and fifty percent in Zimbabwe. The experience of being affected by government corruption is common across all demographic groups, as is the perception that the situation is not improving. In September 2005, Mauritania joined Nigeria in an anti-corruption agreement aimed at stopping the flow of tens of billions of dollars lost to bribery and theft among the African oil-exporting nations. The Extractive Industries Transparency Initiative (EITI), is an effort to disclose contract payment and graft. Unfortunately, thus far Nigeria and Mauritania alone are convinced of the initiative's merits. The other states are in denial.

---

1. Frantz Fanon, *Black Skin, White Masks*, (New York: Grove Press 1967) 11.

2. Osabu-Kle, Daniel, *Cultural Compatible Democracy: The Key to Development in Africa*. (Petersborough, Ontario: Broadview Press, 2000) 274.

3. Maslow, Abraham, *Toward A Psychology of Being* (Princeton: Van Nostrand, 1968).

4. Nyamnjoh, Francis B, "Globalization and Popular Disenchantment in Africa," in *Africa at the Crossroads* in *Africa at the Crossroads: Between Regionalism and Globalism* Edited by John Mukum Mbaku and Suresh Chandra Saxena. (Westport: Praeger Press, 2004) 60.

5. Ibid.

6. C. J. Hamelink, *Cultural Autonomy in Global Communications: Planning National Information Policy* (London: Longman. 1983) 2.

7. Soyinka, Wole (1994) , "Culture, memory and development." in *Culture and Development in Africa*, edited by I. Serageldin, and J. Taboroff, Washington, DC: World Bank.

8. Ibid.

9. Comaroff, J. and J. Comaroff "Alien-nation: Zombies, immigrants and millennial capitalism," *CODESRIA Bulletin* 3-4: 17-28 1999).

10. Sreberny, Mohammadi, A. "The many faces of cultural imperialism," In *Beyond Cultural Imperialism: Globalization, Communication and the New International Order*.(London: Sage, 1997).

11. Ajayi, J.F.A. "The place of African history and culture in the process of nation-building in Africa South of the Sahara," In *Social Change: The Colonial Situation*, edited by Immanuel Wallerstein. (New York: Wiley and Sons, 1966).

12. Mazrui, Ali A. Development in a multicultural context: Trends and tensions. *In Culture and Development in Africa*, edited by I. Serageldin and J. Taboroff. (Washington, DC: The World Bank, 1994).

13. John Reed, 'Taking a cut acceptable, says African minister' *The Financial Times*, October 26, 2006, p. 6.

14. Guy Dinmore, 'Vulture funds under fire for 'feeding upon' African Nations,' *The Financial Times* May 25, 2007. p.6.

15. Giorgio Blundo, and J.P. Olivier de Sardan "Why should we study everyday corruption and how should we go about it?" in G. Blundo & Olivier de Sardan (eds.),

Everyday Corruption and the State: Citizens & Public Officials in Africa (New York and London: Zed Books, 2006) 8-9

16. Lambsdorff, J. G. *The Transparency International Corruption Perceptions Index 1999* Framework Document, TI, October, 1999) *http://gwdu19.gwde.de~UWVW/1999_CPI_FD.pdf.*

17. Blundo and de Sardan, Op. Cit . 11-12.

18. Ottenberg, S, (1967) 'Local Government and the Law in Southern Nigeria', *Journal of Asian and African Studies*, vol. 2, no. 1-2: pp. 26-43.

19. Smith, M.G. 'Historical and Cultural Conditions of Political Corruption among the Hausa', *Comparative Studies in Society and History*, Vol. 6. no. 2: (1964) 164-194.

20. Médard, J. F. (1990) 'L'etat patrimonialisé', *Politique Africaine* 39:25-36.

21. Giorgio Blundo, Giorgio 'A review of the literature' in G. Blundo & Olivier de Sardan (eds.), *Everyday Corruption and the State: Citizens & Public Officials in Africa* (New York and London: Zed Books, 2006). p.25.

22. Ibid. 26.

23. J.M. Mbaku, *Bureaucratic and Political Corruption in Africa: The Public Choice Perspective*, (Krieger: Malabar, 2000).

24. Blundo Op. Cit. 27

25. Ibid.

26. Guha Krishna, 'German group put on graft blacklist,' *The Financial Times*, February 26, 2007. p 7.

26: Diagnosis, Prognosis & Treatment

Every three years Africa receives $ billions dollars in foreign aid. Each year about 1400 NGO aid workers deliver hundreds of thousand tons of food and medicine to Africa. Every five years, over 50 thousand missionaries serve in Africa. There are now 20 thousand churches and 10 thousand missionary hospitals. The UN sends about 50 thousand peace keeping troops every 5 years. Every ten years, the World Bank holds $1 billion in unsecured loans to African states with high interest and default rates. Within in last five years $1 million in micro-loans made to Africans with low interest and default rates have been made to Africans. All this economic and aid activity has done little to alleviate the pain, impoverishment or suffering.

In an article titled, *Explaining African Economic Performance*, Collier and Gunning identified five factors responsible for Africa's poor growth performance: 1) the lack of social capital; 2) lack of trade openness; 3) deficient public service, geography and risk; 4) lack of financial depth and; 5) a high dependence on aid.

Tony Blair's Economic Commission for Africa placed responsibility on Africa's "low productivity and poor competitiveness."[1] There is no doubt that the protectionist economic policies of rich states hurts African producers and exacerbates their impoverishment. It is also true that trade liberalization by rich states is no panacea for African poverty. The primary causes for African impoverishment, and thus the locus of control over these mechanisms, are internal. Absent are the political stability and economic sovereignty required for African governments to address the needs of their people. Africans are criticized for calling for greater access to global markets while avoiding policy reforms and trade openness; for maintaining high tariffs, and not protecting private property rights. A 2005 World Bank study estimated the value of Africa's income growth resulting from full liberalization of global merchandise trade. Taking 2001 as the base year, the authors estimated that by 2015 annual income growth in Africa would be $4.8 billion greater than it would had there been no trade liberalization. Thus, Oxfam recommended that Africans protect their producers from foreign competition.

Critics of African trade policy note that Africa is one of the most trade protected regions of the world. Between 1984 and 2003, the high-income nations of the Organization for Economic Cooperation and Development (OECD) reduced their average applied tariffs by 84 percent (to 3.9%) percent. African countries by contrast reduced their tariffs by only 20 percent to (17.7%). Non-tariff protection in the poorest African countries is four times greater than it is in rich countries. Some of the highest tariffs on African exports are levied by other African states. Accordingly, the World Bank found that income gains from regional trade liberalization in Africa would reach $1.75 billion by 2015, or more than 36 percent of all gains that Africa stands to receive from global trade rounds. In other words, Africa stands to gain almost as much from inter-African trade liberalization as it does from access to the markets of the west.

Opponents of African demands for greater market access rarely consider the myriad consequences of their recommendations. They argue that the potential benefits of increased access for African goods to global markets will remain unfulfilled unless it is accompanied by far-reaching economic and political changes. This includes greater trade openness dealing with corruption, dishonest judiciaries, inefficient bureaucracies and growth-stifling over regulation. The immediate need to address the chronic and acute suffering of the people and the corrosive and corrupting impact of private investment in exacerbating their misery are rarely part of the economic reform calculus. The generation of African leaders who attempted to exercise an internal locus of control over economic development, includes those who nationalized or attempted to nationalize their resources. They include among others, Kwame Nkrumah, Sekou Toure, Julius Nyerere Patrice Lumumba and Robert Mugabe.

Western Prescriptions

The nature of development is complex. Nations with similar preconditions develop quite unevenly. The complex nature of development requires the recognition of certain culturally compatible preconditions. Several internal and external loci of control explanations of the obstacles to African development have been advanced. These views largely ignore the underlying politico-cultural problems, and thus tend to prescribe superficial economic remedies.

Many loci of control explanations blame the African economic crisis on external variables. They focus on structuralists interpretations of development first advanced through the thesis of the Economic Commission for Latin America and later by other Marxist structuralists such Samir Amin in his work *Imperialism and Unequal Development* (1977) and Andre Gunder Frank's essay "The Development of Underdevelopment" (1966).[2] These explanations attribute Africa's impoverishment to the international economic system and many manifestations of globalization: unfavorable terms of trade for Africa; low demand elasticity for African products; substitution of domestic for imported products, including synthetics; economic recession and high interest rates in the developed countries; intractable debt; the overvaluation of the dollar and the consequential asymmetric monetary shocks; and the unexpected events in the international economic and political systems such as oil-price increases and war.

Although these are significant factors, they reflect a deeper problem which is the interaction of forces within and between African countries. Dabiel Osabu-Kle argues that these structuralist interpretations ignore the fact that local actors using failed paradigms can be effectively checked within underdeveloped counties. The fundamental questions are: Can developing countries do anything at all about their horrible situation? Do politics matter at all? Are constraining structures by definition the determining structures? Africa's economic elite are pleased with external locus of control explanations, because these explanations can be used to absolve them of all blame.[3]

For Osabu-Kle, internal locus of control explanations attribute African impoverishment to the irresponsible actions and corruption of political elites, but fail to adequately consider the political-cultural context in which they operate. They blame local actors for the problems associated with the agriculture-industry link. While focusing on the agriculture-industry link they emphasize the inadequate symmetric linkages between agriculture and industry, which contribute to an import-reproduction system with minimal transfer of western technology and little use of local resources as opposed to an import substitution system with a substantial transfer of technology and the use of local resources. The resulting import-dependent industrialization cannot be supported by export earnings, and both the agricultural base and the industrial sector are weakened. The result is economic collapse and perpetual impoverishment. Import Substitution Industrialization (ISI) strategies include tariff protection for the industrial sector which imbalances the internal terms of trade against agriculture and extracts resources from the agricultural sector. Osabu-Kle recommends that African countries proceed slowly on the industrial front and utilize labor-intensive technologies in both sectors. The inward-focused import-substitution industrialization strategy typically did not promote linkages between mass consumption and mass production, but rather was aimed at establishing the local production of luxury goods for small a wealthy elite, especially in South Africa and Zimbabwe, the economies with the most advanced mining sectors. Ironically, as specialization increased, the ISI approach made these countries even more dependent on external sources of advanced technology, machinery and parts and on the export raw materials than ever before.[4]

Another problem is posed by the market, institutional or political structures needed to successfully coordinate agricultural and industrial development patterns. Internal locus of control approaches see a lack of agricultural and economic success in Africa as the reflection of specific political and institutional structures influencing specific polices related to an urban bias. But this approach does not seriously consider the question of how these structures came into neither being, nor their compatibility with African culture.[5] The state-owned African businesses (parastatals), for example, are everything short of profit-making enterprises; they are in fact run as "public-private" businesses for the benefit of patrons and clients in power. Rather than making money for the state, the state is forced to borrow to keep them solvent, for what matters is patronage not prosperity. The state becomes more concerned with obstructing the emergence of popular modes of politics, than with pursuing productive economic policies designed to eradicate poverty and impoverishment.[6]

A problem with internal locus of control explanations is the emphasis on non-food production, which reduces the size of the food surplus provided by those who remain in production. Trade was supposed to minimize this problem. It has not. Africa's acute shortages of foreign exchange are a source of exacerbated hunger and pain. Agricultural growth is stifled through the manipulation of price signals. Prices on the world market are supposed to prevail, but because commodity prices are oligopolistically determined, African producers always lose.

The failure to introduce land reforms supportive of effective production further undermined Africa's agricultural base. In *Beyond Ujamaa in Tanzania* (1980), Goran Hyden suggests that Tanzania's crisis might be attributed to the government's failure to forcibly bring the peasants into the market through a drastic land reform program that would deprive them of land, and theoretically give root to capitalism. Hyden argues that because the peasants were permitted to own their own means of production, they developed a consciousness that the state needed them but they did not need the state. They resisted mobilization under both the capitalist and socialist systems. However, this explanation fails to appreciate what Osabu-Kle terms the African's "economy of affection." Traditional African culture considers it demeaning for a person to think of himself or herself as an individual at the expense and welfare of the extended family.[7]

Political economists such as Robert Bates, the author of *Markets and States in Tropical Africa* and Assefa Bequele, the author of "Stagnation and Inequality in Ghana;" are critical of the World Bank and the IMF because their arguments appease the West's right-wing political actors and financial institutions by propagating an angelic and immaculate image of the West in its relations with the developing world."

Over the past quarter century, there are many internal and external loci of explanations for the impoverishment of sub-Saharan Africa. The socio-economic standard of living fell in many countries during the 1950s. Many countries witnessed extraordinary social, civil and regional conflicts, ranging from genocide to coups in the 1980-90s. Africa's civil wars and adverse climatic conditions are increasingly identified with structural political and economic problems, ranging from post-Cold-War geopolitical fragility to global warming.[8]

In the aftermath of the G8 pledge of 2005 there was no timetable established for African countries explaining to them how their aid levels will rise to meet the 2010 pledge to double aid. Across the continent, African leaders and finance ministers were told by local representatives of the donor agencies that there was no information as to how or when aid levels would increase. In some countries, recipients of US development aid were told that aid other than for HIV/Aids, would be cut as budget priorities were shifted to the war on Iraq.

African governments were explicitly encouraged to increase their investments in disease control, water sanitation, roads, power, schools, clinics and other infrastructure. They were advised to drop user fees in education and health. But they have not been told how, when, or where the aid increases would occur even though 2010 was just two years away. The result, for Jeffrey Sachs of Columbia University's Earth Institute, is a lose-lose situation for both Africa and the donor states. Governments in Africa are unable to plan two years ahead, much less to 2015, when they are supposed to achieve the UN's millennium development goals. Public investment and health are at the core of these goals. Children's lives are saved by preventative health investments such as anti-malarial insecticide treated bed nets, de-worming programs and therapeutic health investments in clinical services. Children are educated when there are trained teachers, adequate classrooms and school lunch programs. Market economies are promoted when roads are paved and power grids and functional ports allow even Africa's land-locked countries to compete in world markets.[9]

Phineas Gage's Story

Phineas Gage is perhaps the most famous patient to have survived severe damage to the brain. He was the foreman of a railway construction gang working for the contractors preparing the bed for the Rutland and Burlington Rail Road near Cavendish, Vermont. On September 13th 1848, the accidental explosion of a charge he had set, blew his tamping iron through his head. He became the first patient from whom surgeons learned something about the relation between personality and the function of the front parts of the brain.

The tamping iron was 3 feet 7 inches long and weighed 13 1/2 pounds. It was 1 1/4 inches in diameter at one end (not circumference as in the newspaper report) and tapered over a distance of about 1-foot to a diameter of 1/4 inch at the other. The tamping iron went in point first under his left cheek bone and completely out through the top of his head, landing about 25 to 30 yards behind him. Phineas Gage was knocked over but may not have lost consciousness even though most of the front part of the left side of his brain was destroyed. Dr. John Martyn Harlow, a young physician from Cavendish, treated him with such success that he returned home to Lebanon, New Hampshire 10 weeks later.

Figure 1
This is the bar that was shot through the head of Mr. Phineas P. Gage at Cavendish, Vermont, Sept. 14, 1848. He fully recovered from the injury & deposited this bar in the Museum of the Medical College of Harvard University. Phineas P. Gage Lebanon Grafton N-H Jan 6 1850 *

Some months after the accident, in the middle of 1849, Gage felt strong enough to resume work. But his personality had changed so much, the contractors who had employed him would not give him his job back. Before the accident, Phineas had been their most capable and efficient foreman, one with a well-balanced mind, who was looked on as a shrewd smart business man. He was now fitful, irreverent, and grossly profane, showing little deference to his fellows. He was also impatient and obstinate, yet capricious and vacillating, unable to settle on any of the plans he devised for future action. His friends said he was "No longer Gage."

As far as known, Phineas Gage never worked at the level of a foreman again. According to Dr. Harlow, he appeared at Barnum's Museum in New York, working in the livery stable of the Dartmouth Inn (Hanover, NH), and he drove coaches and cared for horses in Chile. After he regained his health he worked on a farm south of San Francisco. In February 1860, he began to have epileptic seizures and according to funeral director's and cemetery interment records, died on May 21st 1860.

No post mortem studies of Phineas Gage's brain were made. Late in 1867 his body was exhumed, and his skull and the tamping iron sent to Dr. Harlow. Harlow reported his findings, including his estimate of the brain damage, in 1868. He then gave the skull and tamping iron to what became the Warren Museum of the Medical School of Harvard University where they were thoroughly examined.. They are now on display at Harvard's Countway Library of Medicine. The first newspaper account of the accident appeared in the *Free Soil Union* (Ludlow, Vermont) the day after the accident, and is reproduced here as it was reported in the *Boston Post*.

Surgery is often considered the court of last resort for pain. Among surgeons, it is often said that when all else fails cut nerve endings. Surgery can bring about instant almost magical release from pain. But surgery may destroy other sensations as well. There are several surgical procedures to alleviate pain. The most common is the cordotomy; severing the nerve fibers on one or both side of the spinal cord that travel the express routes to the brain. Besides cordotomy, surgery within the brain includes severing connections at major junctions in pain pathways, such as places where pain fibers cross from one side of the cord to the other, or destroying parts of important relay stations in the brain like the thalamus, an egg-shaped cluster of nerve cells near the brain. Surgeons sometimes relieve pain by destroying nerve fibers or their parent bodies outside the brain or spinal cord. A case in point is the destruction of sympathetic nerves (a part of the nervous system) to relieve pain that sometimes follows a penetrating wound from a sharp instrument or a bullet.

The tropical sub-Saharan region, which needs the lion's share of survival aid, has about 725 million people and will have 775 million by 2010. Perhaps 150 million or more live in countries that will not qualify for much aid due to poor governance, lack of planning or lesser need. By 2010, some 625 million people will share most of the $50 billion or more of aid, leading to about $80 per capita. For many Africans, the appeal of one treatment is becoming increasingly clear.

The conceptualization of the manner in which less developed countries are denied their fair share of trade benefits was described by the economist Raul Prebisch who argued that trade reforms could not and should not be accomplished by reciprocal tariff cuts between Rich (GATT) and poor UNCTAD states. Prebisch was the first secretary-general of UNCTAD. In his writings and through his activities as head of the Economic Commission for Latin America (ECLA), he mobilized considerable political support from less developed countries for an alternative paradigm for viewing their trade difficulties.

Recently, Germany proposed creating a micro-credit fund for African entrepreneurs as an additional effort to promote investment in the continent. Germany's development minister said the fund would be managed by the World Bank and be a "positive signal" to the poorest people in Africa who "often miss out on the effects of investment." Many western donors offer and run programs for women in support of small-scale credits for shopkeepers, crafts people and other cooperative entrepreneurs. The fund would supposedly put additional political weight behind the approach championed by Muhammad Yunus, the Nobel peace-prize winner who pioneered micro-finance in Bangladesh.[10]

African pain and impoverishment might be relieved by the severing of the economic and cultural nerve fibers linking them to their economic centers in Europe and re-routing them to other pathways and junctions such as China and India and Africa. Just as a cerebral cordotomy affects the afflicted body's sense of temperature and pain, an economic cordotomy might alleviate the pain and suffering of intractable debt, accelerated privatization, individual marginalization, internationally facilitated and encouraged corruption, and militarization. The of economic-cordotomy (i.e., de-linking from the West and trading with China) is increasingly a prospect for African states, manufacturers and farmers.

Given the pathological fractures of the infrastructure, the deeply infectious and cancerous corruption, the self-destructive and often pathological social violence, the lack of healthy and sufficient nutrition, the misperception and the often anti-social and anti-national behavior of the military and police forces; the widespread poverty and the resulting social and political illnesses may not be addressed or alleviated by altering or severing some ties with the West.

The recommendations by the Intern and Attending Physician include:

1. The re-development of democratic systems compatible with African culture and history.
2. The creation of a continent wide military force under the command and control of the African Union supplemented by regional units based upon a mix and balance of the local and regional populace. The suspension of all redundant i.e., extra-legal military sales, foreign military and military assistance plans and contracts by individual states. This means the diversion of economic resources to the building of the educational and health infrastructures (major hospitals and clinics in all cities and towns and universal primary and secondary education.
3. The renegotiation of all contracts with external capitalist entities involved in the extraction of African natural and mineral resources. Africa's trade barriers and tariffs are designed to maintain structural imperialism and thereby, a structural violence. African governments have failed to develop strategies for adding value to resources such as, diamonds, coffee, tea, cotton, cocoa, medicinal plants, rare wood and wildlife, thereby encouraging their sustainable utilization. Taking a continent wide inventory, pricing and marketing strategy for all strategic minerals is also necessary. The Development of a continent trade-system which de-links and de-marginalizes Africa. This Africa, could demand equality on the global stage in such fora as the UN Security Council.

Culturally Compatible Democracy?

As the 2008 election violence in Kenyan and Zimbabwe have demonstrated, many African states have failed to develop a culture of commonwealth and public interest that transcends ethnicity. Africa's political and economic marginalization should motivate African social scientists to explore alternative models of political organization that are informed by African historical experiences on the one hand, and the realities of the international political economy on the other. Perhaps the required therapy or treatment involves a return to non-partisan culturally compatible systems of democracy. As discussed earlier, democratic systems existed in Africa long before such systems appeared in Europe. Perhaps these indigenous systems can be rediscovered and modified to meet the needs and of the African people.

Systems based on non-partisan, yet consensual democratic practices that strike a balance between centralization and decentralization would help African societies arrive at consensual decisions forged at the national, local and village levels of government.[11]

Establishing the foundation for culturally compatible democracies first requires an educational system capable of the psychological and ideological transformation of the artificial African created by Europeans. This new cardiovascular system must transfuse or infuse new hope into a new generation of African minds. Osabu-Kle notes this concept and practice of democracy not impoverished liberal democracy must first be established in the minds of African leaders and elites. This means that Afro-centric values and studies must be re-institutionalized in school, home and religion.[12] This will involve the transfer of ideological symbols of unity to a cohesive political entity which constitutes a single national identity and destiny. Given ethnic diversity, until a continent wide system of governance evolves, African governments will have to find sustainable methods and *ad-hoc* means of majority-minority conflict resolution within and between states.

Myriad forms of government in the West are considered "liberal democracies" and those countries are proud of the symbolic and ideological attributes attached to the word "democracy." The same permutations in western system of governance subsumed under the term "democracy" can also be practiced in Africa. Osabu-Kle notes that; this would make Africans proud of their own democracy and accept it as ideologically and psychologically satisfying. The African approach he recommends is referred to as *jaku* democracy. *Jaku* is the Ga word for the common family of Africans, including those inside and outside the continent, as well as an adjective denoting African. He describes such constitutional systems based upon traditional systems mixing styles of leadership as "Jaku." Establishing *Jaku* democratic systems might present the greatest trauma since the arrival of the colonialists and the enslavement of the African. Entrenched internal and external politico-economic forces will not and cannot be expected to readily acquiesce to such revolutionary change. Nonetheless, Osabu-Kle prescribes *Jaku* as the type of culturally compatible democracy most suitable for Africans and that using the term *Jaku* democracy will send the message to the African mind that the continent's people have their own form of democracy which can contribute to their eventual emancipation from mental enslavement.[13]

Any "healing" of Africa requires more than importing missionary and imperialist prescriptions, which were and are designed more to facilitate western religious and political expansion, than to lift Africans from their poverty and make them self-reliant. But, healing Africa also requires more than convincing Africans to be proud of their past and to embrace their indigenous systems. Not only is a Chinese-style "cultural revolution" not possible in Africa, the proposal of such by any African leader would further devastate the impoverished conditions of millions and provide myriad reasons for chaos and war.

A mere awareness of the failed imitation of western democracy and its impoverishing impact on the political-economy of Africans is not a sufficient condition for the establishing *jaku* democracy. Recent history demonstrates that some leaders will resist the consensus-building, selection by merit requirements, checks and balances against corruption and the arbitrary use of power represented by *Jaku* democracy, as a threat to their personal interests. They will naturally resist any major political and economic reform and embrace the status quo. *Jaku* democracy and Pan-Africanism, were the visions of leaders such as Kwame Nkrumah, Julius Nyerere, Patrice Lumumba and Sekou Touré. Its establishment will inevitably result in the confrontation between a new political generation and their opponents. Those seeking change might be supported by the establishment of a Pan-African Youth Organization (PAYO). PAYO would serve as a instrument for cultivating African cadres, a function of the pre-colonial age-sets of traditional African political systems, and prepare them for the daunting task of continent-wide political leadership and economic development.[14]

A Continental Military Force

The Preamble to the US Constitution calls first for provision of the common defense. All nation-states require defense and security systems as a function of self-maintenance. For Osabu-Kle, in accordance with African culture and tradition, all able bodied Africans should belong to an organized, politicized, and compulsory national militia; receive basic military training irrespective of level of education or profession; and perform compulsory police and military duties as part of free national service.[15] Just as liberal democracies and former communist states found it expedient to establish systems of collective security systems such as the Warsaw Treaty Organization (WTO) and NATO, sub-Saharan states may increasingly require a common defense in the widening African-Islamic conflict spreading from such states as Niger, Mauritania, Somalia and Sudan to Tanzania and Kenya. The historic lessons of externally organized coups against Nkrumah and Lumumba should not be forgotten. They led to brutal puppet regimes, decades of military rule, political and economic instability.

The process of *jaku* political re-education, combined with compulsory military service may help reduce the tendency of Africa's auto-immune systems to attack the body politic for externally fomented purposes. As long as Africa remains divided into so many failed states and weak countries, the danger of political penetration via the military will not be eliminated. Thus, Osabu-Kle recommends that political re-education must be reinforced by the African High Command (AHC) of the African Union. With the operational preparedness to swiftly intervene in abort any coup attempt in Africa, the AHC would contribute to continent-wide political stability.

The sharing of military resources and expertise was Nkrumah's vision. It's revival and implementation would discourage coup attempts, because no single state could resist the combined military forces of a continental military-complex. For example, despite the divisions among the Economic Community of West African States (ECOWAS), The Economic and Military Organization (ECOMOG), the military wing of the organization, successfully intervened in Liberia and Sierra Leone returning them to political democracy or "democratic" rule.[16] AFRICOM is the first step. Africa's "peace dividend," the result decreased inter-state and intra-state conflict and thereby decreased military spending; will not be realized increased economic democracy and justice. Conflicts in the DRC, Nigeria, Liberia, and Sierra Leone will not result in a permanent *negative peace*, the absence of conflict, without establishing a *positive peace*, the eradication the structural violence of impoverishment. Food and water security, education, and access to health care inextricable components of peace-building. The development of human capital is a prerequisite of economic development.

The Differential Diagnosis

The intern has taken the patients' vital signs and prepared a diagnosis based on the history of the present illness. The psychological examination reveals the enduring and ubiquitous trauma of slavery, colonialism, economic and political betrayal by those who have historically purported to care. Pain does not kill and it is manageable for Africans have over the centuries learned to endure both the chronic and astute pain that accompanied contact with the West. The accumulated damage is immediately evident as all vital signs and biological systems have been compromised, if not destroyed.

The patient is suffering from chronic disease causing multi-system failure. Failure to appropriately and aggressively treat will lead to the death of the patient and the disease may spread to family members. Failure to treat may lead to civil war and anarchy, genocide, the permanent destruction of natural resources such as rivers lakes and rain forests, the extinction of plant and animal species and the dehydration of water sources. Failure to treat may also lead to increased terrorism, the spread of global diseases, and an accelerated environmental holocaust. It is wise to always give patient the worse case scenario if the condition is left untreated, but room for hope with the proper treatment.

The major complaint and symptom, impoverishment, is the result of many events including the history of slavery and colonialism. But there are other symptoms including corruption, crime, mounting debt and perennial ethnic and religious conflict. One thing is certain; the prescriptions offered in the form of the western nation-state have proven inefficacious. The patient is going into shock, near death and treatments such as debt relief, development aid and missionary activity have failed. There are six treatment priorities.

Treatment

First Priority: The Central Nervous System: treat corruption, establish political accountability and improve multinational political cooperation.
Second Priority: The Auto-Immune System: Preventative multinational economic and military cooperation.
stop the hemmorage of human lives and natural resources
Third Priority: The Gastrointestinal System: Treat pandemic infectious diseases and establish food self suffciency and better water usage starvation.
Fourth Priority: Skeletal System: Improve weak or build or non-existing infrastructures and support growth in cell phones and internet.
Fifth Priority: The Cardiovascular system: Decrease dependency on foreign aid and expertise, by improving educational systems.
Sixth Priority: The Respiratory System: Improve inert resource usage and management.

Paul Collier, the director of the Center for the Study of African Economics at Oxford University, has long tried to answer the question: Why are so many African countries are failing? Collier observed that about 80 percent of the population of developing countries are becoming better off. But almost 1 billion (70 percent of whom live in sub-Saharan Africa), are in economically stagnant or declining countries. Collier refers to this stating: "An impoverished ghetto of people will be increasingly impossible for a comfortable world to tolerate." Collier argues that in these 58 poor countries, 1 billion people fall into one, or more, of four traps from which it is impossible to escape. First, 'the conflict trap' has ensnared 73 percent of the people in this category through civil war. Second, is the 'natural resources trap.' Thirty percent are caught in either or both 'the land-locked resource poor countries trap and the third 'bad neighbors trap.' The fourth the 'trap of bad governance and poor economic policy,' impoverishes 76 percent of the people in these countries.

Many African countries have fallen into more than one of these traps. Collier notes that western prescriptions such as free trade, for all its potential benefits, will not help the bottom billion. These countries are not competitive exporters of labor intensive goods. Moreover, private capital only flows to these poorest countries in exchange for their natural resources. The result is the reverse: huge capital; flight. Collier estimates that 40 percent of Africa's private wealth is invested outside the continent. He argues that debt relief and aid, can and has helped the bottom billion but merely kept them in an economic holding pattern rather than ignite the economic engines required for sustained growth. Aid will not get these countries out of these traps. Aid cannot stop conflict. Aid cannot do nothing about the absence of inert resources. Aid can help land-locked countries improve their infrastructures, but it cannot eliminate bad neighbors. Therefore, Collier makes offers three prescriptive suggestions: first, military intevention; second, laws statutes and charters for improved governance and third; provide trade preferences to these countries.[17]

Marxism, Maoism, Capitalism and all other ideological prescriptions have left the patient with myriad symptoms which manifested in international and intranational wars. Both Marxists and non-Marxists agree that the sequence of modes of production associated with Europe's economic development were made possible by Africa's exploitation but not reproduced in Africa. Revolutionary prescriptions such as 'de-linking,' 'African-socialism' and economic isolation in the form of 'Pan-African development' plans have been tried and failed. None of the "isms" has provided a management strategy for maintaining politico-economic homeostasis.

What if the diagnosis is wrong? What if another hypothesis, i.e., a differential diagnosis is required? In the popular *Fox* television show, *House*, each episode is precipitated on a misdiagnosis of the patient. The main character encourages his colleagues to find a differential diagnosis. In the film *Outbreak*, starring Dustin Hoffman and Morgan Freeman, an African village is destroyed with a nuclear device in order to prevent the spread of a deadly virus throughout the country and continent. This was quite a drastic diagnosis and treatment, but was determined necessary to stop the devastating spread of the virus. Could they have been wrong? In this case, there was no differential diagnosis. In the 48 hour cycle required to diagnose and stabilize the patient, the first twelve hours are devoted to diagnostics. The intern remains with the patient overnight not only to provide less expensive emergency treatment, but to monitor the patient from crisis to stability while learning the art of medicine. What if it is not poverty that threatens to decimate the continent, but extreme climate change? What if the danger is a drug-resistant form of Aids, or a massive outbreak of cholera, Ebola, Marburg virus or H5NI (bird flu)? In short, after 12 hours of monitoring the patient in the emergency room the resident is challenged by the attending physician to shift paradigms and to think outside the box. The attending physician asks; what are you prepared to do now?

The differential diagnosis must consider other forms of treatment that include extreme means of addressing this extremely *dis-eased* and possibly dying patient. Sixty years ago, in an address at Harvard University, US Secretary of State, George Marshall announced what became known as the Marshall Plan for Europe. The plan contained four main elements. First, the US made grants to European governments for restoring production though loans to local business which repaid them to their own governments. Second, each European government spent the repaid funds on restoring the commercial infrastructure to boost production. Third, each European government made economic policy reforms to support their domestic private sectors. Fourth, a regional coordinating body handled the distribution of funds among the countries. Glenn Hubbard and Robert Duggan proposed a new Marshall Plan for Africa with its own institutions along international, regional and national lines. African countries would become eligible through specific policies in place to foster business development.[18] However, in Europe, reconstruction was facilitated by economic and political systems which were already developed. The business class and infrastructure had to be re-constructed, not re-created.

The absence of a pain management strategy guarantees continued chronic and increased acute pain. The absence of a poverty alleviation strategy guarantees more suffering. The African people require leadership with a coordinated strategy that can successfully challenge the structural sources of African impoverishment. This means challenging all who profit from and exploit Africa's social, economic and political debilities including individuals, governments, corporations and the NGO's that depend on the status quo to justify their bureaucratic existence and survival as well as the international economic system which for centuries has been fueled by the exploitation of Africa and Africans. Thus far, Western economic development has meant African impoverishment. And yet, despite the suffering, pain, and misery of cyclic religious and ethnic warfare, foreign and economic exploitation, corruption, widespread and long-term impoverishment; The African people can still manage to smile.

---

1. P. Collier and J. W. Gunning, "Explaining African Economic Performance," *Journal of Economic Literature,* 37: (1999), pp.64-111.

2. Samir Amin, *Imperialism and Unequal Development*, (New York: Monthly Review Press, (1969) and Andre Gunder Frank, "The Development of Underdevelopment." In Frank (ed.) *Latin America: Underdevelopment or Revolution* (New York: Monthly Review Press, 1977).

3. Daniel Osabu-Kle, *Compatible Cultural Democracy: The Key to Development in Africa* (Peterborough, Ontario, Canada: Broadview Press, 1985) 68-69.

4. Patrick Bond, *Against Global Apartheid: South Africa meets The World Bank, IMF and International Finance*, Second Edition, (Cape Town, London and New York: Zed Books Ltd., 2003) 18-21.

5. Osabu-Kle, Op. Cit. 70.

6. J. F. Bayart, *The State in Africa: The politics of the belly.* (London: Longman, 1993).

7. Ibid. 71.

8. Patrick Bond Op. Cit. 18-24.

9. Jeffrey Sachs, "Taking the Guessing Game out of African Aid," Editorial

The Financial Times, March 2, 2007 p. 17.

10. Hugh Williamson, 'Germany proposes micro-credit fund for Africa,' *The Financial Times*, February 14, 2007 p.2.

11. Osabu-Kle, Daniel *Compatible Cultural Democracy: The Key to Development in Africa.* (Peterborough Ontario: Broadview Press, 2000) 273.

12. Ibid. 275

13. Ibid. 278

14. Ibid. 280

15. Ibid. 279

16. Ibid.

17. Paul Collier, *The Bottom Billion: Why the poorest countries are failing and what can be done about it* (London: Oxford 2007 (Reviewed by Martin Wolf) *The Financial Times.*

18. Glenn Hubbard and William Duggan, Editorial 'Why Africa needs a Marshall plan,' *The Financial Times*, June 5, 2007. Glenn Hubbard is dean of Columbia Business School and former chairman of the Council of Economic Advisers under George W. Bush. William Duggan is a former Ford Foundation representative for West Africa at the Columbia Business School.

Bibliography

Achebe, Chinua. *Things Fall Apart*. New York: Anchor Books, 1959.

"The African Charter for Popular Participation in Development and Transformation," International Conference on Popular Participation in Recovery and Development Process in Africa, Arusha, Tanzania. 1990.

Ajayi, J .F. A. "The place of African history and culture in the process of nation-building in Africa South of the Sahara," in *Social Change: The Colonial Situation*, edited by Immanuel Wallerstein. New York: Wiley and Sons, 1966.

Ake, Claude. "Explaining Political Instability in New States," *Journal of Modern African Studies*, Vol. 11 No. 3., 1973.

Ake, Claude. *Democracy and Development in Africa*. Washington, D.C.: The Brookings Institute, 1996.

Amin, Samir. *Imperialism and Unequal Development.* New York: Monthly Review Press, 977

Awolowo, Obafemi. *Path to Nigerian Freedom.* London: Faber and Faber, 1947.

Azikikwe, Nnamdi. *My Odyssey*. New York: Praeger Press, 1970.

Bayart, J. F. *The State in Africa: The Politics of the Belly*. London: Longman, 1993.

Blundo, Giorgio & Olivier de Sardan. *Everyday Corruption and the State: Citizens & Public Officials in Africa.* New York and London: Zed Books, 2006.

Bond, Patrick. *Against Global Apartheid: South Africa Meets The World Bank, IMF and International Finance*. Second Edition, Cape Town, London and New York: Zed Books Ltd., 2003.

Bureau of Intelligence and Research, *Fact Sheet* US Department of State, Washington, DC July 1, 2001.

Burnside, Craig and David Dollar. *Assessing Aid: What Works, What Doesn't and Why*. World Bank Policy Research Report. (Washington, D.C.: Oxford University Press), 1998.

Callaghy, Thomas M. "Africa and the World Political Economy: More Caught Between a Rock and a Hard Place." In John W. Harbeson and Donald Rothchild, eds., *Africa in World Politics: The African State System in Flux*. Oxford: Westview Press, 2000.

Callaghy, Thomas M. *The State-Society Struggle: Zaire in Comparative Perspective*. New York: Columbia University Press, 1984.

Cheikh Anta Diop. *The African Origin of Civilization: Myth or Reality*. Chicago: Lawrence Hill Books, 1974.

Chinweizu. *The West and the Rest of Us: White Predators Black Slavers and the African Elite*. New York: Vintage Books, 1975.

Coleman, James S. *Nigeria: Background to Nationalism*. (Berkeley: University of California Press), 1958.

Collier P. and J. W. Gunning Explaining African economic performance. *Journal of Economic Literature, No. 37,* 1999.

Comaroff, J. and J. Comaroff "Alien-nation: Zombies, immigrants and millennial capitalism." *CODESRIA Bulletin* 3-4, 1999.

Davidson, Basil. *The African Slave Trade*. Boston Atlantic: Little Brown, 1961.

Davison, Basil. *The African Genius: An Introduction to African Social and Cultural History*. New York, Little Brown and Company, 1969.

Davidson, Basil. Can Africa Survive? Arguments Against Growth Without Development. Boston: Little-Brown, 1974.

Davidson, Basil. *The Lost Cities of Africa*. Boston: Little Brown, 1987.

Davidson, Basil. (1992) *The Black Man's Burden Africa and the Curse of the Nation-State*, New York: Random House.

Delgado, Christopher. Jane Hopkins and Valery A. Kelly. (1998), *Agricultural Growth Linkages in Sub-Saharan Africa*, International Food Policy Research Institute, Research Report, 1998.

Diamond, Jared. *Guns, Germs and Steel: The Fates of Human Societies*. New York: W.W. Norton, 2005.

Dudley, Billy. AN *Introduction to Nigerian Government and Politics*. Bloomington: Indiana University Press, 1982.

Dugard, John. *Human Rights and the South African Legal Order*. Princeton: Princeton University Press, 1978

Ellis, Stephen. "Reporting Africa," *Current History*, May, 2000.

Fanon, Frantz. *The Wretched of the Earth,* New York: Grove Press, 1968.

Fanon, Frantz. *Black Skin White Masks,* New York: Grove Books, 1967.

Ferris, E. *Beyond Borders: Refugees, Migrants and Human Rights in the Post Cold-War Era*. Geneva: WCC Publications, 1993.

Fitch, Bob and Mary Oppenheimer. *Ghana: The End of Illusion*. New York: Monthly Review Press, 1968.

Forrest, Tom. *Politics and Economic Development in Nigeria*. Boulder, CO.: Westview, 1995.

Fortes, Meyer and E. E. Evans-Pritchard. eds., *African Political Systems,* London: Oxford University Press, 1940.

Frank, Andre Gunder. "The Development of Underdevelopment," In Frank, *Latin America: Underdevelopment or Revolution,* New York: Monthly Review Press, 1969.

Friedland, William H. and Carl G. Rosberg. *African Socialism*. Hoover Institution Stanford: University Press, 1964.

Gibson, Richard. *African Liberation Movements: Contemporary Struggles Against White Minority Rule*. London; Oxford University Press, 1972.

Gittleman, Richard "The Banjul Charter on Human and Peoples Rights: A Legal Analysis." In Claude E. Welch, Jr., and Robert Meltzer, (eds.), *Human Rights and Development in Africa*. Albany: State University of New York, 1984).

Gray, Henry, T. Pickering Pick and Robert Howden. *Gray's Anatomy: Descriptive and Surgical* New York: Bounty Books, 1977.

Haddad, L. J. Hoddinott, and H. Alderman, eds. "Intra-household Resource Allocation in Developing Countries; Models, Methods and Policy". Baltimore and London: Johns Hopkins University Press for the International Food Policy Research Institute, 1977).

Hammond, Dorothy and Alta Jablow. *The Africa That Never Was: Four Centuries of British Writing About Africa*, Prospect Heights IL: Waveland Press, 1992.

Hamelink, C. J. *Cultural Autonomy in Global Communications: Planning National Information Policy*. London: Longman, 1983.

Harbeson, John W. and Donald Rothchild, eds., *Africa in World Politics: The African State System in Flux*, Oxford: Westview, 2000.

Higgins, P.A. and H. Alderman. "Labour and Women's Nutrition: The Impact of Work Effort and Fertility on Nutritional Status in Ghana." *Journal of Human Resources,* (32), 1997.

Huntington, Samuel P. *The Clash of Civilizations and the Remaking of World Order*. New York: Simon and Schuster, 1966.

International Food Policy Research Institute. "Development Strategy and Governance Division." *Discussion Paper Number 8*. Washington, D.C., 2006.

Osayimwese Izervbuwa, and Sunday Iyare. "The Economics of Nigerian Federalism: Selected Issues in Economic Management." *Publius: The Journal of Federalism* 21 (4) (fall) 1991.

James, A. "Problems of Internal Peacekeeping." *Diplomacy and Statecraft,* 5 (1) 1994.

Janssen, J. *History of the German People at the Close of the Middle* Ages, 16 vols., Kegan Paul London 1896-1910.

Jensen, Mike. "Making the Connection: Africa and the Internet." *Current History*, May, 2000.

Kenyatta, Jomo. *Facing Mount Kenya*. New York: Vintage Books, Random House, 1965.

Khapoya, Vincent. *The African Experience: An Introduction* New Jersey: Prentice Hall, 1988.

Kimani, Martin Mbugua. "Of Darfur and Western Navel-Gazing." *Iko Magazine,* October-December, 2004.

Kuper, Hilda. "'Strangers in Plural Societies: Asians in South Africa and Uganda," In Leo Kuper and M.G. Smith, eds. *Pluralism in Africa.* Berkeley: University of California Press, 1966.

Kwitty, Jonathan. *Endless Enemies: The Making of an Unfriendly World.* New York: Congdon and Weed, 1984.

Lambsdorff, J. G. *The Transparency International Corruption Perceptions Index.* October 1999-Framework Document, http://*gwdu19.gwde.de~UWVW/1999_CPI_FD.pdf.*

Lancaster, Carol. *Aid to Africa: So Much to do so Little.* Chicago: University of Chicago Press, 1999.

Latimer, Elizabeth W. *Europe in Africa in the Nineteenth Century.* Chicago: A. C. McClurg Publishers, 1895.

Loescher, G. *Refugee Movements and International Security.* London: International Institute for Strategic Studies, 1992.

Loescher, G. *Beyond Charity: International Cooperation and the Global Crisis.* New York and Oxford: Oxford University Press, 1993.

Lugard, Frederick D. Lugard. *The Dual Mandate in British Tropical Africa.* Edinburgh and London: Blackwood and Sons, 1923.

Manners, Robert A. "The Kipsigis of Kenya: Culture Change in a 'Model' East African Tribe." In Julian H. Steward, ed., *Contemporary Change in Traditional Societies.* Vol. I Urbana: University of Illinois Press, 1976.

Malawi baseline survey: *Report of Findings.* Prepared for C-SAFE, Tucson, AZ TANGO International, *http:''www.c-safe.org/dwnloads/Mal-baseline%Fin-Report.doc.*

Martin, Guy. "Continuity and Change in Franco-African Relations." *The Journal of Modern Africa Studies.* Vol. 33,(no. 1) 1995.

Maslow, Abraham. *Toward a Psychology of Being.* Princeton: Van Nostrand, 1968.

Mazrui, Ali A. "Development in a Multicultural Context: Trends and Tensions." In *Culture and Development in Africa.* edited by I. Serageldin and J. Taboroff. Washington, DC: World Bank, 1994.

Mazrui, Ali A. "Africa and Other Civilizations." in John Harbeson and Donald Rothchild, editors, *Africa in World Politics: The African State System in Flux*. Oxford Press: London, 2000.

Mbaku, J. M. *Bureaucratic and Political Corruption in Africa: The Public Choice Perspective*. Malabar: Krieger, 2000.

Mbaku, John Mukum and Suresh Chandra Saxena. *Africa At The Crossroad: Between Regionalism and Globalization*. Westport, Connecticut: Praeger Press, 2004.

Mbiti, John. *African Religions and Philosophy*. Garden City, New York: Anchor Books, Doubleday & Co, 1970.

Minter, William. "America and Africa: Beyond the Double Standard." *Current History*, May 2000.

Mohamed Omar Beshir. *The Southern Sudan: Background to Conflict*, London: William Blackwood and Sons, 1968.

Muggah, Robert and Edward Mogire. "Arms availability and refugee militarization in Africa: conceptualizing the issues." In Robert Muggah, ed., *No Refuge: The Crisis of Refugee Militarization in Africa.*, London: Zed Books, 2006.

Niven, C.R. *A Short History of Nigeria*. London: Longmans Green and Co, 1952.

Nyanteng, V. K. and S. Asuming-Brempong. "The Role of Agriculture in Food Security in Ghana." Paper prepared for the FAO for the Role of Agriculture International Conference, Rome 20-22, 2006.

Nyerere, Julius K. *Freedom and Development*. Dar Es Salaam: Oxford University Press, 1973.

Nyerere, Julius K. *Freedom and Development*. Dar Es Salaam: Oxford University Press, 1968.

Nyerere, Julius K. *Ujamaa: Essays on Socialism*. Dar Es Salaam: Oxford University Press, 1968.

Nkrumah, Kwame. *Africa Must Unite*. New York: International Publishers Inc., 1963.

Oginga, Odinga. *Not Yet Uhuru: An Autobiography*. New York: Hill and Wang, 1967.

Osabu-Kle, Daniel. *Cultural Compatible Democracy: The Key to Development in Africa.* Petersborough, Ontario: Broadview Press, 2000.

Ottenberg, S. "Local Government and the Law in Southern Nigeria." *Journal of Asian and African Studies.* Vol. 2. (no. 1-2) 1967.

Pender, John, F. and Simeon Ehui. *Strategies for Sustainable Land Management in East African Highlands.* Washington, D. C: International Food Policy Research Institute, 2006.

Quartney, K. A. B. Jones. *A Life of Azikiwe.* Baltimore: Penguin Books, 1965.
Rattray, R .S. *Ashanti Proverbs.* Oxford: Oxford University Press, 1916.

Reno, William. "Privatizing War in Sierra Leone." *Current History,* Vol. 96. No. 610, 1997.

Reno, William. *Warlord Politics and African States.* Boulder, Co.: Lynne Reinner 1998

Sayigh, Y. *Confronting the 1990s: Security in the Developing Countries.* Adelphi Paper no. 251, London: International Institute for Strategic Studies, 1990.

Schraeder, Peter J. "France and the Great Game in Africa," *Current History,* May, 1997.

Scott P. Layne, M.D., UCLA Department of Epidemiology, "Principles of Infectious Disease: *Epidemiology,"* EPI 2002.

Shepperson, George and Price Thomas. *Independent African: John Chilembwe and the Origins, Setting and Significance of the Nyasaland Native Uprising of 1915.* Edinburgh Press, 1958

Shettima, Kole Ahmed. "Engendering Nigeria's Third Republic," *African Studies Review* 38:3 December, 1995.

Smith, M. G. 'Historical and Cultural Conditions of Political Corruption among the Hausa.' *Comparative Studies in Society and History,* Vol. 6. no. 2. , 1964.

Smith, L.C. "The use of household expenditure surveys for the assessment of food in security" in *Measurement and Assessment of Food Deprivation and Under Nutrition.* Rome: FAO. 2003.

Smith, Lisa C. Harold Alderman and Dede Aduayom. *Food Insecurity in Africa: New Estimates from Household Expenditure Survey.*, International Food Policy Research Institute Research Report 146, 2006.

South African Institute of Race Relations *Survey of Race Relations in South Africa*, Johannesburg, 1979.

Soyinka, Wole. "Culture, Memory and Development," in *Culture and Development in Africa*. edited by I. Serageldin and J. Taboroff, Washington, DC: World Bank, 1994.

Sreberny, Mohammadi. A. The Many Faces of Cultural Imperialism." In *Beyond Cultural Imperialism: Globalization, communication and the New International Order*. London: Sage, 1997.

Stedman, S. J. and F. Tanner. *Refugee Manipulation: War, Politics and the Abuse of Human Suffering*. Washington DC: Brookings Institution Press, 2003.

Thompson, Leonard. *A History of South Africa*, New Haven and London: Yale University Press(1990.

Van Sertima, Ivan. *They Came Before Columbus: The African Presence in Ancient America*. New York: Random House, 1976.

Vogt, M.A. Conflict resolution and peacekeeping: the Organization of African Unite and the United Nations, In *Out of Conflict: From war to peace in Africa*. Edited by G. M. Sorbo and P. Vale. Uppsala: Nordiska Afriakainstistute , 1997.

Wagner, Günter." The Abaluyia of Kavirondo." In Daryll Forde, ed. *African Worlds*. New York: Oxford University Press, 1968.

Wai, Dunstan M., *The African-Arab Conflict in the Sudan*. New York: African Publishing House, 1978.

Ward, W. E. *History of Ghana*. London: George Allen and Unwin, 1958.

Weiner, M. "Security, Stability and International Migration," *International Migration and Security*, 17(3) 1991.

Welch, Claude E. Jr., and Robert Meltzer, eds., "Human Rights and Development in Africa".

Article 2 of the *African Charter on Human and Peoples' Rights*, Appendix One Albany: State University of New York, 1984.

Whitaker, Jennifer Seymour. *How Can Africa Survive?* New York: Council on Foreign Relations, 1988.

Young, Crawford. "The Heritage of Colonialism." in John Harbeson and Donald Rothschild editors, *Africa in World Politics: The African State System in Flux*. Oxford, London, 2000.

Index

A

B

C

D

E

R

S

T

U

V

W

Y

Z

About the Author

Sterling Johnson is Professor of political science at Central Michigan University where he teaches courses in International Relations, American Foreign Policy, International Law and African Political Systems. Dr. Johnson is a former US Foreign Service Officer and has served on the Board of the Directors of the National Council of Africana Studies. He is the author of *Global Search and Seizure: The US National Interest vs. International Law; Black Globalism: The International Politics of A Non-State Nation and Peace Without Justice: Hegemonic Instability or International Criminal Law?*

www.ingramcontent.com/pod-product-compliance
Ingram Content Group UK Ltd.
Pitfield, Milton Keynes, MK11 3LW, UK
UKHW021035150926
475561UK00003B/117

9 780761 843511